Ancient Healing

Unlocking the Mysteries of Health & Healing Through the Ages

Publications International, Ltd.

Louis Weber, C.E.O.
Publications International, Ltd.
7373 North Cicero Avenue
Lincolnwood, Illinois 60646

Manufactured in U.S.A.

8 7 6 5 4 3 2 1

ISBN: 0-7853-2431-3

Library of Congress Catalog Card Number: 97-68862

Note: Neither the Editors of Consumer Guide™ and Publications International, Ltd., nor the authors, consultants, editors, or publisher take responsibility for any possible consequences from any treatment, procedure, exercise, dietary modification, action, or application of medication or preparation by any person reading or following the information in this book. The publication of this book does not constitute the practice of medicine, and this book does not attempt to replace your physician or your pharmacist. Before undertaking any course of treatment, the authors, consultants, editors, and publisher advise the reader to check with a physician or other health care provider.

Picture and illustration credits:

Front cover: **Exley/Image Select International** (bottom right); **Werner Forman Archive/Art Resource** (top right); **Peter T. Furst** (bottom left); **SuperStock:** L. Bogdanov/Hermitage Museum, St. Petersburg (left center & right center); E. Carle/National Museum of Anthropology, Mexico City (center); Museum of History of Medicine, Rome/Canali PhotoBank, Milan (top left).

Back cover: **SuperStock:** Bibliotheque Nationale, Paris/Bridgeman Art Library (bottom); The Lowe Art Museum, The University of Miami (top).

David Agee/Anthro-Photo File: 188; **Ancient Art & Architecture Collection Ltd.:** 220, 231, 305; **Archive Photos:** 356, 359, 365; American Stock: 16 (bottom); Archive France: 361; Rayaz Kabli/Reuthers: 215 (bottom); **Art Resource:** Archaeological Museum, Delphi/Nimatallah: 7 (bottom), 77; Biblioteca Marciana, Venice/Giraudon: 108; Biblioteca de Ajuda, Lisbon/ Giraudon: 113; Borromeo: 201, 223; D.Y./Bibliotheque Nationale, Paris: 106, 109; Werner Forman Archive: 152, 174, 291; Courtesy Enwistle Gallery, London/Werner Forman Archive: Table of contents (center); Giraudon: 122; Musee Conde, Chantilly/Giraudon: 99, 202; Erich Lessing: 44, 65, 75; Erich Lessing/National Archaeol Museum, Athens: 71; Indian Museum, Calcutta, West Bengal/Nimatallah: 230; Iraq Museum, Baghdad/Scala: Table of contents (top center), 12; Museo Nazionale Atestino, Este/Scala: 94; National Museum of Pakistan, Karachi/Scala: 189 (bottom); The Pierpont Morgan Library: 67; Tanzania National Museum, Dar es Salaam/Werner Forman Archive: front end sheets & back end sheets; Yakushiji Temple, Nara: 313; **Corbis-Bettmann:** 51, 74, 103, 190, 207, 245, 249 (bottom); Thony Belizaire/AFP: 348; Reuters: 55, 226 (top), 308, 350; UPI: 257, 263; **Thomas Cranmer:** 7 (top), 13, 31, 49, 69, 100, 145, 169, 187, 278, 323, 340; **Mark De Fraeye:** Table of contents (right center), 273, 299 (bottom); **E. T. Archive:** 93, 283; Aleppo Museum, Syria: 19 (top); British Museum: 6 (top), 19 (bottom), 43, 194, 288; National Museum, Karachi: 189 (top); National Palace Museum, Taiwan: 277; Victoria & Albert Museum, London: 219; **Kevin Ergil:** 272, 298, 299 (top); **FPG International:** Peter Gridley: 127; Robert Holmes: 260; Christian Michaels: 307; Keren Su: 306; **Peter T. Furst:** 128, 129, 132, 133, 135, 136, 137, 138, 142, 146, 149, 153, 154, 159, 163, 164, 173, 175, 178, 179, 181, 182, 244, 246, 247, 249 (top); **Antonia Graeber/Museum of Cultural History at UCLA:** 329; **Paul G. Hackett:** 258, 259; **Historical Collections, National Museum of Health & Medicine:** 95; **Image Select International:** 6 (bottom), 25, 32, 110, 124, 165, 166, 316; Exley: 27; **International Institute of Reflexology:** 36; **John M. Janzen:** 9 (bottom), 10, 326, 327, 331, 334, 335; **Henry John & Margaret Thompson Drewal, National Museum of African Art, Eliot Elisofon Photographic Archives, Smithsonian Institution:** 333; **Craig Lovell/Viesti Associates, Inc.:** 319; **National Library of Medicine:** 309; **Yoshi Miyake:** 40, 284, 285, 291, 294; **Richard T. Nowitz:** 48, 56, 59, 61, 62, 63; **Robert McCracken Peck:** 141, 252; **San Heritage Centre:** 324; **Tibetan Medical Paintings published by Serindia Publications:** 262, 266 (bottom), 270, 275, 276; **Sipa-Press:** Francois Gauthier: 215 (top), 233; Tom Haley: 303; Tony Sevino: 362; **Snow Lion Publications:** 255; **Elisa Sobo:** 342; **SuperStock:** Table of contents (top left & top right), 14, 41, 58, 83, 105, 143, 168, 196, 217, 221, 228, 241, 248, 254, 265, 266 (top), 320, 322; A.K.G., Berlin: 126, 217; American Museum of Natural History, New York/Bridgeman Art Library, London: 172; Archeological Museum, Florence/ Canali PhotoBank, Milan: 90; Bibliotheque Nationale, Paris, France/Bridgeman Art Library, London: 287; Bibliotheque Nationale, Paris/ET Archive, London: 121; C. Bear: 363; L. Bogdanov/Hermitage Museum, St. Petersburg: 29; E. Carle/National Museum of Anthropology, Mexico City: 151; R. Chen: 243; Christie's Images: 33, 54; Deri-ez-zor Museum, Syria/ET Archive, London: 16 (top); Egyptian National Museum, Cairo: 35; Egyptian National Museum, Cairo/ET Archive, London: 47; Explorer, Paris: 26; S. Fiore: Medinet Abu, Egypt: 34 (top); S. Fiore/Valley of the Kings, Thebes: 34 (bottom); C. Harris: 345; Hittite Museum, Ankara/ET Archive, London: 52; Van Hoorick Fine Art: 339; Indian Museum, Calcutta/Explorer, Paris: 208; Kapoor: 226 (bottom); Khuller: 297; R. King: 311; K. Kummels: 156, 234; Library of Decorative Arts, Paris/Explorer, Paris: 162; The Lowe Art Museum, The University of Miami: 131, 160, 161, 167; Manley: 8 (top), 46, 184; Musee Du Louvre, Paris: 22; Musee Du Louvre, Paris/ET Archive, London: 23; Museo Capitolino, Rome/Canali PhotoBank, Milan: 73; Museo Civico, Piacenza/Canali PhotoBank, Milan: 89; Museo del Prado, Madrid/Bridgeman Art Library, London: 117; Museum of History of Medicine, Rome/Canali PhotoBank, Milan: 97; Museum of History of Medicine, Rome/Canali PhotoBank, Milan: 338; G. Ricatto: 354; Rijksmuseum Vincent Van Gogh, Amsterdam: 186; Royal Academy of Arts, London/ET Archive, London: 91; K. Scholz/Valley of the Kings, Thebes: 11, 30; Vatican Museums & Galleries, Rome/Canali PhotoBank, Milan: 68; By Courtesy of The Board of Trustees of The Victoria & Albert Museum, London/Bridgeman Art Library, London: 185, 239; **Giorgio Tavaglione:** 8 (bottom), 237; **Wellcome Institute Library, London:** 9 (top), 280, 281, 301.

Contributors

Contributing Writers

Kevin V. Ergil, M.A., M.S., L.Ac., Dipl. Ac. (NCCA), F.N.A.A.O.M., F.A.A.P.M., Dean and Director, The Pacific Institute of Oriental Medicine, New York (Tibetan Medicine; Japanese Medicine)

Marnae C. Ergil, M.A., Managing Director, Applied Health & Education Systems, Brooklyn, New York (Chinese Medicine)

Peter T. Furst, Ph.D., Research Associate, The University Museum of Anthropology & Archeology, and Adjunct Professor, Department of Anthropology, University of Pennsylvania, Philadelphia (American Shamanism; Aztec, Maya & Inca Healing; Native American Healing; Asian Shamanism)

Nancy Gordon, M.A., writer and editor specializing in history, herbs, and health, Walnut Creek, California (Mesopotamian Medicine; Egyptian Medicine; Hebrew Medicine; Greek and Roman Medicine; Northern European Medicine)

John M. Janzen, Ph.D., Professor of Anthropology, University of Kansas, Lawrence (Sub-Saharan Healing)

Elisa J. Sobo, Ph.D., Visiting Scholar, Department of Anthropology, University of California, San Diego (Caribbean Healing)

Linda Sparrowe, M.A., Managing Editor, *Yoga Journal*, and Editor-in-Chief, *The Herb Quarterly*, Berkeley, California (Ayurveda; Yoga)

Consultants

Darrel Amundsen, Ph.D., Chair, Department of Foreign Languages & Literatures, Western Washington University, Bellingham (Hebrew Medicine)

Clifford R. Barnett, Ph.D., Professor of Anthropology, Stanford University, Stanford, California, and Cofounder & Past President, Society for Medical Anthropology (Native American Healing)

Stephen Birch, Ph.D., Lic.Ac., Acupuncturist and Project Director at Yale University School of Medicine, New Haven, Connecticut (Japanese Medicine)

Frances Cattermole-Tally, Ph.D., Consultant and Instructor for the Archive of American Folk Medicine, University of California, Los Angeles (Northern European Medicine)

Kevin V. Ergil, M.A., M.S., L.Ac., Dipl. Ac. (NCCA), F.N.A.A.O.M., F.A.A.P.M., Dean and Director, The Pacific Institute of Oriental Medicine, New York (Chinese Medicine)

Peter T. Furst, Ph.D., Research Associate, The University Museum of Anthropology & Archeology, and Adjunct Professor, Department of Anthropology, University of Pennsylvania, Philadelphia (American Shamanism; Aztec, Maya & Inca Healing; Asian Shamanism)

John M. Janzen, Ph.D., Professor of Anthropology, University of Kansas, Lawrence (Sub-Saharan Healing)

John Riddle, Ph.D., Alumni Distinguished Professor of History, North Carolina State University, Raleigh (Mesopotamian Medicine; Egyptian Medicine; Greek and Roman Medicine)

William Wedenoja, Ph.D., Professor of Anthropology, Southwest Missouri State University, Springfield (Caribbean Healing)

Kenneth G. Zysk, Ph.D., Assistant Professor of Near Eastern Languages & Literatures, New York University, New York (Ayurveda; Yoga; Tibetan Medicine)

Contents

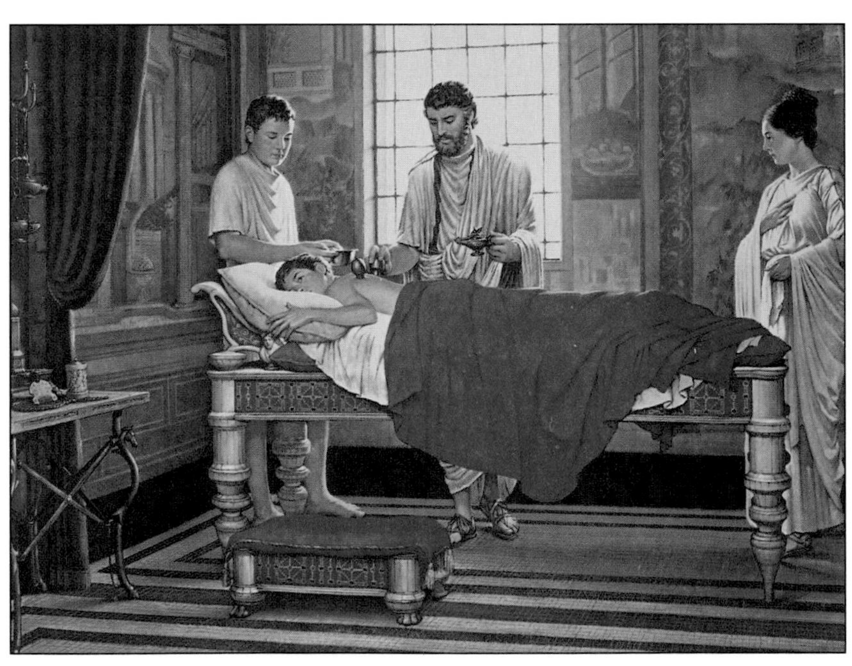

Introduction

How old is medicine? This is a very difficult question to answer. All living creatures have an instinct for self-preservation and take specific steps to treat themselves when their lives are threatened by injury or disease. Among many species, there is a propensity to care for one another in a family or social group: Primates groom one another; cats lick each other's wounds. This seems to be a step above self-preservation, and we might call these behaviors primitive healing. But when does an instinctual health-promoting activity rise to the level of *healing*?

One crucial factor that seems to set healing apart from self-preservation is the element of caring. An individual caring about the health of another and acting to improve it is different from merely trying to keep oneself alive. Healing is a selfless activity—an act of charity and compassion. Indeed, Buddhist medicine (represented in this volume by the Tibetan tradition, pages 254–276) explicitly names compassion as the most fundamental aspect of medicine.

One uniquely human trait (arguably our defining trait, for good or bad) is our ability to, and propensity for, theorizing. Healing and health have certainly had their share of theories. Anatomy, diagnostics, therapeutics, and in some cases cosmology and theology—these theories form a medical system. Not all of the traditions we will explore had codified systems, but all had their theories—some written in great treatises, some passed down orally, and some merely outgrowths of everyday experience—that were the underpinnings of the practical craft of healing.

By this definition, the first time someone brought cool water to a feverish child because she thought it would cool the heat, medicine was born. But can you imagine a time when this would not have been the case? It doesn't even make sense to ask about a mythical first time. So, how old is medicine? It's as old as we are—probably even older.

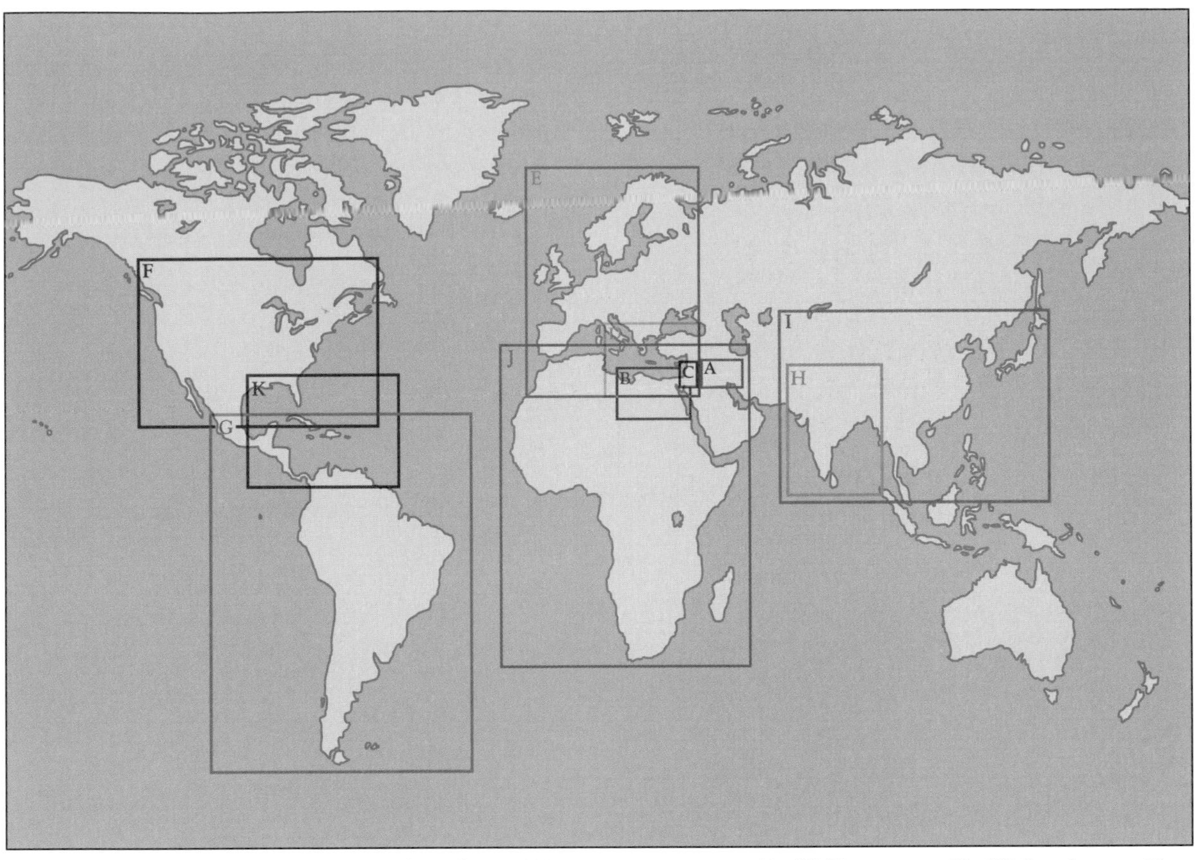

A guide to the maps of areas covered in this volume: (A) Mesopotamia, page 13; (B) Egypt, page 31; (C) Israel, page 49; (D) Greece, page 69; (E) Europe, page 100; (F) North America, page 169; (G) Latin America, page 145; (H) Indian Subcontinent, page 187; (I) the Far East, page 278; (J) Africa, page 323; and (K) the Caribbean, page 340.

The Traditions

Through these untold millennia, people have approached issues of health, illness, and healing in remarkably diverse ways. Despite the common goal of health and longevity, cultures around the world and through time have shown that the paths toward that goal are many and varied.

In this book, we will explore 16 different traditions from around the globe. Some are the ancient roots of systems that persist today; some are now extinct because the civilizations that practiced them died out or were wiped out; and some were forgotten for centuries but have begun to make a comeback. However, each displays a unique approach to the concern for health humans of every generation have always had in common.

THE NEAR EAST The tour begins with the great civilizations of the Near East. Through archaeologic evidence and the existence of written texts dating back to that period, we can glean a pretty good picture of how the ancient Mesopotamians of the Tigris and Euphrates river valley and the ancient Egyptians of the Nile River valley approached medicine some 3,000 years ago. Likewise, we have at least one good historical source for examining the ancient Hebrews—the Bible.

EUROPE The next stop is Europe. Here again we confront two great civilizations with a plethora of archaeologic evidence and written sources. The ancient Greeks and Romans began codifying a system of medicine that would determine the direction of Western medicine right up to the present. In these civilizations we meet Hippocrates, the so-called "Father of Medicine," and Galen, whose medical theories the Western world relied on for more than a millennium. Although their specific theories might not jibe with what we know now, the naturalist approach and scientific method of the Greeks and Romans is still very much with us.

Leaving the great civilizations of the Mediterranean, we come to Northern Europe. We know little about how the disparate tribes of present-day Britain, France, Germany, and Scandinavia conducted their healing practices. Reports from around the time of the Roman Empire give us some clues, and the later practices of the Anglo-Saxons and the early Christian monasteries provide a picture of common folk practices that presumably reflect some of the traditions from early Europe.

THE AMERICAS On the other side of the world, the Western Hemisphere was home to thousands of unique yet subtly connected healing forms. Before the arrival of the Europeans, the

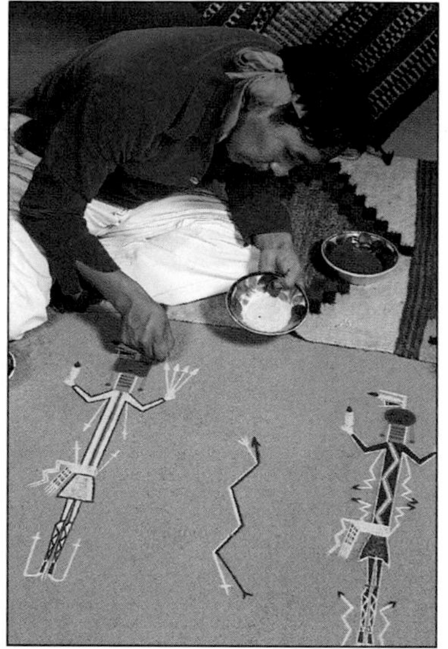

Americas were not by any means "primitive" or "backward" despite what the invading Europeans thought (and perhaps think). Even today, we have trouble comprehending the healing practices of the early indigenous Americans; they are so rooted in a particular worldview, it baffles the modern Western mind. Here we first encounter shamanism, a healing system so connected with every aspect of the religion, culture, and lifestyle of Native Americans it is almost impossible to talk about it as a practice separate from their hunting and agriculture, their statecraft and architecture, or any other part of life.

In the Americas, we also confront the three great pre-Columbian civilizations of Latin America: the Aztec, the Inca, and the Maya. Although hampered by the deep misunderstandings of the invading Spanish, from whom most of our information comes, we get a glimpse of their advanced botanical therapeutics and surgical techniques. The picture, while never entirely clear, suggests a medical knowledge that far exceeded anything the invading Europeans had yet devised.

The North American continent was home to hundreds of different tribes and nations whose therapeutics ran the gamut from herbal remedies to spiritual healing and even what is arguably the first form of art therapy.

The Indian Subcontinent Perhaps one of the oldest and richest traditions of medicine can be found in South Asia. Here, in present day India and Pakistan, the venerable science of Ayurveda was born. Springing from a synthesis of various religious and secular traditions, Ayurveda is probably the most thoroughly structured and empirically rigorous of the ancient medical systems. And yet its apparent complexity does not detract from its elegance or its endurance—Ayurveda is very much practiced and admired today. Yoga—in many ways a cousin of Ayurveda—also has diverse and ancient roots on the subcontinent. And as with Ayurveda, it also has present-day devotees.

The Far East Thousands of years, including some periods of official repression, have not been able to erase the strong healing traditions of East Asia. Beginning with the deep roots of mystical, shamanistic healing in Siberia and moving through the development of medicine in Tibet, China, and Japan, the tour of the Far East is a tour through political and intellectual upheaval. But what springs from it is the medical system that currently provides primary care to more people than any other on Earth—traditional Chinese medicine. Japanese medicine's continuing development and Tibet's distinctive blend of Indian and Chinese influences in one Buddhist tradition demonstrate how East Asia's ancient contributions to medicine remain far from obsolete.

African Traditions Finally, the tour comes to Africa and the Caribbean, where African traditions flourished during and after the time of slavery. Although the healing practices of Sub-Saharan Africa have perhaps the least archaeologic and historical information of any of the regions we explore, it is ironically the place that has the longest history of healing in the world. Fortunately, traditions live on in modern practitioners all across the region. In the Caribbean, too, we see aspects of this age-old medicine with powerful metaphors and surprisingly universal beliefs about health and disease.

The Lessons

Why do we care about the way medicine was practiced centuries and millennia ago? After all, we've made our improvements and no longer need the superstition and misguided notions of the past. There are a number of reasons:

First, the resurgence of so-called alternative medicine has fueled much controversy. Understanding the traditional basis of these approaches—from the theory of specific treatments such as acupuncture to the history and efficacy of more generalized therapies such as mind/body medicine—will allow a more thorough evaluation of their potential.

Second, the history of healing is not just a history of medicine. Healing is a social act, one that helps to define a society; the interaction between the sick and the healthy can reveal a great deal about what a culture values most. It's no accident that religion has almost always been an integral part of healing. Both are expressions of what a culture values in the face of mortality; both show what matters and what a society *does* when the chips are down. Our culture is no different, and we can use the same criteria to judge ourselves and our "superior" reasoning.

You'll find that many of the ancient ways of thinking about illness seem completely absurd. The theory that a disease could be caused by invisible demons seems to be the height of foolishness. And as for blaming ancestors for sickness—a prevalent idea in ancient times from China to the Americas—well, that one fares even worse than the demon idea.

But how different is our medicine from these ancient notions? Are microorganisms any more real to us than spirits were to them? What is the practical difference between bacteria visible only to a scientist with a powerful microscope and spirits visible only to a shaman with the proper drum? Are genetic and hereditary explanations for diseases so different or more understandable than the theories of the ancient ancestor worshipers?

There is a difference, of course. Treating dysentery as an infectious disease caused by a microorganism is much more effective than going the amulet route. Fewer people die. Insulin injections are, without a doubt, a better way to handle diabetes than trying to propitiate an offended ancestor; people live longer and with fewer debilitating complications. And the list goes on: antibiotics, angioplasty, dialysis—these scientific advances save and improve lives.

At the same time, modern Western medicine's successes and advanced methods in no way diminish the power, elegance, and, in some cases, beauty of ancient healing traditions. (Despite the computer-aided color enhancement, does a magnetic resonance image even compare to a Navajo sandpainting?) And all too frequently, modernization has meant the abandonment of valuable aspects of the *art of healing* in favor of progress in the *science of medicine*.

In some respects, we've sacrificed a great deal in the name of longevity, forestalling the inevitable by making treatments more drastic and invasive. In just a few decades, we've seen the virtual eradication of monstrous menaces such as smallpox and polio, only to see the new ones such as cancer and heart disease line up to take their place. Despite our great leaps forward (and they have been great), we ultimately stand as helpless as ever in the face of death. So rather than look with disdain on the misguided ways of past generations, try to put aside your modern bias and see what you can learn from the ever-hopeful ancient healers.

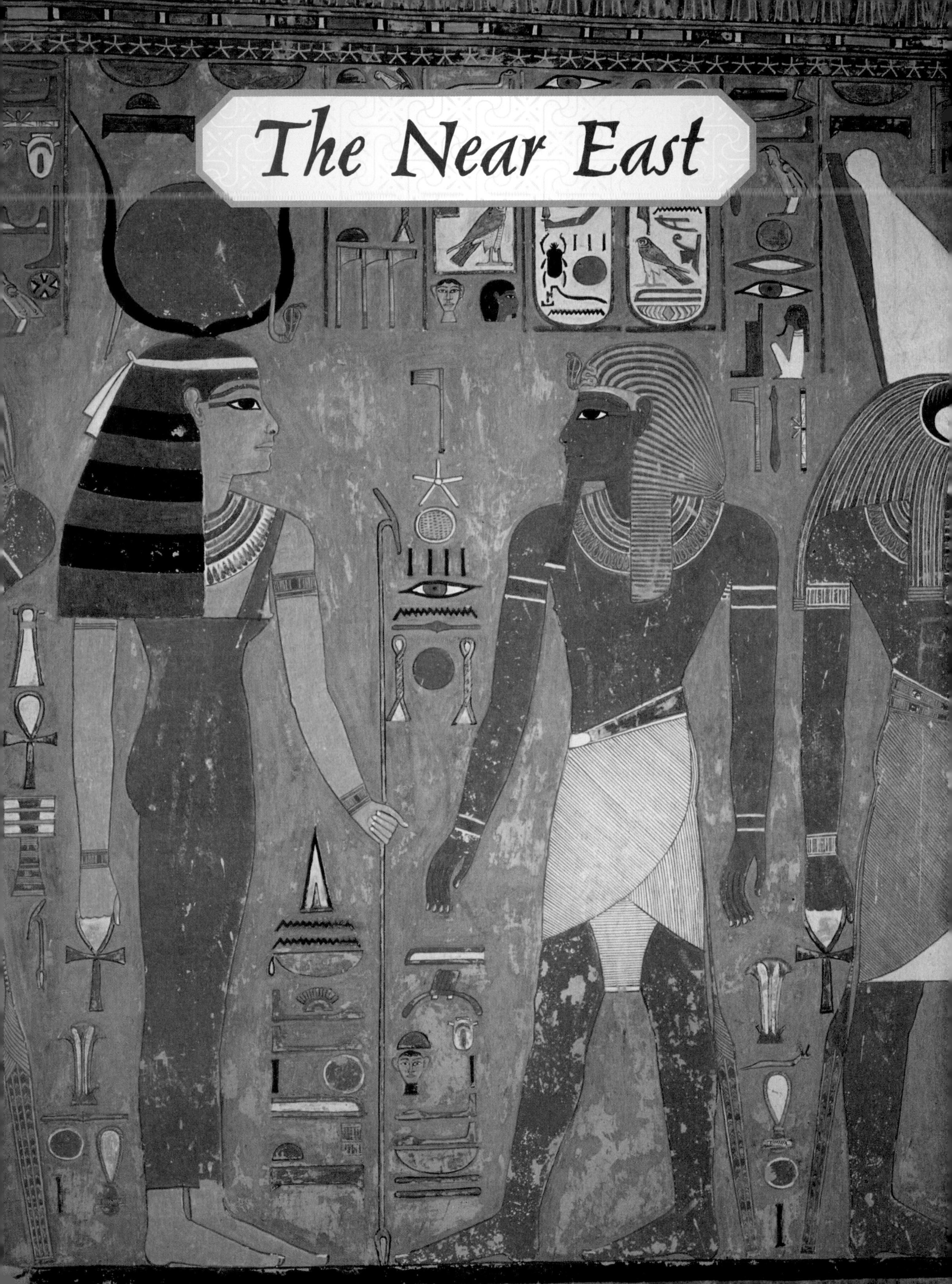

The Near East

Mesopotamian Medicine

TRADITION HAS IT that the beginning of civilization was here. The Fertile Crescent, as Mesopotamia is sometimes called, has been touted by some to be the location of the Garden of Eden and the birthplace of humanity. Although the truth of these assertions will probably never be known, it is true that the ancient civilizations of this region were extraordinary in their culture and accomplishments.

The ancient land of Mesopotamia lay between the Tigris and the Euphrates rivers, in part of modern-day Iraq. In fact, the name Mesopotamia means the land between the rivers. Although their flooding was violent and unpredictable, these two rivers allowed civilizations to grow and flourish, bringing with them all we think of when we use the term *civilization*—cities, monumental architecture, agriculture, the division of labor, art, government, and writing.

The southern part of Mesopotamia, from modern Baghdad down to the head of the Persian Gulf, was the region called Babylonia, which consisted of two areas: Akkad in the north and Sumer in the south. The land known as Assyria lay in the northern part of Mesopotamia, along the Upper Tigris Valley.

Life-size bronze head of an Akkadian king—often ascribed to Naram-Sin or Sargon—from Nineveh, dating to 2350 B.C. The Akkadians conquered Mesopotamia, forming the first unified empire there and pacifying trade routes.

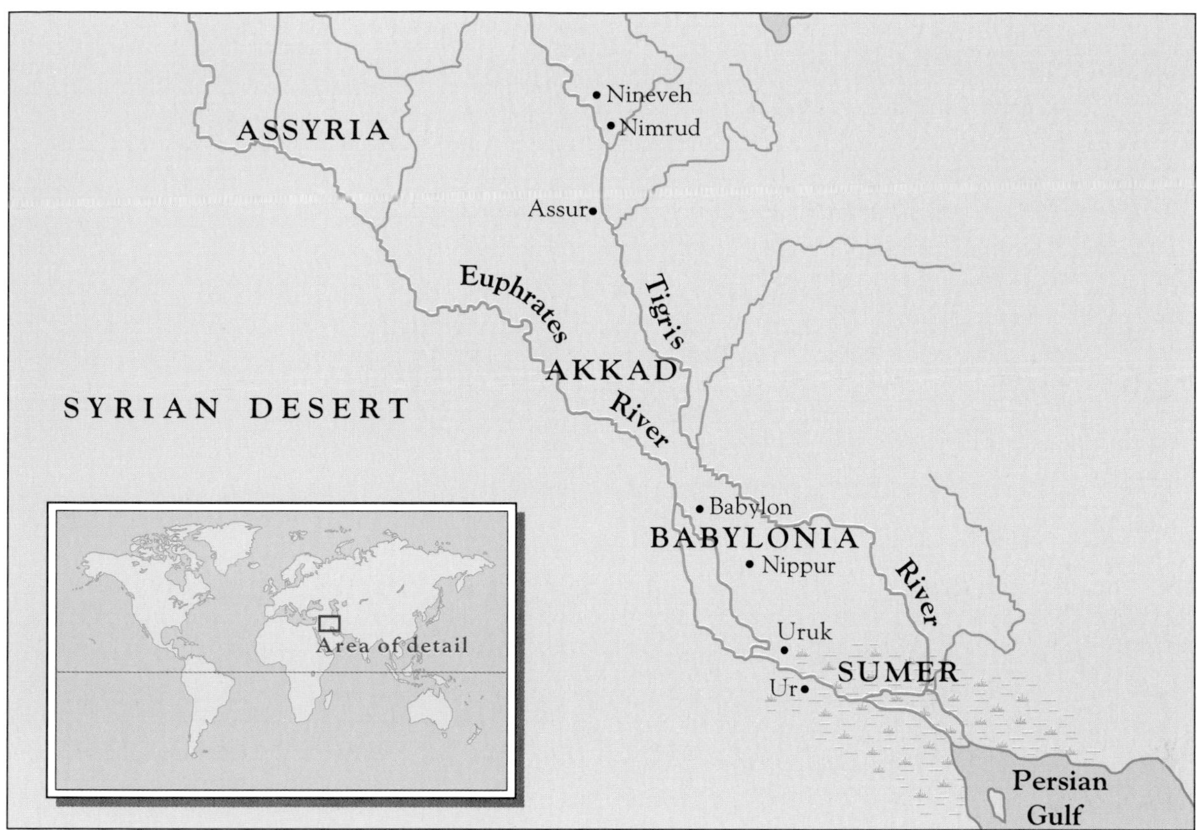

Cuneiform

Writing probably originated in Mesopotamia, with Egypt developing its own system around the same time or slightly later. About 3100 B.C., the people of Sumer (Sumerians) began using pictographs—pictures representing or expressing an idea—to list livestock and agricultural equipment, probably as a business record of some kind. Using a reed, they wrote on damp clay and then let the clay dry and harden. Eventually the pictographs developed into cuneiform writing, done with a wedge-shaped reed. The Sumerians used over 600 symbols to represent the syllables of their spoken language. Because each sign stood for a syllable and not a letter, their writing system is called a *syllabary*, rather than an *alphabet*.

The clay tablets that Mesopotamian scribes wrote on were baked to preserve them. This process was so successful that many tablets survive even to this day. Most of what we know about Mesopotamian civilization we've learned through the translations of these cuneiform tablets, about 1,000 of which deal with medicine. In fact, from the ancient Sumerian city of Nippur comes the world's oldest known medical text—a cuneiform tablet that lists over a dozen prescriptions. The tablets also recorded epic tales of heroes and myths about gods and goddesses, bookkeeping, political documents, letters to and from kings, codes of law, accounts of battles, tribute lists, proverbs, treaties, hymns, and prophecies.

Mesopotamian Religion

The Mesopotamian world was filled with supernatural beings. The people believed in many gods, goddesses, devils, demons,

Important Events in Mesopotamian History

ca. 3100 B.C.: Writing invented

ca. 2630–2600 B.C.: Earliest known Mesopotamian ruler

ca. 2400 B.C.: Ku-Baba, queen of Kish

2334–2279 B.C.: Reign of Sargon, leader of the Akkadians.

ca. 2000 B.C.: Oldest surviving medical text written. The biblical Abraham is born in the Sumerian city of Ur, located in southern Mesopotamia.

1792–1750 B.C.: Hammurabi's reign. He formulates a code of laws, bearing his name and ensuring his legacy—the Code of Hammurabi. Babylon (the Babel of the Hebrew Bible) becomes the head of an empire, a great trading center, as well as a center of knowledge, religion, and literature. The Epic of Gilgamesh, which contains a story of the Flood, and the Epic of Creation represent two of the many works of Babylonian literature. The Babylonians also practiced astronomy and astrology, establishing a network of observatories.

680–669 B.C.: Reign of Esarhaddon

668–627 B.C.: Assurbanipal rules Assyria and collects an extensive library at his palace in Nineveh, consisting of 30,000 cuneiform tablets. Eight hundred of these tablets contain material of medical nature and have supplied us with most of our knowledge of Mesopotamian medicine.

605–562 B.C.: Reign of Nebuchadrezzar II (aka Nebuchadnezzar). Kingdom of Judah defeated and many Jews are taken captive to Babylon. Hanging gardens of Babylon built—one of the seven wonders of the ancient world.

538–530 B.C.: Reign of Cyrus, the Persian king, who conquers Mesopotamia and makes it a small part of his vast empire.

The Ishtar Gate in Babylon, named for the goddess of love, was one of eight gates in the city. This massive 50-foot-high gate was decorated with bulls, the symbol of the lightning god, Adad, and dragons, the symbol of the chief god, Marduk.

and spirits. A major tenet of Mesopotamian religion held that humankind existed to serve the gods. The great temples in the Mesopotamian cities were enormous, complex structures each housing one particular god or goddess. Large staffs of priests and priestesses cared for the gods and performed numerous rituals, including feeding and clothing the image of the deity.

The people witnessed religious processions during festivals, but otherwise their religious practices did not involve the temples. Individuals had a personal god or goddess to whom they made sacrifices, offerings, prayers, and requests. The personal god interceded for the petitioner with the other gods and protected the person from the demons and evil spirits that inhabited the Mesopotamian world.

As is the case with many other ancient civilizations, health and religion went hand in hand in Mesopotamia. Demons, ghosts, or displeased deities were blamed for causing illnesses. A deity may be punishing the sick person because of offenses he or she committed or a demon may be carrying out the curse of the sick person's enemy. Pacifying the unhappy supernatural being or exorcizing the demon would bring relief.

Prayers and offerings were one way to appease the supernatural being causing the illness, if only the deity would listen. One poor sufferer wrote

> My affliction increases, right I cannot find. I implored my god, but he did not turn his countenance; I prayed to my goddess, but she did not raise her head.

Prayers to the gods for the punishment to stop often included confessions, such as, "My misdeeds are numerous, I have transgressed in every way," or "I have knowingly and unknowingly done wrong."

Divination—foretelling future events through signs in nature—represented another form of communication with the gods. Through divination, the diviner could predict the course of an illness and its outcome. Magic and sorcery of this type played an important role in Mesopotamian life, with spells and counterspells for just about everything, especially for healing.

The Doctors

There were several types of medical practitioners in ancient Mesopotamia, from magicians to priests to herbalists. Three types of healers, in particular, were held in high regard: the *asu*, the *ashipu*, and the *baru*. The asu were physicians and pharmacists, as well as members of the priesthood. The ashipu used magic and were also members of the clergy—exorcists, in a way. The baru were soothsayers whose main ability was the diagnosis of disease.

An Exorcist's Incantation Against Demons

Thou art not to come near to my body,
Thou art not to go before me,
Thou art not to follow after me,
Where I stop, thou art not to stop,
Where I am thou art not to sit,
My house thou art not to enter,
My roof thou art not to haunt,
Thou art not to put thy foot in my foot's imprint,
Where I go thou art not to go,
Where I enter thou art not to enter.

Rather than being rivals, though, these three types of medical practitioners sometimes worked together, perhaps with the understanding that illnesses take their toll on an individual both physically and spiritually. A sick man writes in an Assyrian letter, "Let him appoint one ashipu and one asu, and let them together perform their treatment on my behalf."

Sometimes the boundaries between the practitioners became blurred, since the asu occasionally used charms and the ashipu sometimes treated the sick with drugs. We even know of one man who was a deputy of the chief asu. Ten years later this man held the title of ashipu. Twenty-one years after that he was listed as an asu again.

THE ASHIPU Scholars have translated the word *ashipu* as magician, sorcerer, exorcist-priest, and conjurer. These men (women were apparently not allowed to be ashipu) dealt with the world of demons and ghosts, of whom there were many in the Mesopotamian belief system. (Over 6,000 demons have been classified.)

Copper statuette of the demon Pazuzu of the southeast wind, a diety of disease, from Tell Sheikh, Syria. It has the wings, feet, and claws of an eagle and a monster's head. Demons posed threats to health, lying in wait for people in mountains and plains, by rivers and roads, and on rooftops.

Ritual Duties. The ashipu had other duties besides healing, including ritually cleaning temples before religious ceremonies or working in the service of the king as an adviser. The ashipu performed all public acts of magic, overseeing the animals and other materials that were delivered to the palace for use in official rituals. Ashipu may also have visited the sick in their homes, counteracting omens or assisting in difficult times.

Ashipu presided over purification rituals designed to cleanse the patient who had contact with impure substances or people. One very elaborate royal ritual, known as House of Ablution, involved the Assyrian king and his ashipu going outside the city for several days, where the ritual would take place in a series of reed huts. The ritual was very detailed:

> The king enters the fifth hut, while the exorcist recites the prayer formula "Great Lord, Who in the Pure Heavens." The king says the incantation: "Shamash, Judge of Heaven and Earth." You [the exorcist] set up a figurine of the Curse Demon, pierce its heart with a dagger made of tamarisk wood. He [the king] rinses his mouth with water and beer, spits it over the figurine. Then you bury it at the base of the wall.

This and other purification rituals involved water, oil, and other cleansing substances, such as potash, using rational techniques apparently for magical purposes.

Learning and Training. Notes on some tablets mention that an exorcist was the scribe, the owner, or both of medical texts. The ashipu had to be familiar with many different texts: diagnostic omens, texts to quiet babies, magical texts about demons

The Tower of Babel (Babylon) was a seven-story ziggurat (staged tower), a link between heaven and earth. Its summit contained a shrine to the god Marduk, where he descended from the sky to meet his people. On holy days the king and priests sought the favor of the gods there.

and ghosts, and information about plants, minerals, and animal substances and their uses in treatment.

The young student of magic started out as a scribe or apprentice magician, then became an ashipu, and ultimately might make chief exorcist. Sometimes demotions or dismissals occurred. In the city of Uruk, the temple of Anu, the sky god, had seven ashipu. The profession of magician passed from one generation to the next, and at this temple, ashipu came from only three clans.

Omens

The following omens are from a collection from the Akkadian period called "If a City."

- If a man washes himself with water in the corridor of the house: he will become old.
- If he washes himself in the stairwell and lets the dirty water run out into the open: he will die within a year.
- If he washes his toes: he will dwindle away.
- If the washing water looks like beer: he will be well. If it looks like asphalt: he will not be well.

Many of the omens in this series required the careful observation of virtually all kinds of living creatures, such as the sexual behavior of humans and animals and encounters between humans and wild beasts.

The Ashipu Handbook. The ashipu excelled at diagnosis. He interpreted the patient's symptoms and discovered the cause of the illness. He may have taken the patient's pulse, but most of the diagnosis relied on information from the ashipu's handbook. The ashipu referred to the treatise of medical diagnoses and prognoses, comprising 3,000 entries on 40 tablets, divided into five sections—the largest collection of medical texts found so far. The title of this handbook comes from the opening line of the first chapter, "If the exorcist is going to the house of a patient," which was its title in antiquity. The form of each entry is done in the same manner. Starting with "if," the first clause describes the patient's appearance or behavior and the second gives the prognosis, often mentioning the god or demon causing the illness. For example, "If [the patient] grinds his teeth and his hands and feet shake, it is the hand of the god Sin; he will die." Similar statements and omens can be found in some ancient Egyptian texts (see "The Edwin Smith Papyrus," page 44).

The first two tablets in this collection, as the work's title implies, deal with what the ashipu might see on the way to the patient's house. "If the ashipu sees either a black dog or a black pig, that sick man will die. If he sees a white pig, that sick man will live."

The second section (12 tablets) lists the symptoms according to the body parts affected, starting with the skull and ending with the toes. The cause and the outcome are given. "If he is stricken by pain at the right side of his head: hand of Shamash—he will die."

The third section (10 tablets) lists the prognoses chronologically by the daily progress of the illness. The end of this section contains groups of symptoms indicating certain diseases. "If a man's body is yellow, his face is yellow, and his eyes are yellow, and the flesh is flabby, it is the yellow disease [jaundice]."

The fourth section consists of fragments of tablets mentioning treatments and describing certain syndromes. "If a man is stricken with a stroke of the face and his whole torso feels paralyzed, it is the work of the stroke; he will die."

The final section of six tablets seems to be about women's diseases, especially those stemming from pregnancy and malnutrition.

The ashipu's prognoses were not always black and white—"he will live" or "he will die." Sometimes more detailed information is given—"he will live a long time but will not recover" or "he will die in three days."

Gods and demons did not always directly cause disease. Occasionally the patient's behavior brought about his misfortune—"he has had intercourse repeatedly with a married woman," or "he had sexual relations with his mother." The ashipu sometimes correlated the disease with a divinity; the goddess of love and voluptuousness, Ishtar, whose cult involved sacred prostitution, was often considered the cause of venereal diseases—a not entirely baseless assumption.

An Ashipu Treatment

Instructions for the ashipu involved herbal and mineral remedies, rubbing the patient with oil, and reciting an incantation:

> If a man has been seized by a ghost and the ashipu is unable to get it to withdraw, you [the ashipu] crush together the following: [Unfortunately the list of plants is unidentifiable.*] You rub him with oil, you wrap up the herbal mixture in a piece of leather, and you put it around his neck. If "hand of a ghost" is persistent in a man's body and cannot be gotten rid of, to expel it, you take [various minerals] and carob seeds, you char them over coals, you pulverize them, you mix with cedar resin, and you recite the incantation seven times.

*Numerous plants and other drug names are found in the cuneiform tablets from ancient Mesopotamia, but unfortunately, many have yet to be translated. About 50 years ago, a scholar named R. Campbell Thompson undertook the effort of translating Assyrian botanical names based on similar names in modern Arabic or other regional tongues, but his work was just a start. In the decades to come, we can look forward to more scholarly endeavors to reveal more specific information about the substances used in Mesopotamian medicines.

The Methods of the Ashipu. The ashipu relied on incantations to heal. Hundreds of these texts survive, going back to the middle of the 3rd millennium B.C. The practitioner directed these spells against demons, appealed to Shamash, the sun god, or sometimes just spoke nonsense words, like our "abracadabra." The ashipu, or sometimes the patient, repeated the incantation either three or seven times.

The ashipu usually accompanied the incantation with some sort of action, the instructions for which followed the spell in the text. Often these actions involved setting up a brazier (pan of hot coals), preparing a censer (incense burner), or making offerings or pouring libations (drink offerings) to the divinity being addressed. The instructions usually conclude with directions to remove the equipment used in the ritual.

Besides incantations and rituals, the ashipu also used herbal remedies and some form of massage as well.

THE BARU Often another type of practitioner contributed to a patient's case. The baru, or soothsayer, helped determine the cause of an illness, and how long it would last and sometimes determined if the patient should be treated or not. The baru did not form part of the temple priesthood but worked directly for the king as a scholar-in-residence or served local governments or the army. The baru also worked with other practitioners, such as dream interpreters, conjurers, and exorcists, on difficult cases as the following example from one of the ancient sources shows.

This pottery incense burner comes from Tell Fray, Syria. It dates from the late Bronze Age, from the 13th century B.C. *Incense was used in religious rituals and for medicinal purposes.*

> The baru through divination did not discern the situation. Through incense offering the dream interpreter did not explain my right. . . . My omens have confounded the baru. The ashipu has not diagnosed the nature of my complaint, nor has the baru put a time limit on my illness.

Soothsaying, or divination, used a variety of signs from nature to predict the will of the gods or, in other words, what would happen in the future, since the gods shaped the destinies of humankind. The word *baru* means examiner, and these men minutely examined a variety of natural occurrences and used these signs to foretell the future.

A large category of literature from the Akkadian period is the omen collections. These handbooks provided the correct interpretation of signs, organized by topic. Thousands of these signs were collected into different series. One such series deals with the births of malformed humans and animals, and another discusses everyday events, such as the behavior of animals at the gates of a city or events occurring while building a house, performing agricultural tasks, or even washing oneself. Many of these omens predicted the health of an individual.

Liver Divination. Another form of divination also necessitated detailed examinations of nature; this type of foretelling used the internal organs of animals to acquire knowledge of the future. Unlike the omens mentioned above, the examination of animal organs belonged to a category of divination called "solicited omens," those that were actively sought out, rather than things that just happened to occur.

Clay liver models helped determine omens by comparison with a sheep's liver. The baru used models that divided up the organ into rectangular areas with information on each area locating important features. Archaeologists have discovered many such clay liver models throughout Mesopotamia. This one dates from the 18th century B.C.

Extispicy (also called hepatoscopy), or gathering omens from the appearance of a sheep's entrails, was the most common form of soliciting omens. The sheep used for this purpose had to be carefully selected and magically purified. The baru then asked the gods to "write" their messages on the entrails.

Usually the liver of the animal contained the information that the baru sought after the dissection of the body. To help determine the omen from the appearance of the liver, the baru used clay models of livers that divided up the organ into rectangular areas with information written on each area locating important features. Archaeologists have discovered many such clay liver models throughout Mesopotamia. Thirty models came from a site called Mari, along with cuneiform tablets telling how to interpret the signs. The baru's voluminous handbooks listed every possible deformity, mark, or discoloration of the liver, as well as the meaning of such abnormalities.

The interpretation of livers foretold a person's health, as in this example from the handbooks:

> If a fleshy tumor is found at the bottom of the *na* (an unidentified part of the liver), the patient will get worse and he will die. If the liver passage falls to the right, the patient will live. If the gall bladder is long, the king will live long. If the *processus pyramidalis* is shaped normally, he who makes the sacrifice of the sheep will be in good health and live long.

Since divination from livers cost the inquirer the price of an animal, the baru also used cheaper forms of foretelling the future. One method involved the interpretation of the pattern oil made when poured on water.

> When I let oil drop upon water, if the oil sinks and rises to the top again, it means misfortune for a sick man. If the oil forms a ring in the easterly direction, it means that a sick man will recover.

Another inexpensive way used the smoke issuing from a censer to make predictions.

Signs from the Sky. Astronomers or astrologers (they were considered the same thing) studied the heavens, noting celestial movements and weather phenomena, such as solstices, equinoxes, eclipses, thunder, rain, and hail. Predictions made from these observations related to the king, which the state, usually concerning politics or warfare, but sometimes they related to the health of important people.

Observatories throughout Mesopotamia sent regular reports to the king, which included a record of celestial happenings and divinatory interpretations of those events. Even very superstitious kings did not always listen to the omens. One diviner wrote to King Esarhaddon upbraiding him for his disbelief:

> This is what the text says about that eclipse that occurred in the month of Nisan: "If the planet Jupiter is present during an eclipse, it is good for the king because in his stead an important person at court will die," but the king closed his ears—and see, a full month has not yet elapsed and the chief justice is dead.

The Asu In a hymn of self-praise, Gula, the Mesopotamian goddess of healing—often called "Great Physician"—describes herself in her role as an asu, surely reflecting human physicians' activities:

I am a physician, I can heal, I carry around all healing herbs, I drive away disease, I gird myself with the leather bag containing health-giving incantations. I carry around texts which bring recovery, I give cures to mankind. My pure dressing alleviates the wound, my soft bandage relieves the sick.

The asu were probably the closest to what we think of as physicians. Their orientation toward remedies and drugs as therapy sounds more familiar to the modern ear than the magical cures of the ashipu and the predictions of the baru. The asu relied on the correct herbal remedies for cures, along with some incantations.

From the description of Gula, we can assume that the asu probably carried a collection of healing herbs, some incantations in a leather bag, and even some medical texts, as well as dressings and bandages. An ancient story describes a man who disguised himself as an asu by shaving his head and carrying a libation jar (used for pouring drink offerings to the gods) and a censer (a vessel for burning incense). If this was the disguise for an asu, then clearly, the asu used religious rituals as part of their healing practices and considered these spiritual measures as essential as the correct herbal prescription.

Becoming an Asu. Very little is known about the training of the asu. They were probably trained in cult centers—the vast temples to gods found in various cities. The city of Isin was famous as a cult center of the goddess Gula, and a training center for physicians may have been located there. No formal apprenticeship programs existed, and much knowledge was surely passed on orally. However, some hierarchy existed in the profession because we know that the title *physician-in-chief* was used. Some formal approval of training probably also existed because during the Assyrian period, court physicians had to take an oath of office. Asu were usually men, but there is evidence that some female physicians practiced medicine as well.

The medicine practiced by the asu almost certainly arose from a folk tradition of herbal healing. We read in a letter how one young physician gained knowledge of an herbal remedy:

The plants that your physician sent me are excellent. If there is a simmum illness [possibly malaria], that plant cures it immediately. I have just sent Shamshi-Addutukulti, the young physician, to you so that he can examine the plant. Send him back to me.

Private Matters—Saziga Spells

Private individuals also attempted to influence personal health matters. Saziga, or potency rituals, helped those suffering from impotence. Erotic incantations, recited sometimes by the man in question, sometimes by the woman, helped create a certain atmosphere.

Along with incantations, people used herbal remedies, but unique to the saziga texts were prescriptions calling for items, sometimes sex organs, derived from sexually aroused or copulating birds or animals:

If a man loses his potency, you dry and crush a male bat that is ready to mate; you put it into water which has sat out on the roof; you give it to him to drink; that man will then recover potency.

The ashipu may have been involved in administering these prescriptions or it may have been a private matter. Other cures for impotence required the male and female genitals to be rubbed with special oils, occasionally with magnetic iron ore.

Obviously, the asu were willing to learn from their peers and share their knowledge.

An Ancient Prescription

If a man's tongue is swollen so that it fills his mouth, you dry tamarisk leaves, leaves of the *adaru* plant, leaves of the fox grape, and dog's tongue plant; you chop them up finely and sift; you knead them with juice of the *kasu* plant; you rub the top of his tongue with butter; you put the medication on his tongue, and he will get well.

The Asu's Pharmacy. Most Mesopotamian medical treatments consisted of herbal remedies. The medical texts prescribe a large variety of plant products, usually specifying the part to be used—leaves, flowers, seeds, roots—prepared in a number of ways—crushed, cooked, dried, and so on. Pine, fir, and cedar resins were common ingredients. The asu mixed the plant matter with some type of liquid—water, beer, wine, or milk. Often some form of mineral was added as well. Healers used animal parts and even dung in their cures, too. Occasionally prescriptions warned the asu about the toxicity of certain ingredients.

A letter from a physician to a high official shows the importance of obtaining exactly the right herb for a prescription. The doctor writes

> When I assigned a poultice for him, no asu herb was available. And my lord knows that if only a single herb is missing, it will not succeed. I asked the mayor to send word to a gardener. . . . I gave her [a female patient] a potion for constipation to drink. . . but there is no *sarmadu* herb and drawn wine available. Let my lord send some. . . . As to the herbs of which I spoke to my lord, let my lord not forget about them.

Handbooks for the Asu. In about 500 B.C., the asu Nabu-le'u wrote a document that gives us some insight into the medical practice of the asu and how they used their medical texts. The work is divided into three columns. The first column lists over 150 plants, indicating what part of the plant to use and stating any necessary precautions. The second column lists the diseases cured by these plants, and the third column gives details of how the medicine is to be taken—how often, the time of day, and if the patient should fast or not. Scholars call this type of medical text therapeutic because it gives prescriptions for treatment, unlike the diagnostic texts used by the ashipu, which give a diagnosis and prognosis, but no treatment. Some-

This Assyrian priest holds a plant offering, which may represent poppies, the source of opium. Enormous temple complexes had large staffs of priests to perform various rites and rituals, including the care and feeding of the gods. The temple staff consumed food and drink offerings made to the gods.

Hammurabi, king of Babylon, (1792–1750 B.C.), created a code of laws. The 282 laws are engraved on an eight-foot-high block of stone, found in Susa. Some laws mention the asu, what he should be paid, and how he should be punished if he causes injury or death.

times therapeutic texts give a prognosis as well.

The Mesopotamian pharmacopoeia, reconstructed from the tablets of Assurbanipal's library, lists 250 vegetable substances and 150 minerals. Translations are not always certain, but some of the material with known medicinal value may include aloe, anise, belladonna, cannabis, cardamom, castor oil, cinnamon, colocynth, coriander, garlic, henbane, licorice, mandragora, mint, and pomegranate. Other substances used in healing include fats and oils, animal parts, honey, and wax.

The Code of Hammurabi

Hammurabi, king of Babylon from 1792 to 1750 B.C., created a code of laws that now

Medical Laws in the Code of Hammurabi

Law 215: If a physician performed a major operation on a nobleman with a bronze lancet and has saved the nobleman's life, or he opened the eye socket of a nobleman with a bronze lancet and has saved the nobleman's eye, he shall receive ten shekels of silver.

Law 216: If it was a commoner, he shall receive five shekels.

Law 217: If it was a nobleman's slave, the owner of the slave shall give two shekels of silver to the physician.

Law 218: If a physician performed a major operation on a nobleman. . . and has caused the nobleman's death, or he opened the eye socket of a nobleman and has destroyed the nobleman's eye, they shall cut off his hand.

Law 219: If a physician performed a major operation on a commoner's slave. . . and caused his death, he shall make good, slave for slave.

Law 220: If he opened up his eye socket with a bronze lancet and has destroyed the eye, he shall pay one half his value in silver.

Law 221: If a physician has set a nobleman's broken bone or has healed a sprained tendon, the patient shall give five shekels of silver to the physician.

Law 222: If it was a commoner, he shall receive three shekels.

Law 223: If it was a nobleman's slave, the owner of the slave shall give two shekels of silver to the physician.

Law 224: If a physician of an ox or an ass performed a major operation on either an ox or an ass and has saved its life, the owner shall give one-sixth shekel of silver as his fee.

Law 225: If he performed a major operation on an ox or an ass and has caused its death, he shall give to the owner of the ox or ass one-fourth its value.

bears his name. The 282 laws of this code are engraved on an eight-foot-high block of polished black stone, which can be seen in the Louvre Museum in Paris. Several of these laws mention the asu and what he should be paid for certain procedures and how he should be punished if he causes injury or death to a patient (see "Medical Laws in the Code of Hammurabi," page 23).

The Oldest Medical Text

The earliest mention of medicine in the world comes from the southern Mesopotamian area of Sumer. This document, written on a small clay tablet by an unknown Sumerian physician in about 2000 B.C. in the city of Nippur, reveals how physicians treated wounds. The "three healing gestures" used by doctors were: washing (not mentioned in Egyptian medicine), making plasters, and bandaging.

The tablet lists 15 prescriptions using a number of raw materials (see "The Medicine Chest"). Twelve of these medicines were salves and filtrates for external use, and eight were for plasters. One prescription for a plaster called for the physician to pound wine dregs, juniper, and prunes together. Beer would be added to this mixture to form the plaster, which would then be applied to the diseased part of the body.

The other medicines were liquids to be drunk, often dissolved in beer. One such prescription for internal use reads

> Crush to powder the seeds of the carpenter's herb, the gummy resin of the *markazi* plant, and thyme; dissolve in beer and give to the man to drink.

Another prescription reads

> Pass through a sieve and then knead together: turtle shell, *naga-si* plant, salt, and mustard. Then wash the diseased part with beer of good quality and hot water, and rub with the mixture. Then friction and rub again with oil, and put on a plaster of pounded pine.

Note that the physician washed the problem area before applying the mixture.

This little tablet also provides us with evidence for rather elaborate chemical procedures performed at this time. Saltpeter (potassium nitrate), a transparent, white crystalline compound, is mentioned. The physician probably got his saltpeter, used to draw torn tissue together, by crystallizing waste products from the canals. Alkalies, obtained by reducing a plant to ashes, were used to make plant extracts. The raw materials were boiled with salt and alkali and the solution was filtered.

The most amazing quality of this 4,000-year-old medical tablet is that, unlike later

The Medicine Chest

The following are some of the raw materials listed in the world's oldest medical text, originating in Nippur (ca. 2000 B.C.). The translations of plant names are not all reliable but are based on the educated guesses of scholars.

milk	thyme	date palm
snakeskin	willow	oil
turtle shell	juniper	beer
cassia	pear	salt
myrrh	prunes	saltpeter
myrtle	fir	alkalies
asafetida	fig	mustard

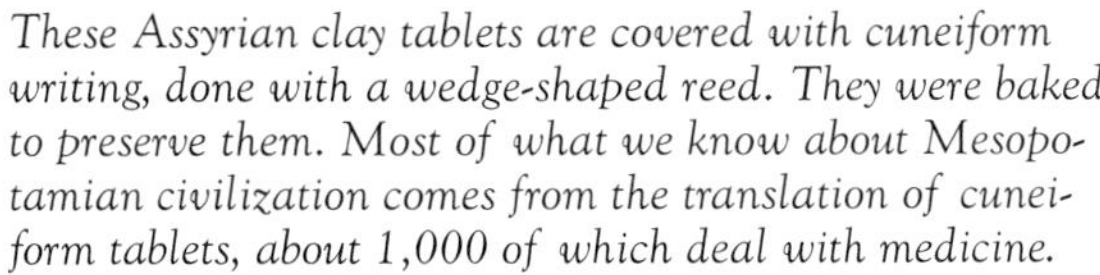

These Assyrian clay tablets are covered with cuneiform writing, done with a wedge-shaped reed. They were baked to preserve them. Most of what we know about Mesopotamian civilization comes from the translation of cuneiform tablets, about 1,000 of which deal with medicine.

texts, nowhere is magic, demons, or sorcery mentioned. Medicine seems to have existed independently of sorcery, even at this early date. In later periods, the ashipu, or sorcerers, appear to have superseded the asu, or physicians, since the asu are not mentioned in later tablets. Although this may reflect the triumph of magic over medicine, it's often difficult to know whether the lack of written evidence means the asu disappeared or whether they stopped writing things down; perhaps the asu stopped recording their "secrets" simply because they didn't want their competitors to get their hands on them.

A Vast Variety of Conditions

What sort of illnesses and conditions did these medical practitioners attempt to cure or treat? In the tablets we read of migraines, insomnia, anorexia, impotence, anxiety, speech impediments, respiratory problems, liver disease, gastric troubles, enteritis, colic, diarrhea, intestinal blockages, dysentery, gout, jaundice, tuberculosis, pneumonia, bronchitis, hemorrhoids, stroke, gynecologic problems (including birth control), venereal infection, and mental illness.

CAUSES Although the Mesopotamians believed that most illness came from supernatural powers, healers ascribed some conditions to natural causes such as cold weather, dryness, dust, putrescence, and malnutrition. They also understood the concept of contagion. Letters from the early 2nd millennium B.C. speak of trying to control the spread of contagious illness by moving whole villages to higher ground.

COMMON DISEASES Eye diseases occurred frequently in ancient Mesopotamia. The medical texts mention them often. Xerophthalmia, an eye disease that causes blindness in children, may have been widespread. This disease results from a lack of vitamin A. Physicians also treated ear problems, such as earaches, ringing in the ears, and hearing loss with pomegranate juice.

A Note of Caution

A letter from Zimri-Lim, the king of Mari (1782–1759 B.C.), to his wife, warning her to limit contact between a sick woman and the other women of the palace reveals some knowledge of contagion:

> I have heard that the woman Nanna is ill with simmum disease, but she has nevertheless been in contact a great deal with the palace servant women and that she has infected many of the women around her. Give strict orders that no one drink from a cup she drinks from, that no one sit on a chair she sits on, and that no one sleep in a bed she sleeps in so that she does not infect any more of the many women around her. That simmum disease is easily caught!

Toothaches, loose teeth, and teeth falling out troubled many Mesopotamians. Healers treated dental problems with incantations and a mixture of beer, malt, and oil. One text gives instructions for driving a pin into the tooth. King Esarhaddon's physician recommended the following:

> The burning of his [the king's] head, his hands, his feet wherewith he burns is because of his teeth. His teeth should be drawn, his residence should be sprinkled. He has been brought low. Now he will be well exceedingly.

Connecting fever with the teeth makes sound medical sense because in certain febrile conditions, a hidden place of infection may be the cause, and today's physicians look carefully at the teeth in such cases.

Healers treated gastrointestinal problems, such as passing blood, rectal stricture, constipation, and flatulence, with suppositories and enemas. They may also have understood that the gallbladder could be involved in jaundice.

An Assyrian tablet mentions thick or cloudy urine, a sign of gonorrhea. Incontinence and gonorrhea were treated by introducing medicine through a bronze tube, a catheter, into the urethra. Many people had skin problems and these were treated with vegetable oils and animal fat applied to the skin.

INJURIES Mesopotamian society seems rather dangerous when looked at through their laws. The code of Hammurabi refers to rape, kidnapping, destroying the eye of another, breaking another's bone, knocking out a tooth, striking a cheek, manslaughter, and being gored by an ox. A

This relief in glazed brick comes from the palace of Darius I at Susa (ca. 490 B.C.). It shows a frieze of warriors, members of the Persian royal guard. The constant warfare in the Near East meant plentiful work for physicians.

man "sick with a blow on the cheek" would receive the following treatment:

> Pound together fir-turpentine, pine-turpentine, tamarisk, daisy, flour of *Inninnu*. Strain; mix in milk and beer in a small copper pan; spread on skin, bind on him, and he shall recover.

Physicians treated hemorrhaging from the nose with dressings, although it seems some asu did not understand the correct use of the dressing. A letter from Arad-Nana, the chief physician, to King Esarhaddon laments that the dressings that he prescribed for a patient were applied incorrectly.

> The Rab-Mugi reported to me: "Yesterday... much blood ran." That is

because the dressings that I had prescribed are applied without knowledge. They are placed over the nostrils, so they only obstruct the breathing, but come off when there is hemorrhage. They should be placed within the nostril; then they will stop the breath and hold back the blood. If it is agreeable to the king, I will go tomorrow and give instructions.

War wounds and other sorts of injuries would, of course, require the services of healers. The king of Mari received a letter from a remote military outpost begging him to send a physician because "if a sling-stone wounds a man, there is not a single physician."

PREGNANCY AND CHILDBIRTH Midwives, called *sabsutu*, and female relatives assisted women in childbirth. Women giving birth used a birth stool; archaeologists have discovered clay models of them. Physicians often treated women for complications after the birth.

Many medical prescriptions existed for helping infertile women conceive and for easing the pain of labor and birth. One text gives a prescription for causing spontaneous abortion; eight ingredients are to be mixed in wine and drunk on an empty stomach.

On the other hand, an Assyrian law called for the death of someone who willfully self-aborted. If a woman had a miscarriage caused by a blow, the guilty party had to pay ten shekels for the loss of the child. The crime was not, however, willful miscarriage or abortion; it was the denying a man the right to sire a child within the marriage bonds that was the crime. If the woman herself died, the person who struck the blow would be put to death.

VETERINARY MEDICINE Veterinarians in ancient Mesopotamia cared for oxen, asses, cattle, and horses. The preparation of cures for animals seems quite similar to that used for humans. To treat illness in horses, one text reads

> These are eight ingredients for equine colic; you mix them with pressed wine; you pour it into his left nostril and he will recover.

DIET Animals served as food for the gods and the wealthy, but most of the population could not afford red meat. Fish and poultry were luxury items for most people. Barley bread and coarse barley meal cooked to form gruel served as the main source of carbohydrates. Sweets were made of flour, oil, date syrup, and lard. Onions, garlic, leeks, turnips, cucumbers, peas, beans, lettuce, and radishes were some of the available vegetables. Seeds such as cress, mustard, cumin, and coriander seasoned food. Pomegranates, figs, grapes, plums, apples, and apricots were part of the diet, too. Beverages consisted of many types of beer, date wine, grape wine, and of course water. Milk spoiled easily, but yogurt and cheese could be kept safely. This fairly limited diet may have con-

Early agricultural people used stone querns and pestles for grinding grain into flour. This example dates from 6000 to 5000 B.C., the time when agriculture and irrigation began in Mesopotamia. Barley and emmer wheat were the first crops cultivated there.

tributed to malnutrition in the poor (especially in women and children), and xerophthalmia, caused by a lack of vitamin A, may have been widespread in ancient Mesopotamia.

Mesopotamian Surgery

As the Code of Hammurabi suggests, physicians were not limited to spells, external treatments, and herbs. Surgery was an option in some cases.

Unfortunately, the medical texts tell us very little about surgery. The clay tablets mention the "bronze knife" only four times. Perhaps the asu learned this skill through observation, rather than by reading about it. The asu probably used his lancet for simple procedures, such as lancing boils, bloodletting, and perhaps cataract surgery. Tantalizing fragments of text describe cutting into the chest and scraping the skull to remove an abscess under the scalp. Even in ancient times, major surgery cost quite a bit. Ten shekels of silver—a not uncommon price—would have paid a carpenter's wages for 450 days!

An Abscess of the Scalp

The following is a description of a surgical procedure that was presumably used to treat an abscess or a cyst of some kind:

> If a man, his skull contains some fluid, with your thumb press several times at the place where the fluid is found. If the swelling gives way, and pus is squeezed out of the skull, you shall incise, scrape the bone and remove its fluid. If, when you press, the swelling does not give way, you will make all around his head an application of hot stones.

The asu must have known that the application of heat would speed up the formation of an abscess by increasing the blood flow to the area.

Some evidence for trephination exists. This procedure involved sawing a square or round hole in the patient's skull to drain fluids and relieve pressure on the brain. Although texts do not mention the practice, trephined skulls have been found; one dating from 5000 B.C. comes from Arpachiya, four miles north of Nineveh.

After surgery on a scalp, the physician practiced a form of postoperative care. The medical text directs him to

> Wash a fine linen in water, soak it in oil, and put it on the wound. Crush powder of acacia and ammonia salt, and put it on the wound; let the dressing stand for three days. When you remove it, wash a fine linen in water, soak it in oil, put it on the wound, and knot a bandage over it. Leave the dressing three more days. Thus continue the dressing until healing ensues.

Veterinary surgery probably included castration, and human medicine may have too; castration was used as a punishment and many court employees were eunuchs.

The Happy, Healthy Life

Adad-guppi, the mother of King Nabonidus of Babylon, wrote an account of the end of her life, illustrating what health and happiness meant to this Mesopotamian queen mother.

> The moon god added many days and years of happiness to my life and kept me alive...104 happy years....My eyesight was good to the end, my hearing excellent, my hands and feet were sound, my words well chosen, food and drink agreed with me, my health was fine, and my mind happy. I saw my great-great grandchildren, up to the fourth generation, in good health and thus had my fill of old age.

Egyptian Medicine

FOR MANY AMERICANS, ancient Egypt means the pyramids, King Tut, and Yul Brynner as the Pharaoh in *The Ten Commandments.* As one of the world's greatest civilizations, it often takes a backseat to Greece and Rome in American classrooms. However, ancient Egypt was a civilization of enormous accomplishments in art, architecture, and especially the sciences—including medicine.

Around 440 B.C., the ancient Greek historian Herodotus wrote, "For the Nile is a great river and does, in fact, work great changes." These great changes made the civilization of ancient Egypt possible. Without the Nile, Egypt would be a desert.

The source of the Nile—a mystery until only about 140 years ago—lies in the highlands of east central Africa at Lake Victoria, where the White Nile begins. For almost three and a half thousand miles, the river flows north as the land's elevation declines. Several smaller rivers flow into the White Nile. At Khartoum, in present-day Sudan, the Blue Nile and the White Nile meet, and north of there, the Atbara River contributes to the Egyptian Nile. At Cairo, the river fans out into many branches, which empty into the Mediterranean Sea. This fan-shaped area, called the Delta, and the narrow Nile Valley below it, constituted ancient Egypt.

This 15th century B.C. funerary stela stood in the tomb chapel of the deceased. It lists his titles and names. The wedjat, or sound eyes of Horus, at the top became quite popular as a protective amulet.

Ancient Egyptian Time Periods

Predynastic Period: 4500–3150 B.C.

Early Dynastic Period: 3150–2700 B.C.

Old Kingdom: 2700–2200 B.C.
- King Djoser, with the help of architect Imhotep, builds the first great stone pyramid, the Step Pyramid.

1st Intermediate Period: 2200–2040 B.C.

Middle Kingdom: 2040–1674 B.C.
- Arts and crafts, literature, and intellectual achievements flourish. The first two Egyptian medical texts are written.

2nd Intermediate Period: 1674–1553 B.C.

New Kingdom: 1552–1069 B.C.
- Tutcankhaten (also known as Tutankhamen, or "King Tut") rules Egypt from 1361 to 1352 B.C. His treasure-filled tomb would be discovered in A.D. 1922.
- Ramesses II begins the second longest reign as an Egyptian king, 1304–1237 B.C. He may have been the biblical pharaoh that enslaved the Hebrews.

3rd Intermediate Period: 1069–702 B.C.
- Shoshenq, the biblical "Shishak," attacks the city of Jerusalem and plunders Solomon's temple.

Late Period: 747–525 B.C.

Persian Period: 525–332 B.C.

Ptolemaic Period: 332–30 B.C.
- Alexander the Great conquers Egypt in 332 B.C. and establishes the city of Alexandria, which becomes a center of learning.
- Greek becomes the official language around 280 B.C.
- Ptolemy II builds the great library of Alexandria and the Pharos Lighthouse, one of the seven wonders of the ancient world.
- The Ptolemaic dynasty ends with the death of Cleopatra in 30 B.C.

Roman Period: 30 B.C.–A.D. 395

Life in the Fertile Desert

Every year winter rainstorms struck the Ethiopian plateau, causing the Blue Nile and Atbara River to rise. These tributaries dumped their swollen floodwaters and rich topsoil into the Nile. The Nile then rose and deposited the water and fertile soil along its banks. Every June the water began to rise. It would reach its high point in the late summer, remaining at that level for two weeks, and then it would slowly recede, until reaching its low point in late May.

AGRICULTURE The Egyptian year consisted of three seasons: flooding, seed, and harvest. When the flood subsided and left the land soaked and fertile, workers cleared the irrigation canals and resurveyed the fields. Before the ground could dry out and harden, farmers planted their crops, mostly emmer wheat, barley, and flax. They harvested crops in the spring and allowed the land to lie fallow for two months before the cycle began again with the flooding.

Wall painting from the Valley of the Kings, Thebes, Egypt. The god Osiris holds the crook and the flail. God of vegetation, judge of the underworld, and king of the dead, his skin is usually depicted as green, the color of vegetation.

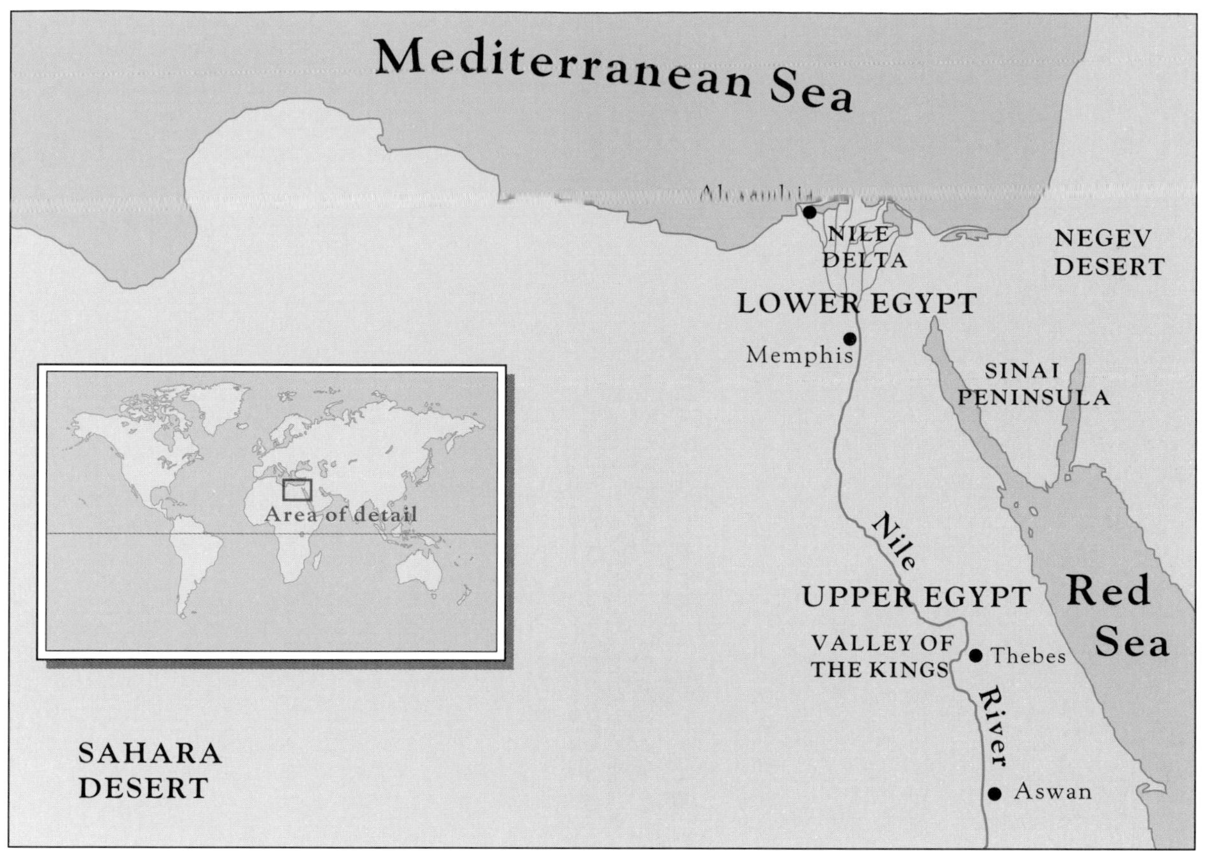

The Egyptians produced two other important agricultural products besides grain—oil and wine. The fruit of the moringa, or horseradish tree, furnished oil. Wine came from dates and grapes. Gardens provided beans, lentils, chickpeas, radishes, lettuce, onions, leeks, garlic, melons, dates, figs, flowers, and herbs. Dill, fenugreek, chervil, parsley, thyme, coriander, cumin, fennel, marjoram, and possibly mint were native to Egypt and would have been cultivated or gathered wild. Also the practice of beekeeping began very early in Egypt's history.

The Egyptians raised cattle, sheep, and poultry for food and sacrifices. From the Nile they received waterfowl, fish, papyrus for making writing material, and mud for brick-making. From the deserts they mined gold, copper, malachite, tin, lead, galena, gypsum, alum, and natron. The Egyptians needed these minerals for metalworking, mummification, beauty products, and medicines.

GROWTH OF A CIVILIZATION This fertile land and abundance of natural resources made possible all the accomplishments of ancient Egypt—art, architecture, and literature. The bounty of the harvest and the river meant that not everyone had to seek out food, and the division of labor allowed people to become priests, scribes, artisans, midwives, magicians, musicians, weavers, brewers, and doctors.

Religion and Health

The ancient Egyptians believed that each person was a product of different spiritual elements. Each person has a *ba* and a *ka*. *Ba* (often translated as "soul") vivifies the person but departs when the body dies; the *ba* is immortal. A person's *ka* is the element that fixes the person as an individual

Discovered in 1799, the Rosetta Stone provided the key to deciphering the ancient Egyptian language. This trilingual stone contains the same material in Greek, demotic, and hieroglyphics, enabling scholars to translate the meaning of the previously mysterious symbols, based on the accompanying Greek translation.

Egyptian Writing

The Egyptians used a form of writing called *hieroglyphs* (from the Greek words *hieros,* meaning sacred, and *glyphein,* meaning to carve). It is a complex system that was not deciphered until the early 1800s when archeologists discovered the Rosetta Stone, which had a passage in hieroglyphics and a Greek translation of the passage.

This writing has more than 700 signs with two main categories: sense signs and sound signs. A sense sign is a picture of a word. For example, a picture of a snake means "snake." But this same picture, used as a sound sign, signifies the sound "dj." The sound signs represent only consonants; the Egyptians did not use vowels in writing. Because of this, we do not really know how to pronounce their language.

instance of their *ba*—a living, breathing animal. When the double spirits—the animal *ka* and the spiritual *ba*—live together in harmony, the individual lives a healthy and rewarding life.

Because both aspects of the person need nurturing, Egyptian medicine integrated physical and nonphysical aspects in its techniques. Prayer, medicine, and magic together played equally important roles in healing the whole person.

The Egyptians worshiped a great number of gods and goddesses. Many deities could assist those in need of medical care. People called upon specific benign deities to prevent or cure diseases and wild animal attacks. They directed incantations to disease-causing malign demons or deities, telling them to leave the body.

Some Egyptian temples were associated with healing and health care. One example is the temple of Hathor at Dendera where the buildings could be called infirmaries or sanatoria. Here the sick were cared for through baths, regimens, and special diets, as well as religious prayers. The temple of Thoueris is where priestesses acted as midwives for gynecologic and obstetric care.

HEALING DEITIES Isis, one of the most important Egyptian divinities, had special powers to ward off evil and to undo the harm caused by malevolent forces. Isis's healing powers stem from the incredible feats she performed in Egyptian mythology, such as reconstructing her husband's chopped-up body and bringing him back to life. Isis showed great sympathy to even the lowliest members of society, and of all the numerous Egyptian divinities, people thought of her as the one most able to understand human suffering.

The son of Isis, Horus, whose eye was torn out (see "The Myth of Isis and Osiris"), also had a role in the healing. He played a dual role as victim and savior. Those requesting medical help identified themselves with the injured Horus whose wound was healed. But Horus himself was also called upon to use his powers to heal. Some of his titles were "the good doctor" and "the savior."

This Ptolemaic statue portrays the goddess Isis nursing Horus. Isis, wife of Osiris, and a very important divinity, could ward off evil. Her healing powers stem from the incredible feats she performed. Isis showed great sympathy to even the lowliest members of society.

Another deity people turned to for healing was Hathor, a sky goddess and the goddess of love, marriage, and motherhood. She was shown in art as a woman when relating to her role as sexual partner or as a cow when in her role as nurturing mother. Sometimes as a cow, she is portrayed with the Pharaoh suckling at her udder. Women giving birth prayed to her. In the Myth of Isis and Osiris, Hathor and the scorpion goddess Serqet attended Isis at the birth of Horus and helped nourish and protect him. Serqet also helped at the birth of kings and gods and protected embalmed bodies; she was a goddess of fertility and the afterlife.

The Egyptians tried to neutralize dangerous forces, such as poisonous scorpions, with kindness. If the goddess who controlled poison was treated well and given a great deal of respect, she could be convinced to use her power against scorpion bites. Some healers held the title "one who has power over the scorpion goddess." They tried to prevent and cure all sorts of stings and bites by persuading gods such as Serqet.

The lioness goddess, Sekhmet, represented the forces of war and destruction, bringing misfortune, often in the form of infectious diseases. The Slaughterers of Sekhmet, dangerous demon messengers, brought

The Myth of Isis and Osiris

The earth god and the sky goddess had four children—Osiris, Isis, Seth, and Nephthys—creating the archetypal dysfunctional family. Jealous of his brother, Seth attacked and chopped up Osiris, throwing his body parts into the Nile. Isis, who had married her brother Osiris and who had a reputation for great cleverness, tirelessly searched for all her brother/husband's parts. Using her vast magical skills, she reassembled the body. In the form of a hawk, she flapped her wings, blowing the breath of life back into Osiris. He revived long enough to impregnate Isis, but then died permanently, becoming the ruler of the underworld.

Isis, prototype of the single mother, raised her son, Horus, with such nurturing compassion that she became the perfect divinity to ask for cure and protection. Isis is usually represented in Egyptian art with the infant Horus nursing at her breast.

As an adult, Horus vowed revenge against his evil uncle, Seth. During a fight, Horus damaged Seth's testicles and Seth tore out Horus's left eye. The god Thoth later restored the eye, which became known as the *wedjat*, or sound eye. The image of the *wedjat* eye became popular as a protective amulet.

This statue of Sekhmet comes from Medinet Habu, Egypt. The lioness goddess, Sekhmet, whose name means power, symbolized might, terror, war, and destruction. Because she brought pestilence and famine, the need to appease Sekhmet gave her and her priests an important role in healing.

flood, famine, and disease. Priests of Sekhmet, who specialized in medicine, tried to please this fearsome goddess with elaborate rituals to ward off plagues and pestilence.

The goddess Thoueris helped women in childbirth. She had the head of a hippopotamus, the arms and legs of a lion, a crocodile's tail, pendulous human breasts, and a prominent (pregnant) belly. Amulets often contained her image. Thoueris's appearance illustrates how the Egyptians combined all the dangerous and protective powers of a divinity in one image.

Thoth, the god of scribes, played a central role in Egyptian medicine and magic. He is portrayed as a baboon or ibis. When a scorpion stung Horus, Isis caused such a disruption to the universe that Thoth cured Horus with a spell. Only Thoth, Isis, and Horus are called "doctor."

Thoth, the god of scribes, played a central role in Egyptian medicine and magic. He had special abilities in writing and reciting and was often called upon in healing incantations. In art, he appears as a baboon or an ibis (a long-legged, heron-like bird). In addition to the time that he restored Horus's eye, he is in the position of healer elsewhere in mythology: When a scorpion stung Horus, Isis made the sun stand still and caused such a disruption to the universe that Thoth went to help this mother in distress. He cured Horus with a spell. Of all the divinities, only Thoth, Isis, and Horus are called *swnw*, or doctor.

The Healers: Swnw, Priests, and Magicians

SWNW The word *swnw* (probably pronounced SUNU or SINU) means "doctor" or "physician" in ancient Egyptian. The *swnw* did not attend medical schools but trained with family members or as apprentices to masters. Their textbooks were the medical papyri (the plural of papyrus, the sort of paper made from the tall aquatic papyrus plant).

Some doctors may have owned their own texts, but since they were expensive, most physicians probably consulted the rolls in the House of Life. This institution, which was attached to various temples, served as a repository of papyri on a variety of subjects, including medical texts and works on purification, rituals, astronomy, and interpretation of dreams. Scribes read, copied, and perhaps composed the books kept there. The House of Life served as a library, scriptorium, and university. Physicians in training learned the art of the scribe in the House of Life, enabling them to read the medical texts kept there.

Physicians had a hierarchy with titles such as *administrator, overseer, inspector*, or *chief of doctors*. Royalty had personal physicians; during the Old Kingdom, almost half the doctors and dentists in Egypt were connected to the palace. Peseshet, a female doctor from the Old Kingdom, held the title of "female overseer of the female doctors." The only other known female physician was Tawe, from the Ptolemaic Period (332–30 B.C.).

We know almost nothing about individual doctors, where and how they practiced, or what they charged. The medical papyri tell us that the *swnw* examined his or her patient by feeling the abdomen or wound, as appropriate to the problem. The most important means of evaluation came from taking the pulses of the wrist, foot, stomach, groin, head, and neck. According to one papyrus, doctors examining wounds would pronounce one of three prognoses: An ailment which I will treat; an ailment with which I will contend; an ailment not to be treated.

PRIESTS Hery-shef-nakht, a physician from the Middle Kingdom, exemplifies how medicine, religion, and magic all formed an integral part of healing. He held the titles of chief of the king's physicians, priest of Sekhmet, and overseer of magicians. His duties included reading the papyrus rolls daily and examining and healing the sick.

The priests of the goddess Sekhmet played a role parallel, but possibly slightly inferior, to the *swnw*. Sekhmet, whose name means "power," symbolized might and terror. She brought pestilence and famine.

The Medical Papyri

Scribes wrote Egyptian medical texts on papyrus, a type of paper made from an aquatic plant. These rolls served as reference works for physicians. The papyri are named either for their original modern owner, the current location of the work, or the place where they were found.

Papyrus	Date*	Subject
Kahun	1820 B.C.	gynecology, veterinary
Ramesseum	1700 B.C.	gynecology, ophthalmology, pediatrics
Edwin Smith	1550 B.C.	surgery
Ebers	1500 B.C.	general medical
Hearst	1450 B.C.	general medical
Chester Beatty	1200 B.C.	rectal diseases
Berlin	1200 B.C.	general medical
Brooklyn	300 B.C.	snakebites

***Dates reflect the appoximate time each papyrus was written. In almost every case, the information probably came from papyri that were, in fact, much older but never found.**

The scorpion goddess, Serqet, assisted the birth of kings and gods and guarded embalmed bodies; she was a goddess of fertility and the afterlife. Serqet protected against scorpion bites. Her priests accompanied mining expeditions into the Sinai because of the great danger of scorpion bites there.

Copy of a wall painting from the tomb of Ankhmahor, a vizier from the 6th dynasty (ca. 2330 B.C.) at Saqqara. The hieroglyphs read "Don't hurt me," and "I shall act so you praise me." Sometimes called manicure *and* pedicure, *the conversation suggests physiotherapy or reflexology is being done.*

The need to appease Sekhmet gave her and her priests an important role in healing. The priests of Sekhmet may also have been veterinarians. *Sunw* and the Sekhmet priests did not compete against each other. In fact, some priests of Sekhmet also held medical titles, such as *Wenen-Nefer*, priest of Sekhmet, and medical inspector.

The priests of the scorpion goddess, Serqet, had a special role in treating the bites and stings of poisonous reptiles and insects. The Brooklyn Papyrus states that the ability to "drive out the poison of all snakes, all scorpions, all tarantulas, and all serpents... and to drive away all snakes and to seal their mouths... is in the hand of the priests of Serqet." The priests of Serqet accompanied mining expeditions into the Sinai because the danger of scorpion bites was so great in that region.

MAGICIANS AS HEALERS The Sinai expeditions also included *sau* (sometimes translated as magicians), or protectors. Magicians were considered on a par with *swnw* and healing priests. Some doctors even held the title of magician. The magicians practiced medicine, but also made protective charms, such as amulets. They were also known to use spoken or written charms. The term *sau* could apply to both men and women. Midwives and nurses in the role of *sau* made protective charms for pregnant women and young children.

SPECIALISTS According to some sources, Egyptian physicians were masters of specialization. Not unlike today, Egyptian doctors specialized in fields such as ophthalmology, gastroenterology, proctology, and dentistry. They apparently had many doctors who would treat only one type of illness. Writing in about 440 B.C., Herodotus, the Greek historian, notes

> Medicine is thereby divided among [the Egyptians] so that each doctor knows but

> one disease and none of the others. All [Egypt] is stuffed with physicians: Some appoint [themselves as experts] on eyes, others do the head, others teeth, others matters having to do with the belly, others specialize in hidden diseases.

Although it is difficult to know whether Herodotus was exaggerating, clearly the Egyptians did make some distinctions among their medical experts.

Knowledge of the Body and Disease

Unlike modern medical practice, which relies heavily on postmortem studies for much of its anatomic knowledge, healers in ancient Egypt probably did not gain an understanding of anatomy from mummification. The Egyptians considered embalmers outcasts and objects of contempt because they came into contact with corpses and the causes of death. Although embalmers had some knowledge of anatomy, they probably had little contact with physicians and little opportunity to share their knowledge.

The Ophthalmologist's War

The reputation of Egyptian doctors was not always an asset. Herodotus reported how the fame of Egypt's eye doctors brought about the Persian conquest:

> Cyrus, the Persian king, asked Amasis, the king of Egypt, to send him his best eye doctor. The doctor chosen was taken from his family and turned over to the Persians. Resenting this and wanting revenge, the doctor suggested to Cambyses, Cyrus's son, that he [Cambyses] should ask for Amasis's daughter in marriage. Amasis sent the daughter of his predecessor instead, and when Cambyses found out he had been tricked, he invaded and conquered Egypt.

Instead, healers would have learned about anatomy from the slaughter of animals and from veterinary medicine, such as the highly prized cattle, which were treated by healers called "one who knows the bulls" and by the priests of Sekhmet. Medical practitioners would also have gained anatomic knowledge from the treatment of battle wounds and accidents that occurred during mining, quarrying, and building.

WEKHEDU IN THE METU The ancient Egyptians had no knowledge of the circulatory system, but instead had a theory about *metu*, usually translated as "vessels" or "tubes." The *metu* included blood vessels, arteries, ducts, nerves, tendons, and muscles. These tubes ran between the heart and the anus and then went to various parts of the body carrying blood, air, mucus, urine, semen, water, and feces, as well as disease-bearing entities and good and evil spirits.

Disease arose when *wekhedu* traveled through the *metu*. Scholars have had a very difficult time translating *wekhedu*, but some suggestions for its meaning are "pain matter", "morbid principle," or "rot." The Egyptian theory of disease was based on the observation that after death, decay began in the bowels and then spread to the rest of the body. In the living, decay occurred in the bowels, therefore this internal decay could spread through the *metu*, causing disease. *Wekhedu* could develop in the body or enter from the outside. Once inside, it could stick to the fecal matter or pus and spread, causing dental problems, stomach cramps, eye infections, fevers, mental illness, and so on.

Because the Egyptians connected the cause of disease with food and digestion, the papyri stress moderation in eating and drinking; overindulgence caused internal illness. Herodotus, who visited Egypt, noted

> For three consecutive days in every month they purged themselves, pursuing after health by means of emetics and drenches; for they think it is from the food they eat that all sicknesses come to men.

The care of the anus—where *wekhedu* was known to develop—and proper elimination to get rid of *wekhedu* formed the basis of ancient Egyptian health maintenance. Most medical papyri discuss the anus, and a large number of prescriptions involved purges. Specialized physicians called "Shepherds of the Anus" gave enemas to ensure that *wekhedu* did not build up in the body.

Beyond the Wekhedu Medical conditions were attributed to other causes, too. Some diseases were known to be caused by dietary or intestinal imbalances. Parasites, specifically worms, were another well-recognized agent of disease.

But there were less tangible factors as well. Ethical or moral lapses could lead to divine punishment in the form of sickness. Magical forces brought about by the devices of enemies were another possible basis. It was also believed that in some cases change in climate could cause disease—a reasonable conclusion that we might attribute to the unfamiliarity of an individual's immune system with the local infectious agents.

Dealing with Disease

Parasitic Diseases Parasites trouble Egyptians, even today. Schistosomiasis is a disease caused by worms that live in freshwater snails found on riverbanks. It causes urine in the blood, anemia, fatigue, loss of appetite, swelling of the scrotum, and can lead to bladder cancer. Schistosomiasis of the rectum, a painful condition, may explain the many remedies for "cooling and refreshing the anus." Many tomb paintings show men with umbilical hernias, scrotal swelling, and enlarged breasts—all symptoms of schistosomiasis.

These conditions appeared mainly in men whose work brought them into frequent contact with river water—fishermen, boat-

Treatment for Parasites

Doctors prescribed many remedies for intestinal parasitic worms.

Herbal Substances	Mineral Substances	Animal Substances	Vehicles
acacia leaves	desert oil	goose fat	beer
barley	malachite	honey	milk
bread	natron	ox fat	wine
carob	red ochre	white oil	
dates	salt		
juniper berries			
pine oil			
sedge			
sycamore figs			
roots of pomegranate			
wormwood/absinthe			

men, and papyrus gatherers. It was once thought that they tried to prevent schistosomiasis by wearing penile sheaths, but this has been discredited; they probably had no idea that it was even transmissible. Calcified eggs of the *Schistosoma* worm have been found in many mummies, including the unembalmed desiccated mummy of the weaver Nakht, from the New Kingdom. Poor Nakht was also infected with tapeworms and *Trichinella*, both caused by eating undercooked meat.

Hydatid disease, caused by eating food infested with the dog tapeworm, was also a problem. The disease causes cysts to develop in the organs, including the brain. These cysts have been found in mummies.

Guinea-worm infestations occur when someone swallows water containing infected cyclops, a tiny crustacean. The worms can grow to as long as three feet. They perforate the skin of the ankle, forming an ulcer. The Egyptians tried to wind the worm slowly around a stick and out of the body when it showed itself at the ankle. This procedure could be dangerous if the worm broke. A mummy found with a calcified guinea-worm had had both legs amputated, perhaps because of a failed attempt at worm removal.

Some experts speculate that this treatment of winding the guinea-worm around a small stick may be the origin of the passage from the Bible in which the Israelites are plagued by serpents during their exodus from Egypt (Numbers 21:6–9). The Lord tells Moses to set a serpent upon a pole to cure the people. Perhaps this is a reference to guinea-worm infection and treatment. It is also possible that this ailment and treatment is the origin of the caduceus—the staff with a serpent coiled around it that has been the symbol of medicine for centuries. It is impossible to verify any of this speculation, however.

The Bowels The Egyptians placed a great deal of emphasis on the idea of cleaning the bowels as a means of preventing disease. *Swnw* quite often prescribed laxatives, not so much for treating constipation but to clear the bowels of wekhedu either as a preventive measure or as a treatment for another ailment because wekhedu was thought to be responsible for almost all illness. These laxatives often involved the use of dates, figs, wormwood, coriander, cumin, juniper, malachite, and other herbs and minerals, combined with things such as honey, dew, wine, milk, or oil. One remedy calls for using the fruits or seeds of the castor-oil plant swallowed with beer. Linseed oil was used as a laxative; in fact, workers on the pyramids were issued a ration of the oil.

Ancient Egyptians' anuses apparently needed a lot of attention. One entire medical papyrus and 81 prescriptions refer only to the anus. Many remedies existed for cooling or refreshing the anus and for driving out heat. A suppository to cool the anus consisted of cinnamon, juniper berries, frankincense, ochre, cumin, honey, myrrh, and three other ingredients that are, unfortunately, as yet untranslatable.

Dental Problems The ancient Egyptians suffered greatly from dental problems. Many mummies show signs of periodontal disease, caused by stress applied to the teeth while chewing and by dental attrition—the wearing down of the teeth.

Periodontal disease causes the teeth to loosen and fall out. Most ancient people had dental attrition, but the Egyptians seemed to suffer from it more than others, probably because the sandy soil contributed to a great deal of sand and grit in their food. Attrition wore down the teeth, exposing the dental pulp, which became infected, leading to abscesses and cysts.

Dentists, called *ibhy*, could also be *swnw*. They used various remedies to make firm or strengthen teeth loosened by periodontal disease. Some of these remedies involved the scraping of a millstone (a form of sympathetic magic) and the use of malachite or honey. A mixture of plants, carob, and honey was applied to ulcers of the teeth. Another remedy was cumin, incense, and carob applied as a powder.

Lung Problems

Sand caused other problems for the Egyptians besides dental attrition. Sand pneumoconiosis—a noninfectious lung disease—occurs when people inhale blown sand. This condition still troubles those living in the Sahara and Negev deserts today. In ancient Egypt, everyone would have been exposed to the blowing desert sand; quarry workers and stone carvers were at even greater risk.

Hieroglyphic Prescription

The Ebers Papyrus contains prescriptions for a wide range of afflictions. The following example shows a remedy for an eye inflammation. A number of the ingredients would, indeed, be helpful for such a condition.

Another [prescription] for driving inflammation from the eye.

Myrrh

"Great Protector's" seed

Oxide of copper

Citron pips

Northern cypress flowers

Antimony

Gazelle droppings

Oryx offal

White oil

Place in water, let stand for one night, strain through a cloth, and smear over [the eye] for four days; or, according to another prescription, paint it on with a goose feather.

Eye Diseases Ancient Egyptian physicians were famous for their skill in treating eye problems, and several of them bore the title "doctor of the eyes." Many eye diseases were prevalent along the Nile. Leukoma, cataract, conjunctivitis, and trachoma (still known as the Egyptian eye disease) troubled people. And at least eight more eye diseases mentioned in the medical papyri have not yet been translated.

Eye treatments consisted of medication applied externally to the eye. Although other cultures seem to have experimented with cataract surgery, eye surgery did not exist in ancient Egypt. Remedies for blindness and poor eyesight included water from a pig's eye, pig bile, eye paint, honey, and fragments from an earthenware jar. One cure—eating liver—may have helped in cases of night blindness or xerophthalmia caused by a lack of vitamin A.

This antelope-shaped ointment vessel may have held an unguent with a base of animal fat, honey, or vegetable oil. People applied ointments externally to sores and wounds.

Medicines for trachoma, a roughening of the eye, included bile of tortoise, laudanum, acacia leaves, carob, ground-up granite, eye paint, ochre, and natron. Eyelashes growing into the eye called for incense, lizard blood, and bat blood.

Medicines

Not only were the eye doctors of Egypt famous for their skill, but neighboring countries held all Egyptian physicians in high regard for their ability to prepare medicines. Ramesses II was asked to send a doctor to the Hittite court to prepare herbs for the king. In Homer's *Odyssey*, the famed Helen of Troy received a drug from the daughter of an Egyptian saying

> For in that land the fruitful earth bears drugs in plenty, some good and some dangerous; and there every man is a physician and acquainted with such lore beyond all mankind.

The Egyptians themselves considered the *swnw* more important than the drug. They had a saying, "A remedy is only effective through the hand of its physician." We don't know if healers prepared the drugs or if pharmacists helped, but most prescriptions start by saying, "You shall then prepare for him. . . ."

Rx Preparations Prescriptions often indicate grinding, cooking, mashing, or straining the ingredients, which many times then "spend the night" in a vehicle such as water, alcohol, or oil. Often the active ingredient in the drug was an alkaloid extracted by soaking in alcohol in much the same way as a tincture. A typical Egyptian prescription follows (the fractions indicate relative proportions):

> You shall then prepare for him to drink: figs, $1/8$; milk, $1/16$; notched sycamore figs, $1/8$; which have spent the night in sweet beer, $1/10$. Strain and drink much. . . .

Doctors sometimes gave patients a container of medicine with the prescription and instructions molded into the clay of the vessel like a prescription label. (Maybe modern prescriptions would be easier to read if they were written in hieroglyphics.)

Egyptian Medicine Chest

Some of the plants or plant products used medicinally in Egypt:

aniseed	date	pomegranate
bean	fenugreek	resins
beer	grape	sedge
carob	hemp	sycamore fig
castor-oil plant	jujube	thyme
celery	leek	watermelon
cinnamon	moringa	wine
coriander	onion	wormwood
cumin	pea	

Incantations reinforced the effect of a remedy. This one was meant to be read when drinking the prescription:

> The remedy comes, and there comes that which drives evil things from this my heart and these my limbs. Strong is magic in combination with a medicine and vice versa.

The author of this spell had great faith in it. He notes that it's "Really excellent; it's worked a million times."

Medicines were also given rectally, vaginally, topically, and by inhalation and fumigation. Suppositories and enemas introduced drugs into the rectum. The gynecologic texts recommend cures and contraceptives for placement in the vagina. Physicians treated wounds with raw meat and then oil and honey. Diseases of the skin, hair, eyes, ears, and anus called for local applications of medicines, which were often bandaged in place.

Patients inhaled medicinal steam by means of a double pot. A liquid herbal remedy was poured over a heated stone placed in the bottom of a pot. Another pot was placed on top as a lid. A hole pierced in the bottom of the top pot allowed the patient to breath in the steam through a straw.

Another treatment, fumigation, involved burning certain remedies and directing the smoke to the eyes, vagina, or any other affected areas.

Egyptian doctors relied on hundreds of ingredients to treat a vast variety of conditions. Unfortunately, many of the names of diseases and about 80 percent of the plant names still cannot be translated from the hieroglyphics.

MEDICINAL HERBS The Egyptians probably had physic, or herb, gardens connected with temples. However, some herbs were gathered wild. The Ebers Papyrus gives us a glimpse into the gathering of a wild herb:

> An herb—*senutet* is its name—growing on its belly like the *kadet* plant. It produces a flower like the lotus. If one finds its leaves looking like white wood, then one should fetch it and rub it on the pelvis.

The Egyptians also imported plant products needed for medicine. Frankincense and myrrh came from Somalia. Pomegranate, olive, and fig trees came from elsewhere in the Near East or the Mediterranean.

MEDICINAL MINERALS Many of the healers' drugs contained mineral products. Natron, an essential ingredient in mummification, drew out fluid and reduced swelling. The physician applied it externally and then placed a bandage over it. Salt occurred frequently in prescriptions and was used orally, in enemas and suppositories, and as an application to the eyes, ears, and skin.

Swnw often treated eye diseases with green eye paint, made of finely powdered malachite, mined in the Sinai. The traces of copper found in malachite would have inhibited the growth of bacteria. Healers also treated eye problems with lapis lazuli, a rare and valuable commodity, which the Egyptians imported from Afghanistan.

Bone cosmetic box in the form of a duck feeding fish to two ducklings. Noble women used many antiwrinkle and cleansing creams, cosmetics, and deodorants, keeping them in various types of containers.

Medicines contained many other minerals, such as alabaster, alum, galena, clay, copper, granite, gypsum, hematite, Nile mud, ochre, and red lead.

Animal Products as Medicine Egyptian prescriptions contained a wide variety of animal products. Hundreds of remedies called for honey, which was used internally and topically. An ointment made with honey probably helped wounds because of honey's antibacterial and antifungal properties. It could also reduce swelling because its high concentration of sugar would draw out fluid.

Many prescriptions contained milk, usually as a vehicle rather than as an active ingredient. However, sometimes a specific type of milk was called for, such as the milk of an ass or human milk from a woman who had recently borne a son. In mythology, Isis brought her son Horus back to life by treating his burns with her own milk; therefore, people believed that the milk of a woman who had recently borne a son could transmit special healing powers.

Some drugs contained excrement from a variety of species, including cats, asses, birds, lizards, crocodiles, flies, and humans. Some treatments for eye problems called for the application of the excrement of a lizard, crocodile, pelican, or human. Rarely, fly and bird excrement was taken internally.

Blood from 21 species formed part of many external medicines. Human urine was an ingredient in enemas and was placed in the eyes. Cat placenta was part of a mixture to prevent hair from turning gray. A mouse cooked in oil also helped with this problem. Healers used goat bile to treat human bites and fish bile to strengthen eyesight. Physicians applied fresh meat to a wound on the first day.

Greasy ointments often included animal fats. A rather surprising remedy for baldness required fat from a lion, hippo, crocodile, cat, snake, and ibex. Considering how exotic these creatures are, this treatment must have been very expensive (at least as much as a year's supply of minoxidil). Ox liver, ass testicles, bird heart, and a variety of brains also played a role in drug preparation.

Medical Procedures

Surgery The medical papyri frequently mention the "knife treatment," but Egyptian physicians performed only minor

This carved relief from the temple of Horus and Sobek at Kom Ombo dates to the 2nd century A.D. (the Roman Period). Shown are women on birthing stools, a washbasin, and a variety of medical paraphernalia, including probes, forceps, a balance, cupping vessels, an instrument case, bandages, and a sponge.

surgical procedures, usually involving swellings, tumors, or snakebites. They did not attempt major operations. No surgical instruments have been found, and the famous carved relief of surgical instruments from the temple of Kom Ombo probably shows Roman, not Egyptian, objects.

Egyptian priests performed circumcision on boys in late puberty, usually as an initiation into manhood. Egyptian doctors rarely performed trephination—cutting an opening in the skull—but three examples of trephined skulls have been found. The trephined skull of a princess had well-healed edges, proving that she survived the operation.

WOUNDS AND INJURIES *Sunw* normally treated a wound, such as a crocodile bite, by bandaging it with fresh meat immediately. After that, the healer bound the wound with oil and honey. Doctors did not use stitches except for gaping wounds, and no mummies have been found with suturing, except for one stitched after death. Sometimes the edges of a gash were drawn together with a bandage, though.

Healers applied a variety of substances to burns, including mud, excrement, resin, dough, oil, carob, papyrus, honey, ochre, malachite, and copper flakes. One burn remedy from the Ebers Papyrus comes highly recommended:

> Barley bread, oil, and salt, mixed into one. Bandage with it often to make him well immediately. A true thing, I have seen it happen often for me.

For dislocated joints and fractured bones, healers used their hands to put them back

The Edwin Smith Papyrus

The Edwin Smith Papyrus lists 48 cases, mostly of trauma. Unlike most of the other medical papyri, this work served as a doctor's instruction book, rather than simply a collection of remedies. Each case entry includes the title of the case, instructions on examining the patient, a diagnosis with prognosis, and the prescribed treatment.

Case 16 from the Edwin Smith Papyrus is an example of wound treatment:

> Instructions for a split cheek. If you examine a man having a split cheek and you find that there is a swelling, raised and red, on the outside of his split, you shall say concerning him: One having a split in his cheek, an ailment which I will treat, you should bandage it with fresh meat on the first day. His treatment is sitting until his swelling is reduced. Afterwards you should treat it with grease, honey, and a pad every day until he is well.

into place. Archaeologists have found two bodies with bone fractures that had splints padded with linen and held in place with bandages.

POISONS The priests of Serqet—the poison experts—consulted the Brooklyn Papyrus for remedies for snakebite. The text gives some spells, but most of this papyrus lists conventional remedies similar to those in the other medical papyri. These remedies are grouped according to the species of snake involved or by the patient's symptoms.

The treatment of snakebites involved the care of the bite, the use of drugs, and the recitation of magical incantations. Sometimes the priest incised the bite "with the knife treatment" and then applied salt or natron, held on with a bandage; this would potentially draw fluid, including the poison, out of the wound.

Many of the remedies for curing or preventing snakebite involved onions. One papyrus reads

> As for the onion, it should be in the hand of the priest of Serqet, wherever he is. It is that which kills the venom of every snake, male or female. If one grinds it in water and one smears a man with it, the snake will not bite him. If one grinds it in beer and sprinkles it all over the house one day in the new year, no serpent . . . will penetrate therein.

Apparently, not every snakebite was treatable. Prognoses consist of blunt phrases such as "he will live," "one can save him," or "death hastens very quickly."

Health Care for Women and Children

Swnw did not specialize in gynecology and did not help women during healthy births. However, the medical papyri do mention contraception, conception, difficult births, and breast-feeding.

The Egyptians did not understand female reproductive anatomy and believed that the womb wandered in the body. The wandering womb caused a number of symptoms possibly along the lines of premenstrual syndrome. It was believed that during the monthly cycle, the womb would travel around the abdomen in search of sperm. Therefore, one treatment for wandering womb was intercourse. Another remedy recommends that the patient drink tar from a ship mixed with the dregs of "excellent beer."

A woman who wanted to become pregnant would drink the milk of a woman who had borne a son. To determine if a woman would bear a child and the sex of that child, one method from the Berlin Papyrus suggested she urinate daily on two different kinds of wheat (regular wheat and spelt wheat) kept in two separate bags. If they both sprouted, she would bear a child. If the regular wheat grew, it would

Ancient Socialized Medicine?

Diodorus Siculus, a Greek historian from Sicily, who visited Egypt in 59 B.C., wrote about the Egyptian physicians of his time:

> On their military campaigns and their journeys in the country they all receive treatment without the payment of any private fee; for the physicians draw their support from public funds and administer their treatments in accordance with a written law which was composed in ancient times by many famous physicians.

This temple of Isis at Philae, near Aswan, was built during the late Ptolemaic and early Roman periods. Scenes on the temple show the king smiting his enemies and offering to the gods. Near the temple is the "birth house," in which Isis was impregnated and gave birth to and suckled Horus.

be a boy; if the spelt grew, a girl. If neither grew, she would not bear a child.

The Ebers Papyrus lists some remedies to hasten a birth. To cause the uterus to contract, hemp ground in honey or celery ground in cow's milk was prescribed. To "release a child from the belly of a woman," plants, resins, onion, beer, salt, and even fly excrement were placed in the vagina.

During childbirth, women squatted on a birthing stool—a seat with a hole big enough for the baby to pass through—or on two large bricks. A midwife helped ease the baby out, then cut the umbilical cord with an obsidian knife.

Mothers breast-fed their children for up to three years. The papyri suggest testing the milk before feeding the baby. Bad milk smelled like fish. To make sure the mother produced enough milk, someone should rub the woman's back with a special mixture or feed her sour barley bread.

Women who wanted to avoid pregnancy placed a variety of remedies in the vagina. To "allow women to cease conceiving for one, two, or three years," lint was moistened with acacia (also called gum arabic), carob, and dates ground with honey. Crocodile excrement features in some contraception remedies; the odor alone may have been enough to do the trick.

Infant mortality rates in ancient Egypt were high. Parents relied heavily on charms, amulets, and spells to protect their children from evil spirits. People made special amulets to protect babies by saying a spell over gold and garnet beads and a seal with the image of a hand and a crocodile. The hand and crocodile would drive away evil spirits that threatened the baby. The beads and seal, strung on a linen thread, were hung around the baby's neck.

This pectoral from the Royal Tomb, Tanis, depicts a scarab, or dung beetle. Scarabs were used as protective amulets because the beetle represented the eternal renewal of life. Funerary scarabs, placed in mummy wrappings or mounted on pectorals, were often inscribed with a quotation from the Book of the Dead.

The Healthy Perspective

In general, the ancient world did not have any illusions about their worldly lot. Few Egyptians could expect to live past 40 years of age, and longevity, although greatly coveted, was rarely obtained. One of the few to reach old age found much to complain about:

Age is here, old age arrived,
Feebleness came, weakness grows,
Childlike, one sleeps all day.
Eyes are dim, ears deaf,
Strength is waning through weariness,
The mouth silenced, speaks not,
The heart, void, recalls not the past,
The bones ache throughout.
Good has become evil, all taste is gone,
What age does to people is evil in everything.

Perhaps because life was so short for the Egyptians, they held elaborate views of the afterlife and felt that in this life one should enjoy oneself to the utmost. The longest-lived and most popular song in ancient Egypt reminded people to take advantage of every moment:

Spend a happy day.
Rejoice in the sweetest perfumes.
Adorn the neck and arms of your wife with lotus flowers
And keep your loved one seated always at your side.
Call no halt to music and the dance,
But bid all care begone.
Spare a thought for nothing but pleasure,
For soon your turn will come to journey to the land of silence.

Love's Cure

A love poem from the New Kingdom refers to both physicians and magicians as legitimate healers (although their usefulness seems somewhat less than optimum):

When the physicians come to me,
My heart rejects their remedies;
The magicians are quite helpless,
My sickness is not discerned...
My sister is better than all prescriptions,
She does more for me than all medicines;
Her coming to me is my amulet,
The sight of her makes me well!

Hebrew Medicine

THE LAND OF ANCIENT ISRAEL lies at the eastern end of the Mediterranean Sea and is a study in contrasts. Except for the narrow coastal plain, the land is mountainous, with summits of over 3,000 feet in most of the country. But this land is also the location of the lowest point on earth, the Dead Sea, with an altitude of 1,300 feet below sea level. A deep rift, the valley of the Jordan River, runs through the land from north of Lake Huleh, through the Sea of Chinnereth (also called the Sea of Galilee or Lake Tiberias), and down into the Dead Sea.

Unlike the civilizations of Mesopotamia and Egypt, which depended on mighty rivers for their very existence, Israel received water in the form of rain brought by westerly winds from the Mediterranean in the winter and heavy dew in spring and summer. Agriculture did not require irrigation, but a drought meant certain famine.

A Jewish scribe working on a Torah. Torah scrolls are made of parchment and are written by hand. The laws of the Torah, the teachings received by Moses on Mt. Sinai, include 613 commandments; 213 of them are rules concerning health, social hygiene, and disease prevention.

The eastern Mediterranean area, besides being geographically and climatically varied, was also an extraordinary nexus of cultures. It is sacred land for three of the world's great religions. The area was a land bridge between Asia and Africa, and the mighty powers of Mesopotamia and Egypt communicated via routes that had to pass through Israel.

The Canaanites

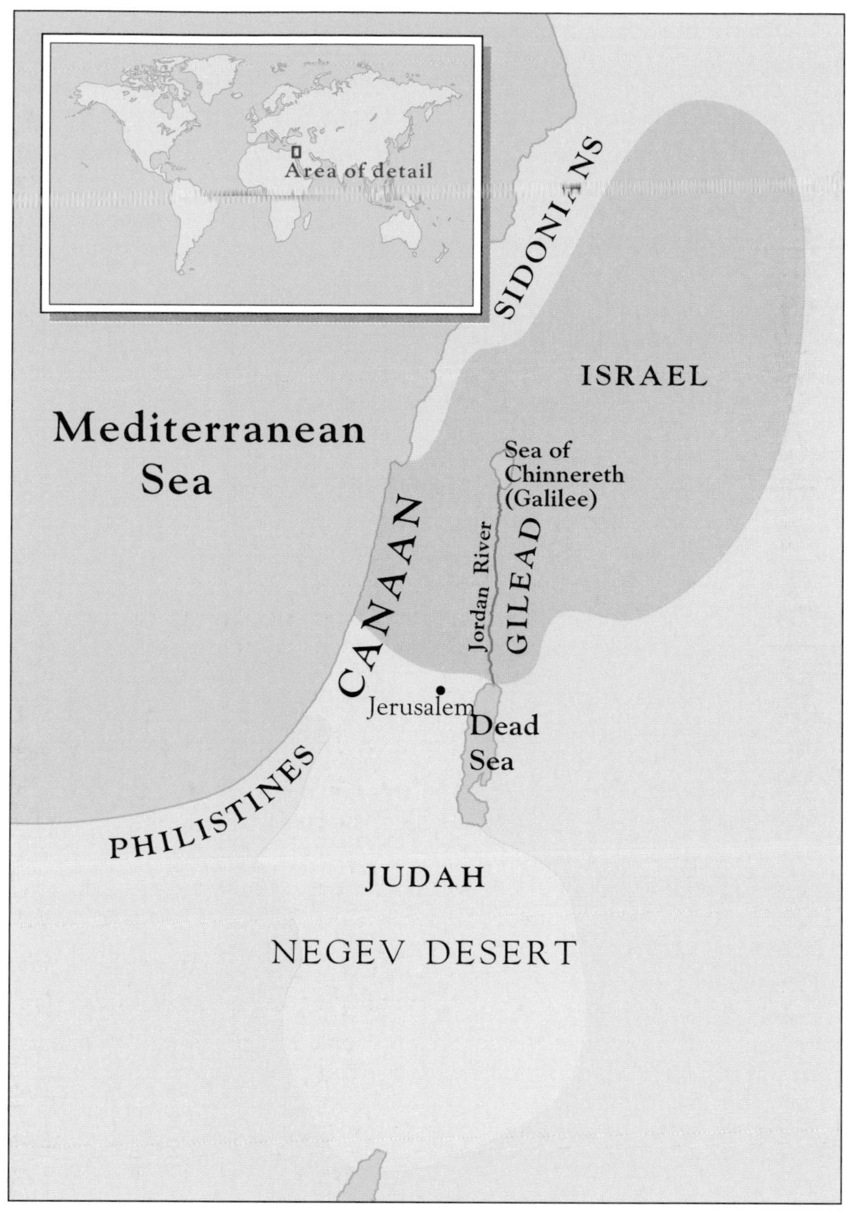

The Canaanites came from the north and settled the area around 3150 B.C. For about 2,000 years, the Canaanites inhabited almost the entire eastern end of the Mediterranean. Finally, invaders pushed them to a narrow strip of coast around 1200 B.C. The Canaanites worshiped hundreds of deities, including El, Baal, and Astarte (the goddess of love) and communicated with their divinities through prayer, sacrifice, and divination.

The Canaanites served as middlemen in diplomacy, trade, and culture between Mesopotamia and Egypt. They lived in independent city-states governed by kings, who ruled merchants, craftspeople, priests, and peasants. Their soldiers used chariots and bronze weapons. These wealthy, walled cities were not united, although they shared a common culture and language and had extensive commercial and social contact.

The Canaanites became well known as ship and furniture builders, using timber from Lebanon. They also processed shellfish into a purple dye, used to make textiles. This purple dye led the Greeks to call these people the *Phoenicians*—*phoinix* means "purple" in Greek. Although their textile work was impressive, the Phoenicians made what one might say was their greatest contribution to humankind by developing a form of writing that led to our modern alphabet.

The Hebrews

The Hebrews first encountered the Canaanites when they migrated to the eastern Mediterranean from Mesopotamia around 1900 B.C. The Hebrew Bible recounts how Abraham, born in the Sumerian city of Ur, migrated with his family to Haran in northern Mesopotamia. When Abraham was an old man, God told him to migrate again with his family and flocks 600 miles southwest to Canaan. Abraham and his people had traveled the entire length of the Fertile Crescent. In Canaan, God commanded him to circumcise all males as a sign of the covenant between them.

The Hebrews settled in Canaan, but soon learned the difference between Mesopotamia—the land with two great rivers—and their new home—a land with no great rivers. Canaan's productivity depended on rain. When that failed, drought and famine drove the Hebrews to the closest area with a reliable water source: Egypt. Abraham had gone there during a famine, but did not stay long. However, his great-grandson, Joseph, moved to Egypt around 1660 B.C., as did many of the Hebrews, settling in the fertile Nile Delta. A number of Hebrews also remained behind in Canaan.

Eventually, the Hebrews in Egypt went from being voluntary settlers to slaves. They built the magnificent cities and temples demanded by the pharaohs. But around 1280 B.C., led by Moses, they escaped slavery and fled from Egypt into the wilderness of the Sinai peninsula. There the Hebrews wandered for 40 years,

Important Dates in the History of Israel

3150–2200 B.C.: Early Canaanite (Bronze Age).

2200–1550 B.C.: Middle Canaanite.

1550–1200 B.C.: Late Canaanite.

1200 B.C.: Beginning of the Israelite (Iron) Age.

1200–1150 B.C.: Arrival of the Sea People (Philistines).

1150–1000 B.C.: Period of the Judges.

1020–1000 B.C.: Reign of King Saul.

1000–960 B.C.: Reign of King David.

960–930 B.C.: Reign of King Solomon.

930 B.C.: The kingdom divides into two: Israel in the north, Judah in the south.

869–850 B.C.: Ahab rules Israel. His wife, Jezebel, encourages pagan worship.

ca. 865 B.C.: Elijah the prophet lives.

850 B.C.: Elisha succeeds Elijah as most important prophet.

723 B.C.: The northern kingdom, Israel, destroyed by Assyria..

715–687 B.C.: King Hezekiah rules Judah.

622 B.C.: King Josiah outlaws worship at "high places."

597 B.C.: Nebuchadrezzar captures Jerusalem. Many Jews taken captive to Babylon.

586 B.C.: Jerusalem and temple destroyed. More Jews exiled.

538 B.C.: Cyrus allows Jews to return to Israel.

520–515 B.C.: Rebuilding of the temple.

445 B.C.: Nehemiah appointed governor of Judah.

332 B.C.: Alexander the Great conquers the area, now called Judea.

164 B.C.: Judah Maccabee rededicates temple.

142 B.C.: Judea becomes independent.

63 B.C.: Romans conquer the area, now called Palestine, after the Philistines.

A.D. 70: Romans destroy the temple at Jerusalem; the dispersal of the Jews (the Diaspora) begins.

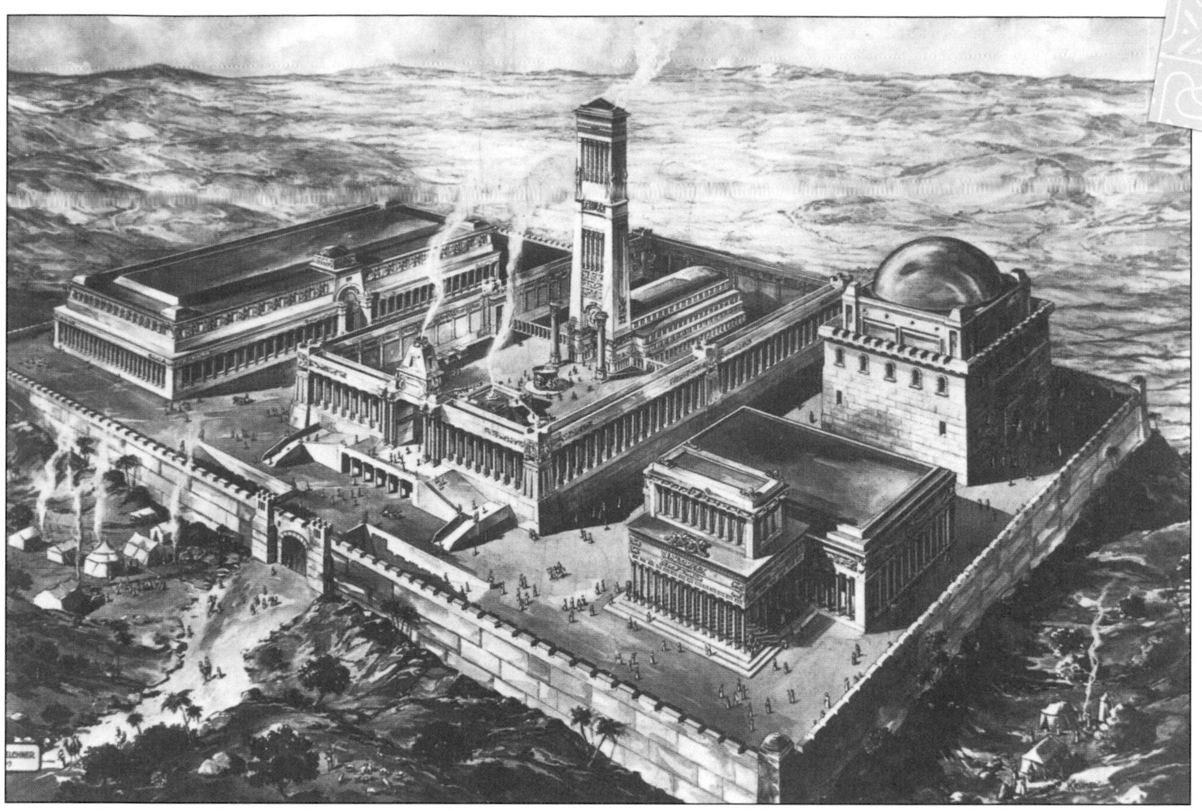

An imaginative reconstruction of the temple in Jerusalem. Jewish temple worship included animal sacrifices and offerings, prayers, readings, singing, processions, and music. King Solomon associated the temple and prayer with healing. He noted that people far from the temple could benefit from prayer by reaching their hands toward the temple.

during which time, God, called Yahweh, communicated with Moses, giving to him and his people the rules by which they should live—the Mosaic Law.

After Moses died, about 1240 B.C., Joshua led the Hebrews, now referred to as the Israelites, in the conquest of Canaan. The Israelites settled some of the land, built hill towns, farmed, and grazed their flocks. By about 1180 B.C., the Philistines settled along the southern coast of Canaan. They brought with them iron and chariots, and like the Canaanites, they fought with the Israelites for territory.

Judges and Kings During the period of the Judges (1150–1000 B.C.), Israel had no single leader. As the need arose, certain people took charge and were referred to as "Judges."

The prophet Samuel anointed Saul king of Israel, the first to hold such a title. King David founded the city of Jerusalem and his son, Solomon, built the temple there. These three kings ruled a united country, but upon the death of Solomon, the country divided into two separate monarchies: Israel in the north and Judah in the south.

The Mesopotamian Conquest The various powers in Mesopotamia sought to control the eastern Mediterranean, which became a battleground. Egypt also became embroiled in the power struggles there. Assyria conquered and destroyed the northern kingdom of Israel in 723 B.C., and in 586 B.C., the Babylonians invaded Judah, destroying Jerusalem—the houses, the palace, and the temple. The Jews were then deported to Babylon; only 20,000 out of 200,000 inhabitants of Judah remained behind. Thus began the period known as the Babylonian Exile, or Babylonian Captivity, which ended in 538 B.C. when Cyrus the Great of Persia occupied Babylon and permitted the Jews to rebuild their temple in Jerusalem.

The Power Shift For over a hundred years, we know little about the kingdom of Judah. No historical records or significant archaeologic finds exist. But a great shift was taking place; the center of political power moved from the Near East to the West. Alexander the Great conquered the known world, and Judah became Judea, a tiny part of Alexander's empire.

Eventually the Jews became independent again, but their freedom was brief—less than 100 years—for in 63 B.C., the Romans conquered the land, renaming it Palestine, after the Jews' enemy, the Philistines. After the Jews repeatedly revolted against them, the Romans destroyed the temple in A.D. 70. Thus began the Diaspora, or the dispersion of the Jews.

Faith and the Canaanites

For the peoples of ancient Israel, as for many other ancient cultures, health and healing was a religious matter, but not everyone in the area had the same religious ideas. The Jewish people worshiped only one god, Yahweh. Although perfectly normal to most of us today, this theology was not the norm in the ancient world, and living among the Canaanites who worshiped a variety of deities, many Jews fell into pagan ways. This must have been a serious problem because the prophets of the Hebrew Bible preached vehemently against adopting pagan ideas.

Fertility Cults The most important Canaanite cult was the fertility cult, whose main deities were Baal and Anat. Archaeologists have excavated fertility figurines throughout Israel and neighboring lands. They were especially common in Judah and were often found there in house remains. These figurines, portraying women supporting their large breasts with their hands, probably represent Canaanite goddesses. They were used in private rituals to ensure fertility or a safe pregnancy and birth.

Temple Worship Although there are some cultural similarities between the Canaanite cults and the Jewish faith, they shared little theologically. Canaanite worship included animal sacrifice, occasionally child sacrifice, and sacred prostitution. The temple cult was a complex organiza-

A fertility goddess from Catal-Huyuk, Turkey. Archaeologists have excavated fertility figurines throughout Israel and neighboring lands. They were especially common in Judah. These figurines, portraying women with large breasts, were probably used in private rituals to ensure fertility or a safe pregnancy and birth.

tion that included priestly families, singers, vestment makers, sculptors, potters, and slaughterers. Jewish temple worship included animal sacrifices, too, and offerings of meal, bread, oil, and wine; prayers; the reading aloud of the scriptures; singing; and sometimes processions and music.

Both Canaanites and Jews worshiped in "high places." The high places were open-air or roofed enclosures that stood on high, tree-covered hills and contained altars, incense, stone pillars, trees or poles, and water. The divinity was worshiped with sacrifices, incense burning, eating, weeping, and praying. Prophets and priests resided there. High places were the centers of private devotion, ceremonies, and festivals.

Divination and Prophecy Like the Mesopotamians, the Canaanites used celestial omens and liver divination to know the will of the gods—that is, to predict the future (see pages 19–20). Divination was probably the only way to diagnose an illness or make a prognosis. Clay liver models have been found in Israel dating from 1550 to 1200 B.C. Liver models were compared with the liver from a sacrificed animal. The meaning of the marks and formations on the real liver were interpreted with the use of the model.

The Hebrews limited official divination to the high priest of the temple, who cast lots to determine the future. Dream divination among the Jews was also an acceptable form of communication with the divine. In the Old Testament, we learn that "When there are prophets among you, I the Lord make myself known to them in visions; I speak to them in dreams" (Numbers 12:6).

Protective Amulets

The people of Israel made use of amulets as protective devices from early on. When the Philistines were being decimated by "mice and tumors"—possibly the bubonic plague, which was spread by rodents and caused lesions—they decided to return the Ark of the Covenant to the Jews. The Jewish priests told them to send it back with five golden tumors and five golden mice. "Then you will be healed" (I Samuel 6:3–5). The gold charms protected against the illnesses that they symbolized.

A fortress in the Negev, from the end of the 9th century B.C., contains magical incantations written on the walls along with alphabetic sequences. The alphabet was used as a magical text since it could spell out the names of divinities, angels, or even demons. The shape of a hand with fingers pointing down was also used as a good luck amulet. From the end of the 7th century B.C., archaeologists discovered two small silver scrolls in Jerusalem. They contain the words "May Yahweh bless you and keep you." These scrolls use the name of God to provide protection.

The Jews and the Canaanites had many prophets, or people who communicated with the divine. Some prophets from the Hebrew Bible are Abraham, Moses, Samuel, Elijah, Elisha, Nathan, Ahijah, Isaiah, and Jeremiah. Miriam, Deborah, Huldah, and Noadiah were prophetesses. God spoke to them in dreams or through the divine spirit. Some of these prophets predicted the outcome of sickness. Others had special healing powers.

When the traditional means of knowing the future (dreams, lots, and prophets) failed him, King Saul resorted to necromancy—the questioning of the spirits of the dead. The medium, or witch, of Endor brought up the ghost of the prophet Samuel, who foretold the death of Saul. This form of divination was forbidden, even by Saul himself who had banned mediums and wizards from the land, but could be used as a last resort (at least if you were king!). We hear of women who practiced magical arts, but sorceresses were absolutely not permitted: "Woe to the women who sew bands on all wrists, and make veils... in the hunt for souls" (Ezekiel 13:18).

Health in the Laws

The Hebrews wrote no medical texts; we have only the Bible and archaeology to inform us of their health practices. The Hebrews felt that health and sickness came from a divine source. People became sick if they sinned. God was considered the physician of his people and healing meant forgiveness of sin. In the wilderness God told the Israelites that if they kept all the commandments, "I will not bring upon you any of the diseases that I brought upon the Egyptians; for I am the Lord who heals you" (Exodus 15:26).

While the Israelites wandered in the wilderness for 40 years, their priests served as health officers. They enforced the laws of the Torah—the teachings received by Moses on Mt. Sinai. Of the 613 biblical commandments, 213 of them were rules concerning health, social hygiene, and disease prevention. Although the health-related purposes of these laws may have been unknown to the Israelites at the time, modern science recognizes that there are many significant health benefits to be derived from following the laws.

NUTRITION The commandments concerning the Sabbath, the day of rest, provided mental and spiritual refreshment and, equally important, relaxation from physical effort to help maintain health and vigor. Animals also had to rest on the seventh day of the week. Even the land itself rested. Every seventh year, farmland had to remain fallow to safeguard against mineral depletion; this practice ensured the continued fertility of the soil and, thus, continued nutrient content in the food supply.

A Scroll of Esther. The story of Esther takes place in Shushan (Susa), east of the Tigris, the winter residence of the Persian king. The king's Jewish wife, Esther, saves her people from Haman, the evil grand vizier, who seeks to destroy all the Jews in the kingdom.

Rules about which foods could be eaten were a major part of the laws. Animals that had died of natural causes could not be eaten. Only animals that chewed cud and had parted hooves could be eaten. These animals were vegetarians. This measure protected against food poisoning, which would be more likely if carnivores were eaten. Pigs could not be eaten; they often served as hosts to a variety of parasites, including those causing trichinosis, toxoplasmosis, tapeworm infestation, and hydatid disease. The laws forbade eating crustaceans, one source of typhoid and paratyphoid fevers. Safeguarding a clean water supply by keeping away unclean objects helped prevent diseases.

An orthodox Jewish boy immerses kitchenware in boiling water. Jewish law requires "kashering," making kosher or fit, all utensils used during Passover. Although unknown to the ancient Hebrews, the process obviously kills any contaminating microorganisms. Kashering stems from the procedures used after the Israelite conquest of the Midianites—passing articles through fire or water to clean them (Numbers 31:21–24).

Hygiene Many sanitary regulations existed that would prevent the spread of infectious diseases. Precautionary isolation and quarantine; the burning or boiling of infected clothing, weapons, or kitchen utensils; the cleaning of houses where infection might be; the examination and purification of diseased people; hand washing; the cleansing of those in contact with corpses or the diseased; and the rules regarding the disposal of human wastes all served to prevent the spread of illness.

Many laws also restricted sexual behavior. Close relatives could not marry, preventing genetic abnormalities. Adultery, homosexuality, and bestiality were forbidden. People had to wash themselves after sexual intercourse. Other practices thought unclean or unhealthy were sexual relations during menstruation, accidental seminal emissions, and coitus interruptus.

The Hebrew Bible contains many references to "clean" and "unclean" people, animals, foods, and objects. The idea of being unclean means to be contaminated by some impurity and to be contagious. Uncleanness could take many forms, seven of which required purification: after childbirth, accidental emission of semen, sexual relations, menstruation, leprosy, bodily discharges, and contact with a corpse. The last three were serious enough to require isolation from the rest of society.

Skin Diseases What is called leprosy in the Bible is not always the leprosy, or Hansen Disease, that we know today. The term was used generally to refer to a wide variety of skin diseases, such as psoriasis. Chapters 13 and 14 of Leviticus—one of the books of laws—deal exclusively with skin diseases. The priests examined anyone with skin swellings, eruptions, or sores. Leviticus provides many fairly detailed descriptions of symptoms, which the priest had to observe carefully in order to pronounce the diagnosis of "clean" or "unclean." If the symptoms did not provide enough information for a diagnosis,

Laws Concerning Health

The pig, for even though it has divided hoofs and is cleft-footed, it does not chew the cud; it is unclean to you. Of their flesh you shall not eat, and their carcasses you shall not touch; they are unclean to you. (Leviticus 11:7–8)

Everything in the waters that has fins and scales, whether in the seas or in the streams—such you may eat. (Leviticus 11:9)

When a man or a woman has spots on the skin of the body, white spots, the priest shall make an examination, and if the spots on the skin of the body are of a dull white, it is a rash that has broken out in the skin; he is clean. (Leviticus 13:38–39)

Every bed on which the one with the discharge lies shall be unclean; and everything on which he sits shall be unclean. (Leviticus 15:4)

If a man lies with a woman and has an emission of semen, both of them shall bathe in water, and be unclean until evening. (Leviticus 15:18)

You shall have a designated area outside the camp to which you shall go. With your utensils you shall have trowel; when you relieve yourself outside, you shall dig a hole with it and then cover up your excrement. (Deuteronomy 23:12–13)

the priest quarantined the person for seven days and then performed another examination.

A person receiving a firm diagnosis of leprosy had to wear torn clothes, let his hair hang loose, and cover his upper lip while crying "Unclean, unclean!" He had to live alone outside the camp. Even Miriam, Moses's sister, had to spend seven days outside the camp when she became leprous, although Moses prayed for her to be healed immediately.

Purification No attempt was made to heal the unclean leper, only to protect the healthy from possible infection. If, however, the leprosy cleared up spontaneously, a priest would go out of the camp to examine the person. If the priest found the person was no longer leprous, a ritual cleansing took place. A living bird was dipped in the blood of another bird, along with cedarwood, red thread, and hyssop. The priest sprinkled the blood over the leper and released the bird. The person being cleansed then washed his clothes, shaved all his hair, and bathed. A week later, elaborate offerings and sacrifices were made and the person was officially declared clean.

The pool of Siloam in Jerusalem provided clean, fresh water to the city and is connected with Jesus healing a blind man. Spitting on the ground, Jesus made clay of the spittle and anointed the man's eyes. After washing there, the man could see.

Purification of those who had contact with the dead involved burning an unblemished red cow along with cedarwood, hyssop, and red thread. The ash was mixed with stream water, forming a mixture called "water for impurity," and was sprinkled from a bunch of hyssop over a person who had contact with a corpse, a human bone, or a grave. The principle of opposites governed the ingredients in the mixture. The red cow and thread suggest blood; the cow is a fertility symbol; the cedar is a long-lived tree; and stream water is "living water." All these "life" elements would counteract the contact with death.

Healing in Israel

THE TEMPLE While traveling through the wilderness, the Israelites complained about the lack of food and water. "Then the Lord sent fiery serpents among the people, and they bit the people, so that many people of Israel died" (Numbers 21:6). Moses prayed for the people. The Lord told him to "make a poisonous serpent, and set it on a pole; and every one who is bitten shall look at it and live" (Numbers 21:8). Moses created a bronze serpent and anyone bitten by a snake had only to look at the serpent and he would be cured of his bite and live (see page 39).

People seeking a cure could go to the temple. The same bronze serpent made by Moses in the wilderness was later placed in the temple in Jerusalem, where people burned incense to it, probably in the hopes of receiving a cure. Archaeologists have actually discovered bronze serpents dating from around 1550 to 1200 B.C. in Israel. At least one came from a temple; they were probably used for healing. The serpent as healer is found in other traditions as well. The ancient Greek stories of Asklepian healing, for example, often mention snakes bringing cures in a dream (see pages 73–74).

Prayer of Gratitude

After being healed by God and being given 15 more years of life, Hezekiah delivered a prayer of thanks for recovery in the temple when presenting an offering to God for his personal deliverance.

I said: In the noontide of my days I must depart;
I am consigned to the gates of Sheol for the rest of my years.
I said, I shall not see the Lord in the land of the living. . . .
Oh, restore me to health and make me live!
Surely, it was for my welfare that I had great bitterness;
But you have held back my life from the pit of destruction,
For you have cast all my sins behind your back. . . .
The Lord will save me, and we will sing to stringed instruments
All the days of our lives, at the house of the Lord.
(Isaiah 38:9–20)

Healing seemed to be naturally connected to the temple. Ezekiel's concept of the ideal temple included trees whose leaves were medicinal. Describing his vision of a restored temple and its garden, Ezekiel stated that

> on the banks, on both sides of the river, there will grow all kinds of trees for food. Their leaves will not wither nor their fruit fail, but they will bear fresh fruit every month, because the water for them flows from the sanctuary. Their fruit will be for food, and their leaves for healing (Ezekiel 47:12).

Praying at a temple often resulted in a cure. Hannah, the mother of Samuel, prayed in the temple at Shiloh to overcome her barrenness. King Solomon associated the temple and prayer with healing. In his speech at the dedication of the temple, he noted that people far from the temple could benefit from prayer by reaching their hands toward the temple.

> If there is famine... whatever plague, whatever sickness there is; whatever prayer... there is from any individual... so that they stretch out their hands toward this house; then hear in heaven... and forgive, act, and render to all whose hearts you know (1 Kings 8:37–40).

PRAYER Prayer without being in or reaching toward the temple also brought cures. A simple prayer to Yahweh gave King Hezekiah 15 more years of life and saved Jerusalem. When the prophet Isaiah told the king he would die soon,

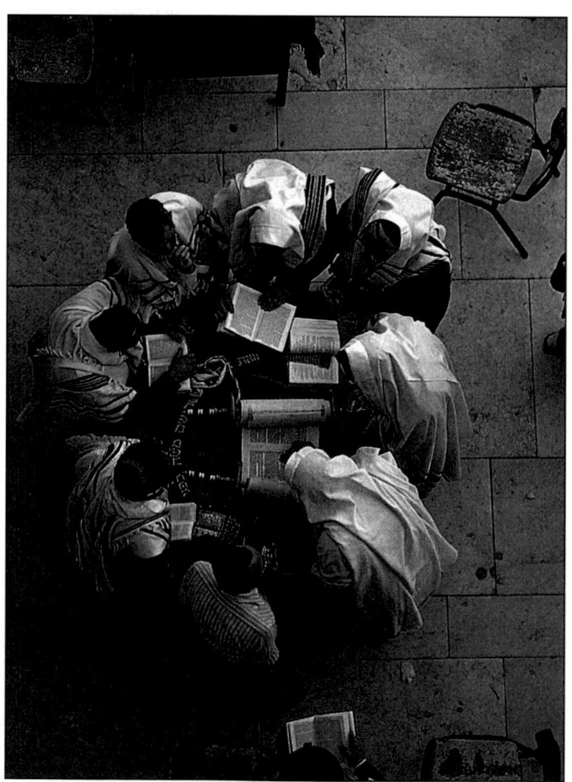

Jewish men praying at the "Wailing Wall," the western side of the wall that bounded the temple mount, on top of which stood the temple. The men wear prayer shawls as they bend over a Torah scroll. Judaism is the oldest continually practiced religion in the world.

> Hezekiah turned his face to the wall, and prayed to the Lord: "Remember now, O Lord, I implore you, how I have walked before you in faithfulness with a whole heart, and have done what is good in your sight." Hezekiah wept bitterly (2 Kings 20:2–3).

God then said

> I have heard your prayer, I have seen your tears; indeed I will heal you; on the third day you shall go up to the house of the Lord. And I will add 15 years to your life (2 Kings 20:5–7).

Prayer and tears saved Hezekiah, who went to the temple to offer thanks for his recovery (see "Prayer of Gratitude," page 57).

The Healing of the Prophets

Although all healing ultimately came from God, his prophets also had healing powers. God responded to Hezekiah's prayers by

The Process of Divine Healing

Although the Hebrew faith emphatically points out that all healing power comes from God, the prophets played several roles in the process. The story of Isaiah and Hezekiah, for example, illustrates some important parts of the process.

When King Hezekiah falls ill, the prophet Isaiah comes to him and tells him that his illness is fatal. Hezekiah then prays to the Lord for healing, and God sends Isaiah back to the King with the cure—a poultice of figs. Isaiah applies the medicine and Hezekiah recovers.

In this one story we can see the whole process of ancient Hebrew healing. First, the prophet assumes the role of prognosticator, revealing the nature and course of the illness. Then, the afflicted person must resort to the power of prayer and ask God directly for healing. God answers—in this case, in the affirmative. And finally, the cure comes in the form of a healing substance from the natural world.

The Jordan River flows from north of Lake Huleh, through the Sea of Chinnereth (the Sea of Galilee or Lake Tiberias), and down into the Dead Sea. The prophet Elisha cured Namaan the Syrian of leprosy by directing him to bathe in the Jordan River seven times.

Then he got up on the bed and lay upon the child, putting his mouth upon his mouth, his eyes upon his eyes, and his hands upon his hands; and while he lay bent over him, the flesh of the child became warm (2 Kings 4:34).

When a group of prophets accidentally cooked a pottage of poisonous wild gourds during a famine, Elisha threw some flour into the pot, neutralizing the poison and allowing the prophets to eat (2 Kings 4:38–41). Elisha cured Namaan the Syrian of leprosy by directing him to bathe in the Jordan River seven times (2 Kings 5:1–27). Even Elisha's bones had healing powers. A corpse thrown into Elisha's grave instantly came back to life (2 Kings 13:20–21).

prolonging his life, but the prophet Isaiah then healed the king's boil with a poultice of figs (see "The Process of Divine Healing," page 58). Several prophets—Nathan, Elijah, Ahijah, and Elisha—had the power of prognostication of sickness, knowing who would die and who would live.

Other prophets actually healed. Elisha, especially, cured many people. He possessed the cloak of Elijah, who had performed miracles with this cloak and had cast it over Elisha, thereby transferring his power to his successor. After inheriting the cloak, Elisha threw saltwater into a spring of bad water making it wholesome, so that the spring no longer caused death and miscarriage. He brought back to life a child who had died, perhaps of sunstroke, while working in the fields. In this miraculous healing, Elisha used mouth to mouth resuscitation:

THE Essenes

From the 2nd century B.C. to the 3rd century A.D. there was a Jewish sect called the Essenes, the writers of the Dead Sea Scrolls. Their name means "healers." They lived in small monastic groups and devoted themselves to handicrafts and healing. Unfortunately, little is known about their specific healing techniques. They gathered roots and herbs to use as remedies, but their main cures came from prayer, mystic incantations, and amulets. They believed that faith could cure common ailments as well as insanity, blindness, deafness, dumbness, and lameness.

Physicians in Israel

Even though some prophets had healing powers, they were not considered physicians. The Hebrew Bible occasionally mentions actual physicians, or *ropheim*. Scholars disagree on who exactly the ropheim were—foreign healers, Jewish healers, secular healers, or healers who prayed to deities other than Yahweh.

THE FORBIDDEN PHYSICIANS Whoever they were, the ropheim were not held in high regard at first. When King Asa, who lived ca. 900 B.C., sought a cure for diseased feet from physicians and not the Lord, he died (2 Chronicles 16:12–13). Although the story sounds like a condemnation of physicians in general, it is more likely that Asa's transgression is more subtle than that. The only physicians, or ropheim, that would have been available to King Asa at the time would probably have been pagan physicians who practiced the type of magic and sorcery that came from Mesopotamian culture (see pages 12–28). This type of supernatural pagan medicine would be, in essence, a recourse to divinities other than the God of Israel, and this is clearly a violation of the Mosaic Law—specifically the first commandment!

PERMITTED PHYSICIANS Feelings about the ropheim changed over the centuries, however, especially as the Jews became familiar with Greek medicine. The Greeks approached medicine—and, indeed, all science—differently from the Mesopotamians and the Egyptians. Although the Greeks were undoubtedly pagan, their thought on the subject of the natural world was not much concerned with theology.

To the Greeks, disease and curing were natural phenomenon that neither denied nor depended on a supernatural being. The natural property of the particular herb or mineral affected the cure, not, as the Mesopotamians believed, the deity invoked during treatment. Therefore, for the Jews, resorting to the extensive knowledge of Greek medicine would not have offended the jealous God of Israel.

By 180 B.C., Joshua Ben Sira, who wrote Ecclesiasticus (not to be confused with the Old Testament Book of Ecclesiastes, which was written by King Solomon) praised physicians, acknowledging that God had created them and the medicines they used. Healing still required prayer and sacrifice, and sin still caused sickness, but physicians were now the instruments through whom cures could come. These physicians still relied on God as the ultimate source of healing, and they prayed for divine guidance in their work.

Ben Sira Praises Physicians and Medicine

Honor the physician with the honor due him, according to your need of him, for the Lord created him; for healing comes from the Most High. . . . The Lord created medicines from the earth, and a sensible man will not despise them. . . . By them he heals and takes away pain; the pharmacist makes of them a compound. . . . When you are sick do not be negligent, but pray to the Lord, and He will heal you. . . . Cleanse your heart from all sin. . . . And give the physician his place, for the Lord created him. There is a time when success lies in the hands of physicians, for they too will pray to the Lord that He should grant them success in diagnosis and in healing, for the sake of preserving life.

An ancient underground olive oil storeroom. Olive oil formed the chief base of ointments and perfumes in ancient Israel. The olive tree and its fruit served for food, fuel, light, carpentry, and medicines in the entire Mediterranean area.

Ineffectual Physicians The Book of Tobit, dating from 200 to 170 B.C., reveals a different view of healing: Demons cause sickness and death, and physicians are ineffective in healing. Tobit's blindness, caused by sparrow droppings falling into his eyes, is not cured by the physicians he consults. God, however, hears his prayers and sends the angel Raphael, whose name means "God heals." Raphael helps Tobias, Tobit's son, to find a cure for his father's blindness, instructing him how to drive away a demon that is bothering Sarah, the woman he wants to marry. Tobias catches a fish and removes the liver, heart, and gall. To drive out the demon, he places the heart and liver on some live ashes of incense and smokes out the demon, who does not like the smell and flees to Egypt.

To cure his father, Tobias sprinkles the fish gall in his father's eyes. When his eyes begin to smart, Tobit rubs them, and the white film scales off from the corners of his eyes.

The cure from God and the uselessness of physicians hearken back to a time before the influence of classical medicine when people were skeptical about the healing abilities of ropheim. The failure and helplessness of the physician also magnifies the glory of the Lord's miraculous healing.

Remedies

God provided the "medicines from the earth" for people to make use of. Ben Sira mentions pharmacists who prepared compounds that would heal and alleviate pain.

Herbal Medicine Herbal cures formed the basis of healing during the time of Ben Sira and earlier. The Hebrew Bible mentions many herbs and plants, but few of them relate directly to healing, with the exceptions of mandrakes, balm, and figs. Leah and Rachel both wanted mandrakes (*Mandragora officinarum*) to cure their infertility. Many cultures valued mandrakes for their supposed aphrodisiac qualities, and the love poetry of the Song of Solomon mentions mandrakes (see "The Magical Mandrake," page 103).

Balsam, or balm of Gilead, was used in healing and as incense. Scholars do not agree on which plant this is, but it might have been gum mastic (from the shrub *Pistacia lentiscus*) or maybe Mecca balsam, or stacte (*Commiphora gileadensis*). Balm is mentioned several times in the Hebrew Bible, starting in Genesis, where Joseph and his brothers see a caravan from Gilead bearing gum, balm, and myrrh. Balm was an aromatic resin used for pain relief, as an antiseptic, and as an astringent for wounds. The balm of Gilead was famous for its medicinal quality, especially in injuries:

An incense burner from Jordan. Incense—burning aromatic plant material—was used as an offering in the temple ritual. In times of plague, incense was thought to sanitize places of slaughter and sacrifice and have purifying powers.

> For the hurt of my poor people I am hurt, I mourn, and dismay has taken hold of me. Is there no balm in Gilead? Is there no physician there? Why then has the health of my poor people not been restored? (Jeremiah 8:21–22).

Plant materials were used to make a variety of ointments, fumigants, perfumes, poultices, and incense. Isaiah used a cake or poultice of figs to cure Hezekiah's boils. Other plants or plant products mentioned in the Hebrew Bible that may have been used medicinally were almond, aloe, barley, carob, castor bean, cassia, cinnamon, crown of thorns (*Zizyphus vulgaris*), cumin, cypress, dill, flax, frankincense, grapes, juniper, leek, myrrh, oil, onion, pomegranate, sweet flag, sycamore fig, tamarisk, thyme, water lily, watermelon, willow, and wine.

ANIMAL AND MINERAL REMEDIES The 2nd century B.C. story of Tobit tells how this blind man regained his sight when fish gall was sprinkled in his eyes. Newborns were rubbed with salt, which may have had medicinal purposes as well as religious or superstitious meaning. Salt had great significance in the ancient world: The people of the Near East used it for ratifying agreements and as a symbol of constancy and fidelity (hence, the "Covenant of Salt" between God and Israel). Eye paint made from stibnite or galena may have been used to protect or heal the eyes, as it was in Egypt (see pages 40–41, 42–43).

Obstetrics

Midwives appear early in the Hebrew Bible (Genesis 35:17, Genesis 38:28, Exodus 1:15–21), and they are the first public health workers mentioned there. In Exodus, their importance is emphasized by the fact that they are named in a passage in which the pharaoh speaks to them directly.

A modern olive press. Olive oil production was a major industry in ancient times. Many stone olive presses have been found. A thick, vertical stone wheel, controlled by a long, pivoted bar of wood, rolled over the olives on a flat circular stone. A groove carried the oil into a basin.

Hebrew women gave birth using birth stools, with the assistance of midwives. The Hebrew midwives in Egypt told pharaohs that the Hebrew women gave birth more quickly and easily than Egyptian woman, indicating that the Hebrew midwives may also have assisted Egyptian women in childbirth.

Pharaoh and the Midwives

The king of Egypt said to the Hebrew midwives, one of whom was named Shiphrah and the other Puah, "When you act as midwives to the Hebrew women, and see them on the birth stool, if it is a boy, kill him; but if it is a girl, she shall live." But the midwives feared God; they did not do as the king of Egypt commanded them, but they let the boys live. So the king of Egypt summoned the midwives and said to them, "Why have you done this, and allowed the boys to live?" The midwives said to Pharaoh, "Because the Hebrew women are not like the Egyptian women; for they are vigorous and give birth before the midwife comes to them." So God dealt well with the midwives; and the people multiplied and became very strong. And because the midwives feared God he gave them families (Exodus 1:15–21).

Two biblical women died in childbirth. Rachel went into hard labor while traveling. The midwife, seeing that she was dying and trying to comfort her, said, "Fear not; for now you will have another son" (Genesis 35:17). The women attending the wife of Phineas said the same thing when she went into labor upon hearing of a tragedy.

Genesis describes two cases of twins. Rebecca overcame her barrenness when her husband Isaac prayed to the Lord. She experienced extreme fetal agitation during the pregnancy, to the point where she wondered why she still lived. Tamar also experienced a difficult birth. One twin's hand appeared, to which the midwife tied a red string to indicate the firstborn. But upon drawing back his hand, the other twin came out. Perhaps the midwife performed some sort of turning procedure to correct the difficult position of the babies.

Care for newborns included cutting the umbilical cord, washing the child with water, rubbing the skin with salt, and swaddling the child with bands.

Medical Procedures

CIRCUMCISION The only surgery mentioned in the Hebrew Bible is circumcision—the removal of the foreskin of the penis. The procedure took place when the infant was eight days old—this procedure was also performed on slaves owned by Israelites. The circumcision probably took place in the home, with the father or other male relative performing the proce-

Illnesses of the Hebrew Bible

The Bible mentions many illnesses, including plagues, consumption, fever, boils, sores, pestilence, leprosy, toothache, infertility, discharges, blindness, and madness. Scholars have attempted to identify these and other ailments when symptoms are described, but they often disagree on the exact identity of the conditions.

- King Asa, who "in his old age... was diseased in his feet" may have had gout or gangrene (1 Kings 15:23).
- The boy who "went out one day to his father among the reapers... [and] complained to his father, 'Oh, my head, my head'" may have had sunstroke or heatstroke (2 Kings 4:18–19).
- Balaam, "whose eye is clear... who hears the words of God, who sees the vision of the Almighty, who falls down, but with eyes uncovered" may have had epilepsy (Numbers 24:3–4).
- King Jeroboam experienced some form of paralysis in one arm. "The hand that he stretched out against him withered so that he could not draw it back to himself.... So the man of God entreated the Lord; and the king's hand was restored to him and became as it was before" (1 Kings 13:4–6). This condition may have been caused by a stroke or transient ischemic attack.
- King Jehoram was punished by God with "a severe sickness with a disease of your bowels, until your bowels come out, day by day, because of the disease" (2 Chronicles 21:15). One modern diagnosis of this condition is amebic dysentery with sloughing of the intestines and massive prolapse of the rectum.
- The skin ailment Job suffered, "loathsome sores from the sole of his foot to the crown of his head," may have been leprosy, elephantiasis, or diphtheria (Job 2:7).

Scholars have come up with some possible diagnoses of other illnesses mentioned in the Hebrew Bible: bubonic plague, jaundice, edema, pemphigus, leishmaniasis, osteomyelitis, gonorrhea, blepharitis ciliaris (inflammation of the eyelids), amaurosis (blindness caused by disease of the optic nerve), ophthalmia, hernia, psoriasis, and boanthropy.

Archaeologists have also discovered evidence for lice, toothache, and a variety of parasites including whipworm and hydatid disease, caused by tapeworms.

dure. The circumciser used a flint knife, even during the Bronze and Iron ages, illustrating the antiquity of the ritual. Metal knives were used starting in Roman times. The Egyptians and most Semites practiced circumcision.

When the Jews became heavily influenced by Greek culture, many men sought to reverse their circumcisions, undergoing a painful procedure called epispasm. The Greeks did not practice circumcision and because those participating in sports in gymnasia had to be nude, the difference prohibited Jews from taking part in this important aspect of Greek life. In 167 B.C., the Syrian-Greek ruler of Judea prohibited circumcision and many mothers who had their sons circumcised were killed.

Trephination Although not mentioned in the Bible, trephination—skull surgery—was occasionally performed in ancient Israel. Twenty-eight skulls have been found there that show signs of trephination, dating from Neolithic times to the 8th century A.D. Amazingly, 77 percent of those undergoing the procedure survived long enough for some bone regrowth to occur. One fascinating skull of a 20- or 30-year-old man, dating to 3500 B.C., found near Jericho, had three separate trephinations performed. He died shortly after the third operation. The operations were probably performed to drain a chronic infection inside the skull. Some scholars believe the term *ropheim*, usually translated as "physician," may actually mean "skull surgeon."

This ivory comb has two sets of teeth, one for straightening the hair and one for removing lice and eggs. Lice infestation was widespread in ancient Israel.

DENTAL PROCEDURES From about 200 B.C. come the remains of a man who had serious dental problems, including abscesses, cavities, impacted teeth, and an additional tooth embedded in the floor of the nose. He also had one of the world's first fillings. A bronze wire 2.5 millimeters in length had been inserted in a tooth canal. The canal had been widened before insertion indicating that specialized dental practitioners may have existed at this time.

PERSONAL HEALTH Archaeologists have excavated many bone spatulas in Israel and several other countries. People probably used these instruments to remove debris from the eyes. Examples of these objects are so numerous that they must have belonged to individuals for household use, rather than to specialists or healers.

The people of ancient Israel suffered from lice infestations. Delousing combs have been found together with 2,000-year-old louse eggs lodged between the comb's teeth. The combs had two sets of teeth, one to straighten the hair and one with tighter teeth, to remove lice and eggs.

Anatomy and Physiology

The ancient Israelites did not know that the blood circulated through the body. Although the word *leb* is usually translated as "heart," it did not mean an organ for pumping blood. The heart, instead, was the seat of the emotions and the place were knowledge, meditations, and moral judgments occurred.

The Israelites had no word for brain and did not connect thinking with the head. Thought, will, and emotions were all intertwined and all occurred in the *leb*. The *leb* corresponded with the functioning of the nervous system and, to many ancient cultures, seemed to be located in what we would call the stomach.

Blood was sometimes linked to the life principle, the vehicle for the soul. But more often, life was in breath. When God formed the first human from dust, he breathed into his nostrils the breath of life.

The Hebrew Concept of the Body and Soul

Body and soul were not two separate entities in ancient Hebrew belief. The word *nefesh*, usually translated as "soul," designates the life principle. A Hebrew person thought of him or herself as being a *nefesh*, meaning a psychophysical organism. A person did not *have* a body, but *was* an animated body—a unit of life.

The Jews must have had some basic understanding of anatomy and pathology gained from animal sacrifice and the ritual slaughter of animals for food. Carcasses had to be examined for disease or blemishes that made them unfit for use. In Talmudic times (100 B.C. to A.D. 500) physiologic studies and experiments were conducted on sick animals before and after slaughter, and postmortem examinations were also done on human corpses.

A Trial by Ordeal

In the only mention of an orally administered pharmaceutical in the Hebrew Bible, the Book of Numbers (5:11–31) describes what to do if a husband suspects his wife of adultery and she is not caught in the act. If the "spirit of jealousy comes upon him," the husband must bring his wife to the priest with an offering. The priest prepares a potion called the water of bitterness, made of holy water, dust from the tabernacle floor, and the ink from the written curse, to which the woman agrees by saying "Amen, amen." The woman drinks the water of bitterness. If guilty, she will experience "bitter pain, and her body shall swell, and her thigh shall fall away and the woman shall become an execration among her people. But if the woman has not defiled herself and is clean, then she shall be free and shall conceive children."

Talmudic Physicians

The Talmudic rabbi-physicians continued the biblical tradition of public health. Believing that "physical cleanliness is conducive to spiritual purity," they formulated rules about city planning, personal hygiene, social relationships, and agriculture. People had to live where physicians and public baths were available, kissing on the lips was forbidden, and food had to be clean, fresh, thoroughly cooked, and served in clean dishes.

The Talmud mentions many medical treatments including diets, compresses, sweating cures, rest cures, sunbaths, a change of climate, hydrotherapy, psychotherapy, massages, exercise, and various herbal remedies.

Neglected Traditions

Strong reliance on God and His omnipotence is one of the great strengths of the Jewish faith but it is also the reason that the Jews in ancient times never developed a medical system in the way other ancient cultures did. By the Middle Ages, even the Talmud had virtually no impact on medical practice, not even among the Jewish physicians of the Middle Ages. However, the structure of the Jewish faith, in which God was the Creator and Sustainer of all nature, made for a perfect fit with the rational, naturalist medicine of the Greco-Roman schools of thought. They borrowed and absorbed the knowledge of cultures around them as long as it did not come in conflict with their religious practices. In Judaism—as in the subsequent monotheisms of Christianity and Islam—science found a place not as a replacement for, but as a tool of, the still omnipotent God.

Even though their therapeutics have long since been supplanted, the healthful dietary laws are still very much in force for many Jews worldwide, and the scriptures—most notably, the Psalms—continue to provide healing power to vast numbers of sick and dying people of many faiths.

Europe

Greek and Roman Medicine

GREECE AND ROME DOMINATE Western ancient history. Western art, literature, architecture, politics, and science all have their roots in these two great civilizations. Their influential legacy includes many of the basics of modern conventional, or allopathic, medicine but also some aspects of therapies now considered alternative. Prescribing plants as drugs, the extensive use of teaching texts, and even the modern conception of the physician as a scientist who trains by internship can be attributed to antiquity. Hippocrates, a Greek physician, is to this day heralded as "The Father of Medicine."

Of course, much of our modern reverence for this period comes from the fact that we have access to so much information about it compared with other civilizations. In classical times, knowledge was routinely recorded in written form and many ancient Greek and Latin texts were preserved through the Middle Ages in monasteries and, later, in universities. Textbooks, treatises, social histories, and even drug catalogs give us a pretty clear picture of medicine in ancient Greece and Rome.

An Etruscan bronze mirror depicting Chalcas, a haruspex, examining a liver during divination. Haruspicy (liver divination) was the most important and widespread means of foretelling the future. After slaughtering the sacrificial animal, the priest inspected the liver and consulted texts to obtain guidance in state affairs or during outbreaks of disease.

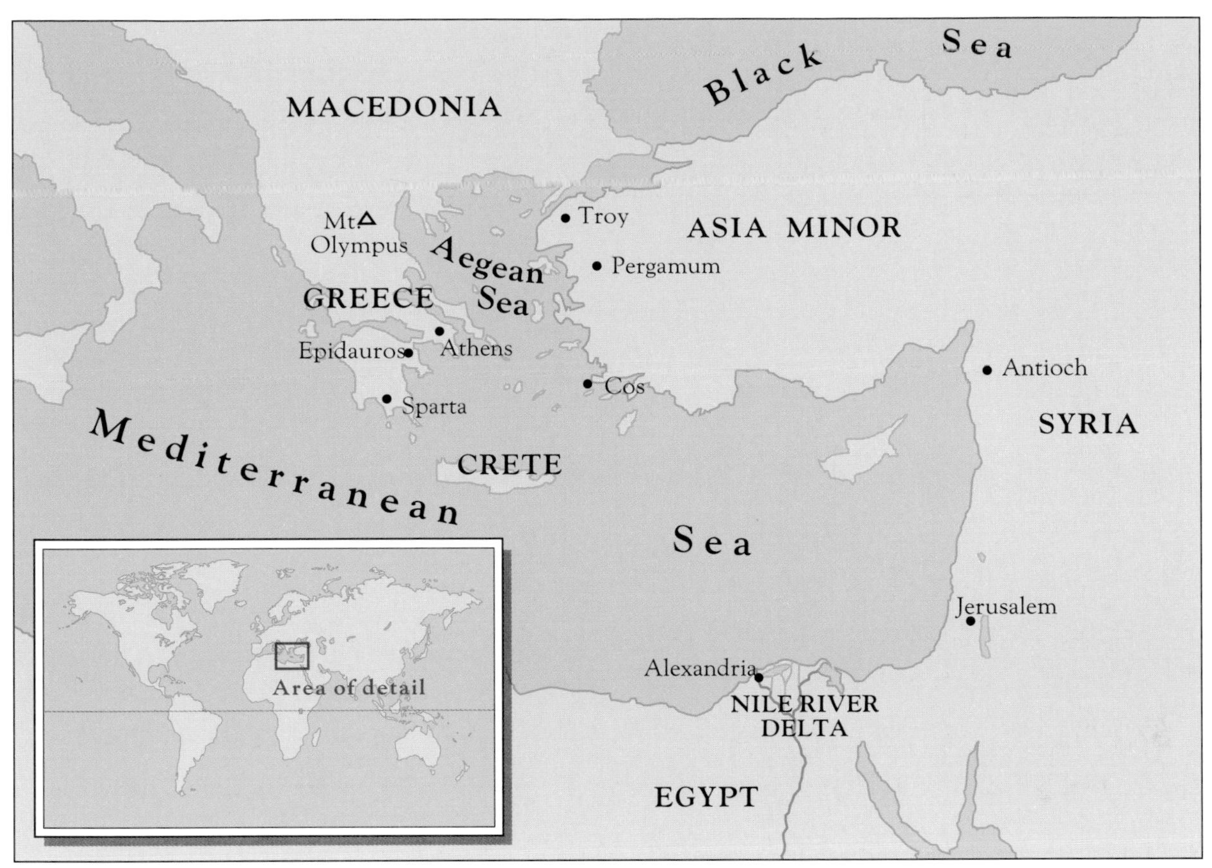

Greece

For a rocky, mountainous country with virtually no important rivers and only a limited amount of arable land, Greece's rise to prominence may be somewhat surprising. In ancient times, Greece consisted of the Greek mainland and the islands dotting the Aegean Sea. This life in and around the sea made the Greeks expert seafarers and traders—necessities that became their greatest strength as they accumulated knowledge and wealth from around the Mediterranean world.

A Brief History Several civilizations called this area home from as early as 3000 B.C. The Bronze Age (3000–1150 B.C.) saw the Minoan civilization flourish on the island of Crete and the Mycenaean civilization on the Greek mainland. Little is known about the Minoans—a relatively peaceful group of traders—but the Mycenaeans—a warlike people who probably gained much wealth from spoils of war—were later immortalized in the works of the poet Homer. The Mycenaeans were the warriors who fought the city of Troy in the *Iliad.* Homer composed the *Iliad* and the *Odyssey* in about 750 B.C., but the events in the poems take place in the Bronze Age, about 500 years before Homer lived. Bards transmitted these poems orally for centuries, and scholars consider the works of Homer a fairly reliable source of information on life in the Bronze Age.

Population movements and large-scale destruction brought an end to the great civilizations of the Bronze Age throughout the Mediterranean world. For Greece, it was the Dark Age, a time of poverty, depopulation, isolation, and vast decline.

A Time Line of Ancient Greece

3000–1150 B.C.: Bronze Age.

ca. 1250 B.C.: Trojan War.

1050–900 B.C.: Dark Age.

900–700 B.C.: Geometric Period.

776 B.C.: First Olympic Games.

ca. 750 B.C.: Homer lives.

700–480 B.C.: Archaic Period.

480–336 B.C.: Classical Period.

469–399 B.C.: Hippocrates and Socrates live.

431–404 B.C.: Peloponnesian War between Athens and Sparta.

430 B.C.: Plague in Athens.

336–323 B.C.: Alexander the Great rules.

331 B.C.: Alexander founds Alexandria, in Egypt.

323–31 B.C.: Hellenistic Period.

During the Geometric Period (900–700 B.C.), the polis, or city-state, began to develop. The population increased, and foreign contacts and trade resumed. The Greeks received the alphabet from the Phoenicians, and Greek literature began with the poets Homer and Hesiod.

During the Archaic Period (700–480 B.C.), political reforms laid the foundation for democracy in Athens.

During the Classical Period (480–336 B.C.), the time we consider the golden age, democracy, architecture, philosophy, and drama flourished in Athens. Socrates, Plato, Aristotle, Hippocrates, Herodotus, Sophocles, Euripides, and Aristophanes all lived in Athens during this period.

Alexander the Great, king of Macedon, conquered Greece and the Persian Empire and reached India. Greek culture, which had been confined to the Greek city-states, was now spread throughout southern Asia and northeast Africa. Alexander founded Alexandria, in Egypt, as well as many other cities.

CENTERS OF LEARNING Although Alexander died young in 323 B.C., he succeeded in spreading the Greek culture and language throughout most of the Mediterranean world, ushering in the Hellenistic (meaning Greek) Period (323–31 B.C.). Although Athens ceased to be the cultural center of the Mediterranean after Alexander's death, various other cities and regions began to rise in prominence: Pergamum in Asia Minor, Antioch in Syria, and Alexandria in Egypt became the new centers of learning, and, thanks to the pervasiveness of the Greek language, these disparate parts of the world could share knowledge and information like never before.

Alexandria's museum and library attracted scholars and writers. The city contained a large, self-governing Jewish quarter and many Jewish scholars contributed to religious and secular learning. Medical knowledge advanced greatly in Alexandria, where the traditional Greek prohibition against dissecting corpses did not apply. Alexandria also became a wealthy city of commerce. The Hellenistic period ended with the Roman annexation of Egypt and the suicide of Cleopatra VII.

MEDICINE IN HOMER The earliest references to the practice of medicine can be found in the works of Homer. Homer wrote in the 8th century B.C. about events that probably took place sometime in the 13th century B.C. Therefore, it is difficult to determine how many of the practices he mentions were in use at the time he was writing about or at the time he was actually writing. Practices probably did not change that significantly during that time, and certainly there is a heavy dose of myth that accompanies the accounts, so the distinction is not crucial.

Marble stele from 4th century B.C. *Athens. The physician Amphiaraos treats a young man's shoulder. The same young man lies on a bed, while Archinos offers him a snake. The snake is the symbol of Asklepios, the Greek god of healing.*

Homer's works mention physicians who were considered professional public servants worthy of honor. In the *Iliad,* Asklepios (a human, not a god, in Homer) could not leave his medical practice to participate in the Trojan War, so he sent his sons Machaon and Podalirios, who also possessed the healing arts. The Mycenaean Greek warriors at Troy considered these physicians more valuable as healers than as fighters: "For a physician is a man worth more than many other men, both to cut out arrows and to spread gentle salves."

Machaon "sucked out the blood and skillfully applied gentle salves which once upon a time kindly Chiron gave to his father." Chiron was a centaur who was famous for his wisdom and knowledge of the medical arts and taught many heroes, including Asklepios. (When Chiron died, he became the constellation Sagittarius.) When Machaon himself was wounded, a woman served him Pramnian wine sprinkled with goat cheese and barley meal and washed his wound with warm water.

The binding of wounds is mentioned twice in Homer. In fact, 147 wounds occur in the *Iliad,* and many are described with great precision, showing a rudimentary understanding of the anatomy of bones, muscles, and joints. When Odysseus received a wound, it was bound up, and a charm was recited to stop the bleeding.

Homer also mentions drugs coming from Egypt. Homer's "Egyptian drug" for wounds was probably opium; although opium does not itself come from Egypt, knowledge of the drug may have. Both the Minoans and Mycenaeans had extensive trade contact with Egypt and probably obtained medicines from the world-renowned physicians there.

GREEK RELIGION As with almost all other cultures, religious beliefs played an important part in the early Greek concept of healing. (We shall see how this changed.) The religion of ancient Greece had two main components: public and private.

The Greek Gods and Goddesses

Zeus: Father of the Greek gods, a sky god who controls storms. Guardian of law, oaths, and morals.

Hera: Wife of Zeus, protector of wives and mothers.

Poseidon: God of the sea and earthquakes, and guardian of sailors and fishermen.

Ares: God of war.

Aphrodite: Goddess of love, beauty, fertility, marriage, vegetation, animals, and the sea.

Apollo: God of music, prophecy, archery, and medicine. (His oracle at Delphi was renowned in antiquity. He is the father of Asklepios, god of medicine. Apollo caused or averted plagues and epidemics.)

Artemis: Goddess of hunting, animals, fertility, and childbirth.

Athena: Goddess of war, wisdom, arts, crafts, and, occasionally, medicine.

Hermes: God of commerce and travelers. He conducted souls to the underworld.

Hephaestus: God of fire and smiths.

Hades: God of the underworld, husband of Persephone.

Demeter: Goddess of agriculture and grain, mother of Persephone.

Hestia: Goddess of the hearth.

Dionysus: God of wine and vegetation.

Eileithyia: Goddess of birth, originated as a Minoan nursing or mother goddess.

Asklepios: God of health and medicine, patron of physicians, son of Apollo and a mortal woman named Coronis.

Public worship centered around the Olympian gods, ruled by Zeus. City-states erected temples to house statues of the deities, and at altars outside the temples sacrifices and offerings were made.

Festivals honoring the gods included processions, dancing, hymns, and sometimes athletic, musical, or dramatic competitions. The gods directed human affairs, so keeping them happy with offerings was of the utmost importance.

By the 4th century B.C., private religion centered around a new religious form: the mystery cults. These focused on a single god, and their membership was restricted to a few by invitation. The mystery cults taught that its worshipers would receive a form of immortality if they lived according to a code of ethical and religious behavior.

The Eleusinian Mysteries was a cult that involved the worship of Demeter. Celebrating at the time of the autumn sowing, initiates took part in processions with torches, purification in the sea, fasting, and drinking barley water mixed with pennyroyal, a type of mint. The rituals culminated in some sort of revelation. Initiation in this cult would ensure happiness in the afterlife.

The worship of Orpheus was also a private religion. Orphism held that the body was evil and the soul divine. Initiates would also be guaranteed happiness in the afterlife. Followers of Orphism did not kill or eat animals.

The cult of Asklepios also formed a part of private religion, providing a close, personal relationship with the divine, not found in the state religion. Asklepios, as we'll see, was an important figure in Greek Medicine.

ASKLEPIOS, THE HEALER The identity of Greece's greatest healer is murky. If he lived at all, it was in the very distant past even to the people of the Classical Period in Athens 1,000 years later. What is certain is that he had a significant influence over the practice of medicine throughout the history of Greek civilization. His fabled techniques seem to be a mixture of incantations and pragmatic remedies—sometimes employing drugs and salves and sometimes invoking mystical powers. But his influence does not stop with knowledge of his renowned techniques.

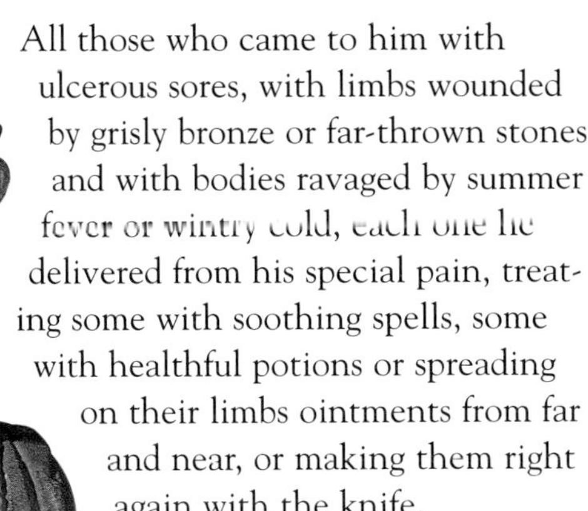

Bust of the Greek Bronze Age physician Asklepios, actually dating from the Roman Empire. Asklepios was mentioned by Homer as a healer, but later was revered as a healing deity.

Although a mortal in the *Iliad*, in later Greek mythology Asklepios (also spelled Aesculapius) was half divine—the son of Apollo, the god of healing, and Coronis. Chiron, the centaur, raised Asklepios and taught him the healing arts.

Pindar, an early 5th century B.C. Greek poet, described Asklepios's career as a physician:

> All those who came to him with ulcerous sores, with limbs wounded by grisly bronze or far-thrown stones, and with bodies ravaged by summer fever or wintry cold, each one he delivered from his special pain, treating some with soothing spells, some with healthful potions or spreading on their limbs ointments from far and near, or making them right again with the knife.

Asklepios's skill even enabled him to resurrect the dead, with the help of a plant that a serpent told him of. Zeus, enraged by the way Asklepios upset the natural order, struck him with a thunderbolt and killed him. After his death, Asklepios became a minor divinity, the worship of whom could bring health and prevent disease—certainly, more than most family physicians can guarantee.

His family also had roles in healing. With his wife Epione, Asklepios had the two

Asklepian Cures

Many of the cures occurring in Asklepian sanctuaries were written down on panels and put on display to advertise the healing power of that sanctuary. Here are four examples:

> A woman from Crete "thanks Asklepios, the Savior, having got a severe ulceration on her little finger and being cured when the god ordered her to apply an oyster shell burnt and powdered with rose salve and to anoint it with mallow mixed with olive oil. And so he cured her."
>
> A woman "slept in the shrine for the sake of children and saw a dream; a snake seemed to lie on her belly, and from this five sons were born to her."
>
> "A dog cured a boy . . . He had a growth on the neck. When he had come to the god, one of the sacred dogs healed him—while he was awake—with its tongue and made him well."
>
> "A man had an abdominal abscess. He saw a vision and thought that the god had ordered the slaves who accompanied him to lift him up and hold him, so that his abdomen could be cut open. The man tried to get away, but his slaves caught him and bound him. So Asklepios cut him open, rid him of the abscess, and then stitched him up again, releasing him from his bonds. Straightaway he departed cured, and the floor was covered with blood."

sons, who took part in the Trojan War as healers, and two daughters who also had healing roles—Panacea and especially Hygieia, the personification of health. (Her name, in fact, is a form of the Greek word for health and is related to the English word *hygiene*.)

Asklepian Sanctuaries This powerful reputation as a healer made Asklepios the object of popular worship. The Greeks built many cult centers to Asklepios where the sick could seek cures. Some of the most famous of the Asklepian sanctuaries were at Epidauros, on the Greek mainland; Cos, an island off Asia Minor; and Pergamum, in Asia Minor. These centers were located outside or at the edge of cities, in areas considered particularly healthful, usually near springs. They contained temples, gymnasiums, theaters, inns, priests' quarters, and baths—much like modern spas or retreats.

Head of Asklepios's daughter Hygieia, the personification of health, attributed to the sculptor Skopas, ca. 360 B.C. Hygieia was closely associated with her father's cult and often appears with him in art. Hygieia had her own cult at Titane. In the Hippocratic Oath, Hygieia's name comes directly after Asklepios's.

Those wanting to ward off illness, to seek a cure for a disease or disability, or to give thanks for health followed a standard procedure after arriving at an Asklepian sanctuary. First, the worshiper bathed in the sea, this outer cleansing symbolizing inner purity. The visitor next offered honey cakes on an altar and performed more ritual bathing at a water basin overseen by the priests.

Those seeking a cure then entered the abaton, a sacred dormitory adjacent to the temple, where they would lie on pallets. Attendants put out the lights and encouraged silence and sleep. This sleep, known as incubation, formed the central part of the cure. During this sleep, Asklepios appeared to the worshiper in a dream or vision, carrying mortar, pestle, and a medicine chest. When the god healed the patient directly, he mixed potions, applied plasters, used the knife, or commanded the sacred serpent to lick the appropriate body part.

If Asklepios did not cure the patient himself, he gave instructions to the patient in a dream, to be performed when the patient awoke. When the god's recommendation was too difficult for the patient to understand, the priests would come in and interpret its meaning, prescribing drugs, a special diet, exercise, or baths.

Those cured by Asklepios dedicated thank offerings to him in the form of sacrificed animals, cakes, money, wreaths, plates or cups of valuable metal, or models of the cured body part.

Hippocrates Besides sacred healing in the Asklepian sanctuaries, Greek patients had access to secular physicians, too. These two healing systems, secular and sacred, coexisted without rivalry. By the Classical Period, the practice of medicine was revered, and doctors, although not deified like Asklepios, were prominent figures in society.

Hippocrates of Cos—now referred to as "the Father of Medicine"—was a famous physician and teacher of medicine in the 5th century B.C. He came to represent the ideal physician—devoted, kind, and skillful. He descended from a family of physicians that traced their roots back to the god Asklepios, and thus were called the "family of Asklepiads." As the family expanded it became a guild of physicians. Two centers, or schools, developed from this group; Hippocrates headed the school on the island of Cos.

Marble bust of the Greek physician Hippocrates. From the island of Cos off the coast of Asia Minor (present-day Turkey), Hippocrates headed a medical school and wrote extensively about the healing arts. His influence on the practice of medicine is felt even today, as doctors still take the Hippocratic Oath (see page 76) when they begin their medical careers.

The Hippocratic Corpus Supposedly, Hippocrates wrote a large body of work, known as the Hippocratic Corpus, which includes the famous Hippocratic Oath. Scholars have argued since ancient times as to how many (if any) of these more than 60 treatises were actually written by Hippocrates himself. Rather than the work of a single author, this group of medical writings is now regarded as the work of many authors and traditions, which had their origins in 5th and 4th century B.C. medical literature. When the librarians of Alexandria, Egypt, received any medical work, it appears that they classified it as having been authored by Hippocrates. It was the practice in ancient times to ascribe the works of an entire school to the founder, and students and disciples often wrote in the name of their master. Therefore, although Hippocrates himself may not have written any of this material, scholars still refer to the body of work as Hippocratic.

The Humors Social taboos prevented human dissection in 5th century Greece, limiting the knowledge of anatomy and physiology. To fill this gap in knowledge, the theory of the four humors was developed later in the Hellenistic period and attributed to Hippocrates along with the theory of pneuma. The four humors—blood, phlegm, yellow bile, and black bile—determined a person's constitution, temperament, and health. Pneuma (literally "air") allowed consciousness, thought, and perception.

Too much or too little of any of the humors, caused by weather or diet, produced sickness. To regain health, seen as balance among the humors, physicians recommended purging, bloodletting, emetics, and dietary restrictions. The Hippocratic Corpus also contains material on herbal medicine, including the popular Greek purge made from black hellebore, parsnip, seseli, cumin, and anise.

Diagnosis and Prognosis Hippocratic medicine was concerned with prognosis, determining the likely course of an illness based on previous experience. Clinical observation of the beginning and progress of the illness took into account the patient's appearance and behavior, noting especially unusual breathing, sweating, excretion, and temperature. The physician looked for hollow, light-sensitive, or red eyes, cold ears, yellow skin color, and a tense face. He asked the patient about sleeplessness, loose bowels, and appetite. Meno, a pupil of Aristotle, wrote that Hippocrates believed that gases emanating from undigested food rose through the body displacing health-giving breath. This theory closely resembles the ancient Egyptian idea of *wekhedu*, which entered Greek medical thought in the 6th century B.C. (see pages 37–38).

The Corpus also discusses diagnosis at length. Diseases are described, classified by

The Hippocratic Oath

Perhaps the most famous part of the Hippocratic Corpus is the Hippocratic Oath. Still used today as a declaration of a doctor's moral responsibility, the Oath is one of the world's first statements of medical ethics:

> I swear by Apollo, the Physician, and by Asklepios and Hygieia and Panaceia and all the gods and goddesses, making them my witnesses, that I will fulfill according to my ability and judgement this oath and this covenant:
>
> To hold him who has taught me this art as equal to my parents and to live my life in partnership with him, and if he is in need of money to give him a share of mine, and to regard his offspring as equal to my brothers in male lineage and to teach them this art—if they desire to learn it—without fee and covenant; to give a share of precepts and oral instruction and all the other learning to my sons and to the sons of him who has instructed me and to pupils who have signed the covenant and have taken an oath according to the medical law, but to no one else.
>
> I will apply dietetic measures for the benefit of the sick according to my ability and judgement; I will keep them from harm and injustice.
>
> I will neither give a deadly drug to anybody if asked for it, nor will I make a suggestion to this effect. Similarly I will not give to a woman an abortive remedy. In purity and holiness I will guard my life and my art.
>
> I will not use the knife, not even on sufferers from stone, but will withdraw in favor of such men as are engaged in this work.
>
> Whatever houses I may visit, I will come for the benefit of the sick, remaining free of all intentional injustice, of all mischief, and in particular of sexual relations with both female and male persons, be they free or slaves.
>
> What I may see or hear in the course of the treatment or even outside of the treatment in regard to the life of men, which on no account one must spread abroad, I will keep to myself holding such things shameful to be spoken about.
>
> If I fulfill this oath and do not violate it, may it be granted to me to enjoy life and art, being honored with fame among all men for all time to come; if I transgress it and swear falsely, may the opposite of all this be my lot.

symptoms, and explained. Along with the descriptions go lists of suitable foods, herbal remedies, and treatments for disease. As the following examples show, this work had elements of modern scientific method and practical applications for specific symptoms:

> A consideration of the diet of the sick, as compared with that of men in health, would show that the diet of wild beasts and animals generally is not more harmful, as compared with that of men in health. Take a man sick of a disease which is neither severe and desperate nor yet altogether mild, but likely to be pronounced under wrong treatment, and suppose that he resolved to eat bread and meat, or any other food that is beneficial to men in health, not much of it, but far less than he could have taken had he been well.... But as it is, if a man takes insufficient food, the mistake is as great as that of excess and harms the man just as much.

Here's another example:

> Hydromel [a honey-water drink], drunk throughout the course of an acute disease, is less suited on the whole to the bilious, and to those with enlarged bellies, than to those who are not such. It causes less thirst than does sweet wine, for it softens the lungs, is mildly expectorant, and relieves a cough.

Another part of the Corpus recognizes the process of healing as a team approach:

> Life is short and the Art (of medicine) long, the occasion urgent, experience deceptive, and decision difficult; yet not only must the physician be ready to do his duty but the patient, attendants, and circumstances must also cooperate if there is to be a cure.

A bronze incense burner from Delphi, Greece, ca. 450 B.C. Incense burning accompanied prayer. The herb thyme was used for fumigation (fragrant smoke offerings) against evil. Pliny believed that burning thyme drove away all venomous creatures.

Banishing Superstition

One aspect of ancient Greek medicine that distinguished it from other early forms of healing was its movement away from the understanding of illness and healing as supernatural occurrences. Despite the Asklepian sanctuaries and various other private cults of healing, many of the great physicians of ancient Greece wrote about a rational, scientifically based view of biology and medicine.

The Hippocratic Corpus developed from observation, reasoning, and philosophy and contains no discussion of magic or superstition. Divinities did not cause disease, as in other medical belief systems. Diseases had their own individual natures and ran their course in a set time period. Humans were products of their environments, subject to the same physical laws as the rest of the world.

A Greek physician who studied at Alexandria, Soranus practiced his art in Rome in the 2nd century A.D. Although he wrote about 20 books, only 2, on fractures and on gynecology, have survived. His works offer rational and practical advice, sound therapy, and a denunciation of superstition. Soranus wanted to remove all superstition from medicine because he felt it was at best useless, and often involved unpleasant, painful, or dangerous treatments. However, he did recognize the value of harmless objects, such as amulets, saying

> One should not forbid their use; for even if the amulet has no direct effect, still through hope it will possibly make the patient more cheerful.

The ancient Greeks believed hysteria was caused by problems with the uterus (*hystera* is the Greek word for uterus or womb). Many Greek physicians treated this condition with unpleasant methods, such as anointing the nose and ears with burnt hair or squashed bedbugs or by blowing air into the uterus. In contrast, Soranus recommended such reasonable treatments as warm compresses and relaxing baths.

THE BOTANISTS, EARLY PHARMACISTS The prescribing of drugs was a significant part of Greek medicine, but drugs in those days were mainly herbs and other plant products. Therefore, herbalists or botanists were the true pharmacists. Several great Greek botanists distinguished themselves, leaving behind a huge body of work on the classification and medicinal uses of various plants.

Theophrastes. Aristotle's pupil, colleague, and successor, Theophrastes was not technically a physician but a philosopher and, one might say, a pharmacist of sorts. He made the first systematic study of plants using observation and classification; his work is considered antiquity's highest achievement in botany. Theophrastes wrote about herbal medicine, detailing the plant parts used, the methods of collection, and the herb's effects on people and animals.

The Herbs of Theophrastes

The following entries are from Theophrastes's botanical writings (when he refers to "they," he is speaking of the various peoples of the empire from whom the recipes and uses were learned):

> The root of cyclamen [part of the primrose family] is used for suppurating [discharging] boils; also as a pessary for women and, mixed with honey, for dressing wounds; the juice for purging of the head, for which purpose it is mixed with honey and poured in; it also conduces to drunkenness, if one is given a draught of wine in which [the root] has been steeped. They say also that the root is a good charm for inducing rapid delivery and as a love potion; when they have dug it up, they burn it, and then, having steeped the ashes in wine, make little balls like those made of wine-lees [dregs], which we use as soap.
>
> The root of wild cucumber [squirting cucumber] is used for white leprosy and for mange in sheep, while the extracted juice makes the drug called "the driver." It is collected in autumn, for then it is best.
>
> The leaves of germander pounded up in olive oil are used for fractures and wounds and for spreading sores; the fruit purges bile and is good also for the eyes; for ulcers in the eye, they pound up the leaf in olive oil before applying it. It has leaves like the oak, but its entire growth is only about a palm high; and it is sweet both to smell and taste.

Diokles. Theophrastes was not the first Greek to write a medicinal herbal. The late 4th century B.C. physician Diokles holds that honor. The Athenians called Diokles a "younger Hippocrates" and credited him with inventing a type of head bandage and an ingenious device for extracting barbed arrows from wounds called the "Spoon of Diokles." Only fragments of his works on animal anatomy, botany, physiology, and dietetics survive, but Theophrastes seems to have used Diokles's material as a source in his own writings.

Dioscorides. Pedanius Dioscorides was a Greek physician and botanist who lived during the 1st century A.D. Dioscorides traveled extensively and discussed cures with a wide variety of people. He matched testimonies with scientific observation and scholarly research into the work of other pharmacy experts whose work is now largely lost. He compiled his knowledge into a systematic, rational treatise on the medical property of 600 plants, 90 minerals, and 35 animal products, including the flesh of vipers. This work, produced in Greek, was translated into Latin, Arabic, and in 1665, into English; it is the most widely read botanical work ever written. Dioscorides's work greatly influenced Islamic, medieval, and renaissance botany and medicine.

LEARNING ABOUT ANATOMY A crucial window of time for the study of anatomy opened up in Alexandria during the Hellenistic period in the 3rd century B.C. Before then, Greek religion and custom forbade human dissection; by the 2nd century A.D. the practice had ended until the 16th century.

Herophilus, the Anatomist. Herophilus (4th century B.C.), a Greek physician, surgeon, and medical scholar trained in Cos, went to Alexandria. There, dissection and even vivisection of condemned criminals was performed. Herophilus applied logic to direct observation and made important discoveries about the eye, liver, brain, and the reproductive, vascular, and nervous systems.

He identified nerves but thought they were channels for pneuma (the word for "air" that also came to mean "thought")—a not altogether wrong assertion. Herophilus discovered that the brain was the location of intellect, believing it the center of the nervous system. He may have been the first to discover the fallopian tubes and ovaries. Herophilus did not simply study the body, though; he tried to use his anatomical knowledge, along with recommendations about diet and exercise, to restore and maintain health.

Erasistratus, Father of Physiology. A contemporary of Herophilus, Erasistratus (born ca. 304 B.C.) was a Greek physician trained at Athens and Cos. After emigrat-

The Wonders of Lettuce

The following are entries from Dioscorides's work *De Materia Medica:*

Cultivated lettuce; good for upper tract, a little cooling, sleep causing, softening to lower tract, increasing lactation. Boiled down it increases nutrition. Unwashed and eaten it is given for upper digestive troubles. Its seeds being drunk are good for [those who] continually dream and [the seeds help the patient] avert sexual intercourse; eaten too often they cause dim-sightedness. They are preserved in brine. The stalk growing up has something like the potency of the juice and sap of wild lettuce.

Wild lettuce is similar to the cultivated, larger stalk; leaves: whiter, thinner, more rough, and bitter to the taste. To some degree its properties are similar to those of opium poppy, thus some people mix its juice with opium. Whence its sap, 2 obols [1.14 grams] in weight with sour wine purges away watery humors through the digestive tract; it cleans away albugo [a white opacity of the cornea], misty eyes. It assists against the burning [of eyes] anointed on with woman's milk. Generally it is sleep inducing and anodyne. It expels the menses; [it is] given in a drink for scorpion and venomous spider bites. Drinking the seeds, similar to that of the cultivated kind, averts dreams and sexual intercourse. Its juice produces the same things [as cultivated lettuce] but with a weaker force. The sap [should be] extracted in an earth bowl, exposed to sunlight first... and stored.

ing to Alexandria, Erasistratus furthered the anatomic researches of Herophilus, advancing knowledge of the brain, heart, and nervous and vascular systems. His primary interest was physiology (the study of the workings of the body), particularly respiration and digestion.

Erasistratus also worked as a surgeon, opening the abdomen to treat the liver and using catheterization to treat slow, painful urination. Going against the teachings of the Hippocratic Corpus, Erasistratus was skeptical of bloodletting and the theory of the four humors.

Theriac—A Popular Panacea

Galen did not invent theriac, but he produced this popular remedy for the Roman Emperor Marcus Aurelius. The name *theriac* comes from the Greek word for wild animal. Theriacs were originally antidotes to both human and animal bites, which the ancients thought to be poisonous. They were then used against poisons in general.

The Persian king Mithridates poisoned criminals to study the effects of antidotes; he compounded the most effective ones into a drug for his own use, which he named mithridatium, after himself. Andromachus, the Roman Emperor Nero's physician, took mithridatium, now called theriac, added chunks of viper flesh to the recipe, quintupled the amount of opium, and brought the total number of ingredients to 64. Galen applied theriac to bites and abscesses and wrote a whole book on the subject. Theriac was a popular panacea through the ages; it remained in the official French pharmacopoeia until 1884.

GALEN—A PHILOSOPHER DOCTOR Galen, the last great ancient thinker in the field of medicine, lived in the 2nd century A.D. A Greek from Pergamum in Asia Minor, he studied grammar, logic, and philosophy before beginning his medical studies at age 16 in Alexandria, Egypt. After leaving Alexandria, he returned to his hometown to take a post as doctor in a gladiator school. From there he moved to Rome where he became physician to the emperor Marcus Aurelius, began a large medical practice, lectured on anatomy, and vivisected and dissected animals, especially apes. Galen performed important work using dissection, proving that both arteries and veins carry blood—a landmark discovery in Greek medicine and medicine in general.

In addition to his contributions to anatomy and physiology, his works contain much information on pharmaceuticals; the term *galenic* refers to his principles of using plant preparations. A galenical is a vegetable remedy or herbal simple. He also concocted a form of theriac, the famous panacea containing almost 70 ingredients in an opium base (see "Theriac—A Popular Panacea").

Galen wrote on many topics, including grammar, philosophy, anatomy, pathology, and therapy. He felt that philosophy and medicine should be integrated. He was a monotheist who felt that the study of anatomy was a way of praising God. Galen's comprehensive system of medical philosophy came to be the embodiment of Greek and Roman medical knowledge; it dominated medicine until the 16th century.

THE HEALTH CARE SYSTEM Although some of their techniques were undoubtedly primitive, the ancient Greek system of health care evolved into one that, in many respects, looks like our modern Western one. Their education and training followed similar lines, and they even had private offices.

Originally, medical knowledge was handed down through the family, and healing was generally a private matter, but medicine slowly developed from a mere skill to a trade. Physicians were eventually considered workers for the public good. They traveled from place to place with a case of instruments, appliances, and drugs, examining patients.

Many physicians had apprentices as nurses and assistants, bound by an agreement. The masters imparted their secrets to their apprentices directly. Then, special centers for the study of medicine began to appear in east Greece at Cos and Cnidus, at Cyrene and Alexandria in North Africa, and in Italy at Croton. These centers were free associations of physicians, teachers, students, and apprentices.

Physicians received employment from rulers or cities as public physicians, or they set themselves up in private practice. Doctors examined and treated the sick in an *iatreion*, or physician's office, equipped with special lights, instruments, bandages, and drugs. They prepared the drugs themselves or with the help of a rhizotomist, or root cutter, who collected, dried, pulverized, and prepared roots and plants for use as remedies—the ancient equivalent of the pharmacist.

GREEK DRUGS Greek physicians prescribed a wide variety of drugs, some effective and some actually harmful. They poured vinegar or wine into wounds and over dressings as a disinfectant. Physicians gave hellebore, a poisonous plant, to patients to induce vomiting and diarrhea. Swollen, inflamed wounds were covered with a plaster made from mullein, raw clover leaves, boiled rock plant, and hulwort.

Greek physicians and botanists ascribed many different uses to hundreds of plants. For example, mustard had more than its share of medicinal duties. Hippocrates recommended white mustard seed taken internally or applied as a counter-irritating poultice made with vinegar. Dioscorides stated that mustard leaves are good for internal pain of long duration. Mustard juice mixed with honey and water was a good gargle for inflamed tonsils. Used as an ointment, mustard cured dandruff and cleared the complexion. Added to figs, it improved hearing, whereas mustard juice in honey helped the eyesight.

Minerals also had a place in Greek pharmaceuticals. Powdered alum, sodium carbonate, copper oxides, lead oxides, and lead sulfate dried and disinfected ulcers and wounds.

Animal products occasionally played a role in drug preparation. Viper's flesh was one of the more popular animal ingredients. It was the main ingredient in theriac, originally a poison antidote. Snake meat pickled in oil, wine, salt, and dill was used to improve eyesight and nerves.

Physicians recommended using drugs in a variety of ways. Patients took them internally, applied them externally as salves, ointments, and plasters, and sat over burning substances or vapor baths containing herbal remedies. Pessaries consisting of remedies wrapped in wool or linen were inserted vaginally, and enemas were used for purging.

The Healthful Regimen Although it seems remarkable how similar ancient Greek medical practices are to our own—or, more accurately, how much our practices are based on the Greek—one aspect of treatment they emphasized that is only now making a resurgence in modern medicine is lifestyle adjustments. Regimens—integrated courses of treatment involving diet, exercise, rest, and personal hygiene—were often part of Greek health practices. And prevention rather than treatment was often the aim of these regimens.

Ancient Greek healers believed the right foods and exercise, applied with attention to the seasons, winds, age, and home situation of the individual, could prevent illness. Humans, being composed of fire and water, had to keep these two elements in balance with a healthful regimen. Foods were considered to have actions congruent with elements, such as cooling, drying, heating, wind-producing, moistening, binding, and so on. For example, barley was considered cooling and drying, millet was dry and binding, fish were dry and light, wines were hot and dry, garlic was hot and laxative, and so on. While recovering from illness, patients were fed barley gruel, honey and water, honey and vinegar, and a variety of wines.

Different forms of exercise also helped keep the body in balance. Running heated and dissolved the flesh and digested the food; wrestling hardened the body. (You could pay a professional trainer to tell you the same today.) Walking, ball playing, sparring, and marching were all recommended. Hippocrates and Galen endorsed massage for toning the body. Strenuous rubbing hardened the body and gentle rubbing relaxed it.

Bathing also kept the body in balance. Freshwater baths moistened and cooled; saltwater baths warmed and dried. Cold baths dried the body. Hot baths and vapor baths reduced pain.

Medical Procedures Greek healers treated a variety of injuries and diseases. The Hippocratic Corpus mentions many war wounds: a man hit high in the abdomen with a powerful and dangerous arrow, someone wounded in the back with a javelin, a man wounded from behind by a broad lance, and so on. Industrial accidents also took their toll: A man who fell on an anchor was wounded in the belly, a loaded wagon passed over a man's chest and broke his ribs, and a cobbler stabbed his thigh with the awl. Often physicians prescribed enemas, purges, and emetics for such injuries. Even minor injuries could lead to death from tetanus or erysipelas—a spreading inflammation caused by bacteria, sometimes associated with gangrene.

Besides purges and emetics, physicians used fomentations (the application of heat), bleeding, cautery, draining of the lungs, and suturing to treat wounds. Skins, bladders, and bronze or pottery vessels held hot fomentations, recommended for pain in the side. Bleeding was achieved by venesection, leeches, or cupping. Greek physicians used bloodletting with cups so frequently that the bleeding cup became the symbol of the physician and was often depicted on doctors' tombstones. Bleeding was used to cure many ailments including eye disease, pneumonia, and lack of nourishment from food.

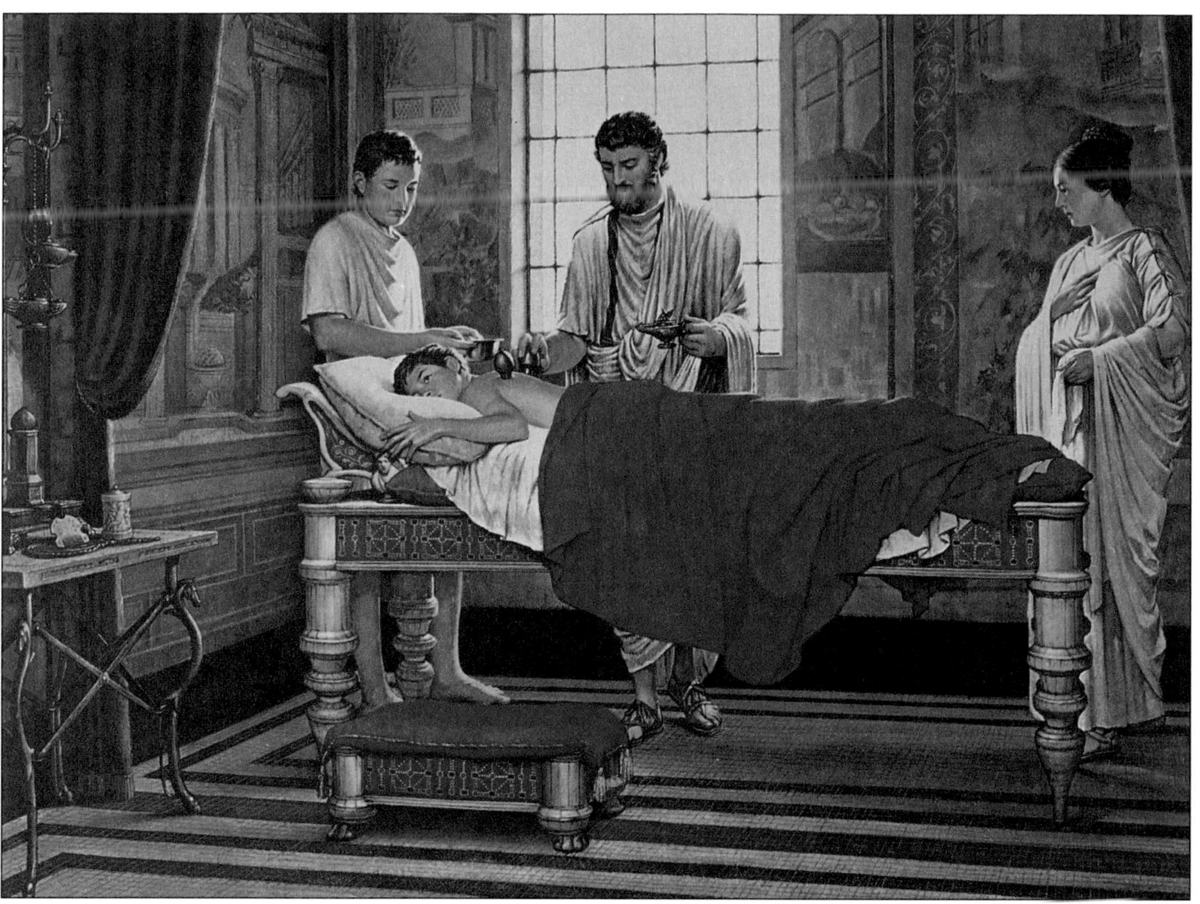

A modern painting by Robert Thom showing Galen, physician to three Roman emperors, cupping a boy. Greek physicians used bloodletting with cups so frequently that the bleeding cup became the symbol of the physician and was often depicted on doctors' tombstones. Bleeding was used to cure many ailments.

Physicians used cauteries, heated irons, for many different procedures, such as destroying abnormal growths, curing or preventing dislocations, stopping hemorrhage, and draining pus from the lungs. The main purpose of cauterization was to drain by piercing a hole or to dry and tense particular parts of the body.

Greek doctors had many appliances to help them restore patients to health. The Hippocratic Bench served to repair dislocated joints. It had many adjustable fittings—levers, crossbars, posts, props, windlasses, straps, and cords to extend and counter-extend fractures and dislocations.

Physicians also performed surgery: amputation, trephination (cutting a hole in the skull to relieve pressure), and other procedures dealing mostly with the bones and their accompanying tissues.

Except for draining the lungs, operations on the soft body parts were avoided. Physicians had a variety of medical instruments to choose from—knives, scalpels, scarificators, needles, probes, forceps, drills, catheters, specula, and more.

WOMEN IN MEDICINE For a male-dominated culture, gynecology received a fair amount of attention, and women were far from absent in the medical field. In the Hellenistic period, women began to study medicine formally. The first female obstetrician in Athens, Hagnodice, studied with Herophilus.

Midwives. Although female physicians were not the norm, the profession of midwife was well respected. Greek midwives were expected to read and study medical texts. Herophilus, Soranus, and Galen all wrote treatises or practical manuals for midwives. Midwives performed much the same service as a doctor, having some knowledge of medical theory. Midwives also worked under the direction of male physicians, serving as intermediaries between doctor and patient. Soranus believed that the best midwives were "trained in all branches of therapy, for some cases must be treated by diet, others by surgery, while still others must be cured by drugs."

Fertility and Childbirth. Of all women's ailments, medical writers mentioned menstrual complaints the most frequently. The pharmacopoeias contained many remedies to cure or ease them. Most Greek medical practitioners believed that menstruation was a purging process that contributed to the health of the female body. Soranus felt that it did not preserve health, but related only to childbearing. He believed that virginity aided female health because pregnancy and birth exhausted the female body and made it waste away.

There seem to have been several theories of the exact mechanism of reproduction. Some Greeks believed that a woman ejaculated female semen into her womb during orgasm and the fetus formed when ejaculate from the man ran together with that from the woman, but Aristotle and others did not believe this. By and large, the idea was that the man's semen stayed in the woman's body until her womb accepted it, combining it with her nourishment to form a fetus—a process that could take days or weeks. The Hippocratic Corpus noted that the best time for conceiving a child was just after the menstrual flow stopped (which is not true, by the way).

Childbirth took place in the home of the pregnant woman. The midwife made sure that all necessary equipment was available. This included a birthing stool, oil for injection and lubrication, warm water for cleansing, warm fomentations to ease pain, sea sponges, pieces of wool, bandages for swaddling, a pillow to place the baby on, and things to smell, such as pennyroyal, apples, and quinces.

Midwives controlled the birth, although a physician might be present to oversee the proceedings. The midwife checked the progress of dilation. When enough space existed for the passage of the baby, the woman got up from her bed and sat on the birthing stool. The seat was crescent shaped; the sides were solid boards with handles

Soranus on Midwives

The midwife must have the right mental, moral, and physical qualifications: She must be literate and study her work theoretically. She must have a keen understanding and a good memory; must enjoy her work and have a sense of honor; must have sound sense, a strong constitution, practical experience, and presence of mind; must not be easily alarmed, but must be sympathetic; that she should herself have given birth is not absolutely necessary. She should further be strong, steady, not given to talk, proof against bribery by those who desire criminal abortion, and free of superstition. She must have gentle hands.

that the woman grasped and pressed while straining. The front and back were open to allow access by the midwife and her assistant.

Contraception. The Hippocratic Corpus mentions numerous methods of birth control and abortion. For example, to prevent pregnancy for one year, a woman should soak a piece of copper sulfate in water and drink the liquid. Copper is used today to make certain intrauterine devices (IUDs) because copper is a spermicide. The Corpus also advocated the Lacedaimonian leap—leaping with the heels to the buttocks, squatting, and sneezing violently to expel the man's seed.

Soranus had more to say on the subject. He recommended that when the man was about to ejaculate, the woman must hold her breath and draw away a little, so the seed would not be hurled too deeply into the uterus. She should get up immediately, squat, induce sneezing, wipe the vagina, and drink something cold. He also suggested smearing the orifice of the uterus with olive oil, honey, cedar resin, balsam tree juice, or white lead. He mentions vaginal suppositories and oral contraceptives containing botanical ingredients such as pomegranate peel, silphium (a now-extinct plant in the giant fennel family—the tree, not the herb), rue, and rocket. Many of the plants that Soranus recommended have been shown through modern testing to have an effect as a contraceptive or abortifacient. Women also used amulets and charms as contraceptives (see "Pliny on the Hairy Spider Amulet," page 96).

For a woman who sought an abortion, Soranus recommended that she should take violent exercise, be jolted in a carriage, and should carry heavy things. Other means of inducing abortion were vigorous massage, the eating of spicy foods, using diuretics and clysters to purge the abdomen, and a variety of poultices and vaginal injections. When all else failed, protracted baths and heavy bloodletting were used.

PEDIATRICS AND CHILDREARING Soranus condemned the custom of Germans, Scythians, and some Greeks of plunging newborns into cold water to toughen them, or worse, to let them die as not worth keeping if they became livid or convulsed from the chilling. However, the Greeks, in contrast to Egyptians and Jews, practiced infanticide. This was done by exposure to the elements. Baby girls, in particular, were left to die because poor families could not afford a dowry, without which the girl could not marry. However, in Sparta, female infants were not exposed; only male infants who would not grow into strong warriors were killed. In Hellenistic times, some exposed infants were collected, wet-nursed, and became slaves or prostitutes.

Children who were kept were well cared for. Soranus gives much advice for swaddling infants and using proper cribs and bedding. He discusses treatment for teething and common children's ailments. Soranus even discusses a "walker," a chair on wheels that helps a toddler learn to walk.

Soranus recommended that women nurse their own children, but not until three weeks after the birth, to allow time for the mother to regain her health. In the meantime, a wet nurse suckled the baby. Soranus felt that a wet nurse should be between 20 and 40 years old, have given birth two or three times, be healthy, and have a large frame with medium-sized breasts. She should not be ill-tempered because

> since by nature the nursling becomes similar to the nurse and accordingly grows sullen if the nurse is ill-tempered.... Besides, angry women are like maniacs and sometimes when the newborn cries from fear and they are unable to restrain it, they let it drop from their hands.

Soranus criticized women who used certain practices to quiet a crying child:

> One must give it milk, but not incessantly, not before the bath, and far less during the bath itself, as women obstinately do who wish to silence an infant that cries easily....

He faults women who give a baby

> three baths a day and night and pour water over it to the point of exhaustion, delighting in the fact that when it has grown weary after the bath it keeps quiet and falls asleep. But this is harmful, for the body becomes weak, susceptible to disease, easily cooled and easily affected by any harm.... If, however, the newborn cries constantly after nursing, the wet nurse should hold it in her arms, and soothe its wailing by patting, babbling, and making gentle sounds....

Rome

To us in the modern Western world, Rome symbolizes the height of ancient civilization and power. Adopting many of the political, philosophical, and scientific aspects of the great Greek civilizations, the Romans built an enormous empire and solidified many of the aspects of our culture that we take for granted.

So closely linked were the Greek and Roman cultures that it is often difficult for us to look back and distinguish exactly who gave us what. Even during the height of Roman power, most of the Mediterranean world they controlled used the Greek language, not Latin. Greek was the common language of the Mediterranean world. In fact, many of the aristocracy in Rome itself used Greek well into the 1st century A.D. Some of the great Greek physicians named earlier—Dioscorides and Galen among them—lived under Roman rule and served, however distant, the Roman emperors.

A BRIEF HISTORY The people of ancient Italy were hardworking farmers and shepherds whose lives centered around the family. Hundreds of small settlements lay

Roman Time Line

753 B.C.: Mythical Romulus founds Rome.

146 B.C.: Rome destroys Carthage.

63 B.C.: Rome annexes Judea.

55 B.C.: Julius Caesar invades Britain.

44 B.C.: Julius Caesar assassinated.

30 B.C.: Antony and Cleopatra commit suicide.

30 B.C.–A.D. 14: Augustus rules.

A.D. 23–79: Pliny the Elder lives. (Wanting to observe the eruption of Mt. Vesuvius, Pliny dies breathing the fumes.)

A.D. 161–180: Marcus Aurelius rules.

A.D. 330: Constantine founds Constantinople.

A.D. 364: Roman empire divides into east and west.

A.D. 452: Attila the Hun reaches the gates of Rome.

A.D. 476: End of western empire.

A.D. 1453: Turks conquer Eastern (Byzantine).

scattered throughout Italy. Eventually the settlements at the mouth of the Tiber River coalesced to form the city of Rome in the 8th century B.C. The Etruscans, a mysterious people whose language is unrelated to any other, had a number of flourishing city-states north of Rome. They greatly influenced the Romans, giving them the alphabet (which the Etruscans had adapted from the Greeks), public buildings, and new forms of social, political, and military organization.

In 510 B.C., Rome expelled its last king and became a republic, ruled by a senate and two consuls elected yearly. By 272 B.C., Rome controlled the entire Italian peninsula. By 167 B.C., Rome dominated the entire Mediterranean.

Julius Caesar ended the Roman Republic in 44 B.C., when he declared himself perpetual dictator, and one month later, a group of senators assassinated him. Caesar's adopted son Octavian emerged the victor from the civil war that followed, and in 27 B.C., he was granted the title of Augustus, becoming the first Roman Emperor.

The rule of Augustus was a Golden Age for Rome. After a century of political turmoil and civil wars, he ushered in a time of peace.The one-man rule established by Augustus saddled Rome with more bad rulers than good, though. Marcus Aurelius exemplified the noble Roman—intelligent, hardworking, and duty bound—but Caligula and Nero were known for their cruelty and excesses.

In A.D. 395 the Roman Empire became officially divided into eastern and western parts. The west came under continued barbarian attacks, until, in 476, the first barbarian king of Italy deposed the last western emperor, bringing about the end of Roman rule there. Constantinople, capital of the Eastern Empire, remained a world power for another millennium, until the Turkish invasion of 1453.

ROMAN RELIGION The Roman religion was a practical one: Divinities protected people in return for the performance of certain rituals. The religion did not demand a love of the gods or moral behavior. A catalog listed the gods' names, their protective powers, their special functions, and the rites that had to be performed to buy their favors.

The Romans felt that spirits were everywhere. Different gods controlled the different parts of life, down to the smallest detail. Divinities existed who prevented wheat rust, watched over tradesmen's profits, protected springs, and saw to the manuring of fields.

To make sure the appropriate gods felt well disposed toward them, the Romans used three main methods in both private and public religion. Prayer communicated a suppliant's request to the god in question. Sacrifice, a gift to the god, could convince the god to grant the request. Divination made known the will of the god.

In the home, the *pater familias* (father of the family) conducted the religious rituals, although some were performed by the *mater familias*. In the state religion, priests came from the political elite. They conducted the yearly rituals in honor of the god during the appropriate festival. The Roman calendar contained about 40 fixed festivals and a number of movable feasts.

The Romans adopted many of the religious practices of the people they conquered. Greek, Egyptian, and Persian cults became popular in Rome, and in the 4th century, Christianity became the official religion.

RELIGIOUS HEALING The early Romans had no specific god of healing. They used divination to determine which god sent a particular disease and had ceremonies to try to placate that god. Sometimes the illness itself became a deity, for whom the Romans built temples and conducted sacrifices. For example, the goddess Febris (the word for fever) had three temples in Rome.

Early Roman healing contained a strong religious element. People who were seeking protection and health would pray

> Father Mars, I entreat and beg you... to keep at bay, repulse, and take away disease, known and arcane... and to give health to me, my house, and my household.

Prayers and offerings were also made for the health of cattle—supernatural veterinary medicine.

Healing sanctuaries existed throughout the lands conquered by Rome. Most centered on hot or cold mineral springs. Ponte di Nona, a healing sanctuary established in the late 4th century B.C. near Rome, contained a temple, a circular pool, a small hostel with baths, and an enclosed mineral spring. People seeking or giving thanks for healing dedicated many votive offerings there, such as terra-cotta hands and feet, heads, eyes, and sexual organs—images of what had been healed or what needed healing.

A popular healing sanctuary at a spring site in Umbria contained a temple to the god Clitumnus. The sanctuary also held small shrines, each with its own god; some of these had their own springs. Archaeologists have uncovered many votive tablets expressing the gratitude of the healed and of those to whom Clitumnus revealed the future.

Roman Divinities

Janus: God of beginnings, doorways, public gates, travel, communication. The first month (Januarius) was named for him.

Mars: Originally, a god of vegetation, fertility, cattle, agriculture, and spring. Later, god of war.

Jupiter: God of rain and thunder, protector of city and state.

Juno: Goddess of marriage, pregnancy, childbirth, and nursing.

Vesta: Goddess of domestic and religious fire.

Saturn: God of agriculture, vine growing, prosperity, and abundance.

Minerva: Protectress of commerce, industry, and schools—sometimes associated with healing.

Mercury: God of merchants.

Faunus: God of fertility and healing.

Angitia: Goddess of healing with medicinal plants, discoverer of poisons and antidotes.

Flora: Goddess of spring, cereals, fruit trees, the vine, and flowers.

Bona Dea: Goddess of women's fertility. (Her temple in Rome was a herbarium where the ill could obtain healing remedies.)

Clitumnus: River god and oracular deity.

Aesculapius: The Roman name for Asklepios, Greek god of healing.

The festival called the Lupercalia, celebrated on February 15, ensured the fertility of the female participants. The priests of the god Faunus, called Luperci, wearing only a goatskin girdle, struck Roman matrons with goatskin thongs. Those who were sterile presented their backs or hands to be lashed. This purification ceremony was intended to drive away hostile spirits that had prevented the women from getting pregnant.

An Etruscan bronze liver model from the 2nd century B.C. The Etruscans practiced divination using the size, shape, color, and markings of the liver of a sacrificed sheep. The model's divisions may have related parts of the liver to areas of the sky, making known the will of the gods.

Agricultural Beginnings of Medicine

The beginnings of Roman medicine come from agriculture. The *pater familias* administered cures to family, slaves, and farm animals. These cures consisted of magical incantations and animal, vegetable, and mineral remedies. Wool was believed to have numerous curative powers when combined with various other ingredients, such as fat, rose oil, honey, sulfur, vinegar, and the herb rue. Cabbage also had many uses as a remedy. Even the urine of a person who had been living on cabbage was used; children who were washed with it would never be weak and puny.

Early Roman medicine involved treatment with simple remedies; issues of prognosis, diagnosis, and prevention were not addressed. The person who administered the cure needed no special training, and doctors played no part in this form of healing.

Greek Healing in Rome

The Romans knew of surgeons and dentists from their neighbors, the Etruscans, who had contact with the Greek settlements of southern Italy. But not until the plague of 295 B.C. did the Romans seek outside help in the field of medicine. At that time, the Greek

A Roman Recipe for the Treatment of Asthma and Poisoning

- ½ hemixeston (about 1 pint) nut grass
- ripe juniper berries
- 12 minas (about 9 pounds) plum raisins
- 5 minas purified pine resin
- 5 minas sweet flag
- 1 mina camel's thorn
- 12 drachmas (1½ ounces) myrrh
- 9 sextai (18 ounces) old wine
- 2 minas honey

Having removed the seeds from the raisins, pound and crush them with the wine and the myrrh, and having pounded and sifted the rest of the ingredients, combine them all to soak for one day; then, having boiled the honey until it has a glutinous consistency, mix it carefully with melted pine resin, and having carefully pounded together the rest of the ingredients, put up for storage in an earthen vessel.

healing god, Asklepios, in the form of a snake, was invited to settle in Rome. His temple stood outside the city on an island in the Tiber River.

Greek physicians came to Rome and were granted Roman citizenship in 46 B.C., although many traditionalists remained suspicious of them. The Roman statesman Cato wrote

> The Greeks... are a quite worthless people, and an intractable one.... When that race gives us its literature it will corrupt all things, and even the more if it sends hither its physicians. They have conspired together to murder all foreigners with their physic.

Despite the skepticism of traditionalists and the common people, aristocratic households often hired Greek physicians or puchased those who had become prisoners of war. Physicians with training and skill served the rich; the poor made due with inferior doctors or even quacks, who put on public recitations to attract crowds and patients.

The Roman public had little faith in the Greek physician, who had acquired a reputation for entering the sickroom, bleeding the patient, laying on a plaster, and giving an enema no matter what the problem. Physicians were known among the general public for pompous verbosity and painful, sometimes deadly, cures. One Greek doctor gained the nickname "executioner" for his savage use of the knife and cautery.

ROMAN PHYSICIANS Eventually, the Romans began to adopt the methods and theories of the visiting Greeks. A Roman physician, like a Greek one, trained with a doctor father or served as an apprentice to a doctor. Sometimes a teacher would take students with him while visiting patients or would give medical lessons in his shop, called a *taberna medica*. Some cities hired doctors to give medical instruction and to treat the needy for free. Most physicians would not have had access to books or drawings but could visit centers of medical studies to consult references.

This 5th century B.C. red-figure crater from Italy depicts soldiers healing their wounds. Bandaging war wounds is mentioned twice in Homer. The Hippocratic Corpus mentions formal bandaging exercises giving physicians practice in various bandaging techniques.

The Roman army offered a young physician the chance to receive valuable experience. Perhaps recalling the praise of physicians in the *Iliad* ("For a physician is a man worth more than many other men.... "), Augustus systematized military medical services. Before then, medical treatment had been haphazard. The duties of the military medical corps, if there actually was a formal corps, would have included treatment of wounds and the control of infectious diseases. On the battlefield, soldiers received first aid from medical assistants. In the field and fort hospitals, a *medicus*, or doctor, would prescribe treatment or perform surgery.

Like artisans, physicians formed guilds, which had their own offices and secretaries. These guilds met to discuss work-related affairs, to give advice and instruction, and to provide meals and burials for members.

Medicine was one of the few occupations open to Roman women. *Medicae* (female physicians) commanded respect, and some became wealthy enough to fund the construction of large buildings and monuments. A few *medicae* became specialists.

PLINY AND CELSUS Pliny the Elder (A.D. 23–79) wrote the *Natural History*, a massive compendium of scientific knowledge covering a number of topics including geography, animals, botany, medicine, art, and architecture. Of the 37 volumes of the *Natural History*, seven cover medical botany. Pliny discusses at length the medicinal qualities of many herbs, vegetables, and minerals.

He had little faith in physicians and herb sellers, many of whom he felt were quacks. Echoing an anti-establishment opinion you're likely to hear from some quarters today, Pliny thought that

> if people sought remedies in the kitchen-garden, medicine would be quite cheap. But herbs are not familiar to most people because experience of them is confined to country folk, who live among the herbs; moreover, nobody wants to look for herbs when crowds of medical men are everywhere.

Aulus Cornelius Celsus wrote his encyclopedia on agriculture, medicine, military science, rhetoric, philosophy, and law during the reign of the Roman emperor Tiberius (A.D. 14–37). Celsus, a wealthy Roman landowner, summarized medical knowledge down to his own time, including the native Latin traditions and the theories of the Hellenistic medical schools. Pliny and Celsus provide us with a look at Roman health, healing, and the various cures and practices available during the 1st century A.D.

PREVENTIVE MEDICINE The Romans excelled at public hygiene as a form of preventive medicine. Since the earliest times, swamps were drained to prevent disease. When building fortified towns, the Romans sought out healthy sites, away from swamps. The Cloaca Maxima, the

A portrayal of the Roman baths at Caracella, Italy, by the 19th century Dutch Painter Sir Lawerence Alma-Tadema. The Romans built public baths in almost every corner of their empire, showing their concern for public health and hygiene.

main sewer of Rome, drained waste into the Tiber River. Aqueducts ensured a clean water supply for the city. Public baths allowed all classes of society to maintain cleanliness.

In addition to public hygiene, the Romans also recognized the influence of lifestyle factors—diet, exercise, habits—on health. Celsus recommended the preventive called "the regimen": regulating food, drink, exercise, bathing, and medicine. Celsus's regimen included moderation in food and drink. Savories or salad should precede a main course of boiled or roasted meat. Dessert, for those who could take it, should consist of dates or apples. For exercise, Celsus favored walking, the strenuousness of which depended on the constitution of the individual. With the exception of the main course of meat, this is much like the advice you'd receive from a modern dietician.

Celsus on Exercise

For the person who has been occupied during the day, whether in public or private matters, should designate some part of the day for the care of his body. His first concern in this regard should be exercise, which ought always to precede the eating of food. The exercise should be greater for him who has worked less and is considered well, and it should be lighter for him who is tired and who has thought less during the day. . . . A healthy man, who is both strong and his own master, ought not to place himself under any arbitrary rules, nor should he have a need for a doctor. . . . His sort of life should give him variety. He should sometimes be in the country, sometimes in the city, more often should he be on a farm. He should sail, hunt, rest from time to time, but more frequently exercise his body. While inactivity weakens the body, work makes it strong; the former gives an early old age, and the latter promotes an extended youth.

Bodywork was another healing art revered by the Romans. They used massage for toning the body, to help in the recovery from fever, and to relieve headaches and partial paralysis. The wealthy had personal physicians and assistants who massaged them at home. Others got massage treatments at public baths where trainers and doctors sold their services.

Roman Drugs

Besides chairs, tables, and couches, a Roman doctor's office would have shelves and cupboards to hold medical instruments and herbs and drugs in jars, pots, and boxes. Equipment for drug preparation, such as mortar and pestle, balances, marble palettes for rolling pills, bottles, scoops, spoons, and spatulas would all be needed. Animal fats, wax, olive oil, wine, water, milk, and honey were used in drug preparation as well.

Besides the pharmacopoeias, which listed hundreds of plants and their uses, the Romans learned of medicinal plants from their foreign allies. In a Roman fortress in Germany, the lid of a lead pot with the words "Extract of the root of britannica" was found. Pliny tells us of a Roman camp where the soldiers suffered from scurvy, their teeth falling out and their knee joints failing. The Frisians, a tribe then loyal to the Romans, introduced them to the plant called britannica, which was good for the sinews and mouth diseases and relieved quinsy and snakebite. This plant has been identified as water dock (from the genus *Rumex*). Seeds of dock have been found in several Roman towns in Britain.

These medical instruments from Italy are probes for pharmaceutical use. The small end was used for stirring medicines and the larger end used for applying them.

Archaeologists have excavated a Roman legionary hospital in Germany and have found hundreds of plant seeds there, including

- centaury, used to heal wounds and snakebites and to cure eye ailments
- fenugreek, used as a poultice and enema
- henbane, a painkiller and sleeping draft
- plantain, given for pulmonary tuberculosis, hemorrhage, dysentery, and elephantiasis
- St.-John's-wort, used to expel bladder stones

Eye diseases troubled many in the Roman Empire to the point where all recruits going into the Roman army had to take an eye test. Eye ointments and salves constituted a major part of ancient pharmacopoeias. Salves were often named for their inventor, such as the salve of Axius or salve of Philo. Some salves contained minerals—copper and zinc hydroxide, zinc carbonate, and mercuric sulfide—that would have been helpful for their antibacterial qualities; the Romans probably got these from the Egyptians who had used them for centuries (see pages 42–43).

Drug makers created dried ointment sticks, called *collyria;* these were short lengths of premixed ingredients that a doctor could easily carry and then dissolve in water, milk, or egg white to make a usable salve. The collyria were usually marked with a stamp to identify the manufacturer. Archaeologists have discovered about 300 of these collyrium stamps, which usually contain the name of the disease, the name of the salve, and a person's name, probably the inventor of the salve or the maker of the medicine—the world's first brand-name drugs.

The great demand for rare herbs and spices from the East needed for botanical remedies gave rise to quack doctors and druggists who took advantage of a gullible public eager for cures. Galen—the Greek doctor practicing in Rome—obtained herbs directly from the emperor's own suppliers to ensure their genuineness. In Syria, he bought balsam of Mecca, and from a passing caravan on the Indian trade route, he purchased lycium, a tannin-rich extract highly effective in treating eye diseases.

Pliny on Quack Druggists

The deceit of men and cunning profiteering led to the invention of the quack laboratories, in which each customer is promised a new lease on his own life at a price. At once compound prescriptions and mysterious mixtures are glibly repeated, Arabia and India are judged to be storehouses of remedies, and a small sore is charged with the cost of a medicine from the Red Sea, although the genuine remedies form the daily dinner of even the very poorest.

ROMAN SURGERY Roman physicians used surgery as a last resort, and those who did so were probably specialists in a particular operation. Anatomical knowledge was limited and anesthetics and powerful antiseptics were lacking; doctors often preferred not to treat a patient at all than to risk their reputations if the patient died. Yet surgery had come a long way since the time of Hippocrates, when only minor procedures were attempted. The breakthrough came in Hellenistic times when the Alexandrian physicians discovered the ligature of blood vessels. With the knowledge of how to tie a bleeding artery came the ability to conduct more complex surgical operations.

Celsus mentions trephination done to remove damaged cranial bone. He advised extreme caution, noting the possibly lethal effects of damaging the cerebral membrane. Physicians used drills and chisels to remove cranial bone. For small areas, they used a specialized instrument, the crown trephine, consisting of an iron or bronze cylinder with a serrated bottom edge, rotated with a strap, bow, or handle. Archaeologists have discovered two such crown trephines along with a large set of medical instruments in a tomb in Germany from the 1st or 2nd century A.D.

Surgery had a place in the treatment of eye diseases. Granular ophthalmia, an infection caused by *Chlamydia* bacteria, was common and often led to trichiasis, or ingrown eyelashes. To remove the eyelashes, they were plucked out with a special type of forceps and the root was cauterized

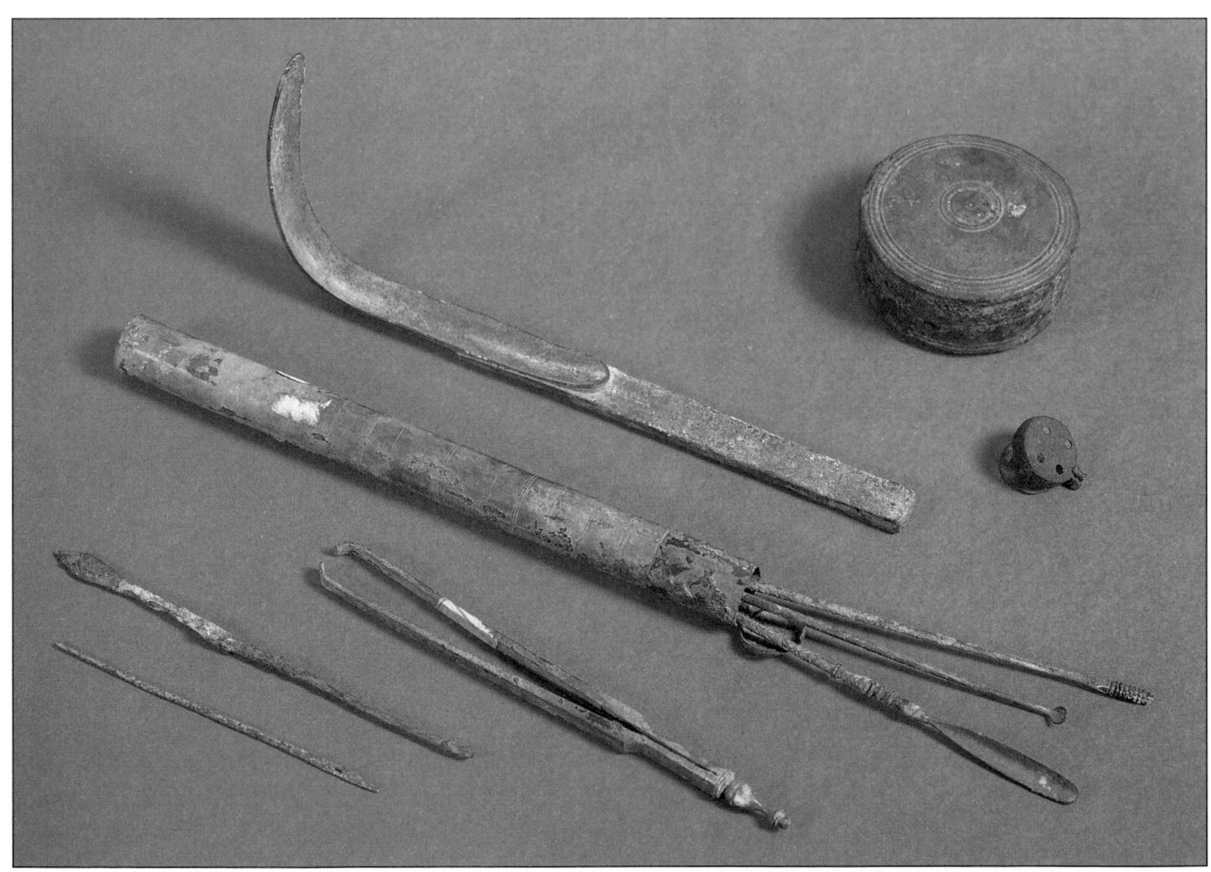

Medical instruments from Italy. The curved strigil was used for warming oil and pouring it into the ear. The medical instrument case contains implements for extracting ointment from tubes and applying it. Tweezers were used for medical and cosmetic hair removal. Needles were used in eye surgery. The larger round object is a bleeding cup.

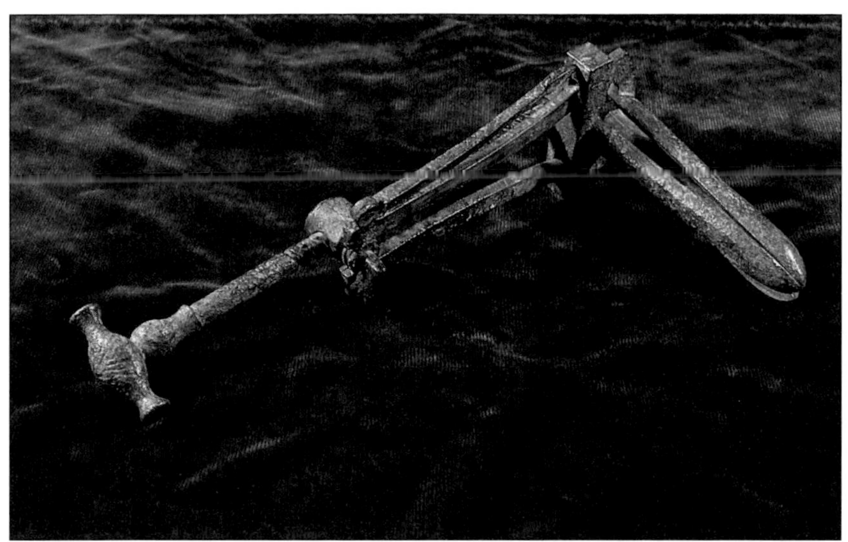

Roman medical instrument from Pompeii. This vaginal speculum used for gynecologic examinations was operated by a screw-threaded handle.

with a very hot, fine iron needle. To cure cataract, the doctor used a needle to move the cataract below the pupil. Sometimes the cataract was cured using needles with special devices that extracted the broken-up pieces of cataract by suction; a similar method is used by modern eye surgeons.

The Roman world allowed for great upward mobility, and some freed slaves often became enormously wealthy. To have their slave brands removed, they would consult a surgeon-physician who specialized in this field. Other former slaves with enlarged ear holes saw a doctor who would incise the excess earlobe, sew up the edges, and cover it with a healing drug. Other forms of cosmetic surgery included counter-circumcision, raising eyelids, and repairing mutilated ears, lips, and noses.

Erysipelas, an acute infectious disease, troubled many people in ancient Rome. One consequence of this disease was an inflamed uvula, which became elongated and diseased and had to be removed. A special forceps, with long slender handles and hollowed jaws with interlocking teeth, crushed the neck of the uvula. This same instrument was also used to strangle hemorrhoids.

Pliny felt the most painful disease was strangury (slow, painful urination) from stones in the neck of the bladder. The Hippocratic Oath forbade Greek doctors from attempting lithotomy (cutting out bladder stones); only specialists in this procedure could perform this operation. These specialists were not members of the medical profession. Physicians did not want to risk their reputations and that of the "art" of medicine by being associated with a practice that lead to the deaths of patients, as this procedure must have done fairly often. But by the time of Celsus, medical advances allowed physicians to undertake this operation. The difficulty of lithotomy probably meant that it was a specialty field within the field of surgery. The surgeon used a lithotomy knife to make an incision and removed the stone with fingers or a scoop.

Military surgeons performed more daring operations because "a doubtful hope is preferable to certain despair," according to Celsus. He describes the procedure for replacing intestines that have rolled out of the body because of a stab wound. More usual battle injuries included flesh wounds; the doctor had to take care to stop hemorrhage, prevent inflammation, and promote agglutination. Special forceps helped with the removal of arrowheads. Infection and gangrene after surgery led to amputation.

For most amputees, a simple crutch, stick, or peg leg would have to suffice, but the wealthy could afford prostheses. From a tomb in Capua dating to ca. 300 B.C., comes a skeleton with an artificial leg made of realistically shaped sheet bronze over a wood core. A veteran of the second Punic War (218–201 B.C.) lost his hand in battle and had an iron one made to replace it.

LEAD POISONING Lead poisoning was a real problem for the Romans. They made must, a wine concentrate used extensively in cooking, by boiling down wine to half its volume. Lead pans were used for this because bronze spoiled the flavor. The Romans were also exposed to lead in their diet through lead pipes. Vitruvius, the 1st century B.C. architect, states that

> water is much more wholesome from earthenware pipes than from lead pipes. For it seems to be made injurious by lead, because white lead is produced by it; and this is said to be harmful to the human body. . . .

He mentions the illness of those who work with lead. Celsus also knew of the dangers of lead; he had an antidote for poisoning by cerussa (basic lead acetate [white lead] made by leaving pieces of lead in jars full of vinegar); he recommended mallow or walnut juice rubbed up in wine.

Despite the concern about lead, lead pipes were widely used in private houses, public baths, and military bases. Women used lead as part of their cosmetic routines. They whitened their foreheads and arms with white lead and dusted their hair with it. Celsus prescribes wound antiseptics containing lead acetate and lead oxide. Pliny says of lead carbonate that since it is

> admitted to be a poison, all the current instructions on employment for medicinal purposes are in my opinion decidedly risky.

One result of lead poisoning would have been gout, caused by an excess of uric acid in the blood. Urate crystals are deposited in the joint tissues, which can lead to the destruction of the joint surfaces, causing swelling, inflammation, pain, and restricted use of hands and feet. The toxicity from lead-adulterated wines could cause kidney failure and an increase in uric acid in the blood. The Romans considered gout a disease that affected the rich, who consumed luxury food and drink with no self-discipline. To treat it, Celsus prescribed bloodletting, diuretics, emetics, and hot fomentations. During remission, he recommended gentle exercise and a spare diet, observing that "some have obtained life-long security by refraining from wine, mead, and venery for a whole year."

CONTRACEPTION Many different physicians had their own methods and formulas for birth control. In discussing contraception, Pliny says "Gossip records a miracle: that to rub juniper all over the male part

Pliny on the Hairy Spider Amulet

There is also a third kind of [poisonous spider], a hairy spider with an enormous head. When this is cut open, there are said to be found inside two little worms, which, tied in deer skin as an amulet on women before sunrise, act as a contraceptive. . . .They retain this property for a year. Of all such preventives, this only would it be right for me to mention to help those women who are so prolific that they stand in need of such a respite.

before coitus prevents conception." Juniper is a strong uterine stimulator that can cause uterine tissue to contract and potentially cause contraception or spontaneous abortion. He warns that pregnant women must take care to exclude rue and water mint from their diet, because they may cause abortion. To induce sterility, Pliny recommends parsley and ferns.

Aetius of Amida, who lived in the 6th century A.D., also mentions some male contraceptives. A man should rub alum, pomegranate, or oak galls with vinegar on his penis and he will not fertilize a woman. He even gives an oral contraceptive for men: the burned testicles of castrated mules drunk with a decoction of willow. For women, Aetius recommends a mixture of aloes, stock seeds, pepper, and saffron in wine. For a contraceptive suppository he suggests white lead with oil. He also considered very effective an amulet made of a lioness's uterus placed in an ivory tube.

By far the most frequently mentioned form of birth control in the Roman world was abortion. A woman who had an abortion might be disapproved of for depriving her husband of offspring or considered selfish for avoiding motherhood, but she would not be breaking any state or religious law. Aspasia, the pseudonym of a 2nd century A.D. writer on gynecology, recommends a sitz bath in a decoction of fenugreek, marshmallow, and artemisia. Following the bath, the woman must rub herself with honey or the juice of rue. Artemisia also prescribes applying a plaster to the abdomen consisting of various herbal ingredients mixed with oil. She notes several other methods of abortion, including pessaries, suppositories, fumigation, vomiting, and drinking strong laxative broths.

Like the Greeks, Roman law allowed for selective disposal of unwanted children through infanticide, exposure, or sale into slavery. The law stated that all male children and the firstborn female child must be reared. No other child could be killed unless it was crippled or deformed at birth. Before a child could be exposed, five neighbors had to agree that it was justified. Many people flouted the law.

CHILDBIRTH Roman births took place in the home, with a midwife presiding over the event and female relatives present. The midwife was the first to inspect the

A Roman depiction of childbirth. Midwives controlled the birth, making sure all necessary equipment was available. The pregnant woman sat on a birthing stool. The front and back were open to allow access by the midwife and her assistant.

infant and advise on its fitness for rearing. The child's father made the final decision as to whether the child would be raised or exposed.

The Romans believed a newborn was unclean. Because of this, a ritual purification took place, on the eve of which a vigil to protect the infant was held. Three men, armed with ax, pestle, and broom struck the threshold of the house and swept the floor. At dawn on the eighth or ninth day after birth, the purification ritual took place, presided over by the appropriate goddess. The child's future was foretold through divination. A protective amulet was placed around the infant's neck and the child officially named.

Wet nurses were bought, if they were slaves, or hired. They lived in the infant's home or nursed the infant in their own home. Babies were usually weaned when they were two or three years of age. The long period of nursing helped protect them from diseases such as dysentery that were transmitted through cow's and goat's milk. Celsus noted that dysentery carried off mostly children up to the age of ten and pregnant women, who, if they survived, often lost their child.

THE ROMAN WAY OF DEATH Relatively few diseases in the ancient world could be cured, and even those with access to the best health care sometimes suffered greatly from their afflictions. Marcus Aurelius, the Roman emperor and stoic philosopher, who suffered from severe chest pains, wrote, "pain is neither unbearable nor unending, so long as you remember its limitations and don't add to it with your imagination."

Pain and hopelessness drove some to suicide, such as Corellius Rufus, who had gout.

> When he grew worse with advancing age, he bore up through sheer strength of mind, even when cruelly tortured by unbelievable agony; for the disease was no longer confined to his feet as before, but was spreading through all his limbs.

Eventually he could no longer stand the pain and starved himself to death.

Those who determined to endure their suffering and avoid suicide were greatly admired. Pliny the Younger wrote of his friend:

> His patience throughout this illness... would fill you with admiration; he fights against pain, resists thirst, and endures the unbelievable heat of his fever.... He sent for me... to ask the doctors what the outcome of his illness would be, so that if it was to be fatal he could deliberately put an end to his life, though he would carry on with the struggle if it was only to be long and painful; he owed it to his wife's prayers and his daughter's tears, and to us, his friends, not to betray our hopes by a self-inflicted death so long as these hopes were not in vain. This, I think, was a particularly difficult decision to make, which merits the highest praise. Many people have his impulse and urge to forestall death, but the ability to examine critically the arguments for dying, and to accept or reject the idea of living or not, is the mark of a truly great mind.

Perhaps Pliny the Elder best summarized the Roman view of life and death.

> I do not, indeed, hold that life ought to be so prized that by any and every means it should be prolonged. You holding this view, whoever you are, will nonetheless die.... Of all the blessings given to man by nature, none is greater than a timely death.

Northern European Medicine

UNLIKE THE WELL-DOCUMENTED and well-studied civilizations of ancient Greece and Rome, the history of the rest of Europe—much of what we now know of as Britain, France, Germany, and Scandinavia—is shrouded in mystery. Records are scarce, and what histories were written were often recorded by Greeks or Romans invading these territories.

Because of this unique perspective, we often think of the peoples of ancient Northern Europe the way the Romans did: "barbarians"—lawless, warlike invaders intent on destroying civilization. Although some of the storied brutality is true, the peoples of Northern Europe also had cultures of their own with religions, laws, and medicine.

Most healing practices in Northern Europe's early history were, predictably, folk remedies, with a great deal of magic and witchcraft mixed in. Greek and Roman medical knowledge, however, did eventually influence the healing arts of Northern Europe with a more scientific approach. And after the fall of the Roman Empire, medicine in Europe advanced with the help of new institutions, such as the Christian monasteries, and outside influences, such as Hebrew and Arab medicine.

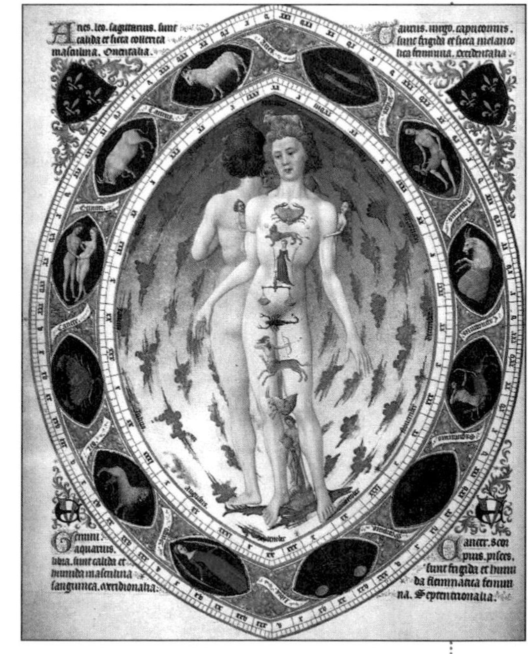

Illuminated manuscript from the Tres Riches Heures du Duc de Berry (15th century France). Books of Hours were personal prayer books made for the wealthy. The design of this image summarizes current medical beliefs regarding the influence of the planets and the zodiac on the various parts of the human body.

The Ancient Tribes

The Northern European peoples were not, by any means, one unified civilization; they were essentially separate tribes. Before we look at their methods of healing, we need to see who these different people were.

THE CELTS The Celts (pronounced kelts) originated in central Europe, but by 500 B.C. they had spread to Spain, Britain, Ireland, and northern Italy, attacking Rome in 390 B.C. Eventually, most of the Celts were either absorbed into the Roman empire or wiped out by neighboring Germanic tribes. Some did survive on the fringes of the empire, however, in Brittany, Ireland, Wales, and Scotland, where people still speak Celtic dialects today.

Although we mainly think of Celts as being residents of the British Isles, they also inhabited continental Europe. In fact, much of our information about the Celts comes from Julius Caesar, who spent ten years in Gaul. The Gauls were the Celts who occupied what is now France, Belgium, Switzerland, northern Italy, and Austria.

The Celts had a distinctive language, beliefs, and art, but they were never unified politically. They were fierce warriors and skilled horsemen. Caesar describes their burning of human sacrifices and their belief in personal immortality, which was so strong that they had absolutely no fear of death in battle.

Their priests, judges, and teachers—the Druids—conducted the religious rites, which included both animal and human sacrifice. The Celts worshiped numerous gods and goddesses and had an elaborate mythology involving divinities and heroes.

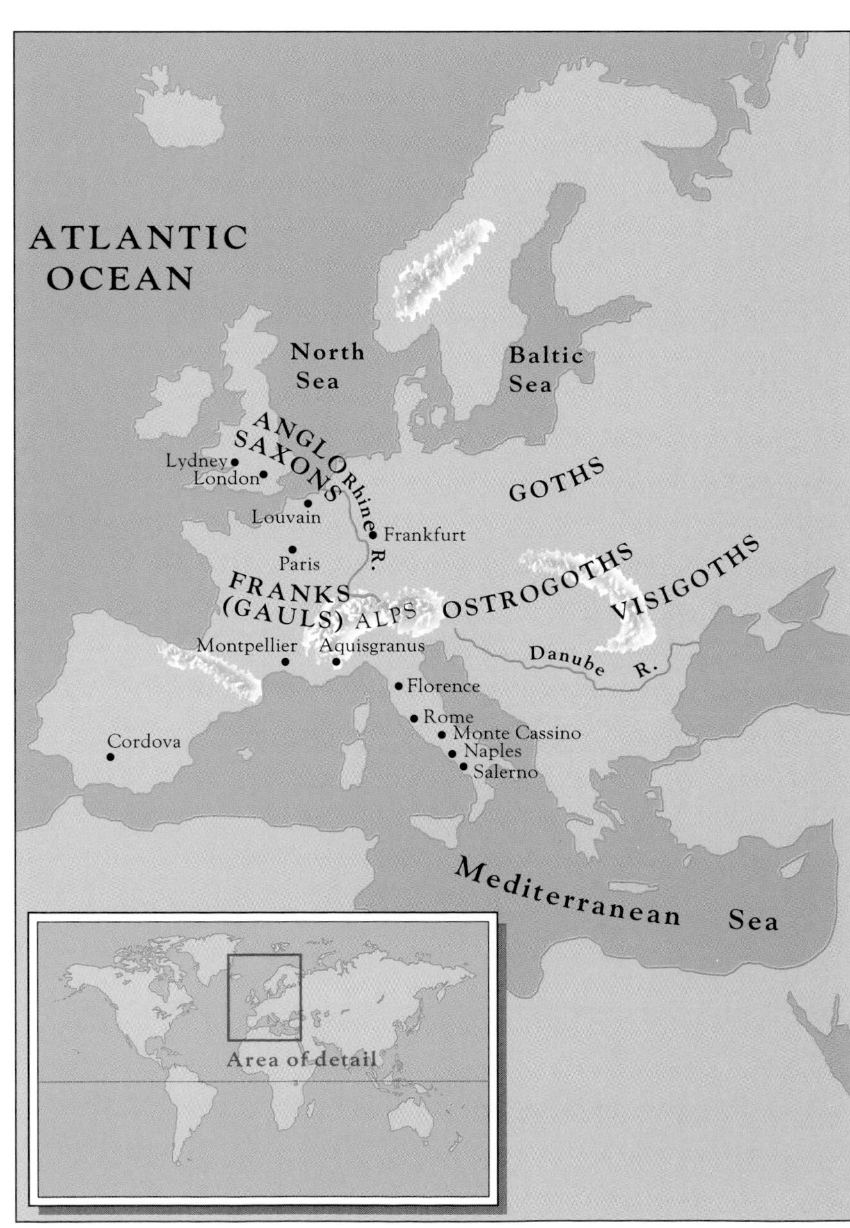

Some of the British Celts had female war leaders and tribal chiefs. In A.D. 60, Boudica, ruler of the Iceni, led her tribe in a revolt against the Romans, who had conquered Britain and made it a Roman province. Cartimandua, queen of the Brigantes, the largest Celtic tribe in Britain, was a Roman ally. Celtic women also functioned as negotiators in war, as prophets and priestesses, and perhaps as Druids.

THE GERMANIC TRIBES The Germanic tribes originated in southern Scandinavia and the north German coast. They later migrated south settling in northern and eastern Gaul. Among the main Germanic groups were the

- Teutons
- Goths (including the Ostrogoths and Visigoths)
- Franks
- Anglo-Saxons

As the Germans moved south, feeling pressure from the Scandinavian tribes, they clashed with the Romans. In the 3rd through 5th centuries A.D., they occupied parts of the Roman empire. Alaric, king of the Visigoths, sacked the city of Rome itself in A.D. 410. The Ostrogoths, under Theodoric, ruled Italy by A.D. 493.

In A.D. 410, the inhabitants of Britain were told they would have to defend themselves from invaders; Rome could not help them. The Anglo-Saxons invaded and ruled Britain by the late 6th century. These Germanic people brought with them to Britain, where Christianity had been established earlier, their worship of Tiw, Odin, Thor, and Frig, and their love of songs and poetry. They also brought their social structure, based on loyalty between personal retainers and their chieftain.

Celtic Women Described by Classical Writers

Various Roman writers communicated what they knew about the strange "barbarians" in the north to their fellow "civilized" citizens. The folks back home must have been amazed:

"Gallic women are not only equal to their husbands in stature, but they rival them in strength as well."

"In a fight a man may call in his wife, stronger by far than he, with flashing eyes; most of all when she swells her neck and gnashes her teeth and poising her huge white arms begins to rain blows mingled with kicks like shots discharged from the twisted cord of a catapult."

"Husbands have the power of life and death over their wives and children."

"The Celtic women arbitrated with such irreproachable fairness that a wondrous friendship of all towards all was brought about. As a result of this they continued to consult with women in regard to war and peace."

CHARLEMAGNE AND THE FRANKS Another highly successful Germanic tribe, the Franks, moved south from the lower Rhine river area and took over Gaul from the Romans. They converted to Christianity around A.D. 500 and had the support of the bishops of Rome. They inherited from the Romans a highly organized system of government, efficient military management, and developed agriculture, trade, and industry.

The king of the Franks, Charles Martel, prevented the Muslims, who had conquered Spain, from expanding into France. The Pope crowned Charles Martel's grandson, Charlemagne, Emperor and Augustus on Christmas Day, A.D. 800. The coronation of Charlemagne was thought to be a revival of the western Roman Empire after an interruption of three centuries.

Charlemagne's empire covered most of western Europe from the Netherlands to northern Spain and central Italy, and from the Atlantic to the borders of Hungary. His interest in education led him to open reading schools for the common folk and cathedral and monastic schools; the palace school educated the emperor's children, sons of the great nobles, and some ecclesiastics. Libraries connected with these schools preserved the oldest existing manuscripts of Caesar, Tacitus, and other Roman authors.

Charlemagne's Estates

Besides education, Charlemagne concerned himself with estate management, since the royal estates provided his main source of revenue. He commanded that 88 species of plants be grown on the estates, helping to disseminate these species throughout Europe.

Seventy-two of the plants were herbs, mostly medicinal, including fenugreek, sage, rue, cumin, anise, pennyroyal, dill, mint, catnip, and others. The vegetables included cucumbers, beans, celery, carrots, parsnips, radishes, onions, and chives. Among the fruit trees were apples, pears, plums, cherries, and peaches.

Charlemagne also had parks and pleasure grounds with menageries. He took a keen interest in wine production, and his vineyards included vines from distant lands.

The abbots of important monasteries, including Alcuin, were probably Charlemagne's chief gardening advisers. These abbots took a special interest in medicinal herbs and exchanged such plants among themselves.

Healing Among the Celts in Britain

The Celtic world involved many gods and goddesses, and worshiping the spirits and gods involved a great deal of festival and ceremony. Strabo, the 1st century Greek geographer, observed that the Celts loved feasts. They had four main yearly festivals—Imbolc, Lughnasa, Beltain, and Samain. All of them had some association with the health of the people, but in particular, the festival of Beltain celebrated on May Day required the lighting of two massive bonfires to ward off evil and sickness. For purification and protection, all of the community's livestock was driven between the two fires. Human and animal sacrifices were made to the gods. Garlanded trees and maypoles ensured continued health and fertility.

THE DRUIDS The Druids were the priests of the Celts. They played a major role in all sacred activities, but they were more than just the clergy. In a way, they were also the lawyers, teachers, and doctors of Celtic society. Because of certain privileges conferred on Druids, such as no taxes and no manual labor, many of the best and brightest of Celtic society may have chosen to enter the profession.

Although they didn't use the written word, some studied for years, committing to memory sacred verses and lore. Perhaps because their religious duties centered around the forest and nature, the Druid's knowledge of both the sacred *and* medicinal qualities of plants was extensive.

CELTIC HERBS Mistletoe figured in the sacrifices of Beltain. A body retrieved from an English bog had eaten or drunk mistletoe as part of his last meal, before his sacrifice. The Roman writer Pliny the Elder reported that the oak tree and mistletoe were very sacred to the Druids, whose name means "knowing the oak."

> They choose groves of oak for the sake of the tree alone, and they never perform any sacred rite unless they have a branch of it. They think that everything that grows on it has been sent from heaven by the god himself. Mistletoe, however, is rarely found on the oak, and when it is, [it] is gathered with a great deal of ceremony... if possible on the sixth day of the moon.

Pliny adds that the mistletoe was cut with a golden sickle by a white-robed Druid, after which two bulls were sacrificed.

An engraving showing Druids gathering mistletoe. Mistletoe was sacred to Druids, the Celtic priests. It was cut with a golden sickle by a white-robed Druid, and after two bulls were ritually sacrificed. They believed that mistletoe made barren animals fertile and was a remedy against all poison.

Herbalists believed that two forms of mandrake existed: the male and the female. Both forms were used for medicine, although some considered the female better, which had sharp leaves. People believed that the roots were shaped like men and women.

The Magical Mandrake

One of history's most revered magical and medicinal plants is the mandrake, or mandragora. The Mesopotamians, Egyptians, Greeks, and Romans all used the healing properties of the mandrake. Supposedly, the mandrake could cure demonic possession, serve as an anesthetic, and determine the sex of a child. Healers also used mandrake to treat arthritis, ulcers, boils, and inflammations. It was used to induce menses, to ease childbirth, and as an aphrodisiac and snakebite antidote.

In Northern Europe, the plant and its healing powers were surrounded by superstition because its root system can resemble the human form. The harvesting of the mandrake was an elaborate affair that took place only in moonlight. After a brief prayer and ritual, the mandrake would be tied to a dog (some say only a black dog), and the dog would uproot the plant. It was said that when it was uprooted, the plant let out a shriek that would make anyone within earshot go insane. Therefore, the harvester would cover his ears and let the dog do the dirty work.

In addition to knowing the magical properties of these plants, the ability to concoct therapeutic herbal preparations appears to have been one of the Druids' specialized areas of knowledge. Pliny reports, "They believe that if the mistletoe is taken as a drink, it makes barren animals fertile, and is a remedy against all poison."

The Druids used other herbs as well. According to Pliny, brooklime—also called water pimpernel or *Veronica beccabunga*—was an important herb of healing, and possibly had nutritional value (it is rich in vitamin C and can be found fresh under the ice of streams in winter). The scientific medicinal value of the plant's properties was probably not the main purpose for its use, though, as can be seen in the ritual way in which it was gathered. A Druid who was harvesting brooklime would first spend several days fasting. He then dug up the plant by its roots, using only his left hand. He placed the herb in a water trough for cattle, and later used it as a healing remedy. It appears that the magic was more significant than the vitamin C.

Woad, a member of the mustard-seed family, was also used by the Celts in the British Isles. Julius Caesar reported that

> All the Britons paint themselves with woad, which gives them a dark-blue color and makes them more frightening in battle.

Other herbs used by the Druids include

- madder
- mandrake
- plantain
- mint
- verbena
- sage

HEALING DEITIES AND SPAS Although little is known about Celtic deities, there appear to have been gods and goddesses that were important to Celtic healing. Sacrifices and prayers to specific healing deities may have been a major part of healing among the Celts. (Later in the history of the Celtic peoples of the British Isles, the Christian Saints—specifically St. Bridget and St. Patrick—took the place of the Celtic gods and goddesses as healers.) Natural spas were recognized for their healing qualities, and these springs and baths were often dedicated as worship sites for the healing deities. Many of the ancient spas are still touted for their miraculous properties today.

Nodens, who appeared as a dog, had a healing sanctuary at Lydney, in Gloucestershire, England, dating to the 1st century A.D. This complex, partially built by the Romans, included a temple, healing baths, an inn, and a long building in which the sick slept in hopes of a nighttime visit by the god. Votive offerings found there include coins, trinkets, a small bronze arm, several stone carvings, and bronze models of dogs. One offering, an engraved bone plaque of a naked woman with her hands on her belly, may have been left by a woman with fertility problems because Nodens's powers were also associated with fertility. Nodens may be of ancient Irish origin. His devotees accepted him as an omnipotent god.

Dian Cecht, the peasant healer of the Tuatha (the People of the Goddess Danu), was another Irish healing god. One of the three goddesses called the Brigits was dedicated solely to healing, perhaps reflecting the importance of the art.

The Druids held oak trees and mistletoe sacred. Pliny recounted that they thought everything that grew on the oak was sent from heaven. Mistletoe was rarely found on the oak, and when it was, they gathered it with a great deal of ceremony, if possible on the sixth day of the moon.

On the European continent, Granus, a Celtic god of light and healing, had a warm sulfur spring dedicated to him at Aquisgranus, meaning the warm spring of Granus. The Romans identified this god with Apollo and rededicated the shrine to him. Later Aquisgranus came to be called Aix, and here Charlemagne built his palace, using the springs for his bathhouse and swimming pool.

The Roman baths in Bath, England, were dedicated to Sulis Minerva, a combination of a Celtic goddess and a Roman goddess. Three vents allow over one-quarter of a million gallons of 120 degrees Fahrenheit mineral water to reach the surface each day. The Romans built public buildings—a temple with an altar in front and perhaps a forum—around the main spring, but people visited these springs as early as 5000 B.C. Celtic silver coins and curses written on thin sheets of pewter containing Celtic names have been found in the spring.

Healing Among the Germanic Tribes

Before the Germanic tribes came into contact with the Roman world, their healing practices consisted of magical rites designed to expel from the body the demons responsible for the sickness. Many spirits and demons inhabited their world, so the exact source of an illness was sometimes difficult to determine. Disease could be caused by elfshot (darts thrown by elves to cause pain and disease) or by the spirits of the fields and woods, who sometimes took the form of insects, moths, and worms to spread illness among humans.

MAGICAL RITES Ridding the patient of the affliction could be carried out in several ways. Animal sacrifice was one way. Sacrifices could appease the gods and restore the stricken person's health. Often, the priest touched the patient with a finger dipped in the blood of the sacrificed animal to mark the person who should receive the benefits of the offering.

Magical healing rites were another treatment. Runes—sacred or magical writings and symbols—were sometimes written in

A medieval medical manuscript showing the gathering of gourds. An English herbal warns that if one wants very large gourds, let women neither touch the young gourds or look upon them, for that will kill them. Gerarde's Herball suggests laying a gourd in a baby's cradle to cure ague (chills).

Women's Role in Healing

Women played an important role in Germanic healing. Tacitus reports that the men went to their mothers to have their war wounds treated. He says that the women sometimes applied their lips to the wounds perhaps to suck out the bad blood and aid in healing—somewhat more than simply kissing the boo-boo, one imagines.

Tacitus described the women of the tribe as indispensible to the men during and after battle:

> Close by them too, are their nearest and dearest, so that they can hear the shrieks of their womenfolk and the wailing of their children. These are the witnesses whom each man reverences most highly, whose praise he most desires. It is to their mothers that they go to have their wounds treated, and the women are not afraid to count and compare the gashes. They also carry supplies of food to the combatants and encourage them... It stands on record that armies wavering and on the point of collapse have been rallied by the women.

red on wooden staffs or small stones and used to heal the sick or protect the vulnerable. Magic stones, soil, and chanted or repeated phrases were also employed in some cases. Sometimes, people wore magical amulets for cure and protection.

The god Odin (or Wotan), the main god of the Germanic tribes, had great magical powers. He granted men heroism and victory, decided men's fate, and could even raise the dead; but most important for healing, he controlled the magic of the runes. In the mythology of the Germanic people, Odin gave up his eye to learn this magic, and in return for his granting a fair wind, a good harvest, victory in battle, or a cure, he required blood sacrifices.

Other gods could also grant health and recovery: Frig (or Frija), Odin's consort, was the goddess of childbirth—a particularly risky event for the health of the mother and the child—and Nerthus was the goddess of fertility—a major concern in any civilization but especially one for which having children was a way to attain status.

HERBAL HEALING Although the majority of healing was probably magical in nature, traditions, legends, and songs told of the healing power of medicinal plants. The Germanic peoples probably didn't differentiate between the magical and medicinal properties of the herbs. The same spirits of the fields and woods who caused disease also knew which herbs could cure disease. Medicinal herbs were usually collected on special days in special ceremonies, revealing that the druglike properties of the plants were probably secondary to their magical ones.

THEODORIC AND THE ROMANS Theodoric, ruler of the German tribe called the Ostrogoths, greatly admired the medical art of the Romans. He assimilated the medical knowledge from all over the Roman Empire. When he took over Italy, he preserved the sanitary administration of the Romans and drained the marshes to prevent disease. He reestablished the office of physician—a position held in high esteem. These healers took oaths before their instructors that they would hate iniquity and love honesty.

Showing that he was well versed with classical medical methods and techniques, which the Romans probably learned from the Arabs and possibly even practitioners from the Far East, Theodoric said:

> Among the most useful arts that contribute to sustain frail humanity, none may be regarded as superior—or even equal—to medicine, which aids the sick with its maternal benevolence, puts our pains to flight, and gives us that which riches and honor are unable to give.... Leave aside, O men of the medical arts, those controversies that are prejudicial to the sick; and if you are not able to come to an agreement, consult someone whom you can question without dislike.... Remember that to sin against the health of a person constitutes homicide.... To the expert physician may the

A Time Line of Europe

2200–1500 B.C.: Neolithic/Bronze Age people build Stonehenge.

500–55 B.C.: Celts establish Iron Age culture in British Isles.

43 B.C.–A.D. 410: Britain is a Roman province.

A.D. 453–1066: Anglo-Saxon period in England.

493: Theodoric, king of the Ostrogoths, conquers Italy.

490–585: Cassiodorus lives.

ca. 500: St. Benedict establishes monasteries.

570–632: Mohammed lives, establishing Islam.

793: Viking attacks against England begin.

800: Charlemagne crowned Holy Roman Emperor.

ca. 900: Medical school in Salerno, Italy, is founded.

ca. 980: Avicenna born.

ca. 1020: Medical school in Montpellier, France, is founded.

1066: Norman conquest of England.

1095–1189: First through third crusades.

1126–1198: Averroes, Arab physician from Cordova, Spain, lives.

1135–1204: Maimonides, Jewish physician from Cordova, Spain, lives.

pulse reveal our internal disorders, may the urines reveal them to his eyes. Enter freely into our palace, with full confidence, and may it be permitted to you to prescribe diets, to say things that one would not dare to hear said, and to prescribe even painful treatment in the interest of our health.

After Theodoric, laws concerning the practice of medicine were codified. Gothic laws prohibited causing abortions and forbade the activities of diviners and sorcerers. Those who placed spells on humans or animals faced severe penalties as followers of the devil. People who asked sorcerers for advice about illness could also be punished.

Under the Visigoths, the law forbade physicians, except in emergencies, to bleed a young girl unless in the presence of a close relative (see "Anglo-Saxon Bloodletting," page 112). No physician could enter a prison alone, preventing him from giving poison to a prisoner. The law also set the prices for operations and medical instruction and stated that no physician could be kept in prison before being examined.

The Rise of the Monastery

As you can tell from the Gothic laws and Theodoric's pronouncements, healing in Northern Europe changed significantly as the influence of the Roman Empire spread. Classical (Greek and Roman) ideas on sickness and health crossed the Alps, but so did Christianity, and this new religion would forever change the way medicine in Europe would be practiced.

Cassiodorus, a Roman politician and writer who had served in the government

This 15th century Italian manuscript shows a physician preparing theriac, originally an antidote to both human and animal bites, which the ancient Greeks thought to be poisonous. Viper's flesh was the main ingredient. Theriac was very popular and remained in European pharmacopoeias until the 19th century (see also "Theriac—A Popular Panacea," page 80).

of Theodoric, retired from public life and founded the monastery of Vivarium in Calabria. He brought to his monastery a collection of ancient manuscripts. He recommended to his monks the study of Dioscorides's herbal, the Hippocratic Corpus, and Galen's writings—Greek works on herbal medicine, anatomy, and general therapeutics. He urged the study of herbal simples and the composition of medicines, while placing all hope in the Lord. Cassiodorus sought to merge classical medical knowledge with Christian belief and philosophy. Although his monastery did not last long, his model for monastic life greatly influenced the founder of one of the most influential monastic orders, St. Benedict.

This medical manuscript illustrates the gathering of balsam resin. Resins trickle out of an incision made in a tree (not to be confused with sap). Balsam resin was probably part of the Balm of Gilead, which is mentioned several times in the Hebrew bible and was famous for its medicinal quality, especially as a wound medicine.

St. Benedict In A.D. 529, on the ruins of a temple to Apollo that lay between Rome and Naples, a highborn Italian named Benedict of Nursia founded the monastery of Monte Cassino. St. Benedict's Rule included the injunction that above all, sick monks must be cared for. Monte Cassino became an important center for scholarship and medicine. Here, the monks kept and copied classical medical texts, and the monastery became the cradle of Western religious medicine. From here, the doctrines and practices of St. Benedict spread to other monasteries, including Oxford, Cambridge, Tours, Fulda, and St. Gall, where the monks acquired simple medical skills, collected medicinal recipes, and grew medicinal herbs.

Over the centuries, Monte Cassino expanded to include a cathedral, a huge library, schools, and infirmaries. Toward the end of the 9th century, Monte Cassino's medical school acquired a great reputation. The 11th century was Monte Cassino's golden age. Constantinus Africanus translated Arab, Jewish, and Greek medical works into Latin, and the sick came from all over Europe to obtain cures. Monte Cassino began to resemble the ancient Greek healing centers of Asklepios (see page 74).

Other Healing Centers Not all monasteries were involved with healing. St. Bernard of Clairvaux (1090–1153) felt it was not proper for Cistercian monks to buy drugs, take medicine, or see doctors. Monks of the Carthusian order were never permitted to consult a physician, and infirmaries were not allowed on the grounds.

In England during the 11th through 13th centuries, most monasteries trained their own physicians to care for the monastic community. They also saw patients outside the monastery and those who came to them for advice. Several monasteries maintained separate infirmaries for the general population. Some monastic physicians attained the highest medical reputations and were sought out by the nobility and the rich.

Contact with luxurious living resulted in a loosening of monastic discipline. In the early 12th century, several papal prohibitions forbade monk physicians from accepting fees for their work. In the middle of the 13th century, ecclesiastical laws forbade the practice of medicine to monks and canons. At that point, monasteries began contracting with physicians and surgeons to care for the ill, on the basis of an annual stipend or, sometimes, per case.

Hildegarde, Abbess of Bingen (1098–1179), cared for the sick. She also wrote on medical causes and cures and magic formulas, medical lore, and medicinal plants. This picture represents her vision of the Fall of the Angels. Her visions may have actually been the auras preceding recurrent migraines.

Monastic Methods

The medicine practiced by the monks during these Dark Ages was often a curious combination of Christian spiritual healing, classical science, and herbal folk medicine. Sometimes conditions were diagnosed using the methods and terms from Roman medicine, the patients were treated with the locally available roots and herbs, and their cure was attributed to the intervention of the Holy Spirit.

Henry II of Bavaria, for example, traveled to Monte Cassino because he was suffering from vesical calculus—a bladder stone that can move into the ureter and cause incredible pain. He received a cure at the monastery; St. Benedict appeared to him in a dream, performed an operation, and placed the stone in Henry's hand.

Some monasteries were more grounded in scientific medicine. The plan for an infirmary drawn up between A.D. 816 and 836 at the monastery of St. Gall in Switzerland looks remarkably like a modern scientific facility. The plan shows the infirmary and its adjoining buildings, including bathrooms, warm rooms with fireplaces, a ward for serious cases (an intensive care unit of sorts), and bloodletting and purging rooms. The physician in charge has a house, a consulting room, and a drug store. In the plan, the infirmary garden contains 16 plant beds, with a variety of herbs including kidney beans, costmary, cumin, fennel, fenugreek, purple iris, lily, lovage, mint, water mint, mustard, pennyroyal, rose, rosemary, rue, sage, and savory.

Another famous religious healer at the time combined the classical approach with a strong dose of folk tradition. Hildegarde, the mystic Abbess of Bingen, cared for the sick and wrote several works, including a book on medical causes and cures and one that included magic formulas, medical lore, and a description of 300 medicinal plants. Hildegarde recommended using fern as an amulet in childbirth. The fern should be placed by the birth canal so that it is the first thing the newborn smells. The odor would prevent the devil from capturing the baby.

Anglo-Saxon Medicine

The Anglo-Saxons were a group of people caught in the middle of a changing Europe. They lived primarily in England after the fall of the Roman Empire's presence there. Although later they would be heavily influenced by classical and Christian medicine, their early practices reflect the local folk traditions of their "barbarian" roots and give us one of our best glimpses at the way healing was accomplished in early Europe.

The people of Anglo-Saxon England had brief, hard lives often interrupted by famine, disease, and war. Their remains tell us of their short life expectancy, their high infant mortality, women dying young in childbirth, and a high incidence of bone and joint diseases. Most people lived in small, dark, damp hovels and probably did not eat a large variety of foods, especially in winter or when harvests were poor. Deficiencies in vitamin A, vitamin C, and niacin were common and led to skin and eye problems. Some of the other diseases affecting the English at this time were dysentery, tertian malaria, toothache, arthritis, and rickets.

EARLY MAGICAL HEALING The Anglo-Saxons practiced a variety of magical healing rites. Healers used amulets, incantations, prayers, and charms to provide cures. Amulets and charms were worn on the body to ward off or cure disease. Nonsense words written on paper and hung from the neck offered a cure for diar-

Easing Childbirth

Among the ancient peoples of Europe, there were many different methods for easing the pain of childbirth and facilitating labor.

In many of these myths, trees appear to have been important in the process. In Sweden, embracing the Vårdträd, or guardian tree, near the house during labor was considered a way to make for an easier delivery. In the British Isles, it was thought that a woman (pregnant or not) who could squeeze through the opening of a tree with a double trunk would be lucky in childbirth. Among the Germanic peoples, passing a woman in labor through the opening of a split tree was thought to ease delivery, but it was a risk because the magic of the split tree could also cause the child to be born a werewolf. Some scholars speculate that the association of trees with childbirth comes from a time when women gave birth outside in the forest, where trees would be the only means of support to a woman in labor, and that the magical properties were incorporated later.

Horses were also valuable magical symbols in the birthing process. One method among the Germanic peoples to facilitate labor when a woman was past due involved having a white horse eat oats directly off the abdomen of the pregnant woman. Another method was for the woman to crawl underneath the belly of a pregnant mare. How the horse got involved with the birthing process remains a mystery.

Anglo-Saxon Bloodletting

Besides using remedies as internal medicines, salves, fomentations, baths, and fumigations, the Anglo-Saxons, like the people of the Mediterranean world, used bloodletting to cure a variety of ailments. The Greeks developed the concept of bloodletting based on their theory that the four humors must be kept in balance to restore and maintain health. In England, the idea became simplified into a concept of "evil" or "harmful" humors that had to be released from the body.

Elaborate charts based on the phases of the moon, astrology, and favorable days told Anglo-Saxon practitioners when they should or should not bleed a patient. *Bald's Leechbook* states, "There is no time for bloodletting so good as in early Lent, when the evil humors are gathered."

Bleeding tables told the physician where to bleed the patient based on the complaint. For example, for "headache or the madness of frenzy," the patient was bled from the middle of the forehead.

Besides bleeding for a specific ailment, bloodletting became a routine health maintenance practice. In some monasteries, the monks were bled on a seven-week cycle. While they received their treatment, the rules under which they normally lived were relaxed somewhat, and the bleeding procedure became a form of relaxation for them.

Many dangers accompanied bleeding, besides the obvious blood loss and weakening. Hemorrhage and sepsis (blood infection) probably occurred often as a result of venesection, and the medical texts offer treatments for "a lancet wound that grows corrupt," "if you cannot stop a gushing vein," and "if in bloodletting a man is cut upon a sinew. . . ."

Scarification was similar to, but less drastic than, bloodletting. The physician superficially scratched or cut the skin, usually on the shoulders, abdomen, and legs and wiped away the flowing blood to slow the formation of a clot. Physicians used scarification as a counter-irritant and for animal bites. Sometimes cupping accompanied bloodletting and scarification. The practitioner placed a heated glass or horn cup over the affected area. As the air in the cup cooled, suction drew blood from the wound into the cup.

rhea. People wore amber beads as protections against disease and danger. Animal teeth and shells were popular amulets. Amulets made from plants were also used often: Betony, vervain, peony, yarrow, mugwort, and plantain were all quite popular.

Rituals and ceremonies also seem to have been popular. A child with epilepsy might be helped by drawing a goat's brain through a golden ring. In a procedure thought to help leg inflammation, a fox tooth was extracted from the living animal—a practice that sounds like a toned-down form of sacrifice.

The color red comes up often in magical healing. For headaches, crosswort placed on a red cloth was bound on the head. To calm a lunatic, clovewort was wrapped in red thread and placed around his or her neck in April or October.

Saliva was used in many magical formulas because it was thought to counteract the worms and serpents that caused disease. A patient being treated for a skin disorder with ointment, scarification, and bleeding had to spit three times saying, "Have this evil and depart with it."

Wood also had healing properties. For certain conditions, a patient was struck with a piece of oak until blood flowed. The wood was then thrown away while the patient sang a magical verse or a spell. For some inflammatory ailments, the patient's name was carved on a stick of hazel or elder. The patient was scratched three times over the affected body part, and the blood from the scratches filled the name on the stick. The stick was then thrown over the patient's shoulder or through his legs into running water.

The Anglo-Saxons occasionally used runes as charms. These ancient Nordic inscriptions, carved on memorial stones, were thought to have healing powers; there were standard runes for health, birth, battle, and victory.

Many of the objects used in magical healing—animals' teeth, head bones, rings, pierced coins—have been found in the graves of Anglo-Saxon and Germanic women. These are often found inside little bags or boxes. Sometimes amber beads had been placed in the graves as well.

This 14th century French manuscript illustrates bloodletting. Healers used bloodletting to cure a variety of ailments. Besides bleeding for a specific ailment, bloodletting became a routine health maintenance practice. Many dangers accompanied bleeding, besides the obvious blood loss and weakening. Hemorrhage and sepsis probably occurred often as a result of it.

Other magical healing rites included placing a child on a roof or into an oven to cure fever. Another means of curing illness in children or stopping crying in babies involved drawing them through an aperture, usually made of earth (compare "Easing Childbirth," page 111). This practice proved so popular that it was banned many times through the centuries.

LEECHBOOK III In Old English, the language of the Anglo-Saxons, the word for physician was *leech*. From this comes the term *leechbook*, for medical text, and *leechcraft*, for the art of healing. To leech meant to heal or to bleed someone with leeches, from which comes our modern term for the bloodsucking aquatic worm, *Hirudo medicinalis*. Strangely enough, the bloodsucking, medicinal leech is not mentioned in any of the Old English medical texts.

Three Old English medical compilations survive nearly intact and are the oldest medical writings, in a native language, to survive from Western Europe. The oldest one, called *Leechbook III*, most nearly reflects Anglo-Saxon medical practice, before it became heavily influenced by classical and Christian sources.

Leechbook III comes as close as we can get to ancient Northern European medicine. A large number of the remedies contain only native ingredients, given their native English names, not Anglicized Latin ones. Some of the remedies include magical charms, but most of the remedies are rational, though not necessarily beneficial. *Leechbook III* contains a head-to-toe list of remedies. One recipe for cough medicine calls for ingredients still used in cough drops today:

Horehound, boil strongly in honey; add a little butter; give three or four slices to eat; after the night's fast sup a cupful of the preceding warm drink with it.

Other Anglo-Saxon Medical Books

There are a number of books that still survive, at least in part, from the Anglo-Saxon period. Some contain folk remedies and some are serious works of scholarship. These works give us a good glimpse of medicine in the Dark Ages of Europe.

The Enigmata. Aldhelm of Malmesbury, who lived in the late 7th and early 8th centuries, wrote another of the earliest surviving works by an Englishman, a series of riddles in Latin, called *Enigmata*. He mentions the use of the medicinal leech for the withdrawal of blood. Aldhelm also includes in his riddles one about the beaver, whose inguinal glands provide castoreum, a valued medicine. He writes that wounds of the entrails and limbs are helped by this medicine. Aldhelm includes three herbs in his riddles: wallwort, celandine, and woody nightshade.

Bald's Leechbook. Quite different from *Leechbook III*, which discussed pre-Christian practices, *Bald's Leechbook* combines Greek, Roman, North African, and Byzantine sources with native medicine. It consists of two sections, one on external medicine and the second on internal ailments. *Bald's Leechbook* was written between 900 and 950 in Old English. A note in Latin states

> Bald owns this book, which he ordered Cild to write; earnestly here I pray... that no treacherous person should take this book from me, neither by force nor by theft nor by any false speech. Why? Because no best treasure is so dear to me as the dear books which the grace of Christ attends.

The Lacnunga. Meaning "remedies," the *Lacnunga* is a rambling, 11th century collection of about 200 prescriptions, remedies, and charms derived from many sources—Greek, Roman, Byzantine, Celtic, and Teutonic. In it are charms to cure pains from the assaults of elves and witches, the Nine Herbs Charm (see below), and other interesting insights into Anglo-Saxon healing. The so-called Omont fragment contains several recipes for ailments of the foot, leg, and thigh. It was also written in Old English.

The Herbarium of Apuleius Platonicus. Also known as the *Anglo-Saxon Herbal*, the *Herbarium of Apuleius Platonicus* is a Latin work that was translated into Old English in about 1000. This collection of remedies uses plants native to the Mediterranean region, adapted for practical use in the English environment. The Anglo-Saxon translator added his own material to the translation. For example, 11 paragraphs were added to the discussion of the plant yarrow. The Herbarium provides information on what a particular herb can cure and where the herb can be found. Cress (nasturtium) is used "in case a man's hair falls out; take juice of the wort [herb], put it on the nose, the hair shall grow."

Excerpt from The Nine Herbs Charm

Chervil and fennel, very mighty two,
These herbs the wise Lord created,
Holy in heaven where he hung,
Ordained and sent into the seven worlds,
For poor and for rich, a cure for all.
She stands against pain, she assaults poison,
She has power against three and against thirty,
Against the hand of fiend and against the
hand of mighty tricks
Against enchantment by evil things.

The original manuscripts contain beautiful color illustrations of the plants under discussion, although they are not all accurate representations.

The Canterbury Classbook and the Ramsey Scientific Compendium. The Anglo-Saxons put together two compilations of Latin works containing medical lore from the Mediterranean area. The *Canterbury Classbook* and the *Ramsey Scientific Compendium* show that the Anglo-Saxons were familiar with most of the minor works in Greek and Latin that circulated freely throughout the Middle Ages. These works mention purging, bloodletting, diet, controlling humors, herbal remedies, and other classical medical practices.

The Healing of St. Cuthbert

A servant named Sibba was suffering a most evil disease. Being near death, he was given water blessed by St. Cuthbert, and after sleeping deeply, Sibba awoke in apparent good health. Abbess Aelfflaed of Whitby, daughter of King Oswiu, could not stand upright or move about except on all fours. Cuthbert sent her a linen girdle to wear, and within three days she had completely recovered. A boy afflicted by a demon was shouting, weeping, and tearing his body. The boy had been taken to the relics of various martyrs, but no cure came about. A priest dissolved in water some earth that had soaked up the water used to wash St. Cuthbert's body. The boy drank the water and was cured of his madness.

THE CHRISTIAN ANGLO-SAXONS Just before the beginning of the 7th century, St. Augustine came to England to convert the people there to Christianity. As with the rest of the "barbarians," the Anglo-Saxons did eventually convert, and the classical and Christian medicine becoming widespread among the monasteries of the continent spread to England.

Showing the blending of superstition, religion, and science going on in so many of the continental monastic infirmaries, Bede also tells of the bishop who discovered that a young nun had been bled on the fourth day of the moon. The bishop reacted:

> You have acted foolishly and ignorantly to bleed her on the fourth day of the moon. . . . It was very dangerous to bleed a patient when the moon is waning and the ocean tide is flowing.

Not only was bleeding practiced in monasteries and convents at this time, but bleeding charts based on phases of the moon indicated when bleeding should be done.

Bede discusses how this same bishop cured a mute boy with a scurfy head (a scalp condition). Through prayer and a form of speech therapy, the bishop restored the boy's speech, but for the scurfy head, the bishop called in a physician. Clearly, religious and secular healing worked side by side among the Anglo-Saxons.

Bede, who lived in the monastery of Jarrow, knew the writings of Pliny and other classical authors. Other English monasteries also had medical texts. Around 755, an English bishop wrote to a German bishop asking for books on medicine, saying, "We have some medical books, but the foreign ingredients we find prescribed in them are unknown to us and difficult to obtain." Not until about 900 did the English write their own medical books.

The people of this time believed profoundly in the personal healing powers of the saints, who may have been regarded by the early Anglo-Saxons as Christianized versions of their recently abandoned pagan gods. Objects such as wood, water, wine, earth, and clothes could bring about healing if they had come into contact with a saint. The saint's personal possessions would be even more effective. But ultimately, Christian healing centered around relics—bits of bone or hair taken from the corpse of a saint.

ANGLO-SAXON PHYSICIANS Scholars know very little about Anglo-Saxon physicians, except what can be learned from the few illustrations that exist in illuminated manuscripts showing physicians at work. Most wear classical dress. A few wear native clothing and are untonsured (they do not have the tops of their heads shaved the way monks do), showing that they do not belong to any religious order. These laymen physicians must have been fairly well educated since so many medical texts were in Latin.

Like other parts of Europe, however, some Anglo-Saxon physicians were probably members of religious orders. Some medical charms required the singing of the mass over the ingredients or the writing of the cross using the oil of Extreme Unction (Last Rites) on the patient's limbs. These actions could only be carried out by a priest.

Anglo-Saxon physicians may have trained medical students. *Bald's Leechbook* has phrases that suggest this, such as "Oxa taught this treatment," and "A treatment for lung disease Dun taught."

HERBAL, ANIMAL, AND MINERAL REMEDIES

Most Anglo-Saxon medicine relied on herbs, with or without magical assistance. At first glance, Anglo-Saxon remedies seem irrational, but a careful examination shows that many elements in a treatment may have benefited the patient. A remedy from *Bald's Leechbook* to cure a sty, for example, calls for ingredients and preparation that may actually have been helpful:

> Make an eye salve for a sty: take onion and garlic equal amounts of both, pound well together, take wine and bull's gall equal amounts of both, mix with the leeks, then put in a brass vessel, let stand for nine nights in the brass vessel, strain through a cloth and clear well, put in a horn and about night time put on the eye with a feather—the best remedy.

Staphylococcal infections of a hair follicle often cause styes on the eyelids. Garlic acts as an antibiotic, inhibiting bacteria growth. Oxgall acts as a detergent against some bacteria. The

Plants and Animals Used in Anglo-Saxon Remedies

The Anglo-Saxons had an extensive pharmacy that included plant and animal sources. The following is merely a partial list:

Plants: agrimony, barley, betony, birthwort, bitter vetch, brooklime, celandine, chamomile, chervil, cinquefoil, comfrey, coriander, cress, dill, dock, elder, elm bark, garlic, garlic mustard, hemlock, henbane, horehound, leek, lichen, lily, linseed, mallow, mandrake, mugwort, oak, onions, parsley, pennyroyal, pepper, periwinkle, plantain, poppy, rue, sage, woodruff, woody nightshade, wormwood, yarrow.

Animals: liver of badger, beaver, buck; eye of crab; urine of goat, cattle, hound, child; dung of dove, goat, sheep, horse, cattle, swine, human; gall of crab, salmon, cattle, goat, swine, bear, hare.

mixture stayed for a limited time in the brass vessel and after straining was kept in a nonreactive horn container until needed. Copper salts would form when the highly acidic wine reacted with the copper in the brass vessel, and copper salts destroy all living cells, including bacteria.

Another eye remedy requiring careful preparation reads

> Medicines for dimness of the eyes: take the juice or blossoms of celandine, mix with bumblebees' honey, put in a brass vessel, make lukewarm skillfully over warm coals until it is cooked.

The heated latex exuded from the celandine removes films or spots from the cornea, and the copper salts and honey are antibacterial. The honey and celandine juice would burn easily, so the author of the recipe indicates that the mixture should be heated carefully over gentle heat.

SURGERY Occasionally Anglo-Saxon physicians performed plastic surgery to correct problems, such as harelip. *Bald's Leechbook* states

> For harelip: pound mastic very fine, add white of an egg, and mix as you do vermilion; cut with a knife, sew securely with silk, then anoint with the salve outside and inside before the silk rot. If it pulls together, arrange it with the hand, anoint again immediately.

The mastic in the salve would be antiseptic. The author of the remedy knew that the tissues in a case like this can sometimes contract, producing deformity, and the practitioner must smooth out the

The Surgeon by Van Hemessen. The education, training, and status of surgeons varied greatly. Heading the hierarchy were skilled, literate surgeons. Empirics—people without formal training, practicing by trial and error—also carried out surgical procedures. Itinerant craftsmen often specialized in a particular operation, such as treating cataracts or bladder stones.

tightened tissues by hand. If the wound had to be handled, the physician then needed to apply the salve again. Scholars have not found a source for this remedy; perhaps its origin is purely Anglo-Saxon, without foreign influence.

Bald's Leechbook also discusses amputations:

> If the livid body is so deadened that there is not feeling in it, then you shall at once cut away all the dead and unfeeling part as far as the living body, so that there be nothing of the dead body left, nor of that which before felt neither iron nor fire.... If you must carve or cut off a diseased limb from a healthy body, then cut it not on the boundary of the healthy body, but much rather cut or carve on the healthy and living body, so that you may cure it better and sooner. When you set fire on a patient [cauterize], then take tender leek leaves and pounded salt, lay over the places; then the heat of the fire is the sooner drawn away.

The care each patient received after the operation varied according to the sex, age, and constitution of the person.

Anglo-Saxon physicians sometimes lanced tumors and abscesses. The Venerable Bede, a historian, teacher, and theologian who lived around A.D. 700, wrote about the physician Cynefrith, who lanced the tumor on the neck of St. Aethelthryth, the abbess of Ely, during the plague of 679. The operation provided only temporary relief (the patient died a few days later), but it is one of the earliest references to surgical procedures and gives us a clue as to the methods being employed at the time. *Bald's Leechbook* gives directions for lancing a lesion as difficult as an abscess of the liver.

Wisdom for Women

Here are some Anglo-Saxon nuggets your OB/GYN is probably not familiar with:

- To treat menstrual flux, a woman should comb her hair under a mulberry tree with a comb used by no one else and never used again. She must then hang on an upstanding branch of the mulberry tree the hair caught in the comb. If her menses are suppressed, she should hang the hair on a down-hanging branch.
- A couple desiring a male child should both drink a potion containing the dried womb of a hare. If only the wife drinks it, the child will be an androgyne.
- If a pregnant woman is offered a choice between a rose and a lily, she is pregnant with a girl if she chooses the rose, and carries a boy if she takes the lily.
- If the womb is carried high she will bear a boy, if low a girl.
- If a woman is four or five months pregnant and she often eats nuts or acorns or any fresh fruit, then it sometimes happens because of that the child is stupid.

Physicians treated fractures with herbal salves, bathing in hot herbal baths, and splinting and/or bandaging. They applied herbal salves to dislocated joints, but the texts do not mention reducing the dislocation using traction or mechanical means.

Gynecology and Obstetrics Little of the Anglo-Saxon writing on gynecology and obstetrics has survived, and most of what we do have can be traced back to classical sources. One medical treatment alone has not been found in other writings.

> If the woman's monthly flow be too great take a fresh horse dropping, lay on hot coals, let steam strongly between the thighs

up under the clothing, so that the patient sweat profusely.

Most of the other Anglo-Saxon material concerning gynecology and obstetrics takes the form of charms or sympathetic magic.

Great Medieval Physicians

Several great physicians from neighboring parts of the world brought their talents to the kings and princes of Europe. They brought with them the techniques and knowledge of medicine in the Near East and the Arab and Jewish world.

A Jewish physician, Isaac Judaeus, was born in Egypt around A.D. 850. There he studied mathematics, astronomy, and medicine, becoming a famous oculist. Relocating to Tunisia, Isaac entered the service of the Caliph, and at his request, composed several medical works. Isaac wrote in Arabic; his works were later translated into Latin and Hebrew. His most important works covered dietetics, urine, fever, and medical aphorisms. Isaac's works were taught in Salerno, Oxford, Paris, and at other universities. His writings led to a greater use of diagnosis based on pulse and urine and an emphasis on diet.

Avicenna (980–1037), a Persian physician, composed his Canon of Medicine to coordinate systematically all the medical doctrines of Hippocrates and Galen with Aristotle's ideas on biology. Avicenna wrote about theoretical medicine, simple medicaments based on Dioscorides, diseases and their treatment, and drugs and their preparation. His work was translated into Latin in the 12th century and became the main text in European medical schools. For 500 years it was required reading in the universities of Montpellier and Louvain.

Averroes (1126–1198), a lawyer and physician from Cordova, Spain, wrote an extended commentary on Avicenna's Canon. This work is more a philosophical treatise than a medical one, although it mentions Galen frequently. When translated into Latin, it became widely used as a university text.

Averroes was considered one of the greatest physicians of his time; he was the first to explain the function of the retina and to discover that a case of smallpox confers immunity. He also wrote commentary on Aristotle and composed his own works in the fields of logic, physics, psychology, theology, law, astronomy, and grammar.

Moses Maimonides (1135–1204) was a Jewish physician and philosopher also from Cordova, Spain. Persecution forced his family to flee Spain and settle in Morocco, and then later in Egypt. Maimonides wrote a number of medical works, all in Arabic. Three became very popular in Hebrew and Latin translations — the *Book on Poisons*, the *Regimen of Health*, and the *Medical Aphorisms of Maimonides*. The *Book on Poisons* was used as a textbook on toxicology throughout the Middle Ages. The *Regimen of Health*, written for a frivolous and pleasure-seeking sultan given to fits of depression, contains abstracts from Hippocrates and Galen; advice on hygiene, sex, diet, and drugs; and Maimonides's concept of a healthy mind in a healthy body. This work was translated into Hebrew and Latin in the 13th century. The *Medical Aphorisms of Maimonides* consists of 1,500 aphorisms based mainly on Greek and Latin medical writers.

The Birth of European Medical Schools

By the 11th century, several major centers of learning were emerging in Europe. Europe had chosen the path for modern Western medicine: Medical schools for the sole purpose of producing practitioners with specialized knowledge.

SALERNO Legend has it that the medical school in Salerno, Italy, was founded by a Greek, a Latin, a Jew, and a Muslim, each teaching in his own language. Although probably not true, the legend exemplifies medical knowledge at Salerno—a blend of Greek, Latin, Arab, and Jewish learning.

Medical teaching at Salerno may have begun as early as the 9th century A.D.; in 904 we hear of a Salernitan physician at the court of the French king but not until the 11th century do we have solid information about the school.

Women studied and practiced medicine at Salerno. In the 12th century, the famous Trotula practiced there and wrote a general work on medicine. So great was her reputation that later gynecologic works were attributed to her.

The "Golden Age" of Salerno, from the late 11th to the early 13th century, arose through the influence of Arab medicine. Constantinus Africanus, from Carthage, North Africa, became one of the most esteemed physicians and professors of Salerno. He translated many works from Arabic, such as the medical works of Isaac Judaeus and Arab versions of Hippocrates and Galen.

Two important developments at Salerno were the study of anatomy and surgery. In the 12th century, dissection, which had not been carried out since classical times, once more took place. Animals, mostly pigs, were used and scholars wrote anatomical texts based on their observations.

Roger of Salerno, who lived around 1170, wrote a manual on surgery. Although based partly on earlier works, it contained much gained from the personal experiences of Roger and his contemporaries. Roger describes herniotomy and recommends mercury salts for chronic skin ailments. He mentions the use of seaweed, which contains iodine, in the treatment of goiter. Roger covers at length wounds to the head and brain. His book proved highly popular; it was published in numerous editions and remained a classic for three centuries.

The school of Salerno's reputation spread far. To this center alone the Holy Roman Emperor, Frederick II,

Quotations from Maimonides

"Medical practice is not knitting and weaving and the labor of the hands, but it must be inspired with soul and be filled with understanding and equipped with the gift of keen observation; these together with accurate scientific knowledge are the indispensable requisites for proficient medical practice."

On astrology he wrote, "It was the first branch of secular learning I had seriously pursued... I had reached the conclusion that the whole science of astrology was baseless foolishness.... Let us never cast our reason back; our eyes are in front and not behind us."

Commenting on a quote from Hippocrates that stated "a boy is born from the right ovary, a girl from the left," Maimonides remarked, "A man should be either prophet or genius to know this."

A Poem About Health—the Regimen Sanitatis Salernitanum

The school of Salerno produced a handbook of hygiene in Latin hexameters, discussing diet, sleep, exercise, work, and play. The poem recommended moderation in eating and drinking, bread dipped in wine for breakfast, chopped onions for hair growth, and prunes as laxatives. Almost 300 editions of this poem exist in five languages. The following verses mention the herbs sage and rosemary and their benefits:

If in your drink you mingle rue with sage,
All poison is expelled by power of those,
And if you would withall Lust's heat assuage,
Add to them two the gentle flower of Rose:
Would not be sea sick when seas do rage,
Sage-water drink with wine before he goes.
Of washing of your hands much good doth rise,
'Tis wholesome, cleanly, and relieves your eyes....
But who can write thy worth (O sovereign Sage!).
Some ask how man can die, where thou dost grow,
Oh that there were a medicine curing age,
Death comes at last, though death comes ne'er
so slow:
Sage strengths the sinews, severe heat doth 'suage,
The Palsy helps, and rids of mickle [much] woe.

The Tacuinum Sanitatum was a book about health based on Arab medicine. Here, women gather sage. People have held sage in high regard since ancient times. A late medieval treatise states that the desire of sage is to render man immortal.

in 1240, gave the right of conferring a physician's license to practice medicine. Students had to complete a five-year course of study and then had to practice medicine for one year under the supervision of an experienced doctor.

MONTPELLIER Montpellier, located on the Mediterranean coast of France, halfway between Marseilles and Spain, was the second-oldest medical school in western Europe, after Salerno. Founded mainly by Jewish scholars, medical teaching began there in the 12th century. A decree of 1180 stated that "whoever or of whatever origin he might be should have the right to give medical instruction without being called to account by anyone."

But by 1220, stricter regulations applied. No one could teach who had not been properly examined and given a license by the bishop. Students attended medical lectures for at least five years, and then practiced medicine for several months, before graduating. After 1340, human bodies, usually of executed criminals, were dissected once or twice a year.

PARIS Medical teaching began in Paris at about the same time as at Montpellier. Medicine was taught along with other subjects, such as grammar, rhetoric, arithmetic, and theology. Ecclesiastical authorities ran the university, but the masters formed a corporation, having common rights and duties.

BOLOGNA At the University of Bologna, the professors organized themselves into guilds, and the students formed unions based on their homelands.

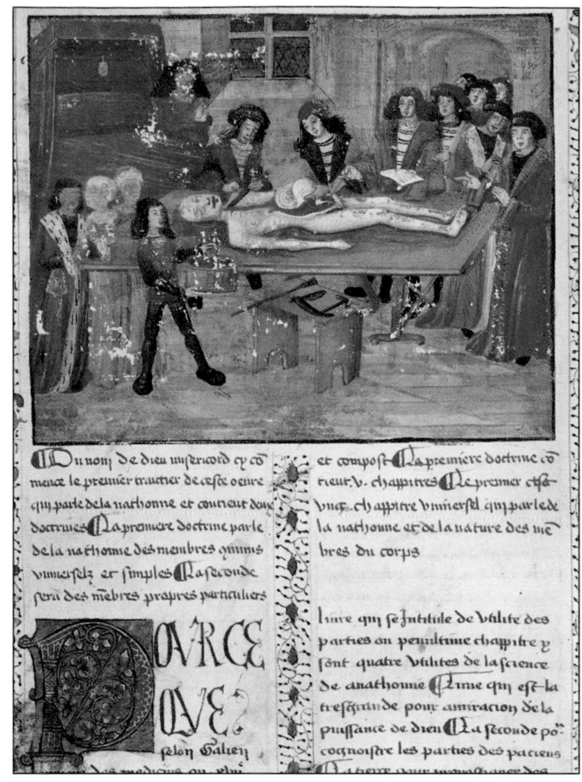

Guy de Chauliac (1300–1368), a famous French surgeon, wrote a textbook on surgery that was the most authoritative one until the 18th century. He operated on hernias and cataracts, excised superficial growths, and treated fractures using slings and extension weights. Here, the "father of surgery" gives a lesson to medical students.

During the 13th century, physicians from the medical school of Bologna contributed to the advancement of surgery. William of Saliceto (1210–1277) favored the use of the knife and downplayed the use of cautery, which was preferred in Arab medicine.

His book on surgery pioneered in including a section on anatomy in a textbook on surgery. He also incorporated regional anatomy into his surgical instruction, warning students to avoid damage to adjacent parts when performing surgery on particular sites. When writing of wounds to the back of the neck, he cautioned his readers to avoid damage to the spinal cord, which might result in paralysis.

William used examples drawn from his own experience to illustrate principles derived from a learned textual tradition. One of William's more remarkable cases was that of a man with a belly wound, whose intestines were hanging out. The first physician called in proclaimed the patient a dead man. William, although extremely concerned because the intestines were damaged and leaking fecal matter, washed the intestines with heated wine and replaced them, suturing the wound. The patient not only survived, but married, had children, and lived long.

OXFORD Oxford University began in the 9th century, but started to flourish in the 13th, when many English students abandoned Paris University and returned home. At this time an independent medical faculty at Oxford began, but throughout the Middle Ages, the medical faculty at Oxford remained small and undistinguished. Those who studied medicine had to become priests, continuing a long tradition of medical practice among the clergy. However, priests were forbidden to lecture on medicine.

Medical Practitioners

University graduates in medicine were the most prestigious practitioners, followed by skilled surgeons, with barber-surgeons and apothecaries at the bottom of the pack—an informal hierarchy of medical practitioners.

The goal of university medical education was to train people to practice medicine. Most of the professors themselves practiced as an economic necessity, since it was their main source of income. Some of the leading professors limited their practices to consultation. Others relied on assistants who performed the necessary procedures.

PHYSICIANS In 12th century Western Europe, the practice began of examining and licensing those who wanted to be physicians. University faculty, political bodies, and ecclesiastical authorities, all licensed people to practice medicine. Craft guilds relating to medicine began in the late 13th century. Florence had a guild of doctors, apothecaries, and grocers established in 1293.

Women also practiced medicine and surgery. Between 1273 and 1410, Naples had 24 female surgeons. Frankfurt had 15 female practitioners, mostly Jewish, between 1387 and 1497. In an agreement from 1326, Sara de Saint Gilles, a Jewish woman, undertook to train a man in the art of medicine and to clothe and care for him for seven months. In return, he agreed to give her all his physicians fees earned during that time.

Advice to the Physician

Don't give your services gratis; let not the wise muse of Hippocrates
Serve the sick in bed without reward.
For medicine bought dearly benefits much;
If something is given for nothing, no good results. . . .
While the patient is suffering let the physician be firm in his demand;
Let him ask for immediate payment or get security;
For the faithful pledge preserves the ancient friend,
But if you seek it later, you will be held as an enemy.

Some practitioners were both doctors and surgeons, especially in Italy. Although their practices overlapped in many ways, such as providing medication and dietary recommendations, only the surgeon sutured wounds, used the knife, and set fractures and dislocations, although bloodletting was done by both. In Northern Europe, physicians and surgeons belonged to separate guilds and surgeons could not serve on university faculties of medicine.

The education, training, and status of people who made their living through surgery varied greatly. At the head of the hierarchy were the skilled, literate surgeons. Empirics—those who acquired medical learning without formal training and practiced by trial and error—also carried out surgical procedures. Itinerant craftsmen often specialized in a particular operation, such as treating cataract, hernias, or bladder stones. One medical student noted that the wandering specialists in couching (treating) cataract were often more successful than the famous surgeons because they had more practice.

BARBER-SURGEONS Barbers in German public baths not only trimmed and shaved their clients, but also let blood, sold ointments, pulled teeth, applied cups, and gave enemas. In about 1100, barbers came into prominence in the monasteries where they tonsured and bled the monks. Surgical experts complained that the physicians did not want to practice surgery, thinking it undignified, so they left it up to the barbers, along with bloodletting.

In England in 1307, the barber-surgeons found themselves in trouble with the mayor of London. He did not like their form of advertising—hanging bloody rags from poles outside their shops and putting buckets of blood on their windowsills. As punishment, their traditional medical privileges were reduced to bloodletting only in the presence of a physician. One year later they again ran into trouble. They were accused of turning the city baths into brothels.

Women could become barbers and were allowed into the guilds. Women barbers usually had taken over their deceased spouse's practice. The records show at least two pairs of mother-daughter barber teams.

APOTHECARIES In the early Middle Ages, practitioners probably created their own materia medica, and they most likely continued to do so later in the countryside. The first public pharmacies were established in Italy around the end of the 13th century. Pharmacists belonged to guilds. Patients often waited for their physician to meet them at the pharmacy and prescribe medication. Many of the drugs prescribed by university-trained physicians consisted of spices, mostly from South Asia. Thus, many of the apothecaries were also spice traders or retailers. In London in 1345, the apothecaries, spicers, and pepperers formed a grocers' company, one of the most powerful in the city. Although the apothecaries ranked below physicians and surgeons, and sometimes even barbers, in the practice of medicine, they were often more successful, influential, and wealthier than many physicians and surgeons.

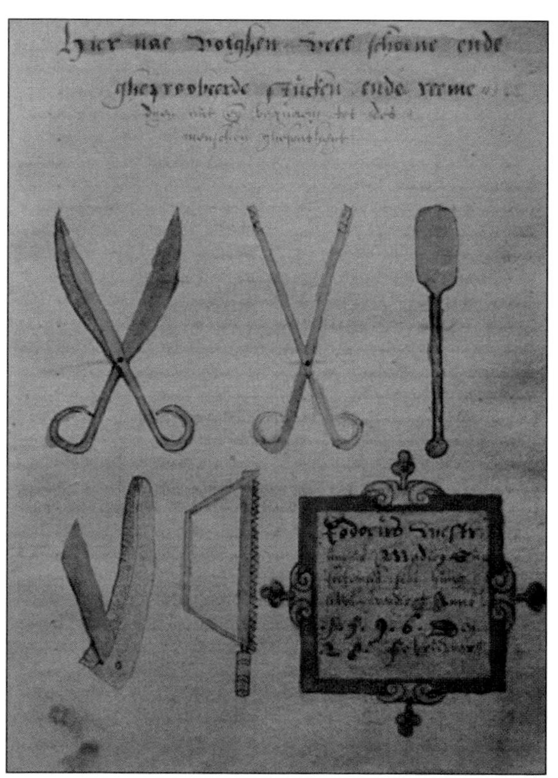

This manuscript illustrates surgeon's instruments. In Northern Europe, physicians and surgeons belonged to separate guilds. Women also practiced medicine and surgery. Between 1273 and 1410 Naples had 24 female surgeons. Women could become barbers and were allowed into the guilds.

The Barber Pole

The medieval barbers advertised their presence by placing the bloody rags that resulted from their surgical procedures, such as tooth extractions, on tall poles outside their shops. The blood from the rags would drip down the pole, causing the pole to become stained with red streaks. According to legend, the modern barber pole with its candy-cane swirl of red is the descendent of these gruesome displays.

The highest honor that any licensed practitioner—physician, surgeon, apothecary, or barber—could obtain was employment in a royal court. Physicians and their underlings, the apothecaries, had the most influence at court. Surgeons and barbers took the fore when the king traveled, especially on a military campaign.

Royal Healing

Edward the Confessor, king of England from 1042 to 1066, seems to have begun a tradition of royal healing. A young woman, who seemed barren and suffered from an infection of the neck glands (probably scrofula, likely related to the deficiency disease rickets) called the King's Evil, dreamed she would be cured if Edward washed her neck. The king actually agreed to it and washed her neck several times, making the sign of the cross. Pus and blood flowed out where the healthy and diseased skin separated. Soon new skin grew, covering the scars, and the woman gave birth to twins.

Edward also healed a blind man named Wulfwin who had been blind for 19 years and had visited 80 churches and their shrines seeking a cure. Edward, dipping his hand in water, touched the man, who regained his sight and gained a responsible post at court, too! Edward also cured cases of quartan fever and tumors. A ring of Edward's, kept in Westminster Abbey, cured epilepsy.

Other English kings also had the healing touch. Edward I (1272–1307) often touched 200 or 300 people in a day. Even medical writers recommended the king's touch. John of Gaddesden (1280–1361) prescribed various diets and drugs for scrofula, adding

> If this does not suffice, go to the king that he may touch and bless you; because this disease is called the royal disease and the touch of the Most Serene King of the English is valuable for it.

The healing of these patients might have had less to do with the power of the king than was thought at the time. Scholars now speculate that the true medicine was the trip to see the king in the first place. To get to the king, most people would have had to make long pilgrimages to London, and pilgrims were usually cared for with a great deal of hospitality. During their jouney, therefore, they were well fed and probably had better care than at any other time of their lives. By the time of their arrival, they were on the road to recovery from any diseases caused by nutrient deficiencies, such as rickets or xerophthalmia. Once touched by the king, though, it was the royalty that got the credit. The last recorded rite of the King's Touch was in 1745

Royal medical service on the battlefield allowed surgeons to gain valuable experience on a large number of patients. War service greatly contributed to the rise of surgery because in civilian life, dissection and experimentation were limited.

Barbers usually just performed the king's toilet; when they performed medical duties, they were limited to minor procedures, such as cupping or lancing. A surgeon had to be present whenever a barber shaved, cupped, or bled the king. Being the king's barber was still a good job, even if it had limited duties, since barbers received many privileges, including land and annuities.

LEECHES Leech, originally meaning doctor in Old English, came to mean an unlicensed village practitioner. Most villages were too small to support any sort of licensed practitioner, even a barber, and thus the village leeches remained important in the countryside. They remained popular because of their low fees, but often had to farm, practice a craft, or serve several villages to make a living. Empirics in the cities faced regulations and fines, but in the countryside, the leech had independence. Leeches trained with experienced practitioners or were self-taught in folk medicine. They created simple medicines from herbs or animal and mineral prod-

A bathing parlor with two doctors in the foreground. Bathing was one of the most popular forms of medical treatment. By the 12th century, bathing had also become a popular diversion. In public baths, the sexes bathed together with only a railing separating them, and spectators watched from above.

Guy de Chauliac (1300–1368), a famous French surgeon, wrote that midwives were also sex therapists of sorts; they administered aphrodisiacs, gave advice, and took part in the procedure known as the "congress." If a couple sought an annulment on the grounds of impotence, a physician or surgeon examined the genitals to see if they were normal. Then a midwife would be appointed to be present while the husband and wife "lie together on several successive days" in her presence. As Guy de Chauliac reports

> She must administer spices and aromatics to them, she must warm them and anoint them with warm oils, she must massage them near the fire, she must order them to talk to each other and to embrace. Then she must report what she has seen to the doctor.

The doctor would then report the findings to the authorities.

ucts. Some leeches were women, many of whom served as obstetricians. Unfortunately for the leeches, people often associated them with quacks, who claimed they could cure using bizarre combinations of potions and charms. Quacks showed up most often in the countryside because in cities they were more likely to be prosecuted. People flocked to them.

MIDWIVES Midwives controlled obstetrics, with male physicians and surgeons rarely involved. Unfortunately, almost no written records preserve information about midwifery. The little we do know indicates that besides dealing with pregnancy and childbirth, they inspected women to check on their virginity.

Uroscopy and the Unheard-of Miracle

Uroscopy consisted of examining a patient's urine for color, density, and content and reaching conclusions about the person's health based on these observations. In fact, practitioners relied so heavily on the inspection of urine for diagnosis, that the urine flask became the symbol of medical practitioners in medieval art. One story was told of a duke who sought to deceive a monastic physician named Notker. The duke sent to Notker, as his own urine, that of a lady of his court. After inspecting it, Notker said, "God is now about to work a portentous and unheard-of miracle, that a man should give birth to a child." The duke was suitably embarrassed.

The Americas

American Shamanism

SHAMANISM is ancient medicine, indeed. It is perhaps the first kind of medicine ever practiced, but it is more than just medicine. Shamanism is a way to see and make sense of the world, and many cultures in all parts of the globe operate with shamanistic beliefs. Although these peoples are often called "primitive," the internal logic of shamanistic culture is far from simple and, in fact, is a truly remarkable way to conceptualize reality. As we will see, shamanism involves spirits, soul traveling, psychic battles, and last but not least, healing.

The Huichols believe that the soul of a powerful ancestor is capable of returning to his or her family from the Otherworld in the form of a rock crystal with divinatory and healing powers. In this wool yarn painting, the late Huichol shaman Ramón Medina depicts a shaman (lower right) embarking on an out-of-body journey to find such a crystallized ancestral soul (white star).

Shamans—sometimes inadequately called "medicine men" or "witch doctors"—are the special members of a tribe or community that have the ability to see the world of spirits. For shamanistic societies, the spirits of animals, plants, and objects, are the true essences of things. Rather than being imaginary or outside of reality, the spirits are actually the true reality. When human affairs are in disarray—when crops fail or illness strikes—it is up to the shaman to right the wrong in the other worlds to heal the disruption in this one. He or she must take this journey often at great personal risk, making shamans some of the bravest and most selfless of healers.

Origins

It has been well known for some time that the peoples of the Western Hemisphere came across the once existent land bridge between Alaska and Siberia millennia ago. The base religion of Siberian peoples was shamanism—as it seems to have been long ago over much of the Eurasian continent—and it was shamanism that the first Americans carried with them into the New World. The techniques of ecstasy and healing that define shamanism have remained at the root of Native American religions ever since.

Central to the shaman's vocation was the ecstatic-visionary trance, or altered state of consciousness. Presumably this was one of its predominant features at least since the Middle Stone Age, even before the appearance of *Homo sapiens sapiens*—the modern species to which we all belong. And it continues to be central to shamanic belief and practice, including the healing arts, among Native American peoples.

Figure believed to represent a shaman in an ancient desert culture rock shelter in southern Texas. The unknown people who occupied these shelters covered their walls with depictions of the spirit world and are known to have used several shamanic botanical intoxicants. Peyote found in the caves has been radiocarbon dated to 5000 B.C.

THE NEW WORLD ESCAPES CHANGE The Old World developed differently, however. As "new" messianic religions (Christianity, Islam) swept across Europe and Asia, the old faiths and practices based on shamanism were suppressed. Shamans were demonized as witches, sorcerers, and frauds, and individual visionary experiences were condemned. Even before the Spanish Inquisition, the knowledge and techniques for contacting the spirit world and healing that had served shamans and their followers for thousands of years were condemned as works of the Devil.

Before the Spanish conquest of the Americas in the 16th century, none of this happened to shamans in the Americas. From the time of the first migrations out of Asia—perhaps as far back as 30,000 or 40,000 years—Native Americans were able to preserve their shamanistic heritage precisely because, before Columbus, the New World never underwent the massive religious transformations that swept across the Old World. On this side of the Pacific, shamans continued to be central to the religious life and physical and mental health of their communities.

ADAPTABILITY As the first Americans, starting in Alaska, gradually came to settle the entire Western Hemisphere, all the way down to the very tip of South America, they encountered forest, jungle, desert, mountains, and plains, each with its own geography, flora, and fauna. Because everything in nature had its own soul and its own relationships to humans and other things, there must have been a great deal for the shamans to learn anew each time they moved to another environment. Clearly shamanism does not,

Hardwired for Shamanism

The remarkable ability of shamanism to survive is not simply because the Native Americans were "backward" or afraid of change. A better explanation is that many of the assumptions of the shamanic worldview correspond to the biology and chemistry of the central nervous system and some of the basic needs of the human psyche. The ecstatic-visionary experience is surely influenced by the cultural setting. However, it is intriguing that many of the compounds that give the psychedelic flora their strange power are structurally related to those naturally occurring in the brain.

and never did, freeze its practitioners or people into one dogmatic, magical worldview that prevented them from practical observation and action.

Shamanism survived despite cultural differences as well. Socially, politically, and economically a great gulf separated the great pre-Columbian civilizations (such as the Aztecs and the Maya) from the agricultural villages out of which they had evolved. Yet we know from the Spanish chroniclers that the professional priests of the Aztecs in Mexico and the Inca in Peru continued to hold the same ideas about the reciprocal relationships among humans, animals, and the spirit world as had their shaman ancestors. In fact, the village shamans who came before continued to flourish alongside the professional priesthood of the urban civilizations.

Understanding Shamanism

Strictly speaking, even if shamanism has sometimes been called humanity's most ancient form of spirituality, it is not a religion per se. It is a religious phenomenon, but it has persisted across a broad spectrum of beliefs and even where the local religion has changed over time. In the Americas, religion—even that of "simple" hunting and gathering societies—can and did take many different forms. The Arctic environment, for example, inspires different ideas about religion than does the desert or the rain forest. Yet there is always this ideologic universal: However they organized themselves—whether in cities, villages, or communal houses; whether they lived in the Amazonian rain forest, in the Arctic, on the plains and prairies, or in the Andes Mountains of South America; whether they hunted seals and walrus, trapped salmon, cultivated maize, or brought down buffalo—there is evidence that all Native Americans shared certain basic and, clearly, very ancient concepts. Even though gods, spirits, legends, and customs vary, the techniques associated with shamanic practice tend to be amazingly similar no matter what the natural or social environment.

The Animate World In the shamanistic world order, all phenomena—everything we can see, hear, or feel; every animal, plant, cloud, rock, and even tool—has a soul. What to us is obviously inanimate, is to the shaman equally obviously a living thing, with a consciousness and an ability to communicate. (The belief that all

Origin of the Term

The word *shaman* came into the European languages in the 18th century from much the same place the original Americans did—Siberia. The word comes from the Evenk—a small offshoot of the Siberian Tungu-speaking people. Samán was their name for the specialist in the sacred.

things have a soul is sometimes called *animism*, from the Latin word *anima*, meaning "soul," which comes from the Greek word *animos*, meaning "wind" or "breath.") To certain species of plants—especially the most important sources of food, intoxicating drink, and the drugs that could trigger the visionary trance—Native Americans even attributed godlike qualities. In shamanism, the soul, or animating force, has the ability to leave the body during life as well as after death.

Eskimo shaman's mask from Nunivak Island representing a spirit. The thin hoops encircling the face stand for the levels of the multilayered universe, which the shaman traverses in his out-of-body journeys.

Reciprocity In this universe of animate things, all relationships are governed by the principle of reciprocity, not only between people but between people and animals, people and plants, and people and the ruling spirits or gods. This type of reciprocity means that all the things in nature are interdependent and each is integral to the whole of the universe. Therefore, shamanic peoples see themselves as parts of the natural world rather than the masters of it.

The Stratified Universe In the shamanistic worldview, the universe is divided into several horizontal levels, with an underworld below, the heavens above, and a middle world inhabited by humans, animals, plants, and their respective spirit "owners," or masters and mistresses. The different cosmic levels, in turn, are connected by a vertical axis known as the *axis mundi*, or shamanic tree, with its roots in the underworld and its leafy crown in the heavens.

The same idea was expressed in sacred urban architecture in the great civilizations in Mesoamerica and the Andes between 1200 B.C. and the Spanish conquest in the 16th century A.D. While these structures also served as the tombs of rulers, the stratification of the universe is the essential meaning of the stepped temple platforms, or pyramids, that annually draw hundreds of thousands of awed tourists from all over the world. They are sacred mountains, whose levels correspond to the particular worldview of their ancient builders. And there are plenty of examples of the shaman's tree in art and surviving rituals.

One of the shaman's unique gifts was his ability to navigate through this stratified universe. For example, the entranced Inuit shaman in northernmost Canada, the Tukano in the Colombian Amazon, or his counterpart in a Mexican Indian village under the sway of the Aztec empire, climbed to the heavens or down to the land of the dead through a series of levels in the stratified universe of the mind. The shaman can transcend the limitations of the human condition by passing safely through monstrous obstacles barring the way to the Otherworld.

TRANCING The ecstatic trance, or altered state of consciousness, is central to the art of the shaman. The shamanic trance is an out-of-body experience during which the shaman feels him- or herself to be in communication with the spirit world. In 1979, a survey of Native North American societies found reports of ritualized altered states of consciousness in no less than 97 percent of them. No doubt, the figure is similar for South America.

To trigger the ecstatic state, the shaman may employ one or more of more than 200 species of hallucinogenic plants, including species of cacti and mushrooms. Not all shamans used the hallucinogenic substances, though. On the Great Plains, nonchemical techniques of ecstasy were sometimes used, such as sensory deprivation, hunger, self-torture, sleeplessness, lonely vigil, exposure to the elements, meditation, yogalike positions, song, dance, drumming, and so on.

The peyote cactus is one of the many hallucinogenic plants used by shamans in the Americas. Huichol Indians have peyote hunts to gather the plant. Peyote plants like these, grown from a single root that was left in the ground on a previous peyote hunt, are considered especially powerful and beneficial by the Huichols.

What the Shaman Does

The abilities and the duties of shamans in various communities were (and are) formidable. Sometimes they were the political leaders. They were the recognized masters of spirits, who assisted the shamans on their out-of-body journeys through the layers of the cosmos and taught them their curing songs. They were believed to be able to metamorphose from human to animal. They served as mediators between human beings and the gods. They were prophets of the weather, the hunt, and with the advent of agriculture some 8,000 years ago, the harvest. And it was these masters of spirits who preserved and passed on the ancient knowledge handed down from the ancestors and who guarded the spiritual and physical equilibrium of their societies and its members. But regardless of the various functions and powers attributed to shamans in different cultures, they were almost always respected as the healers of sickness.

Because shamanism is also performance art, the best shamans were and still are poets and actors able to dramatize in costume, gesture, and word their otherworldly adventures. Traditionally, like their cousins in Siberia, many Native American shamans were distinguished by special clothing, protective amulets, and other symbolic imagery that served to mark their extraordinary social status.

Jack of All Trades

The functions of shamans at the present day are many and various. The Danish anthropologist Knud Rasmussen, writing in 1929 about his Canadian Eskimo shaman friends, outlined the most important functions as follows:

> They must be physicians, curing the sick. Meteorologists, not only able to forecast the weather, but also able to ensure fine weather. They must be able to visit the Land of the Dead under the sea or up in the sky in order to look for lost or stolen souls. Sometimes the dead will wish to have a dear relative who is still alive brought to them in the Land of the Dead; the person in question then falls ill, and it is the business of the shaman to make the dead release such souls. Finally, every great shaman must, when asked, and when a number of people are present, exercise his art in miraculous fashion in order to astonish the people and convince them of the sacred and inexplicable powers of the shaman.

CURING WITH PLANTS As a healer, the shamans of North America had an enormous amount of expertise in different aspects of diagnosis and treatment. Along with the shaman's knowledge of the origin and nature of physical and emotional illness are the theoretical and practical techniques of restoring health and proper balance to the patient and the larger human community.

Although for the shaman most illness may be attributed to supernatural causes, for treatment to be effective it must involve the whole person—mind *and* body. Shamans did and do turn to the spirits for guidance to address the aspects of the illness that involved the mind and spirit. Curing ceremonies involving trances and soul travels were one aspect of most treatments. However, to treat the body, shamans also had command over hundreds—even thousands—of medicinal plants, as well as other physical and metaphysical treatments.

Modern science has confirmed the effectiveness of many of the species of trees, shrubs, succulents, and grasses to which Indian people attribute the power to prevent infection, heal wounds, and cure disease. Not all of the plants shamans used have had such scientific confirmation, by any means, but there are enough to make us admire the pharmacologic abilities and powers of observation that Native American shamans brought to the art of healing (see pages 176–181). Many more species remain to be tested, and many have not even been botanically identified yet.

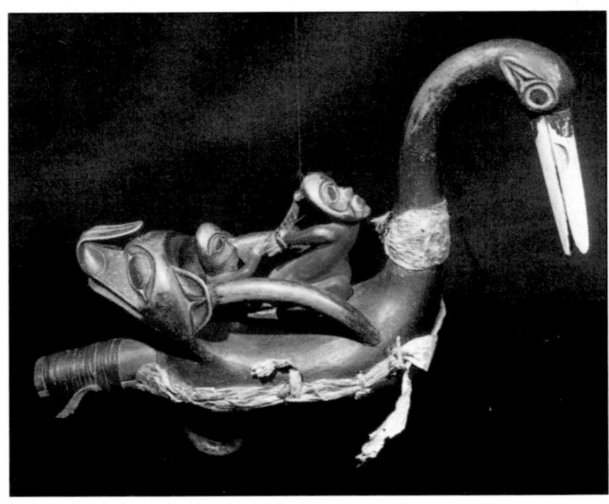

A spectacular Tlingit rattle full of shamanic symbolism, from Yakutat, Alaska. It represents an oystercatcher, a colorful wading bird whose distinctive cry warns other birds of approaching danger, just as the shaman guards his human flock. Riding on the back of the rattle is a shaman (left) who has captured and bound a witch. Witches are much feared as sources of illness and misfortune, and protecting his group against them is an important part of the shaman's art.

CURING WITH SPIRITS Although customs varied across the hemisphere, certain methods and beliefs about curing provide good examples of shamanistic practice in the realm beyond botanical medicine.

There are occasions when shamans call for and conduct dramatic ceremonies in-

Shamanic Transformations

A common theme in shamanic cultures is the close identification of the shaman with certain animals. The identification is so strong that it is believed that the shaman can actually transform him- or herself into that animal. In the tropics, these animals are mainly the jaguar and harpy eagle. The closest connection of the Taurepan shamans of Venezuela is with the jaguar. In fact, so total is the identification of many shamans in the South American tropics with this great jungle cat that the speakers of several Indian languages apply the same or a closely related word to both shamans and jaguars. Shamans are believed to be able to transform themselves into jaguars in life, and after death many appear permanently in that form.

tended to "renew the world" when it seems to have gone out of kilter. Some ceremonies are designed to cure the gods themselves so that, restored to health, they will again provide for humankind. Among many Native Americans, world-renewal ceremonies and their equivalents coincide with the shortest days of the year, the same midwinter period when Christians celebrate Christmas.

OTHER CURING POWERS Shamans generally have significant influence in the spirit world. The shaman has the ability to call allies from the spirit world to help with tasks. He or she can recruit and control helping spirits that will do his or her bidding. Sometimes these spirit helpers come of their own volition to their master's aid because of the mystic bond between the shaman and the spirit.

This power in the spirit world is essential to healing. Because souls can leave the body even during life, the soul of an individual can become lost. Sometimes the soul simply strays; other times it may be abducted by jealous spirits or offended ancestors. The loss of the soul can bring on physical repercussions in the form of disease and even death. It is up to the shaman to restore health and balance by traveling to recover the lost, strayed, or abducted soul. To communicate with the dead and the spirits, the shaman might employ musical instruments and whistle languages; often, the shaman can use a rattle or drum to call the ancestors.

Some shamans also recognize and treat diseases caused by foreign objects (sickness projectiles) magically shot from afar by a human enemy or a neglected or offended ancestor or other spirit. The shaman can restore the patient's health by sucking the sickness projectile from the patient's body.

Another common belief in shamanistic cultures is that the shaman's breath and spittle have restorative and therapeutic power. In some cultures, tobacco smoke blown by the shaman is also thought to have healing properties.

The Shaman as Hero or Spirit

To understand the shaman's world, it helps to see how the legends and stories describe the peculiar position of the shaman in the universe. In the ancient legends, we find the basis of the shaman's healing power. There are striking similarities between the fearsome experiences of shamans, heroes, and the deceased on their spiritual journeys. For a particularly telling example, we go to the Arctic for a story from the Inuit, or "True People," of the shaman's journey

Warao Indian shaman in the Orinoco Delta of Venezuela sucks out a foreign object that has been magically shot into the patient to make him sick. The two common causes of illness in shamanic healing are sickness intrusion and soul loss. In the former, some hostile force has shot a magical projectile into the patient from afar; it is up to the curer to divine the origin of the disease and remove it by sucking.

to the sea spirit Takanakapsaluk—the Mother of Sea Animals.

The Dangerous Passage Like all myths, the Inuit tradition has several versions, no one more true than the others, for, as shamans say, the truth is too big to be contained in only one story. However, one version goes like this:

One day no seals or walrus appeared to offer themselves to the people. Soon there was starvation; men and women went hungry. The milk of the new mothers dried up, and children began to die.

So, the people asked the most powerful and knowledgeable of the shamans to make the perilous journey to the bottom of the sea to discover the reason for the calamity and beg Takanakapsaluk, the Mother of the Sea Animals, to release her charges so the people would again have food. All the people loosened the ties of their clothing so that nothing should bind the shaman to this world, and the shaman went into a trance.

In his trance he took his kayak and pushed off into the icy sea. He paddled mightily all day and all night until he heard a great roaring and crashing sound. Coming closer he saw his way barred by a pair of icebergs that opened and closed in an instant.

The shaman tried desperately to steer his kayak to the left and sail around the fearsome obstacle, but the icebergs shifted position as though alive. As hard as he paddled to one side, they always stayed in front. Finally, he understood that he had

Tlingit "soul catcher" of bone carved into the likeness of a two-headed spirit animal (19th century Alaska). Shamans use these magical tubes to extract pathogens from patients and, more important, to catch and bring back souls that have become lost or abducted by hostile spirits.

no choice but to pass between them. A spirit voice told him to send a seabird ahead to calculate the proper moment for the passage. The bird was one of his spirit helpers. The terrible icebergs opened, and following the shaman's instructions, the spirit bird flew right between them. It made it safely almost all the way through, but as the icebergs closed, some of its feathers were caught and sliced off.

The icebergs opened again, and, paddling with all his might, the shaman pushed forward. He had made it almost all the way through when the icebergs closed on the stern of his kayak, damaging it but allowing him to continue.

On the other side, he saw the whirlpool he knew led to Takanakapsaluk's home. Down and down he slid, as though through a tube. The tube was kept open for the shaman's return trip by all the souls of his namesakes. When he saw Takanakapsaluk, her hair was disheveled, and she was hiding her eyes, and all the offenses committed by the people were gathered as spots of filth covering her body. He took hold of one of the goddess' shoulders and turned her around to face him. He stroked her disheveled hair and with his magic shaman's comb tidied it until it was smooth and shiny. For she, who is without hands and fingers, could not comb it herself. He sang to her until finally she calmed and told him that the miscarriages the women have kept secret and the taboos that have been broken are blocking the way for her animals to reach the surface. The shaman employed all his wiles to put her in a kindlier mood. At last she consented to release the sea animals so they could offer themselves to the hunters.

Only then could he return. The people heard him calling from a long way off. He told them the words of the Sea Mother and one by one all then confessed their offenses, so everyone heard his and her neighbors' secrets. All who were not present were called for, and only when all had confessed their sins to the shaman and one another, did the animals begin offering themselves and life was again assured.

With variations accounted for by local traditions and environments, much the same story is told all over the Americas (as it is also in the Old World).

COINCIDENCE OR EVIDENCE? The Inuit story of the shaman's journey to the sea spirit Takanakapsaluk is remarkably similar to the Greek myth of Jason and the Argonauts and the Symplegades—the clashing rocks at the mouth of the Euxine

Sea through which their ship *Argo* had to pass.

In the Greek tale, Phineus, a blind soothsayer (himself a shaman of sorts) and king of Salmidessus, advises the Argonauts to send a pigeon ahead to test the clashing gateway. The Symplegades would close, and as they opened again, the *Argo* would slip through. If the pigeon were crushed, the *Argo* should turn back. The bird got through, but its tail feathers were caught. The *Argo*, its crew rowing furiously, followed, assisted by a mighty shove from the goddess Athena. The ship made it, but, like the pigeon's tail, its stern suffered damage.

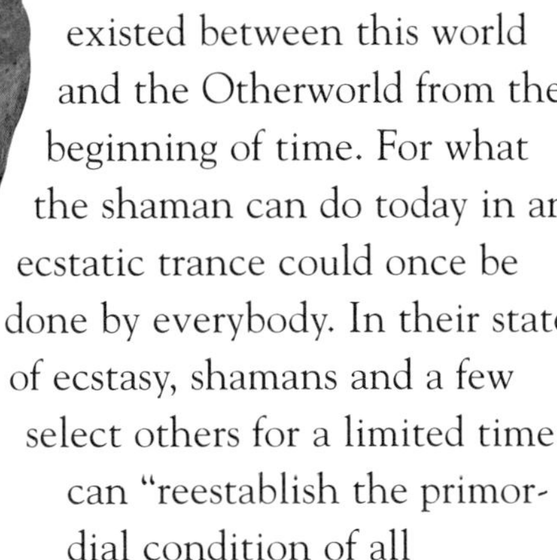

Shamans in ancient Mexico guarded not only the health and welfare of the living but also of the deceased. This explains why 2,000-year-old funerary figurines found in west Mexican tombs are, like this one from the state of Colima, often depict the shaman in a fighting stance.

The story is so amazingly universal that to explain it, someone once dreamed up a theoretical voyage by Alexander the Great far into the Pacific Ocean. There he supposedly shared the classical Greek saga of Jason and the Argonauts with some islanders. They passed it to the north, and this is why the Inuit story is so similar to the Greek story. Of course, there was no voyage far into the Pacific by Alexander to account for the parallels between the Inuit shaman's adventure and that of Jason and his Argonauts, but it is probably no coincidence either. The tale must contain something basic to human nature.

A better interpretation comes from a historian of religion, Mircea Eliade. The message of the widely distributed myths of the dangerous, or paradoxical, passage that opens and shuts in an instant, he wrote, is that "he who succeeds in accomplishing it has transcended the human condition; he is a shaman, a hero, or a 'spirit.'" By crossing the perilous bridge or clashing gate that "connects the two worlds and that only the dead can attempt, the shaman proves that he is spirit, no longer a human being."

At the same time he is restoring the communicability that existed between this world and the Otherworld from the beginning of time. For what the shaman can do today in an ecstatic trance could once be done by everybody. In their state of ecstasy, shamans and a few select others for a limited time can "reestablish the primordial condition of all mankind." Successful passage through clashing icebergs, mountains, thunderclouds, rolling boulders, razor-sharp reeds, the snapping jaws of reptilian or marine monsters, the "mouth of heaven," and a dozen similar gateways that figure in Native American myths is, in Eliade's words, "a return to origins, a reversion to the mystical age of the lost paradise." And that is indeed a universal desire.

And what about the slight injury to the ship, the kayak, the shaman's bird ally, and, in some stories, the shaman himself? Just a gentle reminder that hero or shaman, he is after all not dead, not permanently spirit, but human, and his passage into the Otherworld only temporary.

Becoming a Shaman

Among traditional Indian people in the South American rain forest, it often was, and in a few places still is, the shaman more than the chief who commands the greatest respect and power. In no small measure, this must be because he commands a huge inventory of curing and preventive spells and the myths from which they derive. He knows how to use the therapeutic plants in his environment and when and how to combine them with one another, using the relevant magical spells for greatest effect. Finally, he knows the expectations people and the higher powers have of each other and how to satisfy these expectations.

All this specialized knowledge and more he acquired through instruction by knowledgeable masters and the spirits who volunteered their services to him, or whom he recruited in his training.

THE CALLING Summoned to his vocation by ancestor spirits, usually by means of a near-fatal spiritual and physical crisis he had to overcome, the shaman believed himself capable of projecting his soul on flights to other worlds to retrieve a lost or stolen soul, face down metaphysical enemies, or seek guidance from deities and other supernatural beings. Always and everywhere in the traditional world there was emphasis on the shaman's unique ability to project his soul into other worlds in the ecstatic trance. This is an art the shaman acquired during initiatory training, which typically involved confrontation and even battle with hostile demons and overcoming dangerous obstacles, before he could reach his goal.

It is important to remember that despite what we in the modern world might consider the allure of such a powerful position, the shaman never performed his art for his own benefit, but always on behalf of his clientele, such as an ailing patient or the larger community. Indeed, without a community to recognize and support him and for him to serve, there is neither shamanism nor shaman.

PIASÁN Becoming a shaman often involved elaborate initiations. Although the customs varied from one society to the next, most required intensive physical or mental effort and even danger. Let's see how this was done in one group, the Taurepan of southern Venezuela and northern Brazil.

The Taurepan shaman is called *piasán*, a word derived from that for "ancestor." This title immediately relates him to the deified ancestors, especially Piai'má, myth-

Female Shamans

Although the shamanic vocation is generally open to women, traditionally most shamans have been men, perhaps because men were the hunters and warriors, and with a universe full of disease demons and other potentially hostile spirits, there has always been a combative element in shamanism. Not so any longer. There are now female shamans in many places, including Chile and Argentina, where all the *machi*, the shamans of the Mapuche Indians, are women. And though shamanic folk medicine in highland and coastal Peru used to be a predominantly male vocation, many women have answered the call from the spirits and are practicing their own blend of indigenous ecstatic-visionary shamanism, herbal curing, and imagery borrowed from Christianity and non-indigenous religions.

Shamanism and traditional Indian religion are still strong among the Huichol Indians of the Sierra Madre Occidental of Mexico. Here the highly respected shaman greets the sun god at his first appearance over the horizon.

ical creator of the first shaman. The first thing the novice has to learn is how the first shamans were created, for he will himself have to experience everything that is described in the myth, which goes like this:

In ancient times, some boys lose their way in the forest. After wandering aimlessly about, they find themselves face to face with the great spirit Piai'má, who offers to instruct them in the arts of shamanism. "I will teach you," he says, "so that you will not run around like animals."

As their first ordeal, they have to swallow so much river water that they vomit it up. This is to make their voices beautiful when they sing their shamanic songs.

Next Piai'má gives them powerful emetics made from the crushed bark of different trees. "The emetic I give you," he says, "is not only for now but for always and for all shamans. When they vomit they perceive all that is right in the world." These, then, are the first medicinal plants in what will in time become an enormous inventory of therapeutic species.

Next, they vomit into a waterfall from whose falling and rising sounds they learn magical chants, most of them intended to ward off or cure physical and emotional ills in combination with practical therapy. Then they fall into a deep sleep in which only their eyes show life.

Now their teacher brings tobacco, powerful infusions of which he pours into their nostrils. All this they imagine takes weeks; in fact, it is years. In the meantime they have observed such severe dietary restrictions that they have almost wasted away to a skeletal state. This is to make them light for their first ascent to the heavens, and also to acquaint them with their own skeletons—a common phenomenon of shamanic initiation that South American Indians share with the Inuit and the Siberians.

In their emaciated state, the boys in the myth—and present-day initiates—immediately become intoxicated with the powerful tobacco juice. Then the master braids two ropes from the hair of his wife. He inserts them into their noses and slowly pulls them out through the mouth, making the blood flow. The hair rope symbolizes the ladder on which the shaman's soul ascends to the upper world while his body remains on earth.

The training of the first shamans and all their successors ever since continues with

Tobacco for Health

The tobacco employed in shamanism is nothing like the commercial tobacco of today. The species is *Nicotiana rustica*, which has a nicotine content many times that of ordinary cigarettes. It and the slightly milder sister species, *Nicotiana tabacum*, were first cultivated on the eastern slopes of the Andes over 6,000 years ago and diffused from there, along with its mythology, throughout South America and northward through Mexico as far as Iroquois country in upstate New York.

To Indian people, tobacco was a gift of the gods, who craved it as their proper sustenance, but the gods failed to keep some back for themselves, making them dependent on human beings for their most essential sacred food. To place themselves into the ecstatic-visionary trance, the shamans of certain South American societies consumed tobacco in such quantities they quickly became addicted. If the shamans craved tobacco to the point of feeling sick and anxious when they did not have it, so went the theory, the gods must suffer the same withdrawal pangs. This enabled shamans to manipulate the spirits by threatening to withhold tobacco if they failed to give succor to the patient, the community, or the earth.

further administrations of tobacco. In their tobacco-intoxicated state they hear the spirits, who teach them more and more curing songs. Then Piai'má returns them to their previous condition, fattening them up with good food to prepare them for the return to their own people.

In the meantime, the boys have become elders, assuring them of respect and high repute. As he bids them farewell, Piai'má gives the new shamans tobacco and many magical plants—some for curing illness, others to help them transform themselves, and still others to harm enemies. The spirits of these plants become their helpers and teachers, in much the same way that healing plants and plant hallucinogens are regarded as teachers by modern shamans and folk healers in the Upper Amazon and the Andes.

Preparation for shamanism begins early in a Taurepan boy's life, usually around ages 10 to 12 years. As in myth, training may, in fact, take 10 and even 20 years; the longer the training, the greater his prestige and the greater his knowledge of medicinal plants and sacred geography. Almost always, several novices study together, and because the shamanic vocation is often inherited, wherever possible the young shaman-to-be studies under his father. If a shaman has no son he will select a boy he believes to have the necessary qualities and intelligence, and who does not fear making the necessary commitment of time and the severe physical and psychological ordeals the training entails.

The Taurepan case may be an extreme example, but it does demonstrate, on the one hand, the close connection between mythology and practice one sees in many South American Indian societies; on the other, why more and more young men, as industrial civilization and its ideology make ever deeper inroads into the rain forest and its traditional life ways, opt for wage labor in preference to the enormous time, energy, and physical and mental courage required for the acquisition of the shaman's arts.

An Entire World of Souls

The Inuit, or Eskimos, were the last to arrive in North America from Asia, having settled only about 4,000 years ago in

Venezualen Shaman preparing to enter a trance by inhaling snuff through a Y-shaped double tube. Before him are the "tools" he will need during his ecstatic experience, including a large rattle.

the Arctic environment to which they were so marvelously adapted. Yet their rich and colorful shamanistic mythology sounds as though it preserves more faithfully than any other how the first Americans conceived of the rules of life and of animal and human souls and how the cosmos is structured.

PACIFYING SOULS Propitiating—pacifying or appeasing—the souls of slain game was one of the important ways that shamans preserved the health of the community. When the souls of game were not honored or pacified, they and the spirit masters and mistresses of the species might take offense and revenge on the population.

In Inuit belief, not just seals or walruses have souls, but also each and every one of their inner organs has a soul. So the shaman and the hunter (who are often one in the same because, unlike the priest or the medical doctor, shamans are never full-time practitioners) must propitiate not only the animal's *inua*, the Inuit word for "soul" or "animating spirit," but he must also respectfully address the *inua* of a seal's liver, stomach, heart, bones, even its bladder—everything of which people make use for food, shelter, transportation, hunting weapons, or floats.

Even the harpoon head is alive with its own *inua*, as is the shaft of the harpoon and the sealskin line that holds it to the shaft. And so are the images the Inuit carve of wood to represent an animal, the wind, even the air bubble that rises to the surface from a seal submerged below its blowhole in the ice. As an aged Eskimo shaman named Aua told the Danish anthropologist Knud Rasmussen more than 75 years ago:

> The greatest tragedy of life lies in the fact that human food consists entirely of souls. . . . All the creatures we have to kill and eat, all those that we have to strike down and destroy to make clothes for ourselves, have souls, like we have, souls that do not perish with the body, and which must therefore be propitiated lest they revenge themselves on us for taking their bodies.

A Life for a Life

Reciprocity means that for anything taken—be it a harvested food plant or a life—something must be given in return. The concept is taken very seriously in shamanic religions. An Inuit, Iroquois, or Aztec shaman would make perfect sense out of a story told by a Tukano shaman to the Colombian anthropologist Gerardo Reichel Domatoff: The killing of game diminishes the total supply of energy contained in the environment. To replenish nature with a life force of equal value, when an Indian dies, the shaman presents his or her soul to the supernatural Master of Game, who places the gift within the eternal cycle of life on which the people depend for survival.

INTERCHANGING SOULS A story from the Inuit illustrates the general belief in shamanistic societies of equivalence and interchangeability of all life-forms:

Once there was a woman who suffered a miscarriage. Instead of following the rules of life and ritually disposing of the fetus, she threw it away. A dog ate it and after a time gave birth to the fetus in the form of a dog. It learned how to live as a dog until the *inua*, its soul, grew tired of being a dog and changed into the body of a seal.

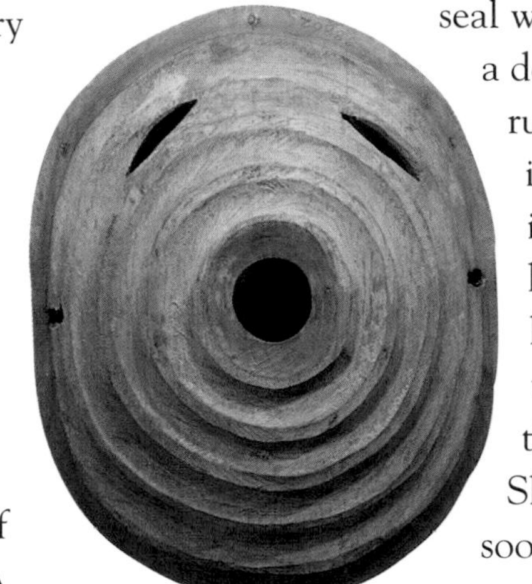

This dance mask, collected on the lower Yukon River in 1879, represents the soul or spirit of the air bubble that rises to the surface from a submerged seal. This spirit belongs to the class called tunghak, which resides on the moon, where shamans visit them in out-of-body journeys to ask for game and health.

It lived as a seal under the ice and had its blowhole like the other seals. The *inua* quite enjoyed the life of a seal, but then it decided to be a wolf instead. It stayed with the wolves for some time, but then it grew weary of always moving about. There was no time to rest, so the *inua* decided to become a caribou.

Again, it was pleasant to live as a caribou for there was plenty on which to graze, but caribou are always nervous, looking about for danger. So the *inua* decided to be a walrus. The walrus were good to live with, but they were always beating up on one another with their tusks, and the *inua* decided to be still other animals. When it had passed through all of them it returned to being a seal, because that was the incarnation that it had enjoyed most of all.

The seals did not fear death and agreed among themselves which hunter they would allow to capture them. One day, the seal who had been a human fetus, a dog, a wolf, a caribou, a walrus, and other animals rose to its blowhole and allowed itself to be captured by a hunter. He took it home to his wife and when she cut it up, the *inua* slipped out of the seal and into her body. She became pregnant and soon gave birth to a boy who became a great hunter, hunting and finding meat for his parents to the end of their days.

This story illustrates the common belief found throughout the native peoples of the Americas: Human beings are not the lords of creation but share the same life essence with animals and plants.

At Least, That Is How It Used to Be...

Some of the traditional shamanic beliefs and practices have managed to survive, and new forms of shamanic healing—both practical and spiritual—have arisen in North and South America, combining old beliefs and knowledge with new. However, in too many places, valuable knowledge is being lost because the old shamans have no successors or no young people willing or economically able to devote years to the acquisition of the vast stores of esoteric and empirical wisdom that were the province of the shaman.

In addition to the loss of valuable knowledge, modern medicine, missionaries, and industrialization have had their inevitable impact. The galloping destruction of tropical forests alone has caused the loss of many plants with confirmed medicinal qualities and countless others not yet discovered and tested.

Aztec, Maya & Inca Healing

THE NOMADIC TRIBES of the Great Plains and the nations of the eastern woodlands were not the only native peoples to inhabit the Western Hemisphere before the arrival of the Europeans. The Americas were also home to three vast civilizations—the Aztec, the Maya, and the Inca—who laid thousands of miles of roads, built towering cities, meticulously recorded the movement of the heavens, and studied the many facets of the art of healing.

A Maya temple pyramid at Chichén Itzá, one of the principal sites of Maya culture on the Yucatán Peninsula. This pyramid, known as the Castle, was built between A.D. 900 and 1200.

The Aztec are perhaps the best known of the pre-Columbian civilizations (termed *pre-Columbian* because they existed before Columbus arrived). Their pyramids in central Mexico are common tourist destinations, and their ruler Montezuma (actually not his name) has gone down in history.

The Maya inhabited southern Mexico, the Yucatán Peninsula, and parts of Central America. They are the oldest and most mysterious of the great civilizations. Their decline and virtual disappearance has fueled outlandish speculation, but their formidable achievements in art, architecture, and the sciences are indisputable.

And, finally, there are the Inca who came to represent the height of the vast civilization of the Andes Mountains. Their high-altitude cities and well-developed trade routes are a marvel even today.

The Aztec

A popular image of the Aztec is that of an imperial people—warlike, fatalistic, fixated on blood and death, and worshiping cruel gods insatiable for human sacrifice.

Imperial they were. Within two centuries of their arrival in the Valley of Mexico, the Aztecs were in control of a vast empire supported by trade and tribute and inhabited by millions of people with different cultural traditions and languages. Founded as a tiny village of reed huts in the great lake covering much of the Valley of Mexico, their capital, Tenochtitlán, grew to one of the greatest and most powerful cities in the Americas, with a population of nearly 200,000.

Warlike? Certainly, but no more so than many human societies have been through history. And fatalistic? Yes, to the degree that the day on which you were born in their 260-day ritual calendar foretold your success or failure in life.

To a certain degree, they were fixated on blood and death, too. For the Aztecs, blood was the soul—the essence that connected the individual to the deities and the universe. It gave a person—and the gods—warmth, health, strength, and vitality. Blood could be decreased or increased

Smallpox: The Spaniards' Deadly Ally

On a night in 1519, known to history as the *Noche Triste*, the Night of Sorrow, the people of Tenochtitlán drove the Spanish invaders from their city. Scores of conquistadors, unwilling to let go of their loot of golden jewels even to save their lives, drowned in the canals. For the Aztec, the bloody expulsion of the Spaniards was to prove no more than a momentary respite, though. Lurking in their midst was an enemy far deadlier than the Spaniards. Unbeknownst to Aztec or conquistador, their unwelcome visitors had left behind a horror beyond imagination.

The Spanish invaders were back in 1521, not as guests but as conquerors. Their once meager numbers were swelled by well-armed Spanish reinforcements and by a large force of non-Aztec Indians who welcomed Cortés and his men as liberators from the heavy burden of Aztec rule and taxation. They blockaded the city on all sides, preventing food from getting in, and cutting off the six-foot-deep aqueduct constructed to carry drinking water from mainland springs into the Aztec capital.

How was it possible that so powerful and populous a city, with an army of brave and seasoned warriors, succumbed so easily to foreign invaders a hundredth, if that, its numbers? Spanish horses against Aztec foot soldiers? The thunder of cannon against the swish of arrows? Swords of steel honed to a razor's sharpness against wooden clubs lined with blades of volcanic glass? Suits of armor against quilted cotton? These all played a part, but the decisive reason for the swiftness of the fall of the Aztec was a virus.

When Cortés fled Tenochtitlán two years before, he left behind smallpox, an acutely contagious disease against which the Aztec had no immunity and in some parts of Mexico was to wipe out up to 80 to 90 percent of the indigenous population. By the time the Spaniards returned to take possession of the capital and make a prisoner of Cuauhtemoc, the last Aztec ruler, half the inhabitants lay dead or dying in their houses and on the streets or floating in the canals and the shallow lake. The Spaniards found the starving survivors reduced to gnawing the bark off trees and too deep in shock at a calamity they could not comprehend, too demoralized by the loss of their loved ones, and too weakened by starvation to dispose of the corpses, much less put up an effective resistance.

by one's actions. Decrease brought sickness, and increase restored health. This is why the gods required blood sacrifice—not because the gods were cruel but because without it their own vitality would be so weakened that they could longer sustain the cycle of life.

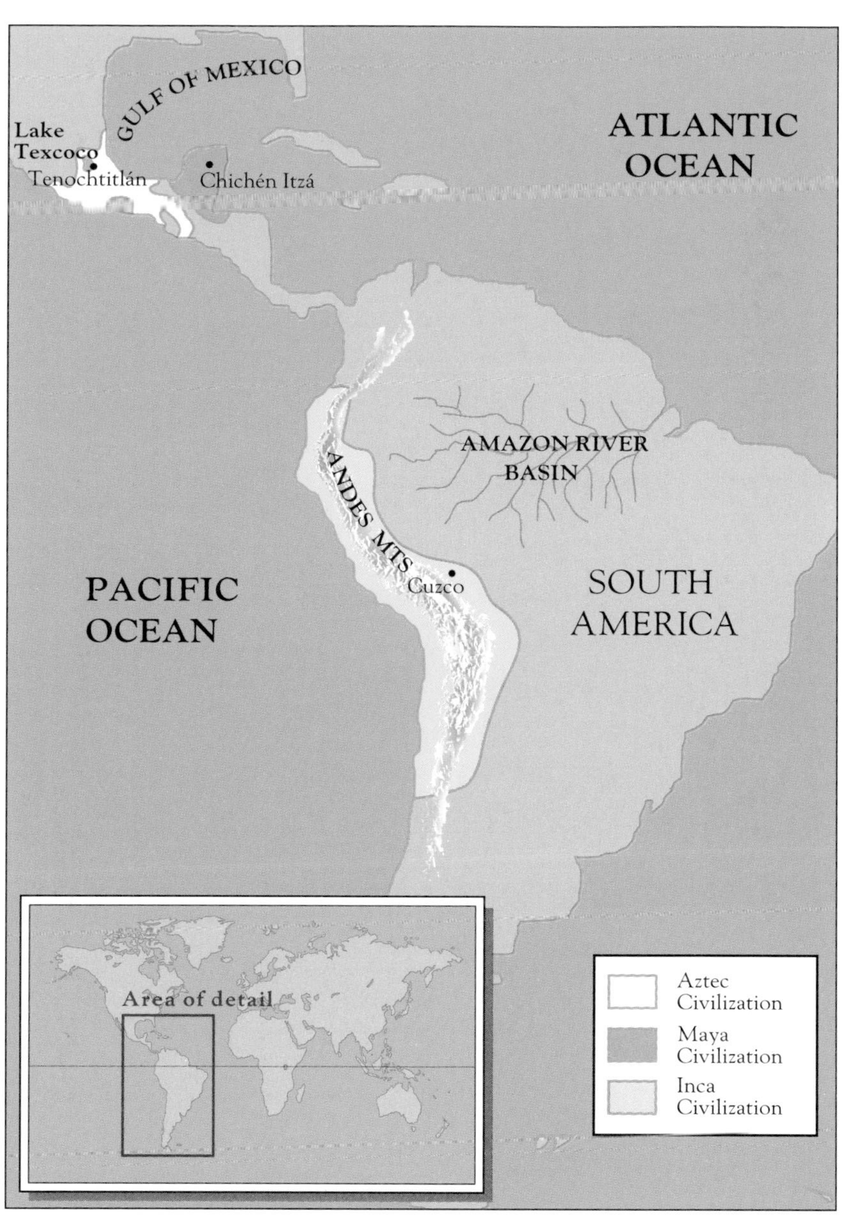

A Jewel in the Valley

When Hernán Cortés and his handful of Spanish conquistadors reached the Valley of Mexico in 1519 after an overland march from the east coast, they saw the Aztec capital, Tenochtitlán, as a sparkling jewel surrounded by lakes, some with sweet water, some alkaline, covering almost 400 square miles. It was connected to dry land by arrow-straight causeways. Like Venice, it was crisscrossed by canals instead of streets. It was a clean, healthful, and beautiful place, with buildings large and small and towering temples more splendid than anything they remembered from their homeland. Its teeming population of nobles and commoners, merchants and artisans, went about their business in blissful ignorance of the impending doom represented by the Spaniards. For a tiny band of Spanish adventurers, illiterate for the most part, with mind-sets barely out of the Middle Ages and fired as much by dreams of uncountable wealth as by religious zeal, it was a dream come true.

This is not a fictional re-creation; this picture of Cortés and his conquistadors coming face to face with one of the great civilizations of the ancient Americas is distilled from the memories of one of their number, Bernal Díaz del Castillo, author of the famous *True History of the Conquest of New Spain*. He wrote it 50 years after the event in righteous anger at those Spaniards who would rob his valiant commander Hernan Cortés of his well-earned credit and deprive him of the fruits of victory (as indeed they did).

HOW WE KNOW WHAT WE KNOW Of all the great pre-Columbian civilizations, we know the most about the Aztecs. We know about their statecraft, their gods and ceremonies, their art and architecture, their ideas about health and illness, their medicine men and medicinal plants, and all the other things that go into making a civilization, because we have several sources—some more reliable than others.

First, there were the chroniclers, the handful of Spanish friars with an inquiring bent of mind, who recorded what they saw and heard with accuracy and a degree of detachment even when what they were observing clashed with their deepest religious convictions. The greatest chronicler of them all was the Franciscan Fray Bernardino de Sahagún, author of the encyclopedic 12-volume *Historia General de las Cosas de Nueva España* (*General History of the Things of New Spain*), better known as the *Florentine Codex*.

Most of the early colonial writers were Mexican-born Spaniards, who approached Aztec medicine from the point of view of their own culture and religion. Exceptions are Sahagún and Martín de la Cruz, the author of the 16th century *Codex Badianus*, an illustrated treatise that lists over 250 Aztec medicinal plants and the ills for which they were employed. An additional 225 medicinal species are described in the *Florentine Codex*. However much these two works are relatively faithful to what the Aztec themselves said, they nevertheless show signs of careful editing, perhaps to avoid problems with the colonial authorities.

Other sources, such as the monumental *Historia Natural* of Francisco Hernández, the learned physician to the king of Spain, owe much to European classifications, particularly the concept of humors and hot-cold dichotomies (see page 75). Still, they provide additional information on the therapeutic uses of plants, animals, and minerals.

Of course there are holes in the record. On some aspects it is maddeningly vague. The early chroniclers inevitably saw the Aztec and their ways through the distorting lens of their own Spanish culture. There was much the chroniclers did not understand. There was much for which they had no model. And, being men as well as members of the clergy, they shut themselves off from women's culture and were, in turn, shut out by it. There was one inevitable conclusion from the writings of the chroniclers about Aztec medicine: In the year 1519, a patient had a much greater chance of dying under the minis-

A drawing of an Aztec physician preparing a medicinal plant remedy. This 16th century illustration appears in Fray Bernardino de Sahagún's Florentine Codex.

trations of a Spanish physician than an Aztec doctor!

Finally, we also know more about the Aztec than other American civilizations because, at least in the countryside, so much of their culture, especially nutrition and medicine, endured through the colonial era into modern times; we can test the early writings against real life among the hundreds of thousands of villagers who still speak Nahuatl, the language of the Aztec, and dialects related to it.

Masters of Public Health To 16th century Europeans convinced that a man should bathe only twice in his life, once at birth and once after death, the Aztec seemed positively fanatical in their insistence on personal and public hygiene. Everyone bathed in hot water, cold water, and super-heated steam.

Human waste, a source of infectious diseases in the cities of Europe, was collected daily by dugout canoes plying the canals of Tenochtitlán. Dried in the sun at special collection points, the waste was spread on maize, amaranth, tomatoes, beans, medicinal plants, and other useful crops flourishing on nearby dry land and on *chinampoas*—the Aztec word for rectangular fields raised in an orderly patchwork above the level of the freshwater part of the shallow lake system.

Balanced Nutrition Everywhere in the world, health and illness are directly linked to nutrition. It was no different for the Aztec, except that, as in China, the key was balance that was important. Foods considered to be "hot" or "warm" were especially beneficial because they added to the heat of your life force.

The Incomplete Conquest

If military conquest of the Aztec was absolute, spiritual conquest was far less of a success. There is plenty of evidence that it was never really completed. After the fall of Tenochtitlán it took Spain generations more, and much blood and treasure, to bring most of what is now the Mexican republic under even nominal control. And the Indian people who made their home in the rugged mountains and valleys of the western Sierra Madre saw few Spaniards until well into the 18th century.

In the northern deserts, seminomadic hunters and warriors who valued their freedom and independence put up a determined resistance for more than a century, succumbing in the end as much to smallpox, measles, and other viral or bacterial infections as to Spanish arms. Even where the invaders had initially met with little resistance, cruel enslavement, heavy taxation, and mass death from foreign diseases provoked revolt. The revolt was almost always under the leadership of the shamans, the guardians of the old traditions.

Armed rebellion was one thing. But there was also quieter and ultimately more successful resistance. Indian people might accept material innovations and even agree to conversion. It was another thing to surrender all the experience of centuries, even millennia. The old holistic ways of diagnosing and treating illness and the reverence for plants whose therapeutic effects were proof of their spirit power refused to wither away and die just because the authorities called it as the Devil's work.

The *chinampoas* supported two cultivated harvests a year. Each was an ecologic mini-universe that sustained a wide variety of foods other than the planted crops, such as migratory waterfowl, native birds, edible insects and their eggs, fish, shrimp, snakes, snails, and larval salamanders.

The salty waters of Lake Texcoco were also part of the Aztec food system, rich in nutritious, popular, and high-status foods, not the least of which were clusters of eggs laid by a corixid water beetle on pine branches the Aztecs stuck in the muddy bottom of the shallow lake. Modern Indians still harvest them as "Mexican caviar" but use them to feed their songbirds rather than to enrich the dinner table as their Aztec ancestors did.

More crucial still to Aztec nutrition and health was one of the world's true miracle foods: the edible one-celled, blue-green alga the Aztec called *tecuitlatl* (literally "excreta of stone"). Scientists identified it 25 years ago as *Spirulina geitlerii*. It attracted millions of migratory ducks, and the Aztec harvested great quantities of the floating mass in canoes, dried it in the sun, and traded it all over central Mexico in the form of flat, brick-shaped loaves the Spaniards said tasted like cheese. It remained for modern nutritionists to discover that an alga some modern writers thought had been no more than a "starvation food" actually contained all the essential amino acids and consisted of 70 percent protein of high biological quality, 18 percent carbohydrates, 8 percent fat, and many important vitamins and minerals, making this lowly one-celled lake product the nutritional equivalent of an egg. *Tecuitlatl* never found favor with the Spaniards, however, and it disappeared from the food trade when the Spaniards drained the lake to protect their capital against periodic flooding. One consequence of this loss of a great food source was the emergence of goiter as a chronic condition in parts of central Mexico, a condition the iodine in *tecuitlatl* had prevented.

CONCEPTIONS OF HEALTH AND DISEASE As among other pre-Columbian peoples, Aztec medicine was a blend of the mystical and the practical. Religion, the calendar, divination, magic, and a relationship of mutual dependence between human beings and the gods all played a part in illness, as they did in curing. The practical consisted of close observation of the natural world and the response of symptoms to treatment by a vast array of medicinal plants, along with physical manipulations of the body and its organs.

Natural and Supernatural. Like other Native Americans, the Aztecs made little distinction between "supernatural" and "natural" causes of disease, although the reality of natural causes—advanced age, for example—was recognized. "Supernatural," in the sense of something outside of, separate from, or, to use the literal meaning, "above" nature, is not part of Native American philosophy. There are realms of the stratified universe that are

The Disease from the Sun

The shamans had no way of accounting for a mass tragedy on the scale of the mysterious epidemics such as smallpox except to lay it at the feet of their gods. It was perfectly logical for the Huichol Indians of the western Sierra Madre, for example, to look to the sun god for the origin of a disease that burned the body with fever and a raging thirst and caused the skin to blister with pustules immeasurably more painful than the severest sunburn. In their own ancient myth, the Sun Father blistered the earth itself when, in the myth of his birth, he came too close and everything—soil, plants, animals—withered under his heat until the shamans put him back into proper orbit.

specific to certain kinds of spirits, such as sky gods and lords of the underworld, but otherwise the spirits are not conceived as apart from the natural world. Rather, they are integral to it. The spirits reside in, and manifest themselves as, natural phenomena that could be observed, touched, smelled, and so on.

Illustration from the 14th or 15th century manuscript called the Codex Vienna. *Here, two minor Aztec deities known as* 7 Motion *(left) and* 7 Wind *(right), standing on either side of Earth's womb (the V-shaped cleft in the ground), hold unidentifiable plants believed to stand for the vast array of botanical medicines known to America's pre-Columbian civilizations.*

For the Indian people, the natural environment consisted both of the seen and the unseen. If an Aztec physician divined a metaphysical cause for a given malady, it did not mean that it came from somewhere out there, beyond the physical world, beyond human understanding, and beyond the reach of empirical treatment. What it meant was that account must always be taken of the spiritual dimension in both illness and cure.

Tonalli. The Aztec world was full of spirits, according to the anthropologist and keen student of Aztec culture Bernard Ortiz de Montellano. Dangerous places and landmarks had "spirit owners," called *chaneques*, as did plants and animals. In addition to the gods, there were lesser spirits of clouds, trees, bushes, springs, crossroads, caves, rivers, lakes, mountains, even anthills. Since the Aztec universe was one of complementary oppositions, "owners" of water and earth were necessarily opposed to those of heat and sky, not as adversaries but as balanced counterparts.

Human beings contained *tonalli*, the immaterial animating warmth that manifested itself especially in body heat and the blood coursing through the body. It was human *tonalli* that the spirits craved to strengthen themselves. (As already mentioned, this also helps explain the phenomenon of human sacrifice: without constant replenishment of their *tonalli*, the gods could not go on.)

The concept of *tonalli* (a word related to the Nahuatl *tona*, meaning "to make warm" or "sun") is extremely complex and would take an entire book to analyze and explain. The Aztec believed it entered the body only at the last moment before birth and left at death as the corpse turned cold. Another Aztec specialist, art historian Jill L. McKeever Furst, defines *tonalli* as the most important of the three souls possessed by each human being (the others being the *yolia* and the *ihiyotl*). Too much or too little of any of these causes illness, but *tonalli* is the most important.

Tonalli extends outward from the individual into the universe and inward from the universe into the body, where one feels it in one's flesh as warmth and pumping blood. It manifests itself in the heat of sunshine and the glow of fire, which is why the patient should be placed close to a fire or exposed to the warming rays of the sun. It is also felt in the joints, the pulse, and the heart. Postmenopausal women are especially rich in *tonalli*, manifesting itself, among other ways, in the well-known phenomenon of hot flashes.

The problem for humans was that the spirits of nature were forever trying to absorb *tonalli*, for example, by drawing it out from people incautious or arrogant enough to approach them in an inappropriate manner. And loss of *tonalli* meant a potentially fatal weakening. Its cure required correct diagnosis, starting with the identification of the offended spirit and the determination of the cause of his or her displeasure, before anything more practical had a hope of reversing the calamity.

Ehecames. Loss of one's animating life force—the weakening, misplacement, or abduction of the *tonalli*—was taken to be one major cause of sickness. Another was "sickness intrusion," meaning the magical invasion of the body by a disease-carrying foreign object. This, in turn, was closely related to the idea of "bad winds," the *ehecames* that survive today as the *mal aires* of Mexican folk belief.

Usually the injection into the body of a foreign disease-carrying object was diagnosed as the work of a disgruntled ancestor or deity, displeased at having been ignored or insufficiently honored with gifts, or as the evil deed of a shaman in the employ of a human enemy. With everything animate, even a tool might avenge itself in this way on its owner if not treated with respect and given food in a ceremony devoted to this duty. The *ehecames* could enter the body through orifices, manifesting themselves as worms, hair, or some other foreign object, and make the person sick.

A major source of these ill winds were the restless souls of the recently departed. Indigenous people still believe that air escaping from someone who died a violent death is dangerous, especially to the unborn, and that dead relatives who feel themselves neglected can return as *ehecames* and try to take the living with them. But there were many other sources of dangerous *ehecames:* the earth itself, the underworld, water, hills, caves, and archaeologic ruins. No doubt these ideas have their origin in pre-Columbian times.

Cannibalism

One of the pervading, fearsome tales about the Aztec was that they were cannibals. One line of reason goes that they were so beset by chronic shortages of food, they had to resort to cannibalism to satisfy their protein needs. However, there is no basis for this theory. The combination of intensive agriculture, tribute in foodstuffs from subject peoples, and a great variety of wild animal and vegetable foods available to the Aztec assured them of all the calories and all the protein they required.

There was cannibalism, yes, but far from serving nutritional needs, it was ritual and fraught with religious symbolism. It was also restricted to specific ceremonies during the year when there were other foodstuffs in plenty, and in which priests and nobles—the only people who took part—partook of the flesh of those victims of sacrifice whose personality and life substance had merged, at the moment of death, with that of the gods. The Spanish clergy understood this very well, taking it to be a cruel parody by the Devil himself of Catholicism's most holy rite.

MEDICAL SPECIALISTS Treating illness often required a two-pronged approach. Recovery of the soul (*tonalli*) and extraction of the pathogen (*ehecames*) by sucking directly into the mouth of the practitioner (a shaman) or through a tube were in the realm of religion and magic. The treatment of the actual symptoms was not, although those who did the curing operated in both the metaphysical and the physical realms.

There was a whole range of specialists. According to Sahagún, built into each practitioner was his opposite, the "good" shaman to cure, the "bad" shaman to make ill. Whether that was how his consultants explained it or the only way he could make sense of what they told him is difficult to say. Perhaps the antagonistic, or complementary, qualities were really present in the same individual.

Aztec stone sun calendar. The calendar was extremely important to the Aztec; the day on which you were born in their 260-day ritual calendar foretold your success or failure in life.

There was, first of all, the *naualli* (the plural being *nanaualtin*). The Spaniards translated it as "sorcerer." We would call him a shaman. Sahagún describes the positive–negative qualities of this type of shaman as though they pertained to different individuals, which was not necessarily the case:

> The sorcerer [is] a wise man, a counselor, a person of trust—serious, respected, revered, dignified, unreviled, not subject to insults.

> The good sorcerer [is] a caretaker, a man of discipline, a guardian. Astute, he is keen, careful, helpful; he never harms anyone.

> The bad sorcerer [is] a doer [of evil], an enchanter. He bewitches women; he deranges, deludes people; he casts spells over them; he charms them; he enchants them; he causes them to be possessed. He deceives people; he confounds them.

A second class of healer, similarly separated into good and bad, read the day's divinatory signs in the 260-day calendar for their negative or positive aspects and revealed the truth to the clients. His opposite was, in the words of Sahagún, "a false speaker, a hypocrite" who "confounds, beguiles, deceives" those who seek his counsel.

Then there was the *tlacateculutl*—from the word *tlacatl*, or "man," and *teculutl* or *tecolotl*, a species of owl. In the words of Sahagún, he was one who "transforms himself, who assumes the guise of an animal. . . . He turns himself into a dog, a bird, a screech owl, an owl, a horned owl."

According to Sahagún, there was nothing positive about this class of transforming shaman. Even his appearance spoke against him:

> He goes about in tatters. He is fatigued; he lives in want, in extreme privation. He causes one to be possessed; he destroys peo-

The Real Spanish Disease

The Aztec ruler Mocetuhzoma (misspelled and mispronounced in the Marine Corps hymn as "Montezuma") received the Spaniards as honored guests, if not quite the gods the omens had told him to expect. When he presented Cortés with green jade and blue turquoise as gifts more precious to the Aztec than the gold their nobles wore as jewelry (because blue and green were the color of life-giving water and fresh vegetation), the conquistador is supposed to have told him, "Sire, the Spaniard suffers from a disease only gold can cure."

> ple; he burns wooden figures of them; he bleeds himself over others, destroys them by deception, depresses their hearts.

Perhaps so, but Sahagún wrote in the second half of the 16th century, when his consultants, and how they remembered the culture of their parents, had been exposed to several decades of missionary instruction. In fact, transformation was, and still is, one of the defining characteristics of the shaman, good or bad, whatever his specialty. Elsewhere Sahagún singles out the jaguar as one of the sorcerer's principal allies, the same role this beautiful and powerful jungle cat fulfills for shamans in the South American tropics (see page 134). Hunters had better take care when shooting arrows at a jaguar, said Sahagún, lest he turn out to be a sorcerer in his animal form and later take revenge.

Finally there is the physician, *ticitl* in Nahuatl, whom the *Florentine Codex* describes as a curer of people and a restorer and provider of health:

> The good physician [is] a diagnostician, experienced—a knower of herbs, of stones, of trees, of roots. He has [results of] examinations, experience, prudence. [He is] moderate in his acts. He provides health, restores people, provides them splints, sets

Small Aztec temple located just north of Tenochtitlán. Although near the capital complex, this temple was probably used only by the local community.

bones for them, purges them, gives emetics, gives them potions; he lances, he makes incisions in them, stitches them, revives them, envelops them in ashes.

And then there is his opposite:

> The bad physician [is] a fraud, a halfhearted worker, a giver of overdoses, an increaser [of sickness]; one who endangers others, who worsens sickness, who causes one to worsen. [He pretends to be] a counselor, advised, chaste. He bewitches; he is a sorcerer, a soothsayer, a caster of lots, a diagnostician by means of knots. He kills with his medicines; he increases [sickness]; he seduces women, he bewitches them.

All in all, he was a prime candidate for a malpractice suit, had there been such a thing among the Aztec. In its absence, there was something much more drastic, such as death by stoning or a sentence of enslavement to the injured party until full restitution was achieved.

Some of the several hundred medicinal plants illustrated in the 16th century Aztec herbal known as the Codex Badianus.

Diagnosis by Hallucination Clearly, there was overlap among the various practitioners of the shamanic and medical arts, just as there was between the spiritual, the pragmatic, and experiential in Aztec medical science. For divination and diagnosis, probably every kind of curer resorted to ritual hallucinogens, including

- the peyote cactus
- *ololiuhqui*—the seeds of the morning glory *Turbina corymbosa*, which contain ergot alkaloids
- one or more species of the *Datura* and *Solandra genii* (from the nightshade family)
- the sacred mushrooms, which contain the hallucinogen psilocybin

The respect accorded to the sacred psilocybin mushroom is self-evident from what the Aztec called them: *teonanácatl*, meaning "divine flesh" or "flesh of the gods." The same plants had no comparable effects on consciousness when used in the treatment of disease, which only goes to prove what modern investigators have known for a long time: The effects of the botanical hallucinogens are as much a function of setting, expectation, psychology, and cultural context as they are of pharmacology.

Medicines We are blessed with a great number of written sources on how the Aztec saw and treated disease. There are lists of virtually every ailment known to the Indians, each with its corresponding medicinal plants. Most of the plants have been identified; the number tested by modern methods is small but growing steadily. The therapeutic effect the Aztec claimed for them has not been confirmed for some, but for others, for which pharmacologic information is available, the results are favorable, attesting to the high state of Aztec empirical medicine.

The plants traditionally used in Mexico for the treatment of dental disease provide

Guadalupe Ríos de la Cruz, widow of the late Huichol shaman-artist Ramón Medina, chanting a protective prayer to a large flowering Datura inoxia. *Huichols identify* Datura *as a dangerous sorcerer capable of bringing sickness and misfortune to his victims. The solanaceous* Datura *played an important part in Aztec medicine, particularly as an analgesic and in sorcery.*

a case in point. Aztec healers and their successors employed 107 species for 17 different oral conditions:

- 27 plants for the treatment of thrush (oral candidiasis), among them the psychotropic peyote cactus, *Lophophora williamsii* (which is known to contain antibiotics effective against several kinds of infections), and several popular ornamentals, such as cosmos, geranium, heliotrope, hibiscus, and bromelia
- 8 plants for local anesthesia, including extracts of croton and species of the pepper family
- 42 plants for toothache, among them three species of tobacco
- 7 plants for dental decay
- 5 for gum disease
- 4 for halitosis (bad breath)
- 10 for gingivitis
- 15 for inflammation of the mouth

Only a fraction of these have been tested, but ten have yielded highly favorable results. It is interesting that in the treatment of thrush, the native doctors also discovered the healing properties of two species of plantain, *Plantago mexicana* and *Plantago lanceolatum*. The latter, and its broad-leaved sister species, *Plantago major*, were also used by Native North Americans, as well as by Europeans since at least the Middle Ages, to speed the healing of cuts, running sores, and other wounds.

Indigenous Medicine after the Aztecs

Aztec civilization came to a bloody end in the first quarter of the 16th century. The professional priesthood was destroyed and its accumulated knowledge suppressed. But much of the knowledge of village shamans—metaphysical and practical—continued to be passed on through the generations into modern times, no matter how hard the clergy and the civil authorities railed against it and punished those suspected of "idolatry." Nothing—not preaching, not imprisonment, not physical torture—seemed able to shake the faith of Nahuatl-speaking villagers in their shamans' access to the spirit world, the magical incantations, and the old plant medicines.

Not only did the village shamans continue to use the sacred hallucinogenic plants to trigger the out-of-body journey but the same species also persisted in medicine, just as they had long before the coming of the Spaniards. In the treatise of 1629 on *The Superstitions That Today Live Among the Indians of This New Spain*, Hernando Ruiz de Alarcón notes that not only were peyote and morning glory seeds accorded the status of divinity by the Indians of his community, but they also administered them as enemas against ailments of the stomach and the intestines.

Another plant used as an enema against similar troubles was *atlinan* (literally, "its mother is water" or "water procreates it"). Its botanical identity was for many years a mystery, but scholars are now convinced that *atlinan* is *Datura ceratocaula*, an aquatic member of the nightshade family. *Datura inoxia* and several other species of this genus—popularly known as jimsonweed—were employed for divinatory intoxication and in internal and external therapy, both north and south of the modern dividing line between Mexico and the United States. How much poetic metaphor and magical incantation were integral to herbal therapy is self-evident from these passages from Ruiz de Alarcón's manuscript:

> The general medicine is the one they call *atlinan*, which means "the water procreates it," and it is thus because it is usually found in the water or in very damp places. This is administered by means of an enema, and they say: "Come, Green Priest [the atlinan]. Here I am stretching you out [injecting you] there in Seven-caves-place [the rectum]. Pursue the green palsy, the dusky palsy [the stomach ache]."

Ruiz de Alarcón set down many spells and incantations in the original Nahuatl. But incantations alone did not do the trick. To effect a cure, in Aztec, as in all Native American medicine, the symbolic and mystical had to go hand in hand with the empirical and practical.

The Maya

To us, the Maya are perhaps the most mysterious of the great pre-Columbian civilizations. They were even somewhat a mystery to the 16th century Spanish. Whereas the Spanish encountered an Aztec civilization at the height of its imperial power, the Maya flourished long before Europeans even knew a Western Hemisphere existed.

The height of the Maya civilization was during the so-called Classic period between about A.D. 200 and 800. They had six or seven centuries in which magnificent architecture, sculpture, mathematics, and both abstract and startlingly naturalistic painting flourished. Along with these arts, they developed the only true phonetic writing system in the Americas.

Even in ruins, this Maya pyramid is quite impressive rising out of the thick Mexican forest. The pyramids were like sacred mountains, whose levels correspond to the multiple layers of the stratified universe (see page 131).

Maya influence stretched across the jungles of the Yucatán Peninsula south through modern-day Belize, Guatemala, Honduras, and El Salvador.

Although the demise of the Maya civilization remains ultimately mysterious, overfarming and overpopulation certainly contributed as their ever-increasing demand for food and land led to large-scale destruction of the rain forest they depended on for their spirituality and their medicine. It was this compromised Maya world that the Spanish found when they arrived in the 16th century.

Lost Information It is hard enough to determine the monumental events of the later part of the Maya civilization, much less piece together the details of everyday living during the height of the Classic period. There are some excellent sources from the years around the time of the arrival of the Spanish—remarkably detailed and accurate documentation on the afflictions that plagued people and on the plants the shamans employed against them—but for the millennia of Maya settlement in Yucatán prior to the 16th century, there is nothing; and there are few, if any, reliable accounts for the southern part of the Maya territory.

The old Yucatecan texts are in European script, and even though the knowledge they contain is obviously far older, none has been preserved that dates earlier than the 18th century. No doubt they were copied from older sources dating to the 16th century, and these from even earlier medical references in hieroglyphic script, but none of these has survived. If they existed at the time of Spanish colonization of Yucatán, they may well have been among the many Maya hieroglyphic manuscripts the 16th century Bishop of Yucatán, Diego de Landa, confiscated and consigned to the flames as "works of the Devil," along with some 5,000 "idols."

Landa made no mention of what might have been in these precious manuscripts lost to religious fanaticism. Very likely he did not know or care. They were works of the Devil, and that was enough. However, because the Maya compiled hieroglyphic books on all kinds of subjects, including, among many other topics, history, calendrics, divination, astronomy, prophecy, and magic, there is little reason why they should not also have had hieroglyphic characters for diseases and the plants to cure them.

MISINTERPRETATIONS In reading the colonial medical texts, we have to separate 16th century European superstition from the Maya system. Curing by bloodletting, for example, smacks of practices the Spanish brought with them to the New World. For the Maya, as for the Aztecs, blood, which they took from the earlobes, the extremities, and the tongue or penis, was a precious and nonrenewable substance. In Aztec belief, blood carried *tonalli*, the warm animating force the Spanish sometimes rendered as "soul." Almost certainly the Maya had similar ideas.

The self-sacrifice of blood was, in fact, common practice among the Maya no less than among the Aztec and other Central and South American peoples. There are plenty of depictions of nobles and rulers piercing themselves to draw blood—women the tongue, men the sexual organ. However, it was always an act of sacrifice to strengthen the gods and add to the spirit power of the universe, not a medical practice in the grossly mistaken European belief that bleeding was somehow good for patients, even those who were already in shock from blood loss.

Clearly, Indian shamans, careful observers that they were of the natural world, were far more aware than European physicians were that the last thing to do to an individual already debilitated by injury or disease was to weaken him or her even further by taking away blood—the very substance of life.

The Lord's Cacao Cup

In the tombs of some nobles and rulers were found elegant cylindrical vases. Some of these works of art have turned out to be nothing less than chocolate drinking cups, their hieroglyphic texts proclaiming, "This is the chocolate drinking cup of Lord. . . ." followed by the name of the owner.

The foamy drink the Maya brewed from the crushed and partially fermented fatty seeds of the cacao tree *(Theobroma cacao)* was an important ceremonial food. And, as with the Aztec and the South Americans, the same plants that figured in ritual or triggered the shamanic state of altered consciousness also had a therapeutic dimension. Cacao was no exception.

The active principle in cacao seeds is theobromine, a bitter alkaloid related to caffeine. Like caffeine, theobromine is an addictive, or at least habit-forming, stimulant. Modern chemistry has confirmed that theobromine also has a protective effect by inhibiting bacteria like *Streptococcus, Shigella, Staphylococcus,* and other assorted pathogens that, among other ill effects on human health, contribute to tooth decay. The precise pharmacology would not have been known by the Maya shaman, but the effects told the story.

Cacao beans have a high content of fat, and this the Maya physician extracted and applied to wounds and infections to speed the process of healing, while an infusion that concentrated theobromine was employed as a diuretic to increase the flow of urine.

Chocolate as medicine—it seems we have a lot to learn from the Maya.

RECONSTRUCTING MAYA MEDICINE That all the written information comes from Yucatán just prior to, and just after, the European invasion does not tie our hands completely. It is probably not far off the mark to assume that Yucatecan Maya medicine in the early colonial period applies as well to earlier times and other places. There was clearly considerable stability to the medical prescriptions of the Maya physicians, for even those written after two centuries of European influence show little alteration from those that date to the 16th century, when Maya medicine was still unaffected by Spanish ideas. So perhaps we can push some of the 16th century Yucatecan medical practices at least back to the glory days of Classic Maya civilization.

Thanks to recent advances in the reading of many of the hieroglyphic texts carved on Maya monuments and painted on pottery, we have learned a good deal about dynastic succession, warfare, conquest, alliances between rival city-states, and the dates when these events occurred. We know the names of rulers and their parentage, their relationships to different gods, and the times of their birth, accession, marriages, and deaths.

In contrast to all this knowledge we could not have dreamed of possessing a few decades ago, everyday Maya life is still a great big blank. We know nothing from the written and painted sources about the one thing that must have most concerned the average citizens of the cities and mini-empires of the Classic period, just as it concerns them and us today: their health. Skeletal remains tell us something of nutritional stress and disease but, except for healed fractures, provide no firsthand evidence of treatment or its effectiveness.

Still, "nothing" may be too broad a term. On rare occasions, we can infer something from what the ancient artists painted on funerary pottery. Almost everyone of high status, especially rulers and their close relatives, was buried with an array of food bowls and ceremonial ceramics. Some are plain, many richly decorated. Most of this art does not bother with daily concerns. Painted vessels depict mythologic events or someone's out-of-body experiences, a mystical encounter, perhaps, between the companion spirit of the deceased and the denizens of other worlds, or a ritual dance in company with the spirits of ancestors and sacred animals. Still, the ancient artists' subject matter is not all beyond our understanding. Sometimes it is almost embarrassingly frank (see "The Therapeutic Enema," page 159).

SPIRITS AND OFFERINGS Like Aztec medicine, Maya conception and treatment of illness drew equally on religion, magic, and science. The Maya believed that death, disease, and other physical and emotional afflictions were almost always punishment for wrongdoings. Before a cure could be attempted, the healer had to discover the identity of whatever spirit the patient might have offended or neglected, and what actions, practical and metaphysical, were required to reverse the victim's ill fortune. However, once that was out of the way, depending on the nature of the affliction, the practical could come into play.

Chief among offenses that could make people sick, requiring the services of the healer, was failure to honor and give sustenance to the gods and ancestors with offerings of ceremonial foods. Suitable gifts included

- heart-shaped cakes molded of maize or pumpkin seeds
- the smoke of burning tobacco and balls of rubber

The Therapeutic Enema

As strange as it may sound, the enema seems to have been a topic of sufficient concern to the ancient Maya to have been memorialized in their art. They, like the Aztec and other Native American peoples, knew all about enemas (or clysters, literally meaning "to wash out"). The cleansing action of the enema was only part of its function; it was also a way to introduce medicines and intoxicants directly into the large intestine. *Euphorbia hirta* (a variety of spurge) was only one of many species of this genus of succulents with milky, latex-like juice that was used to cure a variety of ills in the medical botany of Native Americans.

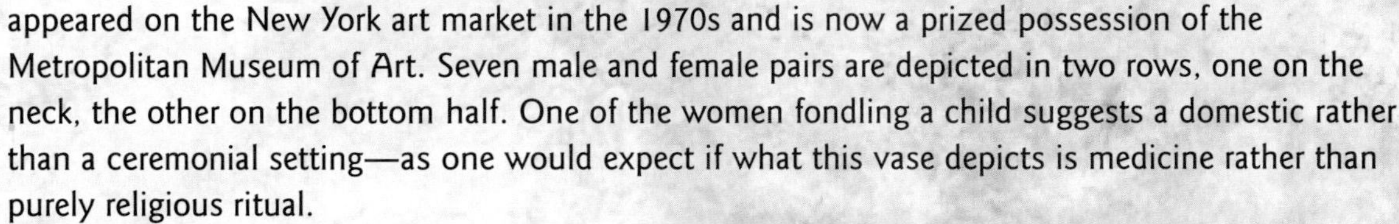

The printed word was one thing. Actually getting a look at the enema in Classic Maya art was another. The piece that, so to speak, broke the code was a large, 1500-year-old painted jar that appeared on the New York art market in the 1970s and is now a prized possession of the Metropolitan Museum of Art. Seven male and female pairs are depicted in two rows, one on the neck, the other on the bottom half. One of the women fondling a child suggests a domestic rather than a ceremonial setting—as one would expect if what this vase depicts is medicine rather than purely religious ritual.

It is what some of the men are doing, or what is being done to them, that caught the attention of art historians and medical historians. Here was visual proof that the Maya practiced what was virtually universally practiced among Native Americans: the medicinal or intoxicating enema. We see men partly dressed, partly nude, in the act of inserting a bulbed enema syringe into their own rectum. In another scene the enema is administered to a man by a woman—presumably a female shaman-physician. (That was another first: graphic evidence that the shamanic vocation was open to women in the ancient past and not just in recent times.) The material of which the bulb was made is unknown, but rubber, which is native to the Maya country, is a good possibility. Another is an animal bladder.

What was injected we cannot say, except for a reference by the 16th century Franciscan Fray Bernardino de Sahagún. He wrote that the Huastecs—the northern-most of the Maya speakers—used enemas to intoxicate themselves with *pulque*, the fermented sap of the agave cactus. However, most other reports from North and South America speak of therapeutic rather than inebriating enemas.

Deciphering the enema scenes on this one vase initiated a whole chain of discoveries. Previously unrecognized enema motifs in Maya art became obvious. On one much-published cylindrical vase the Maya gods themselves own enema paraphernalia, attesting to the importance the ancient Maya placed on the practice.

- perfuming the ground with incense and maize before the sacred idols carved of wood or stone
- human sacrifice (on special occasions)

According to Bishop Landa, the Maya believed that "if they did not perform these ceremonies, certain sicknesses would come on them during the ensuing year."

THE MAYA HEALERS As was the case with the Aztecs the Spaniards made little distinction among physicians, priests, and sorcerers (what we would call shamans). Priests were more concerned with the gods, lofty calendrical matters, and numerology—arranging sacrifices and overseeing the seasonal ceremonies—than with health and other everyday concerns that sent people for the shaman, the midwife, or the bonesetter. Still, the dividing lines between practitioners were probably not always rigid.

Maya rattles from Jaina Island representing the moon goddess and a priestess. All over the Americas, rattles played a part in the shaman's art.

Like the shamans, priests practiced divination. According to Bishop Landa, "it was the office of the priests to discourse and teach their sciences, to indicate calamities and the means of remedying them," whereas "the sorcerers and physicians cured by means of bleeding at the part afflicted, casting lots for divination in their work." But Landa was wrong; there was a lot more to Maya medicine than bleeding.

Bishop Landa admits that "there were also surgeons, or better said, sorcerers, who cured with herbs and many superstitious rites." For Landa and his contemporaries, physicians and sorcerers—*ah-men* in the Maya language, *hechiceros* or *brujos* in Spanish—belonged to the same profession, along with two other specialists: the midwife, called *x-alanzah* in Maya, and the bone-binder, or *kax-bac*. Both of these also used herbal remedies and other therapeutic techniques, the former to ease or speed delivery and alleviate postpartum complaints, the latter to speed the knitting process by massage, manipulation, and poultices of leaves and roots. We even know the identity of the favorite Maya bonesetting remedy: *Ruellia albicaulis*, or *sakal-bac* in Maya.

In the Maya culture, as in the Aztec, the shaman-physician served a double role: to heal physical and emotional illness and to visit a calamity upon his or someone else's enemy by magical means.

NATURAL MEDICINES Whatever "magical thinking" went into Maya medical beliefs and practice, and there was quite a bit, there was much that was clearly practical and effective. The colonial medical literature enumerates a wide range of species we now know exhibit broad-spectrum antimi-

Bathing and Health

Bishop Landa was surprised that among the Maya both men and women "bathe constantly," in cold water as well as hot, the latter more "for the sake of health than cleanliness." Landa was probably thinking of the *temascal*, the saunalike ritual steam bath that is believed to have come into North America from Siberia with the earliest migrations. Whatever its origin and symbolic functions, the *temascal* was of great benefit in terms of hygiene and health. Less successful, not to say downright dangerous, has been the modern use of the *temascal* in cases of measles and some other infectious diseases of foreign origin.

crobial activity, for example. So, if some Maya remedies suggest "superstition," the many detailed descriptions of plants used in 16th century Maya medicine confirm that there was as much that was empirical and systematic.

The point is not whether there was a religious or magical component to Maya medical practice; it is that the Maya had a broader concept of naturopathy than we do. The healing power of plants came from and belonged to the realm of the spirits. As in South America today, certain species were identified as plant deities and teachers of herbal expertise. For the medicine to work, the shaman had to give it its proper psychological and spiritual dimension.

Maya incense burner from Honduras (ca. A.D. 600–900) representing a shaman wearing a jaguar headdress. The jaguar was one of the Maya shaman's principal allies and animal equivalents.

There was no shortage of medicinal plants or of expertise in their effects. In 1931, the scholar Ralph L. Roys was able to discern 447 separate medical conditions, together with their corresponding herbal prescriptions and other therapeutic techniques. For asthma, the medical tracts prescribed the crushed leaves and bark of *Coc-che* (*Conocarpus erecta*, or button tree; also called *botoncillo* in rural Mexico). Among the several cures for blood in the urine was an astringent tonic made from, among other healing plants

- the bark of *chim-tok* (*Krugiodendron ferreum*, or black ironwood; also called *Quiebra hacha* in Spanish), a hardwood tree with dull green leaves
- the *plumilla* (*Trixis radialis*, called *hierba del aire* in Spanish)
- *sanguinaria de flores negro*, roughly meaning "the one with the black flowers that is thirsty for blood" (*Sanvitalia procumbens*, or creeping zinnia; also called *ojo de gallo* ["rooster's eye"])
- the boiled leaves, stalks, and root of *Melochia tomentosa* and *Cenchrus echinatus*

Some of these were also used for a variety of other ills, alone or in combination. So, for example, *Trixis radialis*, another species of the same genus as *Trixis inula*, has 12 different medical uses, internal and external, including those for open sores, edema, swollen feet, and pneumonia.

An important beverage in Maya ritual was *balché*, an alcoholic drink made of fermented honey and an extract of the bark of the purplish-flowered *balché* tree (*Lonchocarpus longistylus*). It may have figured in enema rites as well. The Maya medical texts prescribe the crushed leaves of the tree as a poultice for smallpox (a disease unknown in the Americas before the European invasion; see page 144) and an infusion to cure loss of speech. Many Maya still use the *balché* drink today ceremonially, recreationally, and medicinally.

The intoxicating morning glory seeds the Maya call *xtabentun* (not to be confused with a commercial liquor of the same name sold in Chiapas and Yucatán) were also used as medicine, possibly in enemas. Morning glories are plentiful in their environment, especially along stream and river beds, and we know they used the seeds. There is no information on *xtabentun* as a hallucinogen, but one of the earliest Maya medicinal texts credits it with beneficial effects in, among other ailments, kidney stones and disorders of the urinary tract.

THE PROOF OF THE PUDDING To claim that Maya medicine was all, or even mostly, "science" would be an exaggeration. However, like that of the Aztec, it stacked up favorably against European medicine of its day and for centuries thereafter. No Maya physician would have accepted on faith that men have one less rib than women because God had taken one of Adam's ribs from which to fashion Eve. And no Maya would have taken Aristotle's word for it that women have fewer teeth than men.

Besides, against whatever "irrational" aspects there were in Maya medicine, a surprisingly large number of Maya medical texts describe the treatment of symptoms based on objective observation of the effects of certain plant preparations on the human system. As Roys writes, Maya medicine

> was at least not hampered by the theories of humors and distempers which so long continued to be the basis of European medical science.... Even when the Maya doctor borrowed from the Spaniards, he usually adhered to his own methods and adopted their simple remedies rather than their pseudo-scientific theories.

The Spanish saw their newly conquered land through the lens of their own history. This 18th century European rendering of an ancient Peruvian priest worshiping the sun probably bears little resemblance to any actual ancient Andean. In fact, the clothing and the vessels look remarkably Roman.

The Inca

The Inca empire was a vast multiethnic state, stretching for thousands of miles along the west coast of South America. A technologically and administratively advanced civilization, they built an impressive highway system—over 15,000 miles of roads—along the coastal desert and high in the Andes Mountains. The Inca, like the Aztec and the Maya, also eventually fell to the invading Spanish, but not before they had developed a culture—and a medical tradition—as rich as any other in the Americas.

THE KALLAWAYAS, HEALERS OF THE ANDES There are still some 13,000 people in and around La Paz, Bolivia, that are called *Kallawayas*. They are not of the same ethnic stock as the Inca, and they were probably originally speakers of a dialect of Aymara (the language of most Bolivian Indians) not Quechua (the language of the Inca and of many Peruvian Indians today). *Kallawaya* literally means "Land of the Medicine," and these natives have given us a good look at what medicine was like during the days of the empire.

Five hundred years ago, the Kallawayas played a key role in Inca medicine, in trade between the highlands and the tropical lowlands, and in the expansion and consolidation of the empire. They were considered by the Inca rulers to be the direct descendents of the Sun. It was their role as healers and herbalists to be the bearers of all Inca rulers and other nobles as they traveled across their far-flung empire and into unknown territory, just as a doctor accompanies the president of the United States on all his travels.

At the beginning of this century, the former priest and anthropologist Joseph E. Bastien wrote

> Kallawaya curers can, for example, calm mental illness by *floripondio* [datura], set bones with plaster of Paris casts, and stretch muscles with frog skins. . . . Their pharmacy includes remedies that are nature's equivalent of aspirin, penicillin, and quinine and others that have yet to be discovered by modern medicine. . . .

Selfless Chronicler

Some of the best evidence we have of daily life and religion in the time of the Inca is not words but pictures. In the second half of the 16th century, a half-Inca, half-Spanish native of the Peruvian city of Cuzco named Felipe Huaman Poma de Ayala felt himself commissioned by God to write a history of the Inca before and after the Spanish conquest. Before he was through he had covered 1,000 sheets with words and full-page pen and ink illustrations.

Huaman Poma de Ayala had a Spanish father and was educated in Spanish schools. But his mother was a direct descendent of the tenth Inca emperor, Tupac Yupanqui. It was clearly to her side of the family that his heart belonged. We do not know how long it took him to complete his illustrated manuscript. By one account it was decades. Surely it was years. He sent this labor of love to the king of Spain, apparently in the hope that learning something of Inca history and daily life, and of the cruelties and exploitation the Indian people had suffered since the Spanish Conquest, would move the Crown to ease their misery.

We do not know—nor did he—whether the Spanish king ever even saw it. Certainly it did not have the effect he hoped for. Nor do we know how and when the manuscript got from Spain to Denmark, where a German professor named Richard A. Pietschmann discovered it in 1908 in the Royal Library of Copenhagen. It was not until 1936, when the French scholar Paul Rivet published a facsimile edition that it became available to a wider audience. Ever since, no work on Andean civilization in the time of the Inca would be complete without some attention to Huaman Poma de Ayala's charming pictorial record of his mother's people.

> These mysterious medicine men, who are rapidly passing from the scene, nevertheless remain the hope of incurables and are the healers of the Indian.... Because doctors and nurses are scarce in the Andes, traveling curers treat the sick in places where doctors refuse to live.

The Kallawayas descended regularly from the highlands of the Andes to the tropical jungle, where they gathered their medicinal herbs to take back and treat the sick. (They continue to do so to this day.) According to Bastien—who was able to identify more than 100 medicinal species in use today by Kallawaya herbalists—they were still at the beginning of this century taking their healing herbs and their knowledge all through the Andean nations: Bolivia, Chile, Ecuador, Peru, and Argentina—all the places that once came under Inca influence.

AN ANCIENT SHAMAN'S GRAVE Kallawayas have been practicing their brand of medicine since at least 1,000 years before the conquest of Peru in the 16th century, but as is the case with the other pre-Columbian civilizations, finding evidence of their ancient practices is difficult.

A few years ago there was a lucky archaeologic discovery in Kallawaya territory: an undisturbed medicine man's grave dating from A.D. 400, a time when the Andean culture was rapidly expanding. The male occupant of the grave was accompanied by a typical shaman's kit: carved wooden snuff tablets and tubes; a gourd container with remains of an hallucinogenic snuff powder; leaves from a species of holly (*Ilex guayusa*); a trephined skull; and enema syringes, one consisting of a hollow reed with a bulb of animal intestine tied to it with cotton string.

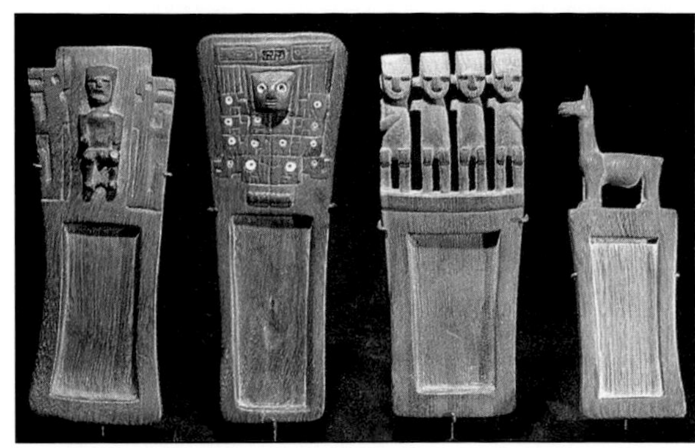

A group of 1,200-year-old wooden snuff tablets believed to have been used by the shaman healers of northern Chile. These were probably used to administer the powerful inebriating powder made from the crushed seeds of a leguminous tree in the mimosa family (Anadenanthera colubrina).

Holly. Tea brewed from *Ilex guayusa* and its sister species, *Ilex paraguariensis*, is still drunk in great quantities by many South American people. It is used as a pick-me-up in the morning, to relieve fatigue after heavy labor or long journeys, and to settle the stomach or calm the nerves. Kallawayas also use preparations made from this and related plants for sunburn, to reduce inflammation, and to cleanse and dry infected wounds. The leaves accompanying our ancient Kallawaya shaman were carefully prepared in groups of three and five for his final journey. No one knows

A Miraculous Kallawaya Cure

Kallawayas claim remedies for ailments against which modern medicine is helpless, and against which the invading Europeans certainly were. There are, in fact, historic examples of such "miracle cures." Bastien mentions the cure by Domingo Flores, a famous Kallawaya herbalist, of the daughter of Augusto Leguía, a former president of Peru. The best doctors in Lima had diagnosed her condition as incurable and dying. It took Flores 15 days to cure her with his herbs. President Leguía awarded him an honorary M.D. and publicly recognized the effectiveness of traditional Kallawaya medicine.

the uses to which the ancient shaman put his leaves, but there is little question that he and his contemporaries recognized their healthful properties.

Trephination. Trephination is a surgical procedure of which there is ancient evidence found in most parts of the world. It involves the drilling of a small hole or holes in the skull to relieve pressure or allow illness out. The trephined skull found in the shaman's grave is the earliest evidence we have for skull surgery in the Andes. The traditional procedure had become almost extinct in the Andes early in this century, but from this ancient grave, it seems it was already highly developed by A.D. 400. The skull found with the medicine man had three openings drilled with flint or obsidian, for what reason we do not know. However, we do know that the patient survived; the bone around the openings shows signs of healing.

Trephined skull from ancient Mexico. There is evidence that trephination was practiced by the Aztecs of Mexico and by the people of the Andes.

The art of trephining became highly developed in Inca times, probably because of the need to repair damage from war clubs to the heads of warriors during their conquest of more than 5,000 miles of mountainous territory in the 100 years before the Spanish conquest. (Some of the ancient Mexicans, too, made successful use of trephining, as shown by, among other evidence, skulls found at Monte Alban, Oaxaca, on which the bone had grown back around the surgical openings.)

Enemas. Medicinal enemas also have a long history in the Andes. Huaman Poma de Alaya mentioned their use in strengthening Inca warriors in preparation for battle. Early in this century, some Andean shamans were reported to be still using enemas with infusions of psychoactive plants to enhance their spirit powers. Bastien reported that Kallawaya herbalists recommend enemas for curing the sick:

> Kallawayas conceptualize the body as a skeletal-muscular framework with openings, conduits, and processing organs. Fluids enter and are processed into other fluids. From distillation, poisons develop that must be periodically cleansed.... Therapeutically, Kallawayas employ enemas, emetics, and sweat baths to cleanse the body of these fluids.

The type of enema apparatus found in the shaman's grave also occurs among the Amazonian Indians and has a long history in Peru, at least as far back as the 1st century A.D.

A Wealth of Botanical Knowledge The Spanish conquistadors were mightily impressed by the wealth of medicinal plants known to Peruvian healers and attempted to obtain as much information

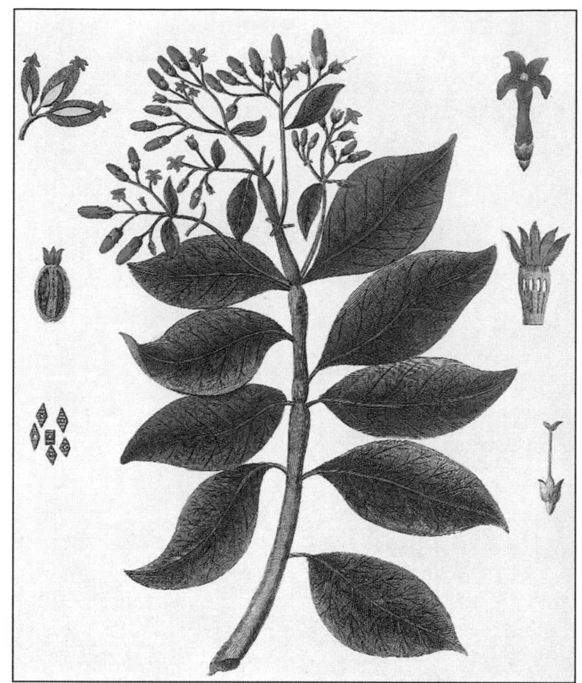

Cinchona—also known as Jesuit's Bark or Peruvian Bark—was the source of the miraculous antimalarial drug quinine. Although not used by the pre-Columbian peoples because malaria was unknown before the Spanish conquest, quinine is just one of the thousands of medicinal substances to come from the forests of Latin America.

on them as possible, without regard to the natives' magical explanations of their effectiveness. Even though purification and public confession of transgressions, such as neglect of ancestor worship, was widely considered essential to a cure, the early chroniclers mention only native decoctions made from the plant kingdom for numerous common afflictions, from rheumatism and flux to depression, epilepsy, dropsy, and scabies. Indeed, the discoveries of the medicinal properties of plants by Andean and lowland South American Indians have resulted in some of the most dramatic improvements in modern therapeutics.

Where would surgery be without the coca plant, *Erythroxylon coca*, a cultivated native of the Amazon basin and the Andes, which some native peoples held, and still hold, to be holy? The plant—the source of cocaine—is not known in a completely wild state; it has been cultivated and used against numerous conditions, including altitude sickness (the majority of the Inca population lived at an altitude above 10,000 feet), hunger, fatigue, sore throat, and stomach and intestinal ills and for increasing the nutritional value of a high-starch diet. These uses date back at least 2,000 years and probably before that.

Modern medicine uses countless other medicines—or, more precisely, synthetic versions of them—that were commonplace to the healers of the Andes. Ipecac, curare (a potent arrow or blowgun dart poison that has resulted in major discoveries in physiology), sassafras, cascara, and balsam now have their synthetic equivalents but are still important in modern medicine. Essential oils, alkaloids, flavonoids, saponins, and other chemicals have been iso-

The Disappearing Pharmacy

The total number of the world's higher plants has been estimated at about 500,000. Of these, perhaps 80,000, or 16 percent, live in the Amazonian rain forest. The types utilized for medicine, food, shelter, and other purposes by the native peoples of South America numbers in the many thousands. But only about 1500 species native to northwestern Amazonia, representing 596 genera in 145 plant families, have been described by plant explorers; of these, only half have been scientifically investigated for their pharmacologic and chemical properties.

With every day that passes, more of the forest falls to the axe, the bulldozer, and the flame. With it go as yet unknown and untested medicinal plants that may well hold the key to the cure of AIDS, cancer, and other scourges whose cure and eradication have thus far eluded the world's best minds.

lated from *Chenopodium linneus* and its sister species, from which Andean and other South Americans decoct effective purgatives and vermifuges. One species, *Chenopodium quinoa*, is the source of a nutritious Andean seed crop available in many health food stores. Nor must we forget tobacco—one of the most prominent and most sacred plants in South American shamanism that also has a major role in native therapeutics, especially as a fumigant.

Finally there is quinine, the most effective of all remedies for malaria—indeed, the most important medicinal plant Peru gave to the world. Therein lies an interesting story. Quinine is an alkaloid extract from the bark of the *cinchona* tree or shrub mentioned in the 17th century Spanish colonial literature as *arbol de calentura*, or "fever tree." The first Europeans to describe *cinchona* were struck by the fact that the Indian people not only professed ignorance of its antimalarial qualities but refused to take it. Nor did the Kallawayas know anything about it. The reason, of course, was not some sort of "blind spot" in native plant therapeutics, but the fact that malaria was one of those dreadful foreign scourges the Europeans introduced into the Americas.

This vessel from the Moche Civilization of the north coast of Peru (ca. 200 B.C–A.D. 600; before the Inca empire) represents an owl and a sea lion. Vessels like this, with their characteristic stirrup spout, were used as fine-quality water jars.

Public Health. Perhaps the most noteworthy aspect of Inca medicine was their public health policy. Herbalists and other healers received public remuneration, and the poor and disabled were fed from communal lands. There was a law that every surgeon and other nonherbal medical specialist should be fully trained in medicinal plant lore. A kind of genetic engineering was practiced, in that congenitally malformed individuals were required to marry only among themselves. Houses were well constructed against heat, cold, and vermin, and cities were supplied with ample and healthful water. People who failed to observe hygiene regulations were publicly excoriated and subject to penalties. Diet and work were highly regulated, and although whole populations were transplanted by the totalitarian Inca regime, attention was paid to the association between health, climate, and altitude.

Finally, the fundamentally social and religious attitude toward health and illness was confirmed by the annual public celebration of a great prophylactic ritual, known as *citua*. It was held in September at the onset of the rainy season, which was regarded as the season of disease, just as it still is today by the Warao Indians of South America. On this occasion, the statues of the deities were paraded around Cuzco, the Inca capital, after which the emperor dispatched four parties of warriors to the four directions to drive out the disease spirits. The entire population, meanwhile, shook the demons of illness out of their clothes and took part in ritual bathing and fumigation with tobacco smoke, coating their faces and houses with a sacred paste made from ground maize.

Native American Healing

DESCRIBING the healing traditions of Native North Americans is not as simple as describing those of, say, the ancient Egyptians. The people that inhabited the continent before the arrival of the Europeans came during three different migrations from at least three different areas of Asia, each with different traditions. Over a period of at least 12,000 years, they spread down and across the continent, adapting and developing hundreds of different cultures, as rich and varied as the lands the people came to inhabit—from the soggy, wooded Northwest Coast to the forests of upstate New York to the desert of the Great Basin.

Painting entitled Medicine Man *by the 19th century American artist Joseph Henry Sharp, depicting a Native American shaman in a deep trance.*

Many tribes did use similar methods; shamanism, herbal remedies, healing ceremonies, and other forms of spiritual healing seem to be found in most North American tribes. However, different underlying beliefs led to an amazing array of approaches. Instead of trying to describe all of them—a daunting, if not impossible, task—we'll look at a few examples:

- The spirit dancing of the northwest Salish
- The False-Face Society of the New York Iroquois
- The herbal healing of the Chippewa
- The sandpaintings and chants of the Navajo

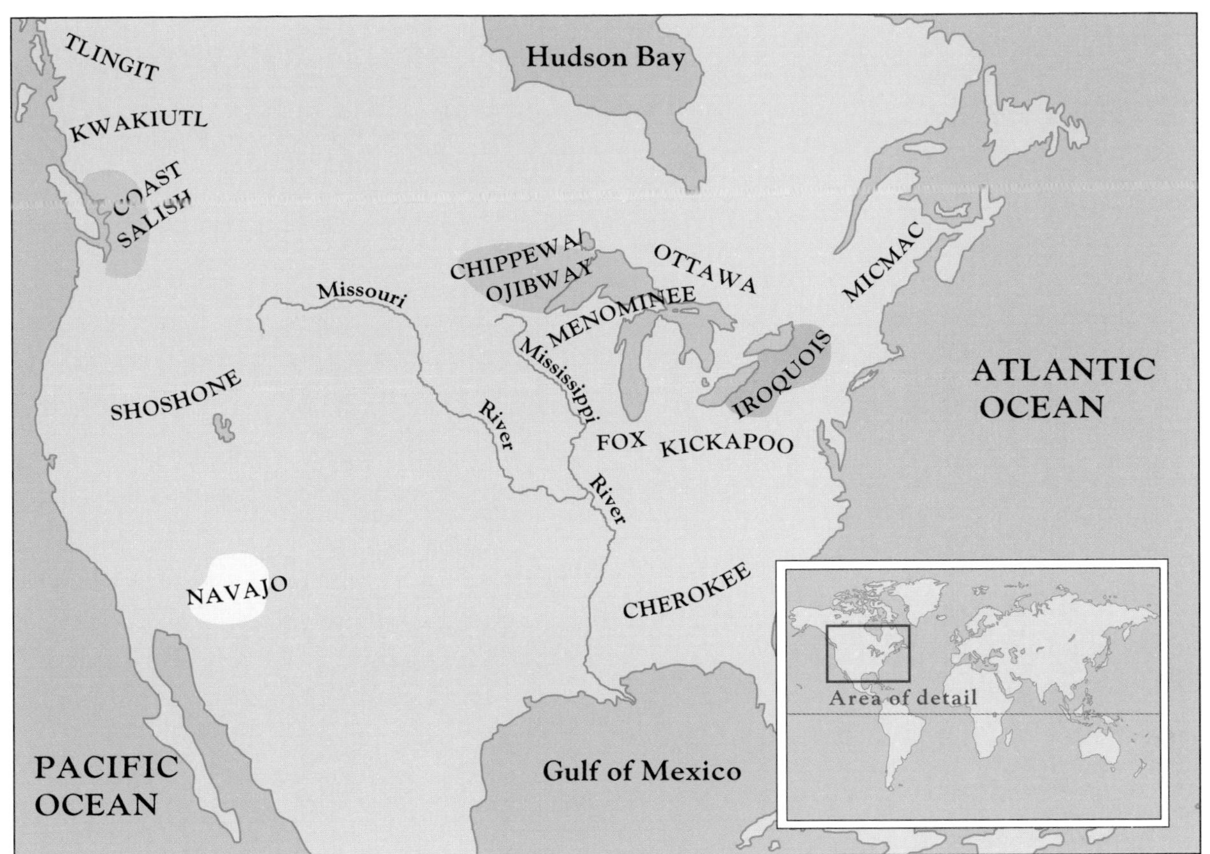

Spirit Dancing Among the Salish

Because Native Americans had extensive knowledge of botanical medicine, it is easy to see why other aspects of indigenous medical practice sometimes receive relatively little attention. The theory and practice of Native American psychological healing challenge modern Western medicine's focus on the mind and body as mutually exclusive and subject to different kinds of treatment.

Among the scores of different Native American cultures that still survive today, one could pick examples almost at random and come up with lessons for modern medicine. There is no culture of any social and economic complexity that has not discovered the medicinal qualities of plants, but there is also no culture whose healers do not pay attention to both physical body and the psyche, as well as social context, in seeking the causes and cures of illness. Some of the systems of symbolic healing that these cultures have developed are very beautiful and moving, with both the visual and the literary arts as indispensable components.

The spirit dance of the Salish of northern Washington and southern British Columbia is called the *Tamanawas*. The word is a corruption of *tomanoas,* meaning "guardian spirit" in Cowitchan, one of the indigenous languages of the Northwest Coast. The word became shorthand for the spirit dance. As its name implies, one of its purposes was acquisition of a guardian spirit who would stand at your side and help you through life's crises and illness. The idea of a guardian spirit can be found in virtually every Native American culture, but in British Columbia and northern Washington it took a much more dramatic and public form.

The spirit dance involves a severe psychological and physical trauma in which the patient is "killed" before he or she can be reborn, recharged with spirit power, and healed. Centuries old and nearly extinguished during years of official repression (see "Punishable Medicine"), the Salish rite has proved its modern worth in treating drug and alcohol addiction, depression, and other ailments of the spirit, which are aggravated, if not actually caused, by the relative deprivation, discrimination, unemployment, colonialism, hopelessness, anger, and other negatives of modern Native American life.

One aim of the dance was recovery of personal spirit power, the loss of which made one vulnerable to invasion by disease agents. This loss of spirit power might even lead to death—just as the loss of *tonalli*, or essential life force, did in Aztec medicine (see page 149). A man or woman could lose personal spirit power through inappropriate behavior toward family or community, an encounter with and possession by a hostile spirit, or even the inadvertent acquisition of the wrong kind of spirit song—a ritual song associated with certain spiritually derived powers.

GRUELING TREATMENT Spirit dancing is drastic medicine. Preparation of participants can take weeks of purification and psychic and physical training. It means fasting to the point of hallucination, seclusion in total darkness, alternate periods of sensory deprivation and overload, instruction in tribal lore and community values, physical and psychological pressure, and, most dramatically, the initiate's symbolic death by "clubbing," also called "doctoring up" or "grabbing." Usually this leads to

Punishable Medicine

> Every Indian or other person who engages in celebrating the Indian festival known as the Potlatch or in the Indian dance known as the Tamanawas is guilty of a misdemeanor, and shall be liable to imprisonment for a term of no more than six nor less than two months in any gaol or other place of confinement, and any Indian or other person who encourages, either directly or indirectly, an Indian or Indians to get up such a festival or dance, or to celebrate the same, is guilty of a like offense, and shall be liable to the same punishment.

The above quotation, shocking to us now in a more enlightened age, is taken from a section of Canada's Indian Act of 1886 that was not repealed until 1951. In British Columbia, in the meantime, it had been used to suppress indigenous ceremonies, from the much-misunderstood reciprocal chiefly giveaways of property, known as the potlatch, to midwinter world renewal rites and the spirit dance. Little did the authorities care that in addition to reaffirming traditional religious and social values, the outlawed spirit dance had powerful therapeutic dimensions.

We should not congratulate ourselves for greater respect for Native American religion and techniques of healing body and soul south of the Canadian border. In northern Washington before the turn of the century, for example, the churches and the Indian Agency actively discouraged social ceremonies that once were integral to indigenous medicine and spirituality. Punishment ranged from confiscation of costumes and ritual paraphernalia to public shaming of participants, fines in goods and cash, and forced labor. The result: Many of the old rituals became forgotten through enforced disuse. It is only in the last 20 years or so that the spirit dances, once so essential to Native psychotherapy, have made a real comeback.

temporary loss of consciousness. Taken together, these ordeals have the purpose of personality depatterning and reorientation, intended to make the initiate forget and abandon his or her former self and shortcomings.

The initiate falls into the kind of ecstatic trance that is one of the universal characteristics of the shamanic journey. In this altered state of consciousness, the spirit dancer travels to the underworld, the land of the ancestral dead. In the process he or she acquires a spirit song, new self-knowledge, and the restoration or enhancement of personal spirit power that may have become lost or weakened.

Already shaken to the core in anticipation, the candidate spirit dancer is kept in the longhouse, secluded in a dark cubicle, or "smokehouse tent," for a period of usually ten days, which may be reduced to four days or prolonged for several weeks or even the whole season. The length of this seclusion seems to depend mainly on the novice's motivation and his conscious or unconscious cooperation in "finding his song and dance," which is the professed purpose of the initiation process. The principal therapeutic functions of this process—personality depatterning and reorientation—are not unknown to the ritualists. In the words of a senior participant:

> It is an Indian treatment, it is a kind of brainwashing, four to ten days of torture. Through this torture they soften up; their brains get soft. During this time you're the weakest and your brain is back to nil; anything you are taught during those ten days is going to stick with you; you're never going to forget it. There is always someone with you during that time, always telling you to change your life. This is when you are taught all rules of your culture . . . the harder the torture, the stronger you get.

Or, as one Salish man put it

> They kill you as an evil person. They revive you to a new human being. That's why when they club you, you just go out and pass out, but you come back. . . . There is not to be evil thinking after they are through with you, all you think is, I'm starting life all over again.

THE JOURNEY The spirit journey of the novice reenacts a familiar drama: A shaman travels to the land of the dead to recover the lost or stolen soul of his patient and return it to the land of the living and the healthy. In the Salish version of this virtually universal shamanic experience, the shaman makes his journey in a spirit canoe. He faces west on his way to the underworld, and east on his return to the land of the living. When he has located the soul and placed it in his canoe he poles as hard as he can upriver against a fast-flowing cur-

The Support of Public Healing

The curing traditions of the Salish—and, indeed, most of the native cultures of North America—often consist of public or semipublic events. They involve, if not require, much of the community. What this does for the public, most of whom are actual or potential patients, is demystify what goes on in a curing ceremony, so that when they are in need of care, they know what to expect. Furthermore, the participation of the community means that the sick individual receives a great deal of social support from family, friends, neighbors, and so on—the very kinds of healing that we have more recently learned to supply by creating "support groups" for patients with particular illnesses.

rent "toward light and life." In fact, this essential element of shamanic practice—traveling to other worlds to recover abducted or otherwise lost souls—is implicit in the Salish word for shaman, which in English roughly translates to "the one who travels."

The shaman's canoe journey to recover the soul from the realm of the dead used to be reenacted in Salish ceremonialism. Playing himself, the shaman would carry a long magical pole which he manipulated like a canoe pole or paddle. This aspect of Salish shamanism survives mainly in the spirit journey of the novices and of mature spirit dancers who repeat the therapeutic experience every year during the winter ceremonies.

A mask with two faces, the second attached by hinges, known as a revelation mask; from the Kwakiutl people of the Northwest Coast.

Between their symbolic death and rebirth the novices are conceived of as "babies" unable to fend for themselves. They are given special protective clothing or "uniforms," a staff, and "babysitters" who help keep them safe along the way. Like newborn babies, but also like the shamans on their trance journeys to the Land of the Dead, the novices are very vulnerable.

Traveling in an altered state of consciousness that simulates death, they must overcome numerous obstacles and resist all manner of temptations, such as foodstuffs offered to them by the spirits—an especially difficult ordeal after their long fasts. They also emulate the shaman on his spirit canoe journey by wielding their staffs to "pole themselves upstream" toward the land of the living. But they can return fully to earthly existence only when they have achieved their goal: the acquisition of their healing songs, guardian spirits, and personal spirit power.

Spirit Illness A condition known as "spirit illness" that does not yield to scientific medicine also plays an important role across the entire area of northwestern North America where spirit dancing was practiced. This seasonal condition is akin to another shamanic phenomenon: initiatory illness, or "sickness vocation." Initiatory illness is supernatural recruitment of a candidate to the shamanic profession by gods, spirits, or ancestor shamans. The advent of the winter season, with its spirit dances, is heralded by the visible sickening of all those who have acquired the will and the power to dance. They become distraught, anxious, depressed, despondent, anorexic, emaciated, and weak, and they suffer local and general pains. These conditions require the intervention of experienced shamans as mediating therapists, but they may also yield to the sympathetic ministrations of experienced spirit dancers and members of the community.

The False-Face Society

Among the greatest works of Native North American artists are the masks that Alaskan Eskimos, the Salish of northern Washington and southern British Columbia, the Tlingit of Alaska, and the Haida, Tsimshians, Kwakiutl, Bella Coola, and other indigenous peoples of the Pacific Northwest made to represent animal spirits and ancestors in ceremonies. But 3,000 miles to the east, the Iroquois of upstate New York and the Canadian province of Ontario have an old masking tradition that for centuries has been a crucial element in traditional doctoring.

Medicine "Faces" representing spirit beings continue to be carved of basswood by men who dance to the sound of turtle-shell rattles in dramatic midwinter rites to drive away disease, purify houses, and cure their occupants. The women of these matrilineal societies, meanwhile, braid another kind of forest and vegetation spirit face of dried cornhusk.

The curing function of the masks comes into play not only in the midwinter ceremonial and other seasonal observances but at any time of the year when someone dreams of a mask and feels the need of a cure by a member of the Society of Faces. Following a successful cure, the dreamer may himself join the Society; most of its members join after seeing a "face" in a dream and being healed by it. A new member may ask an experienced carver to make a mask for him or her representing the spirit that appeared in his or her dream. But owning a mask is not a requirement. Many members, in fact, borrow masks from friends to participate in a curing rite.

Some masks depict animals, but most represent mythologic beings that appeared to the Iroquois in ancient times while hunting or gathering food or, more recently, in a dream. With their sometimes grotesquely distorted features, long manes of horsehair, and shiny metal rings around the eyes, the "faces" are not intended to disguise the wearer but to give substance to ephemeral

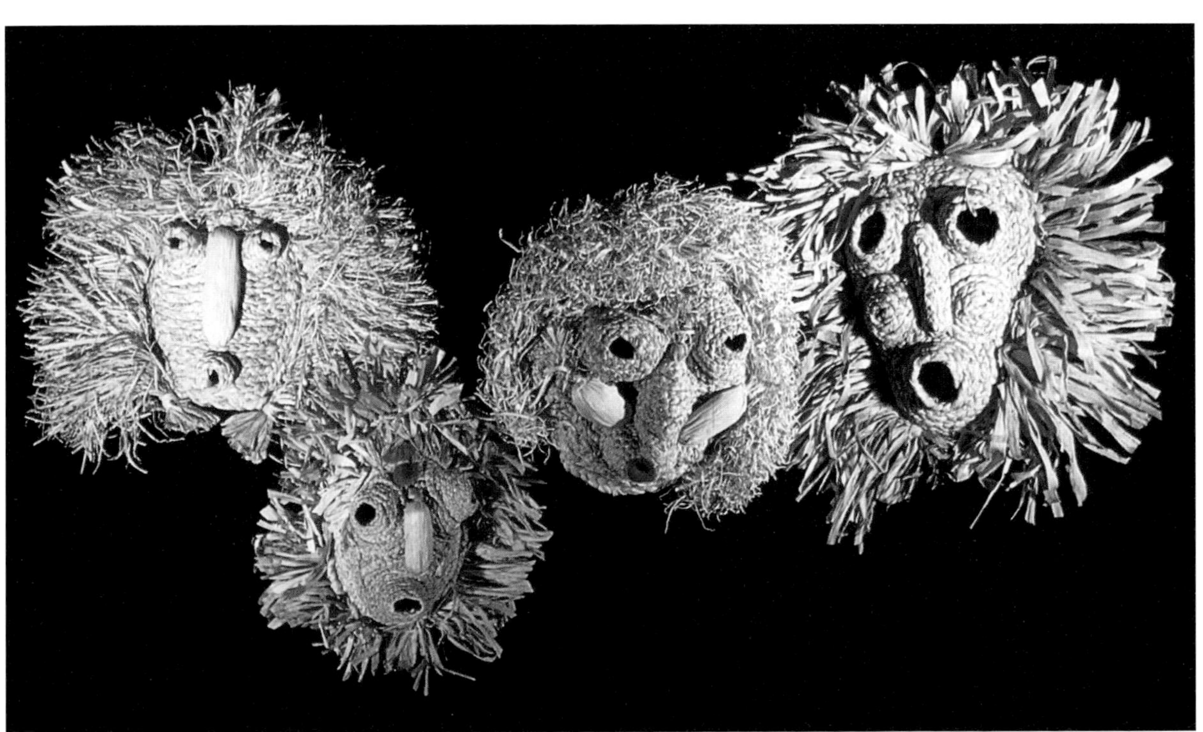

Braided cornhusk masks made by Iroquois women represent vegetation spirits. Those who wear the masks function as doctors, visiting and treating people in their own homes. They also assist in driving out spirits of disease and misfortune from the community in seasonal ceremonies. Wooden masks are only for men, but the Husk Face society is open to both sexes.

beings the hunters might have seen flitting from tree to tree or hiding beneath waterfalls and rocks.

WHIRLWIND The power of some masks goes far beyond individual or communal curing. Suspended from trees in the forest, or even thrown into the face of an approaching storm, they are believed capable of turning away blizzards and tornadoes. There is an old tale told by the Cayuga, another of the Iroquois peoples, that accounts for the origin of the first mask of Whirlwind—a spirit so dangerous that even such powerful beings as Lightning and Thunder failed to strike him down. The story recalls a sickness that can be cured only by the patient's agreeing to become a shaman:

One day a hunter stalking game with a companion in the forest inadvertently glimpsed the face of the Whirlwind spirit. Blood began to spurt from his nose and when it would not stop, he fell over dead. The second man was luckier, escaping with his life even though he, too, saw the Whirlwind face peering at him from behind a tree. Back in the village he asked a shaman to divine what had happened to him and his friend. He was instructed to return to the forest with a tobacco offering for the Whirlwind spirit. In this way he would himself become a curer.

The man returned to the forest with his offerings, but try as he might, the man failed to get another glimpse of the Whirlwind face. At last he fell into a deep

Sapling and the Rim Dweller

There are many stories that account for the origin of the masks and their distinctive features. The mask the Seneca Iroquois call Great Defender and their Onandaga cousins call Great Humpback has a broken nose and a mouth twisted to one side. It is also known as Rim Dweller because before the spirit was tamed and turned to humankind's benefit, he was thought to live on the very edge of the world, where he caused storms and other calamities. There are different traditions to explain his misshapen face and the birth of the Society of Faces. They differ in detail but generally agree on the basic elements:

One day the Iroquois creator/hero, whose name was Sapling, or Sky Holder, was wandering about inspecting his handiwork when he encountered a giant carrying a long staff and a rattle made from the shell of a mud turtle. They challenged each other to a contest to determine who was more powerful. Sapling suggested they both try to move a mountain. The giant tried first, but failed to move the mountain more than a few inches. Sapling then ordered the mountain to come right up behind his adversary. It did so with a sound like a great wind. When the giant turned to see what was making the noise, he smashed his face against the mountainside and had to acknowledge defeat.

Magnanimous in victory, Sapling ordered Rim Dweller to mend his ways and from now on use his spirit power not to harm but to help human beings and drive away the diseases that threatened their health and well-being. In exchange, the people would give him offerings of tobacco and sacred foods and carve his features—broken nose and all—from the wood of living basswood trees. And that was the beginning of the shamanistic curing Society of Faces.

sleep, and in his dream he saw a man carving a Whirlwind mask intended for him. When he awakened he sought out the carver and obtained the mask. A few nights later his wife dreamed of a terrible approaching storm that would surely kill them unless her husband hung the mask from a tree and burned a tobacco offering to Whirlwind. The storm passed over them without harm, and in gratitude, the man, now a full-fledged curing shaman, carved the spirit's likeness in three sizes: one life-size to be worn in the curing ceremonies, a second smaller one to be carried for protection, and a third in miniature. This one he suspended from the largest mask as its companion.

In fact, miniature replicas of the larger masks serve some vital functions. They can be substituted for their life-size prototypes and they are thought to protect their owners against illness just as well as the full-size masks. They are also thought to be effective in curing their owners from troubling dreams caused by a hostile Mask Spirit.

Stone pipe represening an owl. In the Hopewell Culture (the Native culture that covered much of North America 2,000 years ago), massive sculptural pipes like these were used in shamanistic tobacco ceremonies. With a nicotine content many times that of modern commercial tobacco products, Nicotiana rustica *tobacco was capable of triggering altered states of consciousness.*

Cures of this kind are part of the so-called dream-guessing ritual that was traditionally held during the midwinter ceremony. The dream-guessing ritual was first described in the 17th century by French Jesuit missionaries, who were astonished by the sophistication with which the Iroquois treated emotional ills, their understanding of unconscious causes, and the effectiveness of the treatment prescribed by the elders. As anthropologists have pointed out, the Iroquois's dream-guessing rite was a primitive but very effective form of psychotherapy that recognized, long before Freud, the latent and manifest content of dreams.

Ancient But Still Living How old is the Iroquois tradition of representing forest spirits with wooden masks and using them to drive away disease spirits and restore individuals and the group to health? No one can say. During the American Revolution, the Iroquois allied themselves with the British, from whose colonial officials they had received greater respect and better treatment than from the Yankee settlers. The result was scorched-earth destruction of the Iroquois's crops and villages and, with the American defeat of the British, dismemberment and alienation of much of their traditional land in New York. Out of the ashes of defeat came spiritual rebirth with the new religion of the Longhouse, a blending of older pre-European indigenous beliefs with the reformist message of the Seneca prophet Handsome Lake. Ever since, the society of the curing masks and its traditions and rituals have been firmly embedded in the Longhouse Religion.

But like the Iroquois Longhouse itself, mask healing in Iroquois culture is clearly much older. One authority was convinced that the masks and their ritual context belong to a very ancient woodlands tradition. Miniature "faces" similar to the life-size masks are modeled on clay tobacco pipes dating to the 16th and 17th century. This suggests an antiquity reaching at least as far back as late precolonial times, some 450 years ago. As for the cornhusk masks that mainly depict vegetation spirits, corn, or maize, these originated many millennia ago in Mexico. It reached the Iroquois about 1,000 years ago, along with *Nicotiana rustica* tobacco, a South American hybrid first cultivated, along with its sister species *Nicotiana tabacum*, perhaps 7,000 years ago on the eastern slopes of the Andes. The Iroquois still tie small bundles of *Nicotiana rustica* to the masks and burn them as sacred offerings to the spirits the masks represent.

To the Iroquois, the masks are not objects of worship. They are alive, capable like any human being of seeing, hearing, and feeling, so much so that when not in use, they are supposed to be kept lying face-down and wrapped up lest they see and hear things that might offend them. They are not art for art's sake, carved to decorate the home or fill out a museum exhibit. Rather they make visible and concrete the ephemeral spirit beings that are very real and sacred to the Iroquois. Their representations in wood and cornhusk are imbued with a beneficent life force not unlike that attributed to the several hundred medicinal plants that continue to play a role in traditional Iroquois healing.

Likewise, dancing with the mask in the midwinter rites is not nostalgic reenactment of an ancient shamanistic curing ritual that has lost its meaning in the face of modern medicine. It is a living tradition in every sense. The masks are not the icons of a bygone faith, but a vital component of an ancient art of healing the spirit when it is most in need of community support and sustenance.

The Healing Herbs of the Chippewa

It is often said that the indigenous peoples of North America were in touch with their natural environments to an extent unknown to the peoples of Europe. Certainly in the realm of medicine and, particularly, the use of botanical medicine, Native North American peoples had extensive knowledge. North American Indians put to use thousands of plants and their different parts—roots, flowers, stems, seeds, leaves—in the internal and external treatment of hundreds of ailments, from snakebite and skin rash to hepatitis and broken limbs.

Although medicinal herbs play a part in the Salish spirit dance and the Iroquois had extensive herbal pharmacies, medicinal flora really came into its own among the Chippewa and other Algonquin-speaking adherents of the now-defunct Midewiwin, or Grand Medicine Society. It was in their initiations into the several grades of the shamanistic Mide organization that initiates acquired expertise in the therapeutic properties of plants. The other side of the coin was that the natural world also provided the means to make people sick and to kill. This dangerous knowledge was also among the secrets imparted to the initiates into the Midewiwin, contributing to the suspicion and hostility it fostered over time and its ultimate demise.

The number of medicinal plants used by the first Americans is so vast it defies counting. In 1977, a book called *American Medical Botany: A Reference Dictionary* listed 1,288 different species belonging to 531 genera in 118 different families employed in 48 different cultures. Two additional studies done in the 1970s—one on the medicinal plants of the Cherokee by Paul B. Hamel and Mary U. Chiltoskey and a doctoral dissertation on the medical botany of the Iroquois by James W. Herrick—added more than 4,000. Thousands more have since been added to the list.

The Extensive Tribal Pharmacies

According to *Medicinal Plants of Native North America*, the result of a huge 1986 study conducted by Daniel E. Moerman of the University of Michigan, the various tribes of North America had over 18,000 medicinal uses for plants. The Iroquois, the Cherokee, and the Navajo seem to have the most extensive botanical pharmacies, but as this list shows, the healing power of plants was no secret to the rest of indigenous America.

Tribe	Region	Number of Plants Used
Iroquois	Northeast and Great Lakes	2,325
Fox	Northeast and Great Lakes	426
Micmac	Northeast and Great Lakes	330
Chippewa/Ojibway	Northeast and Great Lakes	883
Menominee	Northeast and Great Lakes	297
Mohegans	Northeast and Great Lakes	265
Potawatomie	Northeast and Great Lakes	217
Cherokee	Midwest	2,722
Navajo-Ramah	Southwest	1,037
Navajo-Kayenta	Southwest	400
Paiute	California and the Great Basin	770
Shoshone	California and the Great Basin	730
Coastanoans	California and the Great Basin	296
Kawaiisu	California and the Great Basin	293
Thompson	Pacific Northwest	513
Kwakiutl	Pacific Northwest	284
Bella Coola	Pacific Northwest	186

Significantly, no matter how distant from one another in geography, language, and culture, the healers of some of these indigenous populations often hit on the same or closely related species for similar ailments. These similarities arose even in the absence of contact, leading to the conclusion that healers probably used close observation and experimentation—empirical methods—to develop their herbal pharmacies.

THE BEAR WHO GAVE PEOPLE HEALING HERBS

The bear is quick-tempered and very fierce, a Great Lakes Chippewa Indian told ethnologist Frances Densmore many years ago, but with respect to herbal medicine, the Chippewa consider him to be the chief of all the animals. "Therefore it is understood that if a man dreams of a bear he will be expert in the use of herbs for curing illness."

Densmore wrote, Health and a long life

> represented the highest good to the mind of the Chippewa, and he who had knowledge to that end was most highly esteemed among them.... He who treated the sick, by

whatever means, claimed that his knowledge came from *manido* (spirits), and those who saw a sick man restored to health by that knowledge readily accepted its origin as supernatural.

Cherokee bear shaman costume of bear fur with the mask carved of wood. The Cherokee considered the bear to be chief among all animals when it came to knowledge of medicinal herbs.

Two methods were used by Chippewa medicine men and women to treat the sick. Both depended on supernatural assistance, but medicinal herbs were used in one and not the other, depending on whether or not the curer was a member of the powerful society known as the Midewiwin. It was usually only they who used material remedies that "were among the secrets of that organization."

LEVELS OF THE MIDEWIWIN The Midewiwin, or Grand Medicine Society, was a secret society open to both men and women among such Algonquin-speaking eastern woodlands peoples as the Chippewa (or Ojibway), Ottawa, Sauk, Fox, Winnebago, Potawatomie, and Kickapoo. It was divided into four grades in ascending rank order, and its members, dressed in festive clothing, met in a specially constructed lodge to dance, make offerings, and pray to different *manidos*, under the leadership of initiated Mide priests. The society was named for a magical white shell, *mide* in the indigenous language, which members newly initiated into the first grade were taught to control and use to "shoot" into other members, as it had been shot into themselves, to give them sacred power.

Acceptance into the different grades involved payment by the initiate who, in turn, was presented with the skins of mink, otter, fish, and other animals and a special medicine bag in which he or she kept the magical shell. Those newly initiated were also taught the properties of medicinal plants and how to cure with them. Over time this special knowledge came to be so feared as sorcery and witchcraft by nonmembers that the Grand Medicine Society fell into disrepute and was even outlawed; their initiations were stopped by one group after another.

MYTHICAL BEGINNINGS Today only memories survive of the Mide among the Indian people of the Great Lakes region. But in its glory days, its origin was credited to none other than the divine hero and sometime trickster known variously as Manabozho, Mänabush, Nanabozho, or Winnebajo. According to the story of the Mide, the sky gods gave the hero the Grand Medicine lodge and its secrets to comfort him after the underwater *manidos* killed his younger brother and inseparable companion Little Wolf. (In Great Lakes native mythology, the underwater monsters were the sworn enemies of the Thunderbirds, the *manidos* of the sky.)

The hero brought the medicine lodge down to earth from the sky and taught human beings the Mide secrets so that they might cure disease, defeat their enemies, and enjoy a long and healthy life and abundant foodstuffs. These included wild rice, an important staple that was eaten seasoned with maple sugar or combined with duck or venison broth.

STILL IN USE Among the hundreds of plants used as medicine by the Chippewa, at least 69 have been identified and recognized by whites for their medicinal value, including several that made it into various editions of the United States Pharmacopoeia (USP). Others have been accepted by at least some physicians or long been used as family remedies by Europeans who had settled near or in the native communities. Some examples include

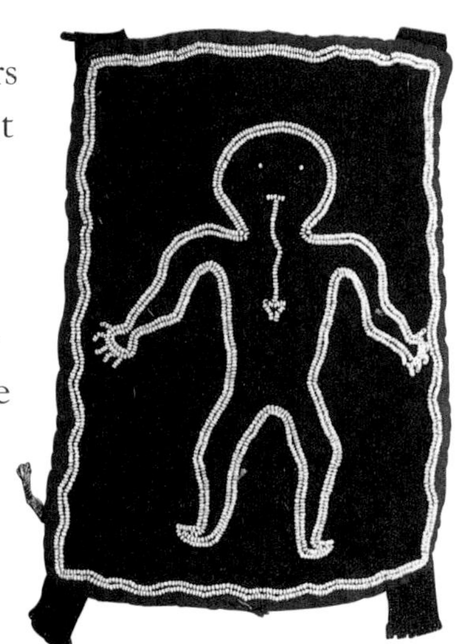

Ojibway cloth Mide bag with the figure of a Mide (healer), or perhaps his spirit helper, outlined with tiny white beads. The "life line" from the mouth to the center of the body where Mide initiates are "shot" with the sacred white shell also represents the healing power of the Mide's breath.

- Seneca snakeroot (*Polygala senega L.*)—The roots were used as a decoction for coughs and colds and the leaves as an infusion for sore throat. In the USP from 1820 to 1936 and in the National Formulary (NF) from 1936 to 1960, the plant was listed as an expectorant, cough remedy, emetic, and diuretic.
- Wild cherry (*Prunus virginiana L.*)—The steeped bark can be taken as a tea for coughs and colds, and by some, also for lung trouble. The USP (1820–present) lists it as a sedative and pectoral and the syrup as a flavoring agent.
- Tall cinquefoil (*Drymocallis arguta*)—This plant was used as a styptic to stop bleeding. Various species of puffballs also were used as hemostatics to stop bleeding or hemorrhaging.
- Balm of Gilead (*Populus candicans Ait.*) and Balsam poplar (*Populus balsamifera L.*)—The buds were boiled in fat to make a salve. The ointment was placed in the nostrils to relieve congestion from colds, bronchitis, and other respiratory ailments. These were listed in the NF (1916–1965) for their use as a stimulant and expectorant. (Although the Balm of Gilead shares the same name as the biblical remedy, they are not the same.)
- Blue Flag (*Iris versicolor L.*)—The root of this plant was steeped and used for colds, for lung trouble, and as a burn and sore dressing. In the USP (1820–1895) and the NF (1916–1942), the blue flag root was said to be a cathartic emetic and diuretic.

SHARING THE INFORMATION One of the fundamental teachings of the Midewiwin was that no tree, bush, or herb was without use and that many, even those used mainly as food, had curative properties. Nevertheless, the extensive Mide pharmacopoeia was not shared by all members, at least not immediately. Instruction on the practice of medicine, with the identification and uses of a number of different therapeutic species, took place whenever an initiate advanced from one grade to the next.

In addition to these times of special instruction, a Mide curer might go to an older man or woman to buy additional knowledge. In the old days, a person would not share any facts about medicinal plants, even with a family member, without compensation, apparently for fear that information given freely would not be accorded the proper respect. Also, names were rarely given to plants; rather, a fresh plant would be shown to someone seeking knowledge. In addition to those herbs that formed part of the secret Mide knowledge, each Chippewa household had its own supply of herbs for common ailments. If these failed, a Mide specialist would be called in.

PREPARATION AND ADMINISTRATION The part of the plant most commonly used was the root because it was considered to contain the greatest healing power, but stalks, leaves, and flowers were also used. Usually, these plant parts were dried for storage and pulverized for use. Mide curers might use only one plant for treatment or combine several. Some preparations included as many as 20 different species. Usually, a Mide doctor would collect, prepare, and store medicinal herbs for the entire season, sometimes traveling to distant places where certain species were known to grow in greater abundance than at home.

Birch trees (trees of the genus *Betula*), were highly valued in Native American medicine. Decoctions of various parts of the birch were used by native doctors for stomach cramps, as teas for postpartum tonics, as medicinal seasoners, as incense for people suffering from catarrh, to treat tuberculosis, and as stimulants, diuretics, astringents, parasiticides, antiseptics, and counterirritants. In a 17th century account of a voyage through New England, John Josselyn said this about the birch as native medicine:

> The bark of the birch is used by the Indians for bruised wounds and cuts—boyled very tender, and stamped betwixt two stones to a plaister, and a decoction thereof poured into the wound; and also to fetch the fire out of burns and scalds.

In short, this common tree served as a virtual panacea.

As among other Native American peoples all over the Western Hemisphere, herbal remedies were often administered as enemas. The Chippewa apparatus consisted of a syringe made from a deer bladder, a small birchbark tray on which the syringe was laid, and two measures for the medicine, a larger one for adults and a smaller one for children. A carefully measured amount of the medicine was put into the bladder, and a short piece of hollow reed was tied in the opening by means of a strip of slippery elm bark. The reed, about an inch long, was used only once and then burned—remarkably similar to the single-use, disposable medical equipment used in modern Western medicine.

The principal medicine administered in this way was the inner bark of the common white birch that was scraped and steeped in water. An astringent decoction of the wood of the ash tree was also used. White ash, mountain ash, black ash, and red ash were also widely used.

MORE THAN DRUGS Medicinal plants were treated with great respect: Before taking one from the ground, a little hole would be dug beside it and an offering of tobacco placed in it. Meanwhile, the plant would be respectfully addressed with a little speech, thanking it for giving its curative powers for the benefit of the people. Tobacco would also be offered to trees, such as the chokecherry (*Prunus virginiana*) or wild black cherry (*Prunus serotina*), whose bark was to be used as a medicinal decoction.

Was every remedy effective? No. Was all treatment pragmatic, based on experiment and observation? No. Magic played its role, for example, in the use of plants both as internal medicine and as prophylactic charms. As elsewhere, including Europe from the time of the ancient Greeks to the 19th century, the so-called "doctrine of signatures" played a role in Chippewa plant herbal medicine: Certain plants whose leaves or other parts resembled an afflicted organ were thought to be effective in restoring that organ to health.

Among the Mide religion of the Ojibway and related Algonquin-speaking Indians of the Great Lakes region, costumes such as these representing forest spirits and spirits of animals were worn in firelit dances at great communal initiation and healing rituals.

If these proved to be of therapeutic value, it was by coincidence. Nevertheless, Mide curers achieved some remarkable cures with an extensive herbal pharmacopoeia based, in the absence of scientific knowledge of their active medicinal constituents, on observation and experimentation, reinforced by faith in the supernatural or spirit power the *manidos* invested in the natural environment for the benefit of human and animal life.

Symbolic Healing in Navajo Medicine

The Navajo—or, as they prefer to be known, the *Diné*, meaning "People" or "True People"—practice a form of symbolic curing that aims to reestablish beauty and balance. Through chant and pictorial art, the Navajo re-create the world as it was in the beginning, when the Holy Ones, by defeating the monsters of disharmony, made the earth fit for human life. It has rightly been called one of the great healing systems of the world.

THE BEAUTY PATH When the Diné speak of *hozho*—the desirable and the natural condition of the world—they mean health, beauty, and harmony. Roughly translatable as the "Beauty Path," *hozho* is the natural, desirable way of the world. Disturbance or lack of *hozho* means sickness, disharmony, and ugliness. *Hozho*, then, is the condition that must be restored whenever a person, a family, the community, or the natural environment has fallen out of balance.

Sickness, of whatever kind, disrupts balance, within the self and between the afflicted individual and everything that makes up the social, natural, and spiritual environment: family, friends, the community, plants, animals, geologic features, and, most important, the vast array of spiritual forces that inhabit and enliven the Navajo universe. In consequence, Navajo medicine is directed not toward an afflicted organ or a specific symptom but toward reestablishing the equilibrium—the condition of *hozho*—that has been disrupted by pathology, be it physical, mental, or social.

THE PRIMORDIAL DRAMA The Diné have blessing and curing rites for virtually everything: physical or emotional sickness; a soldier leaving for, or returning from, war; animals; places such as houses; crops and livestock; and even starting a new business. For the Diné, making things right, restoring health, or putting the individual and the group back on the beauty way, involves both the literary and visual arts. Together they re-create the world when the twin sons of Mother Earth and Father Sky have battled and defeated the Monster Spirits that represented darkness, ugliness, evil, and disharmony, thereby readying the earth for its human inhabitants. It was the Holy Ones and the Hero Twins who gave the Diné the stories to be sung in the curing chants. They also instructed the Diné how to represent themselves, the Hero Twins, the Monsters (also called Enemy Gods), the sacred animals and plants, and all the other participants and events in the primordial dramas.

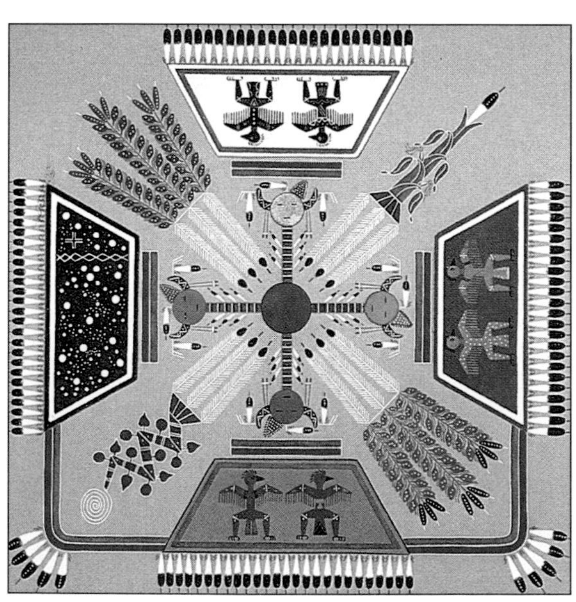

A two-foot-square sandpainting made in 1979 by one of the greatest of Navajo artists and shaman-singers, Herbert Ben, Sr. Called "Homes of the Buffalo People," this sandpainting depicts the buffalo brought back to life in their houses in the Otherworld and harmony restored after a near-fatal encounter with the Hero Twins, children of Mother Earth and Father Sun.

The sandpainting depicting the adventures of the ancient ones along with the words of the chant wipe away the boundaries between the now and the mythologic past. The patient for whom the ceremony was called is seated in the center of the painting so that he or she may absorb its healing power. At the same time the Holy Ones and the mythical events depicted in the painting draw out the disharmonious forces that caused the illness or imbalance.

ARTISTIC AND LITERARY SKILL To accomplish the rigorous requirements of the ceremonies takes years of instruction under knowledgeable elders. Some curing rituals extend over many days and nights, requiring the creation (and destruction once they have done their job) of 50 or more consecutive sandpaintings. There is an enormous amount of artistic and literary skill involved, including the expertise and intimate knowledge of content and meaning of the ancient stories.

Altogether, the complete repertoire of symbolic healing numbers some two dozen different chants, each with scores and even hundreds of songs, and a total of perhaps 500 specialized sandpaintings. For example, the Hail Chant, which counteracts illness caused by cold and frost, is one of the *shortest* in the extensive inventory of Diné curing chants, and yet it consists of more than 400 songs!

The Sand Paint

White is made from ground-up limestone.

Red and yellow is made from ocher.

Black is made from charcoal.

Pink is a mixture of red and white.

Blue is made from lime and charcoal.

Brown is a combination of white with yellow and red.

To the Diné these are not dead minerals but the living substance of Walking Rock, the last of the monsters slain in primordial times by the elder of the twin sons of Father Sun. For that reason he is called Monster-Slayer or Slayer-of-Enemy-Gods. Although it was their destruction that made human existence possible, they are nevertheless honored as having been essential to the origin of the world, and they are treated with respect.

The Plant People also play their part in the ritual, for the roots of different species are burned and their ashes mixed with the minerals not only to give them bulk but also to invoke their healing powers. Thus the popular name "sand painting" is not strictly correct; more appropriate terms would be "dry painting" or "ground painting."

A Cure for Many Ailments A curing chant may be requested by an individual who feels him- or herself (or, more often, is perceived by others) to be out of balance with the social, natural, and supernatural environment. Dreams can also be signs that a chant is required. The worst kind of dream would be one in which the dreamer encounters a *chindi*, the restless spirit or ghost of a dead person. In such a case, a "sing" or curing chant is definitely indicated, lest the dream turn out to be prophetic and the dreamer fall victim to the unpacified spirit. Illness, dispute, injury, a relative's death—all these and more can cause disruption of the essential equilibrium, a divergence from the Beauty Path, a loss of *hozho*.

Some chants are intended not to expel illness but to secure benefits, such as protection by the Holy Ones for a journey or some other enterprise fraught with peril. The Diné fear contact with the dead, and there are cases on record where veterans returning from war asked for curing chants to cleanse themselves and heal spirits disturbed by the sight of so much carnage.

To determine the cause of the malady, a shaman must be consulted. These shamanic diagnosticians are different from the "singers" who do the curing ceremonies. They are not trained or taught as the singers are, but rather their powers of diagnosis often come to them unannounced. The diagnostician might simply start to tremble and go into a trance, performing a "handtremble" over the patient. While in the trance, they may trace various designs on the floor; these designs are interpreted later after the trancing.

Once the cause had been divined, the diagnostician prescribes the appropriate chant to cure it. The patient or family engages the healer skilled in the proper songs and the accompanying artworks and provides the assistants that will help the specialist in the creation of the many different designs. The patient's family must also provide food for the large number of relatives and friends who will observe the ritual so that they, too, may share in its blessings. The singer himself requires a fee, which may be substantial but which is always adjusted to fit the patient's purse; the Diné say no chant is ever refused because the patient is poor.

The curing takes place in a specially prepared and consecrated *hogan*, the traditional eight-sided Navajo dwelling similar to the *yurts* of central Asian and Siberian nomads. Offerings for the Holy Ones, including feathers, turquoise, tobacco, cornmeal, and other consecrated foodstuffs, are placed outside the *hogan* so that the ancestor spirits will see them and be pleased.

The rituals of the first night are repeated on three successive nights, while the patient is instructed in the sacred lore, purified with steam baths, and given aromatic and medicinal herbs. There is always a prescribed order for the different actions of the curing drama; deviation can render them ineffective. The making of the first sandpainting does not begin until the fifth day. By nightfall it must be wiped away and its materials, which have soaked up the negative forces troubling the patient, returned to nature.

For the Navajo Indians of Arizona and New Mexico, restoration of health and harmony and the control of evil involve the invocation of the heroes of the mythical past and their heroic deeds in song and pictorial art "drawn" on the bare earth with colored sands and other materials.

The making of these sacred designs is a marvel to behold. First the healer lays down a bed of fine light-colored sand, which he makes level and smooth with a weaving batten. He holds the pigment in the palm of his hand and allows it to trickle out between his first and second fingers, using his thumb as a guide. For every change of color he cleans his hand by rubbing it with sand. The flat colors are laid down first, with details of costumes and accoutrements added in other colors, always working from large areas to small, and from the inside to the outside. Blue and black are generally used for male figures, while female figures are white and yellow. Some of these sacred curing designs are small, perhaps a foot across, others can take up virtually the entire floor of the *hogan*, measuring as much as 18 feet from end to end. Often the scene is encircled by a protective snake, or, more commonly, the elongated rainbow guardian.

The sandpainting and chanting represent a kind of healing that is foreign to most modern nonindigenous Americans. It is mythical healing, in which the implications of illness and disease are grander than simply the symptoms of the illness. In his book *Navajo Symbols of Healing*, Donald Sandner writes

> There is no question that often the time and resource necessary for a chant prevented or delayed the timely use of a specific, effective scientific remedy. . . . If I had tuberculosis or appendicitis, or cancer in its early stages, I would be quick to avail myself of modern medicine. But if I had one of those maladies for which science has no specific cure, like cancer in its later stages or some psychiatric illness, I would prefer the symbolic healing of the Navajo.

The Indian Subcontinent

Ayurveda

ANCIENT INDIA is one of the few places in the world that developed a coherent medical system whose tenets remain in practice today. Ayurvedic medicine is still practiced throughout the Indian subcontinent and is enjoying a burgeoning popularity in the West.

In the ancient Indian language Sanskrit, *Ayurveda* means "the science of longevity" and is sometimes translated more broadly as "the science of life." The system seeks to restore harmony and balance to the body, mind, and spirit through a system of diet, herbal medicine, massage, purification, and lifestyle discipline.

A bronze sculpture depicting Shiva as Nataraja, Lord of the Dance. This incarnation of Shiva was particularly popular in the early Tamil tradition, where it is told that Shiva invented 108 different dances.

In Ayurvedic medicine, the patient is active in his or her own preventative therapy and restoration. In this sense, Ayurveda is much more concerned with health than with disease—with the healthy person rather than with the unhealthy patient.

Although one of the features that makes Ayurveda so popular today is its "holistic" approach, the truth is Ayurvedic medicine is firmly grounded in empirical observation and scientific theory. And while its ancient development and practice are not entirely devoid of magical charms and incantations, some of the earliest treatises on Ayurveda are remarkably rational and scientific.

Diverse Beginnings

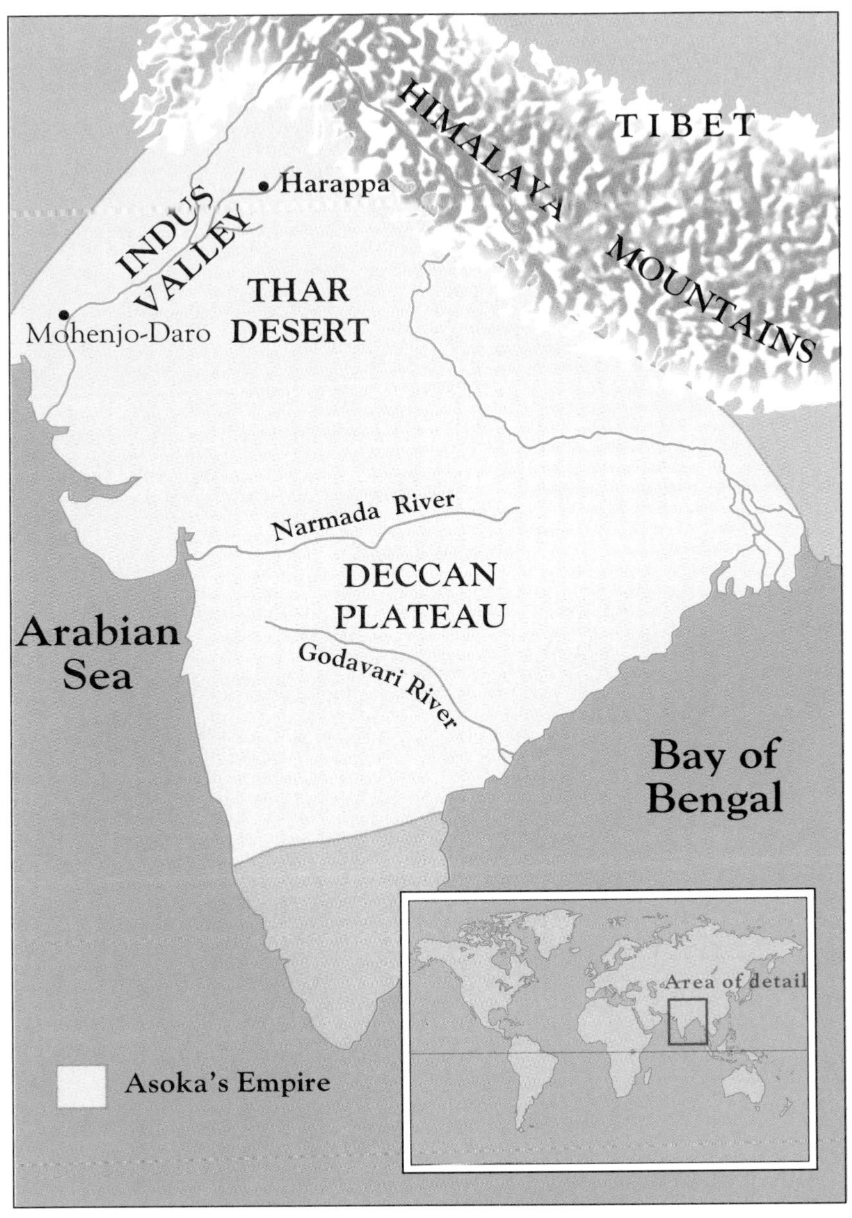

Scholars of Indology cannot determine the exact origins of Ayurveda, but we can see how many different traditions combined to create it over the millennia. The magical, religious lore of early Indian civilizations, the more empirical and practical approach of the so-called wandering ascetics, the medical traditions of the early Buddhist monks, and possible additions from neighboring traditions all work together to provide the basis of what we know as Ayurveda.

Out of these traditions emerges a system eventually codified in the two great Ayurvedic medical treatises—*Caraka Samhita* and *Susruta Samhita*. Although these two works, which provide the basis for the entire system, are considered Hindu, the information in them clearly developed over the centuries with significant help from the Buddhists and other religious and secular traditions.

The Indus Valley

To begin, we need to go back at least 4,500 years to the Indus Valley civilization on the banks of the Indus and Ravi rivers in present-day Pakistan and western India. It was here that two cities—Harappa in the north and Mohenjo-Daro in the south—reflected a highly developed civilization. (The entire Indus Valley culture is often called simply *Harappan*.) This society, which extended well beyond the two cities, was probably built by inhabitants who had lived there for centuries and continued to flourish largely unchanged for over a millennium.

Not much exists today to shed light on the life of the Indus Valley inhabitants. Their

The ancient city of Mohenjo-Daro in present-day Pakistan was part of a highly developed civilization known for its sophisticated urban planning and centralized government. Oriented on a north-south axis, its streets were designed on a grid, and mounds walled off by bricks dominated the city.

language remains locked up in an undeciphered pictorial script, so information can only come from archeologists unearthing examples of their material culture. A centralized form of government helped create a stable society that featured a standardized system of weights and measures, an elaborate sewer and waste-disposal system, and a uniform layout of its cities. Particularly noted for their realistic human figurines as well as their seal engravings of gods and animals, the Indus Valley inhabitants demonstrated an impressive attention to detail. However, for some reason they seemed content to leave their buildings and homes largely unadorned, preferring to build plain, utilitarian structures. Even the bricks used to build their structures were all the same size and shape.

The Harappans come across as conservative and hardworking. Artisans and farmers formed the basis of the society but were known more for their practical inventions than their artistry or ornament. They traded their goods for metals and semiprecious stones as far away as Afghanistan and Tibet.

A Sense of Public Health Although no evidence of temples or large religious structures remain, one impressive building merits attention. Archeologists have uncovered a huge bathhouse near the citadel area of Mohenjo-Daro. This structure, housing a 39 x 23-foot bathing pool 8 feet deep, contains several small rooms (possibly home to the city's priests) opening out onto a cloister. The townspeople higher up on the social ladder may have used the bathhouse for purification rituals the way tanks and pools served the same purpose for Hindus in more recent times. Although its exact use is unclear, its existence reflects the general population's attention to cleanliness and personal hygiene.

This concern is certainly clear in the elaborate, sophisticated sewer system built into their cities—a system unparalleled until the Roman Empire. The system provided drains in every bathroom to remove human wastes, which would flow through covered sewers under the main streets of town and into large soaker pits. Human wastes and tainted water are still major health concerns in many parts of the world. With little or no concept of infectious diseases and how to treat them, the urban Harappans had to rely on scrupulous public health measures to avoid the ravages of hygiene-related diseases and epidemics.

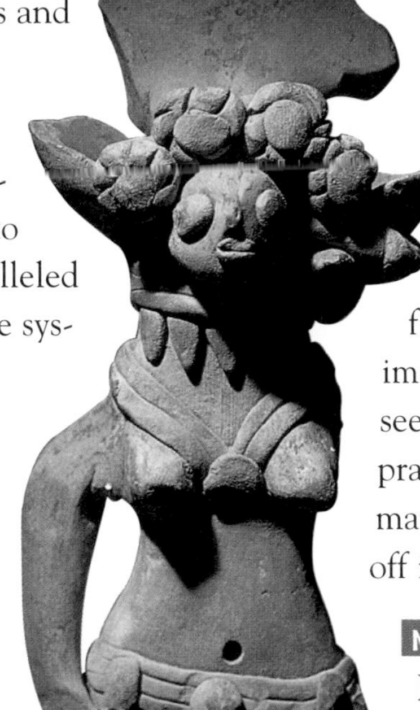

Found in the excavations at Mohenjo-Daro, this rough terra-cotta figure of the Mother Goddess dates back to approximately 2000 B.C. This partially naked woman with an ornate headdress was a very common icon among the lower classes of Harappa culture.

Religious Practices Even their religious observances bordered on the practical. Relying heavily on agriculture to sustain an urban society, Harappans revered the earth as Mother Goddess and the sky in the form of a bull or a horned god, a common fertility symbol. By performing sacrificial rituals to the Earth Mother and the Sky Father, the farmers might have sought to produce abundant yields of their crops. Plants and animals received reverential attention as well, and elaborate rituals—probably using fire, water, and magical incantations—might have sought to ensure a good harvest.

This sculpture of a bearded man, from the city of Mohenjo-Daro, dates back to approximately 2000 B.C. An example of portraiture, this figure is quite possibly a priest in a meditation pose.

Archeologists have discovered thousands of terra-cotta figurines and small seals with images of animals and plants. These seem to have had both religious and practical functions, used perhaps to mark property or as amulets to ward off illness and evil spirits.

Magical and Religious Medicine In addition to the hardworking, practical folk of Harappan culture, there seems to have been an ascetic side as well. There is evidence that at least a certain segment of the population chose asceticism, adopting a life of austere spiritual self-discipline. Some seals show figures in yoga poses; one, in particular, illustrates a yogin (one who practices yoga) in a meditation posture. Another common figure, a male yogin adorned with a horned animal mask, sits surrounded by a number of wild animals, emblems of masculine fertility.

In all probability, the ascetics performed shamanistic functions—healing by means of magical, spiritual rituals. Although they might have used plants and potent herbs as medicine, they likely believed that the power to heal came more from worshiping the plant and its connection to the earth than from what we would consider its chemical constituency. They seem to have used elaborate ritualistic dances to exorcize the body of evil spirits, which they thought caused disease; they probably chanted powerful mantras or incantations; and they may have used water in purification ceremonies. By and large, the community probably awarded these shamans or ascetics with great status and respect.

Aryans and Vedic Culture

No one really knows the exact reasons Harappan civilization began an erosive decline around 1500 B.C. Some say erratic changes in the ebb and flow of the Indus and Ravi rivers contributed to poor crop production and reduced water supplies. This would have disrupted the region socially as well as economically. Others feel that the culture was simply not prepared for the military might of the chariot-riding barbarians who invaded with more sophisticated weapons and the dreaded horse.

Whatever the reason, these Aryan invaders took little time in abandoning the highly developed and rigid organization of the Indus cities and the carefully orchestrated rules governing law and order. They were essentially nomads and probably had no use for the developed urban culture of cities like Harappa and Mohenjo-Daro.

Brahmanism and The Vedas The Aryan invaders brought with them Brahmanism, a complex, sacrificial religious tradition

In this 19th-century painting, a student, sitting at the feet of his guru, learns to memorize the mantras and ancient teachings found in the Vedas.

that can in many ways be considered a prototype of Hinduism. Much of the religious complexity of modern India is due to the blending of religious traditions, and the Brahmanism of the Aryans probably incorporated some Harappan beliefs into its own.

The sacred scriptures of Brahmanism are known as the *Vedas*. Chanted in Sanskrit and eventually written down, the Vedas are a mixture of prose and verse, the oldest being poetry similar to hymns or psalms. Initially three books—the *Rgveda*, the *Yajurveda*, and the *Samaveda*—made up the sacred scripture. The *Rgveda* and *Samaveda* are sacred poetry; the *Yajurveda* contains prose hymns devoted to sacrificial ritual. All three were primarily for the use of the Brahmans, or priestly class. However, a fourth book was later added to the triad: the *Atharvaveda*. This was the book of the atharvans—the magicians skilled in the art of fire and magic. Unlike the very sacred first three Vedas, which were intended for the Brahmans, the fourth book gave advice to the householder by way of spells, incantations, and magical charms useful for a host of problems, including medical conditions.

MEDICINE IN THE VEDAS In addition to their spiritual significance, the Vedas also contain many references to medicine and healing. Like the Indus Valley civilization it replaced, however, Vedic society continued to view disease as a result of diabolical conditions and looked to healers to exorcize through magic, ritual, and herbal medicines the spirits that inhabited the sick person's body.

Some medical references exist in the *Rgveda*, but they're mainly hymns to the healing deities the Ashvin twins (known as the "physicians of the gods") or to gods and goddesses that personify aspects of nature. A better source for medical information is the *Atharvaveda*.

The diseases discussed in the *Atharvaveda* can be divided into three types:

1) internal ailments caused by unseen sources

2) external afflictions brought on by injury or insect infestation, which include broken bones, loss of blood or hair, skin disorders, or flesh wounds

3) those illnesses caused by poisoning, which manifest themselves both internally and externally

Treating the diseases was again a matter of using the proper incantation from the *Atharvaveda*. In general, the *Atharvaveda* separates chants and incantations into two divisions—*bheshaja* (that which cures) and *adhichara* (sorcery). The bheshaja chants cover everything of a healing, medicinal nature—cures for fever, leprosy, jaundice, dropsy, and difficult childbirth. It also adds love charms and incantations to secure wealth, good fortune, and virility. There's even a spell to put an entire household to sleep so a lover can slip into the house undetected and join his beloved!

Adhichara spells bring bad luck or illness to one's enemies. A woman might, on occasion, cast a spell on a rival to make her a spinster forever or seek to destroy the virility of a man who had done her wrong. Replete with black magic and sorcery, adhichara spells provided hymns of praise to demons and serpents to garner their favor.

THE BHISHAJ Medical practitioners in Vedic culture were called the *bhishaj* and their methods were derived principally from the *Atharvaveda*. It was the job of the bhishaj to rid his patient of disease. This might entail anything from exorcizing the disease demons from inside the body to mending a broken bone.

Much like the shamans of the early Indus Valley civilization, the bhishaj understood medicinal plants, knew the proper spells and incantations, and, if necessary, could go into trances. He would use amulets and talismans made of plants and animal horns or burn a fragrant plant to ward off an evil spirit or to prepare the healing site. He also used water, which consistently offered healing properties for many diseases.

Divine Intervention. No matter what plant, fragrance, or surgical procedure the bhishaj used, the cure invariably came from the specific magical use of mantras, or spells. Reciting the proper hymns, using the correct incantation, invoking the right deity all gave power to the plant—and to the bhishaj—to cure an illness. Although it can't be known for sure, the bhishaj may have called upon the Ashvin twins for help when problems were serious. Likewise, he might invoke the particular god or goddess controlling the illness or the demon causing the problem in the first place. For example, if a patient suffered from dropsy (an excess buildup of fluids in the connective tissue), the bhishaj might invoke princely Varuna, the ruler of the waters, or call on Barahindevi, the demoness who caused the disease.

Transference. The bhishaj would sometimes rid the patient of a disease by transferring it to an animal, plant, or even a stone. He could do this in one of two ways: He could either manufacture a replica of the animal or plant by making one from wood or clay or choose another living entity for the transference. If he chose a replica, he would transfer the disease to it by using specific incantations and spells, and then he would throw it away or bury it. The living animal that received the disease by transference was driven away from the area or drowned, whereas a plant was burned.

Healing Substances. The *Atharvaveda* mentions several classifications of medical substances. Under the heading of animal substances, a bhishaj might choose rotten fish, animal saliva, tooth scorings, feathers, insects, frogs, or lice. There were various plants at his disposal and he used every part of its substance: the flower, root,

Vedic Cures

It is difficult to know the exact prescriptions that the bhishaj used, but the *Kausika Sutra*, written around the 3rd century B.C., is a treatise in the tradition of the *Atharvaveda* and gives us some picture of what early Vedic medicine might have been like:

akshata (tumor)—Tickle the area with the hair of a bull's tail; rub with dirt from the roots of a neem tree.

kasa (cough)—Drink clarified butter (ghee) in which dog's hair has been boiled.

kilasa (skin rashes)—Rub the area with a mixture of dog saliva and bull urine.

pakshabhata (paralysis)—Rub entire body with earth from inside the footprint of a dog; rub affected area with the ashes of an insect taken from a dog.

takman (fever)—Tie a frog to the leg of the patient's bed with red thread.

leaves, thorns, bark, seeds, fruit, and sap. There is even mention in the *Atharvaveda* of using mineral substances to heal, including gold, silver, stones, and salt. The bhishaj always took great care in how he harvested his medicine; some of the rules make good botanical sense and others are incomprehensible. The ground in which the plant grew must be free of molds and large animal burrows or holes; the harvester must pick it while facing north and never use a weapon of war to cut it down. The plant itself must be healthy, devoid of blemishes, rot, and insect contamination.

Anatomy. Although the bhishaj was often called on to perform primitive surgery, he never possessed much more than a superficial knowledge of human anatomy. This was not because such information was lacking. Indeed, the Vedic scriptures contain very precise anatomical instructions. However, anatomy lessons remained solely the privilege of the priestly class, the Brahmans, and even they only really knew the anatomy of animals—especially horses. Such knowledge was esoteric, to be used only to perfect sacrificial rituals. During sacrifices, the priests had to be familiar with anatomical parts because as they butchered the animal, they recited the name of each body part and tossed a ball of rice into the sacred fire.

The Pariah. Although Vedic society looked upon the bhishaj as an indispensable part of the community, he was not considered pure enough to join the sacrificial rituals. Since bhishaj was not a religious position, they remained outside the circle of priests, barred from the ceremonial sacrifice. The Brahman class knew that the bhishaj probably traveled far and wide, healing the sick. Many of their patients were non-Aryans and, therefore, looked on as impure or defiled. The bhishaj himself was also considered impure and tainted to the Brahman not only because he associated with and cured inferior human beings who were non-Aryans but because in doing so he came into contact with polluted bodily fluids. Choosing to surround himself with the sick and the dying didn't help matters either.

A bhishaj could never quite be relegated to the status of an outcaste, however, because he performed a necessary service and could justify his actions as a way to make a living. Even then, it didn't matter how you felt about doctors; you still needed them. A later verse of the *Rgveda* explains it this way:

> A poet who is a poet, physician, and apothecary in one person travels around the country carrying with him a wooden box full of all sorts of healing herbs and practicing his profession, not without humor and with a frankness that deserves recognition. He does not hide the fact that it is not philanthropy that motivates his practice, but that his main inspiration is gain.

The Wandering Ascetics—the Sramana

After the Aryan invasions were long forgotten, while Brahmanism was still dominant and the bhishajs were working their magic, another cultural movement was emerging that would change the face of healing in India. For ages, asceticism—the practice of self-denial and spiritual self-discipline—was revered in India. We've already seen evidence of ascetics in Harappan culture, and the practice con-

The earliest Ayurvedic physicians most likely were the wandering ascetics. Today India boasts of thousands of wandering ascetics, called sadhus, *whose austere and sometimes bizarre practices draw seekers from all over the world.*

tinued in Vedic culture. Ascetics were wanderers—spiritually and literally—and although they were never shunned, it can be said that they lived on the fringes of society, certainly not in the mainstream. In the 6th century B.C., many of these ascetics were adherents to the nascent ascetic religions of Buddhism, Ajivika, and Jainism. It seems that at least some were well versed in the healing arts, and because they traveled extensively, exchanging ideas with other ascetics about what works and what doesn't, they soon developed an impressive array of therapeutics.

These wandering ascetics were called *sramanas*, or "strivers." Although some of the Vedic bhishaj could be numbered among the sramanas, the medical practices of the sramanas generally offered a much more empirical, less magical, view of healing than either the Vedic tradition or the earlier Harappan culture; the ascetic healers relied on observation to diagnose and treat illness. They prescribed certain foods to cure internal diseases and applied plant-based poultices for external injuries.

Unlike their bhishaj brethren, the sramanas did not believe in charging for their services. As "strivers," the sramanas were more concerned with the accumulation of knowledge rather than material gain; their path to understanding was based largely on experience. Because they did not ascribe to the taboos of their Brahman counterparts, they could entertain an interest in human anatomy.

The Proper Method of Dissection

According to the *Susruta Samhita,* a physician must supplement what he learns in textbooks with practical, hands-on experience to truly understand the human body:

> After having cleaned the entrails, one should let decay a body with all its limbs intact, which has not been severely infected with poison, which has not suffered a prolonged illness, which is not badly injured, and which is not too old. Wrap [the corpse] in any of the coverings of munja grass, tree bark, kusa grass, hemp, and so on; place it in a cage and in a concealed spot in a driving, flowing [stream]. Then after seven nights, the completely putrid body should be removed [from the stream]. Thereupon, one should very gradually scrape off the layers of skin, and so on, by means of any of the bunches of vetiver grass, coarse animal hair, bamboo, or balvaja grass and should identify with the eye all the various major and minor parts [of the body], both external and internal . . .

It is interesting to note that a similar technique was employed in medieval Europe; in Europe, the corpse was usually that of a person who had been crucified.

They believed that humans were the epitome of nature and, as such, demanded direct observation. Theirs was, in truth, a philosophy of humanity. In fact, one of the ways in which a Buddhist ascetic contemplated impermanence and sought enlightenment was to meditate on a decomposing human body, focusing on every aspect not only externally—on hair, skin, bones, and teeth—but internally as well—on the blood, bile, liver, kidneys, spleen, and heart. They even meditated on bodily discharges and wastes. Although this direct scrutiny of a corpse—either in the mind or in the flesh—and meditation on bodily processes had more to do with religious observance (experiencing the impermanence of human form) than with medical research, on some level it gave the ascetic healers a clear understanding of the internal and external structures of the human body.

Buddhist Influence

Perhaps no other culture influenced the early medical lore that was to become Ayurveda more than the Buddhist monks. The knowledge the sramanas shared made up a rich oral tradition of healing, though nothing was written down or collected in any systematic way. About the middle of the 5th century B.C., many Buddhist ascetics—monks and nuns—began to organize into spiritual communities called *sanghas*. Membership in these sanghas was open, and the monks encouraged other wanderers to seek shelter there, especially during the rainy season. Again, the primary reason for this seems to be as a means of acquiring knowledge. Visiting ascetics, eager to debate and exchange information, brought new ideas and healing strategies, which they debated with apparently great devotion.

The Buddha and the Sick Monk

As the story goes, the Buddha arrived for a visit at a certain sangha, calling upon the monks in their cells. During his inspection, he came upon a certain monk suffering from dysentery and lying in his own excrement. Because the monk was so ill and weak, he could not perform his duties and was, therefore, of no use to the other members of the sangha. No one came forward to nurse him back to health. The Buddha then knelt down and began to wash the man's body from head to foot. He covered him in clean cloths and laid him in bed. Turning to the other monks, he declared, "You have neither mother nor father to care for you when you fall ill. If you do not nurse one another, who will nurse you? Whosoever would care for me should care for the sick."

MONK-HEALERS Upon entering the sangha, all monks and nuns received a bowl for begging, robes to clothe themselves, a place to sleep, and putrefied cow's urine for medicine. The urine came in handy for snakebites and other ailments, and since it was readily available without killing anything or having to purchase it (who would pay for it?), the monks could get it easily. A very popular antidote, putrefied urine appears in the sramanas culture and in later Ayurvedic texts.

At first, sangha members concentrated on healing their fellow monks and nuns. Even though the Buddhists did not strictly adhere to the Vedic taboos surrounding disease and bodily fluids, they still had trouble overcoming the unavoidable conception that nursing the sick was somehow personally defiling. At any rate, it was not

The original stupa, a singularly Buddhist phenomenon, was erected over the ashes of the Buddha during the reign of King Ashoka. Later on, stupas contained the ashes of many revered monks and bhishajs. This particular stupa, Kanakhepa, is located in Sanchi, Nepal.

a task anyone pursued enthusiastically. To make it somewhat more appealing, anyone nursing a terminally ill patient received his or her possessions—a rice bowl and robes—once the person died.

Medicines In later sangha life, monks were given five basic medicines—clarified butter, fresh butter, oil, honey, and molasses. At first, a patient was only allowed to consume these medicines twice a day—no more frequently than taking meals. In the Buddhist tradition, monks were not allowed to have any food after midday. According to the Buddhist scripture *Vinaya*, when Buddha discovered that some of the monks were not getting better, he decreed that these medicines could be administered more frequently. When he learned that these five cures still didn't do the job all the time, he added more medicines into the pharmacopoeia: roots, extracts, fruits, gums or resins, leaves, fats, and salts. These medicines, although food and plant based, could never be used to satisfy hunger—only to cure.

Doshas and the Understanding of Disease

As the sangha population stabilized, the monks and nuns began to standardize and codify all the medical information they had gathered. Much of this material can be found in the *Vinaya Pitaka* of the Buddhist Pali Canon, devoted to the code of conduct for the Buddhist monk.

The chapter on medicine represents the earliest form of Buddhist healing and closely parallels some of the information that would later be set down in the *Caraka Samhita* and the *Susruta Samhita*. Once written, this Buddhist "order of things" became the first step toward an Indian medical system. The Buddha identified the causes of disease as falling into one of the following categories:

- a change of season
- past actions (*karma*)
- unusual or excessive activities
- violent, external actions (being robbed or attacked)

Sramanic and Buddhist healers believed that humans represent or reflect the whole of nature—a belief also found in the Vedas. In other words, humans are microcosms of the universe, containing the same elements that make up all of creation. These elements—space (or ether), air, fire, water, and earth—are combined into three biological forces, or *doshas*, in humans—*vata*, *pitta*, and *kapha*.

- Vata is space and air.
- Pitta is fire and water.
- Kapha is water and earth.

The doshas came to be seen as responsible for all the functions of our bodies and minds. (They are often called "humors" because of the similarity between this system and the biological understanding of the ancient Greeks who recognized four humors [see page 75].) English has no adequate translation for the word *dosha*. Although you'll often see them referred to as air, fire, and water, respectively, or (less delicately) wind, bile, and phlegm, the concept of the dosha is more than that; for example, vata has windlike qualities, but it is not simply wind.

Five Medicinal Foods

The Buddhist texts, as well as the *Caraka Samhita* and *Susruta Samhita*, outlined the five basic medicinal foods and their effects on the doshas. Using these medicines, the healer could manipulate the doshas and undo the disruption causing the disease.

Food	What It Does
Clarified Butter (ghrta, ghee)	Alleviates vata and pitta
Fresh Butter (navanita)	Removes vata and pitta
Oil (taila)	Alleviates vata and kapha; promotes digestion
Honey (madhu)	Increases vata; decreases pitta and kapha
Molasses (phanita)	Beneficial for all doshas

The Buddhist canon, and later Ayurvedic medicine, views disease as a disruption of the doshas. Each dosha has its own seat, where it naturally resides in the body. Disruption of the dosha—its migration to, and accumulation in, another part of the body—will cause illness. For example, if vata is unseated from its seat in the lower bowels and moves to and accumulates in, say, the joints, arthritic symptoms may appear. It would be, therefore, the job of the medical practitioner to evaluate the problem and prescribe a treatment to rid the joints of excess vata.

Vata. Vata comes from the Sanskrit word *vayu*, meaning "wind," and indicates movement. Made up of air and ether, vata governs everything in the body that pertains to movement: blinking of the eyes, pulsations of the heart, and movement of the muscles. Its primary site in the body is the colon in the lower digestive tract, but it's also found below the navel in the thighs, hips, pelvis, bone marrow, bladder, large intestines, and nervous system. It governs the sense of touch. In the brain or nervous system, vata is responsible for anxiety, nervous energy, fear, and muscle spasms, as well as adaptability and comprehension. When vata accumulates, a person can suffer from flatulence, nervous disorders, insomnia, and confusion.

Pitta. Pitta is made up of fire and water. Located in the small intestines, blood, lymph, lower stomach, liver, spleen, eyes, skin, sweat, and sweat glands, pitta's fire controls digestion, absorption, assimilation, nutrition, bodily warmth, thirst, hunger, intelligence, and courage. Its primary site in the body is the stomach and the small intestines. Pitta brings about jealousy, anger, and hatred, as well as compassion, understanding, and perception. Excessive pitta causes inflammation, infections, indigestion, and jaundice.

Kapha. Kapha means phlegm. This dosha, composed of water and earth, denotes stability and solidity. Although its primary seat is in the lungs, kapha is also found in other parts of the upper body—the chest, throat, sinuses, head, upper stomach, fat tissues, nose, and the areas between the joints. It is responsible for maintaining lubrication and the body's immunity, strength, and sexual power. It keeps the skin moist, helps wounds heal, and provides energy to the heart and lungs. Its sense of calm and stability keeps vata and pitta under control. Kapha elicits avarice, greed, and attachment, as well as love, patience, and forgiveness. When kapha accumulates, a person suffers from excess mucus, swelling, nausea, lethargy, asthma, and depression.

An Individual's Constitution. Each one of these doshas by itself and in combination with the others is vital to the health of the body. Without vata, for example, kapha and pitta could not move. Kapha, which is part water, keeps vata from fanning the fire of pitta out of control and burning up the bodily tissues. Without pitta's fire, the digestive process in the body could not take place.

Each person is made up of a unique combination of vata, pitta, and kapha. This combination, created at conception from the combined doshic makeup of one's parents, is called the *prakriti,* or constitution. To preserve good health, a person must maintain the same ratio of doshas he had when he was conceived. As a person grows up and responds to daily stresses and environmental changes, his or her doshas are stimulated and move. The predominant dosha is generally the one that fluctuates the most, so knowing the patient's doshic makeup is the first step in diagnosing any health problems. When a particular prakriti is out of balance, symptoms resulting from an excess dosha or a combination of doshas will manifest themselves. By understanding a person's doshic makeup, a physician can help anticipate potential problems before they arise and more accurately assess the nature of an illness when it occurs.

Rarely does a person have a predominance of only one dosha, although it is possible. Besides the monotype vata, pitta, and kapha constitutions, there are the duotype combinations of vata-pitta, pitta-kapha, vata-kapha, and the very rare tri-doshic vata-pitta-kapha, sometimes called *sama.* The following is a brief description of each doshic type. These descriptions are based on monotypes and do not include influ-

Determining Doshic Type

To diagnose and treat an illness properly, the healer would have to figure out which of the three doshas predominates in the patient. One way of doing this is to pay attention to the patient's physical and psychological attributes. The doctor puts a check mark on each word or phrase that accurately describes the patient. The body type with the most check marks will be the predominant dosha.

Vata

- thin, has a hard time gaining weight, small-boned, underdeveloped
- cold, dry, rough skin
- dark, coarse, kinky hair on the head that tangles easily
- eyes small, dull, dry, with bluish whites; dark brown, gray, or slate blue
- teeth protruding, crooked, with receding or emaciated gums
- digestion irregular, with dry, hard stools
- appetite irregular; cannot fast without feeling weak
- sexual appetite varies; has many fantasies, but tires easily
- thinks quickly, darts from idea to idea
- grasps concepts quickly; forgets just as quickly
- generous with money; can't save easily
- loves change; moves around a lot
- hates cold weather, wintertime; loves the sun
- dreams often; has trouble remembering them
- anxious under stress; gets excited or irritated easily
- living space messy
- changes mind on a whim; easily swayed

Pitta

- medium build, athletic body, average weight
- complexion fair, ruddy or freckled, or soft and oily
- sharp, penetrating eyes; green, hazel
- moderate sized teeth; yellowish in color
- good appetite; seems to be always hungry and thirsty
- digestion strong
- active, aggressive mind; competitive and ambitious
- easily irritated, overly critical; often jealous
- sharp memory; retains information well
- self-disciplined; good planner, organizer
- gets overheated and tires easily
- enjoys mental and physical challenges; loves to win
- doesn't need a lot of sleep, but sleeps soundly
- dreams can be fitful, violent, fiery; usually remembers them
- hates hot, humid weather; sweats profusely
- spends money on luxuries

Kapha

- powerful build, often bulky, sometimes overweight
- large features; big, beautiful eyes (often blue) with long lashes
- graceful movements; slow and deliberate
- dark, lustrous hair
- strong, white teeth
- digestion slow but good
- appetite moderate; tends to gain weight easily
- enjoys creature comforts, including gourmet foods and luxury surroundings
- does not enjoy exercise much; tends to be lethargic
- mind is slow, steady, but excellent memory
- dreams are of romantic nature; soft, water images
- hates being uncomfortable
- loves to sleep
- emotional, can be overly protective, possessive, and greedy
- saves money easily
- slow, deliberate speech patterns

ences from the other doshas that help make up a particular constitution.

Vata Types. Remembering that vata is the dosha composed of air and space, it is apparent that vata personality types tend to be fast-talkers, quick-thinkers, and have extreme characteristics—very tall with protruding joints and bones and dry, rough skin. Motion through space (mentally and physically) characterizes vatas, who go unburdened. No excess weight gets in their way—they are generally thin and wiry. Since air (or wind) dries out whatever it comes into contact with, vata types may suffer from digestive problems such as constipation—there's not enough lubrication to loosen things. They don't always take the time to eat, and their appetite varies.

Mentally, vata types move at a rapid pace. With no time to sit around and ponder, they grasp concepts readily, have thousands of ideas every minute, and possess a creative, active imagination. Unfortunately, they often forget things almost as quickly as they grasp them and have trouble putting their ideas into practice. In business, they make great brainstormers and, with a characteristic generous nature, can spur coworkers on to great things.

Pitta Types. Pitta, on the other hand, is ruled by fire primarily. Unlike the element of air that flits from one place to another, fire is rooted in one place and burns steady and long. The heat of fire in itself can dry things out. Fueled by fire, pitta types have a strong metabolism and can digest their foods readily, but they can suffer from acid indigestion from a digestive system that's too aggressive. Pitta types tend to be thin and delicate, though not to the extreme of their vata brethren.

Mentally, pitta types share some traits with vata types. Like vatas, they master concepts quickly, enjoy a lot of activity, and are very intelligent. However, with their fire aspect burning steadily, pitta types have no trouble concentrating on the task at hand. They enjoy the challenge of working through a problem, and their good, quick memory comes in handy. In business, pittas make good planners and have the staying power to see those plans through. Their fiery dispositions, however, cause them to be short-tempered and quick to jump to conclusions; pittas are hotheads.

Kapha Types. Water and earth govern the kapha dosha. The qualities of water (lubricating, cool, soft, and shapeless) and earth (heavy, inert, dry, calm, and solid) show up in people with predominantly kapha personalities. These "salt-of-the-earth" types tend to have well-developed physiques and strong appetites.

Mentally, kapha personalities exhibit the characteristics of both water and earth. They are calm, even-tempered, loving, dependable, and forgiving. Unlike vatas, whose beliefs change with the wind, and pittas, whose convictions are extremely strong and passionate, kaphas exhibit deep, solid beliefs that don't change readily. In business, they are loyal and dependable organizers.

THE REIGN OF KING ASHOKA By about the 3rd century B.C., the monk-healers extended their medical care to the general population, possibly at the behest of King Ashoka, the famous Buddhist ruler who reigned from approximately 269 to 232 B.C. King Ashoka began his reign as a tyrant, and it is said that his prisons were

An architectural column with a majestic lion on top—a symbol of King Ashoka's reign. King Ashoka's greatest triumph was his renunciation of war and his dedication to nonviolence. His compassion extended to the treatment of animals as well as his human subjects.

equipped with the most modern torture equipment. He commanded that hundreds of animals and birds be slaughtered daily for his royal kitchen, and no tactic was too despicable as he conquered kingdoms far and wide.

Then, about eight years into his reign, he had a complete change of heart. Shocked by the amount of suffering he had caused as a result of his conquests, he resolved to change his ways. He converted to Buddhism and embarked on a policy of humanitarian ethics. In matters of conquest, he abandoned aggressive warfare and replaced it with a commitment to *ahimsa*, the doctrine of nonviolence. His new resolve benefited his subjects, and he declared them his "children" and vowed to care for them compassionately.

This compassion radically changed life in his kingdom. For one thing, he no longer tolerated animal sacrifice and set up strict rules regulating the killing of animals for food, even banning the murder of certain species altogether. He replaced sport hunting, a popular pastime, with pilgrimages to Buddhist holy spots and boasted of single-handedly reducing meat consumption in the palace to the bare minimum. Although vegetarianism did not become the order of the day in India until much later, many feel that King Ashoka's encouragement helped spread the idea.

As part of his commitment to Buddhist doctrine, King Ashoka insisted on free medical treatment for all his subjects—humans and animals alike—and looked to the monasteries to provide it. He even issued an edict proclaiming that if the necessary herbs, roots, and flowers were not available, they were to be imported and planted for medicinal use. He also ordered his subjects to plant fruit trees along the roadsides to provide sustenance and shade for weary travelers.

Indeed, the number of Buddhist monasteries expanded rapidly. Usually found along trading routes, these monasteries offered both solace and medical care for travelers from far and wide. Wealthy merchants likely supported the monasteries in exchange for a place to rest and refresh themselves during their often arduous travels. And Buddhists found outsiders much more willing to receive a little spiritual guidance if it came with medical advice as well.

Although there is evidence that King Ashoka set up free hospitals for both humans and animals, that's probably not the case. It's more likely that Buddhist monasteries and sanghas continued to provide a place for the sick to get well. It probably wasn't until the 2nd or 3rd century A.D. that compounds specifically designed to house the sick became more common. Again, Buddhist in nature, these institutions provided both medical care and charity for all who needed it. There was never a cost involved for the medicines and food dispensed.

The Emergence of Ayurveda

By the first few centuries A.D., Hinduism—the legacy of the Brahmanic and Vedic religion of the ancient Aryan people—was once again ascendant in India. Buddhism found adherents to the east in Tibet and China, and Hinduism absorbed a great deal of theology and science from the Buddhists.

In medicine as religion, the Hindus incorporated what they valued from the Buddhist tradition into their emerging system. Elaborating on earlier concepts and finally codifying what was probably common, orally transmitted knowledge, Indian physicians were finally setting down the tenets of Ayurveda.

THE SAMHITAS The *Caraka Samhita* and *Susruta Samhita,* the sacred medical texts, represent the first true codification of the Ayurvedic system. The *Caraka Samhita* is primarily a clinical medical text; the *Susruta Samhita* is primarily a surgical text. The *Samhitas* make up the basis of Ayurveda and are still considered authoritative on many issues today.

It's hard to say exactly when the *Samhitas* were written down. Some scholars say the *Caraka Samhita* dates from the 2nd century A.D. and the *Susruta* from the 4th. It's also likely that both works represent a compilation of data that spans several centuries, beginning a few hundred years B.C. What we do know is that both texts include medical information from the early wandering physicians as well as revisions added during a much later era to incorporate Hindu medical lore. The later Hindu, or Brahmanic, additions (around the 4th or 5th century A.D.) reflect a desire to justify the art of healing and incorporate it

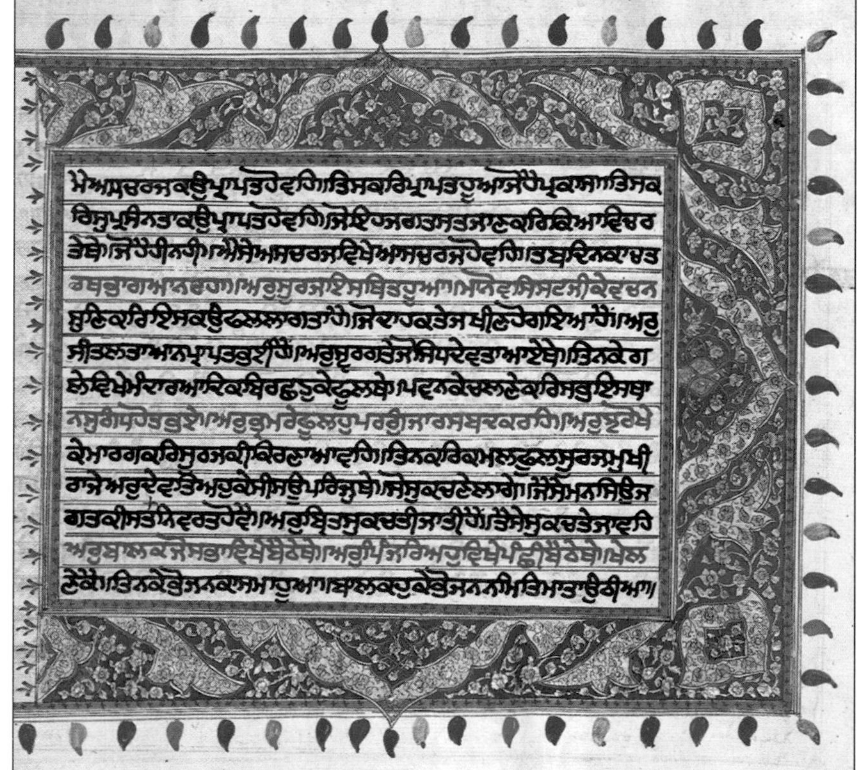

Here is an example of Sanskrit, the ancient language of the Vedas. Known as the "language of the Gods," Sanskrit's alphabet is organized according to where the sounds originate in the throat and the mouth. Daily chanting of Sanskrit mantras is said to result in improved health and ultimately enlightenment.

Rules of Conduct—Practitioner

Both the Buddhists and the early medical treatises (the *Caraka Samhita* and *Susruta Samhitas*) map out a physician's code of ethics not unlike the Greek Hippocratic Oath (see page 76). The Buddhist doctrine insists that the monk-healer be competent, kind, and generous, never refusing medical care to anyone.

The *Caraka Samhita* reminds the physician to be current in his medical knowledge, never betray his patient's trust, "pray each day for the welfare of all beings . . . and strive with all your heart for the health of the sick." In the *Susruta Samhita*, physicians must be intelligent, have practical experience, and hold fast to the principles of *satya* (truth) and *dharma* (duty). Their attendants must give affection to the patient, never grow tired, and carry out the wishes of the physician.

into their religious tradition—the tradition of the Vedas.

Although the Buddhist monk-healers prided themselves on using only the most empirical and rational means to cure the sick, magic never truly disappeared from the Indian medical scene. The *Samhitas* do, in fact, contain some magical and religious doctrines, showing that the Vedic culture of the bhishaj still had a strong hand in Indian medicine despite the influence of the Buddhist's more scientific approach. The *Caraka Samhita* recognizes its power to heal and defines "divine source" as one of the three forms of therapy. It explains that sometimes a physician needs to resort to reciting mantras, using amulets, making fire offerings, invoking the name of certain deities, or embarking on a pilgrimage to rid his patient of a tenacious disease.

Despite the presence of some magical charms and a general gloss of Brahmanic religion, the two texts are still mainly scientific treatises. They continue and expand the work of the Buddhists, recording more classifications as well as giving specific diagnoses and treatments.

THE BODY AS MICROCOSM Like the Buddhists before them, the early Ayurvedic physicians believed that the human body contains the same elements as the universe around it.

The Gunas. In the *Samhitas*, this concept is best exemplified by the three *gunas*. According to one of the earliest of the orthodox philosophies of Hinduism, the primordial energy involved in creation was made up of three distinct attributes or gunas—*sattva* (goodness or essence), *rajas* (movement or passion), and *tamas* (darkness or inertia). The interaction of these three attributes caused the evolution of the universe. The gunas—sattva, rajas,

Rules of Conduct—Patient

Both the Buddhist *Vinaya* and the *Samhitas* clearly lay down rules of behavior for patients to follow. The Buddhists remind patients never to be disagreeable; to always communicate with the healer, telling him where the pain is, what feels better, and what feels worse; to always take their medicines; and to endure any discomfort bravely. Both the *Caraka* and *Susruta Samhitas* have similar requirements for patients—self-control, courage, attentiveness, knowledge of his or her condition—with one interesting difference: It's important that the patient have a disease that's curable! In fact, only if the disease is curable and the patient can afford to pay should one go to a physician. Otherwise, the physician can lose prestige and risk "universal censure."

and tamas—create all existence as we know it, and also manifest themselves as emotional and mental predispositions that make up our character.

- Sattva, or essence, expresses goodness, compassion, and clarity. Generally, sattvic people are charitable, intelligent, religious, strong, and courageous. Sattvic foods are easy to digest and generally bland—milk, clarified butter (ghee), wheat, and certain fruits and vegetables.
- Rajas suggests passion, movement, transformation, and aggressiveness. Rajastic people tend to be good in business dealings, forceful, political, and extroverted. Taken to an extreme, they can suffer from jealousy and selfishness. Rajastic foods include meat (except beef) and fish and can be salty, pungent, and bitter.
- Tamas denotes inertia, gloom, darkness, and laziness. A person who is overly tamasic is dull, slow-witted, and selfish. It drives sexual energy and material desires. Tamasic foods include onions and garlic, beef, alcohol, and mushrooms.

The Elements. The five gross elements of ether, air, fire, water, and earth that make up the external universe and inorganic matter manifest in our bodies as the senses—hearing, touching, seeing, tasting, and smelling. They help us perceive the world in which we live.

- Ether, or space, enables the ear to function and manifests as sound. It is light, cool, elastic, mobile, and exists everywhere. Sound expresses itself through speech, so the ear and the mouth are connected.
- Air relates to the skin and manifests as touch. The hand is the organ of action, enabling the body to experience the tangible world, through giving, holding, and receiving. It is not only light and cool like ether, but dry and clear as well.
- Fire enables the eye to see, bringing color and form to the forefront. It is hot, dry, and bright, with upward movement, and it manifests as sight. The sense of sight also connects to walking, giving the walker a sense of direction. Therefore, fire is also related to the feet, and controls movement.
- Water is the element of taste and of the tongue. Its attributes are liquid, cold, and downward movement. (In Ayurveda the tongue is closely related to the genitals and controls the act of reproduction.)

Gross Elements—Inside and Outside

Operating on the principle that the human body reflects the makeup of the universe, each gross element in nature is associated with various organs and functions of the body:

Element	Dosha	Sense Organ	Motor Organ	Governs
ether	vata	ear	mouth	speaking
air	vata	skin	hand	holding
fire	pitta	eyes	feet	moving
water	pitta	tongue	genitals	reproducing
earth	kapha	nose	anus	eliminating

• Earth is the element of smell and the nose. It is heavy, rough, inert, and hard. The function of the nose closely relates to the excretory action of the anus and therefore controls elimination.

AGNI: THE FIRE INSIDE The *Caraka Samhita* introduces the concept of *grahani*, the seat of digestive fire, or *agni*. This internal organ "seizes" the food and releases the power of the fire. Located above the navel, this phantom organ, according to Caraka,

> checks undigested food and releases the digested [food] from the side; but when the digestive fire is weak, it [the grahani] becomes defective and gives off undigested food.

In Ayurveda, agni governs metabolism, breaking down the food we eat and turning it into energy and waste products that we can absorb and eliminate. Of course, there's more than one agni in the body; in fact there are 13 of them. (Modern Ayurvedic practitioners identify these 13 agnis with what we call digestive enzymes.)

THE THREE MALAS Vital to health in Ayurveda is proper elimination of the three *malas* or waste products—feces, urine, and sweat. Urine and feces form during digestion, so it's imperative that agni, the digestive fire, works optimally. Ayurveda sees a connection between sweat and urination, which are both pitta related and reduce water content in the body. Modern Ayurvedic physicians believe diabetes, dropsy, and skin diseases such as psoriasis result from an accumulation of pitta in the skin, causing it to be out of balance with the kidneys.

THE SEVEN DHATUS The *dhatus* loosely correspond to the body's tissues and fluids. They are responsible for the entire structure of the body.

The order of the dhatus is especially important. The health of a particular dhatu depends on the health of the previous one since each dhatu is formed and receives its nourishment from the one before it. Here are the dhatus in serial order:

1. *Rasa—plasma and lymph.* Sanskrit for "sap" or "juice," rasa includes tissue fluids, chyle, lymph, and plasma and contains all the nutrients from digested food. Rasa, which circulates through the body with the help of the vata dosha, serves to nourish all tissues, organs, and systems in the body. Governed by kapha, rasa's byproducts include menstruation blood and breast milk. Rasa flows from the heart through 24 ducts—10 going up, 10 going down, and 4 going sideways—feeding the whole body. It takes five days to convert rasa into blood and a month to transmute it into sperm or ova.

2. *Rakta—blood.* More than just the blood that flows through the body, rakta, which comes from rasa, serves to invigorate the system and maintain life. Its action is governed by pitta. Ancient Ayurvedic physiology believed that a disruption of pitta, therefore, spoils the blood and makes it black, blue, frothy, green, too slow or too fast, and toxic.

3. *Mamsa—muscle and flesh.* Including all the muscle tissue, tendons, and flesh that cover the body's organs, mamsa functions to stabilize the system. Connected with the element earth and the kapha

The Seven Dhatus

Dhatus	Balanced	Excessive	Deficient
Rasa	glowing, healthy skin; clear, focused mind; vitality	aches, pains, and heaviness; increased saliva	heart arrhythmias
Rakta	healthy nails, lips, tongue, ears, hands, feet, genitals	red, swollen eyes; skin rashes; jaundice; poor digestion	dry, rough skin; pale, wan, cold complexion
Mamsa	strength, stability	lethargy, fatty tissue	weakness in muscles; sense of fearfulness
Meda	healthy glow, compassion, honesty	upper respiratory problems; fatty tissue around breasts and middle	cracking of joints; sagging middle or face
Asthi	strong bones, joints, and skull; optimism	protruding teeth, bony prominence of skull and joints	stiff, painful joints; brittle nails and teeth
Majjan	strong voice, supple body	chronic bone pain, fatigue	joint pains, fragile bones
Shukra	good sexual desires, fertility, and physical/spiritual energy	oversexed, heavier menses, spontaneous lactation	impotence, irregular menses, chronic fatigue

dosha, mamsa controls the movement of the joints and maintains the body's strength. Mamsa is simply blood heated by agni (fire) and condensed by vata (the bodily winds).

4. Meda—fat. Oily and kapha (water and earth) by nature, fat works to "oil" the system and keep the tissues lubricated. Meda is mamsa (or flesh) further transformed and deposited under the skin and under the belly.

5. Asthi—bone. This dhatu gives support to the whole system and includes bone and cartilage. Governed by air and earth, asthi is meda (fat) heated by the natural fires (agni) and dried by the bodily winds (vata) until it hardens.

6. Majjan—marrow and nerve tissue. The bone marrow is what the ancient texts referred to as the "oily perspiration of the bones," and includes red and yellow marrow. This "oily perspiration" congeals to fill in the spaces between the bones. Majjan also carries motor and sensory impulses to the brain.

7. Shukra—reproductive. According to Ayurveda, shukra originates from the bone marrow and contains the ingredients of all tissues. Concentrated in the reproductive organs, shukra includes male and female sexual fluids and governs reproduction and immune functions. Shukra comes from the bone marrow and produces the essence Ayurveda calls *ojas*—a substance difficult to translate, but loosely described as vitality or bodily strength (see page 208).

THE SROTAS The physical body produces nutrients it must transport to its various tissue sites and waste products it has to expel. To do this, it needs avenues to transport them all. These avenues or channels are called *srotas*. There are 13 of them: big channels with large passageways (large and small intestines and the uterus, for example); small channels with narrow passageways (blood vessels); and subtle channels that don't appear to have any physical opening but that allow for transportation anyway (nerves). Improper flow as well as excessive buildup of doshas in any of these channels causes disease.

The Picture of Health Good health means that the entire body is working efficiently. The mind discriminates effectively when the three gunas of balance, energy, and inertia (sattva, rajas, tamas) are in equilibrium. The body is healthy when

- the digestive fire (agni) is burning properly
- the three doshas are working together optimally
- the seven dhatus are functioning properly
- the 13 srotas are open and flowing properly
- the three malas—urine, feces, and sweat—are efficiently eliminated

In other words, everything must function in harmony. When everything is in tune, the immune system can then offer natural resistance even to contagious diseases, and a person's mental and emotional health will be strong.

Shri Dhanvantari, an incarnation of Lord Vishnu, symbolizes divine consciousness and has come to epitomize the healing tradition of Ayurveda. Often found at Ayurvedic clinics and schools, this statue represents the spiritual side of healing.

Classification of Disease

The earliest Ayurvedic texts identify disease in terms of an eight-fold classification system. The Buddhists attributed four of the eight causes to doshic disruption (vata, pitta, kapha, and a combination of the three). The other four causes included changes of season, stressful or unusual activities, violent or traumatic events, and past actions (karma). But Ayurvedic medicine divides the eight-limbed system into three broader categories. *Adhyatmika* takes into account the four doshic imbalances and karma; *adhibhautika* includes stressful activities and violent events; *adhidaivika* includes the change of seasons and supernatural causes. Although adhidaivika is somewhat contrary to early Buddhist medical doctrine, it reflects early Ayurveda's unwillingness to let go of the magical and religious causes of disease completely.

Ayurveda equates all disease with doshic disruption, without negating the age-old premise that disease stems from internal, external, and unexplained causes. It simply says that everything in the universe has doshic properties. These properties and the way in which a person interacts with his or her environment can affect health: the food eaten, attitudes held, the people associated with, the time of year, and even the time of day. In other words, a person's internal environment constantly interacts with the environment around him. When the two are out of balance, a person gets sick.

Internal Factors Weak digestive agni prevents food from being broken down properly, causing it to remain in the system. This undigested or improperly digested mass accumulates in the srotas, blocks them, and putrefies into a sticky substance called *ama*. Ama is basically made up of undigested or improperly digested food and any external toxins the body cannot expel. Ayurveda considers the accumulation of ama to be one of the major causes of disease.

Ojas

The Ayurvedic concept of ojas is very hard to define. It's not a physical substance, and it cannot be measured by instruments. What comes closest to it in the West would be vitality or vigor. Governed by kapha, ojas is fluid—cool, transparent, and white or pinkish in color. According to the *Caraka Samhita*, an abundance of ojas can only be produced by a true *brahmacarin*—one who abstains from sexual activity (usually a prepubescent boy). Too much physical exercise, pain, grief, anxiety, anger, hunger, overwork, or loss of blood or semen, all contribute to a loss of ojas in the body. Eating foods like milk, ghee, or special tonic herbs or engaging in meditation or yoga practice will help replenish ojas.

Symptoms of ama accumulation are a coated tongue, bad breath, headaches, body odor, and a general feeling of heaviness or dullness. Ama affects the entire body. Not having been broken down properly, ama is thick and dense, so it ends up clogging the channels, preventing them from contributing to the formation of the subsequent channels.

Diseases from ama accumulation vary according to the three doshas. This is to say, an Ayurvedic physician must take into account which dosha-ama is dominant so as to determine how to treat the resultant disease. A kapha-ama (or toxic water) condition, for example, will manifest as indigestion and congestion with thick mucus that is difficult to expel. A pitta-ama (toxic fire) condition also manifests as indigestion with the addition of fever and diarrhea. Vata-ama (toxic air) conditions bring indigestion, bloating, constipation, gas, and arthritis.

Another internal factor can be depleted ojas. Ojas—the essential energy produced by the seventh dhatu—gives vitality and health to the body and mind. When ojas is reduced, disease follows. Diseases that stem from low ojas generally are difficult to cure and include most infectious and nervous disorders. (Today's Ayurvedic physicians see HIV and AIDS, hepatitis, premature aging, and chronic fatigue as prime examples of ojas-related conditions.)

Lord Shiva, a later incarnation of the earlier Vedic god Rudra, sits atop his bull and shoots his famous bow.

Negative or repressed emotions, according to Ayurveda, can also contribute to ill health. All emotions (present or the results of past karma) remain imprinted in our muscles and certain organs and correspond to particular doshas. Repressed anger, for example, aggravates pitta, changing the balance of the gallbladder, bile duct, and small intestines. Ayurveda recommends that emotions never be held inside (see "Conditions Caused by Suppression of Natural Urges," page 211).

EXTERNAL FACTORS The most common external factors affecting health are diet, environmental toxins, and lifestyle stress. Ayurveda also understands that the passage of time affects the body's ability to stay balanced. Eating at the right time, going to bed by a certain hour, pacifying the body at the right month of the year, all have beneficial effects on a person's health.

Dietary Factors. There's a Western adage that aptly describes the Ayurvedic understanding of food: "You are what you eat." What a person puts into his or her body and how the body responds to and digests it can adversely or positively affect health. Certain foods aggravate certain doshas. For example, popcorn, which is dry and full of air, doesn't digest well in a person whose vata is out of balance. It can cause bloating and excess gas. Kaphas who feel sluggish and possessive should stay away from kapha foods such as ice cream, avocados, or winter squash. Pittas, especially in the heat of the summer, should refrain from adding hot chili peppers or onions to their food.

Planetary Influences. The ancient healers believed that the planets and other heavenly spheres influenced the body and, particularly, the mind of human beings. Physicians sometimes asked the patient to have his or her astrologic chart read, or they would interpret his or her dreams to pinpoint the exact cause and placement of the disease.

Biological Time. Childhood, adulthood, and old age are all ruled internally by the doshas. Kapha governs the first 16 years of life. During infancy, a child depends on her mother's milk for sustenance; later childhood years are marked with kaphalike diseases: colds, flu, congestion, and ear infections. Throughout these years, children are growing and developing strong tissues, and their bodies need constant nourishment. Adulthood lasts until age 55 and is governed by pitta. These are the most active, vital years of a person's life, a time when the body needs stability. When pitta is out of control, teenagers tend to suffer from acne (strong pitta) and older adults are plagued with digestive disorders. Vata controls the later years, of a person's life 56 and older or, for a woman, when she enters menopause. This is the time when metabo-

Time and the Doshas

A person's doshic makeup changes with age, season, and time of day. Although not a rigid rule—just because it's summer, for example, not everyone is dominated by pitta—doshas do increase during their corresponding period.

Dosha	Biological Time	Chronological Time	Season
kapha	infancy to 16 years	6 A.M.–10 A.M. 6 P.M.–10 P.M.	winter/ early spring
pitta	17 years to 55 years	10 A.M.–2 P.M. 10 P.M.–2 A.M.	late spring/ summer
vata	56 years to end of life	2 P.M.–6 P.M. 2 A.M.–6 A.M.	fall/ early winter

lism slows and the tissues are not replenished as readily. Vata disorders in old age include arthritis, poor memory, tremors, and wrinkles.

Chronologic Time. The doshas also govern chronologic time. Early morning belongs to kapha. It's a time of awakening, stretching, and beginning the day. A person may feel somewhat heavy, slower than other times during the day, but fresh and alert. Midday is pitta time—when the digestive juices start flowing and a person gets hungriest. This is the time of day when Ayurvedic practitioners would recommend having the main meal of the day, when the digestive agni is at its peak. In the afternoon, vata takes over. This is the time of activity and high energy. In the evening, kapha comes back. This, according to Ayurveda, is the time to slow down, relax, and prepare for sleep. Pitta kicks in again around 10 P.M. and works to digest the day's food until 2 A.M. when vata resurfaces. Vata time—between 2 A.M. and 6 A.M.—is the time for dreaming and beginning the process of awakening. Ayurveda believes a person should wake up before 6 A.M. when vata is still active so that he or she can arise refreshed and energized, and so that elimination of waste products will happen easily.

Seasonal Time. Knowing the aspects of the three doshas, it's easy to see how they are related to the seasons of the year. The autumn months through early winter—a time of windy days, the dropping of leaves, falling temperatures—are a vata time, the air dosha. With winter in full swing, plant life dies, animals migrate to warmer climes or hibernate, and people come down with colds and other upper respiratory ailments. This is the time of kapha, ruler of the lungs and the dosha of water and earth. The transition between winter and spring still sees the influence of kapha as the effects of winter begin to thaw—snow melts, the earth softens, animals give birth. As the earth and air heat up, pitta takes over. Late spring and summer bring a host of pitta-induced ailments like rashes, diarrhea, allergies, and sunburns.

Diagnosing Disease

Diagnosis takes on a much different meaning in Ayurveda than it does in Western medicine. Western physicians seek to identify disease after it produces symptoms; Ayurvedic doctors prefer to monitor the body before illness is manifest. They pay attention to the interaction between wellness and illness, between order and disorder. This way, when an imbalance occurs in the body, the doctor can more easily detect its nature and administer the proper treatment.

OBSERVATION For thousands of years, Ayurvedic healers have relied on their keen powers of observation and their knowledge of the interactions of micro- and macroanatomy to diagnose disharmony in the body. Through an elaborate interview process, urine and feces analysis, and observation of the tongue, skin, eyes, nails, and other physical features, Ayurvedic doctors can determine which doshas, tissues, channels, and organs are affected. To find the disturbed dosha, a physician needs to establish the patient's individual prakriti (constitution). Like any good doctor anywhere, an Ayurvedic physician takes into account a patient's mental and emotional condition as well as the physical.

When diagnosing an illness, according to the *Caraka Samhita*, a physician must take into account the following items:

- patient's condition
- family background
- heredity and caste (social class)
- climate, food, and water in the country of the patient's birth
- character and temperament
- physical constitution
- whether the disease is hot or cold

The *Caraka Samhita* also specifies the proper physical examination, which should include

- general appearance of the patient
- the feel of the patient's skin (checking temperature)
- examination of eyes, tongue, feces, and urine
- tasting the secretions of the patient, when appropriate

An Ayurvedic physician observes the body with care. This ancient diagnostic tool is still relied on by physicians to give them the information they need. For instance, noticing that a person's skin is rough, cracked, or chapped, a physician could ascertain a vata imbalance. If a patient is hot to the touch and flush of face, a physician would diagnose a pitta imbalance; a pale, drawn complexion of a patient who feels cold would indicate aggravated kapha.

Face. A physician can tell a lot from a face. Ayurveda teaches that emotions can lodge in the tissues, most evidently in the face. Worry lines, bags under the eyes, and cheek discoloration all indicate general constitution as well as emotional state.

Conditions Caused by Suppression of Natural Urges

Suppressing biological urges also contributes to disease formation. The *Caraka Samhita* lists 13 different biological urges and the problems that ensue when any one of these urges is habitually suppressed. Treatment involves expressing the urges appropriately and pacifying vata through diet and lifestyle changes.

Urge	**Problems Resulting from Suppression**
vomiting	nausea, itching, rashes, skin disorders, anorexia
sneezing	migraine headache, facial twitching, stiff neck, impaired sense organs
tears	inflammation of nasal passages, eye disorders, giddiness
sleep	body aches and pains, heavy eyes, yawning, nervousness
thirst	dry throat and mouth, depression, heart pain, hearing loss
hunger	weakness, body aches and pains, poor complexion, anorexia
defecation	cramps in abdomen and legs, colic, headache, flatulence
urination	headache; stiff groin; pain in the bladder, urethra, and kidneys
flatulence	pain in abdomen, more flatulence, exhaustion
ejaculation of semen	pain in penis and scrotum, obstruction of urine, body aches
breathing after exercise	fainting and heart irregularities
burping	hiccups, shortness of breath, nervous twitching
yawning	convulsions, numbness

Eyes. The eyes are also good indicators of health and well-being. The eyes may be the windows to the soul, but they also provide another diagnostic tool for physical illness. The condition and coloration of the eyes, as well as any abnormalities, are indicative of a variety of problems.

Tongue. The doctor observes the size, shape, color, and contour of the tongue. If the tongue has a white coating on it, toxins may be present. If the tongue's coloring is pale, the patient could be anemic; a yellowish color indicates problems in the liver or gallbladder; a bluish cast points to heart problems.

Lips and Nails. The condition of both the lips and the nails can also help a physician ascertain an imbalance in the patient. Like the tongue, the physician pays attention to color and size. However, general appearance and consistency can be equally informative. A nutrient deficiency will cause white spots on nails; ridges indicate malabsorption, and, of course, bitten or torn nails can show that the patient is nervous or anxious.

PULSE DIAGNOSIS Most Westerners are familiar with checking their pulses by putting their two fingers against the pressure points on either side of their wrists or throat. Persian healers probably introduced a much more elaborate system of pulse reading to Ayurveda around the 14th century. Physicians learned to read the pulses on the nose, neck, armpit, inner arm above the elbow, wrist, groin, and ankle to determine the strength or weakness of the pulse, its character, and the number of beats per minute. Pulse readings inform the practitioner as to disruptions of the doshas and even the presence or diminution of ojas, that untranslatable term we call life force, energy, or vitality.

URINE EXAMINATION Like pulse diagnosis, urine examination as a diagnostic tool probably did not arrive in Ayurvedic circles until the 13th or 14th centuries. Color, clarity, consistency, and odor can

Outside Influences

Despite the fact that Ayurveda already had such diverse contributors, it was also open to input from still more sources. Other traditions that influenced Ayurveda include Persian (Unani) medicine and quite possibly Greco-Roman medicine and classical Chinese medicine.

The Persian wandering physicians probably contributed several remedies to the Ayurvedic arsenal. Pulse examination could have come from the Persians—but not until much later. In fact, Ayurvedic physicians did not really embrace that particular diagnostic tool until around the 14th century A.D. Classifying diseases into hot and cold and treating them with opposite medicines and diet (hot diseases need cold foods and cold drugs; cold ailments need heat) quite possibly came from either the Persian (Unani) or Greek healers, but it was not used in India until the 14th century either.

Some scholars speculate that the tri-dosha classification system (vata, pitta, kapha) may have evolved from a similar Greek theory of the four humors (blood, phlegm, yellow bile, and black bile), though no one really knows for sure.

It is almost certain that Indian medicine had an influence on the development of Chinese medicine. Chinese wandering healers almost certainly traded their secrets with the healers of India. Some of the Chinese influence may have resulted in the belief in alchemy (the discovery of a universal cure for disease) and the use of elixirs for prolonging life.

indicate of doshic imbalances. Sometimes, the physician puts a drop of sesame oil into the urine sample and holds it up to the sunlight for inspection. If the drop diffuses quickly, the disease is easy to cure; if the drop sinks to the middle of the urine, the illness is more serious and difficult to cure; if the drop sinks all the way to the bottom, the disease is very difficult to treat.

A physician can also tell from the urine sample what type of imbalance a patient suffers from. If the drop of sesame oil spreads in wavy patterns like a snake, too much vata is present; if the drop breaks up into colors like a rainbow pattern, pitta is indicated; if the oil drops like a pearl, it suggests a kapha imbalance.

Treatments

Since all disease stems from a disruption in the doshas, treatment must begin to return the body to a state of doshic harmony. Ayurvedic physicians use diet, herbs, and cleansing techniques to counteract the manifestation of disease in the body.

Ayurveda believes it is vital to eliminate the toxins that are causing the disease before attempting to pacify or temper the body. The reasons are simple: First, if a doctor prescribes a treatment that merely attends to the superficial symptoms of an ailment, the disease may go further into the tissues and move away from the treatment. So while the symptoms may get better temporarily, in the long run the disease will manifest elsewhere in the body, causing further debilitating symptoms. Second, an accumulation of undigested foods or toxins (ama) prevents the body from absorbing the herbs and foods designed to treat the disease.

There were and are several primary means of treatment to prepare or tone the body. To eliminate disease from the tissues, Ayurveda uses a two-step approach: palliation and purification. In a way, palliation therapy is similar to the Western-style approach called detoxification and cleansing. Purification therapy, however, goes beyond the Western understanding of elimination. Ayurveda believes no treatment can successfully eliminate the toxic wastes from the body without first directing these toxins to their proper channels of elimination. If disease manifests in the body because of an imbalance in the gastrointestinal tract (the first stage of disease), an Ayurvedic physician will almost always perform purification therapy. If the disease has already entered the tissues, however, palliation techniques must precede purification.

PALLIATION Palliation means "to pacify." The herbs administered during this phase attempt to break up the toxins and calm the doshas enough to expel the excesses when purification therapy begins. The *Ashtanga Hridaya Samhita*, an Ayurvedic text from around the 7th century A.D., explains how palliation therapy uses "herbs to burn up toxins, herbs to stimulate digestion, fasts, and exercise" to strengthen agni, the digestive fire, which in turn destroys the toxins.

Also called *purvakarma* and sometimes alleviation therapy, this treatment program can be administered by a doctor or sometimes by the sick person him- or herself. To loosen toxins and cleanse the body, the physician would use honey, clarified butter (ghee), long pepper (if the patient can't tolerate ghee), or sesame or castor oil.

Palliative Therapy

Although palliative therapy can last from one week to a few months, one example of a short-term pitta-eliminating palliative therapy would be:

Day One: Take one tablespoon of ghee first thing in the morning followed by a cup of warm water. Drink several cups of warm water throughout the day. Eat lighter meals than normal.

Day Two: Take three tablespoons of ghee upon rising; drink several cups of warm water throughout the day. Eat lighter meals than normal.

Day Three: Take six tablespoons of ghee in the morning; drink several cups of warm water throughout the day. Eat lighter meals than normal.

Day Four: Take nine tablespoons of ghee in the morning; drink several cups of warm water throughout the day. Eat lighter meals than normal.

Day Five: Do not take any additional ghee. Drink warm water throughout the day. Eat light, preferably vegetarian meals.

Day Six: Take several capsules of senna leaf as a laxative. Do not eat any food until most of the cleansing has subsided.

Honey works to eliminate excess kapha; ghee, long pepper, or castor oil gets rid of pitta; and sesame oil eliminates vata. Purvakarma has to begin about five days to a week before purification therapy. Other palliative therapies include massage and heat, which are external treatments to cause the patient to relax or sweat.

PURIFICATION THERAPY Purification therapy, or *panchakarma*, includes a five-step approach to healing. According to the *Ashtanga Hridaya Samhita*, "cleansing enemas, nasal medication, purgation, vomiting, and blood-letting," were the five methods of purification. These five actions were designed to rid the body completely and finally of the excessive doshas and ama causing an acute disease. If a patient is in a weakened condition, usually a physician modifies the panchakarma therapy, often leaving out the more severe methods.

Therapeutic Vomiting (vanuna). Generally the patient drinks three or four cups of a strong tea made from licorice root, salt, calmus root, or lobelia. If that doesn't do the trick, a couple glasses of salt water first thing in the morning should. Physicians never prescribe vomiting for those who are weak, too old, too young, or who suffer from a hacking, dry cough.

Purgation Therapy (virecana). This therapy is used to rid the body of excess pitta from the small intestines, colon, kidneys, liver, and gallbladder. Purgation, or laxative, therapy treats constipation, diarrhea, dysentery, and food poisoning. Lots of different herbs are used as mild laxatives: castor oil, senna leaf, dandelion root, psyllium seed, cascara sagrada, and flaxseed husks.

Enema Therapy (basti). Enemas are used to rid the body of excess vata. Castor oil is sometimes used, but dry enemas are sometimes used with it in an alternating fashion.

Nasal Therapy (nasya). Ayurvedic physicians swear by nasal application of herbs, and it is mentioned often in the ancient texts. It works well for sinus conditions, dry coughs, scratchy throats, migraine headaches, and feelings of nervousness, anxiety, and fear. The physician places a few drops of herbal oil on his or her finger and inserts it as far into the nose as possible. Then the physician massages the nose, helping the medicated oil to reach far into the passages. The use of a *neti* pot is another form of nasal therapy. It involves pouring warm, salted water up one nostril and out the other.

This type of nasal therapy, or nasya, involves filling a neti pot with warm, salted water. The water is then poured into the right nostril and allowed to pour out the left. This ancient practice is still used today for relief of colds and sinus infections.

Bloodletting (raktamokshana). Although not popular in the West, bloodletting is an ancient form of Ayurvedic treatment employing leeches to purify the blood. A gentler, effective method of purifying the blood is burdock root tea. A patient begins by clearing out the system with a gentle laxative. For the next two to three months, the patient then drinks burdock root tea every evening, allowing the action of the herb to purify and tonify the blood.

DIET Besides prescribing purvakarma and panchakarma treatments, an Ayurvedic doctor takes care to monitor a patient's diet. There would be no use in going through an intensive series of elimination and tonifying treatments if the patient plans to return to a poor diet and an unhealthy lifestyle. All

A powerful blood-purifying herb that helps rid the body of excess toxins, saffron requires labor-intensive harvest of its delicate threads. Here a whole family chips in to collect the stamens before the bees get there first.

foods (and medicines) affect the doshic makeup of the individual, and it is critical to eat the foods that do not promote or exacerbate a doshic imbalance. For example, a person suffering from excess vata may feel dry, cold, nervous, and agitated. To eat foods that are also dry, cold, or bitter would only exacerbate the situation. So a physician would prescribe vata-suppressing foods such as seaweeds (formed from fire and water) that clean out the tissues or would prescribe sour foods such as miso and lemons that would aid digestion.

Physicians classify foods by taste (*rasa*), by potency (*virya*), by qualities or attributes (*guna*), and by aftertaste (*vipaka*). One popular Ayurvedic method of classifying food and medicine is by how they taste on the tongue: sweet, sour, bitter, pungent, salty, or astringent. Like the doshas, each taste, or rasa, corresponds to two of the five gross elements: Sweet comprises earth and water; sour is a combination of earth and fire; bitter combines air and ether; pungent comprises fire and air; salty combines water and fire; and astringent brings together earth and air.

With the understanding that "like increases like," it's easy to see how a physician would need to know the qualities of any medicine he or she would want to prescribe. A pitta imbalance, for example, may bring on an ulcer, result in excessive sweating, or create acidic urine, all of which point to too much heat in the body. The medicine prescribed would need to be cooling, dry, heavy, and dull (the opposite of pitta) to be effective.

PREPARATION OF MEDICINES Once the doctor determines the medical problem and its characteristics and attributes, it is time to choose and prepare the medicines for use. For the physician to use a medicine, it must pass several tests:

- Does it cure more than one disease?
- Will it treat the disease both at its site of origin and at the site of manifestation?
- Can it prevent the disease from spreading any further?
- Can it be prepared in several ways to accommodate the patient's needs?
- Will it produce any adverse side effects?

Botanical-based Medicines. There are several ways to prepare the hundreds of botanicals Ayurveda uses as medicines, such as the following:

- Extractions are juice or sap extracted from plant parts.
- Infusions are plant parts or herbs steeped in boiling water.
- Decoctions are plants or herbs simmered in water until the water is reduced and the plant part softened. (Decoctions can be quite bitter and were often sweetened with honey after they cooled or combined with ghee or oils to make them more palatable.)
- Powders, or *churnas*, are pulverized dried plant parts or herbs.
- Pastes, plasters, or oils are made from plant or herbal extracts, similar to the powders with the addition of a liquid. These were especially useful for external injuries such as sprains, broken bones, or joint problems.
- Herbally infused oils—sesame, coconut, sunflower, or olive—are used for enemas, massages, or dry or itchy scalp conditions.
- Pills or suppositories are herbs or plant extracts usually ground up and inserted into vegetable-based capsules or suppositories for internal use.

- Boluses are pulverized herbs or plant parts placed in a muslin sack, dipped in very warm water or milk, and rubbed over the body. (These are used in some panchakarma treatments.)
- Alcoholic extracts are herbs boiled then distilled or simply added to the alcohol.

A common herb in Ayurvedic healing, cinnamon acts as a stimulant, giving heat to the body. According to Ayurvedic physicians, it is beneficial for vata and kapha disorders, but too warming for pitta. Cinnamon aids digestion by increasing the digestive power of agni, and it relieves congestion in the lungs.

Mineral-based Medicines. The use of minerals and metals is almost as old as Ayurveda itself. At least four types of medicines were prepared this way. The first are called *sublimates*, which are medicines made by sublimating sulphur (taking it from its solid state to a vapor quickly) in a glass container. The second group are called *bhasmas*, which are ash residues from metals, gems, plants, and animal by-products. Mercury is the most common bhasma and contributes to the increase of red blood cells. The third group, called *pishtis*, combine pulverized gems with juices and extracts. The fourth group of mineral-based medicines, *collyrium*, is the residue of antimony powder, lead oxide, or lamp soot mixed with castor oil and used to improve eyesight.

Tonics. After treating a particular ailment, a physician would often recommend tonics, or *rasayanas*, to keep the body functioning optimally. Rasayanas are herbal elixirs or tonics used to tone and strengthen the body's tissues and keep the doshas in balance. They promote longevity and youthfulness, two important goals of health in Ayurveda.

Surgery

Surgical procedures were not foreign to Ayurvedic practitioners even in ancient times. Indeed, one of the two great *Samhitas* is a surgical text. The *Susruta Samhita* describes many types of surgery for tumors, bone fractures, dental problems, and eye diseases, among other conditions.

Some of the techniques were not uncommon in other parts of the ancient world—cautery, bloodletting, cupping—but some were well ahead of their time. Grafting of tissue was used to repair wounds and congenital defects. Susruta discusses the surgical repair of ears and noses damaged by accident or as a form of punishment. This type of advanced plastic surgery was not developed in the rest of the world for centuries.

Patient care before, during, and after the operation was not neglected. Preparatory measures—actually a form of *purvakarma*—included waiting for the astrologically auspicious moment and ensuring the proper deities were honored and all the surgical instruments were clean and within reach. During the surgical treatment (*pradhanakarma*), cold water sprayed on the face was used for the patient's pain, and the surgeon was instructed to move swiftly and surely so as not to prolong the procedure. Postoperative care (*pashcatkarma*) included such familiar modern procedures as observation in a special nursing chamber (a recovery room) and frequently changed wound dressings.

Susruta on Baldness

Among the many surgical treatments for various conditions, the *Susruta Samhita* includes a treatment for total baldness. According to Susruta, baldness can be cured by this relatively simple procedure:

- Scrape the surface of the scalp until bleeding occurs.
- Cover the area with a paste made of gunja seeds (*Abrus precatorius*) until it heals.
- When fine hairs reach the surface, massage regularly with oil made of karavira (*Nerium odorum*), malati (*Aganosma caryophyllata*), agni (*Plumbago zeylanica*), and naktamala (*Pongamia glabra*).

The surgeons were acutely aware of the dangers of such procedures. Susruta carefully instructs the surgeon to keep instruments clean and sharp and even to apply alcoholic liquids to the incision site (despite the fact that they had no knowledge of microorganisms). Certain mortal points, or *marmans*, were to be avoided at all costs; these 107 marmans were areas where veins, arteries, or nerve bundles were particularly vulnerable to damage, with very serious repercussions. Wounds were constantly monitored for postoperative infections, and many poultices and other medicines were used to prevent them.

Lifestyles and Wellness

Ayurveda firmly believes in preventative health care. Many physicians advocate panchakarma (purification) treatments at the change of each season, but certainly in the springtime. This helps clean out the system and prepare the body for the new season. They will caution that their patients pay particular attention to their diet and their daily routine, taking care to listen to their body's needs. Ayurvedic recommendations act as a reminder to stay in sync with the rhythms of the external world, which is also governed by the five gross elements—ether, air, fire, water, and earth—and, in turn, relate to the three doshas—vata, pitta, and kapha. Only by maintaining this balance can we maintain health. If the biological balance is upset, Ayurveda can restore doshic harmony. Knowledge of the causes of illness, how it is manifested in the humors, and the tissues and pathways affected are crucial to maintaining this equilibrium.

An Evolving Medical System

Ayurvedic medicine has existed in different forms and stages of development, evolving over centuries not merely as a healing method, but as a school of thought on medical science. It is a set of principles that can be used as a method of studying human anatomy and biology. As a means of maintaining and restoring health, Ayurveda has developed into what is today a sophisticated philosophy, combining an understanding of physiology with remedial diet and treatments. For these contributions, Ayurveda will doubtless continue in its evolution as both a scientific school of thought on physiology and a discipline for daily health for centuries to come.

Yoga

Most Westerners' conception of yoga is of people meditating in the traditional lotus position and reciting a mantra. While this image is not entirely incorrect—yoga does involve meditation, poses, and sometimes mantras—it is a rather limited picture. Yoga is much more.

Although yoga is not a "healing" system like Ayurveda or traditional Chinese medicine, it strongly encourages and promotes the good health of its practitioners for higher purposes. To combine and advance body, mind, and spirit, humans need health, enlightenment, and inner peace. To this end, yoga uses a psychological and physiologic system to gain control of and exercise both the body and mind, thereby freeing the spirit.

Lord Krishna bends down to paint the toenails of his beloved Radha. Krishna was known to captivate the attention of many women and it is said that, although Radha was his favorite, he had 16,108 wives and 108,000 sons during his lifetime.

Yoga sees health as a state of bodily harmony that cannot be taken for granted and, as such, demands serious discipline. Falling ill usually denotes a false relationship to one's life and to other people. Feeling ill at ease or alienated from society contributes to creating disease in the body. To return to good health, a yogin must return to a moral and happy life, understanding his or her interconnectedness to all beings. And it cannot be denied that yogic disciplines impart great health benefits to its practitioners.

A Long Development

From ancient times the practice of yoga has sought to deliver its practitioners from the cycle of birth, death, and rebirth that characterizes many Indian worldviews and lead them toward self-realization and ultimate liberation. To attain enlightenment, the yogin (male) or yogini (female) had to strive to keep the body as healthy and as strong as possible through a successive series of techniques, which include postures, breathing, and meditation or contemplation.

ROOTS IN THE INDUS VALLEY Yoga's rich history begins in India perhaps as early as 2000 B.C. Although yoga did not develop as a codified system of philosophy until around the 2nd century A.D., there's evidence of yogic postures dating back to the Harappan culture of the Indus Valley.

Unfortunately, the language of the Indus people is still undeciphered, and we do not know how they used these postures. However, we do have examples of some of their seal engravings that show men and gods in traditional yogic postures such as the lotus position. Some seals depicted animals or human figures. One famous seal shows a yogin in meditation pose with a trident behind his head (an important symbol of yogic transcendence). Another figure, a male yogin or fertility god adorned with a horned animal mask, sits surrounded by a number of wild animals. The figure is nude and has his legs drawn up close to his body with his heels touching—a familiar pose used even today.

This 15th-century sculpture depicts Narasimha-Vishnu as a fierce man-lion, protector of humankind. Seated in lotus posture, this horned god epitomizes the devotional aspects of yoga.

YOGA AND THE VEDAS The earliest form of yoga practice appeared in the *Rgveda*, the oldest of the ancient Vedas, dating back to about 1500 B.C. The Vedas are the original scriptures of the Brahmanic people of India who succeeded the Harappans (see page 190). The *Atharvaveda*, the Vedic book of magic spells and incantations, mentions a group of men called *vratyas*, who were possibly fertility priests whose unorthodox ways also made them outcastes among the Brahmans. These vratyas probably used *pranayama*, or breath control—one of the eight steps of the later, Classical Patañjali yoga tradition (see page 223)—which they used in conjunction with the singing of songs they composed and performed.

THE YOGA OF THE UPANISHADS Yogic techniques appear many times in the *Upanishads*, treatises that date back to between 800 and 500 B.C. The authors of these mystical teachings believed that liberation came through knowledge. The word *Upanishad* comes from the root *upa* meaning "near," *ni* which means "down," and *sad* meaning "to sit." This refers to the way in which the Upanishads were taught. The student sat down near his or her teacher, or *guru*, who, in turn, imparted the secret doctrines of these texts.

Definitions of Yoga

The word yoga comes from the Sanskrit root *yuj*, which means to "yoke," "harness," or "bind together." Other connotations include "union," "team," or "spiritual endeavor." The first mention of the word appears in the *Taittiriya Upanishad*—a sacred text dating from around 700 B.C. In it, yoga refers to both getting the senses under control (to control desires) and releasing the bonds that unite the spirit to the material world.

The *Yoga Sutra*—the first systemization of yogic practice, written sometime in the 2nd century A.D.—evokes the same concept from a different metaphorical approach: "Yoga is the stopping of the movement of the mind."

The truth of the Upanishads destroyed ignorance and helped the pupil attain spiritual liberation.

According to the Upanishads, unhappiness and even illness come from desire and the false understanding that one's self is separate from the universal self, or Brahman. In these texts, yoga provides a practical method of harnessing the senses and the mind, releasing them from the power of transient thoughts and desires and creating a unity with the universal Brahman.

The Importance of a Guru Yoga requires guidance from a teacher, or guru. During the Upanishadic Age (800–500 B.C.), yoga epitomized the mystical sacrifice inherent in the philosophical texts of the *Upanishads:* the internalization of Vedic sacrifice and ritual. Even to begin the study of yoga back then, a student had to be ready to forsake the everyday world of family and

Bathing Ceremony. Water, particularly from the River Ganges, is viewed as a special elixir, cleansing and purifying the yogin of all diseases and imperfections. This bathing can wash away the effects of past actions and bring good karma. These students stand in the river while they listen to the lessons of their guru.

work and, with the help of a guru, learn the self-discipline and self-denial—the ascetic ways—of the yogin.

A guru helped his student learn the secret knowledge of the *Upanishads* and the meditation techniques that would still the mind and hold the body steady. Sure signs that a student was on the path toward liberation included

- clearheadedness
- steadiness
- lightness of body

MYSTICAL SOUNDS Throughout the history of yoga, meditation on the sound of *Om* was probably the most popular teaching method for liberation. In the *Maitri Upanishad*, by meditating on the sound of *Om*, one enters the world of nonsound. By closing one's ears with the thumbs, one can hear the sound inside the body: the heart, the pulse, the breath. This sound is variously compared to the ringing of a bell, the rushing of a river, the croaking of a frog, or the falling of a spring rain.

During Vedic times, the primordial sound of *Om* accounted for all of creation. Much like the Christian proclamation, "In the beginning was the Word," the Vedic seers understood that the subtle vibrations of the primordial sound formed the basis for all of creation. Later, during the Upanishadic times, the primordial word *Om* came to exemplify the inner meaning of a person's actions, and speech became the vehicle by which to express the words behind those actions.

The power of the Word continues in yoga teachings today. The guru transmits instructions to his students, and in the more devotional aspects of modern-day yoga, repeating the name of a god or goddess remains the most powerful link between an individual and the divine.

In the *Upanishads*, meditation on the "mystical sounds" is equated with the practice of yoga and the attainment of liberation. The *Maitri Upanishad* states

> Whereas one thus joins breath and the syllable *Om*
> And all the manifold world...
> Therefore it has been declared to be Yoga.
> The oneness of the breath and mind,
> And likewise of the senses,
> And the relinquishment of all conditions of existence,
> This is designated as Yoga.

This *Upanishad* goes on to declare that if a yogin (or yogini) practices diligently for only six months, successfully freeing himself from all attachments to the senses and to sensory stimuli, he will realize perfect union.

The Early Philosophy of Yoga

SAMKHYA CREATION Much like the science of Ayurveda, yoga is based on Samkhya, one of the earliest of Hindu's philosophical systems; yoga added the notion of God, however, a concept not found in Samkhya. The two main categories of existence for Samkhya are *Purusha* (pure, transcendental spirit or self; male) and *Prakriti* (nature or matter; female). Purusha has no beginning and no end; it simply is. Prakriti, on the other hand, is dynamic, creative, and distinct; it is in constant motion.

Prakriti creates three distinct manifestations of itself, called *gunas*. These manifestations exist at the same time, but in differing degrees, in everything that makes

The god Vishnu lies atop the serpent Sesha in this close-up of the Temple of Vishnu in Rajasthan, India. Vishnu, an ancient Vedic god, represents the concept of preservation. His followers practice bhakti—the yoga of devotion.

up the cosmos. An understanding of the three gunas helps to explain how each relates to existence:

- *Sattva*—This guna manifests the mind and the five cognitive senses. The mind coordinates all biological and psychic activities and controls the subconscious. The cognitive senses (eyes, ears, nose, tongue, and skin) help us acquire knowledge and put us in touch with the external world.
- *Rajas*—When rajas is in control, the senses of yearning manifest: the voice, hands, feet, anus, and genitals. Rajas makes motor energy and physical experience possible. It controls passion and the activity of the body.
- *Tamas*—Tamas is darkness of consciousness. When this guna predominates, the five subtle elements appear. These are the *potentials* of sound, sight, taste, touch, and smell, which give rise to all structures.

The Cause of Delusion or Suffering

According to the Samkhya system, suffering, disease, and confusion all come from the misguided understanding that the cosmos is real. Existence is, in fact, a manifestation of imbalance, just like disease is. In other words, when one guna predominates over the others, it gives rise to the appearance of phenomena, including the senses.

If a person becomes attached to phenomena or their effects, falsely believing that what he or she sees, hears, tastes, touches, or smells exists in and of itself, he or she becomes deluded. This delusion creates further attachments and confusion and pushes the person further away from the higher self. Yogic philosophy strives to keep the gunas of mind, body, and spirit in balance and maintain equilibrium so that the practitioner can reach the higher self, seeing and knowing the truth without the false distractions of one guna or another.

Classical Yoga: Patañjali

Classical yoga of *Patañjali*, written down sometime around the 2nd century A.D. in the treatise known as the *Yoga Sutra* (but no doubt much older than that), was the first systemization of yoga. It is based on the Samkhya philosophy of creation and consciousness but goes a step further. Where Samkhya taught

Patañjali's Yoga Sutra

A collection of 195 aphorisms, or "terse statements," written in the 2nd century A.D., Patañjali's *Yoga Sutra* provided a philosophical guide for how to live in the world. Because Patañjali believed one could not attain liberation without the aid of one's guru, his aphorisms were more like shortcuts for teaching than a step-by-step guidebook.

that spiritual knowledge is all that is necessary to attain final liberation, Patañjali asserts that no one gets there through study alone. It takes hard work, in the form of ascetic practices and austere meditation, to ascend to a higher level of consciousness or cosmic understanding.

This work was not only mental but physical as well. Just because the work was difficult, however, did not mean the yogin should get agitated or strive to complete a goal at any cost. Yoga exercises were never about satisfying particular ambitions, but stemmed from a calm desire to pass over the human predicament and onto a higher plane.

This yoga also differed from Samkhya by introducing a god into the mix. Isvara was not a creator-god but rather an entity that existed for all eternity without being caught up in the illusion of being part of Nature. Like the sound of *Om*, Isvara acted as a vehicle to aid meditation and help the yogin attain liberation.

MENTAL FLUCTUATIONS: CITTAVRITTI The goal in Patañjali's *Yoga Sutra* is for the yogin to suppress his or her mental states or activity (*citta*) through a series of physical exercises and breath control designed to conquer all mental activity and physical desire. These mental states produce a series of fluctuations (*vrittis*) that impede the yogin's ability to transcend human suffering. These states include ignorance, the feeling of one's own individuality, passion, disgust, doubt, sorrow, and love of or attachment to life or the will to live. As soon as the yogin understands that the cittavritti binds him to the pain of the human condition, the cittavritti can be suppressed. However, to prevent its inevitable return, a strong and continual discipline is required. Only through the rigors of yoga, says Patañjali, can a person break this "circuit of psychic matter" and stop repeating painful actions.

THE CESSATION OF CITTAVRITTI The goal of yoga, therefore, is to stop the flow of cittavritti, or mental fluctuations. In other words, a yogin strives not to think and to stop random thoughts, sensations, memories, and words coming at him from external stimuli, as well as from his subconscious. The second thing a yogin attempts to quiet is the activity of his subconscious or the indelible imprints left behind in our subconscious through our daily experiences. According to yoga philosophy, the activity in the subconscious is responsible for propelling one's consciousness into action.

CLASSICAL YOGA'S EIGHTFOLD PATH To help stop the flow of cittavritti, the yogin learns to concentrate on a single point or object. This object can be imaginary or concrete: a point between the eyebrows, a statue or painting, a mantra, a thought, or a color. This one-pointed concentration, called *ekagrata*, prevents the yogin from allowing his mind to attach itself to every object or thought that comes along.

Ekagrata is not easy to achieve. If the body, for example, is tired or unhealthy,

Establishment of Opposites

Patañjali cites doubt as the most serious obstacle facing a beginning yogin. To erase doubt, a yogin should dwell on the opposite feeling or thought. This works for all feelings and sensations that might crop up in one's meditations. For example, if one feels hatred, one should immediately focus on love; if one is agitated, one should focus on being calm.

ekagrata is impossible to attain. Patañjali outlined a series of techniques—physical and spiritual—designed to prepare the yogin for ekagrata and ultimately for final liberation, or *samadhi*. These stages include

- *yamas* (restraints or moral observances)
- *niyamas* (disciplines or practices)
- *asanas* (postures or poses)
- *pranayama* (breath control)
- *pratyahara* (withdrawal or sensory inhibition)
- *dharana* (concentration)
- *dhyana* (meditation)
- *samadhi* (final liberation)

The first two groups—the yamas and niyamas—are the preparatory exercises every yogin must adhere to before he or she is ready to embark on a yogic path.

Yamas. Sanskrit for "restraints," the yamas are the yogic equivalents of the Ten Commandments and serve as the foundation of all spiritual discipline. Patañjali defines five yamas as follows:

- *Nonviolence* means that the yogin will abstain from harming anyone in any way, through words or actions. Nonviolence became associated with the spread of vegetarianism and nonviolent protests in India. Mahatma Gandhi was the most famous example of someone who practiced nonviolence both personally and in his political life. According to Patañjali, it was the great vow that should pervade all other actions.
- *Truthfulness* means that one should never speak with the intent of harming, deceiving, or confusing another. According to the *Yoga Sutra*, a yogin should speak only to impart the truth and to share his or her knowledge with others.
- *Nonstealing* not only means to refrain from taking anything that doesn't belong to you, but to refrain from coveting someone else's property, even in his thoughts.
- *Sexual continence*, or chastity, is another key. Any yogin who forswears sexual intercourse (even thoughts of a sexual nature) gains vital energy. A later text, the *Agni-Purana*, defines it as the "renunciation of the eight degrees of sexual activity": fantasizing, glorifying the sex act, foreplay, eyeing the opposite sex, love talk, longing, deciding to break one's vow of chastity, and making love.
- *Nongreed* came to mean in later texts giving up all your worldly possessions, but in the *Yoga Sutra* it meant one should only keep what's necessary and, more important, not become attached to the possessions. Patañjali taught that strict adherence to nongreed awarded the yogin knowledge of his past lives.

Other texts list as many as ten yamas, which include sympathy, patience, steadfastness, proper diet, living in solitude, cleanliness, devotion to the guru, moral integrity, and dispassion.

Niyamas. The second limb of Patañjali's eightfold path, niyamas are disciplines. Like the yamas, the niyamas constitute five practices.

- *Purity*, or cleanliness, taken to an extreme may lead to a repulsion toward the body—one's own and other people's. In the *Yoga Sutra*, cleansing the body meant both external and internal purification rituals. The external rituals included washing the body with water and sometimes with mud or earth; eating foods that promote lightness, clarity,

Covering his matted hair and body with ash, this Naga sadhu—a Hindu ascetic, or yogin—prepares for the Kumbha Mela festival held every 12 years in Allahabad, India. The act of smearing ashes on the body is a type of bathing ritual considered to be an important niyama, or self-discipline, in the Raja yoga tradition of Patañjali.

strength, and happiness; and purifying the organs to eliminate toxins and alimentary residues. Internal cleansing meant paying attention to one's mental impurities, too. These purification rituals took on a larger role in the later Tantric practices of Hatha yoga (see page 233).

- *Contentment*, or serenity, is defined by Patañjali as the "absence of the desire to increase the necessities of life," and says that perfecting it leads to "unexcelled joy."
- *Asceticism* has had several interpretations. Whereas some yogic traditions revile the body and define asceticism as allowing the body's desiccation, or emaciation, Patañjali's definition is more positive, teaching that asceticism leads to "perfection of the body and the senses." It leads to the transcendence of opposites or extremes and the control over oneself. A yogin who perfects the discipline of asceticism feels neither heat nor cold; the desire to sit is the same as the desire to stand; and the desire to speak is kept to a minimum lest the yogin reveal the inner secrets of the mind.
- *Study* is not just book learning or memorization. It constitutes learning from one's guru the sacred knowledge needed for self-understanding and liberation. It also includes reciting the mantra *Om*.
- *Devotion to Isvara* (God) means that the yogin desires to make God the object of all his or her actions. In exchange, Isvara bestows on the yogin a special love that aids him or her in practice.

Many other niyamas show up in later yogic texts. Some of these include mod-

This yogin, a Hindu ascetic, sits in full lotus, deep in meditation. Many perform austere practices they believe will help them attain great powers and eventually liberation.

esty, conviction, hospitality, fasting, bathing, silence, control of the penis, and following the teacher's footsteps; the more devotional disciplines include worship, pilgrimages, affirmation of the existence of the divine, and adoration in their niyamas.

Asanas. Once the student begins the practices of restraint and discipline in earnest, the real yoga techniques can begin. Asana in the *Yoga Sutra* of Patañjali refers to postures designed to give the body stability and strength and to help establish control of the physical body. Patañjali doesn't go into much detail about such postures except to say that the yogin should be able to hold the body in a particular position for long periods of time without effort. It's only when one no longer feels fatigue or pain in certain areas of the body that one can give up paying any attention to the body itself and devote oneself completely to meditation, or ekagrata.

Asanas became much more important in later yoga schools where elaborate postures were developed both to prevent disease and conquer death and to confer magical powers. For most beginners, asanas are uncomfortable and sometimes even unbearable. To further meditation, or ekagrata, yogins must perform their asanas without effort so that all movement in the body ceases and all pairs of opposites (pain and pleasure, for example) no longer bother them.

Pranayama. After a yogin has begun to perfect his asana practice, he is ready to conquer the breath. Pranayama (literally meaning "breath extension") in the *Yoga Sutra* prolongs life itself and rejuvenates the body. The goal in practicing pranayama is to calm the breath and make its rhythm as slow as possible. By concentrating on controlling the movement of the breath (retaining the breath between the inhalation and the exhalation—inhale, hold; exhale, hold), the yogin slows and ultimately steadies the movement of the mind and the senses.

Asana: The Seat of Yoga

Originally the word asana meant "seat" and referred to the type of surface the yogin sat on. This seat must be neither too high nor too low, neither too soft nor too hard. Asana also meant the cover of the seat, which was often made from grass, animal skin, wood, or cloth.

Patañjali's classical yoga does not put any emphasis on the physical postures we've come to know as yoga in the West. What he meant by *asana* was the seated pose the yogin assumes for meditation. Today that pose is called padmasana, or lotus pose. To do the pose, place your right foot on top of the left thigh and your left foot on the right thigh. Hands should rest on the top of the knees with the tips of the index fingers touching the tips of the thumbs and the other fingers outstretched. Or wrap the arms around the back and catch hold of your big toes.

The first step in learning pranayama is to perfect the three phases of breathing: inhalation, retention, and exhalation. More advanced yogins can retain the breath at will. Later yoga schools (Tantric and Hatha) believed that practicing proper pranayama techniques cured a multitude of physical ailments.

Pratyahara. This fifth stage of Patañjali's eightfold yogic path is the beginning of the path that tames the senses and the mind. The first four stages on the eightfold path prepare the yogin for the rigors of this and the next three stages. Literally meaning "withdrawal," pratyahara enables the yogin to separate his or her senses from the tangible world. This means that yogins make a conscious effort to draw their senses and attention away from the external world and become less distracted by outside stimuli. They remain keenly aware of all the senses but cultivate a feeling of detachment at the same time. Directing attention inward, yogins quiet the mind and begin to observe their minds and bodies more objectively. It's a time for them to take a look at habits that may not only be detrimental to their physical health but their spiritual pursuits as well.

Dharana. The practice of pratyahara helps the yogin to prepare for dharana, or intense concentration. The yogin has now learned to rid him- or herself of all outside distractions. Now he or she must train the mind to rid itself of all scattered thoughts and feelings. Practicing asana and pranayama helped the yogin pay attention, first to the body and then to the breath. Pratyahara helped slow activity even more, and the yogin became more focused. Now dharana allows the yogin to concentrate on a single point, that is, to practice ekagrata. As we learned earlier, that focal point can be anything: the navel, the space between the eyebrows, a flower, an image of a guru, Isvara, or a sound or phrase (mantra).

Dhyana. The ability to concentrate on a single point prepares the yogin for the next two stages. Dhyana is the uninterrupted flow of concentration, a deepening of dharana. Patañjali allows the yogin to use any object as a prop for meditation, as long as it isn't taboo or doesn't arouse the yogin (like a naked figure). Although Patañjali allows the yogin to use props, such as diagrams or images of Sanskrit symbols, the goal of dhyana should be complete quieting of the mind.

Samadhi. During samadhi, or ultimate liberation, the yogin becomes one with the point of focus and transcends the self altogether. Union of opposites becomes possible—life is no different from death,

This sadhu from Katmandu meditates in the lotus position, with his few belongings nearby. The trident at his side is an ancient symbol that represents the transcendence of the seven stages of existence.

emptiness equals abundance, subject and object merge, and being and nonbeing are the same thing.

This is a very hard concept to understand, especially for the Western mind. Basically, the yogin realizes that all entities are interconnected and the individual self returns to its primordial place in the higher self. Another way of explaining it is that the yogin understands there is no separation between the one meditating and the object of the meditation. Also the yogin is no longer troubled by external tensions and is impervious to hot and cold, light and darkness; he becomes stronger and more self-contained and able to protect himself from any outside stimuli. Consciousness becomes absorbed, and the spirit is in a state of truth and bliss.

Postclassical Yoga

The postclassical period of yoga extends from around the 2nd century A.D. through the end of the 19th century. During this time, yoga changed dramatically. The *Yoga-Upanishads*, one of the later *Upanishads*, describe the techniques of yoga, adhering pretty much to Patañjali's eightfold path: restraints, disciplines, postures, breath control, sensory withdrawal, concentration, meditation, and liberation. But they go further and are more sophisticated than Patañjali.

Most of them mention particular postures (asanas) by name; they define different schools of yoga: Mantra yoga, Laya yoga, Raja yoga, and Hatha yoga; they talk more about breathing techniques; and they glorify yogic abilities. The *Yoga-Upanishads* discuss physiology in great detail and explain how the macrocosm (the universe) is inherent in the microcosm (the body). It is during this period of yogic development that the overall health of the yogin becomes an important prerequisite to attaining enlightenment.

MANTRA YOGA Mantra yoga is a relatively late development of yoga. Reciting various mantras made up of sounds or syllables from the Sanskrit alphabet enables the yogin to attain liberation. We know from the *Rgveda* that mantras have long been invoked for their magical powers and as a means to perfect sacrificial rituals. Mantra yoga is said to be good for beginning yoga students.

LAYA YOGA Helpful for the intermediate student, Laya yoga uses hand gestures (*mudra*), pranayama, and meditation on the body (particularly the immortality of the body) to attain physical and psychological control, longevity, and ultimately liberation. Its goal is to dissolve the individual ego, or conditional mind, and absorb it into the Absolute.

RAJA YOGA Raja yoga is the so-called royal yoga outlined in Patañjali's *Yoga Sutra*. In the later *Yoga-Upanishads*, Raja yoga was compared to Hatha yoga (see page 232), which was merely the means of preparing the body for the higher spiritual practices of Raja yoga.

Tantric Yoga

By the middle of the 4th century A.D., Tantric yoga became incredibly popular. With its emphasis on the physical body, Tantra was a departure from the classical and postclassical schools of yogic meditation. Tantric philosophy was not new, however; many scholars believe its roots date back to the practices of the early Brahmanic people or even the Indus Valley culture. Tantra was always an esoteric movement, and it reached its height by the 17th century.

Rejection of the Vedas We have seen throughout Indian history a reverence for the Vedas as the sacred canon of Hinduism. By the 4th century A.D., Tantric yogins, however, believed that the Vedas were no longer relevant. They felt that humans no longer possessed the discipline necessary to follow either the Vedic teachings or the rigorous path of the ascetic yogin. In fact, Tantra was decidedly antiascetic, antispeculative, and sometimes even antimeditation. It was more important than ever to have a strong, healthy body in order to withstand the rigors of Tantric practice.

The Union of Opposites Like in most yogic traditions, Tantra teaches that primordial consciousness (Purusha) contains within itself all sets of opposites (all polarities, or dualities); it is unity. Humanity is caught up in the illusion of opposites. Becoming attached to the objects that he or she perceives as separate from the self brings suffering, delusion, and illness. The goal of the tantrika (one who practices Tantra), then, is to reunite the opposing principles in one's own body.

The Role of Sex Most yoga practice espouses abstinence and sees sexual intercourse as sapping a man of his vitality and preventing him from transforming his personality and achieving union with the Absolute. Most schools of Tantra, however, while agreeing that orgasms deplete a man's vitality, see sexual activity as a positive practice. In left-hand Tantra—the more radical approach—a man and woman can achieve samadhi, or liberation, through sexual pleasure and physical union.

Tantric Meditation Practices Before a male or female practitioner can delve into practices to attain liberation, he or she must be well-versed in the yamas and niyamas, as well as the poses and breathing practices we learned about from Patañjali's eightfold yogic path.

The first place to begin for a practitioner is with concentration and meditation on an icon of a deity. Although this seems easy enough, it isn't; it requires intense, uninterrupted concentration and a summoning of spiritual energies.

After the practitioner perfects the ability to meditate on an icon, the next step is visualization. This allows the student not only to see and feel the sacred force of the deity as a mental exercise but to experience its divinity.

When the student is ready, he incorporates the deity into particular parts of his body in ritual projection. For example, associating the five fingers of one's hand

Kali, the "black" goddess of Hinduism and one of the wives of Shiva, represents the destructive aspect of the divine. This bronze sculpture of the fierce goddess is one of the more benign depictions. She generally is shown with her eyes bulging out of their sockets, her tongue hanging out of her mouth, and severed heads dripping blood from her hands.

The Kinds of Tantra

Right-Hand Tantra

Conservative approach to Tantra; works with asana, pranayama, mudra, and bandhas to awaken the female Kundalini serpent (Shakti), draw it up through the body, and unify it at the crown of the head with the male energy of Shiva.

Left-Hand Tantra

Known for its practices that make use of forbidden pleasures such as sexual intercourse, eating meat or fish, or drinking alcohol, left-hand Tantra teaches that the yogin should participate in all forbidden pleasures to transcend this life and attain liberation.

with the five gross elements (ether, air, fire, water, and earth).

Mantras—mystical sounds—take on a whole new meaning in Tantra. Imparted only by a guru, mantras assist the practitioner in his meditation. A mantra is generally just a syllable or a string of syllables and may not have any translatable meaning. The use of mantra is very ritualistic. It's not enough in Tantra simply to recite the mantra in one's meditation. One must purify one's thoughts first, be alert and physically strong, and begin to dissect the mantra, letter by letter. Invoking a mantra awakens the corresponding parts of the body and the forces of the universe it represents.

Mandalas are used to help the yogin become one with his deity. Mandalas are drawings on wood, cloth, or paper—sometimes simple, other times quite complex—of circles and geometric elements. In the center of all mandalas resides the "seed" that represents the point of true realization, the union of the cosmos and the mind. Surrounding circles depict all the levels of existence. The mandala represents the outside world and the cosmos; by entering the mandala through meditation and visualization, the yogin enters sacred space and sees the gods residing in his own heart. He understands there is no separation between the individual and the Absolute.

The Shri Yantra, or blessed wheel, is the most common symbol of Tantra yoga, a visual representation of creative sexuality. Its nine interlocking triangles are positioned so that four point up, representing male energy (Shiva), and five point down, symbolizing feminine energy (Shakti).

The Shri Yantra

The most common mandala is called the Shri Yantra, which represents all existence—the manifestation of duality. Very complicated in its design, the yantra has nine interlocking triangles, four pointing up—representing the male principle of Shiva—and five pointing down—the feminine principle of Shakti. All the deities that rule over certain aspects of human existence reside in the 43 triangles that result from the original nine. Two concentric circles surround the geometric design; two lotus patterns encircle the triangles, which are further enclosed by four more concentric circles. The entire mandala is protected by three parallel lines forming a fanciful square shape. The point in the center is the primordial unity (Purusha), or the undifferentiated Brahma; the triangles represent the interconnectedness of existence, or the duality of Shiva and Shakti.

Hatha Yoga

In yoga, health and physical conditioning have always been a means of controlling the body to discipline the mind. While the body and mind were seen as microcosms of the universe even in Vedic times, most yogins disdained the body, seeing it as the source of great pain and a hindrance to their goal of final liberation. Other yogins understood the necessity of keeping a strong, healthy body to enable them to withstand the pressures of meditation practice. Patañjali, while acknowledging the importance of the physical body, believed that the purer a yogin's consciousness became, the more the yogin viewed the body as defiled and the more he shunned others for fear of becoming contaminated by their physical presence.

The popularization of Tantra changed all that. Its practitioners revered the physical body and saw it as a means of conquering death. Tantra taught that one attained liberation through experiencing life to the fullest. But of all the schools of thought in yoga, Hatha yoga was the one that focused on physicalness the most.

Hatha taught a systematic approach to mastering the body: One must learn the complete physiology (organs, energy channels, tissues, and the presiding divinities) to transform the physical body into the subtle, divine body and thereby attain liberation. As in Tantra, sexual practices also come into play in the Hatha yoga texts as means of unifying the male and female energies. But in general, Hatha yoga is associated with strenuous physical postures (asana practice) as opposed to the sex of the Tantra.

Goraksha: Father of Hatha Yoga

Not much is known about Goraksha, a semi-mythical yogin who probably lived around the 9th or 10th century A.D. (possibly as late as the 11th) in Punjab, India. Folklore offers the account of his birth as arising from the sweat of Shiva's breast. Others say he was the product of Shiva's union with a cow. Although he became known for his rather extreme Tantric practices and his utter disregard for convention, Goraksha was considered the founder of Hatha yoga and one of the 84 great adepts who not only possessed magical powers, but attained final liberation and immortality.

There are not many texts remaining from the Hatha yoga school of thought. Of those that do exist, only three shed any light on its practices. The earliest one, the *Hathayogapradipika*, was probably written around the 14th or 15th century A.D. and describes approximately 15 postures (asanas), most of them variations of the lotus position. The *Hathayogapradipika* includes techniques to

- purify the body and bring it into balance
- control and extend the breath
- increase digestion
- aid concentration

The second text is the *Gheranda Samhita*, probably a late 17th-century Hatha yoga treatise, which describes 32 different postures and 25 seals (*mudras*). The sage Gheranda focused on purification rituals called *shodhanas*, part of his sevenfold discipline of yoga.

The third treatise, the *Shiva Samhita*, is the most extensive. Possibly written around the late 17th or early 18th century A.D., it gives us an elaborate breakdown of yogic physiology and describes five different types of prana, or life breath, and how to regulate them through pranayama, asanas, and mudras. Eighty-four different asanas are mentioned, but the *Samhita* gives detailed accounts of only four of them. The physical postures are touted for their ability to cure diseases, bestow longevity, and confer magical powers.

One of the six kriyas, or cleansing techniques, this dhauti is a rather intense practice. The practitioner swallows a long piece of cloth, leaves it in her stomach for a while, and then slowly pulls it out. This is said to cure digestive problems, diseases of the stomach, leprosy, and other skin disorders.

Purification Rituals

Before a yogin can even begin the physical practice of Hatha yoga, he or she must purify the body. The following are six techniques his guru would employ.

Dhautis. These purification rites concentrate on internal cleansing, dental cleansing, rectal cleansing, and purifying the heart.

> **Don't Try This at Home!**
>
> One extreme purification ritual involves a yogin standing in water up to his navel. He gently, "by means of ether power," takes out his large intestine, squeezes it to remove all contents, washes his bowels, and then puts it all back by drawing it up into the abdomen. This should only be done under direct supervision of an experienced guru and takes years of practice to perfect.

- Internal cleansing practices range from simple techniques, such as belching or passing gas; to more challenging ones, such as pushing the navel back toward the spine 100 times to stimulate the digestive fires in the belly; to rather severe ones, such as washing one's prolapsed intestines—not something one would want to do unsupervised! (see "Don't Try This at Home!").
- Dental cleansing involves brushing the teeth, the tongue, the ears, and the sinuses. Cleaning the ears promotes the ability to hear inner sounds.
- Rectal cleansing by means of a turmeric stalk helps the breath to circulate freely.
- Cleansing the heart is an intense practice. The first part includes taking a stalk of turmeric, placing it down one's gullet, and slowly drawing it out. This helps remove excess pitta (bile) and kapha (phlegm) from the mouth and chest. The second technique is "cleansing by vomiting," a rather indecorous way of removing kapha from the stomach and chest, which comprises eating a full meal, drinking water until it fills up to the throat, gazing up between the eyebrows, and throwing up the water. The third part is the most difficult to perform:

Swallow a long, thick piece of cloth and leave it in the stomach for a while before pulling it out again. This is said to help reduce fever and cure diseases of the stomach and large intestine, leprosy, and other skin disorders.

Bastis. The bastis are nothing but enemas—dry or water-based. The dry enema works in the seated, forward-bent position, contracting and dilating the sphincter muscle and pressing down hard on the intestines. The water enema also calls on the yogin to contract and dilate the sphincter muscle, but this time he or she squats in water up to the navel in the chair pose. This is said to cure urinary and digestive troubles.

Netis. The netis clear out the nasal passages and the sinuses. These days people use a neti pot to pour salted water in one nostril and allow it to drain out the other side (see page 215). Another method works by inserting thin threads into the nostrils and pulling them out through the mouth. This is said to improve vision and clear the sinus cavities.

Nauli. The nauli is actually a yoga pose designed to balance the digestive system. To perform nauli, sit in the lotus pose, bend forward slightly, and release the shoulders forward (hollowing out the chest). Isolate the *rectus abdominis* muscle (the large, straight muscle in the abdomen), lock it in place, and then rotate it vigorously for several minutes.

Trataka. Trataka is designed to cure diseases of the eye and to encourage clairvoyance. It involves sitting in the lotus pose and staring at a small object directly in front of one's feet. One should stare at the object, without blinking, until one's eyes begin to tear uncontrollably.

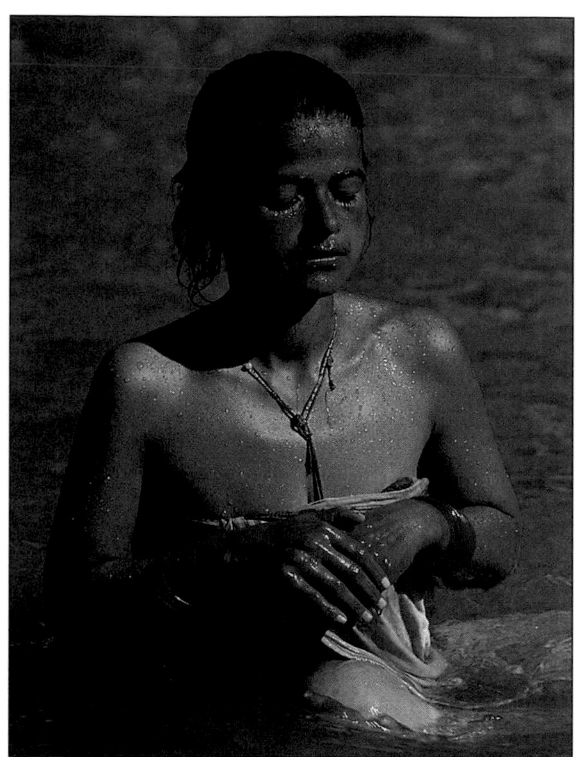

Wading waist-deep into the Bagmathi River in Kathmandu, Nepal, this young pilgrim prays that the cleansing effects of the river water will heal his wounds.

Kapala Bhati. The sixth cleansing act helps clear out the nasal passages. It is usually made up of three separate practices. In the first practice, or left process, the yogin inhales repeatedly through the left nostril and exhales through the right. In the second practice, the yogin draws water up through the nose and expels it through the mouth. The third technique works the opposite way: The yogin draws water into the mouth, holds his breath for as long as possible, and expels the water through the nose, making the sound "sheet" as he exhales. This practice claims to control hunger, thirst, and sleep.

Hatha Yogic Physiology

Before we go on to describe the effects of asana and pranayama practice on the mind and the body, it's important to understand how yogins viewed the body. In Ayurvedic medicine and perhaps as far back as the Vedic period, physicians understood something about basic anatomy. No doubt most yogic gurus were also well-versed in scientific physiology, but for purposes of meditation and to awaken "primordial consciousness," the yogins used a more spiritual or mystical physiologic model. Instead of talking about muscles, veins, nerves, and organs the way a medical scientist would, a yogin would expound on the theory of the nadis, the chakras, the physical body, and the subtle body.

BODY AS A MICROCOSM Just like Ayurvedic practitioners, Hatha yogins viewed the body as a microcosm of the universe. They all saw the five elements—ether, air, fire, water, and earth—absorbed in the body. For example, the cosmic winds (*vayu*) are incorporated into the body as air or breath (*vata*); fire (*agni*) becomes the digestive fire. In Hatha yoga, the spinal column is a miniature Mount Meru—the mountain at the center of the Earth. Therefore, the spinal column is seen as the central axis of the body that controls everything. Yogins see this axis as one large bone that is fixed and motionless. The seven worlds of Hindu cosmology are represented in the seven *chakras*, or psychoenergetic centers, in the body.

Meditation on the Body as Microcosm

Meditating on the body as a microcosm of the universe helps the yogin realize the body as part of the entire concept of cosmic delusion. Therefore, if the yogin succeeds in transcending the body, he will transcend the universe. For example, the yogin sees the spine as Mount Meru (the mountain at the center of the Earth); the arms and legs as the continents; the eyes as the sun and the moon; the head as the realm of the gods; the toes, knees, and thighs as home of the seven hells; and the soles of the feet as home to the mythical tortoise that holds up the universe.

THE NADIS The central axis of the body is just one of a multitude of veins, arteries, and nerves present in the body. Yogic texts differ on the number of these channels, or nadis, that help transport the life force (*prana*), which flows through the physical body. Estimations vary from 10 to 700 million of these vessels. The three most important of these are the *sushumna*, the *ida*, and the *pingala*.

- The ida nadi, also called the "channel of comfort," is responsible for cooling the body and encouraging it to exhale. It moves the down-breath of the body during the exhalation or during suspension of the breath at the bottom of the exhale. The ida nadi is said to begin just above the sex organs and terminate under the left nostril. It controls the lower half of the body, from the navel down to the feet.
- The pingala nadi's nature is strong, expansive, and energizing, encouraging the yogin to inhale. This nadi moves the life force through the body, on the inhalation or during breath retention at the top of the inhalation, creating heat and light and invigorating the whole person. A clear pingala nadi optimizes respiration and cardiovascular functioning.
- The sushumna nadi is, for the physical body, the central axis (or spinal column), which transports the life force from the base of the spine up to the crown of the

The Elements of Prana

Throughout Vedic history, prana, or life force, has had five aspects:

Prana (the out-breath)—This part of the life force is associated with the sun, resides in the heart, and stimulates the body to exhale. It is light and energizing and moves through the body by way of the pingala nadi on the right side of the spine. It governs the torso, chest, and stomach and controls respiration and cardiovascular health.

Apana (the in-breath)—This part of prana is associated with lunar energy and, as a result, is gentler and contracting. It has a grounding effect on the body and is connected to the inhalation. It moves through the body via the ida channel on the left side of the spine. Residing in the lower half of the body—from the belly down to the feet—it governs digestion, elimination, and sexual functions. It mixes with prana and agni (digestive fire) in the belly to arouse the Kundalini serpent.

Vyana (the diffuse breath)—This part of prana helps circulate life force throughout the body and most particularly in the joints, the eyes, ears, and throat. Some yogins believe vyana activates speech.

Udana (the up-breath)—This part of prana also helps circulate the life force in the body and is responsible for digestion. Some texts say it resides in the throat, others find it in the palate.

Samana (the breath of food)—This part of prana distributes food throughout the body, normalizing all body functions. Some say it lodges in the heart; others say the navel.

head. Inside the sushumna is a thinner, finer channel; and inside that is a channel as thin as one-thousandth of a hair width, where the chakras are said to attach (see page 237–238).

PURIFYING THE NADIS All humans contain within them a multitude of nadis that transport the vital energy to all parts of the body. It's important to keep these channels of transportation pure and unobstructed, otherwise illness occurs.

The most common and effective purification practices are called *nirmanu* and *samanu*. Nirmanu is the same as the dhauti practices discussed earlier: cleaning the teeth, the gastrointestinal tract, the nasal passages, and the heart (see pages 233–234). The samanu practice involves breathing practice, which a yogin performs while seated in the lotus pose. During the exercise, the yogin must visualize his or her guru, bringing the teacher into his or her heart. It begins by meditating on the syllable *yam* (symbol of the cosmic wind).

- First inhale through the left nostril while silently chanting *yam* 16 times.
- Hold the breath while silently chanting *yam* 64 times.
- Exhale very slowly (32 repetitions of *yam*) through the right nostril.
- Concentrate on the fire in the belly, drawing it up to the heart.
- Inhale through the right nostril while silently chanting *ram* (the fire syllable) 16 times.
- Retain the breath while silently chanting *ram* 64 times.
- Exhale very slowly (32 repetitions of *ram*).
- Meditate on the reflection of the moon—the nectar of immortality—at the tip of the nose.
- Repeat inhalation on the left side using the syllable *tham*; retain the breath for

64 counts while meditating on the immortal nectar; and then exhale for 32 counts, silently chanting to oneself the syllable *lam*.

- Perform the adept's posture—similar to the lotus pose but with the left heal against the anus and the right one above the genitals. Rest the chin on the chest and gaze at a point right between the eyebrows.

A representation of the seven chakras, or psychoenergy centers, where the subtle body meets the physical body. Six of these chakras can loosely be associated with the various nerves and blood vessels in the body; the seventh resides above the crown of the head, transcending all existence.

THE CHAKRAS Deep within the sushumna channel lie the chakras: psychoenergetic centers where the subtle body meets the physical body. Basically these centers house all the energy necessary for a human to live, and they distribute that energy through the thousands of nadis. Most texts agree that there are seven main chakras, including the sahasrara chakra, which resides above the crown of the head and transcends all physical existence.

The chakras are a type of internal map that a yogin uses as he or she meditates on the body. The yogin meditates on each chakra as a lotus blossom with a certain number of petals, each with a Sanskrit letter imprinted on it. Each chakra has a corresponding color, a ruling god or goddess, and a "seed syllable" from the Sanskrit alphabet. Each chakra also relates to one of the five gross elements.

Beginning with the base of the spine, the seven major chakras are as follows:

- Muladhara chakra—this root chakra resides at the base of the spine. Its element is earth; its sense is the sense of smell; its organ of action is the feet; and its sound is *lam*. This chakra is the source of desire, and Dakini is the goddess that presides over it.

- Svadishthana chakra—Situated in the genital area, this is also known as the pleasant chakra. Its element is water; its sense is taste; its organ of action is the hands; and its sound is *vam*.
- Manipura chakra—This chakra sits right in the lumbar region of the spine, at the level of the navel. Its element is fire; its sense is sight; its organ of action is the gastrointestinal tract; and its sound is *ram*. It governs the breath and the emotions of fear, jealousy, and shame. To contemplate this chakra successfully is said to bring the yogin freedom from disease and pain and the ability to make medicinal remedies.
- Anahata chakra—Located at the heart, this chakra has been known as a powerful center of the body since Vedic times: the seat of the Divine and the place of the primordial sound of *Om*. Its element is air; its sense is touch; the organ of action is the penis; and its sound is *yam*. It is the seat of the individual self. Isvara resides here. It governs emotions such as hope, anxiety, doubt, remorse, duty, and egotism.
- Vishuddha chakra—This is the throat chakra, whose color is gold. Its element is ether, or space; its sense is hearing; its organ of action is the mouth; and its sound is *ham*.
- Ajña chakra—Situated between the eyebrows, this chakra governs the realm of understanding and the power of concentration. It is sometimes known as the third eye. It has no element; its sense is the sense of cognition; its organ of action is *yoni*, or female genitalia, and its sound is *Om*.
- Sahasrara chakra—Beyond the crown of the head sits the "Lotus of One Thousand Petals," the place of transcendence. The sahasrara chakra represents pure consciousness. It encompasses all colors, all sounds, all organs of action, all functions of the mind and body. It symbolizes the final union of Shiva (male) and Shakti (female).

Kundalini—Yogic Union

Tantra and Hatha yoga took two basic, ancient principles of Indian philosophy—Samkhya philosophy and the body as a microcosm of the universe—and expanded upon them. In Samkhya, Cosmic Consciousness (Purusha) was masculine, formless, immobile, and omniscient Matter, and Nature (Prakriti) was feminine, creative, and the ever-moving Spirit. In yoga, the god Shiva personifies the Purusha, and the goddess Shakti is the feminine form, Prakriti. The union of these two aspects of the Divine represents the reunion of all opposites and the libera-

The Union of Opposites

The physical postures of yoga continue the philosophy that the creation of opposites promotes pain, delusion, and disease. All asana and pranayama exercises contain opposing energies; it is through practice that the yogin brings these opposite motions into balance. In every pose, practitioners find expansion and contraction, active and passive, effort and relaxation, prana (up-breath) and apana (down-breath). In a yoga class, students perform what yogins call pose and counterpose—that is, for every action, there is an automatic reaction. If you perform a forward bend, your body will need the opposite movement—a backbend; if you twist one way, you'll need to twist back the other way; if you perform a seated pose, you'll also need a more energetic standing pose.

Lord Krishna and his consort Radha, seated in a grove. Krishna, an incarnation of the ancient Vedic god Vishnu, is seen as our protector and mediator between good and evil. His union with Radha represents the mystical union between an individual and her personal god.

tion from the cycle of birth, death, and rebirth.

Viewing the body as a microcosm of the divine dance, Tantra and Hatha yoga saw the Shiva and Shakti residing in all of us. Kundalini yoga saw that the path to uniting these opposites was to combine sexuality and spirit in the human form. The union of Shiva and Shakti awakens the yogin, destroying any sense of the individual self and flooding his or her entire being with indescribable bliss. To prepare the body and mind for this union, the yogin must practice

- asanas
- pranayama
- selected mudras (seals or gestures)
- bandhas (locks)

Asanas Though the primary goal of these practices is to release the flow of life force in the body, the asanas bring health benefits as well.

Originally mentioned in Patañjali's *Yoga Sutra* as a way of sitting for meditation (the body should be steady, relaxed, and comfortable; the posture straight and in proper alignment), asana in Hatha yoga acquired a variety of therapeutic effects. Most of the effects stemmed from stress tolerances, increasing the digestive fire, stimulating the liver, and releasing phlegm from the lungs and intestines. Modern yoga mentions as many as 200 postures, which claim benefits ranging from increased circulation to restoring health and relieving premenstrual syndrome.

Benefits of Asanas

Several asanas also work to balance the body and mind:

Padmasana, the lotus pose, is said to help overcome all manner of disease.

Muktasana involves a similar seated pose in which the left ankle sits above the groin and the right ankle above that.

Vajrasana is a pose in which the yogin grips the thighs "like a thunderbolt," and places his or her legs underneath the anus. It works to strengthen the body.

Bhujangasana is known today as cobra pose. Lying on the stomach and pressing up through the arms, the yogin lifts the body from the navel up, arching the back and raising the head like a snake. The cobra pose is said to increase body temperature, cure myriad diseases, and awaken the Kundalini or "serpent" energy.

Mritasana, or corpse pose, involves lying supine on the ground, completely relaxed, to overcome fatigue and regenerate energy after practicing asanas.

PRANAYAMA Also mentioned in Patañjali's *Yoga Sutra*, pranayama became the principal way to awaken Kundalini energy and unite the higher consciousness for Hatha and Tantric yogins. Pranayama, when practiced properly, helps cure hiccups, asthma, headaches, earaches, and congestion in the lungs. It also strengthens the body, invigorates the mind, and makes the practitioner feel younger. Pranayama's purpose is to expand the life force through inhalation, retention, and exhalation.

MUDRAS AND BANDHAS Once the yogin is able to open the channels in his body (the ida, pingala, and sushumna nadis) to allow for the unimpeded flow of energy, he is ready to learn to control where the energy goes. There are two ways to do this: through the practice of mudras, or seals, and by creating bandhas, or locks, which prevent the energy from entering a particular chakra or area in the body. Paramudras—practices that combine asana, pranayama, bandhas, and mudras—are highly esoteric practices, the details of which have never been written down. It has been claimed that these can only be transmitted orally and performed under the supervision of an experienced guru. A sampling of paramudras are as follows:

- Mahamudra (the Great Seal)—The yogin sits with the right leg outstretched and the left foot pressing against the perineum, holding the right foot with his hands. He then closes off all orifices of the body (ears, eyes, nose, and mouth) using his powers of concentration, and contracts the throat by placing his chin on his chest snugly while gazing between the eyebrows and retaining the breath. This activates all the nadis and stops the flow of semen, which increases vitality. Modern yogins believe this paramudra relieves constipation, hemorrhoids, and indigestion.
- Khecharimudra (the air-moving seal)—There's some preparation involved before the yogin can perform khecharimudra. He first must cut the tongue's frenum (the connecting membrane that keeps the tongue in place), and massage the tongue with milk, stretching it out (sometimes using an iron tool) until it is long enough to reach a point between the eyebrows. Then the yogin must loosen his soft palate by hooking a piece of metal onto the palate ridge and gently drawing it forward. After he is ready (and

Unlike the yogins in southern India, this pilgrim from the mountains of Nepal is dressed warmly in brightly colored clothes, bedecked with jewelry from the surrounding lands.

the procedure could take several months), the yogin draws his tongue back down his gullet, blocking the nasal passages that open into the mouth, silently repeats the mantras his guru has given him, and fixes his gaze between his eyebrows. This supposedly blocks the flow of semen; prevents fainting, hunger, thirst, old age, and death; and makes the yogin immune to snakebites.

- Vajrolimudra (the thunderbolt seal)—This practice is said to enable the yogin to combine (in his own body) the male and female fluids, thereby uniting all opposites. Months of preparation are necessary for this one, too. The man must cleanse and strengthen his penis, making it as strong and hard as a thunderbolt. He then practices dipping it into a bronze vessel of cow's milk, sucking the milk up with his penile shaft, and releasing it again. The bandha he perfects is called the *medhra bandha*, or phallus lock, by which he causes the penis to stay rigid for an indefinite period of time. When he is ready, he ejaculates his semen into a woman's vagina where it mixes with her fluid. He then sucks the two fluids back up into his body. This mudra, not surprisingly, is said to be very deleterious to the female volunteer.

Other mudras and bandhas help the advanced practitioner to seal off the left and right channels (the pingala and the ida nadis), forcing all the Kundalini power to surge up through the sushumna nadi and head straight for the sahasrara chakra above the crown of the head.

Yoga and Western Medicine

Yoga came to America with the arrival of Swami Vivekananda over 100 years ago. It wasn't the physical style of Hatha yoga that so intrigued the participants that day at the World Parliament of Religions, but it was the merits of Patañjali's ancient eightfold path of practice. It took many years for the practice to catch on, and it took many years after that for its health benefits to be noticed by the medical establishment.

Vital Points

Certain gurus use their special, secret knowledge of the vital spots in the body (called *marman*) to cure ailments in almost the same way traditional Chinese doctors use pressure points. These gurus focus their breath and their concentration on each pressure point to free the life force and allow it to flow throughout the body. Western scientists have looked on as one guru cured his patient of a toothache by massaging one of her ribs; another teacher relieved a patient of asthma by gently pressing a point behind the ears.

Yoga, for millennia, has taught that the body, mind, and breath are inexorably linked. Yogins discovered as they worked to attain liberation, one side benefit they produced was a physically fit, healthy body free of the normal aches, pains, and afflictions. Modern Western medicine saw this side effect as one of primary importance to a people whose lives are filled with stress, poor eating habits, and little time to exercise. Besides toning and strengthening, yoga benefits all the systems of the body: muscular, skeletal, circulatory, respiratory, digestive, reproductive, endocrine, lymphatic, and nervous. The combination of posture, movement, and breath also affects the emotions and the mind. Actions, knowledge, and spirit form a harmonic trinity.

Mainstream medical practitioners and researchers have begun to take a serious look at the benefits of yoga. They have found that heart patients who stick to a combined regimen of yoga, meditation, and a low-fat diet can reverse coronary artery blockage. Combinations of yoga and other meditation have been shown to help patients manage stress and chronic pain and even reduce blood pressure.

Yoga and yoga meditation help the practitioner not only manage stress better but to change the stress-producing patterns the mind sets up. They remove the obstacles—the causes—of the stress and discomfort, and they help the practitioner develop a deeper insight into what causes agitation in the first place.

Some of the other benefits that modern Western medicine has begun to recognize in yoga are

- increased immune system functioning
- increased musculoskeletal flexibility (aiding in the treatment and prevention of arthritis, multiple sclerosis, scoliosis, fibromyalgia, and injuries)
- decreased discomfort in premenstrual syndrome and menopause
- enhanced mood and stability in mental illnesses such as depression

Yoga's Definition of Health and Disease

In Hatha yoga, health is defined as "the ability to hold one's breath as long as one wishes, to increase digestive fire (agni), and to hear inner sounds." Yoga took a very practical view of illness: One could not meditate or practice yoga (and thereby attain final liberation) if one was distracted by pain or fever. It saw disease, much like Ayurveda did, as a disruption of the bodily humors (doshas and dhatus), the organs, and the bodily secretions. It is best, a guru will tell his student, to realign the body through practice of asana and pranayama before seeking outside help in Ayurveda.

Health and Liberation

Whether a practitioner chooses yoga as a system of health maintenance or as a spiritual philosophy to pursue the ultimate liberation of self is an individual concern. As such, the benefits are also only limited by the individual. Concentrating the mind gives the adept mastery over matter and immunity to karma and illness; the yogic exercises help harness life energy.

To whatever end the yogin strives, yoga itself remains a discipline of mind and body in a union that can lead to a recreation of the body, command of the mind and senses, and an eventual withdrawal from illusory experience.

The Far East

Asian Shamanism

THERE WAS A TIME when historians considered Siberia to have been the birthplace of shamanism. This was because here, among the reindeer nomads and the small settlements of hunters and fishermen of northern Siberia and along the Arctic Ocean, the shaman seemed to be more central to the life of his people than anywhere else in the world.

Here, too, many of the universals of shamanism appeared to have their most dramatic expression: supernatural calling, initiatory sickness, ecstatic trance, out-of-body journeys of the soul, spirit helpers, transformation, animism, magical drums, ritual costumes, cosmic levels, the shamanic tree, mystical numbers, symbolic dismemberment, rebirth from the bones, bird symbolism, flight to the heavens, descent to the underworld, soul loss, sickness projectiles—in short, everything that is central to shamanic religions.

In fact, the very word *shaman* comes, via the Russian, from the language of the Siberian Tungus, who call the specialist in the sacred and master of spirits *samán*. And there are also powerful traces of traditional shamanism in the Asian religions of Buddhism and Lamaism.

Shaman's mask from the Maritime Koryak people of eastern Siberia. This wooden mask found in 1900 was used in masking ceremonies to drive kalas, or evil spirits, from households.

An Art Older Than Humankind

It sounds attractive and logical to place shamanism's origins in Siberia and northeast Asia, but scholars now agree that the origin of shamanism cannot be sought in any one region. Rather, it was the common heritage of the Stone Age way of life across Europe and Asia and in other places of the world, including the Americas. Even the Neanderthals, whose culture goes back more than 100,000 years, conceived of an afterlife—burying their dead with offerings of food, tools, and medicinal plants and constructing shrines to honor the spirits of the giant cave bears they had slain.

Where but in the spirit universe of shamanism do we find such ideas? Who else but the shaman has the human soul in his care and knows how to placate the supernatural? It is reasonable, then, to suspect that even the Neanderthals, whose rituals argue for religion and a belief in souls, shared in an early form of the shamanic heritage. Shamanism is so old and so universal in human societies, to speak of a geographical birthplace would be meaningless.

The Sickness That Makes a Healer

Being called to the shamanic profession is a trial in almost every shamanic culture, and nowhere is this more true than among the Samoyed peoples of northern Russia and western Siberia. Some of the sicknesses that mark the future shaman (called *initiatory sickness*) can be truly frightening. The candidate might experience dismemberment, the flesh scraped from his bones, his bodily fluids drained, or his eyes gouged out. He dies and the spirits put him back together. This type of sickness is also therapeutic, for the shaman is one who has been struck with sickness and has learned to heal himself.

Take the case of a Samoyed shaman whose shamanic calling, or sickness vocation, was an ordeal that contained many of the elements common to becoming a shaman in other parts of the world. The man was struck by smallpox, became unconscious, and appeared so nearly dead that his relatives almost buried him. When he came to, he recalled being taken to the middle of a sea. There he heard the spirit of his sickness speak:

> From the Lords of the Water you will receive the gift of shamanizing. Your name as a shaman will be *Huottarie* [meaning "diver"].

The First Physician

One of the earliest known representations of a shaman is this 20,000- to 25,000-year-old painting of the so-called "Sorcerer of Trois Frères" discovered on the wall of a cave in France. It is possibly a depiction of the shaman as his animal alter ego or spirit helper—in this case a stag with paws and a feline face. Some have referred to this portrait (or possibly self-portrait) as "the first physician." The fact that it is found in France calls into question where shamanism originated and lends credibility to the assertion that shamanism may, in fact, be a universal human phenomenon.

Learning About Disease Then the spirit of smallpox roiled the waters. The future shaman climbed out and went up a mountain. There he met a naked woman who said,

> You are my child; that is why I let you suckle at my breast. You will meet many hardships and be greatly wearied.

The woman was the Lady of the Waters. Her husband, the Lord of the Underworld, gave the future shaman an ermine and a mouse to guide him to the underworld. There he met disease spirits living in tents. The spirits tore out his heart and threw it into a pot. Passing through other tents he met the Lord of Madness and the lords of all the nervous disorders. In this way he learned all the diseases that torture humankind.

Making the Drums Still led by his animal guides, the candidate came to the Lord of the Female Shamans, who strengthened his voice. Then he was carried to the shores of nine seas. In the center of one was an island, and in its middle there was a young birch tree that rose to the sky. This was the tree of the Lord of the Earth. Beside it grew nine herbs that were the ancestors of all the plants on Earth. The candidate visited all nine seas, of which some were very salty, others so hot he could not go near them. Then in the top of the birch tree he saw men of all the Siberian nations: Yakut (Sakha), Samoyed, Dolgan, Tungus, and Russian. He was told to make three drums from the branches of the birch tree: one drum for shamanizing women in childbirth, a second for curing the sick, and a third for finding men who had become lost in the snow.

A lithograph from 1861 depicting male and female Siberian Tungus shamans dancing in full costume and bearing their tambourine-style drums. Note the small, round, possibly copper ornaments akin to toli, or mirror disks. The lithograph comes from a volume about the peoples of Russia published for the court of Czar Alexander II.

Forged Anew Then he learned the secrets of medicinal plants and flew through the sky in the company of birds. After many other adventures—some troubling, others benign—he came to a desert, where he saw a mountain in the distance. It took him three days of walking to reach it and enter it through an opening. Inside the mountain he met a blacksmith working a bellows to heat a fire under an enormous cauldron, the size of half the earth. The smith cut off the candidate's head, chopped his body into pieces, and boiled them for three days in his cauldron.

There were also three anvils. On the third, the smith forged the candidate's new head. This was the one on which the best shamans were forged in the manner of iron. The smith then threw the candidate's disembodied head into one of three pots. This one contained the coldest water. The candidate's spirit was then instructed that if he was called to cure someone, he should test the water in a ritual pot. If it was very hot, it would be useless to shamanize, for the patient was already doomed; if the water was warm, the patient was sick but would get well; and if the water was cold, the patient was healthy.

Now the candidate saw his own fleshless bones floating in a river. The blacksmith fished them out, put them together in their proper order, and recovered them with flesh. He changed the new shaman's bodily eyes to mystical ones to see the spirits when shamanizing. He pierced his ears so he would understand the language of the healing plants. Then the candidate found himself on the summit of a mountain and finally awoke in his own *yurt*, or hut, among his family. Cured from his initiatory illness, he could now sing and shamanize for hour after hour without getting tired.

This story has everything that is typical of the initiatory sickness experience of the Siberian shaman (and often also of candidate shamans in North and South America; see pages 128–142): supernatural selection through sickness; loss of consciousness; skeletonization; dismemberment, death, and resurrection; celestial flight and passage through the different cosmic levels; acquisition of animal spirit helpers; encounters with the masters of water, the dead, the animals, and the healing plants; ascent of the cosmic mountain and world tree; shamanic drums; spirit teachers who instruct him in the different diseases and their cures; and replacement of ordinary organs for magical ones.

The Shaman's Tools

In the old days, the novice shaman also received some of the power objects he would later use in his vocation, such as one or more shamanic drums and objects that would be part of the special costumes for which Siberian shamans were famous before the turn of the century. The shaman would be festooned with shiny metal mirrors, feathers, bird skins, symbols of skeletonization, and different kinds of amulets made of metal, leather, bone, or wood that embodied spirit helpers.

One of the earliest European portraits of a Siberian shaman is this Dutch illustration by N. Witsen dated 1672. This Tungus shaman dances with his drum and reindeer-antler headdress.

THE DRUM Of all the shamanic trappings, the shamanic drum has remained a central element in northern Asian shamanism from the Pacific Coast to the country of the Sámi—the reindeer-herding people of northern Finland, Norway, and Sweden. Despite the enormous physical distance separating them from, say, the reindeer Koryak of northeastern Siberia, the Sámi—better known as Laplanders—share more than a few beliefs and practices basic to shamanism virtually everywhere, including those of the Native Americans.

The earliest mention of the shamanic drum as an instrument of ecstasy among the Sámi is a 13th-century chronicle in the Latin language known as the *Historia Norwegiae*. In this early manuscript the deeds of a shaman—*noaide* in the Sámi language—who pounded his drum to place himself into a trance are recounted. In this condition, he would change himself into an animal and travel to other worlds on behalf of his clan. Here, as in Siberia, Mongolia, and Nepal, making a drum required not only technical skill but also so much specialized knowledge that the drum makers themselves had to be shamans.

Among villagers in Nepal, for example, the shamans divine the proper tree, cut strips from its trunk or branches, and then carefully bend the strips to make a circular frame. The tree is a living being capable of hearing and feeling, so its spirit is propitiated, fed, and thanked with prayers and offerings for giving its wood for the shaman's drum. So is the animal whose skin will be used for the drum head.

But the drum itself is always more than just an instrument whose steady pounding puts the shaman into an altered state of consciousness. It embodies the multilevel universe and serves as the shaman's "mount" (the spirit animal he or she rides on out-of-body journeys in search of lost souls).

Once Christianity took hold in the Scandinavian countries, the missionaries saw clearly how central shamanism was to Sámi religion and how central, in turn, the drum was to shamanizing. And so to eradicate shamanism, they first went after the drums, burning them publicly wherever possible, along with other implements associated with the traditional rites, just as they did in Siberia. In reaction to the systematic destruction of

The Fly Agaric

Part of the Siberia-as-cradle-of-shamanism myth is that the most ancient form of shamanistic ecstasy had to be the "spontaneous" kind, like that of the Arctic Eskimos, whose shamans used drumming, sensory deprivation, and other *nonchemical* techniques to trigger the out-of-body experience. In this view, the shamanistic use of plant hallucinogens and other intoxicants—widespread in the Americas and represented in Siberia by the fly agaric mushroom (*Amanita muscaria*)—represented a "degeneration" of "true" shamanism.

But that was before radiocarbon dating established that in North America, the Pleistocene hunters of giant bison and mammoth were using intoxicating plants in shamanistic rituals more than 10,000 years ago. And it turns out, the fly agaric was being used as an intoxicant by some Siberian shamans much more recently than thought.

A shaman's drum from Altai, Siberia, with a three-dimensional image of the shaman's principal spirit helper on the reverse side.

their drums, the Laplanders would hide them in the mountains or even put them underwater. The Sámi considered such places sacred and dangerous, and they feared coming too close to them, lest there be serious mishaps.

The Mirrors In some traditions, the origin of the mirrors found on the special costumes of the shaman is closely linked to the origin and knowledge of death itself. This, in turn, helps explain why shamans—such as those of the Amur River region of central Asia, for example—who accompanied the dead to the underworld had the greatest prestige, while those who only cured illness had the least.

In the mythology of the Nanai, one of the peoples of the Amur, long ago near the beginning of the world there was a man named Kado. He was the first person to die and enter the *buni*, or the underworld, becoming its lord. The people, meanwhile, remained in ignorance of the road to the *buni*. Kado's father missed him very much and went to find the hole that was the entrance to the underworld. When he found it, he decided to go no further. Hoping to stop mortality, he plugged the hole with his clothing.

For a while everything was fine and few people died. In time, however, the clothes that barred the gateway to the land of the dead rotted and mortality returned. People started dying in greater numbers than before, but the dead were not always able to find the entrance to the *buni*.

Then Kado's father fell asleep and dreamed of an enormous tree. Its tangled

Photograph of a shaman during a horse sacrifice. Dressed in his ceremonial costume, he is festooned with amulets and brass bells and carries his drum (see photo at upper left). The sound of the bells is meant to call the attention of the gods to the sacrifice.

Portals to Other Worlds

So many peoples of the world share the idea of mirrors as portals into other worlds and reflections of the soul that it must be very ancient. The metal mirrors of Siberian shamanism almost certainly have their origin in the polished bronze mirrors of ancient China, particularly those of the Han Dynasty (206 B.C.–A.D. 220) that are often embellished with representations of the celestial dragon and other spirit beings. Like the circular disks of polished obsidian and metallic minerals found in archaeologic sites in Mexico, most of the Chinese bronze mirrors probably also served magical and shamanic purposes more than they did cosmetic ones.

roots were snakes, and its leaves were *toli*, mirror disks made of shiny copper. The tree's flowers were rattles, and the uppermost branches were antlers made of iron. This, he recognized, was the shamanic tree. The following morning Kado's father went into the forest to search for the tree he had seen in his dream. At last he found it with the help of his magic arrows. He took many of the copper mirrors, rattles, and iron antlers off the tree. In time these objects multiplied in a magical way and spread among all the Nanai clans. This gave them the possibility of having their own shamans who could lead the souls of the dead to the underworld.

Then Kado's father had another dream. In it he met a very old man who instructed him in the proper manner of dressing and how to use the metal mirrors, the rattles, the iron antlers, and the other shamanic instruments he had taken from the tree. "Go into the forest," the old man told him, "and get the furs of a bear, a wolf, and a lynx, and make a special cap out of these. You shall apply the iron horns and the main rattle to the cap; on your chest and on your back you will hang the *toli* that will protect your body from the arrows of the shamans' enemies. Then you will make a belt out of the rattles; this belt and the drum will take you to the *buni* whenever you want; you will be helped by the spirit Butchu and by the bird Koori, who will always bring you back from the *buni*."

In Siberia, Manchuria, and Mongolia the many meanings of shamanic mirrors differed from group to group. But their connection to souls was universal. In fact, the Manchurian-Tungusic word for the shamanic mirror is *panáptu*, from *paná*, meaning "soul" or "spirit," and *ptu*, meaning "receptacle"; so *panáptu* translates to "soul receptacle."

By looking into a mirror, the shaman could peer into the universe and into the

Attracting Souls from the Sky

The key to human fertility and the transfer of souls from the Otherworld to human mothers is the sky goddess, Aiyyhyt, who shares many attributes with similar fertility goddesses among other central Asian peoples. In the old days, there were different shamanic rituals to combat problems of infertility or the death of infants by convincing the sky goddess to move souls from the care of the sky god, Aiyy Toion, to the uterus of an infertile mother. Shamans considered to be especially effective in conducting such rituals were often women. In one case, a young woman who had lost many children asked a shaman for help. To attract the souls of a potential newborn, he prepared a small bird's nest for her and placed it in a sacred tree in the forest. Soon after she bore a child who, unlike her previous children, lived to adulthood.

souls of the dead. His mirrors reflected the deeds of people, both good and evil. They served as containers for the shaman's spirit helpers or for the souls of animals, such as dogs or reindeer. They were also used to transport the souls of the dead to the underworld.

The Three Souls of the Sakha Shaman

Like the ancient Aztec, the Siberian Sakha conceived of three kinds of souls, which each play their part in animating the body and keeping it healthy and whose welfare is in the charge of the shaman. These are the *iiè-kut* ("mother soul"), the *buor-kut* ("earth-clay soul"), and the *salgyn-kut* ("air-breath soul").

For future shamans, individuals who have shamans in their family trees, or those who are incarnated shamans, the three souls have special destinies and require special training. For its training and its acquisition of knowledge of diseases connected with water or those caused by shamans, for example, the earth-clay soul becomes a fish.

The air-breath soul might take the form of a cuckoo or sandpiper, nestle in the hollows of a larch tree, and feed on the eggs of a raven or eagle. This is to learn diverse shamanic tricks because the sons and daughters of one of the sky gods, Ary Darkhan, often turn themselves into either eagles or ravens.

The most interesting fate is that of the shaman's mother soul. It is taken away to a land that lies parallel to the earth in the middle world, where it becomes the *iiè-kyll*, or "mother beast spirit"—the most important of the shaman's alter-ego helpers. It lives a separate physical existence from the shaman, who may see it or take its form on different occasions (some say three times in a lifetime, others once a year, and still others whenever the shaman feels a critical need). The mother beast spirit shares the shaman's fate. In the Sakha republic, when his mother beast alter ego dies so does the shaman.

The mother beast double often takes the form of an eagle. But bear, elk, deer, raven, and crane are also reported. Stronger shamans have an eagle or bear, less powerful ones may have a wolf or dog.

Birds as Spirit Helpers

Birds often serve shamans as a helping spirit and mediator between the seen and unseen worlds. This understanding of birds is one of the phenomena that links Siberian shamanism and mythology to North America. On the northern Pacific Coast, from Alaska to British Columbia and south to northwestern Washington, the raven is as big in the old stories as it is across the North Pacific.

And it is hardly alone. The feathered kingdom in general has played a crucial role in shamanism on both sides of the Pacific not only as spirit helpers and the shaman's double but as winged manifestations of the human soul.

Raven, swan, crane, snow goose, eagle, loon, hawk, grouse, and even smaller birds, such as the lark or cuckoo, have all served as mediating spirits for the shaman on out-of-body flights to the upperworld, while those that dive deep down into the water facilitated the journey to the underworld.

The Raven

The raven has always been one of the main shamanic helping spirits in Siberia. But as a helping spirit, the raven is a mixed blessing. Many people in Siberia are a little afraid of this intelligent scavenger with its shiny, coal-black plumage because they also take him to be a harbinger of ill fortune and death. That explains why shamans who have the raven as their principal spirit helper were not only respected and revered for their power but also feared and even pitied for the troubles this paradoxical spirit helper could bring. The raven is clever, resourceful, and powerful as a helping spirit to shamans, but he is also a foolish trickster whose pranks more often than not backfire.

An American anthropologist named Marjorie Mandelstam Balzer writes,

> As birds help shamans ascend through difficult, multilayered cosmic terrain to capture lost souls or find spirits of sickness, they loan shamans their qualities—for example, the eagle's piercing eyesight and endurance.

This is why bird symbolism has been such an essential part of the traditional Siberian shaman's costume and why feathers, talons, bones, and all kinds of other objects symbolizing birds and flight are so important in Native American shamanism as well.

But if bird spirits have almost always been an essential element in the shamanic curing rite, and remain so today, the array of a shaman's spirit helpers could change several times over a lifetime. The list could include not just high-soaring and diving birds, or birds of lesser prestige, but bears, wolves, dogs, foxes, and even bulls. Typically there were from three to nine of these animal spirit helpers, though an especially powerful shaman might have as many as 47!

Invoking the Spirit Helper

There is considerable variation across Siberia in how the helping spirits and the shaman interact with one another in the seance. When a shaman starts speaking as his spirit helper, he is already in an altered state of consciousness, if not actually in a trance. He might even take a rest from time to time to recharge, so to speak, his state of ecstasy. The shaman can identify so completely with his helping spirit that not only he but the audience comes to see him as spirit, a common phenomenon especially in eastern and central Siberia.

A Mongolian shaman in full costume beats his drum as he enters a trance. In many parts of Asia, the shamanic trance is triggered by nonchemical means, such as the hypnotic beating of a drum.

The Russian ethnographer Jochelson described a Yukaghir shaman thus:

> The shaman half-opens the door and inhales his spirits in deep and noisy breaths. Then he turns to the interior of the house [and] holds his hands like claws, rolls his eyes upwards so that only the whites are seen, sticks out his tongue, curling it under the chin and, without uttering a word, walks to the center of the house and sits down on the ground. Having sat down, he straightens his hands and pulls his tongue in with his eyes still turned upwards and [with] a blown up belly he sits there and already one of the spirits speaks through him.

During the seance, the Yukhagir shaman identifies both with his own helping spirit and the spirit responsible for the disease, alternately speaking as one or the other. If the shaman loses himself completely in his animal spirit helper—if he becomes that spirit—an assistant may take over his role as mediator, followed by a dialogue between him and the shaman-as-spirit to discuss the illness.

The area of Siberia in which shamans identify totally with the spirit helper is also the area where the spirit of an ancestral shaman may continue to serve as the new shaman's principal helping spirit. This is especially important in central and eastern Siberia where illness is typically explained by a disease spirit having entered the patient's body.

Shamanic Sickness and the Soviets

In the summer of 1994, an American anthropologist named Marjorie Mandelstam Balzer visited the grave of a famous Sakha *oiuun* named Tokoyeu (*oiuun* is what the Sakha, or Yakut, call their shamans). This *oiuun* died in 1959, but his deeds were still famous. Tokoyeu's grave was fenced in, sitting by itself a little way off from the other burials in the Russian Orthodox cemetery outside a small village in the northern Sakha Republic. This was because the graves of especially respected or feared shamans were kept apart from those of ordinary folks.

In accordance with local custom, Dr. Balzer tied some horsehair to a nearby tree as a gesture of respect. When she turned to look back at the shaman's grave, she suddenly saw a large black raven fly up and land in a nearby larch tree. For some minutes the raven stared at her. One of Tokoyeu's principal spirit helpers had been a raven. And so she said silently in her own mind, "If you are who I think you are, please help your grandson."

Tokoyeu's grandson was born in the same year his shaman grandfather died. As a teenager, Tokoyeu's grandson was struck by a mysterious illness in which he felt himself being tortured and tested by the spirits—all the symptoms of shamanic sickness vocation. Dr. Balzer writes that in another time, Tokoyeu's grandson "would have accepted the spirit helpers of his grandfather and become a leader and spiritual helper of his people," just as his grandfather had. In the Soviet era, however, shamanic sickness was regarded as mental illness—both politically and socially dangerous. And so, instead of taking his grandfather's place as a respected healer and leader of his community, the unfortunate young man was twice imprisoned in psychiatric institutions, where he was subjected to sadistic treatment with debilitating drugs.

He still showed shamanic talents, however, and he visited a distant shaman whose spirit helper was also a raven. Thus, there was hope that with the support of a loving family Tokoyeu's grandson might still become part of the renaissance Yakut shamanism and culture have been experiencing since the collapse of the Soviet Union.

Tibetan Medicine

TIBETAN MEDICINE is an ancient tradition whose roots penetrate deep into many of the healing traditions of Asia. It is called the *So Rig* in Tibetan, which means the "Science of Healing." The *So Rig* represents the accumulated knowledge of centuries of exploration by Tibetan physicians—exploration that included the observation of what worked locally and the examination of healing traditions from many other parts of the world. In this regard, Tibet was fortunate to have neighbors with strong healing traditions—China and India—that could be readily adapted to the specific environment found on the Tibetan plateau.

Two Tibetan monks in ceremonial clothing sound sacred conch trumpets adorned with silver and precious stones. The sound of the conch is used as a musical offering during sacred rituals and as an announcement of auspicious events.

The Tibetan ability to integrate the knowledge and traditions of healing from their neighbors goes hand in hand with their acceptance and embrace of Buddhism. Because Buddhist medicine views all knowledge about healing as the gift of a compassionate Buddha to a suffering world, Tibetan physicians have always felt comfortable exploring and integrating the knowledge of different traditions without regard to their origins. Tibetan physicians see compassion as the very heart of their medical tradition—it is considered the prerequisite for effective medical practice.

Spiritual Origins

Many Asian medical traditions have stories that describe their origins in supernatural or spiritual terms. Tibetan medicine is no exception. And like other myths, these stories tell us about events that seem to be nothing more than fairy tales. Although these stories cannot be considered the "real" history of the medical tradition, they can tell us a great deal about what the tradition and its practitioners valued. In the case of Tibetan medicine, there are interesting parallels between its mythologic origins and the ways in which its practice developed over the centuries.

For the practitioner of Tibetan medicine, who is typically a Buddhist, the world is seen as one among many and the present as a mere moment in a cycle of creation and destruction that extends through vast reaches of time. Throughout all these worlds and times there have been many Buddhas, or enlightened beings, who have, because of their compassion and wisdom, come to help humans and all beings reach enlightenment. Furthermore, these Buddhas always provide their knowledge in ways that are the most helpful and appropriate to the needs of the people.

*The Medicine Buddha is known as the Buddha of Lapis Lazuli Light because of his vivid blue color, which is said to be like that of the precious stone. In his left hand is a bowl of life-giving nectar and in his right is the flower and fruit of the myrobalan (*Terminalia chebula*), one of the most important medicines in the Tibetan and Ayurvedic traditions.*

The Medicine Buddha According to the scriptures of Buddhism, it was a great Buddha of the past—Kasyapa Buddha—who taught medicine to Brahma, resulting in the tradition of Ayurveda (see pages 186–218). By tradition, the teachings of Tibetan medicine spring from a similarly divine and enlightened source. In Tibet, it is believed that Sakyamuni Buddha, who lived and taught his path to enlightenment around 600 B.C., appeared to many gods, sages, and students of medicine in the form of the Medicine Buddha.

The Medicine Buddha is known as the Buddha of Lapis Lazuli Light because his skin is a deep, radiant blue color. This color is associated with the power of healing. In his right hand the Medicine Buddha holds the fruit of the *Terminalia chebula* (sometimes called myrobalan)—a healing plant—and in his left hand he holds a bowl of life-giving nectar. This was the vivid and mystical form that the Buddha adopted to teach medicine.

The scriptures tell us that the teachings took place in a celestial palace of medicine called *Tanadug*, which was located on a hill surrounded on all sides by different medicinal plants and substances. The Medicine Buddha appeared before Buddhists and non-Buddhists, gods, and sages in this dazzling blue form and caused two accomplished physician-sages, or *rishis*, to appear—one from his heart and one from his mouth. The two began a dialogue based on question and answer that resulted in the teaching of the core text of the Tibetan medical tradition: the *Four Tantras*.

COMPASSIONATE ACTION According to tradition, each group of beings listening to these teachings heard them in a way that was most meaningful and appropriate to them—in a way that related to their medical traditions. Accordingly, many Hindu practitioners who were there are said to have heard teachings on sacred Hindu texts, whereas other sages heard teachings from Caraka, one of the fathers of Ayurveda (see page 202).

These powerful stories link Buddhist healing with all medical traditions in Asia. Scholars generally believe that the Buddhist scriptures that describe these events and the medical teachings were written in about A.D. 400, long after the passing of Sakyamuni Buddha. However, the image of the Medicine Buddha teaching many medical traditions was a way of indicating that, as a compassionate human activity, there was no separation between methods and types of medicine. There was no need to draw a distinction between the medicines of Ayurveda, the medicines of China, or the medicines of Tibet. From the perspective of Buddhist medicine, all medicine was an expression of compassionate action.

Historical Origins

Historians know very little about Tibet before A.D. 600. There are legends of kings extending back into the past, but they are historically unreliable. What we do know is that the Tibetans lived in groups organized along family lines and herded yaks and sheep across the vast Tibetan plateau. They engaged in trade with their neighbors and used the horse as an important means of crossing long distances, rounding up livestock, and communicating with other clans.

In the 7th century A.D., Tibet began to emerge as a significant force in central Asia. Songtsen Gampo, Tibet's 33rd king, was able to unite many small tribal factions into a military force capable of projecting Tibetan power into neighboring countries, including China.

ACQUIRING KNOWLEDGE FROM NEIGHBORS Tibet has a long history of absorbing ideas from outsiders, and the study of medicine

The Country at the Top of the World

Modern Tibet, or the Tibetan Autonomous Region as it is known today, lies north of India and Nepal and west of China, although technically within the political boundaries of the People's Republic of China and under the control of its government (see map, page 278). Tibet is the world's most elevated country, with communities over 10,000 feet above sea level and roads traversing steep mountain passes.

The country is bounded on three sides by mountains: to the south, the Himalayas; to the north, the Kun Lun and Tang La ranges; and to the west, the Karakoram and Ladakh mountains. Because of changes in elevation and terrain, Tibet presents a tremendously varied landscape. In addition to the steep mountains, Tibet has lush forests, vast tracts of grassland, and areas of farmland and pasture.

Tibet shows evidence of having been inhabited since 2000 B.C., but little is known of its history prior to the 6th century A.D. Until 1959, when it was invaded by the Chinese Army, Tibet considered itself an independent country and maintained a distinctive political system.

The Potala Palace, overlooking the Tibetan capital Lhasa, has been the home of Tibet's Dalai Lamas from the late 17th century to the middle of the 20th century, when the 14th Dalai Lama was forced to flee from Chinese troops. The hill that the palace occupies had been the site of forts, palaces, and monasteries since the reign of Songtsen Gampo (ca. A.D. 635).

in Tibet benefited greatly from this habit. According to historical writings, two Indian doctors came to visit Tibet and teach medicine around A.D. 400. This was probably not the first time foreign doctors shared their wisdom with the Tibetans. Young Tibetan nobles often went to China to study in the years preceding Songtsen Gampo's reign, and it would be safe to infer that they brought home many ideas about Chinese medicine.

During the reign of Songtsen Gampo, though, Tibet's influence in Asia and its military successes against the Chinese cleared the way for even more exchange of ideas. For example, Songtsen Gampo was able to demand the hand of a Chinese princess, Wen Ch'eng, in marriage, and she brought with her a Chinese medical text called the *Great Analytical Treatise on Medicine*. During Gampo's reign, a written form of language was developed, Buddhism was introduced, and most important from our point of view, the first of two international medical conferences were held.

THE FIRST MEDICAL CONFERENCE Just as they sought knowledge about Buddhism, language, law, and technology from all over Asia, the Tibetans were also interested in medical developments in neighboring countries. Two early kings invited learned physicians from other parts of Asia to share their knowledge, and Songtsen Gampo invited three physicians from India, China, and Persia to come to the Tibetan court to give lectures on their methods and systems. These doctors translated works into Tibetan and then, richly rewarded by the king, returned home. The Persian physician Galenos, however, stayed behind and created a family lineage of medical practice in Tibet.

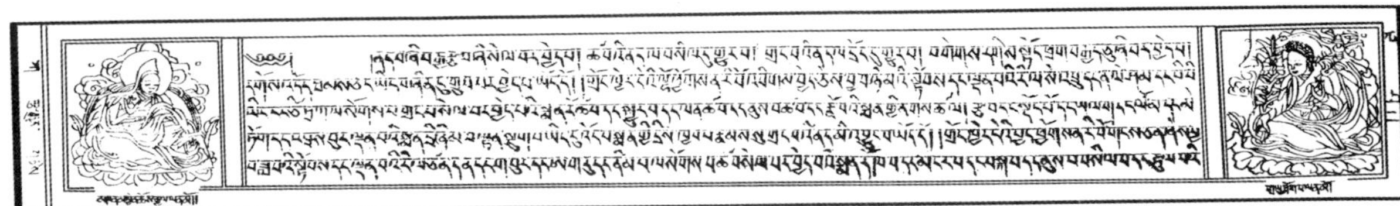

The first two pages of an edition of the Four Tantras *that dates to the middle of the 18th century. The* Four Tantras *form the basis for the theory and practice of medicine in Tibet.*

In the 8th century, King Trihsong Detsen continued the tradition of inviting foreign physicians to teach their knowledge of medicine to the Tibetans. During his reign, he sent messengers with gold to bring doctors from India, China, Persia, Nepal, and other countries to translate their works into Tibetan. The reign of Trihsong Detsen also saw Buddhism flourish in Tibet and the translation of the core texts of the Tibetan medical tradition—the *Four Tantras*—from Sanskrit into Tibetan.

Over time, Tibet was transformed from a powerful military state with ambitions outside its borders to a religious state under the guidance of a succession of enlightened kings, the Dalai Lamas. In this environment the medical traditions that had been imported and integrated were lovingly nurtured in monasteries, medical schools, and in the family lineages of generations of Tibetan doctors.

The Eight Branches of Medicine

The division of medical practice into eight branches derives from the Ayurvedic tradition. The Tibetan tradition absorbed this and many other ideas from the Ayurveda. In a way, the branches bear a great deal of similarity to some of modern Western medicine's categories, with at least one notable exception:

- Physical ailments
- Pediatrics
- Gynecology
- Men's ailments
- Diseases caused by spirits
- Wounds from weapons
- Geriatrics
- Reproductive medicine

Medical Education

The study of medicine in Tibet occurred through traditional systems of apprenticeship, with students studying with private physicians, and through organized schools. Yuthog the Elder founded what is thought to be the first medical college in Tibet. This school bore the name of the mountain on which the Medicine Buddha gave his teaching on medicine: Tanadug.

The 5th Dalai Lama established three medical schools during his reign, including the famous Chag Po Ri, or iron mountain. This medical school became the source of physicians for each of the districts throughout Tibet. During the reign of the 13th Dalai Lama (1895–1933), a famous physician named Kenrab Norbu established the Medicine House in the city of Lhasa, which became another center for medical education.

THE FOUR TANTRAS Today and since the 8th century, the most important medical book in the Tibetan tradition is a compilation of knowledge about the body, diagnosis, and healing called *The Four Secret Oral Tantras on the Eight Branches of the Essence of Nectar.* Also known by the shorter names, the *Four Tantras* or the *rGyud-bzhi* (pronounced GYU SHE), this text is said to have been taught by the Medicine Buddha through the manifestation of the sages. The text is actually thought to have been written in Sanskrit about A.D. 400 and translated into Tibetan. A short time later, it was edited and supplemented by the court physician Yuthog Yontan Gonpo (708–833), who integrated the teachings of the physicians who came to the great medical conference convened by King Trihsong Detsen. The *Four Tantras* continue to be used as the basis for teaching, learning, and practicing Tibetan medicine.

The *Four Tantras* is divided into the *Root Tantra,* the *Explanatory Tantra,* the *Information Tantra,* and the *Final Tantra.* For centuries, the study of Tibetan medicine has begun with the memorization of these texts. Usually the first two and the last are studied first and committed to memory; the third—an extensive discussion of curing many different diseases—is studied later. Together these four texts comprise 156 chapters that address the eight branches of medicine.

The Tree of Medicine, or Three Roots, is a traditional way of organizing the knowledge of Tibetan medicine. The Three Roots are the Situation of the Body, Diagnosis, and Therapy. This elegant metaphor for the organization of the healing arts in Tibet is described in the sixth chapter of the Root Tantra, one of the Four Tantras. *Pictured here is the First Root composed of two trunks: the healthy body and the body in illness.*

Because the *Four Tantras* are meant to be committed to memory, they are organized systematically to make the process of learning them easier. The *Root Tantra,* which contains the essence of the *Four Tantras,* is composed of six chapters. The first describes how the Medicine Buddha taught medicine. The second describes the organization and contents of the 154 chapters that follow. The third, fourth, and fifth chapters discuss the general practice of Tibetan medicine. But the sixth chapter describes the three roots of medicine and the tree that grows from them, known as the Tree of Medicine.

THE TREE OF MEDICINE The tree described in the sixth chapter of the *Root Tantra* represents the entire practice of Tibetan medicine. It is the central image used to help practitioners of Tibetan medicine organize their knowledge and commit it to memory.

Each of the roots of the tree represents one of the three sections of Tibetan medical practice:

- Root 1: *The Situation of the Body*—the basic concepts about the working of the body in health and disease
- Root 2: *Diagnosis*—the process of determining what has disturbed the normal equilibrium and health of the body
- Root 3: *Therapeutics*—the methods used to restore the body to harmony

The Tree of Tibetan Medicine

Root 1: The Situation of the Body
- Trunk 1: The Healthy Body
- Trunk 2: The Body in Sickness

Root 2: Diagnosis
- Trunk 3: Observation
- Trunk 4: Palpation
- Trunk 5: Questioning

Root 3: Therapeutics
- Trunk 6: Diet
- Trunk 7: Behavior
- Trunk 8: Medicine
- Trunk 9: External Treatment

The image of the tree works like an outline: Each root gives rise to a specific number of trunks from which branches and leaves sprout, producing a detailed image of the entire practice of Tibetan medicine.

STUDY AND MEMORIZATION Even today, a medical student will begin his or her studies by progressively committing the *Four Tantras* to memory. Traditional education in Tibet has always been linked to the process of memorization. A child would learn the Tibetan alphabet and, as soon as he or she could sound out words, would begin memorizing texts on grammar and religion. Medical education would build on this foundation, and a medical student would use these very developed abilities to memorize and absorb medical knowledge by rote. Once memorized, these texts provided the basis for future study and learning. Oral commentary, the observations of experienced teachers, and the study of healing methods would all rest on the solid foundation provided by the memorized *Tantras*.

The Tree of Medicine was an important tool in this practice. Medical students in Tibet would study elaborate paintings that

The high altitudes and soaring vistas of the Himalayas provide the southern barrier to Tibet. The environmental conditions and distinctive plant life have had a definite influence on the development of Tibetan medicine.

depicted the tree, or the Three Roots as it was sometimes called. They would go to the market and buy buttons and colored thread to trace out the roots, trunks, branches, and leaves of the tree. As they did this, their understanding would grow firmer. The classification and structure of the Three Roots became the basis for the memorization and understanding of future medical learning.

A Universe of Elements

The fundamental ideas that create the foundation for Tibetan medical theory and practice come from ancient Indian systems of philosophy. Although contemporary practitioners of Tibetan medicine recognize these ideas as being quite different from modern scientific perspectives, these ancient views are important to the medical system and have formed its basis for centuries.

According to the traditional Tibetan view, the universe and the body are both a result of the existence and interaction of the five elements: air, fire, water, earth, and space. The Tibetan term *jung wa* can be translated as "element," but it also has the sense of a "source" or "origin." Hence, the five elements are, in effect, the source of all phenomena. Everything that we experience is created by the interplay of earth, water, wind, and fire within the vastness of space.

Just as the universe originates from the activity of these elements, so do we. In fact, the five elements are the foundation for understanding much of what is done in Tibetan medicine. Everything consists of the five elements in different proportions, and that is what gives things their distinctive features. A cup of coffee, for instance, has proportionately more wind and fire in it than other elements. A peach has predominantly water and earth elements.

Development of the Human Body

The various stages of fetal development are dealt with extensively in the medical texts and with a level of detail and accuracy that can be quite surprising. Each part of the body corresponds to one of the parents and to the element that forms it.

- Father's sperm: bones, brain, and spinal cord
- Mother's blood: flesh, blood, solid organs, and hollow organs
- Earth: flesh, bones, the organ of smelling, and odors
- Water: blood, the organ of taste, tastes, and moisture
- Fire: warmth, clear coloration, the organ of sight, and form
- Wind: breath, the organ of touch, and physical sensations
- Space: cavities in the body, the organ of hearing, and sounds

The system of elements permits interactions among phenomena to be understood in terms of their elemental composition. They govern the birth and death of the body; their disturbance produces disease; and by using them properly, health can be restored. The five elements constitute the body that the Tibetan doctor seeks to heal, and they are contained in the medicines that he will use to accomplish the healing process.

The Healthy Body

Blooming at the top of the first trunk of the Tree of Tibetan Medicine are the results of good health: the two flowers—

The first root of the Three Roots of Tibetan medicine is Situation of the Body. It has two trunks: one shows the constituents of a healthy body, and the other shows the causes and processes of disease. In addition, two flowers, representing long life and freedom from illness sprout from the first trunk and are said to ripen the three fruits of dharma (the sacred teachings of the Buddha), wealth, and happiness.

health and longevity—and the three fruits—spiritual accomplishment, wealth, and happiness. From a Buddhist perspective, being born as a human being is an exceptionally fortunate event that gives us many opportunities. A long and healthy life affords the greatest range of possibilities. With a healthy body, we can pursue wealth and happiness, and we can also look beyond this life to spiritual accomplishment and liberation from an endless cycle of rebirth.

Despite the grand metaphors and the spiritual definitions of health, what it means to be healthy in Tibetan medicine is very well defined by physical phenomena. The basic elements and the structures and substances of the body form the basis of the Tibetan understanding of health. Borrowing from their Chinese neighbors to the east and their Indian neighbors to the west, Tibet devised an elaborate system of anatomy and physiology to describe the healthy body.

THE THREE HUMORS Although the five elements make up everything in the universe including the body, when it comes to health and disease, Tibetan medicine uses three slightly more complex substances called *humors* to talk about the day-to-day functioning of the body. The three humors, which correspond to Ayurvedic medicine's doshas (see page 196), are

- wind (Tibetan: *rlung*; Sanskrit: *vata*)
- bile (Tibetan: *mkhris pa*; Sanskrit: *pitta*)
- phlegm (Tibetan: *bad kan*; Sanskrit: *kapha*)

The Tibetan word for the humors is *nyeba*, meaning "fault." Just as the original Sanskrit term *dosha* suggests a defect, *nyeba* is used in Tibetan medicine because the humors, or faults, are integral to the normal functioning of the body but they also carry the seeds of illness in them. It is in their nature to become disturbed by environmental factors, by diet, and by emotions.

The humors are discrete physical substances, each performing specific functions and having specific locations in the body. When a humor becomes unbalanced—that is, increased, decreased, or moved to an inappropriate location in the body—illness results. (Ultimately, the only true solution—the only way to get away from the faults and the suffering that their perpetually potential disturbance imposes—is the achievement of enlightenment.)

The idea of the three humors comes directly from India and the Ayurvedic tradition, but Tibetan medicine often considers blood almost as if it were a fourth humor. Some consider blood's mention in the Tibetan system to be an example of the influence of the ancient medical traditions of Greece and Persia, because these other systems used four humors to describe the body and accorded blood a significant place in the consideration of the body's processes.

A Tibetan monk sits holding prayer beads in his right hand. His shaved head and bare right arm express the standard for Buddhist monks since the Buddha gave his instructions on their conduct (ca. 600 B.C.). Although heavier to accommodate the colder climate at high altitudes, his robes are patched and dyed in earth tones to express renunciation of worldly decoration and costly garments.

Humors and Elements. As in Ayurveda, the basic elements make up the three humors in the following manner: earth and water form phlegm; fire is the basis of bile; and air is the basis of wind. Space provides an environment for the activities and interactions of the elements. This elemental makeup gives us clues to a humor's attributes and behavior. For example, phlegm has the combined qualities of earth and water and is increased by the presence of these elements; phlegm is considered to be cold in nature. Bile, made up of fire, has a hot nature.

The Locations of the Humors. The humors have fundamental associations with specific parts of the body and are said to "reside" in these places. Phlegm is said to reside in the head and chest; bile resides in the abdomen; and wind resides in the hips and legs. This structure parallels the makeup of the universe in Tibetan thought, with earth and water resting on the fire, which rests on wind.

Subcategories. Each humor is further divided into five different types, or subcategories. Each subcategory is located in a different part of the body and has a different function, yet each displays the quality of its corresponding humor. For example, each of the three humors has subtypes that pertain to the process of digestion, and each of these expresses the nature of its humor. Decomposing phlegm breaks food down into a semiliquid state; the earth and water aspects of the phlegm soften, moisten, and unite the food that has been eaten. Digestive bile, using its fire, transforms the partially digested food into substances that can be used by the body. The wind involved in digestion—the fire-equalizing wind in the

The Humors and Essential Temperature

The categories hot and cold are critical to understanding the body, diagnosis, and treatment in Tibetan medicine. Hot and cold are a set of fundamental and opposing qualities that are used in the classification of medicine to understand the relationship of the humors. (In a discussion of medicines, hot and cold are called potencies.) Two humors are considered cold in nature, and one humor and the blood are considered hot:

HOT	COLD
Bile	Phlegm
Blood	Wind

lower part of the stomach—separates wastes from nutrients and conveys these nutrients through the body.

Bodily Constituents The ancient Tibetan view of anatomy integrated both Ayurvedic and Chinese notions. The idea of seven bodily constituents, or *dhatu* in Sanskrit, comes directly from the Ayurvedic tradition, whereas the notion of solid and hollow organs, or *zang* and *fu* organs, comes from the Chinese system of medicine (see page 295). The idea of the solid organs that the Tibetans use is a little different from contemporary use in Chinese medicine, suggesting that these ideas were borrowed and integrated early on.

As the five elements of the body increase, the seven constituents of the body are nourished by the nutrients, or chyle, carried to them by the fire-equalizing wind. As in Ayurveda, the constituents are ordered, reflecting the nourishment of the body. Thus, (1) chyle contributes to the formation of (2) blood, which develops (3) muscle tissues. The essence of these tissues forms (4) fat from which (5) bone is nourished. The essence of bone forms (6) marrow, whose essence forms the (7) regenerative, or reproductive, fluids. (For Ayurveda equivalents, see page 205.)

Excretions The three impurities are feces, urine, and sweat, which correspond to Ayurveda's malas (see page 205). They are composed of the wastes separated out of the digested food by the fire-equalizing wind and expelled from the body by the subcategory of wind known as the downward-moving wind.

Personal Qualities Besides physical processes, the humors also influence personality and constitution. Each human being reflects a distinct elemental and humoral blend that influences his or her growth, development, and personality. For example, a person whose constitution is dominated by wind is said to be lively and talkative, to enjoy laughter, to be graceful, and to sleep poorly. All of these traits pertain to the light and mobile aspects of wind. Sleeplessness is typically associated with wind. (For more on personality types in humoral theory, see page 198.)

Causes of Disease

The cause of all disease in Tibetan medicine is a disruption of the humors. Although a seemingly simple theory, the factors that can cause disruption and the patterns of disruption that can occur are many and varied. The humors exist in a delicate state of balance. One humor can be diminished, two humors can be diminished—in fact, any logical combination is possible.

Emotional Disturbance Tibetan medicine is definitely Buddhist medicine. Buddhism is concerned with past actions, specifically actions in past lives, known as *karma*. Therefore, Tibetan medicine's appraisal of illness and disease also takes into account an individual's karma. And because all actions occur under the influence of a mental state, the fundamental causes of disease (disturbances of the humors) are the emotional afflictions of desire, anger, and ignorance.

Desire is related to wind, anger to bile, and ignorance to phlegm. These three mental states are seen as the actual causes of disease. Factors such as an unbalanced diet, inappropriate behavior, climate, and

A Tibetan sits engaged in the accumulation of merit, or the accumulation of good deeds, to help ensure a happy rebirth in future lives. The "mala," or rosary, in his left hand is used to count the number of times he recites a mantra or prayer. The prayer wheel in his right hand holds slips of paper, each with a mantra or prayer written on it many times. Each time the prayer wheel spins, the prayers written on the paper inside are considered recited.

harmful influences (such as spirits and inauspicious days) are considered secondary causes that create the potential for negative actions in past lives to produce illness in the present.

The negative activities of the mind can also be an immediate cause of illness since violent desire or anger can substantially disturb wind and bile. The activity of the mind either in past lives or in the present lays the foundation for disturbances of the humors.

ELEMENTAL DISTURBANCE Because the different emotional afflictions have qualities similar to the various humors, they can stimulate some humors and thus unbalance them. Similarly, some conditions depend on exposure to a particular elemental configuration, which affects a humor. Once again, through excessive stimulation or diminution, the humor becomes unbalanced.

For example, if an individual partakes of sweet foods to excess, the presence of earth and water elements in the sweet-tasting food increases the earth and water elements that constitute phlegm. Increasing phlegm causes an imbalance between the humors. An overabundance of phlegm can lead to a decrease in digestive heat (water quenches fire) and result in indigestion. In another case, one of the specific subcategories of the humors can be disturbed. For instance, the connecting phlegm that is responsible for the smooth action of the joints can become disturbed, causing the joints to thicken and causing pain in the shoulders and hips.

AGES, TIMES, AND SEASONS Besides their interaction with elements and emotions, the different humors also correspond to different times of the day, times of the year, and times of an individual's life. For example, wind accumulates in the early summer because that season is characterized by qualities of lightness and roughness. These seasonal qualities of early summer are similar to the qualities of wind and, therefore, cause wind to increase. (Ayurveda recognizes a similar relationship between different times and the doshas; see page 209.)

Distinguishing the periods during which a humor will predominate permits the physician to anticipate occasions when specific diseases will flourish. The patient can also be on guard against the dangers of the sea-

Like the smaller prayer wheels, these larger wheels hold many slips of paper on which prayers and mantras are written. On the outside of each brass drum is inscribed the special mantra of Chenresigs: Om Man Padre Hum. *Each time a wheel turns, the positive expression inscribed on the wheel and on the paper within is mobilized, bringing its benefits to all beings.*

son or the time of day and plan activities and diet accordingly.

Diagnosis

The root of diagnosis has three trunks in the Tree of Medicine: observation, palpation, and questioning. Observation is the examination of the tongue and the urine. Palpation, or feeling, is checking the pulse. Questioning is used to evaluate behavior and symptoms. These three diagnostic techniques allow the physician to understand the nature of the disease.

OBSERVATION Observation refers to the examination of the tongue and the urine, although in practice other aspects of the patient's appearance are examined as well. The tongue can reveal much about the humoral imbalances affecting the patient. When a humor is disturbed, it produces a distinctive appearance on the tongue.

Urine diagnosis has been used for centuries. Its practice has long been surrounded by strict traditions, but these traditions really serve to keep the experiment strictly controlled. The ancient texts describe many preliminary compliances, which are to be observed by the patient; actions that are thought to alter the condition of the urine are forbidden. For example, the patient is not to consume tea (which can affect wind urines), whey (which can affect phlegm urines), or foods with a hot taste (which can affect bile urines). Strenuous activity is also forbidden, possibly because it leads to excess water excretion.

Diagnosis is the second root of the Three Roots of Tibetan medicine. This root has three trunks describing diagnosis by observation, by palpation, and by questioning. The colors used to paint the trunks represent the different humors: wind, bile, and phlegm.

Urine is traditionally observed in the morning before eating. (The medical scriptures state that the best time for examination is at dawn.) There are no stipulations concerning the length of time that may elapse before the urine itself is examined.

The changes observed in the urine immediately after it is stirred indicate the nature of the patient's humoral disturbance. For example, a sample of urine taken from a patient who has a combined disturbance of bile and phlegm would have a comparatively dark color and show thick, medium-sized and small bubbles. A few moments after being stirred, the bubbles vanish and this sign—the rapid disappearance of the bubbles combined with the darkish hue—suggests the bile disturbance. The thick clustering of the bubbles would suggest phlegm. Consequently, this urine would be interpreted as indicating a combined disturbance of bile and phlegm.

The Trunk of Observation

Padma Karpo, a 16th century commentator, wrote this as a way of explaining the first trunk on the second root of the Tree of Medicine:

> The first trunk has two branches: the branch of observing the tongue and the branch of examining the urine.
>
> The first branch has three leaves. The wind tongue is red, dry, and rough. The bile tongue is covered with thick, pale-yellow phlegm. The phlegm tongue is pale, lusterless, soft, and moist.
>
> The second branch has three leaves. Wind urine is like water with big bubbles. Bile urine is red-yellow with much steam and a strong smell. Phlegm urine is white, having little vapor or smell.

PALPATION: PULSE DIAGNOSIS The Tibetan term *tsa* means "root" or "channel." To palpate the channels is to feel a pulse. Often the term *tsa* is translated directly as "pulse," but the term can also indicate many other types of channels in the body. In Tibetan medicine, pulse reveals much more than just the speed of the heart's pumping; it is a window to the dynamics of the humors and the quality of the pulse. Pulse diagnosis is considered the most difficult medical skill to acquire.

Wind produces movement in the body. Wind moves through certain channels by itself. In others, it is responsible for the movement of the substances the channel carries, such as blood. Although wind and blood flow together, pulse diagnosis can discern the quality of the wind (assessing the quality of the motion displayed by a channel in which the wind flows).

Pulse diagnosis is one of the most esoteric arts in Tibetan medicine. According to both ancient texts and modern practice, the pulse is taken at the radial artery on the wrist to avoid the interference from the noise of the lungs and heart, and it

The Trunk of Palpation

In his commentary on the *Four Tantras,* Padma Karpo describes the second trunk of the second root of the Tree of Medicine this way:

> The second trunk has three branches: the first is the branch of feeling the wind pulse, the second is the branch of feeling the bile pulse, and the third is the branch of feeling the phlegm pulse. There are three leaves, one on each branch. The first leaf describes wind pulse, which is full and stalk like; it stops abruptly. The second leaf describes the bile pulse, which is quick, strong, hurried, and forceful. The third leaf describes the phlegm pulse, which is sinking, thin, and slow.

usually takes place in the morning before breakfast when it gives the truest representation of the patient's condition. Three fingers of each hand are used. It is said that the index finger should rest lightly on the skin, the middle finger should feel flesh, and the ring finger should feel bone. The need for this variation of pressure, it is said, derives from the shape of the channel, which is compared to a radish or carrot that tapers as it goes deeper into the ground.

The Tibetan medical texts explain that a healthy individual may be characterized by one of three pulse types: male, female, or neuter. Each of these has its own particular beat.

- A male pulse indicates a constitution with a predominance of wind. This pulse beat is rough and thick.
- A female pulse indicates a constitution with a predominance of bile. This pulse beat is rapid and thin.
- A neuter pulse indicates a constitution in which phlegm predominates. This pulse is smooth and pliable.

These pulses are *constitutional* in that they describe the dominant humor (as a trait) of an individual's body. The Tibetan physician recognizes the constitutional pulse through experience and familiarity with the patient. These pulses are not to be confused with the pulses of wind, bile, and phlegm disorders.

In addition to revealing the constitutional makeup of the patient, pulse diagnosis is used to assess the condition of the major organs in the body. The six hollow organs—the stomach, large intestines, gallbladder, small intestine, urinary bladder, and reproductive organs—and the five solid organs—the lungs, heart, liver, spleen, and kidneys—are each related to a point on the doctor's fingers. The "organs" that are being assessed through palpation are different from those modern biomedicine concerns itself with. The organs that a Tibetan physician is concerned with might best be viewed as spheres of physiologic function—categories of function throughout the body—rather than individual, localized clusters of tissue.

The pulse can also reveal whether the patient's disorder is hot or cold (one of the most basic distinctions) and many other pieces of information about the patient and his or her condition. For example, pulses felt along the ulnar artery (in the forearm) can be used to address esoteric issues such as the involvement of spirits, the health of relatives, and the life span of the patient.

There are a rather substantial number of descriptive terms for the types of pulse, each signifying a specific sort of imbalance. There is nothing ambiguous about this to the system's practitioner. The pulse is regarded as a messenger that tells the physician what the condition of the body and the organs is.

The value of the information derived from the pulse can be immense. When the modern Tibetan physician Yeshe Donden examined a patient at an American hospital not too long ago, he took a great deal of time feeling the pulse. Afterward, Donden correctly described the patient's condition as a congenital heart disorder. He also used metaphor to describe the state of the heart in a fashion that was strikingly consistent with the biomedical

A Visit to a Tibetan Doctor

Because we know little about the exact ways in which clinical practice was conducted in ancient times, except for what is written in the scriptures of Buddhism, we must rely on the living presence of physicians who are the present expression of an unbroken lineage dating back to the great ancient healers of Tibet.

Yeshe Donden was born in 1929 and received ordination as a Buddhist monk at the age of six. He entered the school called the Medicine House at Lhasa, Tibet, at an early age and gained great proficiency in the medical system. Although he left Tibet for India with other refugees in 1959, he reestablished the Medicine House for the Tibetan community in exile and served for over 20 years as personal physician to the 14th Dalai Lama. He now has his own clinic in a small community in Himachal Pradesh, India, and treats patients all over the world.

Generally, urine inspection is the first event in the diagnostic routine. If the patient has brought urine, Yeshe Donden proceeds outside with it to a small concrete sink equipped with a water tank that is used specifically for urine examination. This event provides the clinic with a bustle of activity. Often he forms the head of a little procession as he rustles along in his maroon robes followed by the patient, the patient's retinue, and any students who happen to be present. The urine is poured from its container into an enameled cup where it is agitated with a long, thin section of bamboo. He inspects the bubbles, the color, and any particle content. Sometimes questions ensue at this point, sometimes not. The doctor and patient return to the consulting room for the pulse taking and the questions.

In pulse taking—the second of the three diagnostic trunks on the Tree of Medicine—the doctor feels the pulses at both of the patients wrists in a subtle and sensitive process that can take a few seconds to many minutes depending on the situation. Once this is done, Yeshe Donden asks the patient to describe factors such as diet, behavior, and climate that make the condition better or worse. In the case of a complex condition, this may be an extensive process during which the doctor may even review the medical records that the patient has brought with him.

Once he reaches a diagnosis, Yeshe Donden prescribes medicines and other forms of treatment for the patient. The medicines are usually provided in the form of small spherical pills made of herbs to be taken three times each day with warm water until the next visit.

diagnosis: congenital interventricular septal defect (heart defect) with resultant heart failure.

Questioning A Tibetan physician's repertoire of diagnostic techniques includes the use of the "29 questions." By determining what diet and behaviors the patient has engaged in, what symptoms the patient is experiencing, and what experiences give relief, the physician can determine the nature of the patient's illness. These questions allow the doctor to determine if the patient has engaged in activities or consumed a food that may have unbalanced a humor.

Whether they be dietary, behavioral, or environmental, causes have qualities in common with the humors they disturb, and the disturbed humors have symptoms that are similar to their essential qualities. Heat produces bile disease; windy places engender wind; and cold, moist environments produce phlegm. When disturbed, wind produces restlessness, agitation, and sighing; questioning will reveal the origin of such problems.

The Trunk of Questioning

The third trunk of the second root of the Tree of Medicine describes a basic set of questions that are used to establish whether the disease is primarily caused by a disturbance of wind, bile, or phlegm. The questions are used to establish both causes and symptoms. Padma Karpo wrote

> The third trunk has three branches: the first is the branch of questions [about] the customary state of illnesses conditioned by wind, the second is the branch of questions about the customary states of illness conditioned by bile, the third is the branch of questions about the customary states of illness conditioned by phlegm.

When the text refers to "customary states of illnesses conditioned by wind," it refers to causes and symptoms that are typical of wind. For example, light and coarse food or emotions might be implicated as causes of wind disorders. Typical symptoms might include yawning, shivering, sighing, mental agitation, and insomnia. Bile disorders could be caused by sitting in the hot sun or engaging in violent behavior, and their symptoms might include a bitter taste in the mouth or a severe headache. Phlegm disorders could be produced by the consumption of heavy greasy food or sleeping in damp environments.

With these questions, a practitioner can verify the results obtained by means of observation (tongue and urine examination) and palpation (pulse diagnosis). If the results of these or other methods are not clear, the process of interrogation can help him reach a definitive diagnosis.

Therapeutics

Diagnosis attempts to get a clear picture of the humoral imbalances affecting the patient and the way in which they impact the body. Once this is done, appropriate healing methods can be selected. Treatment in Tibetan medicine can draw on many methods of eliminating the imbalance of the humors and the symptoms of disease. The root of therapeutics is the most dense and complicated of the roots of the Tree of Medicine. It is a summary of the myriad therapeutic possibilities that are available to the clinician. The root of therapeutics has four trunks:

- the trunk of diet
- the trunk of behavior
- the trunk of medicine
- the trunk of external therapeutics

These trunks are all systematically organized according to their application to the three humors. In practice, which is based on the contents of the *Information Tantra* and on many other texts and traditions,

The third root of the Three Roots of Tibetan medicine describes methods of healing. From the root sprout the four trunks of food and drink, behavior, medicine, and external treatment. From each of these trunks sprout branches and leaves that describe ways of treating disease. The first trunk, for instance, has six branches, which describe the correct foods and beverages for people with diseases caused by wind, bile, and phlegm.

the matter becomes quite complex. The texts describe food and behavior first because these are considered fundamental to establishing and maintaining good health.

DIET An initial examination of the trunk of diet is a little shocking (see "Food and Drink That Treat Humors"). It mentions quite a few foods and beverages that we as modern Westerners would be very unlikely to recognize, much less eat. It is important to remember that these are foods from a very different cultural and physical environment. Year-old meat, for example, sounds a bit unappetizing but actually refers to meat that has been aged and dried, not unlike beef jerky. Horse and yak meat rarely find their way onto our tables, but among the nomadic Tibetan clans, horse and yak would have been staples.

Despite their apparent oddness, all of the foods described represent the application of the principles provided by their elemental qualities and relationship to the humors. The meats are chosen for their oily and heavy properties, whereas garlic and onion both have the property of settling wind. Similar principles apply in the selection of foods and drink for bile and phlegm. These principles can be applied to any food based on tastes and qualities. There is an intimate relationship between the elements and the tastes and qualities of foods and medicines.

BEHAVIOR The adjustment of behavior has always been considered critical to preventing, managing, and curing illness. The essence of this form of therapy is engaging in behaviors that act to sooth the overacting humor while avoiding those behaviors that exacerbate existing imbalances.

Food and Drink That Treat the Humors

In his commentary on the *Four Tantras,* Padma Karpo lists the basic foods and beverages that can be used to treat humoral imbalances.

Foods and beverages that clear wind:

horse meat	treacle
donkey meat	garlic onion
marmot meat	milk
year-old meat	grain beer containing *Bletia hyacynthum*
human flesh	beer
seed oil	bone beer
year-old butter	

Foods and beverages that clear bile:

yogurt	ground grains
goat's yogurt	dandelions
fresh butter	hot water
deer and antelope meat	cool water
goat meat	cooled boiled water

Foods and beverages that clear phlegm:

mutton	warm porridge of an old grain
meat	yogurt
yak meat	whey
the meat of wild carnivorous animals	strong beer
fish	boiled water
honey	

A patient with a wind imbalance who shows signs of restlessness, sleeplessness, and frequent yawning might be advised to seek out a warm place and pleasing friends. A patient with a bile imbalance might be asked to counter the sense of irritation and heat by finding cool environments and cultivating relaxed behavior. A patient with a phlegm imbalance who shows signs of corpulence, lassitude, and chill might be told to stay in a warm place and cultivate strenuous activity. For this last patient, resting or sleeping during the day would be discouraged, whereas it would be recommended for the patients with wind.

MEDICINE Since the very early days, Tibetan practitioners have made use of many minerals, animal substances, and herbs as medications. The application of specific medicinal substances in Tibetan medicine is quite complex. The theory that underlies the practice of prescription is based on the intricate relationship that exists between a medicine's powers, potencies, qualities, tastes, and influence on the elements and, hence, the humors of the body.

Jivaka and Medicines

In Buddhist medicine, there is little that is not of medicinal value. One famous story that comes from a tradition in India illustrates this.

Jivaka—a legendary Buddhist physician—was one among many of his master's disciples. One day, his teacher, a well-known physician, sent his students into the fields telling them to bring back plants and substances that had no medicinal value. Some students returned quickly bearing plants. The rest came back late that night with various substances. Jivaka remained gone for nearly a week. When he returned he explained that he had walked for several days in various directions and had been unable to find anything that could not be used as medicine. His teacher was very pleased with him and explained to his students that there was no plant that did not have value as medicine.

*Myrobalan (*Terminalia chebula*) after being processed by Tibetan physicians for the preparation of medicines. In the foreground, a brass tray holds the seeds that have been removed from the fruit, which lies in another brass tray in the background. The stone block and pestles are used to remove the seed from the fruit. Myrobalan is said to increase digestive heat and to help cure all diseases arising from wind, bile, and phlegm.*

First of all, foods and medicines can be divided into the categories of hot and cold. These are called potencies in Tibetan medicine. Hot and cold reflect the general tendencies of a medication. Medicines having a hot potency are pomegranate and black pepper; white sandalwood and camphor have cold potencies. A medicine with a hot potency would be used to treat a cold disease such as one caused by the overabundance of a cold humor such as phlegm.

The tastes of medicinal substances are also extremely important. There are six tastes: sweet, bitter, sour, salty, astringent, and hot. Each of these tastes is associated with two of the basic elements:

- sweet = earth and water
- sour = earth and fire
- salty = water and fire
- bitter = water and air
- hot = fire and air
- astringent = earth and air

If this list is compared with the elemental components of the three humors, you can see that the humors are controlled by tastes not similarly constituted. That is, wind is composed of the air element and pacified by tastes of substances containing earth, water, and fire elements. This reflects the essential intention of Tibetan therapeutics: to remove a condition by affecting the factors (the humors and their elements) that have caused it to develop. The object is to restore bodily balance by the application of an opposite force.

Like the 2 potencies and the 6 tastes, there are also 8 powers and 17 qualities that can be attributed to different medicines. These, in turn, relate to the elements and the humors. These attributes—potency, taste, power, and quality—provide the physician with a method of evaluating medicines and discerning which ones would be most appropriate for a given patient's condition.

Choosing the Prescription. The selection and prescription of Tibetan medicines is a complex activity. The selection of an appropriate medicine for a disease according to its heat or coolness (potency) is crucial. It is said that if this diagnostic determination is not done properly, the treatment has no hope of succeeding.

Once the appropriate medicines are chosen, they are given to the patient at specific times of day, according to the dominant humor. Thus a patient with a bile disease might receive a strong medicine to reduce bile at noon when bile is most in the ascendant (see page 209).

Tibetan Medicinal Plants

Long Pepper (*Piper longum*)—Treats cold, wind, and spleen disorders.

Aloewood (*Aquilaria agallocha*)—Treats heart fevers, diseases of the life channel, and wind disease.

Pomegranate (*Punica granatum*)—Treats cold wind and cold phlegm diseases, and increases digestive heat.

White Sandalwood (*Santalum album*)—Treats fevers.

Myrobalan Fruit (*Terminalia chebula*)—Treats diseases caused by wind, bile, and phlegm.

Fennel (*Foeniculum vulgarae*)—Treats wind fevers, eye disease, and improves appetite.

Adhadota (*Adhota vasica*)—Treats hepatitis and inflamed blood vessels.

Saffron (the stigmas of *Crocus sativus*)—Treats liver disease and constricts the openings of channels.

Nutmeg (*Myristica fragrans*)—Treats wind and heart fever.

Costus (*Saussurea lappa*)—Treats abdominal distension and wind, blood, and lung disorders.

Scute (*Scutellaria baicalensis*)—Treats all types of fevers.

Modern production methods now play a role in Tibetan medicine. Medicinal pills are shown here being poured into drying trays after being polished in the large electric polishing units arrayed nearby. Polishing, the final step in pill production, permits a longer shelf life and a more pleasing appearance.

Medicines are spiritual as well as material substances. Physicians will have Lamas come to their pharmacies and perform rituals and prayers to bless the medicines with the power and spirit of the Medicine Buddha.

Tibetan Medicines and Their Uses

- Aquilaria 31 treats insomnia and dizziness.
- Carthamus 7 treats acute abdominal pain, colic, and pain in the area of the liver.
- Pomegranate 13 strengthens digestive heat; benefits the appetite; and treats indigestion, phlegm accumulation in the epigastrium, bleeding ulcers, and phlegm disorders.
- Swertia 8 treats bile diseases with heat: headache, fever, thirst, nausea, bitter taste in the mouth, sleepiness in the daytime, yellow sclerae, and yellow tongue.

Once we move from the therapeutic uses of single substances to the compounding of medicines, the matter becomes much more complex. Generally, texts such as the *Information Tantra* provide detailed instructions concerning the selection of medicinal compounds for specific conditions. The compounding of medicines is carried out in a variety of ways. The ingredients are often measured, powdered, and made into pills. This is currently the most popular style of medication, although powders and decoctions are still used.

Most Tibetan medicines are named according to the principal ingredient and the total number of ingredients in the medicine. For example, one famous medicine, Aquilaria 31, is made from *Aquilaria agallocha* and 30 other substances including *Terminalia chebula, Terminalia belerica,* cardamom, sausurea, and sandalwood. This medicine is used to treat a wide variety of disorders where an imbalance of the wind humor is indicated. These include emotional disorders, disturbances of sleep, or symptoms such as dizziness. In these cases, the powder prepared from the above ingredients is burned and inhaled. When mixed with melted butter it may also be applied as an ointment to be massaged into related areas of the body. In this form, it can be used for back pain.

External Therapies

Therapy for Wind

- Anointing and rubbing—rubbing the body with medicinal oils
- Moxibustion—warming points on the body or burning them with powdered herbs
- Mongolian burning—applying a compress of hot oil and caraway seeds to the skin

Therapy for Bile

- Sweating—wrapping the patient in warm clothes to induce sweating
- Venesection—taking small amounts of blood from suitable veins after giving herbs
- Cold-water compress—applying cold water to the patient in various ways

Therapy for Phlegm

- Burning—applying heated instruments made of iron or other metals to selected points of the skin
- Moxibustion—warming points on the body or burning them with powdered herbs

EXTERNAL THERAPEUTICS The fourth trunk of the root of the therapeutics has three branches: wind therapy, bile therapy, and phlegm therapy. As with the other therapeutic methods, these methods are selected according to their qualitative effects on specific humors. Rubbing the body with oils and applying gentle heat is selected for wind. Sweating, bleeding, and applying cold compresses are the methods chosen to release the heat of bile. Phlegm is treated with strong burning therapy and moxibustion. There are detailed divisions of all of these therapies. Burning therapy can involve the use of a gemstone heated with friction or the application of a heated iron to specific points on the body.

One famous method of external treatment in Tibetan medicine is the use of the so-called golden needle. In this method, a short gold needle is placed shallowly in the crown of the patient's head. Once this is in place, a dry herbal tinder is burnt on the head of the needle. The method helps to treat disturbed wind and can be used for severe headaches. During this treatment, the physician will invoke the Medicine Buddha and use his mantra to contribute to the healing process.

External therapy includes techniques such as surgery, which was once practiced extensively in the Tibetan tradition but is now limited to minor surgery. Legend has it that the mother of one of the ancient Tibetan kings lost her life during surgery that was intended to cure her. The son forbade the practice of surgery, and so from that time on most surgery in Tibet was minor surgery. Given the great variety of medical practices in Tibet and the distribution of doctors across vast distances, we have no way of knowing whether the king's ban was entirely honored. Other opinions exist: Some authors believe that surgery was never extensively developed in the Tibetan tradition except for minor surgery, the treatment of wounds, and the surgical treatment of hemorrhoids, bullet wounds, and infections.

Acupuncture was also used as a method of external treatment in Tibetan medicine, although possibly less routinely and extensively than in China. However, moxibus-

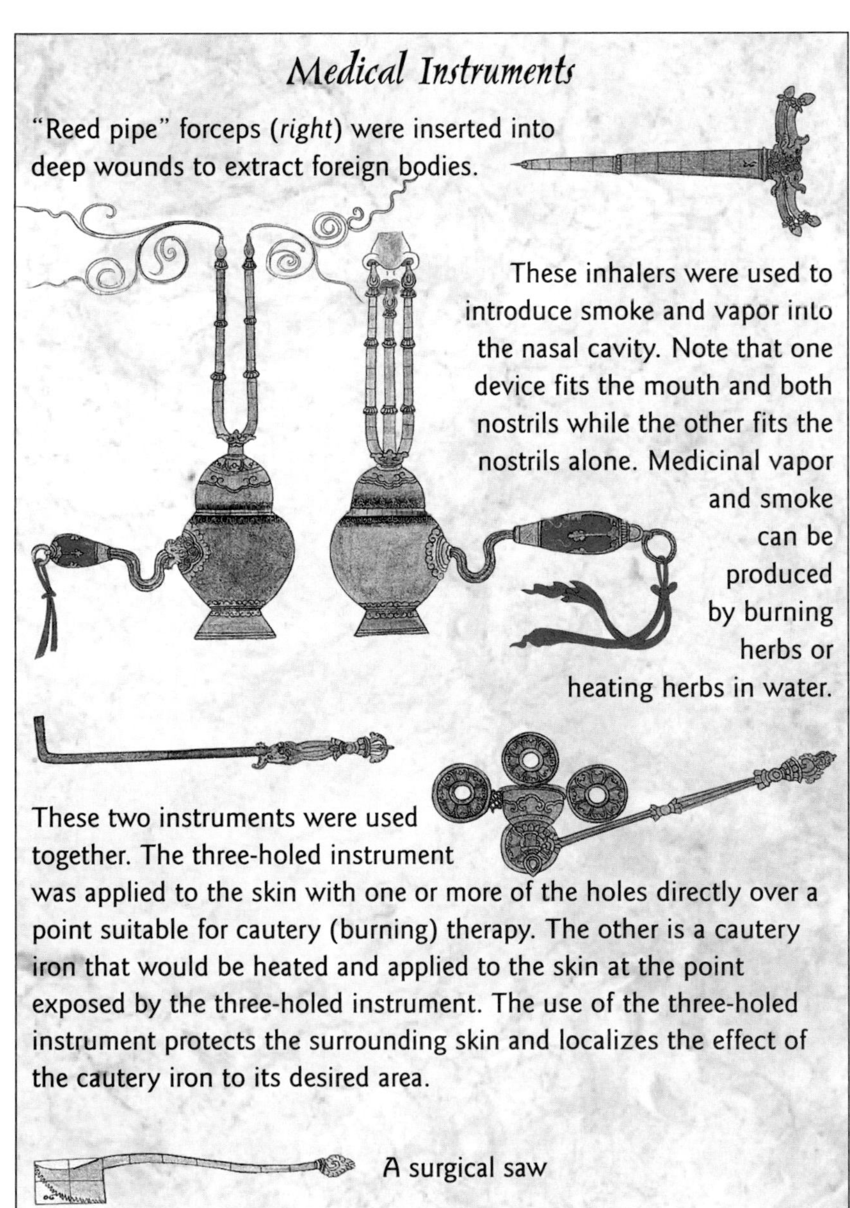

Medical Instruments

"Reed pipe" forceps (*right*) were inserted into deep wounds to extract foreign bodies.

These inhalers were used to introduce smoke and vapor into the nasal cavity. Note that one device fits the mouth and both nostrils while the other fits the nostrils alone. Medicinal vapor and smoke can be produced by burning herbs or heating herbs in water.

These two instruments were used together. The three-holed instrument was applied to the skin with one or more of the holes directly over a point suitable for cautery (burning) therapy. The other is a cautery iron that would be heated and applied to the skin at the point exposed by the three-holed instrument. The use of the three-holed instrument protects the surrounding skin and localizes the effect of the cautery iron to its desired area.

A surgical saw

tion and other types of burning therapy seem to have been widely used. Points suitable for acupuncture, moxibustion, and bleeding are vividly described in ancient medical paintings.

Ultimately, all therapeutic methods in Tibetan medicine are linked directly to the physician's understanding of the patient's elemental and humoral situation. The method of treatment will be selected according to how these are understood. The goal of treatment is to bring the humors, or faults, into balance again and to remove the disease that their imbalance has engendered.

A rendering of the Palace of the Buddha of Lapis Lazuli Light, or Medicine Buddha. The palace is adorned with precious healing jewels, which dispel the 404 diseases that arise from wind, bile, and phlegm. The palace lies in the center of the village of healing, which is inhabited by sages. On each side of the village lies a mountain on which healing plants grow and medicinal substances are found.

Contemporary Practice

In ancient times, Tibetan doctors performed surgery and traveled extensively in the care of their patients. Today, although minor surgery and bonesetting is still practiced, the surgical tradition is no longer carried out. Tibetan doctors will use a range of external therapies including massage, acupuncture, moxibustion (heating the skin with burning herbs), bleeding, and various therapies using heat and water.

Today, as in the past, the formal knowledge of the Tibetan doctor is organized around fundamental concepts that are presented in the *Four Tantras* and that serve as the basis for all therapy. Tibetan medicine is practiced in a surprising number of places today. Its traditions, which embody the blending of practical therapy and compassion, are kept alive by Tibetan physicians in exile in India and Nepal. The government of the Dalai Lama has made extensive efforts to preserve the traditions that were almost destroyed by the Chinese.

Most individuals who encounter the Tibetan tradition feel that this ancient tradition still has much to offer the modern world. Not only do its theory and techniques offer unique insight, but modern medicine has much to learn from its Buddhist emphasis on compassion.

Chinese Medicine

THE HISTORY of Chinese medicine is a history of China. As political, social, and religious trends developed, declined, and died out, aspects of them were incorporated into a constantly changing and continually developing medical system. From the ancestor worship of the earliest documented dynasty of China to the systematization of Confucian thought and the Daoist search for immortality, from the reinterpretation of ancient classics in the 11th century to the introduction of Western medical thought, the traditional medicine of China is one of the richest traditions of healing arts in the world.

This Sung Dynasty painting depicts a country doctor burning moxa directly on the skin of a man's back. This technique, though painful, can be used for a variety of internal conditions and is still in use today.

Today, a medicine that retains many aspects of these historical developments is practiced in China (including Hong Kong), Taiwan, Singapore, Japan, Korea, and more recently, Europe and the United States. As this medicine has matured and traveled across the world, it has incorporated new theories and continued to change and develop.

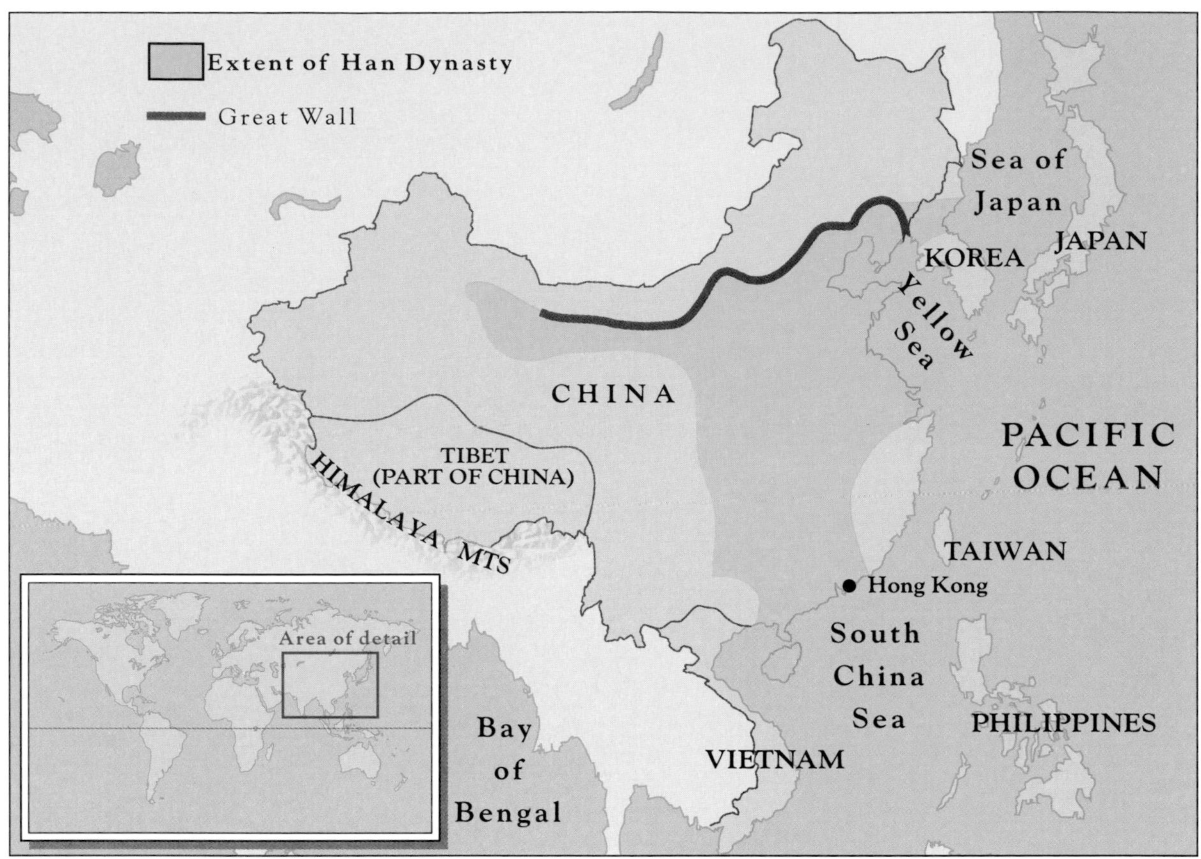

A Glorious History

The lengthy history of civilization in China is a source of great pride to the Chinese people, and their tradition of a systematic medicine is one aspect of that pride. Statements concerning the age of Chinese medicine vary, with some sources drawing a relatively unbroken line from 5,000 years ago and others pointing to a time approximately 2,000 years ago. Archaeologic evidence indicates that some type of systematic therapeutic activity was taking place in China as long ago as 1700 B.C.

However, it is not the actual age of the system that is so important to the Chinese but the sense of history embodied in Chinese medicine. And this history continues into the present. Today, there are many aspects of Chinese culture and medicine that bear more than a passing resemblance to the culture and medicine of the people living in China 2,000 years ago.

The history of Chinese medicine is intertwined with the country's political and economic history. The medical system that developed into traditional Chinese medicine primarily stems from the Han Dynasty (206 B.C.–A.D. 219). During this time, the major texts that would go on to influence Chinese medical thought were written or compiled; right up to the present, all subsequent practitioners have referred to these age-old writings to validate their theories.

Mythical Origins

As is true of any culture, there is a creation myth to explain the origins of the Chinese people, and this story is integral to their understanding of health and dis-

A Comparative Time Line

Year	China	West
21st–18th century B.C.	**Mythical Xia Dynasty**	
18th–12th century B.C.	**Shang Dynasty**	
	Ancestor worship	Stonehenge built
	Oracle bone divination	Trojan War (ca. 1200 B.C.)
	Beginning of *wu* shamans	
12th century–256 B.C.	**Zhou Dynasty**	
	Ancestor worship continues	Homer lives (ca. 750 B.C.)
	Wu shamans more prevalent	Rome founded (ca. 753 B.C.)
	Demonologic therapy	
	Magical correspondence	
	Confucius lives (551–479 B.C.)	
475–221 B.C.	**Warring States Period**	
	Continued chaos/unrest	Buddha lives (560–480 B.C.)
	Demonologic therapy	Plato lives (ca. 428–347 B.C.)
	Development of yin-yang school	Aristotle lives (ca. 384–322 B.C.)
	Development of five-phase school	
	Development of Daoism	
221–206 B.C.	**Qin Dynasty**	
	Reunification of China	Hannibal crosses the Alps
202 B.C.–A.D. 220	**Han Dynasty**	
	Nei Jing, Nan Jing, Shang Han Lun, and *Shen Nong Ben Cao* all written	Julius Caesar lives (ca. 104–44 B.C.)
	Systematic Correspondence developed	Jesus lives (ca. 4 B.C.–A.D. 30)
	Buddhism comes to China	
220–280	**Three Kingdoms**	
265–420	**Jin Dynasty**	Rome adopts Christianity
420–581	**Northern and Southern Dynasties**	Sack of Rome (410)
581–618	**Sui Dynasty**	
	Government herb farms established	Mohammed lives (570–632)
618–907	**Tang Dynasty**	
	Rank of Imperial Physician established	Charlemagne lives (768–814)
	Imperial school of medicine founded	
907–960	**Five Dynasties**	
960–1279	**Sung Dynasty**	
	Medicine becomes more specialized	Magna Carta (1215)
	Bronze figurines made to teach acupuncture	
1271–1368	**Yuan Dynasty**	
	China taken over by Mongols	Gunpowder comes to Europe (1313)
1368–1644	**Ming Dynasty**	
1644–1911	**Qing Dynasty**	
	Influx of Westerners into China	
1912–1949	**Republic of China**	
	Chinese medicine nearly lost	
1949–present	**People's Republic of China**	
	Mao proclaims Chinese medicine a "treasure house of knowledge"	

ease. In China, the legend is the story of Pan Gu.

PAN GU In the beginning, the cosmos was a gas that slowly solidified into a colossal stone. Out of a cosmic egg was born a creature named Pan Gu, who lived for 18,000 years, growing at a rate of 10 feet a day and spending his time chopping the stone into two parts, one of which became the heavens and the other the earth. Other stories say that the heavens were his father and the earth his mother and so, consequently, he was named the Son of Heaven—a name that was later given to the emperors of China to show their close relationship with the heavens.

When Pan Gu completed his work and died, his head became the mountains, his breath the wind and clouds, his voice thunder, his left eye the sun, and his right eye the moon. His muscles and veins became the matrix of the earth, and his flesh became the soil. His hair and beard became the constellations, and his skin and body hair became plants and trees. His teeth and bones became metals, and his marrow became pearls and precious stones. The seat of his body became the rain, and the parasites upon him were impregnated by the heavens and became humans.

This myth is important for two reasons: First, it is interesting to note that, unlike many creation myths that suggest a given people traveled from some faraway place, the Chinese myth assumes that the Chinese people originated in China. Second, and more important for our story, is the use of Pan Gu's body to create the environment for life. One of the fundamental aspects of Chinese medicine is the recognition of a very close relationship between the human body and the world. As we look through Chinese history, we shall see that the health of the emperor's body, in particular, was closely related to the health of the world. Natural disasters, for example, meant that the emperor's relationship with the heavens was out of balance, causing illness or destruction on Earth. This relationship of the earth to the body is an important element of the philosophy of Chinese medicine and one that appears not only in medical theory but also in political action and the stories of common people.

Fu Xi was one of the three "founders" of medicine in China. Said to have lived in 2953 B.C., Fu Xi was the first of five rulers of his time. He is thought to have been miraculously conceived and was born after 12 years' gestation. He is responsible for establishing rules of marriage and teaching fishing, the rearing of domestic animals, cooking, and the making of musical instruments. His connection with medical history is based on his construction of the Ba Gua, *or Eight Trigrams, on which were based the* I Jing, *or* Book of Changes, *and the principles of medical philosophy.*

THE ORIGINS OF MEDICINE

Beginning in approximately 2900 B.C., five legendary rulers were said to have governed China. Three of these figures are closely associated with the creation of the Chinese culture and Chinese medicine. These are Fu Xi (the Ox-Tamer), Shen Nong (the Divine Husbandman), and Huang Di (the Yellow Emperor). Although it is likely that none of the three actually existed, they

Herbs in the Shen Nong Ben Cao

Chinese Name	Common Name	Use
hou po	Magnolia Bark	Relieves abdominal fullness, loss of appetite, and diarrhea
ren shen	Ginseng Root	Treats a weak pulse, shallow breathing, and fatigue
wu wei zi	Schizandra Fruit	Relieves wheezing, diarrhea, and fatigue
ling zhi	*Ganoderma lucidum*	Strengthens the constitution and reduces signs of aging
da huang	Rhubarb	Acts as purgative and laxative; drains heat from the blood
xie bai	Macrostem Onion	Relieves pain in the chest from cold, abdominal pain, and dysentery

serve the important function of explaining the origin of Chinese medicine.

Fu Xi is said to have lived around 2953 B.C. and was highly influential in the establishment of the Chinese civilization; he is also said to have invented the earliest written picture symbols as communication. His contribution to medicine is said to be the construction of the *Ba Gua*, or Eight Trigrams, on which the *I Jing* (*The Book of Changes*) and many of the principles of medical philosophy were based. The trigrams were drawings that represented aspects of nature according to their yin and yang qualities (see pages 291–292). The drawings could be arranged to form hexagons, which, in turn, became the basis of various divination techniques.

Shen Nong, the Divine Husbandman, was considered the father of Chinese herbal medicine. He was the mythical author of the earliest materia medica, the Shen Nong Ben Cao (Divine Husbandman's Materia Medica). *Shen Nong is thought to have been a Daoist recluse who gave up the world to seek immortality. Here he is seated at the mouth of a cave, dressed in clothes made of leaves, with herbs that he has been tasting by his side and in his hand.*

Shen Nong is said to have reigned from 2838 to 2698 B.C. Along with the social and agricultural advancements he made, he was the legendary author of the first materia medica, the *Shen Nong Ben Cao*. Evidence indicates that the text was not actually written until sometime in the 1st century A.D., during the Han Dynasty, but it is attributed to Shen Nong because of his prowess in the art of herbal medicine.

Shen Nong is said to have tasted 70 different kinds of plants, animals, and minerals in a single day—surely a day that changed the art of healing in China forever by establishing the art of herbal medicine. Shen Nong was the patron god of herbalists and is still revered by many Chinese herbalists. On the 1st and 15th day of each month, incense and offerings are traditionally put before his shrine, and in some places, herbs are discounted ten percent on these days.

Huang Di, the Yellow Emperor, is perhaps the most widely recognized culture hero of Chinese medicine. Said to have lived from 2698 to 2598 B.C., he is the mythical author, along with his minister Qi Bo, of the *Huang Di Nei Jing*, or *Yellow Emperor's Inner Classic*. Almost every future generation of medical theorists have linked their ideas to this text, and it continues to be cited today to support the modern practice of Chinese medicine. The *Inner Classic*, as it is often called, is probably a compilation of writings written by many different people around 200 B.C., but regardless of its actual origin, this book is where traditional Chinese medicine is first expressed in a form that remains familiar to us today.

The text is divided into two books: the *Simple Questions* (*Su Wen*) and the *Spiritual Axis* (*Ling Shu*). The *Simple Questions* deals with medical theory, such as the principles of yin and yang and the five phases; the *Spiritual Axis* focuses primarily on the techniques of medicine, such as acupuncture and moxibustion. The two texts are written as a series of questions and answers between the legendary emperor Huang Di and his minister Qi Bo (see "A Dialogue on Longevity").

Credit for being the inventor of the traditional medicine of China is variously ascribed to any one of these three legendary rulers. Shen Nong and Huang Di and the texts that bear their names continue to be important to the basic theory of Chinese medicine and are constantly referred to by modern authors to give support to theories and practices.

A Dialogue on Longevity

The following is from the *Yellow Emperor's Inner Classic*, a text that is framed as a conversation between the legendary emperor Huang Di and his minister, Qi Bo.

> Huang Di to his minister: I have heard that in ancient times, the people lived to be over 100 years, and yet they remained active and did not become decrepit in their activities. But nowadays, people reach only half of that age and yet become decrepit and failing. Is it because the world changes from generation to generation? Or is it that mankind is becoming negligent of the laws of nature?
>
> Qi Bo replied: In ancient times those people who understood Dao [the Way], patterned themselves upon the Yin and the Yang, and they lived in harmony with the arts of divination.
>
> There was temperance in eating and drinking. Their hours of rising and retiring were regular and not disorderly and wild. By these means the ancients kept their bodies united with their souls, so as to fulfill their allotted span completely, measuring unto 100 years before they passed away.

The Shang Dynasty

The Shang Dynasty (1766–1122 B.C.) is the first Chinese dynasty of which there is clear archaeologic evidence of any kind. Among the evidence of the Shang are many artifacts indicating that some sort of therapeutic activity did take place. The Shang people were still tribal, however, so very little is actually known about the practice of medicine during this time.

Although not much is known about the Shang as a people, it is important to understand a little bit about them to understand the medicine that began to develop. There was a king and a class of nobility. Perhaps most significant, though, is that the people of the Shang period were no longer nomadic as earlier peoples in the area were; they had settled down.

The Importance of the Ancestors

During this period, there appears to be a definite understanding of the interdependent relationship between the living and the dead: The dead depended on the living for food, and the living depended on the dead for health, well-being, success, and the stability of nature. This relationship developed into the beginnings of ancestor worship and served as the early basis for medicine.

The scapulae, or shoulder bones, of oxen were used for divination in the Shang and Zhou dynasties. Everything from the weather to the health of the emperor and his family could be divined using the oracle bones. The oracle bones are the earliest evidence of the Chinese beliefs concerning the cause of disease. The bones mention the ancestors, wind, and snow as the main causes of disease.

Essentially, the Shang believed that the dead, if neglected, would curse the living, and these curses could involve major crises such as crop failure or individual crises such as illness. The curse of crop failure would indicate a huge problem, possibly a rift between the living and the dead that involved the entire community. Illness, on the other hand, involved only the dead and the family of the individual who was sick. In a very general sense, it appears that the ancestors could be appeased with food or more attendance at the grave sites. (At present, evidence of therapeutic activity exists only in relation to the king, his family, and those in his immediate circle. It is not known how the lower classes of Shang society dealt with physical illness.)

In addition to the ancestors, there is some evidence that the Shang believed there were environmental causes of disease, such as snow and wind. Both ancestral and environmental factors remained important to Chinese medicine for hundreds of years, and environmental factors, most especially wind, remain important to this day.

Diagnosis via Oracles

The king was the only person who was able to consult with the ancestors. This he did through the mediation of oracle bones—usually either the scapula (shoulder bone) of oxen or tortoise shells. Holes would be drilled into the bones or shells and a question inscribed. The bone or shell would then be heated to a very high temperature and quickly cooled, creating cracks between the drilled holes. The cracks could be read and interpreted to know the will of the ancestors.

Questions posed to the ancestors ranged from inquiries about the weather, hunting, or dreams to illness, war, and the future. In one tomb, more than 100,000 oracle bones were found with questions such as "Will the king's child be a son?" or "The king has a headache, has he offended the ancestors?"

TREATMENT OF DISEASE Because the main cause of disease during the Shang Dynasty was offense to the ancestors, the treatment was relatively straightforward: appease the offended ancestors. Unfortunately, it is not at all clear how this was done.

We do know that individuals called *wu* (essentially a shaman of some sort) were somehow involved in expelling the wind and snow from people to relieve them of environmentally caused disease; however, like most early cultures, therapy in the Shang Dynasty was less concerned with treating the sick individual and more focused on resolving conflict with the ancestors. It is likely that there were rituals managed by the king and the nobility to communicate with the ancestors so that whatever diseases, social ills, or natural disasters confronting the people could be diminished. Based on our understanding of the rituals of other early sedentary groups, therapy was probably a social event or ritual designed to create a change in the relationship between man (specifically the king) and the ancestors.

Because the king was the only person who was able to communicate with the ancestors, he was the only healer; his clientele was limited to himself and his family or the nobility. In the event of a major social or natural catastrophe, he would be called on to heal the community; but in general, the diseases of the people were out of his scope of attention unless they became so severe as to threaten his authority. It was the ruler's ability to communicate with the ancestors that gave him his authority and on which his continued leadership depended. If he lost this ability to communicate, then he could lose his power. In fact, this became the guiding principle by which dynasties were created and defeated until the final Imperial Chinese Dynasty fell in 1911. If the ruler lost his ability to communicate with the ancestors and to heal the people of social and natural disasters, then he could be replaced by someone who had that power.

Wng

The character for king, written above, shows the relationship of the king, or emperor, to heaven and earth. The horizontal line on top depicts the heavens, the bottom is the earth, and the middle is the king. The line connecting the three indicates that the king, in the middle, is the mediator between heaven and earth.

Here we can see the close relationship between the ruler, the ancestors, the health of the nation, and emerging medical therapeutics. Over time, a medical system developed that was more directed at preventing disease or treating the individual, but that system still retained much of the underlying structure of its political roots.

The Zhou Dynasty

Clearly, during the Shang Dynasty, ancestor worship and maintaining the health of the king were the primary health care goals. In the Zhou Dynasty (1100–256 B.C.), however, ancestor worship led to the development of many complex philosophical systems. One such system, *Feng Shui* (wind and water), began as a method of divining the winds and waters so that the graves of ancestors were placed in propitious places. Many of the ideas of Confucius, who lived in the middle of the 6th century B.C., were also to develop out of this concept of ancestor worship, especially his emphasis on filial piety and the veneration of one's ancestors.

Throughout most of the Zhou Dynasty, the system of consulting oracle bones or tortoise shells remained very similar to that used in the Shang Dynasty. However, in the early Zhou Dynasty, the *wu*, who during the Shang Dynasty had primarily focused their energies on the healing of environmental diseases, became more involved in the interpretation of the oracle bones, and the king, or ruler, was further removed. As the Zhou Dynasty continued, the loss of a centralized power—and a central healer—seems to have created a change in attitude toward the dead.

As more chaos was created among the living and power became more transient, the importance of individual ancestors in the health of the people diminished, and greater emphasis was placed on the idea of demons being responsible for illness or misfortune. Toward the end of the dynasty, the *wu*, who had primarily been members of the royal family, lost much of their power. They were able to establish themselves as healers among the ordinary people, but they never again wielded the same authority to influence the fate of the nation.

Yi *Wu*

The character for medicine (*yi*) and physician, or healer (*wu*), may have been created during the Zhou Dynasty. The character for medicine originally had the character for *wu* *(at right)* on the bottom with the upper half depicting a quiver with an arrow on the left and a spear on the right. Later, the bottom half of the character was changed to depict the character for alcohol, an important component of medicinal wines.

Demonic Medicine To understand the rise of demonic medicine during the Zhou Dynasty and the Warring States Period that followed, it is important to understand the chaos that existed in the land. There was no clarity about who was in charge, and natural disasters—usually attributed to heaven's displeasure with the prevailing earthly affairs—took on major political significance; the people were confused. Without any one leader, they could not know what was right and what was wrong, nor could they be sure that anyone was truly in communication with the celestial deities.

Similar to ancestor worship, demonic medicine is also based on the idea that there are beings living in the world who cannot be seen but who nevertheless influence the state of the world. The difference exists in the nature of these beings. The ancestors were associated with specific individuals who had issues that would cause them to become angry. The demons, on the other hand, were not directly connected to an individual; rather, they were evil spirits who might cause illness or disaster on a whim. Because it was no longer clear if the king had direct contact with the beings of the other world, the *wu* took on the role of interpreting the demons' desires and exorcizing the demons and evil winds from the sick.

It is possible that the concept of demons not associated with individuals sprang from the development of the concept of the human soul during the Zhou Dynasty. In fact, the Zhou conceived of man as having two souls: the *hun*, or ethereal soul, and the *po*, or corporeal soul. The corporeal soul exists in the body from birth and dies at death. The ethereal soul, on the other hand, enters the body some time after birth and can leave the body during sleep to wander through the world. After death, the ethereal soul continues to travel the world until it finds another body to enter. The *wu* had the power to exorcize these homeless souls and banish them from the world of the living, but adherence to proper social norms no longer protected people as it did when the ancestors prevailed.

TREATING DEMONIC DISEASE Although the belief that demons could cause disease is clearly documented in archaeologic artifacts of the late Zhou Dynasty and Warring States Period, what the actual treatment was is less clear. There is some evidence that the *wu* attempted to treat demons in the same way as leaders attempted to expel invaders: by attacking them with spears. The *Book of Rites* of the Zhou Dynasty states that

> several times a year and also during certain special occasions, such as the funeral of a prince, hordes of exorcists would race shrieking through the city streets, enter the courtyards and homes, thrusting their spears into the air, in an attempt to expel the evil creatures.

In addition to using spears and fear, the *wu* also used medicinal drugs to expel or destroy demons. Some of the drugs used include "aromatics, prepared animals or parts of animals, herbs, a woman's menstrual cloth, and others." However, very little evidence from the Zhou Dynasty exists concerning actual treatment measures used to relieve suffering or to expel demons. It is likely that the methods of the *wu* were passed down orally, and as the *wu* consolidated their positions as healers, the methods remained secret so that the *wu* would not lose their hold on power.

Any Number of Souls

During the Zhou Dynasty, man was thought to have two souls: the *hun*, or ethereal soul, and the *po*, or corporeal soul. Over time, the concept of the souls was expanded, so that by the time the *Huang Di Nei Jing* was written, man was thought to have five souls, each of which was related, according to the theory of the five phases, to one of the viscera, or zang organs (see page 295). As the *Huang Di Nei Jing* states:

> The five zang organs have their corresponding attributes of spirit. The heart houses the *shen*, the governing spirit. The lungs house the *po*, or courage and boldness. The liver houses the *hun*, or intuition. The spleen houses the *yi*, or intellect. The kidney houses the *zhi*, or willpower and volition.

Warring States: Creating Order from Chaos

The final years of the Zhou Dynasty were filled with wars and battles, and in the end, all semblance of order disappeared. From 475 to 221 B.C., there was no central authority in China. Out of this chaos came many attempts to bring order to life and society. Perhaps the most influential of the philosophies to emerge at this time was the philosophy based on the writings of Confucius and his students. These writings created a philosophical doctrine that was to influence every aspect of the Chinese people and culture right up to the present day.

Confucius and the Health of Society

Kong Fu Zi, better known to the West as Confucius, was born in 551 B.C. and died in 479 B.C. He was a scholar who failed the examinations to become an official. During his life, he did not wield much influence at all; however, many years after his death, after his students had written down his thoughts, he was to have immense influence on every aspect of Chinese life, including the traditional medicine of China.

Essentially, Confucius believed in a natural order to things that was also a moral order. The decay and chaos of the nation was due to inferior men who were not performing the rites of the feudal society correctly. His answer to the chaos of the world was virtue. If all men were virtuous and strictly observed the rites of the ancients, then the country would be orderly.

Confucius's influence on medicine began with his writings on the immorality of "professionals" and the higher virtues of the scholar-bureaucrat. In his view, it was the job of the scholar-bureaucrat to learn medicine so that he could offer his services to his family, his ruler, and his circle of acquaintances. However, to use medicine as a profession—as a way of earning money to support oneself—was not virtuous but immoral. These ideas created a constant strain on the practice of medicine in China. Should medicine be something that was learned as an art and practiced out of the goodness of one's heart, or should it be developed into a profession and offered for a fee to anyone in need? This essential problem was to bother medical practitioners and scholars for many years to come. It contributed to the use of the traditional medicine of China only by the elite, but also to the development of other folk, or regional, health care modalities throughout China. As we look at the emergence of the traditional medicine of China, it will become clear that Confucian thought permeated every aspect of medicine and medical texts even beyond this one dispute.

Confucius was a scholar and teacher who lived in the Warring States Period, a time of chaos and disarray. Although his writings did not pertain directly to medicine, his political ideas concerning morality, correct behavior, and each man's position in the world were taken by medical practitioners and used to understand the proper functioning of the world and the human body.

The Reunification

For a brief period (221–206 B.C.), China was reunified under the Qin Dynasty. Although there were no great advances in medicine during this time, the emperor known as Qin Shi Huang Di created China's first truly centralized government. To do so, however, required complete obedience to the central government. Therefore, Qin Shi Huang Di prohibited philosophical discussion and forbade both criticism of the current government and praise of earlier governments. In 213 B.C., all writings other than official Qin historical documents and treatises on divination, agriculture, or medicine were collected and burned. Copies were maintained only in the Imperial Library.

During this period, major unification projects, such as roads, waterways, irrigation systems, canals, and the Great Wall, were begun with the help of forced labor. The Qin did not last long, however, and the dynasty fell apart under the second emperor, the son of Qin Shi Huang Di, who was too weak to maintain the central government.

The Han Dynasty and Systematic Correspondence

In 202 B.C., China was reunified under the Han Dynasty. During the Han Dynasty, a stable aristocratic order was established, and China expanded geographically, economically, and politically, influencing what is now Vietnam and Korea. This dynasty is considered by many as the beginning of civil society in China, and even today, the Chinese call themselves *Han ren*, or "people of the Han," after this dynasty. The Han Dynasty was a period of great advancement for China. During this period, the medicine of systematic correspondence, which bears a relationship to the medicine we are familiar with today, evolved.

As its name implies, the medicine of systematic correspondence was not a magic-based system designed to drive out evil, but rather a rational system intended to bring order to chaos. The medicine of systematic correspondence was composed of six major components. With the exception of concepts of demonic medicine, these

This 17th-century painting depicts the God of Longevity, with his elongated head, leaning on a staff and accompanied by his stag, contemplating the yin–yang symbol. A child hands him a peach, a symbol of longevity and immortality. The peach is thought to be one of the main ingredients of one of the Daoist elixirs for immortality.

components have been retained in the traditional medicine of China as it is practiced today. These six components include

1) certain concepts of demonic medicine
2) a belief in the unity of man and nature
3) the theory of yin and yang
4) five-phase theory
5) the concept of *qi* as the basis of life
6) the theory that a united, harmonious, smoothly functioning empire is mirrored in the healthy body, and a fragmented, unbalanced, stagnating empire is mirrored in the sick body

Supernatural Medicine We've seen that from the time of the Shang Dynasty, disease was thought to be caused by certain environmental factors (wind and snow), the influence of the ancestors, and the influence of demons.

Wind was seen both as a natural phenomenon and also as a demonic phenomenon—an evil that lived outside the body and could invade the body. The wind evil lived in caves or tunnels and could invade the body through caves or holes on the body. All of the texts that discuss the influence of external pathogens on the body use the term *xie*, or evil, to discuss these pathogens. During the Han Dynasty, though, as medical concepts developed, the idea that these evils were demonic played a lesser role, and wind became more associated with an influence of the natural world on human health.

In addition to the external evils, there is also written discussion of 13 ghost or demon acupuncture points on the body that could be used to exorcize demons. The needles used to penetrate these points were considered analogous to the spears used by the *wu* to exorcize demons from the villages.

THE UNITY OF MAN AND NATURE As we saw with the story of Pan Gu and the creation of the world, the unity of man and the natural world is an elemental component of the traditional medicine of China. Essentially, this aspect of the theory states that there is a relationship among the environment, the state of the world, and the state of the body. This is most commonly and clearly expressed in terms of the natural environment and its effect on the body. On a very basic level, for example, exposing oneself to wind can result in being "struck by wind," which can manifest as a common cold or as facial paralysis. Another example would be internal wind that can be stirred up if there is an insufficiency of fluids causing dryness. This may result in spasms, seizures, or even paralysis. This reflects the state of the real world, where drought causes great winds that can create sandstorms and cause an insufficiency of food.

This unity, however, does not apply only to the natural environment but also to the social environment. If one's social relationships are inappropriately maintained,

Han Dynasty Practitioners

There are several stories of great physicians from the Han Dynasty. One legendary hero of Chinese medicine, Hua Tuo (A.D. 110–207), is said to have discovered the first anaesthetic and used it in surgical practices. He supposedly had a secret powder that produced numbness, thus allowing him to open the abdomen and remove any diseased organs. He was also an acupuncturist and an herbalist. He developed some of the early forms of *qi gong* based on animal postures. Unfortunately, it seems that either Hua Tuo failed to pass his knowledge on to anyone else, or the story of his surgical prowess postdated his life, as the art of surgery never developed to any great extent in China.

Another physician of the time was Chun Yu Yi, who was the first known physician to record his personal observations of clinical cases. In a suit against him for malpractice, he indicated that he had used acupuncture to change the flow of *qi*. As acupuncture was still not widely accepted at the time, his choice of treatment modalities was probably the cause of the malpractice charges.

Also during the Han Dynasty, there is mention of at least one female physician who was called to the palace to treat the empress. Other stories say that she was an obstetrician, but there is no extensive biography of her or record of her medical practice.

then one's emotions are affected—anger rather than love between husband and wife, for example—which is then reflected in one's body, manifesting as headaches, palpitations, and so on. Therefore, maintaining the appropriate relationship to the natural environment and maintaining appropriate social relationships are equally important to the maintenance of health.

The theory of Chinese medicine discusses the relationship between man and the universe in terms of the causes of disease, which can be broken into three classes: the six excesses, the seven affects, and the neither internal nor external causes. The development of this theory began in the Han Dynasty and was first expressed in the *Yellow Emperor's Inner Classic*.

The Six Environmental Excesses. The ancient Chinese observed six different environmental conditions: wind, cold, summer heat, dampness, dryness, and fire. In nature, these are known as the six *qi*. When they cause disease, they are referred to as the six excesses. The diseases caused by these excesses are, to a certain extent, seasonal in nature: cold diseases occur more often in cold weather, and dryness diseases occur more often in the autumn (the dry season). However, any person's constitution or psychological makeup or any given environmental condition may cause one or more of these diseases to occur at any time of year.

The signs and symptoms of any one of these external causes of disease will generally correspond to its nature, so diagnosis of the disease will be based on the nature of the symptoms. In other words, if a person has a cold accompanied by chills and fever (with fever predominant), sore throat, and sweating, it is more likely to be a cold due to wind and heat than if the person had chills and fever (with chills predominant), no sore throat, and no sweating. Treatment of diseases caused by the six excesses would be based on the theory of opposites. In a cold condition, warming techniques would be used, and in a warm condition, cooling techniques would be used.

In addition, some diseases that are, in fact, attributable to organ dysfunction will present signs similar in their nature to those of external diseases. Although these are considered internal diseases because they mirror the nature of the external excesses, the same terms—wind, fire, cold, and so on—are used to describe them, and similar treatment methods would be used.

The Causes of Disease According to Traditional Chinese Medicine

I. The Six External Excesses
- Wind
- Cold
- Summer Heat
- Dampness
- Dryness
- Fire

II. The Seven Affects
- Joy
- Anger
- Anxiety
- Thought
- Sorrow
- Fear
- Fright

III. Neither Internal nor External Causes
- Dietary Irregularities
- Sexual Intemperance
- Taxation Fatigue
- External Injuries
- Parasites

The Seven Affects. The seven affects are joy, anger, anxiety, thought, sorrow, fear, and fright. These are an individual's normal reactions to the environment. However, when these emotions are excessive, persistent, or out of the ordinary, they may disturb the balance of yin and yang and affect the body's internal organs. As we will see with the five phases, each emotion is related to one of the organs, and too much of any given affect will cause a reaction in its related organ. In addition, all of the emotions can damage the heart. In general, treatment for conditions related to the affects include changing the environment causing the excessive affect.

Neither Internal nor External Causes. The neither internal nor external causes of disease include dietary irregularities, sexual intemperance, taxation fatigue (both overworking and underworking the body), external injuries, parasites, and so on.

YIN AND YANG The third element of the medicine of systematic correspondences is the understanding of yin and yang. The theory of yin and yang is the most fundamental concept in the philosophy of Chinese medicine. Originally, the two characters signified no more than the sunny side of a hill (yang) and the shady side of a hill (yin). The very different environments that exist on either side of a hill—the brightly lit, warm, and active side and the shaded, cool, and quiescent side—came to represent a set of opposites that (1) must always be present simultaneously, (2) each contain elements of the other, and (3) can transform into each other.

The yin–yang school explains the world in terms of these paired oppositions. The theory was later applied to the body to express ideas about both normal physiology and disease processes. One of the most important aspects of yin–yang philosophy is that each phenomenon must be identified as yin or yang in relation to something else. In terms of the body, the outside of the body (the skin and hair) are yang in relation to the inside of the body and the organs; the upper part of the body is yang in relation to the lower part of the body; and the back of the body is yang in relation to the front of the body. Yin and yang can be defined only in relation to each other, not as individual entities existing without each other. So, for example, autumn is yin in relation to summer because it is cooler and more quiescent, but autumn is yang in relation to winter. Thus the yin or yang nature of any phe-

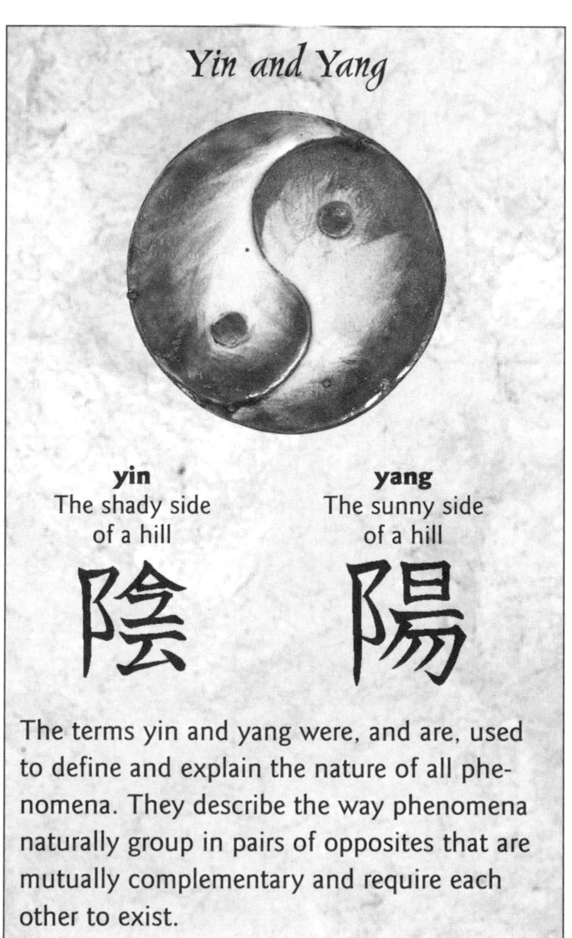

The terms yin and yang were, and are, used to define and explain the nature of all phenomena. They describe the way phenomena naturally group in pairs of opposites that are mutually complementary and require each other to exist.

nomenon is not definite but ever-changing in relation to the environment.

One of the discussions of the yin–yang school is the debate over the physical existence of yin and yang. Are yin and yang merely concepts used to organize phenomena in relation to each other, or are they actual, tangible phenomena that wax and wane?

In medicine, yin–yang is both of these: The body can be organized in terms of yin and yang, and disease can be organized as varying imbalances in yin and yang. A body that is healthy will have an appropriate balance of yin and yang: neither too cold nor too warm, neither too active nor too quiet, and so on. In a sick body, yin and yang will be out of balance, and it is necessary to determine whether one is overabundant or whether one is insufficient.

Yin–Yang Correspondences

All things can be described in terms of yin and yang, but yin and yang are descriptive of phenomena only in relation to each other. For example, the sun is considered yang in relation to the moon, and the moon is considered yin in relation to the sun. But the sun is not yang in and of itself and the moon is not yin in and of itself; yin and yang can only be applied when two things are in relation to each other. The meaning of this relationship is often illustrated by a chart that presents phenomena or conditions in yin and yang relationships.

Yang	Yin
Light	Dark
Heaven	Earth
Sun	Moon
Day	Night
Summer	Winter
Hot	Cold
Fast	Slow
Male	Female
Up	Down
Inside	Outside
Fire	Water
Bowels	Viscera
Qi	Blood

Determining overabundance or insufficiency can become confusing as the signs of an overabundance of one are often similar to an insufficiency of the other. For example, the signs of an overabundance of yang (fever or heat, activity, red face) can, on initial observation, be similar to an insufficiency of yin (afternoon fever, feverish activity, flushed red cheeks). Differentiating the cause of the imbalance is vital so that proper treatment can be administered.

FIVE-PHASE THEORY Another system the ancient Chinese used to understand the world around them was the five phases. Called the *wu xing*, literally meaning the "five movements," they are typically translated as the "five phases," or sometimes the "five elements." The phases—wood, fire, earth, metal, and water—are not static but dynamic, constantly changing in relation to each other and to the environment.

Five-phase theory is closely related to Confucian thought in that it is based entirely on definite lines of correspondence into which all things in the universe can be placed. If the proper relationships between these lines of correspondence are maintained, then there is harmony in the universe and health in the body.

Included in the theory of the movement of the five phases is an engendering cycle, in which one phase is responsible for produc-

Five-Phase Correspondences (Wu Xing)					
Category	**Wood**	**Fire**	**Earth**	**Metal**	**Water**
Viscera	Liver	Heart	Spleen	Lung	Kidney
Bowels	Gallbladder	Small Intestine	Stomach	Large Intestine	Urinary Bladder
Season	Spring	Summer	Late Summer	Autumn	Winter
Time of Day	Before Sunrise	Forenoon	Afternoon	Late Afternoon	Midnight
Climate	Wind	Heat	Damp	Dryness	Cold
Direction	East	South	Center	West	North
Color	Blue-green	Red	Yellow	White	Black
Taste	Sour	Bitter	Sweet	Astringent	Salty
Sense Organ	Eyes	Tongue	Mouth	Nose	Ears
Odor	Goatish	Scorched	Fragrant	Raw Fish	Putrid
Vocalization	Shouting	Laughing	Singing	Weeping	Sighing
Tissue	Sinews	Vessels	Flesh	Body Hair	Bones
Mind	Anger	Joy	Thought	Sorrow	Fear
Soul	*Hun*/Ethereal	*Shen*/Spirit	*Yi*/Reflection	*Po*/Corporeal	*Zhi*/Mind

ing the next; wood engenders fire, for example. There is a restraining cycle, too, in which one phase is responsible for restraining another; wood restrains earth, for example (see "The Cycle of the Five Phases," page 315).

Because each organ in the body is related to one of the five phases, an imbalance in that organ can be expressed in terms of the five phases. So, for example, if a person suffers from frequent colds and cough, then there could be insufficient metal (the phase that is related to the lung) in the body. To treat this, one could either supplement the metal element directly or, in what some consider to be a more supportive method, one could supplement the earth phase because in the engendering cycle, earth is the mother of metal. If the mother is strong, then she can produce more of the son, thereby strengthening the son. If there appears to be too much fire in the body, then a patient might experience insomnia, restlessness, dream-disturbed sleep, and thirst. In this case, there may be too much of the fire phase (related to the heart) or an insufficiency of the water phase (related to the kidney), and so the water is not properly controlling the fire.

There is some similarity in the theories of yin and yang and the theory of the five phases—and, indeed, many other ancient systems—in that both are concerned with the fundamental balance of substances in the body. When these substances become out of balance, then illness is manifest in the body and must be treated.

Qi—the Basis of Life During the Warring States Period, *qi* seems to have had the meaning of vapors, breath, life, and that which makes up all tangible matter. Thus, *qi* was both what formed us and what kept us alive. Over time, the idea of *qi* has become extremely broad, encompassing almost every aspect of all natural phenomena. It is common to see the term translated as "energy," but this translation does not embody the distinctly material aspects of *qi*.

Like yin and yang, or the five phases, *qi* is something in the body that can become out of balance. An insufficiency of *qi* can cause myriad symptoms, including fatigue, shortness of breath, and a pale complexion. Alternately, a relative abundance of *qi* can also occur in a particular location, commonly referred to as *qi* stagnation; most traumatic injuries or painful conditions are due to some form of *qi* stagnation. *Qi* moves through the body, bringing warmth, nourishment, and protection to all areas of the body. If *qi* becomes stagnant, then there is no movement, and so there is pain.

There are many different types of *qi*. In general, *qi* is classified according to its source, its location, and its function. Organ *qi* functions within the organs;

Qi

The character for *qi* is made up of the symbol for rising vapors above with the character for cooked rice below. Therefore the character represents "vapors rising from food"—or life.

Moving Qi

qì tong zé bú tòng, qì bú tong zé tòng

This play on words in Chinese translates as: "When *qi* moves, there is no pain. When *qi* does not move, there is pain." This concept is fundamental to understanding *qi*. If *qi* becomes stagnant anywhere in the body, then the proper flow of *qi* through the body is disrupted and there is pain. This can be applied both to the pain of traumatic injury and to the pain of organ disharmony, such as dysmenorrhea.

channel *qi* moves through the channels to warm the body; defense *qi* is in the outer part of the body and serves to defend against the invasion of external evils; and construction *qi* is internal and supports and nourishes the body. In essence, the functions of *qi* in the body are

- activation
- warming
- defense
- transformation
- containment

Healthy Body, Healthy State The theories of yin and yang, the five phases, and *qi*—the bases of traditional Chinese medicine—were, in essence, philosophical responses to political strife occurring between 700 and 220 B.C. It is important to remember, however, that these ideas did not emerge first as theories of medicine but rather as ideas that could be applied to the political chaos existing in China so as to unify the nation.

This idea is expressed in the language that permeates Chinese medicine. Organs are referred to in military terms as the ruler (the heart), the general (the liver), and so on. And the body is viewed as a microcosm of the state, with channels (rivers, streams, and canals) for movement, organs of storage (or granaries of storage), and organs of consumption of waste (the palaces). Essentially, all of the important elements of the economy (storage, consumption, and transportation) are represented in the body, so that a body in balance and functioning properly is a mirror of the healthy state; a body out of balance and not functioning properly reflects a political state in need of attention.

The Inner Classic and Commentaries

All of the ideas of Chinese medicine discussed so far can be found in the *Yellow Emperor's Inner Classic*, which was compiled during the Han Dynasty. All of the texts of Chinese medicine after the *Inner Classic* would continue to develop and expand these and other ideas as they were discussed in the *Inner Classic*.

The Han Dynasty was a very important time for Chinese medicine; this is when most of the important texts of Chinese medicine were written. However, the *Inner Classic* is not a classic from which a homogeneous system of ideas can be understood. Rather, it is a collection of the ideas and teachings of various schools and teachers of various times. It includes ideas popularized through demonic medicine as well as ideas about *qi*, yin and yang, the five phases, the relationships of the viscera and bowels (see "The Viscera and Bowels"), the circulation of *qi* in the channels, and about 300 acupuncture points (see pages 297–298). The *Inner Classic* also discusses diagnostics and refers to both tongue and pulse diagnosis (see pages 300–302).

The Viscera and Bowels

The anatomy of human beings in Chinese medicine is understood to have six viscera, or organs of storage, and six bowels, or organs responsible for the decomposition and removal of waste. Although these organs carry names that are familiar to us and the functions seem similar, they each have further functions that Western medicine does not recognize. The organs are paired in yin–yang relationships, viscera being yin and bowels being yang.

6 Viscera	6 Bowels	Phase
heart	small intestine	fire
spleen	stomach	earth
lung	large intestine	metal
kidney	urinary bladder	water
liver	gallbladder	wood
pericardium	triple burner	fire

The organs are also understood in terms of the five phases. For example, in ancient medical thought, the spleen and stomach were associated with the earth. According to the five-phase relationship, this pair can be affected by a disturbance of the wood phase, which is associated with the liver. A simple instance of this relationship is the disturbance of digestive processes in certain kinds of liver disease. This relationship can also work in a more abstract fashion. The metal phase can be damaged by the fire phase. If there is an abundance of fire or if there is an insufficiency of metal, this can affect both the lungs and the large intestines, causing cough, frequent colds, and perhaps, constipation.

In addition to the actual text of the *Inner Classic*, commentaries were added over the centuries. One of the more important commentaries on the *Inner Classic* is the *Nan Jing*, or *Classic of Difficulties*, which takes the discussion of channels and points begun in the *Inner Classic* and expands on

The Emperor Inquires About the Depots

The 12 organs recognized by the ancient Chinese have names that sound familiar to us, but their functions were and are much broader for the Chinese. In this selection from the *Yellow Emperor's Inner Classic*, the emperor's minister, Qi Bo, explains the significance of the organs, or depots.

> The Yellow Emperor asked: "I should very much like to hear about the relative importance of the 12 depots and their mutual relationships?"
>
> Qi Bo replied: "That is truly an informed question! Let me answer it immediately. The heart is the ruler; spirit and enlightenment have their origin here. The lung is the minister; the order of life's rhythm has its origin here. The liver is the general; planning and deliberation have their origin here. The gall is the official [whose duty it is to maintain the golden] mean and what is proper; decisions and judgements have their origin here. The heart-enclosing network [pericardium] is the emissary; good fortune and happiness have their origin here. The spleen and stomach are officials in charge of storing provisions; the distribution of food has its origin here. The small intestine is the official charged with collecting surpluses; the reformation of all things has its origin here. The kidneys are officials for employment and forced labor; technical skills and expertise have their origin here. The triple burner is the official in charge of transportation conduits; water channels have their origin here. The urinary bladder is the provincial magistrate and stores body fluids; once the influences [of the latter are exhausted through] transformation, they may leave [the bladder].
>
> If the ruler is enlightened, peace reigns for his subjects. He who carries out his life on these principles is assured of longevity; he will never be in danger. He who rules the empire in accordance with these principles will bring forth a golden age. If, however, the ruler is not enlightened, the 12 officials are endangered; streets shall be closed and all traffic interrupted. Form will suffer great harm. He who carries out his life on these principles will bring down misfortune. He who rules the empire on such principles shall endanger his entire clan.

it greatly. In the *Classic of Difficulties*, the focus is on the concepts of systematic correspondence. The body is presented in a more coherent, functional whole, and for the first time, the practical application of the theoretical system—in the form of acupuncture—is directly discussed. Although not as culturally important to the story of the traditional medicine of China as the *Yellow Emperor's Inner Classic*, the *Classic of Difficulties* is considered by many practitioners to be a more complete, useful, and mature text.

Acupuncture, Moxibustion, and the Channels

Acupuncture and moxibustion are the two clinical techniques that have become the most well-recognized Chinese treatments today. The two can be used independently of each other but are so closely connected that the term we translate as acupuncture, *zhen jiu*, literally means "needles and moxibustion." Both techniques are used to provide stimulus to specific points (*xue*, literally "caves") that lie along channel pathways.

There are 12 channels described in the *Inner Classic*. The channels are a network that serves to move *qi* over the entire body. The 12 main channels are considered the largest channels of this network, and then there are progressively smaller and smaller related channels, which form connections between the main channels and various areas of the body. Each major channel is related to one of the viscera or bowels. Stimulus on any given channel is thought to affect the channel pathway itself, any disharmonies in the pathway,

The Rudiments of Acupuncture from the Inner Classic

Huang Di asked: Could you please tell me the important principles of acupuncture?

Qi Bo replied: In disease one must differentiate between the external and internal location of the illness. In acupuncture, there are differentiations of deep or shallow insertion. If the illness is on the *biao*, or external level, one should insert superficially; if on the internal level, one should insert more deeply. The location of the illness must be reached; but it is important not to insert too deeply so as not to injure the five zang organs. Inserting too shallowly, however, will not allow the physician to reach the area of illness, and the *qi* and blood can be disrupted, which allows an opportunity for evil *qi* to enter. Acupuncture performed without a guiding principle can be dangerous or damaging.

and the organ it is related to. So, again, if there is a disharmony of the metal phase, a practitioner might stimulate points on either the lung or the large intestine channel to influence the organs.

ACUPUNCTURE The therapeutic goal of acupuncture is to regulate the *qi* in the body. When the flow of *qi* is impaired by an evil, by trauma, or by a mental state, then illness and pain result. Acupuncture is used to remove the obstruction or evil, allowing the *qi* to flow correctly or to where it is needed. When the disharmony in the body has been determined, acupuncture points on the channel are chosen to help move, supplement, or drain the *qi* of the channels to resolve the disharmony.

Each acupuncture point has specific indications associated with it based on the empirical experience of generations of practitioners. Points may be selected because of their location on a channel or simply because they are tender to the touch. Once a point is selected, it is correctly located and then properly stimulated with an acupuncture needle. The needle is inserted rapidly through the skin and then adjusted to an appropriate depth. The point is then stimulated by rapidly rotating the needle or by carefully manipulating it.

The aim of the acupuncturist when needling a site is to "obtain *qi*." The signs that *qi* has been obtained are both subjective and objective. The acupuncturist may feel a gentle tugging on the needle as a fish tugging on a line or there may be redness around the point. The patient may feel itching, numbness, soreness, or a swollen feeling at the site of insertion, and the sensation may travel up or down along the channel pathway.

Manipulation techniques vary depending on the location of the point and the desired effect, but the two fundamental techniques are draining and supplementing. One simple way to do this is to adjust the direction of the needle either to follow the flow of *qi* in the channel (supplement-

Patients receiving acupuncture and moxibustion at a hospital of traditional Chinese medicine. Burning the moxa directly on the needle is a technique for warming the needle that is used in cold conditions. Burning moxa daily on a point located just below the knee (as seen here) is considered to be one of the best methods of disease prevention.

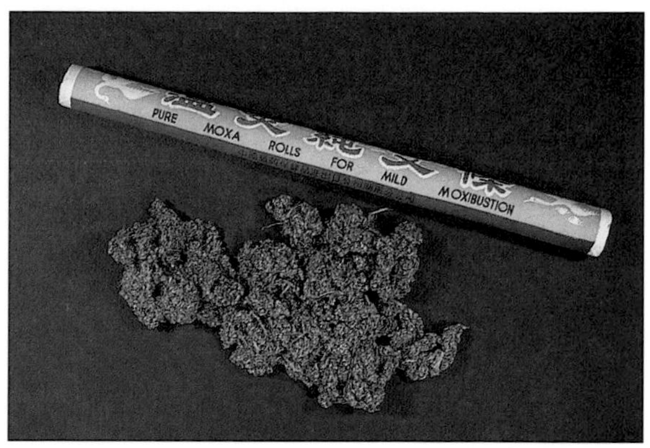

Two types of moxa used in moxibustion. The loose moxa can be burned on the needle, directly on the skin, or with a barrier, such as garlic or ginger, between the skin and the moxa. The rolled moxa is lit and used to gently warm acupuncture points. Although unclear, some evidence suggests that moxibustion as a healing technique actually preceded acupuncture.

ing) or to go against the flow of *qi* in the channel (draining).

MOXIBUSTION Moxibustion is the burning of the dried and powdered leaves of the plant *Artemesia vulgaris* (*ai ye*) either on or near the skin to affect the movement of *qi* in the channel. Moxibustion as a treatment modality is mentioned in some of the earliest Chinese medical texts, such as the texts excavated at Ma Wang Dui (ca. 163 B.C.), which do not discuss acupuncture at all but do cover moxibustion.

CHANNELS AND POINTS How to use the points on the channels was not discussed very much in the *Inner Classic*, but the *Classic of Difficulties* did discuss the actions of particular points in much greater detail and categorized points in ways that helped to explain their functions. The point categories discussed in the *Classic of Difficulties* are still used today to aid the acupuncturist in determining treatment.

Several texts unearthed from three tombs in the Hunan Province, called the Ma Wang Dui tombs, identify 11 vessels, described as being either yin or yang vessels (6 of which originate on the feet and 5 of which originate on the hands) through which vapor (it is not called *qi* in these texts) flows. The Ma Wang Dui texts also mention moxibustion and the use of heated stones, but they do not speak about acupuncture or about specific acupuncture points—an omission that has led to the hypothesis that the channels of the body may actually have been recognized and described before the recognition of acupuncture points.

The Dao and Herbalism

Herbal medicine is an integral part of the Chinese culture and medical practices that, until the 9th century A.D., developed very separately from the medicine of systematic correspondences and the therapeutics of acupuncture. At least part of this separateness comes from herbalism's association with Daoist rather than Confucian thought.

THE WAY Both Lao Zi and Chuang Zi, two of the heroes of the Daoist movement, are thought to have lived at about the same time as Confucius. The development of Daoism, like the Confucian philosophy, was also a response to the chaos of the late Zhou and early Warring States Period. But whereas Confucian thought was concerned with how man should behave in society, Daoist thought emphasized how man could best conform to the laws of nature. Although the two systems may once have been mutually exclusive, they evolved to appeal to two different sides of the Chinese character, and it appears that after serving for years, many Confucian scholars and officials retired to seek the Dao—"The Way."

Early Daoist writings were not so much about a search for immortality as about a return to a simpler, even primitive life in which man was in harmony with nature and death was a natural event. It was a prevalent idea during the chaos of the late Zhou and early Warring States periods that humans used to live longer and fuller lives in "ancient" times. As Daoism developed, it became a doctrine of individualism in unity with nature. For some Daoists, the unity with nature evolved into a search for immortality, which led to a great involvement with medicine and therapeutic practices.

SHEN NONG The Daoists had a great influence on the development of herbal medicine as they searched for an herb that would allow them to live forever. Shen Nong was probably declared divine by the Daoists, and the organization of his materia medica (*Shen Nong Ben Cao*) was probably created by the Daoists.

The *Shen Nong Ben Cao* was divided into three sections:

- superior herbs that could be taken in the long term without harm and had rejuvenating properties
- medium herbs that had tonic effects but could be toxic if taken in the long term
- inferior herbs that were used for curing disease but were considered poisonous and not to be taken in the long term

In addition to herbal therapeutics, the Daoists also developed many breathing exercises to keep the circulation of *qi* smooth. They greatly developed the idea of man's unity with nature, with the environment, and with the rhythm of the seasons.

A ceramic mural from the museum of Chinese medicine in Chengdu, China, depicts several traditional physicians out gathering herbs for their pharmacies. It is important that herbs be harvested at the correct time of year so that they retain their nature and temperature.

The development of the herbal pharmacopoeia by the Daoists led to the writing of many texts on the theory and practice of herbal medicine. One of the most famous and important herbal texts, the *Shang Han Za Bing Lun*, or *Treatise on Cold Damage and Miscellaneous Disease*, was written by Zhang Zhong Jing during the Han Dynasty. This text was an herbal medicine text based on Zhang Zhong Jing's clinical experiences and observa-

Once a formula is written for a patient, it must be prepared by the herbalist or pharmacist. Many herbs are much more potent if they are first ground. This traditional grinder would be used to break up herbs before giving them to the patient. The drawers in the background each contain different herbs, and the contents of each are written on the drawer.

> ### *The Fundamental Categories of the Materia Medica*
>
> Throughout the history of Chinese herbal medicine, there have been many methods of organizing herbs and herb formulas into categories. One might organize them according to the conditions treated, for example. Very early texts such as the *Shen Nong Ben Cao* used three major categories: upper, middle, and lower. Upper-grade substances were said to nourish life; middle-grade substances were said to nourish constitutional types; and lower-grade substances were used to eliminate disease.
>
> By the 12th century, the organization of medicinal substances was being linked to therapeutic principles with categories such as "purging" and "lubricating," and by the early 17th century, 14 categories were in place. Today, modern practitioners use about 18 categories to organize the extensive materia medica of Chinese medicine. Although they are expanded, the categories are quite similar to those used in ancient times.
>
> Exterior-resolving
> Heat-clearing
> Ejection or vomiting
> Precipitant or purgative
> Wind-dispelling
> Water-disinhibiting
> Interior-warming
> *Qi*-rectifying
> Food dispersing
> Worm-expelling
> Blood-rectifying
> Phlegm-transforming or cough-suppressing
> Spirit-quieting
> Liver-calming or wind-extinguishing
> Orifice-opening
> Supplementing
> Securing and astringing
> External use

tions. Like the *Classic of Difficulties*, this text studied disease from a more clinical standpoint, placing emphasis on the physical signs and symptoms, the course of disease, and the method of treatment. He was especially interested in fevers because his family and two-thirds of his village were wiped out by fever epidemics (possibly typhoid). Unfortunately, Zhang's work was not well received at the time he wrote it, and it was not until much later (A.D. 960) that the ideas in this text were recognized as clinically important.

The traditional Chinese materia medica contains over 5,000 substances, including herbs, minerals, and animal parts. While the *Shen Nong Ben Cao* divided herbs into three categories, later developments divided herbs into 18 basic categories based on their nature and their actions (see "The Fundamental Categories of the Materia Medica"). These categories are based on the eight methods of treatment, including sweating, clearing heat, ejection or vomiting, precipitation or purgation, harmonization, warming, supplementing, and dispersing. Zhang Zhong Jing's work was one of the earliest texts to organize the multitude of herbs into clearly organized formulas. However, it was not until much later in the Sung Dynasty (A.D. 960–1279) that physicians became interested in this type of practice and in relating herbal practice to a systematic theory.

Diagnosis

In a system as complex and intricate as that of traditional Chinese medicine, properly diagnosing the illness or imbalance is clearly the crux of the matter. In his *Treatise on Cold Damage*, Zhang Zhong

Jing considers diagnosis to be of primary importance. The most important element of the diagnosis was being able to see symptoms as manifestations of a root cause and determine what that root cause was.

Diagnosis in Chinese medicine did, and still does, include four aspects:

- inquiry
- listening and smelling
- observation
- palpation

The inquiry phase conducted by a practitioner is extensive, including all aspects of a person's bodily functions and subjective sensations. Listening and smelling refers to the practitioner observing, hearing, and smelling any anomalies in the patient's voice, breath, body odor, and so on. Observation includes observing the patient's demeanor, spirit, complexion, and especially tongue. Tongue diagnosis is extremely important to Chinese medicine; the state of the internal organs, the blood, and the *qi* are all reflected in the tongue. Finally, there is palpation, which includes feeling any areas of pain, touching the channels, and examining the pulse. Like the tongue, the pulse reflects the state of the internal organs as well as the state of *qi* and blood. While tongue and pulse examinations are the best known of the diagnostic methods, all four are extremely important, and a correct diagnosis cannot be made without the thorough use of all four examinations.

In traditional practice, taking the pulse of a woman was extremely important as the physician probably would not have been able to ask her the type of intimate questions he might ask a man. In some cases, the woman might even be hidden behind a screen and all the physician would see of her were her wrists. This 19th-century depiction of a physician taking a woman's pulse epitomizes the serenity and calm the physician required to take a pulse.

After completing all four of the examinations, a diagnosis can be made. A diagnosis may be based on the six evils or on dysfunction of *qi* and blood, disharmony of the five phases, some channel pathology, a disharmony of the viscera and bowels, or one of the more complex categories developed by Zhang Zhong Jing and later commentators.

The Ten Questions

The inquiry phase of diagnosis consists of ten basic questions from which the practitioner can glean valuable information. The practitioner should

1) Inquire about cold and heat
2) Inquire about perspiration
3) Inquire about the head and body
4) Inquire about stool and urine
5) Inquire about food and drink
6) Inquire about the chest
7) Inquire about hearing and vision
8) Inquire about thirst
9) Inquire about old illnesses
10) Inquire about previous medication

For women, the physician would also ask about menstruation; for children, the physician would ask the parents these questions.

Once a diagnosis has been made, the practitioner must then determine an appropriate treatment, which could include acupuncture, moxibustion, an herbal formula, or breathing exercises to improve *qi*, known as *qi gong*.

Buddhist Influences

Another element that had some influence on medicine during the Han Dynasty was the introduction of Buddhism from India. Buddhism was probably introduced to China sometime around A.D. 100. Unlike Daoism and Confucian thought, Buddhism never had a very strong following in China. Around A.D. 400, it began to make some inroads into popular Chinese culture, but in a much different form; more as only one element of the already eclectic religious pantheon of China at the time.

Even if Buddhism was not a huge influence on Chinese culture, its influence on Chinese medicine was significant. Many aspects of the extensive Indian pharmacopeia of botanical medicine were integrated into the Daoist herbal arsenal, but the theory of Indian medicine never became important to the medicine of China.

The medical system that developed in China and is described in the ancient texts of the Han Dynasty was the medicine of the elite, of the gentry, and not the medicine of the general population. Eighty percent of the total population of China in the beginning of the 1st century A.D. consisted of farmers and peasants living at a subsistence level and dependent on the soil for their life. These people developed their own traditions, primarily based in eclectic religious beliefs and herbal lore, but they did not, for the most part, participate in the development of the traditional medicine of China and were not privy to the secrets of acupuncture and moxibustion, much less the esoteric theories of channels and *qi*. What the Buddhists did was introduce to China the concept of

The Great Medical Works

Chinese Name	English Name	Date Written	Subject Matter
Huang Di Nei Jing	*Yellow Emperor's Inner Classic*	ca. 200 B.C.	Yin–yang theory; five phases; acupuncture and moxibustion
Shen Nong Ben Cao	*Divine Husbandman's Materia Medica*	ca. 100 B.C.	Herbal medicine
Nan Jing	*Classic of Difficulties*	A.D. 200	Systematic correspondence; acupuncture
Shang Han Za Bing Lun	*Treatise on Cold Damage and Miscellaneous Disease*	A.D. 220	Systematic relationship between diagnosis and herbal therapy
Mai Jing	*Pulse Classic*	A.D. 280	Pulse diagnosis
Zhen Jiu Jia Yi Jing	*Systematic Classic of Acupuncture*	A.D. 282	Acupuncture
Qian Jin Yao Fang	*Thousand Ducat Prescriptions*	A.D. 652	Ethics and herbal medicine

hospitals and medical care for the peasant. Buddhist monasteries were also hospitals, and the monks were willing to treat anyone who needed their services. To prevent the Buddhists from becoming too influential among the people, other medical practitioners eventually had to follow their path and treat the common man as well as the elite.

The Maturation of Chinese Medicine

As we have seen, the Han Dynasty is the time period to which most of the ancient traditions of Chinese medicine can be traced. During this time, the groundwork was laid for the rest of the development of medical practice in China. This is not to say that the traditional medicine of China remained static from A.D. 220 to the present, but rather that the foundation for further examination and development was created.

The first mention of acupuncture as a therapeutic modality and the first herbal prescriptions were written during the Han Dynasty. However, the actual practice of Chinese medicine was limited to a few scholar-officials who found the topic interesting. Throughout the next 1,800 years, new theories would continue to be presented and old ideas would be reexamined, but the texts of the Han Dynasty, especially the *Inner Classic*, the *Shen Nong Ben Cao*, the *Classic of Difficulties*, and the *Treatise on Cold Damage and Miscellaneous Disease* (later divided into the *Shang Han Lun—Treatise on Damage by Cold*—and the *Jin Gui Yao Lue—Prescriptions of the Golden Cabinet*) were to remain the core of traditional medicine in China.

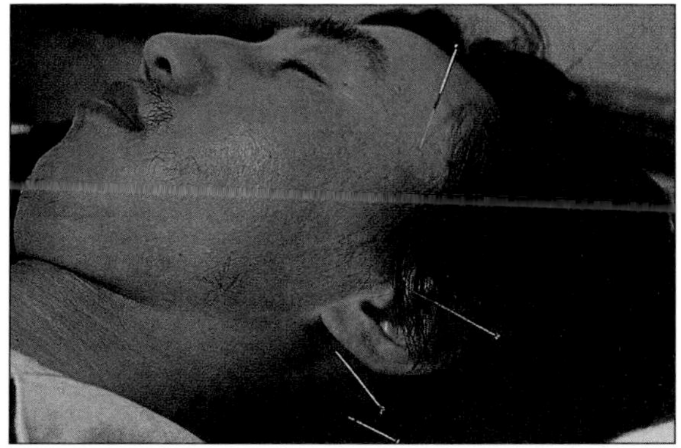

Patient receiving acupuncture at points on the gallbladder and triple burner channels. He is likely being treated for some type of hearing disorder such as tinnitus. Local and adjacent points on the channels would be chosen so that the qi could move smoothly through the channels, thereby eliminating the cause of the problem.

The Han Dynasty fell in A.D. 220 and was followed by another long period of strife and unrest. During this time, the medicine of systematic correspondence continued to develop, as seen by the publication of Huang Pu Mi's (215–286) *Systematic Classic of Acupuncture* (*Zhen Jiu Jia Yi Jing*) and Wang Shu He's (210–285) *Pulse Classic* (*Mai Jing*), which was a greatly expanded discussion of pulse diagnosis.

In 581, the Sui Dynasty reunified China and again began the outward expansion of the empire. The next stage of development in Chinese medicine revolved around a reexamination of the classics and the creation of treatment principles or strategies based on a new interpretation of the fundamental concepts that had evolved during the Han Dynasty.

MEDICAL EDUCATION Short lived as it was, the Sui Dynasty did not see a large contribution to the development of medicine. Rather, this dynasty was focused on unifying China under a single political structure and developing a strong bureaucracy. However, there are records of the Sui Dynasty that indicate a certain amount of government support for farms for the cultivation of herbs. In 618, the Sui Dynasty was succeeded by the Tang Dynasty, considered by many to be the height of China's cultural development. The Tang Dynasty continued to spread the influence of China through Vietnam and Central Asia, and into Korea and Japan. During this period, both Buddhism and Daoism strongly influenced medical thought.

Several important steps in the development of medicine occurred during the Tang Dynasty. First of all, educational ranks were developed for imperial physicians. While most Confucian, Daoist, and Buddhist scholars had a certain amount of medical knowledge, it was not until the 7th century that an imperial school of medicine was founded in the capital and medical institutions developed in other major cities. Medicine, which had been a pastime or sideline for scholar-officials, became a path toward advancement in the imperial bureaucracy. Medical students were required to study the *Yellow Emperor's Inner Classic*, the *Shen Nong Ben Cao*, the *Pulse Classic*, the *Systematic Classic of Acupuncture*, and other fundamental texts, after which time they could specialize in any given course of study.

In the Tang Dynasty, medicine was broken into four main specialties:

- Internal Medicine
- Acupuncture
- Massage
- Incantations

Within each specialty, students were required to study the following:

- Therapeutics (7 years)
- Pediatrics (5 years)
- Dermatology (5 years)
- Eyes, Ears, Nose, Mouth, and Teeth (4 years)
- Horning or Cupping (3 years)

Still, the imperial schools were founded primarily for the training of physicians to the emperor and his family and officials. These physicians were also Confucian scholars and bureaucrats. It was not until the Sung Dynasty (960–1279) that schools were established for the training of physicians for the average citizen.

MEDICAL ETHICS The other important development of the Tang Dynasty was the beginnings of thought concerning medical

From "On the Absolute Sincerity of Physicians" by Sun Si Miao

Whenever a Great Physician treats diseases, he has to be mentally calm and his disposition firm. He should not give way to wishes and desires, but has to develop first of all a marked attitude of compassion. He should commit himself firmly to the willingness to take the effort to save every living creature.

If someone seeks help because of illness or on the ground of another difficulty, [a great physician] should not pay attention to status, wealth, or age, neither should he question whether the particular person is attractive or unattractive, whether he is an enemy or a friend, whether he is Chinese or a foreigner, or finally, whether he is uneducated or educated. He should meet everyone on equal ground. . . . Finally, it is inappropriate to emphasize one's reputation, to belittle the rest of the physicians, and to praise only one's own virtue. Indeed, in actual life someone who has accidentally healed a disease [and] then stalks around with his head raised shows conceit and announces that no one in the entire world could measure up to him. In this respect, all physicians are evidently incurable.

ethics. Sun Si Miao (581–682) was a famous physician of the period who was well versed in both Daoist and Buddhist practices. One of his books, the *Thousand Ducat Prescriptions* (*Qian Jin Yao Fang*), contains a section entitled "On the Absolute Sincerity of Physicians," which established him as China's first medical ethicist.

His commentary sparked further discussion of appropriate behavior for physicians, whom they should treat, and the fees they could accept. He also addressed the need for continued scholarship among physicians and for compassion and high moral standards toward the patient.

Specialization and Systemization

In the Sung Dynasty, another major change occurred in the bureaucracy of China. The hereditary aristocracy was entirely replaced by the scholar-official, whose position was based on merit. Individual merit became the criterion for advancement in the bureaucracy, and civil servants became the elite of China. The Sung also saw an increase in literacy due to the spread of printing, the establishment of systematic educational institutions, and the complete acceptance of civil service examinations as the method of entry into the bureaucratic system. This increase in literacy led to a profusion of new texts in all areas, including medicine, and to even greater attempts to return to and reinterpret the classics.

During the Sung Dynasty, medicine became much more specialized. Texts on specific diseases and their treatment were published, and the first practical handbook on acupuncture and moxibustion was compiled. There was more focus on the treatment of symptoms rather than the root cause of disease. Although, theoretically, understanding the root of disease was still important, the alleviation of symptoms took precedence over the root problem as medicine became a more widespread practice. In 1027, the emperor had two bronze figures made to illustrate the location of acupuncture points. The models had holes drilled at the location of the points. For study purposes they would be covered with wax and then filled with water. When a point was correctly located, water would drip out of the hole.

Qing Dynasty replica of the bronze figurine used to study the location of acupuncture points. In the original models, holes were made at the acupuncture points, and then the figure would be covered in wax and filled with water. Students would practice their location and needling skills on the models. If they inserted the needle into the point correctly, then water would come out of the hole.

Officially Rediscovering Herbs

One of the most notable shifts that occurred in the Sung Dynasty was the incorporation of herbal therapeutics into the medicine of systematic correspondences. Until this time, herbal medicine had remained a field separate from the more systematic medicine of the imperial schools, but now there were huge advances in the field of herbal medicine, and several extensive herbal pharmacopeias were published under imperial decree.

This is when tastes and temperatures were assigned to herbs according to their yin or yang nature, and specific functions were assigned to individual herbs. Herbal medicine, once the property of the Buddhists and Daoists, was now integrated into the Confucian system.

A traditional herbal pharmacy in China will usually have over 300 different herbs available for filling formulas. Formulas generally contain 5 to 20 substances with different functions. A formula may be based on a traditional formula from a historical text, or it may be written to fit the exact condition of the patient.

As a part of the revision of herbal medicine, the theories of Zhang Zhong Jing, the author of the *Treatise on Cold Damage*, were also revived. This revival had a huge influence on the theory of herbal medicine, and several hundred years later, it was to precipitate the formation of a new theoretical school, the school of warm diseases.

SUNG CONFLICTS While the theoretical underpinnings of Chinese medicine lie in the Han Dynasty, the form which we recognize today really began to be established during the Sung Dynasty with its emphasis on classification and order. Thus the five phases were further developed as were the functions of the organs. The emphasis on systematic correspondences stems from the Sung Dynasty as well as attempts at reconciliation of opposing theories.

Despite all of the advances that occurred during the Sung, there were also struggles, most notably in the realm of education. A large number of schools of medicine opened during the Sung Dynasty. Who would be permitted to attend these schools and whether attendance at these schools was mandatory to practice medicine was, however, at issue. Much of the conflict stemmed from differing views between imperially trained physicians and independent physicians on the use of medicine as a livelihood or as a natural outgrowth of scholarly pursuits.

By the 12th century, given the emphasis on neo-Confucian thought and order and the growing importance of the examination system for entrance into the official class, the imperially trained physicians won the argument. Attendance at medical schools was again limited to the classically trained Confucian scholar, and the practice of medicine was limited to those trained in the medical academies. This system effectively limited the resources and abilities of the lay physician and jeopardized their ability to continue to practice medicine.

This decision also institutionalized a certain amount of disdain for anyone who chose to practice medicine as a vocation rather than an avocation—as a profession rather than a diversion. The result was that Buddhist and Daoist monks continued to practice medicine for the people and to include the use of incantations and exorcisms in their practice, while the neo-Confucians rejected these supernatural elements of medicine and focused on the physical rather than the spiritual.

Of course the medicine of systematic correspondences continues to recognize the influence of the emotions on the health of the body, but the more spiritual aspects of medicine, such as the influence of the soul or of the spirits, was exorcized from the medicine of systematic correspondences. Thus, when we hear today that Chinese medicine lost its "spiritual" aspect with the advent of the Communist party, this simply is not true. In fact, the dropping of spirituality from Chinese medicine began in the 11th century, long before the Communist revolution.

The Continuing Tradition

The academic medicine and systematic therapeutics of the Sung Dynasty continued through the next dynasties, adding to the already extensive list of therapeutic herbs and the refinement of techniques whose roots remained firmly planted in the age-old theories of the Han Dynasty.

The introduction of Western influence, technology, and medicine into China created some problems of legitimacy for the traditional physician during the Ming and early Qing dynasties (the infiltration of Western medicine was such that in 1822 acupuncture was formally eliminated from the Imperial Medical College), but the return to the classics continued even beyond the dynastic age, which ended with the fall of the Qing Dynasty in 1911.

Finally, with the collapse of the Qing and the formation of the Republic, the groundwork was laid for the total elimination of Chinese medicine from the landscape. Sun Yat Sen, the father of the Chinese Republic, was trained in Western medicine in Japan, and there was a series of clashes over the regulation, establishment, and elimination of practitioners of Chinese medicine. In the end, to salvage the profession, practitioners from a variety of schools and traditions came together to create a unified medical system. It was at this time that the heterogenous traditional medicine of China came to be termed *traditional Chinese medicine*, or *Zhong Yi*, to

The physician feeling a patient's pulse in a modern hospital of Chinese medicine. Feeling the pulse is one of the four methods of diagnosis in Chinese medicine. Taking a pulse involves feeling the rate, depth, force, rhythm, and quality of the radial artery in three positions on either wrist. Each position is related to an organ and can give the physician information about the overall state of health.

differentiate it from Western medicine. However, the Nationalists disdained the medicine because of its lack of scientific proof, and the Communists disdained the medicine because it referred back to the feudal period in China to support its theories. The period from 1911 to 1958 was, therefore, a difficult time for practitioners of Chinese medicine, and extinction seemed imminent no matter which political party won. Finally, in 1958, after the Communist Revolution, in an attempt to find a medical system that would bring primary health care to all Chinese, Chairman Mao declared that "Chinese medicine is a great treasure house! We must uncover it and raise its standards."

Japanese Medicine

THE ANCIENT HEALING TRADITIONS of Japan are closely connected to those of China. Starting in the 6th century A.D., an extensive cultural exchange existed between Japan and China. Ideas about medicine, religion, philosophy, and even the method of writing were transmitted to Japan by the Chinese. Therefore, much of the traditional medicine practiced in Japan relies heavily on traditional Chinese theory and technique.

Before this period of interaction with China, however, Japan's history is somewhat shrouded. Our understanding of medical practices and beliefs before that time are based on records of ancient tales and legends that were not systematically compiled until the 8th century A.D., and even these are of questionable reliability.

Shinto priests walk to a ceremony to prepare for the New Year at the Meiji shrine. Shinto is the most ancient healing tradition in Japan, and it is still used today as people participate in Shinto rituals and visit shrines to pray for their health and prosperity in the year to come.

Japan is also unique in relation to other countries in Asia in that it adopted western European medicine and made it a matter of national policy in the mid-19th century. In doing so, Japan deliberately relegated the medical traditions that it had relied on for centuries to second-class status.

Japanese woodblock showing the development of a fetus (right to left) *set in the scheme of the changing seasons.*

Practices in Prehistory

The origin of the Japanese people continues to be a topic of debate. One perspective is that two successive waves of peoples came to settle these remote islands. One wave from northern Asia is associated with the Jomon period (2000–200 B.C.) and another group of peoples from southeast Asia is associated with the Yayoi period (200 B.C.–A.D. 200).

Little is known about the most ancient medical traditions of Japan in the periods preceding the 6th century A.D. Since writing first arrived in Japan from China in the 6th century and was not routinely used by the Japanese until the 7th century, many of the descriptions of ancient practices had only been transmitted orally. And when they were finally written down, the political and cultural perspectives of the writers clearly influenced the way these traditions were recorded.

The compilations of ancient histories, tales, and legends—known as the *Nihongi* and the *Kojiki*—and accounts of early life in Japan—the *Fudoki*—describe some of the beliefs and practices of the early Japanese people, at least as they were understood in the early part of the 8th century. The Chinese also recorded observations about their neighbors to the east, and from these accounts we know a little about the preliterate period of Japanese society.

According to the *Nihongi*, two divine beings—Opo-kuni-nushi and Sukana-biko-no-mikoto—joined their powers to build the universe. These two beings

> also determined the method of curing illnesses for the race of mortal man and for animals; they also determined magical methods for doing away with calamities from birds, beasts, and creeping things.

Ancient tales describe the use of native plants to treat disease, sometimes in a magical context. One tale that is often referred to and was recorded in the *Kojiki* describes the instructions given by a divine being, or *Kami*, to a rabbit who had lost his fur in an unhappy encounter with a crocodile. The rabbit is sent to the river

A Japanese Explanation

In the early 19th century, Hirata Atsutane wrote about the relationship between the ancient gods of Japan and the medicine and philosophy of China. In his statement, one can see his perspective on the fact that the Japanese did not develop their own distinctive system of medicine; one can also see his nationalistic views on the value of the Chinese philosophies of Confucianism and Buddhism:

> The art of medicine, though introduced to Japan from abroad, appears originally to have been taught to foreign countries by our own great gods. Later, because of the special needs it meets, this art came to be widely practiced in Japan, and though it may be said to have once been of foreign origins, we are not obliged to dislike it for that reason. Nevertheless, it is true that the art of medicine developed to such a high degree in China by way of a quite natural reaction to the rampant and pernicious maladies which resulted from the evil character of the country itself. The spread in Japan since middle antiquity of Confucianism and Buddhism, both of them exceedingly troublesome doctrines, has worsened and confused men's minds, and as a result of the attendant increase in the number of things to worry about, various maladies which were unknown to [Japan in] ancient times have become prevalent. The Chinese methods of treatment were perfectly suited to deal with such maladies and are, therefore, now in general employ.

to bathe his body with water and then to roll in the pollen of the *kama* grass that grows at the mouth of the river. Throughout the centuries, similar plants such as kudzu would be used both in the folk traditions of herbal medicine in Japan and in the formal herbal traditions imported from China.

Impurity and Cleansing Rituals The early Japanese view of the world made no clear distinction between gods and men. Human beings were seen as essentially good, but transgressions and misdeeds could allow evil spirits to cause disease and calamities. The misdeeds and, hence, the illness could be remedied through rituals of purification.

Purification had other uses as well. Contact with polluted people or things, such as blood, corpses, and people with skin diseases, could produce the condition of "having a spirit polluted by bad poison." The ideas of physical injury and uncleanliness were closely linked; the expression *kega*, for example, has the meaning of both a "wound" and a "defilement." As a result, association with the ill, the dead, and the dying was potentially very problematic—a belief not conducive to recruiting medical practitioners. However, contact with defiling objects, people, or situations could be counteracted by cleansing rituals such as bathing the body and rinsing the mouth.

Ancient ideas of illness included the notion of contact with, or even penetration by, the unclean, which would have to be removed forcefully and definitively. Consequently, medicines that produced sweating, purgation, and vomiting were popular. The idea of certain situations and contacts as dangerously impure continue to be prevalent in contemporary Japan, although in less extreme forms.

Shinto Shinto (or *Kami-No-Michi*, meaning "the way of the gods") was the name given to the indigenous religious traditions of Japan. It became necessary to define these traditions when other beliefs, such as Buddhism, began infiltrating Japanese society from China. (In fact, the name *Shinto* is borrowed from the Chinese language.) Shinto continues to express the idea of a world where men and gods live in

Shinto shrines are often placed in locations of immense natural beauty. The Shinto deities, or Kami, prefer to inhabit beautiful natural settings, often dwelling in trees, mountains, and streams.

close proximity and where every facet of nature is endowed with divine significance.

The influences of Shinto were not that significant in the development of traditional medicine in Japan, but they were important to popular ideas associated with healing, such as bathing practices and spiritual interventions for disease. Japan has a long history of incorporating the advances and practices of other cultures into its own—in medicine, it was no different. When the more medically significant Buddhist practices arrived in Japan, they intermingled with Shinto and were often used simultaneously or interchangeably, eventually leading to distinctive adaptations of Chinese practices.

Chinese Medicine Comes to Japan

The ancient medical traditions of Japan are so closely linked with Chinese medicine, it is typical for many discussions of traditional medicine in Japan actually to begin with a description of traditional medicine in China. (Although some of these will be discussed here in the context of Japanese traditions, you may want to read more about Chinese medicine in chapter 13, pages 277–307.)

Kon Mu is said to be the first physician to come to Japan using Chinese methods. He was sent in A.D. 414 by the king of Silla, in southeast Korea, to treat the emperor Inkyo Tenno. It is quite possible, though, that there was some degree of medical exchange prior to this date, because there is evidence of some interaction between the people of the Japanese islands and the people of the mainland from about A.D. 57.

In 562, Zhi Chong (*Chiso* in Japanese) came from southern China with more than 100 books on the practice of Chinese medicine, including the *Systematic Classic of Acupuncture* (*Zhen Jiu Jia Yi Jing*) and probably the *Classic of Difficulties* (*Nan Jing*). These exchanges coincide with the adoption of Chinese characters as the basis for Japanese writing and the gradual expansion of literacy throughout the elite of Japanese society.

With the establishment of direct contact between Japan and China in the 6th century, Japanese physicians traveled to China to learn more about its healing traditions. The movement of information was no longer in the form of texts and a few physicians arriving from China or Korea. By 608, young Japanese physicians began to travel to China for long periods to study these medical texts and examine patients with Chinese physicians.

Medicine was not the only thing Japan appropriated from China. In the early centuries of the exchange, Japan made an effort to model its social organization and imperial administration on those of China's. One effort to emulate the bureaucratic structures of China was the creation of the Taiho Code in 702. This code made provision for a ministry of health to be composed of specialists, physicians, students, and researchers.

The Chinese model proved to be difficult for the Japanese, not because of the science, but because of the different social and political natures of the two countries. One striking feature of China, for example, was the extensive use of examinations and other merit-based competitions to ensure that individuals achieved rank and authority based on competence. Because social rank was based on inherited position in Japan, the exam-based approach was

The Ministry of Health

In the early part of the 8th century, Japan established a Ministry of Health. With the exception of the magicians, the staff of the ministry looks extraordinarily modern and complete for such an early foray into public health. The extensive specialization reveals the complexity of the medical establishment and its classification systems. (The titles are listed in English with the Japanese in parentheses.)

Minister of Health
Vice-minister (*Suke*)
Secretary (*Jo*)
Senior Assistant (*O-sakan*)
Junior Assistant (*Ko-sakan*)
10 Physicians (*I-shu*)
Doctor of Medicine (*I-hakase*)
40 Students of Medicine (*I-sei*)
24 Doctors of Internal Medicine (*Tairyo*)
6 Pediatricians (*Sho-sho*)
6 Surgeons (*Soshu*)
4 Doctors of Ears, Eyes, Mouth, Teeth (*Ji-moku-ko-shi*)
5 Acupuncture Practitioners (*Hari-shi*)
Doctor of Acupuncture (*Hari-hakase*)
20 Students of Acupuncture (*Hari-sei*)
2 Massage Practitioners (*Anma-shi*)
Doctor of Massage (*Anma-hakase*)
10 Students of Massage (*Anma-sei*)
2 Magicians (*Jugon-shi*)
Doctor of Magic (*Jugon-hakase*)
6 Students of Magic (*Jugon-sei*)
2 Herbalists (*Yakuen-shi*)
6 Students of Herbology (*Yakuen-sei*)

not adopted. Also, the strong central authority of the emperor, which was an important factor in China's development, was not a feature of Japanese life. The emperor was of important symbolic value, but the power was held unequally by a number of feudal lords who did not fall under anything resembling central authority until the 16th century.

Buddhism offers many healing rituals associated with many specific Buddhas, or enlightened beings. Devotees would say prayers and recite mantras to invoke the healing power of the Buddha. This 9th-century statue in a temple in Nara, Japan, is of Yakushi—the Healing Buddha (see also page 255).

Despite these challenges, Chinese medicine was well established in Japan by the early 8th century. Medical exchange continued during this period. One notable event involved the Chinese Buddhist monk Jian Zhen (*Kan Jin* in Japanese) from Yang Chow who moved to Japan in 753 along with 35 disciples, his medical books, and many herbs. Among these disciples were physicians who shared their medical knowledge with the Japanese monks and students. Jian Zhen is said to have created a charitable clinic where he and his disciples treated patients for free. Because of these actions, he came to be worshiped as a saint in Japanese temples.

Important Medical Books from China

Between the 6th and 9th centuries, many important and famous medical texts arrived in Japan from China. These included books such as the *Yellow Emperor's Inner Classic* (*Huang Di Nei Jing*), which may have been compiled as early as 100 B.C.

The *Divine Husbandman's Classic of Materia Medica* (*Shen Nong Ben Cao*) appeared in Japan about this time as well. This text is the first known appearance of a formal presentation of medicinal substances considered individually. Working over the centuries, writers in both China and Japan would produce many texts describing the uses and properties of these and other medicinal substances.

The *Classic of Difficulties* (*Nan Jing*) was compiled sometime during the 1st or 2nd century A.D., although its authorship is attributed to the legendary physician Bian Que. This text has had, and continues to have, a marked influence on the practice of Chinese medicine and, to an even greater extent, on the practice of Chinese medicine in Japan.

Truly Ancient Herbs

When the Chinese Buddhist monk Jian Zhen arrived in Japan, he brought many Chinese healing herbs. Shortly after the death of Emperor Shomu, 60 of the herbs were placed in the Storehouse of the Todaiji Temple called Shosoin in Nara, Japan. Interestingly, these have remained relatively undisturbed and intact for the last 1,200 years. Among them was a sample of ginseng that has been used to compare the biochemical properties of ancient with modern ginseng roots.

The *Classic of Difficulties* marks a drastic shift in medical thinking. It constitutes a systematic discussion of the theory and practice of therapeutic acupuncture. It is almost entirely devoid of magical elements. Because of its succinct and organized approach to therapy, this text retained its popularity in Japan in a way that it did not in China.

The *Treatise on Cold Damage* (*Shang Han Lun*) and the *Survey of Important Elements from the Golden Cabinet and Jade Container* (*Jin Gui Yao Lue*) were published in the 2nd century A.D. by Zhang Zhong Jing (also known as Zhang Ji). Chinese medical texts of this period were primarily philosophical (except for the *Classic of Difficulties*), but Zhang studied disease more from a clinical standpoint, laying emphasis on the physical signs, symptoms, and course of disease, as well as the method of treatment. (He was especially interested in fevers because most of his village was wiped out by fever epidemics, possibly typhoid.) The *Treatise on Cold Damage* became, perhaps, the single most influential text on the practice of herbal medicine in Japan. It came to function as the core text of herbal medicine, or *kanpo* (Chinese method), in Japan. Zhang's book was theoretically and diagnostically sophisticated, but its emphasis on therapy rather than theory made it popular with practical-minded Japanese physicians. The *Treatise on Cold Damage* inspired many commentaries and an entire school of medical thought in the 17th century. Today many of its formulas are approved for insurance reimbursement by the Japanese government.

Fundamental Concepts

With some slight variations, most of the theory underlying traditional Japanese medicine is the same as traditional Chinese medicine. Yin and yang, the five phases, and *ki* (the Japanese version of the Chinese *qi*) came to be the important organizing principles just as they did in China.

YIN AND YANG Yin and yang express the idea of opposing but complementary phenomena that exist in a state of dynamic equilibrium. The most ancient expression of this idea seems to have been that of the shady and sunny sides of a hill. The sunlit southern side was the yang side and the shaded or northern side was the yin side. The contrast between the bright and dark sides of the hill portrayed the yang and the yin (see also "Yin and Yang," page 291). Yin and yang are always present simultaneously; there is no absolute yin or absolute yang. There is no yin without yang; something is yin only in relation to something else being yang and vice versa.

The *Yellow Emperor's Inner Classic*, the oldest text to discuss the medical application of yin and yang, tells us that "yin and yang are the way of heaven and earth." This text used yin and yang to express ideas about normal physiology and disease processes as well. Yin and yang were applied to the organization of phenomena in many ways.

The ideas and properties associated with yin and yang are often illustrated with lists of associated terms. Yang, for example, is considered to be hot and rapid and to move upward. Yin is cold and slow, and it moves downward. These contrasts allow the physician to organize his thought about the body in a systematic way. Thus, a yin or cold condition such as arthritis would be treated with yang or warm therapies such as moxibustion and warming herbs. (For more about yin and yang, see pages 291–292.)

THE FIVE PHASES Another idea that has played a significant part in the development of some aspects of Chinese medicine is that of the five phases (*wu xing*): earth, metal, water, wood, and fire.

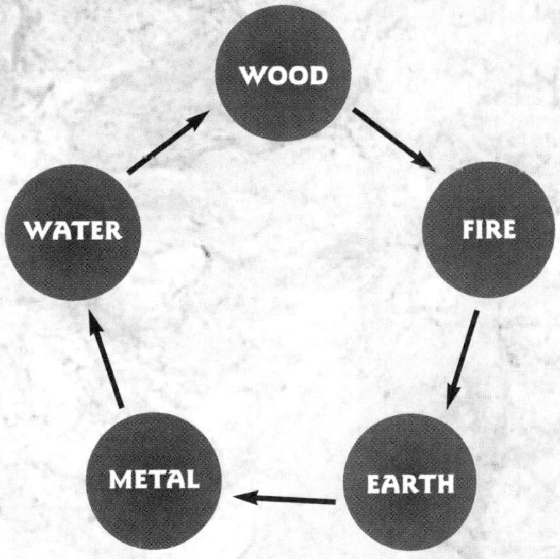

The five phases are connected with all phenomena. Each phase has an associated taste, organ, emotion, food, and season (see "Five Phase Correspondences," page 293). The relationships that exist between the phases also exist between the phenomena that are associated with them, and these ideas extend to diagnosis and therapy. For example, the kidneys, which are associated with water, are thought to nourish and support the liver, which is associated with wood accord-

Cycle of the Five Phases

The five phases are connected to each other. The fire phase produces earth, which produces metal. Water is produced from metal, and wood comes from water. Finally, the cycle is complete with wood producing fire. This cycle, known as the cycle of generation, is one of four relationships that occur between the five phases. The other important relationship is control, in which fire controls wood and so on. These relationships describe a process in which the five phases maintain a balanced and harmonious dynamic.

ing to the cycle of generation. Therefore, a problem with the kidneys might also go on to affect the liver.

The *Classic of Difficulties* made extensive use of the five-phase theory in the development of a system of pulse diagnosis that allowed the practitioner to diagnose disturbances in the channels and the organs and then use acupuncture to treat them. In ancient acupuncture traditions, each phase was said to relate to many different phenomena—everything from weather to seasons. By observing these relationships and understanding the interplay among the five elements, the ancient Japanese physician could understand the illnesses that afflicted his patients and prescribe the most effective treatments for them. (For more on the five phases, see pages 292–293.)

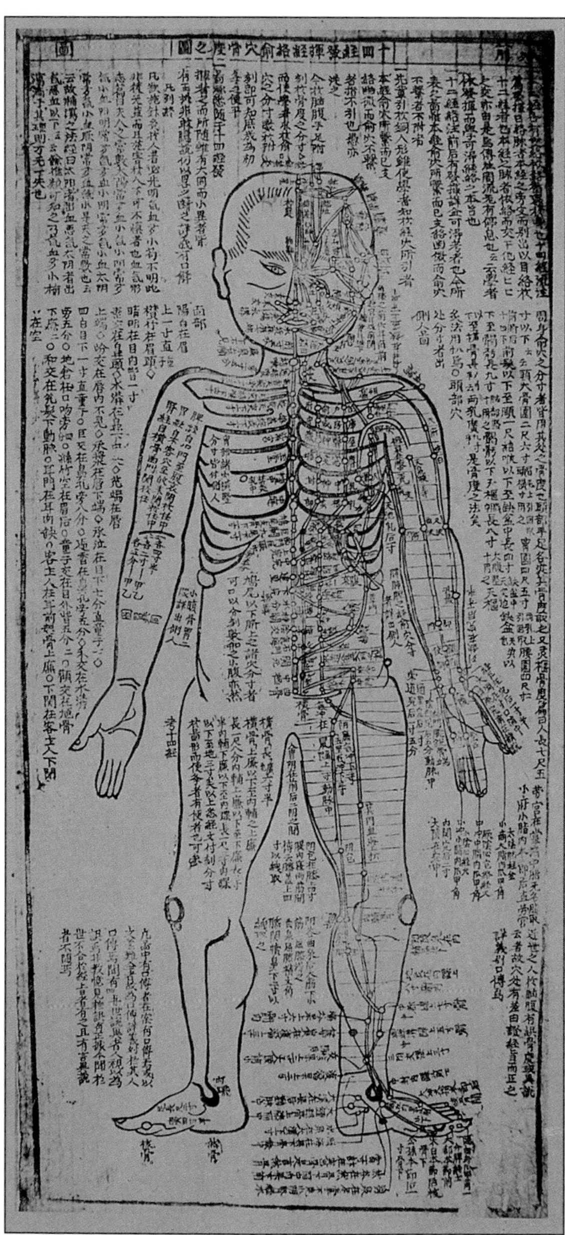

This 19th-century Japanese acupuncture chart shows some of the channels (keiraku) *and the points used in acupuncture therapy.*

KI AND THE ESSENTIAL SUBSTANCES Apart from the ideas of yin and yang and the five phases, there is no concept more crucial to Chinese medicine than *qi*. In Japanese, the character is pronounced *ki*. *Ki* is the subtle force that drives physiologic functions and maintains the health and vitality of the individual.

The idea of *ki* is extremely broad, encompassing almost every variety of natural, living phenomena. *Ki* was said to be produced as a result of normal physiologic processes and to circulate through *keiraku*, or channels. There are many different types of *ki* in the body, but in general, *ki* has the functions of activation, warming, defense, transformation, and containment. (For more on *ki* [or *qi*], see page 294.)

Diagnosis

A great deal has been said about diagnosis in the chapter on Chinese medicine (see pages 300–302). Traditionally in China, the idea of diagnosis included four methods: inspection, listening, palpation, and questioning. These ideas persist in Japanese therapeutic traditions, too. Over time, the Japanese medical tradition placed greater emphasis on palpation, or pulse diagnosis, than the Chinese, and sometimes, palpation alone was considered enough for a diagnosis. It is interesting to note that at different times, certain practices were emphasized or de-emphasized in Japan. For example, some traditions of Japanese acupuncture entirely dispensed with pulse diagnosis in favor of palpating the abdomen, whereas others retained the pulse diagnosis as a key diagnostic tool.

Therapeutics

Japanese approaches to therapy mirrored many Chinese practices and developed new ones (as we shall see). For example, acupuncture—the insertion of fine metal needles into the body to adjust the functioning of the channels and organs—was frequently used. Moxibustion—the burning of the plant moxa on or near certain points on the body—was also practiced.

Although originally similar treatments, these forms of therapy were elaborated on extensively by the Japanese. The trends toward specialized development became so pronounced that by the 20th century, the practices of acupuncture and moxibustion became separately licensed in Japan. This development has permitted the folk use of moxibustion by monks in Buddhist temples to persist.

In the middle part of this century, aspects of the Japanese *amma*, or massage, were adapted and integrated with acupuncture concepts in a formal way to create the system of massage known as *shiatsu*. Massage was typically practiced by physicians and specialists.

One problem that Japan faced with the expanded introduction of Chinese medicine was the difficulty of getting the raw materials. While many herbs in the Chinese pharmacopeia grew in Japan, many did not. Herbs such as cinnamon, rhubarb, and ephedra were difficult or impossible to cultivate in Japan and needed to be imported.

The result of this lack of access was that in many areas, Japanese folk medicine practices were, out of necessity, combined with Chinese herbal medicine. The scarcity of ingredients for the preparation of Chinese herbal formulas may have led to the lower doses typically seen in Japanese herbal prescriptions.

Blind Acupuncture and Guide Tubes

In the 17th century, a blind man named Waichi Sugiyama began to train the blind in acupuncture using very fine needles and guide tubes. Sugiyama received a high official rank as an acupuncturist possibly as a result of successfully treating the Shogun (the military ruler of Japan). Since it had become customary in the earlier part of the Edo period for the blind to do massage, both massage and acupuncture now became associated with blind practitioners. This contributed in the long run to a lowering in the social position of acupuncture practitioners and to the further specialization in medical practice.

The guide tube that Sugiyama developed was a hollow metal cylinder that held the acupuncture needle upright against the skin. The tube allowed for finer needles to be inserted into the body and for needles to be inserted with less discomfort for the patients. The prevalent use of fine needles and the guide tube continue to be distinctive features of Japanese acupuncture even today.

In modern Japan, both the blind and sighted continue to practice acupuncture, although as a result of Sugiyama's contribution, there are many schools of acupuncture for the blind.

Chinese Medicine Becomes a Japanese Tradition

During the Nara period (A.D. 710–794) medical knowledge from China had been actively assimilated in Japan. But by the early part of the 10th century, contact with China began to diminish, and the medical practices adopted from China began a course of independent development in Japan. Up until this time, Chinese medicine had been, by and large, the province of Buddhist monks; now, however, fewer monks became involved in medicine, and provincial officials and other educated members of the upper classes began to take over.

THE FIRST JAPANESE TEXT In 982, Yasunari (Yasuyori) Tamba, a Japanese physician, composed a 30-volume compilation of medical knowledge at the direction of the emperor. His book *Ishinho* is considered the first Japanese medical text. It contains detailed discussions of the practice of *kanpo*, or Japanese herbal medicine. The text recommends acupuncture and moxibustion for many conditions. Based on Chinese medical theory, it quotes extensively from Chinese texts. It describes hygienic practices, acupuncture, moxibustion, magic, and many other topics, even the proper regulation of sexual activity.

The use of moxibustion was indicated for many conditions including the treatment of abscesses. Herbs, such as coptidis (*huang lian*), that we know today have marked antibiotic properties were recommended to treat infections.

GREATER INDEPENDENCE The Kamakura period (1190–1333) saw the conclusion of a period of civil war with the establishment of a strong military rule. While the rulers in earlier periods had looked to China for guidance in the organization of the political world, this period revealed a distinctively Japanese approach to these matters. Similarly, the Japanese physician began to show a greater independence in medical thought: Books and ideas continued to be imported from China, but these were now responded to more critically. According to the perspective of a contemporary acupuncturist, the practice of acupuncture and moxibustion began to decline in Japan. At the same time, moxibustion became part of the practices offered at Buddhist temples, and the knowledge of physicians (often *samurai*, or members of the privileged warriors class) became restricted to the feudal lords they served.

Japanese and Western Medicine Through a Foreigner's Eyes

These are excerpts from a series of observations made by Father Luis Frois, a Jesuit priest who lived in Japan in the 16th century, comparing the practice of medicine in Japan with the practice of medicine in Europe:

> We use Bleeding; the Japanese, buttons of fire with herbs.
>
> Our physicians take the pulse of men and of women first on the right arm and afterwards on the left; the Japanese, for men, first on the left and, for women, first from the right.
>
> Amongst us wounds are sutured; the Japanese place on them a little adhesive paper.
>
> Amongst us, if a physician is not examined, there is a penalty and he cannot practice; in Japan, in order to make a living, whoever wants to can be a physician.

A pharmacist's display in Takayama, Japan, has herbs in various jars as well as the heads of monkeys. Certain varieties of monkey flesh are said to have medicinal properties.

Western Europe Encounters Japan In 1542, three Portuguese sailing on a Chinese junk were beached on Japan's shore by a typhoon. Within a few short years, Portuguese traders and Jesuit priests began to visit Japan with their minds set on trade and spiritual conquest. The Portuguese—and later the Spanish, Dutch, and Germans—established an extensive exchange of goods and ideas. Dutch and German physicians contributed ideas about medicine to the Japanese, and the Japanese exposed them to new ideas as well. "Dutch medicine," as western European practices came to be called in Japan, became increasingly important, culminating in an imperial decision to require that all doctors study Western medicine.

The political stability of the Edo period (1615–1867) supported a series of creative initiatives on the part of Japanese physicians. For example, guide tubes were developed to aid in the proper insertion of acupuncture needles. The Edo period also saw the continued introduction of Western medical ideas into Japan, especially anatomy. Medical knowledge continued to develop both through the independent efforts of Japanese physicians and through the arrival of new materials from China.

Thought on medicine continued apace in various schools throughout this long period. The Koho School called for a return to older principles of therapy and diagnosis. Yoshimasu Todo (1720–1773)—a noted exponent of the Koho school—proposed that all disease resulted in poison being lodged in the body. He developed a system of abdominal diagnosis to assist in this task stating,

> The abdomen is the source of life and, therefore, the myriad diseases have their root here. The abdomen must always be examined in order to diagnose disease.

Another physician named Goto Gonzan (1659–1733) proposed the theory of *ikki-ryutai-setsu*, which suggested that the sole cause of disease was stagnation of *ki*. One pupil reports that he said:

> All diseases occur from the stagnation [of ki], and not from anything else. Wind and cold cause the stagnation [of ki], food and drinks cause the same, and seven kinds of emotions do the same, too. If the stagnation [of ki] takes place in one meridian or somewhere in the skin, it finally always infiltrates into the viscera.

Herbs and teas continue to be prevalent in Japanese society and Japanese therapeutics. Shops devoted to selling these products are very common.

What can be seen here is a characteristically Japanese desire to eliminate theoretical elaborations in favor of simple and practical therapeutic ideas.

One distinctive contribution to Japanese perspectives on diagnosis and therapy was made by a 17th century acupuncturist named Mubunsai. In 1685, he published a book called the *Compilation of the Secrets of Acupuncture*, which addressed the systematic diagnosis and treatment of disease through the abdomen. In his system, the abdomen was divided into specific regions, each associated with an organ. According to Mubunsai, the presence of evil *ki* can be felt in the abdomen, and where this is felt, the abdomen should be needled. Mubunsai developed a distinctive technique of *dashin*, in which a small wooden mallet was used to stimulate gold and silver needles that are held at the surface of the skin or slightly inserted.

Traditional Medicine in the 20th Century

Traditional medicine in Japan has experienced something of a renaissance in the last 50 years. Despite significant Westernization in the country generally, Japanese medicine has seen the continuation of focused specialization, innovative exploration, and expansion of traditional acupuncture concepts.

The trend toward specialization has continued to the present day with the official division of acupuncture, moxibustion, and massage into separately licensed practices (although many individuals hold all three licenses), and the actual practice of herbal medicine is retained in the hands of medical doctors. Pharmacists are allowed to recommend herbs in modern Japan, but not to touch their patients. Interestingly, a large number of Chinese herbal prescriptions are recognized as appropriate therapy for certain medical conditions under government regulations governing health care in Japan.

African Traditions

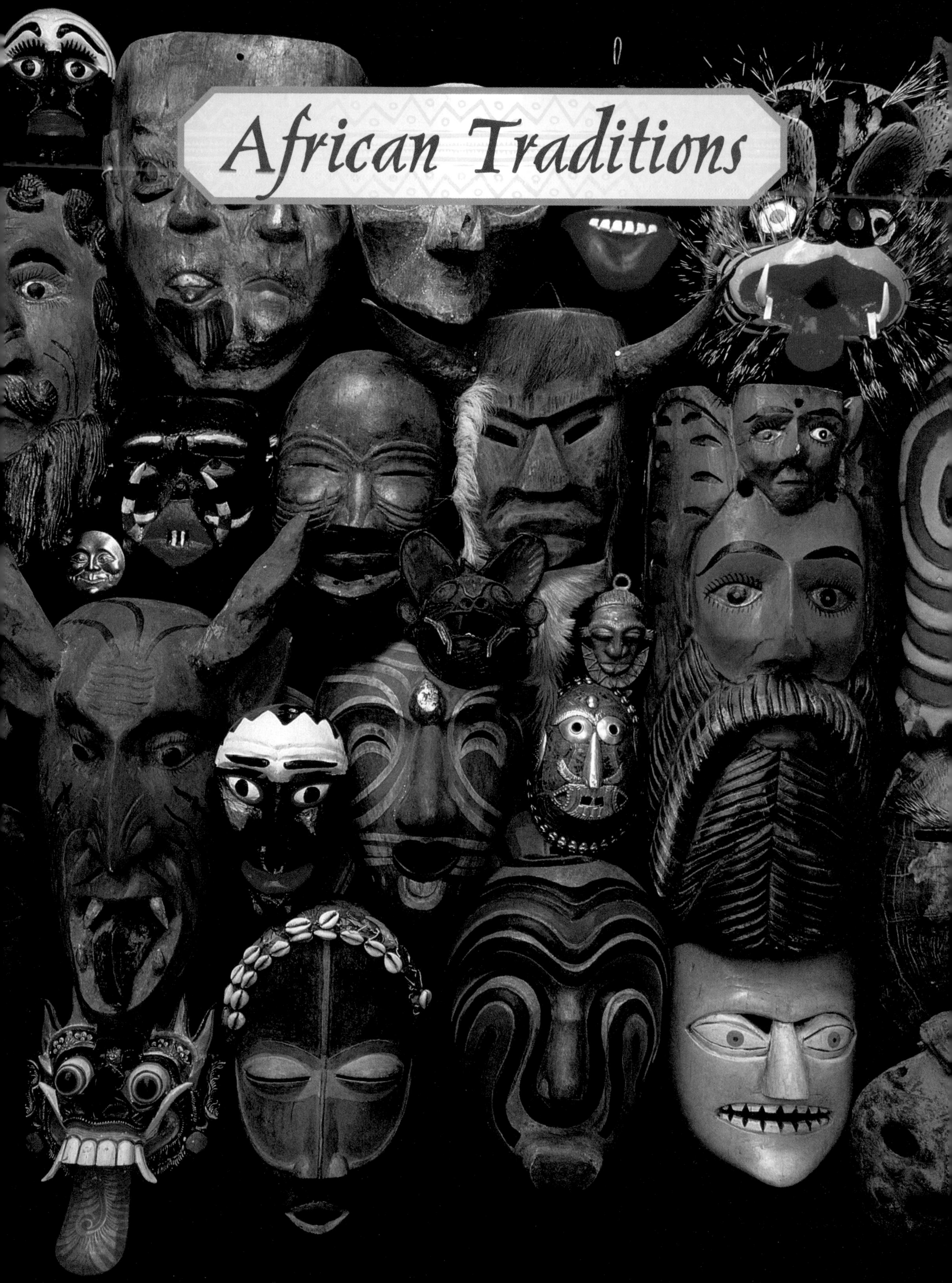

Sub-Saharan Healing

THE ANTIQUITY of African ideas about health, disease, and healing takes us further back in history than anywhere else in the world—back toward the very origins of humanity. The teachings and traditions of Africa's ancient hunter-gatherers reflect a deep history, spanning several hundred thousand years of human civilization.

However, this very distance in time and culture is what makes these practices very difficult to discern. Therefore, the medicine from Sub-Saharan Africa (the region of Africa south of the Sahara Desert) that we will examine will be the traditional healing we see today in the region. There is reason to believe that these modern traditional practices have their roots in the settled way of life that began around 4,000 years ago and spread throughout the continent.

The truly remarkable practices of Sub-Saharan healers have a great deal in common with traditions found a world away. Aspects of shamanism, herbalism, divination, and community healing can all be found in the traditional diagnostics and therapeutics of this vast and varied region.

Ashanti fertility doll, worn at one time by pregnant women to ensure a handsome and healthy child and an easy delivery. A highly abstracted form of human anatomy, the figure accentuates flesh neck rings, a sign of beauty in West Africa.

Maintaining a Distinctive Character

The name *Africa* originated at about the time of the Roman Empire in a region of Carthage named *Ifriqiyya*. Only in the past 500 to 600 years has the name *Africa* come to be applied to the entire continent. The regions we now call Sub-Saharan Africa have been referred to, among other names, as Ethiopia, Guinea (roughly, West Africa), and Sudan ("the land of the blacks" to the south of the Sahara). Herodotus, the ancient Greek historian, spoke of the region near the source of the Nile River as the land of the "Mountains of the Moon" (probably the volcanic peaks of Rwanda). Beyond these places were the "Empty Lands," too hot to be inhabited. We know today, however, that those lands were inhabited by ancestors of the Mbuti pygmies of the rain forests and the Khoi-San-speaking hunter-gatherers of southern Africa.

The Sahara Desert was not always the barrier it now seems. As recently as 3,000 years ago, the region that came to be known as the Sahara Desert featured lush grasses, teeming herds of cattle and wildlife, and cities full of people. Even as the rains diminished and the great desert formed, the camel allowed long-distance trade between the people who withdrew southward and the people who moved northward toward the Mediterranean. This ancient communication is why many ideas of health and healing in the Sub-Saharan region resonate with those of civilizations in the Mediterranean, the Near East, and Asia.

The medicine of ancient Egypt, for example, had significant influence in shaping

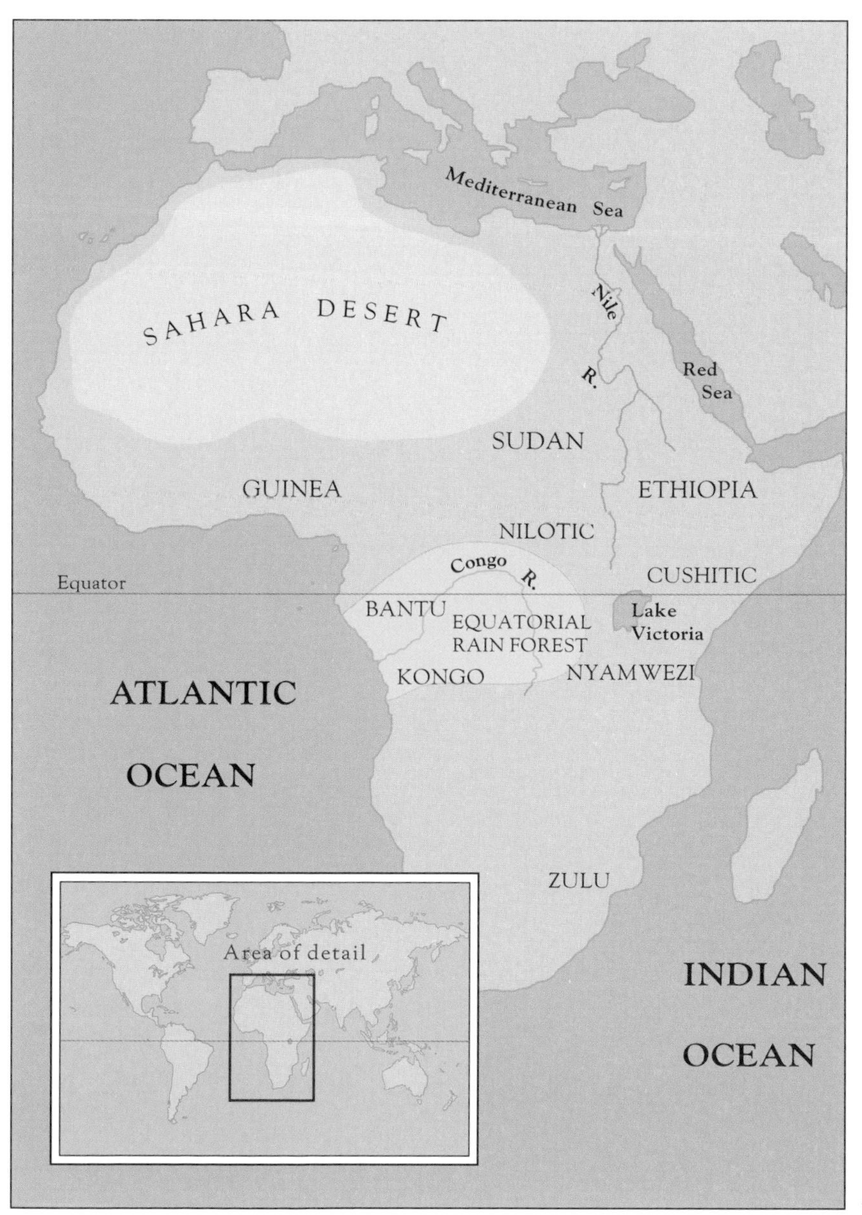

the ideas of civilizations around it, including the medicine of classical Greece and Rome. Their ideas on medicine spread abroad to other African regions, especially through the influence of Islamic medicine and Galenic medicine—the medicine of humors associated with the Greco-Roman physician Galen (see page 80). Christian faith healing also spread into Africa, first across North Africa and Ethiopia, then later with European influence to Sub-Saharan Africa.

This scene of a Natal, South Africa, rock painting is, like many, enigmatic. But it is reminiscent of the spirit dance of Khoisan-speakers in contemporary southern Africa. The dancing group surrounds the healer who, in a trance, raises the spirit to bless his community and heal the sick.

Despite the commonalities African medicine has with other traditions and despite the influx of influence from Europe and the Near East, Sub-Saharan African medicine maintains a distinctiveness. The application of these foreign ideas to the particular climates and diseases of Sub-Saharan Africa reflects the social patterns and technologic developments unique to Africa.

Ancient Roots, Modern Branches

It is likely that some of the features of current Sub-Saharan healing are adaptations of ancient hunting and gathering practices that were retained. For example, until recently, most healers collected their medicinal plants from the wild, assembling medicines fresh for each case. Now, however, some enterprising healers incorporate the cultivation of medicinal plants into their practice. Modern scientific analysis of medicinal plants in Sub-Saharan Africa continues to yield an understanding of the applications and effects of its ancient materia medica.

The Spread of Domestication In West Africa, the domestication of plants and animals in sedentary settlements—as opposed to nomadic hunter-gatherer societies—was well underway by 2000 B.C., giving rise to numerous local healing traditions. Urban centers emerged in the savanna by the first few centuries A.D. Along with the stable settlements came trade routes that linked West Africa with the Mediterranean and Europe. By early in this millennium, the influences of Islam and Arabia were felt in the savanna, without fully supplanting the earlier healing practices.

The spread of food cultivation and sedentary society southward through and around the rain forest came to be associated with the spread of the Cushitic, Bantu, and

Nilotic cultures and languages. The Cushitic culture spread from the Horn of Africa and Ethiopia southward with cattle and farming as its economic basis. The Bantu had begun to spread from the border area of Cameroon and Nigeria as early as 1000 B.C. The Bantu languages ultimately came to be spoken throughout the whole of central, eastern, and southern Africa.

Food production and ironworking spread rapidly through this area during the first millennium A.D. The Nilotic societies and languages spread southward from the Sudan. Because of the common linguistic and cultural backgrounds, many health-related terms and concepts are comparable with the rest of Sub-Saharan Africa (see "How We Know What We Know").

SPECIFIC ECOLOGIC SETTINGS Ecologic settings have shaped many of the ideas and practices in African healing. Depending on the ecology of an area, residents had two main options for their livelihood: cultivating crops (agriculture) or raising livestock (called pastoralism). These two modes of livelihood can be practiced together in areas that have adequate rainfall for crops and the absence of certain diseases that can wreak havoc on livestock; however, these conditions are not present everywhere in equatorial Africa. Sleeping sickness (trypanosomiasis) carried by the presence of the tset-se fly was especially devastating to cattle. Throughout the forest region of equatorial Africa and parts of West Africa, the menace of the tset-se fly prohibited pastoralism.

How We Know What We Know

One of the best methods for reaching back through African history to find the faint images of ancient thought and practice is through language. How people talk about health, disease, and healing can be very telling. Sub-Saharan healing is not codified in written texts, but it is transmitted through rich oral instruction passed from generation to generation. In many ways, these instructions and their vocabulary are even more durable than the papyrus or parchment of other cultures—especially in the tropics.

Examining language for clues to history is called *historical linguistics*, and it works, in part, by examining similarities in vocabulary from one group to another. For example, the root term for "suffering" in west African Yoruba society is the same as that used in Kongo society of Central Africa. Linguistic analysis of these two and many other languages in between shows that this term is part of a broad west-coast language family that spread southward about 2,000 years ago.

Part of the historical linguistics approach is based on the premise that the core vocabulary in any language remains relatively constant and can be traced by comparing other historically similar languages. Core vocabulary shows a change at a rate of about 20 percent per 1,000 years. Thus, if two languages are shown to have 60 percent of their core vocabularies in common, they are about 2,000 years apart in their history. This historical linguistic method permits scholars to study concepts up to 5,000 years old.

A similar analysis of medicinal substances (materia medica) offers another approach to the understanding of African healing. A study of the distribution of terms for diseases, conditions, techniques, and botanical identifications can give clues to the ancient spread and development of practices. Unfortunately, this approach has barely begun, although it holds much promise.

Where the tset-se fly was absent—as across eastern Sudan, in the lake region of East-Central Africa, and into moderate southern Africa—pastoralism conveyed a distinctive set of ideas about health, sickness, and medicine. For example, in the lake regions where the agricultural and pastoral traditions overlap, nearly as many medicinal plants are used for animal husbandry purposes as for human healing. Similarly, other environmental zones of desert, tropical rain forest, and savanna have exerted their influences on health and healing. In many markets of West and Central Africa, sections are devoted to the medical plants of the rain forest on the one hand and to the arid regions on the other.

Kongo healer Kitembo stands at forest's edge with plants he has collected. Many of the substances in the Sub-Saharan materia medica derive from "wild" plants, suggesting a cultural history of this art within foraging hunter-gatherer society. Some healers and scientific research institutes, however, keep "gardens" of important plants.

The Fig First

In Kongo society of western equatorial Africa, whose ancestors began to settle in villages and cultivate plants for food about 2,000 years ago, each prospective new village site was opened with the planting of an *nsanda* fig tree (*Ficus bubu*). One explanation for this is that the site's nature spirits require this; another reason is that the fig's roots grow deep quickly to reveal the adequacy of groundwater at the site, thus revealing the soil fertility that makes for a successful settlement site.

Over the centuries, the development of cultural traditions in response to ecologic settings and conditions has slowly but surely created distinctive emphases within the common core of medical ideas and practices. These patterns have also determined how the medical traditions from the Mediterranean North, the Islamic East, and the Christianized and scientized West would later be received.

The Common Core of Ideas

Across the vast area of Sub-Saharan Africa, there are, of course, many diverse healing traditions. Despite differences, however, understandings of health, sickness, and healing are often couched in a basic set of ideas about the nature of the world. And as with many other cultures worldwide, Sub-Saharan peoples offered powerful metaphors to make sense of the senseless suffering and uncertainty of illness. These ideas have a deep history and broad geographical and cultural distribution, and they are still used in diagnosis and treatment in many parts of Africa.

WHITE, RED, AND BLACK The first example of an organizing idea enveloping health, sickness, and healing defines health as the ideal, ordered structure of the body as a whole. Any disruption, negation, or distortion of this ideal suggests sickness. This idea is often expressed through the use of colors: In the Yoruba medicine of Nigeria, for example, the color of chalk (white) represents purity and wholeness; red (such as blood or the appearance of redness on the skin surface) represents transition and danger; and charcoal (black) represents human chaos. This expression of order and chaos in health and disease through a kind of color code is very widespread. It appears again and again in connection with sickness, healing, and the order of the human and natural universe.

An epileptic depicted in a Pende mask, with twisted lines dividing the white half of the face from the black half, in keeping with the Sub-Saharan color code relating the visible and the invisible.

White is associated with goodness and the legitimacy of the created order. Examples include

- chalk smeared onto the face and body
- white beads strung around the body or the head
- flour or some other white powder used to trace the outlines of sacred space
- allusions to milk or semen, symbolized by white sap

Chalk, taken from the riverbanks, is said to represent the realm of the water, the spirits, and the beyond. It stands for the clarity and goodness of the spiritual world, where human life is ultimately rooted.

In a related way, redness—marked by camwood smeared on the face and body, dyed into cloth, or covering a ritual object—often appears alongside whiteness to denote transition and danger. It is a color and sign of power—power that can build up the created order but can also destroy it.

Charcoal, the remains of fire, often represents the chaos and destructiveness of human life left to itself. Charcoal is the destructive potential of power that is not balanced by the whiteness, or clarity, of chalk.

This color system is widely invoked in unspoken actions about health and disease and used in the return to health through healing.

Health as Harmony, Disease as Disharmony

The second idea that organizes thoughts and actions of health and healing is based on balance, or harmony. Balance is thought to be necessary in the relationship between an individual and the surrounding community, as well as between the community and the natural and spiritual environment. One of the terms expressing this sense of balance or harmony in life is *lunga*. Appearing in the vocabulary of the Zulu of southern Africa and also in the vocabulary of the Kongo of Central Africa, *lunga* is also used as an attribute of God. Indeed, the idea of balance as health and imbalance as illness is not limited to Africa. The balance between the humors and natural elements in ancient Greek medicine (see page 75), the doshas in Ayurveda (see page 196), yin and yang in Chinese medicine (see page 291), and even the concept of *hozho* in Navajo healing (see page 181) testify to this concept's virtual universality.

The idea of balance is a profoundly ancient African idea expressed in many origin stories across western, central, and southern regions. In ancient creation myths, you can see how the very beginning of the world depended on the balance between the two opposing forces:

In the beginning, these stories recount, a sky force and an earth force existed. (Usually the sky force was male, and the earth force was female.) A bolt of lightning or a stormy wind generated the movement to bring the two together. Out of this encounter came the combination of heat and coolness and the rhythm of light and darkness. Light and heat are found in the characters of the sun, the moon, and the stars; the earth is identified with moisture and coolness. From the encounter of these opposing spheres and forces—sky and earth, hot and cold, male and female, dry and moist—emerged the reproductive potential of the world and its creatures, bringing life into being. And the health of this life depends on maintaining the balance of the two.

Health as Coolness, Disease as Heat

The thermal concept of health and ill-health is also widespread in Sub-Saharan African thinking. "Coolness" is grace, style, and health; "heat" is conflict and disease. (This notion of the "cool" is one of the most prominent features of African culture brought to the New World and infused directly into popular culture in North America.) In curing techniques, the heat of conflict-caused disease is "cooled down" through herbal baths and rituals.

Health as Purity, Disease as Pollution

A fourth idea used in the organization of health and disease may be expressed as purity and pollution. Purity is a ritual state in which the human world is in order. Pollution is an impersonal condition that can be righted by ritual or curative intervention. There is some similarity between this notion and the first mentioned above—order versus disruption. Purity and pollution represent a traditional set of natural contrasts that may have served as a foundation for understanding health and the prevention of disease.

Health as Flow, Disease as Blockage

The concept of flow and blockage is the closest to a classical African anatomy. Furthermore, health as flow and disease as blockage has clear implications for therapeutic practices. The prevalence of purgatives and emetics, fertility medicines, and herbal drinks in the African tool kit

Helping the Newborn to Flow

According to Nzoamambu, a Kongo healer, a newborn child should receive three purges to cleanse its abdomen after birth. Before it can begin to nurse, it must produce its first excrement to get rid of *ndumba*, a problematic stomach condition. As it begins to nurse, it sucks wildly about at first, getting too much air with its mother's milk, so that its stomach puffs up. It should then receive a purge made of the *vamu* plant extract (possibly a plant of the Euphorbiaceae family) to make its stomach flow and recede. After another month has passed, the child may develop "elephant stomach." This is best treated with a purge prepared from *nsudi* tree leaves (*Gossypium barbadense*), again permitting the stomach to flow. In due course, a third purge becomes necessary, because careless parents feed their child just about anything, or the child picks up and eats dirt or whatever else it gets its hands on. This time, leaves of the *lubota* tree (*Millettia versicolor*) may be used with good results.

reflect this conceptual scheme. However, what flows and what is blocked are not necessarily the physiologic structures we might imagine; they are usually linked to the wider world of a person's relationships in society, if not to society itself as a body.

In fact, there seems to be a clear analogy between the physical realm of the body and exchanges in society. Both are seen as needing to flow openly to live and thrive. Just as food and fluids need to be taken in and ingested for the physical body to be healthy, the social body needs to be "fed" with reciprocal gifts and gestures of goodwill. Grudges, envy, and ill-will in the social body are, in this thinking, seen to cause blockage in the physical body. In Rwanda, for example, one observer suggests that flow and blockage is a metaphor in which flow within the social and physical body contribute to health, whereas blockage—through envy and ill-will—may lead to constipation, infertility, witchcraft, and disease.

Protection Versus Vulnerability

What modern medical scientists call contagion—the spread of infectious disease—is, in fact, a relatively old idea that dates from well before the theory of microorganisms. The idea that sickness spreads and infects is widely held in traditional Sub-Saharan medicine. The actual cause spreading the sickness, though, was thought to be ill-will, poison, malicious medicines, or any of a variety of forces that can cause harm. Quite possibly, this thinking was applied to specific diseases. For example, it is well known that smallpox-infested communities were quarantined and that the healthy were immunized with a bit of fluid from the pustule of an infected individual (see page 338).

Applying the Principles

The principles of health and disease just enumerated—harmony versus disharmony, coolness versus heat, flow versus blockage, and so on—were used to base many of the practical diagnoses and treatments in a whole host of ailments: broken bones, fever, rheumatism, intestinal disorders, parasites, lactation deficiency, earache, toothache, headache, epilepsy, menstrual disorders, and more. Medications were based on a wide array of mineral, animal, and especially vegetable substances reflecting the desert, savanna, and rain-forest ecologies.

A few examples illustrate the ways in which these higher-level principles were often combined to organize practical insights into treatment techniques and the curative powers of plants. Although modern Westerners will probably recognize the matter-of-fact treatment of herbal medications in the following examples, classical African medical thought often added dimensions that Westerners might call "symbolic" or "social." In the two examples of treatment by modern healers using traditional techniques, the fusion of the natural and the human dimensions is evident.

Kongo consecrated medicine statue called Nkisi Makongo. Iron nails and wedges driven by the healer into the body of this 19th-century figure identify the points of many sufferers' afflictions. The wounding of the figure in a public ritual of song and incantation heightens the belief that Makongo protects the sufferer by its "anger" at the perpetrator.

TWO TYPES OF BODILY SWELLING Mama Mankomba of Mbemba village in the Luozi region of what is now the Democratic Republic of Congo (formerly Zaire), was well known for her treatment for bodily swelling. She distinguished between two types of swelling: One was thought to be caused by heart congestion; the other was thought to be caused by "poisoning," the result of anger growing out of the animosity of one individual for another.

Simple swelling was dealt with by an initial emetic from the drops of sap of the finger cactus (*Euphorbia tirucalli*) with a soapy base to keep the toxic sap from harming the body. This was followed by a potion made from the roots of six savanna plants taken three times daily: *Psorospermum febrifugum*, *Annona arenaria* (a relative of the custard apple), *Crossopteryx febrifuga* (a member of the madder family), *Syzygium guineense* (a member of the myrtle family), *Hymenocardia acida*, and *Maprounea africana* (members of the spurge family). Dietary restrictions against sugar, salt, and pepper were also imposed.

Poisoning cases received the same initial purge, but were followed by a second purge of the bark scrapings of only the *Maprounea africana* plant with salt and palm oil to provoke diarrhea and vomiting. Although Mama Mankomba treated the physical manifestations of anger illness, she refused to become involved with the deeper causes of anger, which required conflict resolution and judicial action. The disharmony aspect of anger illness was a dimension that herbs could not cure.

Cures That Work

Several researchers have examined traditional African cures and found that many have merit and can be shown clinically effective.

One such cure is a treatment for intestinal microorganisms practiced by Mirau, an herbalist of the Meru people. One of Mirau's 200 single-plant treatments is for children's diarrhea—a serious problem in many regions of the continent where infant mortality reaches more than 100 per 1,000 births. Using the plant known locally as *mamiso* (*Bidens pilosa*, a relative of the beggar tick), Mirau takes 15 to 20 flowers and boils them to obtain one dose, which is given twice daily as oral medicine. Although not necessarily known to the healer, this plant actually carries antibacterial substances (some unknown to Western science) against microorganisms, including five organisms that cause gastroenteritis. The same plant is used against dysentery and colic in other regions of eastern and southern Africa.

In another well-documented and researched study from the National Zairian Research Institute, the work of six healers in Kinshasa was examined for effectiveness in 22 diabetes cases. Independent examination of blood sugar levels revealed that after treatment, which lasted a week or longer, 17 of the cases experienced a significant decline in average blood sugar levels. Although a surprisingly large diversity of plants was used in preparation of the oral medications, several plants stand out for their repetition from healer to healer, including *Crossopteryx febrifuga*, *Nauclea latifolia* (both members of the madder family, Rubiaceae), *Anchonames difformis* (from the Arceae family), and *Bridelia feruginea* (from the Euphorbiaceae family), the latter of which is also used in Ghana for diabetes therapy. Some of the Kinshasa treatments were accompanied by dietary prohibitions against salt, ripe mangoes, pepper, beer, manioc (cassava), and mushrooms.

Treating Madness Another example is the specific treatment for madness (*lauka* in the KiKongo language of western Congo), which was part of Kongo healer Bilumbu's longer regimen; it is the sedative for an episode of psychotic agitation. The medicinal portion of the sedative consisted of an extract prepared from the foliage of four plants: *Brillantaisia patula* (called *lemba-lemba*, a member of the acanthus family), *Virectaria multiflora* (called *kilembe-lembe kia mbwaki*, a member of the madder family), *Erigeron floribundus* (called *kilembe-lembe kia mpembe*, a relative of horseweed and part of the Compositeae family), and *Piper umbellatum* (called *lemba ntoko*, a member of the pepper family). The extract, probably thinned with water, was administered orally to the sufferer several times per day to assure sedation, but according to the healer, it should not be continued indefinitely because of the danger of "intoxication." (Incidentally, in a field study, this cure was clinically confirmed to be very effective.)

Ofoe—the messenger of Ogiuwu, god of death—in Yoruba religious thought. An ominous head with legs and no body, Ofoe pursues humankind relentlessly, reminding those who see this figure of their mortality.

However, there is more to this treatment than the chemotherapy of herbs; its symbolic superstructure is intriguing. The indigenous names for all four plants bear the word *lemba* or *lembe*, which means "to calm" or "to cool." Furthermore, the part of the landscape from which these plants are gathered is important: *Lemba-lemba* grows in the domestic realm of the village; *lemba-ntoko* comes from the wild realm; and the two remaining plants—one "red" and the other "white"—originate in the gardens (in a sense, the temporary domestication in the wilds). The cure then suggests the sufferer's wild behavior is being domesticated or calmed.

At the chemical level, the "white" garden plant, *kilembe-lembe kia mpembe* (*Erigeron floribundus*), like many plants of the Compositeae family, has been discovered to contain volatile oils and alkaloids that may have psychoactive and analgesic properties. The symbolic and social dimensions in this treatment include extensive support by kin and healer, analysis of dreams, and a culminating "banquet," which features the successful re-entry of the sufferer back into public life and normalcy. So the cure for madness in this case combines social therapy, four symbolically charged plants, and a clinically demonstrated sedative. Which, then, is the "active" ingredient?

Natural Versus Unnatural

In African thought about disease, now as in the past, there is a split between what we might call natural causes and unnatural causes. It is a dichotomy dividing one source of illness and misfortune in the routine, ordinary, and predictable nature of life from another in which misfortune is catastrophic, not understood, or seen to be the result of the chaos of underlying affairs in the human and mystical realm.

In African thought, though, *natural* and *unnatural* have a meaning that may be somewhat unfamiliar to us. Whereas we tend to call gods, spirits, and so on *supernatural*, in African thought it's the *natural* that would be associated with God or caused by God. God-caused misfortune is widely seen to be the created order of things, such as the seasons and the rhythms of birth and death in society and the surrounding world. The death of an elderly person would be "in the created order," whereas the death of a childbearing mother would be seen as unnatural or due to some other human- or spirit-caused force.

The unnatural source of misfortune, then, is either a human or a malicious spiritual agent or condition. Many ills are attributed to human error, malicious motive (both conscious and unconscious), or the deceptive, opportunistic antisocial nature of some individuals. This view of humanity often includes the ancestors or demigods who have a vested interest in the outcome of human affairs, especially in their clans and localities.

In some of the deep civilizations of West Africa, a host of demigods named *orishas* represent varied societal and environmental forces. The ambiguity of human nature filled with pitfalls is represented by Eshu-Elegba, the trickster; the ferocity of nature is represented by Shango, whose hammer produces peals of thunder when thrown across the heavens; the worst diseases such as smallpox are represented in Ipoona; and death, known as Ogiuwu, is represented by his messenger Ofoe.

According to the late Rwandan scholar Pierre-Claver Rwangabo, the causes of disease in traditional Rwandan medicine are divided at a general level between physical and mystical causes. Diseases can be attributed to either category or to both. Disease classes include parasitic diseases, microbial diseases, systemic diseases and bodily accidents, gynecologic and obstetric diseases, and psychological and behavioral diseases. The last group, however, includes diseases believed to be caused by broken prohibi-

A Genetic Response to Malaria

The peoples who inhabited the parts of Africa where malaria is endemic developed a unique genetic adaptation to the high death rates caused by the disease. This adaptation was a form of anemia now called sickle-cell disease. The disease offered resistance to malaria infection to some individuals with the right combination of the sickling gene.

However, the sickling gene offered immunity to malaria only among people who received the gene from only one parent (heterozygous offspring). People who received the sickling gene from both parents (homozygous offspring) experienced the debilitating and lethal effects of the disease. This genetic quirk, then, created the potential for disastrous effects: For example, if two sisters carry the sickling gene and one marries a man with it and the other marries a man without it, all the offspring of one sister might be heterozygous and hence all survive; whereas children of the other sister all die because they are homozygous. This tragic circumstance required a philosophy of misfortune that explained two so perplexingly different outcomes from otherwise identical personal stories; it required divination to answer the question, Why me?

tions and beliefs about ancestors and other spirits.

The Purpose of Divination Divination is a sort of diagnostics. Discerning the difference between that which "just happens" and that which has a "human cause"—the natural versus the unnatural—is the province of the diviner. The pervasiveness of divination in diagnosis attests to the importance of the general question of which kind of cause is it: that which "just happens" (sometimes translated as "of God" or "caused by God") or one of the more difficult malicious causes. The diviner may tell the client that his or her case does not entail anything to worry about, that it is "of God," or in the nature of creation. This is helpful to the client, for it lifts the case and its diagnosis to a more general level of thought and opens up many healing approaches.

Usually, consultation with a diviner is not undertaken until there is sufficient reason for the sufferer or his family to suspect causes other than the natural. Reasons might include a sharp decline in a person's health, a sudden and mysterious death, the coincidence of a sickness with a social conflict, or the occurrence of a disease on only one side of a family (see "A Genetic Response to Malaria," page 332). In these tragic and perplexing cases, the clients are looking to the diviner for an answer to several questions: Why did it happen? Why did it happen to us? Who caused it? What should we do about it?

Most often these questions will be answered by pointing to the human causes of a misfortune, including error in judgment, excesses of various kinds, inconsistencies, contradictions, rivalries and conflicts, willful gossip, the power of harmful words, poisonings, and attempted mystical killings.

The modern advancement of health and scientific understanding in a community may not necessarily lay to rest these questions. For example, a community may know very well that malaria is caused by a microorganism transmitted by the bite of a mosquito, but the diviner may shed light on the question of why some people in the group were infected and others were not, or why some infected people died and other infected people got well.

Ifa in West Africa As pervasive as divination is across the African continent, the particular manifestations of divination vary enormously. In the broad belt from

*The ancient art of West African Ifa divination. Visible in this recent picture are the shells and nuts that are thrown onto the tray to determine the appropriate verses. White chalk, red, and black or blue are color symbols of the cosmos. The tray features the face of Eshu-Elegba, the trickster—*orisha*, or god, of misfortune and fate.*

central Nigeria to Ghana, the prevailing mode of divination is known as Ifa, or Fa. A cup or tray bearing a set of usually 16 cowries, or pods, is thrown out into a divination tray. The combination of "ups" and "downs" is coded to indicate a set of verses, numbering in the thousands, which illuminate the life situation involved in the affair.

The tray or the cup usually bears the image of Eshu-Elegba, the trickster, who is believed to somehow hold in his hands the fates of individuals and families. At least, he ceaselessly attempts to surprise humans with contradictory and unintended turns of events, often for the worse. Thus, he and his character of trickery, deceit, and surprise embody the essence of what divination seeks to illuminate.

The Ngombo divination basket operated by a Chokwe diviner on the Congo-Angola border region of Kahemba. Symbols representing social life, the ancestors and spirits, and the natural world emerge as the basket is shaken to indicate to the diviner and his client the constellation of the case before him.

NGOMBO BASKET On the southern savanna, from the Kongo coast southeast to the Copper Belt, the Ngombo basket mode of divination is common. Its distribution and thorough integration into the societies where it has been represented suggest that this form of divination may well be at least 1,000 years old. Carved figurines and natural objects, representing human situations and predicaments, lie together in the basket. As the basket is shaken, one of the objects emerges to the fore at the basket's rim between two lumps of clay—one red, the other white. As noted earlier, this gateway of white and red suggests the threshold between the visible and the invisible spirit world. The diviner "reads" the case before him in the light of the emerging object or the constellation of objects in the basket.

CASTING THE BONES In southern Africa, a common mode of divination is a bag of animal vertebrae. The bag is shaken, and the bones are thrown out onto a mat before the diviner and the client. The arrangement of the bones represents issues in human life, relationships, and the world of spirits. Sometimes the diviner will go into a trance for the reading.

These types of divination in Sub-Saharan Africa, as well as many others, are based on the assumption that sickness or other misfortunes may be caused by an untoward turn of events in the human or related spirit world. The immediate cause or agent, such as the sign or symptom of disease, is thought to require interpretation in the light of the ultimate natural, human, or spirit agents. Thus, despite widespread acceptance of modern science in Africa, divination continues to be a

A sangoma/tukoza diviner at work near Mbabane, Swaziland. The diviner "reads" the pattern of vertebrate bones and other objects thrown on the mat before her while an assistant (left) responds with "I agree" or "I do not agree" to questions posed by the diviner. The client (right) has told her concern to the assistant. The beaded strands across the diviner's shoulders in red, white, and black represent the categories of spirits by whom she is inspired.

typical method for discerning the dividing line between that which "just happens" and the human or mystical factor.

The Social Fabric of Health

The texture of human society is extremely rich and nuanced in Sub-Saharan Africa. As we have seen, misfortune and disease can be shown by divination to be directly related to human affairs. Health is widely perceived to be affected by social rules, and there are health consequences for breaking them. Besides breaking social rules, disease can be seen as a consequence of words and ill-will.

Breaking Social Codes Represented in several languages by the root term *-gidu-*, this concept refers to the role of social prohibitions, taboos, and the consequences of their violation. Sometimes this is mentioned with reference to the restriction on eating or killing one's clan. Other observers note that these prohibitions help individuals adhere to social codes in general, including health-promoting restrictions on such things as overconsumption of alcohol, overeating, or health-destroying excesses of any kind. Indeed, breaking these codes does have a direct effect on health.

The Power of Words Another notion of the human cause of sickness or misfortune encompasses both the anger or ill-will toward another and the instrument expressing it, be that an injurious word, a blow to the head, or a bit of poison. This notion is, in fact, so ancient in Africa that its linguistic root (*-dog* or *-dok*) can be found in the Proto-Bantu language of at least 3,000 years ago. Because of its centrality to the African worldview, modern derivations of it are found from Cameroon and the Kongo coast in the west, to the Swahili coast in the east and the Nguni speakers in South Africa. However, the notion is not always associated with ill-will. Sometimes it is used simply to refer to the power of words, or the use of powerful words in oaths or spells.

In diagnosis, victims will often identify a string of misfortunes and try to recall the exact words spoken by others surrounding the events, drawing the logical inference that these specific utterances had caused, or could have led to, the misfortunes. Words of warning or injurious words spoken in anger are especially suspect. Therefore, in divination, these moments are recalled so that the individuals or the relationships may be repaired. For without treating the root cause, the surface signs and symptoms cannot be permanently overcome.

The Healing Orders

In the history of most African regions, there were communities, or orders, of healers based on common afflictions or common beliefs about the gods or spirits considered the cause of these afflictions. Communities of people devoted to these gods have arisen and declined over time as particular afflictions have come and gone. Often these communities have been a kind of barometer of the major diseases in a region. Orders were devoted to, for example, reproductive issues, the fertility of the fields, the success of hunters, or particular environmental hazards or epidemics. These orders sometimes had established priesthoods, but in less organized societies, they were more like a loose network of people.

Shrine Communities In West Africa, shrine communities and cults were often associated with major shrines or cults to Earth, water, nature, or the sky. Some shrines were addressed to specific conditions, such as being a twin, or particular diseases, such as the shrine complex to the god of smallpox (variously named Ipoona, Shapanna, or Shapata). These shrine communities addressed many aspects of health and the public good, such as instruction of the youth, midwifery, and hygiene.

Drums of Affliction Across equatorial Africa, a type of ritual assembly was used therapeutically. The assemblies often centered around particular issues, such as fertility, women's reproductive issues, the health and well-being of infants and children, debilitating chronic conditions, fortune and misfortune for men in hunting, mental illnesses, and a range of social and even environmental issues such as poisonous snakes. Membership was usually made up of the afflicted and formerly afflicted who had undergone a therapeutic initiation with stages from sufferer-novice to healer-priest—a progression similar to shamanic beliefs elsewhere in the world (see pages 138 and 245).

These assemblies were dubbed "drums of affliction" by the researcher Victor Turner because they centered around the type of drum known as *ngoma*. The sound of this drum is believed to be the voice of the ancestors and spirits. These ancestors and spirits inhabit the participants and express themselves in the songs and dances at the core of the ritual.

Often the mark of growth, or healing, in the sufferer-novice is the articulation of a personal song based on the ordeal of suffering, a dream vision, or other moving experiences. The song constitutes a unique set of powerful words (recalling the *dok*, see page 335) that can overcome the disintegration, misfortune, sickness, and chaos of the previous period of the individual's life.

Where the drums of affliction address community issues, the healing ritual may be directed to the community, and society becomes the body that is cured. Leaders or segments of society, such as households, may be the "sufferers," and the "medicines" may be symbols of authority or titles of leadership.

Public Health and Preventing Disease

Although very little is known about how ancient African peoples perceived the health of their communities and how they dealt with disease, some inferences suggest an approach to what we today term "public health." In some cases, the ancient practices still survive and provide clues to early concerns.

MAINTAINING A BALANCE Even in the 20th century, the Khoisan speakers of southern Africa were still reported to practice infanticide and birth-spacing of up to four years between children—age-old techniques of population control. We do not know how widespread these approaches may have been in early African society, but if they were, they represented conscious techniques for maintaining a harmonious balance between the human society and its food source in the environment.

CONTROLLING EPIDEMICS With the transition to cultivation and larger, sedentary communities—first in the Sudan then across the continent—major new diseases made their appearance. We have some evidence of public health techniques that must have existed in ancient times in response to at least three diseases: sleeping sickness, malaria, and smallpox.

Some examples are straightforward: Hunter-gatherers, such as the Khoisan speakers of southern Africa, were known to pick up camp whenever diseases broke out or when there were deaths in an old settlement. Given the small population concentrations, leaving ensured contagious diseases did not have a chance to take hold and become endemic. But some public health problems were more difficult.

Tset-ses and Mosquitoes. As noted earlier, livestock herding spread southward about 6,000 years ago, skirting the rain forest area. (The boundary between pastoral and nonpastoral societies has historically been approximately the distance between the rain forest and the savanna.)

This boundary coincided with the boundary between two very different food production systems: On the one hand, the cultivators without large livestock had to emphasize crop fertility, soil fallowing, and the importance of rainfall; the pastoral cultures, on the other hand, had to manage their herds, concentrate on good breeding, and learn the politics of being good neighbors while on their annual treks to find seasonal pasture lands. But they also had to understand where the danger zones were—the habitat of the sleeping sickness-causing tset-se fly—lest they loose their cattle and their food supply.

Another insect-borne scourge native to the area was the variety of malaria carried by the anopheles mosquito. It is known to have become a problem for certain African cultivators about the time sedentary communities appeared and the forest began to be cleared for crops. One response was to avoid the mosquitoes. Breezy hillsides rather than the mosquito-infested quiet thickets are known to have been preferred sites for villages and towns (doubly so in areas inhabited by the tset-se fly). Thus, long before quinine and the late 19th-century association of mosquitoes with malaria, breezy hilltops were preferred settlement sites, provided they were near sources of good water.

Smallpox. Smallpox has been a widespread scourge not only in Africa but in the Old World ever since large concentrations of people began settling together. The earliest appearance of smallpox in Sub-Saharan Africa is not known, but Ipoona—the god of smallpox—is a central figure in West African religious beliefs, suggesting that smallpox has a history of millennia rather than centuries.

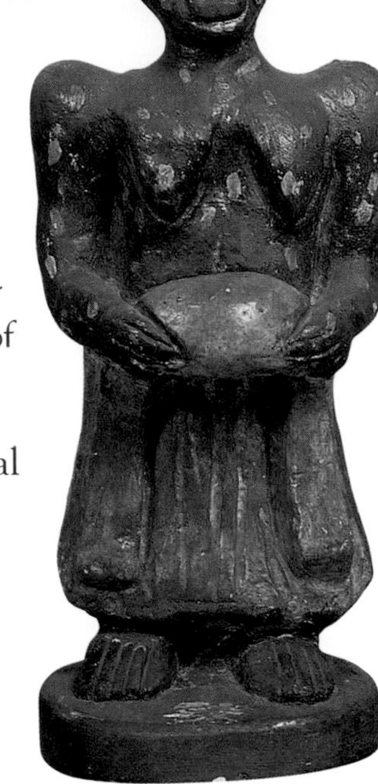

Ipoona (also Samponna), god of smallpox in Yoruba religion and medicine, is depicted in this powerful shrine figure by all the signs of the horrible disease that once ravaged the Sub-Saharan world.

Sub-Saharan peoples took several approaches to smallpox. Sacrifices were made to the angry god Ipoona, who had the power to kill. But actions of another sort during smallpox epidemics suggest an acute public health consciousness. Reports from both West and East Africa mention the separate burial of victims, the abstinence from mourning in close proximity to the victims' bodies, and the quarantine of entire infected households or settlements.

Perhaps the most intriguing response to smallpox was the attempt to immunize those not yet infected by taking puss from the poxes of infected individuals and introducing it into scratches in their skin. However, despite the similarities to modern immunization, this ancient technique probably had less to do with inducing an immune response and more with a broader symbolic principle of confronting the evil of the disease or threat head-on.

Vipers. The manner in which some other health threats were dealt with resembled the approach to smallpox. Several kinds of poisonous vipers have for ages posed a serious problem in the lands of the Nyamwezi and Sukuma peoples of western Tanzania. Organizations of snake-handling experts actively promote the encounter with these poisonous vipers and other snakes through public dance performances in which they demonstrate that they can come to terms with the threat. The demonstration includes allowing the otherwise venomous snakes to bite them.

However, the snake handlers are immune to the venom because they have been inoculated with small doses that they milked from the vipers. This understanding of immunization is a closely guarded secret available only to those who have been appropriately initiated to the Snake Handling Order. In its organization, the snake-handling fraternities resemble the *ngoma* "drums of affliction" made up of the commonly afflicted—in this case those bitten by dangerous snakes who survived.

These examples of immunization to smallpox and snake venom are part of the much wider notion across ancient Africa of the need to incorporate or confront the disease to overcome it. Snake-handling *ngoma* members sing to the spirits of the vipers to placate them and to stay in touch with them. This is not unlike the manner in which people placate with song and dance ancestral spirits that visit the living in dreams or through misfortune—public spectacle for public health.

Caribbean Healing

ALTHOUGH THEY CANNOT be said to be "ancient" in the same way, say, India's Ayurveda is, the healing systems in the Caribbean have ancient roots extending beyond a history of slavery and colonialism to places as far apart as Africa, Europe, and Asia. There are significant regional variations across the Caribbean, due mostly to differences in the mixes of people who ended up in each specific location, but the various healing systems all express the same set of underlying principles.

This artistic rendition of a Vodun service in a forest was painted by Jean-Pierre. While much of Haiti is now quite barren, forests are known as places that harbor spirits: Each loa, *or spirit, has a favorite type of tree. Certain trees are known as particularly spiritual places. Worshipers burn candles at their roots, leave small sacrifices, and even take small chips of bark home with them as protective charms.*

The records kept by colonists, diaries kept by slaves or freed men and women who taught themselves to read and write, and old newspaper articles and ads provide the majority of our information on the region's traditional healing systems. Research carried out with the descendants of slaves, colonists, and other immigrants helps fill in the gaps, since many of the ancient traditions brought to the region long ago have been adapted and passed down over time by word of mouth—in fact, many are still in use.

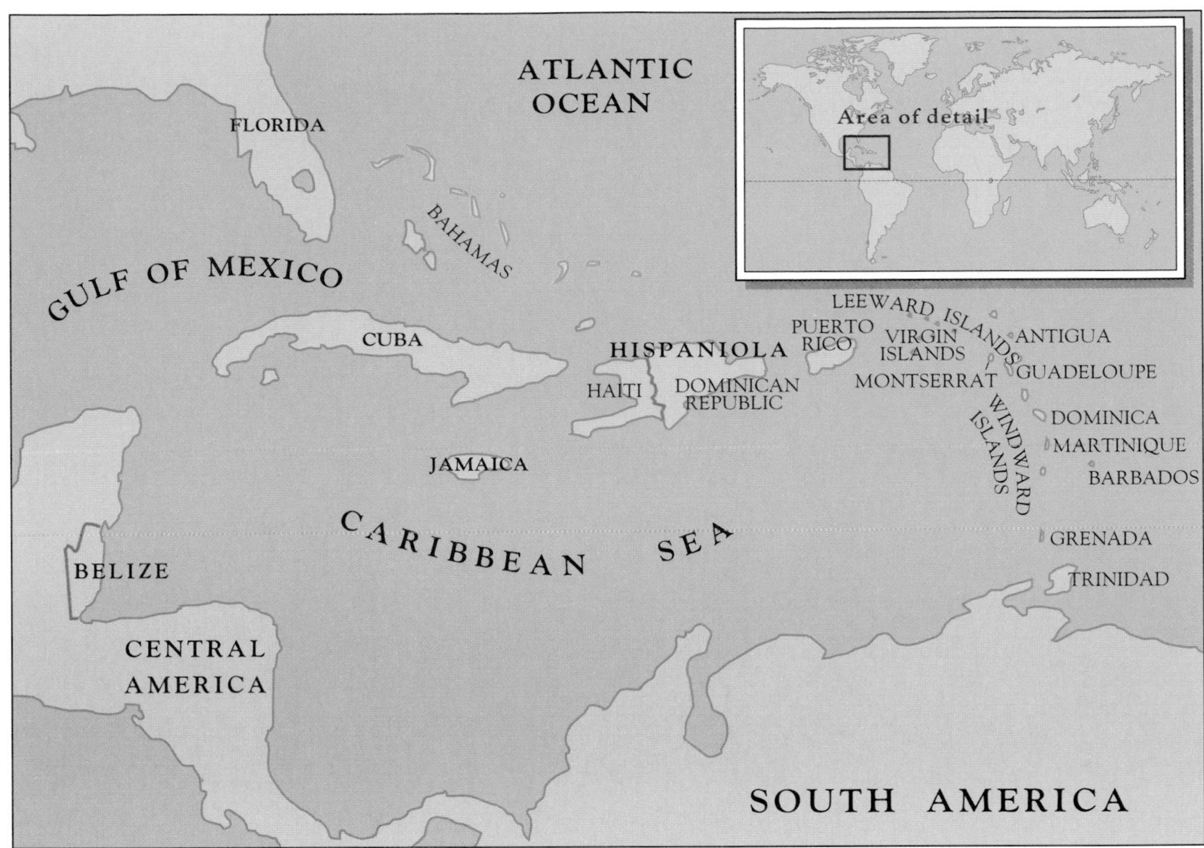

The majority of information we have on Caribbean medical practices comes from Jamaica, one of the biggest, most politically and economically significant Caribbean islands. Jamaica played an essential role in the success of the colonial sugar and slave economy and has long supplied low-priced labor to Britain and North America.

Jamaica is but one island in a region that spans the sea between South and North America on Central America's east side. Other main islands include Cuba, Hispaniola (the Dominican Republic and Haiti), Trinidad, and Puerto Rico. The Bahamas and the Virgin Islands are groups of smaller islands. Other small islands can be found on the Atlantic edge of the region. These include Grenada, Barbados, Martinique, Dominica, Guadeloupe, Montserrat, and Antigua. Belize, Guyana, Surinam, and French Guiana, although on the mainland, also form part of the contemporary Caribbean, largely because they were colonial plantation societies with African slaves.

Invasion and Colonization

While Britain's power in the region today remains the strongest of the old colonial regimes, Spain was the first to enter the region. Spanish colonization followed the late 15th-century voyages of Christopher Columbus (he called the islands the "West Indies" thinking they were off the coast of India). The Spaniards and other colonists found the region attractive for a number of reasons besides its lush, natural beauty and tropical climate. The islands proved useful bases for mounting exploratory and, later, military expeditions into the continents. But first and foremost, colonists entered the region in search of resources.

Gold and other precious metals were what interested the Spaniards most. Others saw in the Caribbean the perfect location for sugar, tobacco, and coffee plantations and for foresting precious hardwoods. And, as there turned out to be little precious metal in the region, agriculture was what paid off. The agricultural plantations and their profits provided Europe with much of the human energy (as spurred by sugar, coffee, tobacco, and rum) and financial capital to support the industrial revolution.

The Spaniards' claims on the Caribbean made their European neighbors quite jealous. The English and French established their own colonies with the assistance of the Dutch, who not only helped them to bully the Spanish but also sold them slaves and provided estate supplies and knowledge of sugar cultivation. Eventually, the French and English began to resent the Dutch monopoly on the transport of goods and slaves, and they passed laws forbidding trade with them. Having no major Caribbean plantation settlements of their own, the Dutch returned their attention to their eastern empire. English and French pirates continued to strike at the Spanish, raiding their cities and sacking their ships.

Columbus's Caribbean Visits

Columbus made four voyages to the Caribbean. The names he gave to various islands, capes, gulfs, and other land formations reflected his devout Catholicism and his Spanish patrons.

1st Voyage (1492–1493): Visits the Bahamas, the north coast of Cuba, the north coast of Hispaniola (the island shared by Haiti and the Dominican Republic).

2nd Voyage (1493–1496): Visits the Leeward Islands; sails the north coast of Hispaniola, the south coast of Jamaica, and the south coast of Cuba before landing at St. Ann's Bay, Jamaica, in May 1494.

3rd Voyage (1498): Lands at Galeota Point, Trinidad, in July; sights some of the Windward Islands in August; sails the south coast of Hispaniola.

4th Voyage (1502–1503): Sails the Central American coast; passes to and from it via the gap between Jamaica and Cuba.

Slavery

Agricultural enterprise could not have been possible without a cheap and reliable supply of labor. When first eyed by Columbus, the Caribbean region already was home to various groups of Arawak and Carib Indians; the region's official name commemorates the latter. The Spaniards immediately put the Indians to work. However, the brutality of the early regime as well as the influx of Old World diseases that came with it nearly killed off the native population. Those who survived were absorbed into the populations brought into the region to replace them: poor indentured or enslaved whites, white convicts, and, most of all, slaves from Africa.

Slaves were culled from a variety of West African societies, especially the kingdoms of Ashanti, Oyo, and Benin and, later, from Sierra Leone. But slaves were taken from any village between Senegal and Angola. Originally, the Portuguese held the monopoly on the African slave trade, and all slaves had to be procured through them. They negotiated with representatives from the aforementioned kingdoms, where domestic slavery had long been

The End of Legal Slavery

	Abolition of Slave Trade	Emancipation of Slaves
British Colonies	1807	1834
French Colonies	1818	1848
Spanish Colonies	1820	1873
United States	1862	1865

practiced. But when the demand for slaves rose, the Portuguese "exclusive" was broken by the Dutch, French, and British. Techniques of procurement grew less gentlemanly and, as moral and ethical doubts stirred, a newly virulent form of racism provided justification.

Most slaves who survived the overseas journey to the Caribbean were put to work on plantations. Some escaped to remote regions in the jungly island interiors where they formed or joined bands of Maroons, as the runaways were known. Some met and teamed up with groups of natives who, earlier, also had fled to the hills. Some Maroon settlements declared themselves independent nations and waged war on colonial forces. A number of the villages founded by runaway slaves are still inhabited by their descendants. Their traditions retain recognizably African elements.

In the words of Peter Ashdown, "The West Indian sugar and slave society was unhealthy and unstable." In addition to making efforts to escape, slaves resisted by staging rebellions. The pressure of revolts and the abolitionists' efforts led to the emancipation of the slaves in the mid-1800s. For some Caribbean nations, independence soon followed: Haiti became the first Black republic in the world in 1804. But most Caribbean nations did not gain their independence until just a few decades ago.

The Caribbean healing traditions discussed in this chapter developed during what some contemporary Caribbean people call "slavery days" and are relatively new. However, they are extensions of some very ancient ways.

Picking Up the Pieces

The slave trade undermined the traditional basis of the health care of the enslaved and encouraged the emergence of new, blended forms of healing through a process sometimes called *Creolization*. This is a fancy term for mixing bloodlines and the cultures linked to them. People born in the Caribbean, as opposed to those who migrated or were brought there, were

A woman tends her garden in Jamaica. Gardens or farm plots are generally located up in the hills behind villages. Most farmers grow food crops. While some may grow medicinal herbs, most do not because many "bush medicines" can be found growing wild, and others are easily purchased in the markets.

The Accumulation or Diffusion of Healing Knowledge

One way to classify healing systems is to plot them along a continuum between two opposing types: "accumulating" and "diffusing" systems.

Accumulating systems involve the collection of knowledge over time, generally in written form. Practitioners share knowledge at conferences and through professional associations, and they have institutions for formal training. Modern scientific medicine is a good example of an accumulating system. Traditional Chinese medicine, Ayurveda, Egyptian, and Galenic medicine, discussed in previous chapters of this book, also are accumulating systems.

Diffusing systems, on the other hand, do not have forums for exchanging and discussing information or for systematizing their knowledge. Practitioners generally specialize in particular healing techniques or problems; they treat their cures as trade secrets, sharing knowledge only with apprentices (if they have them). Diffusing systems are fragmented.

Although many factors underlie how healing knowledge accumulates or diffuses, the existence and use of a written system of record is key. For the most part, Caribbean healing knowledge was shared and passed down orally. Oral culture can accumulate if those who pass it down organize themselves to this end. But the cultures slaves came from generally had not done this. Moreover, oppressive colonial rules outlawing meetings among slaves meant that practitioners had few forums to gather and share knowledge. Much of what they did had to be done covertly. They were not in the position to create an accumulating system.

referred to as Creoles. A Creole culture emerged over time as various ancestral African cultures blended. As part of the Creolization process, bits and pieces of healing practices from here and there were layered, adapted, and combined to form a number of useful healing systems.

The Merging of Traditions The first bits of these systems were chiefly African, traded between slaves who shared quarters and who needed help when sick. Some parts were indigenous to the islands, acquired from the few surviving natives. After a few generations, a solid knowledge base emerged. African bits continually diffused into it as newly arrived slaves with fresh memories of the traditions of their African kin entered the established Creole slave communities. Some European practices were appropriated, and after the slave trade ended and indentured servants from China, India, and the Middle East began to arrive, Asian traits were added to the various island mixes. Initiated under the difficult circumstances of slavery, Caribbean healing systems were—and still are—extremely open to new ideas and to change.

The invention of Caribbean healing was no simple feat. New slaves often were separated from close kin and fellow tribespeople. When an individual felt ill, he or she would not have the old familiar helpers to turn to. Generally, in the past as now, people tried to treat themselves or their children when they first fell ill. Mothers and grandmothers provided the first—and, frequently, the only necessary—treatment for the sick worldwide. But slavery divided kin. Indeed, the primary ailment of many slaves was the broken heart caused by grief at the loss of family ties.

Many slaves forged new kinshiplike bonds with the people they found themselves living and laboring with. New companions helped each other when they could. However, while many ailments were successfully treated in the home or quarters and many home remedies were common knowledge, certain ailments needed specialized treatment, and specialists were very hard to come by. For one thing, West African specialist healers were often older, and older people would have been left behind by slave traders. Even where specialists were available, whole traditions would not have been carried by them; different people specialized in different techniques or diseases. So on each plantation, people had to cobble together a system of healing from the bits and pieces to which they had access.

EARLY CHALLENGES Even where specialists were present or where memory could serve as a guide, people could not necessarily put knowledge into practice. The Caribbean wasn't West Africa, and some ingredients could not be procured; substitutes for many of the old familiar medicines had to be discovered or invented by trial and error. The timetable of plantation life also posed a problem: Any long ceremony had to be truncated so that the cure could be effected in time for the slave to get back to work.

Other challenges stemmed from language differences. Sick people and their helpers often had to rely on what could be expressed through gestures and body language to communicate symptoms or instructions. Cultural diversity among the enslaved also made it hard for people to agree on the right treatment sometimes. But West African traditions had much in common, and these commonalities enabled the slaves to develop coherent healing traditions based on a cultural logic that made sense to people from diverse backgrounds.

Colonial Contributions

In addition to African understandings, the practices of colonists also influenced Caribbean healing. Sick slaves generally relied on themselves for cures, but sometimes they approached their masters when ill. Overseers and other European plantation occupants would try to help by drawing on their own health traditions. If their advice proved helpful, the slaves would later disseminate it.

PLANTATION PRACTICE In some cases, European plantation doctors treated sick slaves. Large plantations sometimes had infirmaries where sick slaves stayed until well or dead. Slaves who worked in the infirmaries could watch and learn from the European-trained doctors they assisted. But the services the European doctors provided were not always helpful. Their bosses, the plantation owners, pressured them to get their charges up and working rather than perfecting the quality of their services. Often, they sent genuinely sick slaves back to the fields to labor.

The abolition of the slave trade in the early 1800s exacerbated this tendency, as now new replacement slaves could not be readily purchased. Sometimes plantation owners took matters into their own hands even when they weren't trained to administer medicine: One Dr. Craig wrote in his hospital log that the proprietor of a Jamaican estate killed a slave by administering an overdose of medicine, ostensibly to cure him in less time than a hospital stay would have involved.

Caribbean people, especially women, carry heavy loads upon their heads. Women often coil some leaves or vines into a sort of crown that sits under the load to steady it. While this woman carries chickens, more often people carry water, fruit, or vegetables, and rather than baskets, plastic tubs or large cast-off cans generally serve as containers these days.

Even top-quality medical attention might not have cured the slave in question. European doctors in slavery days would not have known about microorganisms; they would not even have known to wash their hands or to practice other basic sanitation. They relied on bloodletting, leeching, poultices, hot-spring baths, and other primitive cures. Even the most modern physicians' practices and theories of the time still had much in common with European folk healing traditions.

Furthermore, there were no real standards in medical education until the early 20th century. Some plantation doctors had no official training at all; others had set up practice in the Caribbean because they were barred from Europe. In any case, European training and experience could not prepare doctors for many of the problems they would encounter in the Caribbean.

STRIKING OUT ON THEIR OWN Once the slave trade was abolished and slaves were freed, plantation doctor services were no longer available. While many ex-slaves moved off into the mountains or other remote locations, the European doctors tended to stay put or even go home to Europe. For their part, ex-slaves did not necessarily trust European doctors anyway. They knew their growing corpus of medical knowledge could serve them well enough. They continued to patronize their own healers.

With a natural human desire for good health and the need felt for following the fashions of the Europeans, ex-slaves formed a lucrative market for European and European-style medicines. Retail druggists stocked a range of then-modern medicines, including chemicals that we now know are quite dangerous and substances that we now use for completely nonmedical procedures, such as cleaning.

Druggists (or apothecaries or chemists, as they also were known) carried many kinds of patented or proprietary medicines. Vague and optimistic claims, generally lacking ingredient information, suggested that these medicines could offer complete cures for all manner of maladies. For example, a double extract of witch hazel would remedy bleeding lungs, sore throats, piles (hemorrhoids), burns, and the tendency to vomit blood. Jeye's Sanitary Compound and Perfect Purifier could preserve the teeth, purify the breath, and abolish odors from city drains. Henry's Number 2 Vigor Pills, a male medicine, could strengthen the brain and nerves, cure impotence and emission problems, and restore any weaknesses associated with "indiscretions."

Most drugs worked—or claimed to work—to purify the blood, expel toxins from the body, or relieve congestion in the liver. Anyone who purchased Dr. Frank's Genuine Grains of Health could look forward to being cured of "all complaints connected with obstruction of the bowels including congestion of the liver, lungs, and brain." Mother Seigel's Operating Pills cured cold, fever, and constipation. Although based on European folk medical traditions, these types of drugs fitted neatly with existing Caribbean health traditions and so proved quite popular.

European-style medical practices and products legitimized the Caribbean beliefs and practices that they fit with. They encouraged an emphasis in Caribbean tradition on purifying the blood and cleansing the bowels. The association between nerves and sexual fluids, seen for example in the ad for Henry's Pills, also was perpetuated. Patent and proprietary medicines were eagerly absorbed into the home remedy range, and traditional healers prescribed some of them with regularity.

Traditional Understandings of the Body

Because of variations in each Caribbean society's history and because all illness types are not alike, a number of healing systems evolved in the Caribbean. Each had a different explanation for the ultimate causes of sickness and, as a result, each system's healing recommendations differed, too. To gain a better understanding of the various treatment systems, and to appreciate why dispensary remedies such as vigor or operating pills proved so popular, we need to examine in greater detail Caribbean understandings of how the body works.

The outline below is built largely around Jamaican research but would have applied throughout the Caribbean (it is important to note that because of tradition—and because of their usefulness—a great many people still swear by the following beliefs). Significant regional and local differences could, of course, be found, but generally these were merely differences of degree or point of focus. Some related to environmental conditions: For example, people living near the sea made greater use of sea water in their remedies than those living in the central mountains, and people living where certain ailments were more common developed methods to treat them.

Traditional Medicinal Chemicals

Proper Names	Folk Names
Ammonia solution	Horsehorn
Codeine or Aspirin	Surgical pain tablets
Copper sulphate	Blue stone
Ferric chloride solution	Steel drops
Mercury	Quicksilver
Mercury ointment	Blue butter
Precipitated sulphur	Milk of sulphur
Rock sulphur	Brimstone

Body Basics In Caribbean tradition, the body existed as an open system whose equilibrium had to be maintained. Ideally, the body maintained itself at a certain warm temperature. But because it has pores and is permeable, the body's temperature could be thrown off by thermal changes in the external world. A cool breeze, for example, could enter the unprotected body through the pores and chill the innards. People were also at risk for the intrusion of harmful substances or essences and from the untimely loss of valued ones. Although potentially dangerous, permeability was seen as necessary for proper heat exchange and for the elimination of wastes.

In addition to keeping the system thermally regulated and clean, it had to be kept properly moist. The ideal body was plump with vital fluids, and good health depended on maintaining the flow of substances throughout the body. Cross-culturally, a developed emphasis on maintaining a continuous, unimpeded flow of fluids through the body was most common among those who valued reciprocity and emphasized the obligation kin have to share with each other, which Caribbean peoples did (and still do). Sickness occurred in such systems when flow was blocked; individual ills mirrored social ills, caused by disturbances in the flow of mutual support and aid (see also pages 328–329).

In Caribbean tradition, people were physically linked by bodily liquids—fluids such as semen, the blood that flows from mother to fetus during gestation, and the milk the child drinks after birth. People also were linked through food that was shared. Both vital bodily fluids and foods fattened the body, making plumpness an indicator of the quality and extent of one's social relations as well as of good physical health. It was good to be fat. Although the scarcity of food and other resources no doubt supported this view, the social necessity and cultural value of cooperation underpinned the idea.

Blood Once ingested, different foods turned into different bodily components as needed, whether for growth or to replenish substances lost through work and other activities. Blood was the most vital and the most significant bodily component, and it came in several types. When unqualified by adjective or context, the word "blood" meant the red kind—built from thick, dark liquid items, such as red pea soup, stout, or old-fashioned porridge, and from reddish edibles such as tomatoes. Red wine, sometimes called "tonic wine," could also be used to build blood, which was itself sometimes called "wine." The juice from pork, beef, or other flesh foods was also thought to be directly incorporated in blood through digestion.

Blood's importance stemmed in part from the fact that it cleansed the body as it

Connected Bodies?

The concept of bodies linked by fluids or food may seem foreign to readers who view the body like they view the self: autonomous, individual, and independent. In the context of current Western values, bodies serve primarily as vehicles for the expression of the individual self. Traditional Caribbean peoples, however, viewed the body's shape as reflecting aspects of the social network in which a person was enmeshed and of those individual character traits affecting a person's social connectedness, such as his or her ability and willingness to share and give.

A Haitian woman prepares to sacrifice a chicken during an annual ceremony celebrating the Vodun god of war. Propitiating this god is essential for the continued health and well-being of the members of this particular congregation.

moved around inside. To ensure blood could serve this function, and to ensure good health, people monitored and adjusted blood's various qualities. These included blood's

- thickness or thinness
- quantity or volume
- location
- purity

Variations in these qualities could affect blood's color, which itself served as a quick index of the blood's state. Blood's temperature also was important; it varied with the thermal situation of the body as a whole and with the blood's purity.

Blood could be too thick and abundant or too thin and lacking if a person took sick or simply did not take in the right amount of blood-building nutrients and fluids. Unattended to, blood that became too thin or low in volume could lead to a condition sometimes known as "low blood." People with low blood lacked energy. Low blood was similar to, but not the same as, the condition we call "low blood pressure." Likewise, conditions that Caribbean peoples referred to as "pressure" are not the same as our "high blood pressure." While some of the symptoms match, the mechanisms understood to underlie the conditions differ. This becomes obvious when traditional cures are taken into account. For example, for pressure, people drank garlic tea to thin the blood, or eliminated blood-building foods, such as dark soups, from their diets.

Caribbean peoples did experience a condition called "high blood," which they distinguished from pressure. It had to do with blood's location. Ideally, blood was distributed equally throughout the body, but this could be affected by various forces. For example, blood could be drawn toward a weakened or injured body part or location to cleanse it of poisons causing or resulting from the distress. Another example would be blood moved to the head to treat a headache. If a headache lasted too long, too much blood could get stuck up there (and thus be "high"). Of course, if there was not enough blood, it could never flow to the body's higher or furthest reaches. A blockage, the blood's own overthickness, or the effect of gravity on a person spending too much time upright, also could account for this. "Low blood" could refer to blood's placement in the body as well as its thinness.

Blood that did not flow properly due to problems in volume or viscosity and blood not located evenly could not be pure; it would pick up too much of the body's natural waste (or the waste generated by illness) at the points in which it concentrated. Furthermore, blood with flow problems could not move the waste to expel it, whether via the pores (in sweat), the vagina (in menses), the urinary tract (in urine), the rectum (in feces), or any of the body's other permeable orifices.

Even blood that flowed properly sometimes became dirty. This was, in part, a function of blood's age: New blood, which was bright red, eventually dirtied over time. Old blood, which was dark brown, could be expelled in the feces or, when necessary, through menstruation or afterbirth. New blood replaced it. A bad diet, too, could dirty the blood.

While Caribbean healing systems focused a great deal on regular red blood, another equally important type of blood existed. It was built from okra, fish eyes, and other pale slimy foods, such as egg white or the gelatinous portions of boiled cow skin or hoof. This class of blood included, among other substances, the joint lubricant that scientific medical specialists call synovial fluid, which resembles egg white. It also was associated with the nervous system and with procreation. Sexual fluids and breastmilk contained it. Many called this class of blood "white blood" as opposed to red.

THE BELLY Although blood was the primary bodily component, the belly was the most important part of the inner body. This big cavity, or bag, extended from just below the breast to the pelvic floor. The belly was full of bags and tubes, such as the womb and the intestines. Stringlike fibers held these slippery structures in place, but only loosely. Tubes sometimes tied themselves up so that nothing could pass through them; in Trinidad and Jamaica, "knot gut" referred to a fatal kind of constipation. Moreover, tube and bags were not tightly coupled. A substance improperly propelled might meander off course and slide into an unsuitable tube or bag and get lodged there.

Most sickness started in the belly. Sometimes, sickness occurred when something made its way into the wrong bag or tube and rotted there or clogged the digestive system. Other times, disagreeable foreign substances caused a bad reaction in the belly. Eating habits that made the blood dirty, too full of sugar, too thick, and so on could also cause problems. Since what happened in the belly could make people sick, what happened there also could make them well again. Many remedies for illness and preventive actions relied on medicines absorbed through the belly and on changes in diet.

One of the most basic belly problems was gas generated as food was digested and the belly emptied out; small belches signaled hunger and an empty belly. Generally, the belly made gas in manageable amounts. Still, if the belly was empty too long, excess gas could accumulate. In addition to causing pain, it could dampen the appetite, taking up the space that food would otherwise fill. (Worms, which everyone was thought to have, worked in the same fashion, dulling the appetite by occupying the belly and tricking the body into feeling full; they were worse than gas, however, because they also ate whatever food did get ingested, leaving the sufferer extremely malnourished.) Hot beverages or warm, fermented beverages, especially ginger beer, were useful for helping people to belch off excess gas. Some mint teas could "turn it down" (into flatulence, for example) and re-empty the stomach. Eating on time could also prevent problems with gas.

Waste and Washout Not all things taken into the belly were transformed into specific components like red or white blood; some things were not used in the body at all. Extra liquids became urine, and solid food turned to feces. People who did not use the toilet often enough, whose digestive systems were sluggish, or who had blockages in the bottoms of their bellies, literally filled up with waste. Blood washing through their bodies would quickly dirty. Whatever was lodged inside would rot and fester. The belly could even burst from buildup.

A body that did not efficiently rid itself of excess and waste could turn rotten inside. With particular medicinal bush, or herbal, teas, toxins left behind in the belly and those that entered the blood could be forced into the feces or urine and cleansed

Pilgrims honor the Vodun goddess Erzulie, associated with the Virgin Mary, in a rite of purification in the sacred waterfalls of Saut d'Eau. This is the home of many aquatic spirits, and the water is healing and life-giving. A huge fig tree near the falls is home to Damballa, the serpent god.

away. The bitterness of a brew often indicated how effective it would be. Most tea brewed for breakfast had a degree of preventative blood-purifying action. Cerasee (*Mimordica charontia*) tea was a Jamaican favorite.

The most popular Caribbean cure-all in this regard, the washout or laxative purge, was taken to eliminate blockages and harmful waste directly from the belly while also purifying the blood. A washout once a month—a schedule modeled on the menstrual cycle—was advised. Every household medicinal supply included, if nothing more, the ingredients for a purge.

Temperature and Cold Temperature could also affect internal flow. For example, when warmed, whether through physical exertion or overexposure to the sun, blood grew thin, and blood too warm and thin could run out through a cut too fast, bringing sickness or death. Blood also got hot if it tried to wash away an unusually high level of toxins, leading to fever as the body tried to regain equilibrium. Purgatives could be taken to clear the toxins; lime juice was used to cool the hot blood. On the other hand, a person with a fever might have tried to heat his or her body further to assist it in its self-cleansing efforts. One could sit over a tub of steaming water laced with herbs such as fever grass to encourage the body to sweat out the blood-heating toxins, for the heat opened the body, increasing its permeability, making it very vulnerable to cool air or the intrusion of dangerous substances or essences.

In contrast to hot blood, blood too cool was thick and ran slow. It could pool and coagulate, forming a blockage. Blockage also would have occurred from the overproduction of mucus, or "cold," which could coagulate. Normally, mucus was generated in the body in manageable amounts, but certain conditions, such as overexposure to cool weather or drafts, could cause the body to make excess. Going from a hot, pore-opening task such as ironing to a cold bath could cause excess "cold" formation as the cool air or water penetrated the body. For example, simply sitting on cold ground would cause "cold" to form in one's bottom, leading to constipation because "cold" not expelled in a timely fashion would clog the body's conduits. It could also wrap around organs and bind joints, as in arthritis.

Anything that helped the body expel coagulations of "cold," wherever such coagulations might occur, was called "cold medicine." Many cold medicines worked by heating the body. For example, people could take medicines or teas made of thyme, cinnamon, or pepper, or they could drink hot beverages or rum to loosen or melt "cold." Loosened cold could be coughed up or blown out, and it could move into the urine or feces and be expelled.

The importance of keeping clean inside so that a proper, balanced flow could be maintained paralleled the importance of keeping goods and services flowing through networks of kin, which corresponded in a number of ways to people's abhorrence of hoarding. An overabundance of perishable resources not passed on would rot. Hoarding generally led to hardship and damaged social relations.

Reproduction Kinship involved interdependence and obligation. People determined kinship through blood ties. Male and female sexual fluids were thought of as parallel types of white blood, and mingling white blood led to conception. Pregnancy was believed to occur when discharged male semen met discharged female white blood in a woman's reproductive tract. Because conception was a process of accretion, all men who had intercourse with a woman in the early days of conception could, as long as their fluids were all compatible, be fathers to her child. Generally, however, each child had one father.

Compatibility between male and female fluids was important if they were to mix well and form into a child. Because of compatibility issues, a nursing mother could only have intercourse with men whose sperm helped conceive the nursing child. Otherwise, the child would get sick from drinking breast-milk that contained sperm foreign to its constitution. Contact with, or the ingestion of, any foreign sweat that remained on the mother's breast after sex with the nonfather also was harmful. The baby would then fail to thrive.

A woman with a small, slow child risked being accused of adultery or of having a new partner. People often surmised that economic instability forced her into the liaison. This shamed her, and it shamed the child's father by indicating that he failed to provide for his child. Through early weaning, women with new lovers could avoid harming their babies, their reputations, or their conjugal relationships. Early weaning also helped women maintain health as well as youthful figures, as prolonged nursing taxed their bodies.

DISCHARGE AND DECAY Sexual fluid, like fatness itself, was good; here again, however, too much could be harmful, and balance had to be maintained. A buildup of unreleased sexual fluid, or "discharge," was thought to cause pimples as excess sexual fluid worked its way out through the pores. Youths, whose caretakers could afford to provide them with expensive, rich foods but who also insisted that they remain celibate in keeping with the behavioral expectations for the elite, were said to suffer more from such skin problems.

To maintain bodily equilibrium, sexual fluids had to be discharged now and again, as through orgasm. Without ejaculation, excess amounts of undischarged semen would harden up in a man's spine, causing back pain and sexual problems. Drinking helped promote the flow of fluids through the penis.

Celibate women or those with poor lovers also could become sick through the retention of too much sexual fluid. They could grow mad or develop problems with their nerves, as the nervous system contained white blood. People—mostly men—used this knowledge to justify frequent sex and to coerce others into partnership.

Women were thought to expel fluids at orgasm, and they took in men's discharge during intercourse, when their bodies were hot and open. Like their own sexual fluids, sperm taken in fattened women and made them sexually appealing and attractive. A teenage girl's increasing plumpness was perceived as much a result of her becoming sexually active as it was a positive result of her own growing fertility. Then again, discharge taken in improperly or excessively could work as poison.

When conception did not happen, discharge could lodge in spaces not accessible to the red blood that might otherwise have cleared it away. It would rot quickly, and turn toxic and polluting. Menstruation served as a purifying washout for the female reproductive system.

Body and Mind Health was not only a bodily process. Or, more precisely, the body was not something that could be divorced from the person who inhabited or used it. His or her feelings or emotions were part and parcel of his or her body and, consequently, of his or her health and well-being.

In Caribbean tradition, emotions originated in the heart. Emotional changes were first sensed there; the chest tightened or felt as if it was filling up. Too much of an emotion could fill and enlarge the heart or otherwise strain it. Grief could burst the heart if it did not gain expression through tears, which carried out the waste related to, or caused by, the grief. A person overcome with sorrow and longing could die of a "broken heart."

Besides harming the heart, certain emotions, when chronic, caused weight loss. A worried mood, which generally reflected a worried social context, worked as an oven's heat, melting away vital bodily fats and juices. Sexual feelings and anger heated the body, too, but these were generally short-term feelings, cooled down through action (in the case of anger, one could drink cold water to cool down).

Worries also could eat away at or dry the nerves out, as they did fat. Nerves were understood as anatomical structures filled or lubricated with white blood. The state of one's nerves underwrote one's daily reactions to the stresses of life; dried out or overfull nerves could not function properly.

In a person with nerve problems, the white blood supply had come unbalanced, generally being too low. This happened sometimes because of worries, but often because of environmental factors. A person who spent too much time in the sun could melt out all of his or her white

The Universal Nature of Equilibrium Systems

That European and Caribbean folk medicine matched so well was not mere coincidence. Both have historical ties to humoral medicine, which has its roots in ancient Greece. Humoral medicine, sometimes called Galenic after the great classical physician Galen, emphasized balance and recommended the release of toxins and congestions so that healthy flow of humors, or substances such as blood and sexual fluids, could be maintained (see page 75). In Europe, the historical ties to Galenic medicine are direct; modern scientific medicine grew out of Galenic teachings over the centuries. Greek-influenced Muslims moving westward through North Africa around the 7th century helped spread Galenic teachings to West Africa (as well as to Spain and Portugal). Enslaved Africans carried Galen's influence to the New World.

But equilibrium notions (notions of balance) also existed in West Africa before any contact with European teachings (see page 327). Cross-culturally, all health systems and concepts of the body (those of modern medicine included) emphasize balance of some kind. Equilibrium beliefs stem ultimately from universal embodied experiences; for example, the feeling of hotness that accompanies fever, the bloated feeling of a very full stomach, the sense that a full bladder may burst or overflow, and the emptiness one feels after emptying the bowels. So even without the diffusion of Galenic beliefs, we would expect to find equilibrium notions in all healing systems worldwide, past and present.

blood. Sometimes the nerves lost white blood because of a blow to the body. The loss of white blood also could be a function of age, as people ran low on it when they got older.

Dim vision and other eye problems were symptomatic of nerve trouble (healthy eyes are filled with white blood and glide around in the head with its aid) as well as aching teeth. Nerve problems left people feeling jumpy, itchy, and restless. They had trouble sleeping. Jerky movements, shaky hands, and clumsiness were attributed to bad nerves as well (the lack of lubrication at the joints caused the trouble). Nerve problems caused life's stresses to register with greater impact than they should; people with nerve problems could not do too much physical labor nor could they cope with social stresses, such as uncooperative neighbors.

People troubled with nerve problems drank milk mixed with orange or soursop juice, rum, and gooey things such as honey, egg whites, and aloe vera gel. They also drank the oily tea made of boiled peanut skins (the thin membranes covering the nuts within their shells) and a drink made from Irish moss (seaweed); they ate coconut jelly (the white, gellike fruit of green coconuts), too. Anything that resembled white blood could help build it back up.

Traditional Healing Systems

Caribbean tradition assumed that sickness had impersonal natural causes, or that it was created through supernatural means, spiritual intervention, or some kind of active manipulation of nature. Natural sicknesses stemmed from impersonal forces such as excess food waste or environmental fluctuations upsetting the body's balance, as we saw earlier. They were not intentionally inflicted but simply the outcome of natural circumstance, accident, or chance. Although it always benefited a person to keep his or her social and moral life in order, natural sicknesses could be treated without social, supernatural, or spiritual intervention.

A boy in Barbuda chops the tops off of green, or water, coconuts, opening drinking holes. These coconuts contain liquid, which makes a very refreshing drink. Some say that "coconut water" washes over the heart and other internal organs when drunk, helping to ensure inner cleanliness.

While sickness was natural by default, when naturalistic treatment failed, when sickness after sickness befell a person, or when a condition just did not seem typical or normal—when it looked "funny"—an interpersonal cause involving an active external agent was suspected. The agent who created the sickness could have been human (a sorcerer) or nonhuman (an ancestral ghost, an evil spirit, or a deity).

Sometimes, a person just happened to find oneself the victim of malicious magic or interference. But often, the purposive acts that brought on created sicknesses were provoked by the individuals who found themselves sick. That is, they were acts of retribution. The agent involved in retribution was either a neighbor angered by some antisocial behavior, an ancestral ghost put out by a lack of attention to his or her memory, or a punishing god angered by a moral infraction (see also page 329).

What Caribbean peoples called "created" or "spiritual" sickness anthropologist George Foster calls "personalistic." In personalistic sickness, Foster writes, emphasis is placed on

> the need to make sure that one's social networks, with fellow human beings, with ancestors, and with deities, are maintained in good working order.

For, if not retribution, behavior that is out of order surely will provoke at least a warning, in the form of ill health, meant to push a person back into line. People know this and so try to behave; fear of sickness, or anxiety over the possibility of punishment for breaking social and moral rules, served as a mechanism for maintaining social order. This was especially so in societies that have few or no formal methods for settling disputes or enforcing conformity. This would definitely have been the case for Caribbean peoples living during a time when the only legal institution they could call on belonged to, and worked solely for the good of, colonial interests and not their own.

Conforming to this cross-culturally common pattern, Caribbean healers were, then, either personalistic or naturalistic in their approach to sickness. After trying home remedies, people consulted either a naturalistic or a personalistic healer depending on what they saw as the particular cause of a given condition.

ROOT DOCTORS Because good health depended on the quality of the blood, people took blood-building tonics as a general preventive measure and for specifically blood-based problems. The word "tonic" referred to any bottled liquid or syrup thought to build the blood, promoting health. Tonics were purchased from druggists in prepackaged form or made at home. Homemade versions generally involved boiling a selection of roots to obtain a brownish liquid medicine.

While most people knew a basic tonic recipe, many villages had one or two root doctors—men or women known for their special tonic blends. Some root doctors specialized in particular sicknesses, but many had a wide range of recipes and could cure any ailment based on poor blood. The main active ingredients in roots tonic came from plant roots gathered during the full moon, when they were plumpest and most powerful.

The specific needs of an individual, his or her palate, the roots at hand, and the root doctor's preferences determined the mix, but tonic recipes almost always included roots such as chainey root (*Smilax balbisiana*), sarsaparilla (*Smilax ornata*), and any number of plants with names such as

These paquettes are charms, or "guards," made of padded cloth, feathers, and other materials. They contain a sacred mixture. Prepared under strict ritual conditions, they are passed over a patient's body to excite and strengthen the attending loa, or spirit, so that the spirit can help the patient. The power of the paquettes themselves is maintained by exposing them to flames burning in sacred pots.

strongack, blood wiss, raw moon, and tan deh, or "stand there," buddy (buddy meaning penis). The properties of evenly numbered combinations canceled each other out, but an extra root served as a catalyst: root doctors only boiled odd numbers.

To make the tonic, the root doctor chipped, mixed, and boiled roots, bark, and vines. After about an hour, when the water had boiled down halfway and looked bloody or brownish-red, the root doctor cooled and strained the liquid. Most sweetened their "roots juice" with honey and other strengthening ingredients such as molasses before pouring it into an old gourd or bottle. The power of "the roots" could cause bottles to explode and lids to pop.

Roots tonic was taken in small measures, once in the morning and once at night, for a period related to the ailment being treated. People could take roots tonic also at wider intervals to promote good health in general. Roots tonics energized the body by building, cleansing, and mobilizing the blood. Because of its blood-building power, too much roots tonic could dangerously overheat the body, but it took a lot for this to happen.

Roots tonics increased sexual potency as well as enhancing health. Sexual potency often served as an index for good health in general. Dry spine, a male ailment related to sexual overindulgence, showed itself in ejaculation problems, impotence, and infertility. Men with dry spine also grew thin as their stores of vital juice dried out and depleted. Recovery demanded total sexual abstinence so that the body could renew its store of white blood. A man with dry spine took roots tonic once every morning and night for at least a year to replenish and enrich his blood stores. After that time, his body would have grown moist and full with vital fluid.

Roots tonics were also used for sexually transmitted infections. A Trinidadian recipe called for yon tasso, sarsaparilla, minnie, gully, zeb-a-femme, and wild coffee roots as well as graveyard bush leaves,

St. John's leaves, senna leaves, the inner scrapings from a young calabash, and the bark of sosofa. The roots doctor added salt physic (Epsom salts) to the mixture and let it stand for three days. Another recipe boiled redhead roots with ti mawee leaves and thorns. This recipe specified that after the symptoms had disappeared the patient was to drink tea made from senna pods and salt physic, ostensibly to wash away leftover toxins.

So while for some ailments roots tonic alone was all that was needed, others called for additional measures. For dry spine, men also took lime juice, as it drew out heat and dissipated the libido. They generally added plenty of slimy okra and other sinew-building foods to their diet, such as drinks made from milk mixed with soursop (*Annona muricata*) juice or from the seaweed Irish moss (*Gracilaria* species), which resemble semen, and the white, gel-like meat of young coconuts. If this sounds like one of the cures for nerve problems, it is because they, too, related to depleted supplies of white blood.

Leaf or Bush Doctors Doctors whose medicines used mostly the leaves of locally available plants or bushes were called "bush doctors," or "leaf doctors," rather than root doctors. While root doctors could deal with general or chronic health ailments and sexual dysfunctions, people sought bush doctors for help with specific and acute complaints such as toothaches, stomachaches, or fevers. But the line between the two types of practitioners was quite fuzzy, and many ailments could be treated either way.

Bush doctors generally recommended teas brewed from specific plants, fortified with a bit of milk and sugar. Sometimes, they soaked whole or crushed leaves in alcohol or oil, creating medicines that patients would take by the spoonful or rub on affected body parts. Baths, too, were often recommended. Plants were boiled or soaked in water, and the patient's body or injury was bathed with the mixture. Bush doctors sometimes also added substances available at the apothecary to their medicine mixes or recommended dietary supplements. Sometimes, a prescription of sorts would be written for additional medicines that the patient could take to a druggist.

People knew many bush medicines for curing common ailments or for preventing them; most tea brewed for breakfast had some medicinal value. Ganja (marijuana) was a popular cure-all when prepared as tea or in a tincture. However, in tough or worrisome cases or in regard to uncommon problems, the bush doctor provided expert advice and supervision. Bush doctors also prepared abortion-inducing medicines as well as gentler medicines for menstrual regulation. Menstrual regulation and abortion techniques followed from ideas about healthy menstruation and so they worked by inducing a washout. The concoctions traditionally used to induce abortion caused the body to break up and purge the blockage that a fetus posed. In many cases, the bush doctors who offered this type of assistance also worked as midwives.

Granny Midwives More often than not, midwives, or grannies, were older women who had already borne children. They not only attended births but also provided prenatal advice and even helped new mothers with household chores in the days that followed a new baby's arrival.

Before birth, women ate foods such as okra to make their vaginal passages slippery and to aid in the expulsion of the baby. Thyme tea and castor oil were regularly used to speed delivery after the onset of labor. The vaginal area was washed and massaged with oil (perhaps reducing tearing in the area between the vagina and anus during birth). Pain was expected, but labor was hastened by the fact that women were not confined to their backs, a position that compresses spinal nerves and limits the blood and oxygen supply to the lower body.

Birth was not complete until the placenta had come down, and women took washout to ease this process and to make sure that nothing was left behind. The placenta and umbilical cord were buried, generally under a special tree in the family's yard, rooting the baby to the family and to the new homeland—an act that has special significance in light of the legacy of slavery.

Midwives knew how to handle problem pregnancies, too. Those who were personalistic healers in addition to being regular, naturalistic midwives could even deal with the monster, or "false belly," pregnancies that resulted when a woman was raped by a ghost or hexed by a neighbor. Generally, washouts and prayer were called for. The washouts purged the nonbaby from the womb and then washed the womb completely. The prayer enlisted the assistance of spiritual forces in ensuring the woman's delivery from sickness. Sometimes, a midwife or a healer dealing with false belly lit candles, burned incense, fumigated the house with incense, anointed the gates of the yard, rubbed the mother with magical oils, and conducted other rituals to help call forth good powers and rebuke destructive ones. Midwives might have done this for normal births, too, just to be on the safe side.

PERSONALISTIC HEALING False or monster babies, like other "funny" sicknesses, were created actively through sorcery, by a troublesome spirit, or by a punishing deity. Created sicknesses arose when people offended others—living or dead, mortal or immortal—enough to provoke retaliation. They, therefore, called attention to the fact that some kind of social or moral infraction had taken place. People could live upstanding lives to try to ensure that they were not hit with created, personalis-

Magic or Religion?

Magic involves manipulating the forces of nature to make certain results happen. Through magic, humans put supernatural or extraordinary pressure on nature so that things that would not normally happen do occur. In religion, on the other hand, higher powers control the turn of events. So in religious healing we must try to persuade god(s), spirits, or spiritual forces to grant a cure on our behalf.

In magic, one's actions lead directly to the result (for example, burning some herbs and chanting a spell to reverse a cancerous growth); in religion, one's actions only lead the higher powers to consider bringing about the result (doing good deeds and praying for the reversal of a cancerous growth). Magic does; religion asks.

One further difference is that religious action by definition involves adopting a moral stance that is pleasing to the higher powers. Magical action need not make reference to ideas about good and evil. However, magic carried out secretly with the aim of harming someone is recognized as evil and generally termed "sorcery."

tic sickness. But sometimes even the most upstanding person could encounter a run of bad luck.

The actual mechanics of the disease process (a buildup of blood-heating toxins, a blockage of flow, festering waste, and so on) were the same for personalistic and natural ailments but the ultimate cause was different. In the case of personalistic illness, the suffering was provoked; it was not due to pure chance. Further, the toxins causing personalistic problems were often unnatural as, for example, when a destructive essence was sent to harm someone's body.

Even so, all things destructive to the body were treated by the body in a similar fashion. The body treated destructive essence exactly as any other noxious substance: It heated itself and otherwise tried to purge the poisonous spirit substance from its system. Practitioners treating personalistic sicknesses could use naturalistic cures; but even when they did, the cures were augmented with magical and religious practices. If they did not augment the cures, the ailment would persist.

SOCIAL HEALING Sometimes personalistic healers in the Caribbean sent any destructive forces back to where they came from (to the person who paid the sorcerer to set the hex, for example). Retribution helped victims release anger and assuage feelings of powerlessness, even if this meant scapegoating weaker members of the community, such as blaming an illness on an unpopular neighbor. But healers often avoided practicing "turnback" medicine, refusing to support a cycle of vengeance between community members. Especially in areas under heavy Protestant influence, many healers chose to promote harmony and forgiveness rather than divisiveness.

Three women prepare the compound for a Vodun service by drawing and consecrating vévé *for the* loa. *Each* loa, *or spirit, has his or her own* vévé*—seal or insignia—and worshipers draw them with corn meal. The* vévé *are then consecrated, and offerings (the spikes, which are perhaps for the war god) may be added to them. The* vévé *attract the* loa *and thus help to ensure a ritual's success.*

Often enough, patients who complained to healers that they had been hexed actually were mistaken, and some healers spent a great deal of time convincing people that their distress actually had to do with poor life conditions and troubled social relations. Life in the Caribbean was indeed difficult; most people were (as many still are) very poor and had little privacy, a trifling amount of autonomy, and almost no room for personal advancement. Healers provided a form of psychotherapy, persuading sick and demoralized individuals to have hope and to adopt an optimistic outlook. Where sickness represented a breakdown in an individual's adaptation to the stressful social environment, personalistic healing strengthened self-esteem and built up an individual's ties to a supportive group of people who had been healed by similar methods. Most personalistic healers had followers who assisted them in their work, often forming a church of sorts. Indeed, much healing was carried out in the context of religion.

Esoteric Traditions

Despite their differences, the groups the slaves came from had many religious customs and beliefs in common. Most shared a belief in one supreme and distant deity existing with many lesser, yet powerful, spirits close at hand. The lesser spirits and not the supreme one concerned themselves with the daily affairs of the slaves, as did ancestral ghosts. Many groups practiced ancestor worship and had experience with spirit possession by which the lesser spirits "mounted" and "rode" people as if horses, bearing messages to, simply visiting with, being entertained by, and entertaining their mortal hosts. Sorcery and fetishism, herbalism, and personalistic curing also were common.

In many Caribbean settings, the disintegration of kin groups meant that, in some locations, ancestral spirits, so important when lineages were intact, lost their traditional position as cult figures. They became simply ghosts, often referred to as *duppies* or *jumbies*. But the ideologic principles behind ancestor worship still prevailed; that is, ancestors (now ghosts) continued to have an influence in the lives of the living. In any case, organized public spiritual events such as those that might have accompanied ancestral worship were outlawed because the slave owners feared they might encourage revolts.

OBEAH Despite the suppression of ancestral worship, magicians whose activities traditionally were secret, such as the Ashanti *obayifo*, thrived. In addition to assisting people, they could cause severe misfortune and even death. They were thus feared, not only by slaves but by slave owners as well. Demand for their sorcery practices gained momentum in the socially divisive slavery context, and soon an indigenous sorcery system known as obeah developed. Obeah practitioners aided slaves seeking vengeance through magic—one of the only means the enslaved ever had for altering the conditions of their existence or of getting even.

African religious traditions do not divide the world into good and evil as Christian traditions do. Caribbean obeah practitioners may have been sorcerers, but they could also cure and divine. Each had his or her own specialty, for instance, in curing by sucking out sickness or through the

Obeah in Trinidad

In his 1886 *Guide to Trinidad*, published after Emancipation, James Henrey Collins had this to say about obeah:

> When a peasant, stepping out of his hut one morning finds a sealed bottle lying at the entrance, containing abominations as horrid as those of Macbeth's witches, his heart sinks within him, for he feels that calamities dire and untold are looming ahead. Somebody, one of his enemies, is working "obeah" on him. His children will get "yaws," his cow will dry up, his crops will fail, goodness knows what may befall him. One thing is certain, all will go wrong with him; unless he can counteract or overcome the evil.

use of herbs, or in preventing illness and misfortune by offering protection in charms, fetishes, and tonics. But because of colonial law they did not—indeed, could not—do so in a public fashion, and the secrecy they surrounded their actions with fueled the anxiety and suspicion that the condition of slavery engendered.

MYALISM In Jamaica there existed a religious practice called Myalism. It takes its name from the Myal dance, introduced by obeah specialists to ensure immortality in the dancer as a means for destroying slavery. While our information on the Myal dance is sketchy, it seems that during the dance, which included much singing and stomping, the obeah specialist administered, in a ritual fashion, a drug that induced a comalike state in the initiate. Then an antidote was administered, again in a ritualized fashion, complete with gestures and spells, and the initiate awoke, revitalized, impervious to any death that might otherwise have been inflicted in the course of a slave rebellion. This was the ultimate in preventive medicine.

Myalism was at first seen by plantation owners as merely a dance, and so it was tolerated as a form of entertainment. It persisted until about 1850, when it was absorbed into emerging African-Christian cults. But even by the 1830s, Myalists had lost their revolutionary tendencies, leaving behind the simplistic obeah immortality ritual and taking on a subtler orientation to fighting oppression. Myalism provided a form of solace, functioning for the oppressed as a coping mechanism and a way of letting off steam.

One of the West African cultural traditions that survived slavery held that illness

Vodun worshipers "salute" drums before they are played. They are paraded, offered libations, blessed with plants and song, and otherwise sanctified. The worshipers' uniform dress suggests that they will welcome a particular loa, *or that this is a particularly special ceremony. The nature of the ceremony may have been indicated in the symbols, or* vévé, *that their feet seem to have already wiped away.*

could be caused if the soul or shadow were lost or stolen—a belief similar to many shamanic cultures (see pages 134, 149, 170). Generally, this happened through obeah sorcery. Myalists, originally assisted by obeah specialists and therefore familiar with their methods, knew how to recover lost shadows, and so they could restore good health. They developed many other anti-obeah techniques. Obeah became associated simplistically with the oppressor.

When Christianity was introduced, Mylalists embraced it, perhaps seeking to improve their position by association with this white power source. Christian belief in baptism, prophecy, vision, revelation, sacrifice, possession, demonism, and healing fitted well with Myalist sensibilities. The Christian dichotomy between good and evil was appropriated and applied in relation to obeah. Many Myalists considered themselves now as Christians with angel guides; some even acted in vigilante fashion to stamp out obeah.

Revival Zion Myalism was eventually replaced by or renamed "Revival Zion," a Christian-style religion whose practitioners also generally practiced the healing art called "Balm." Balm, which is still practiced today, took its name from the healing herbal baths patients were given. Generally, healing takes place on specified days in the church, or Balmyard, associated with a given group. The head healer, usually called to her vocation by a vision, was called "Mother," and a nurturing parent–child relationship ensued between her and her patients or helpers (cured ex-patients often became helpers). Balmyards served as therapeutic communities and provided supportive social networks, which helped cure many of the sick.

Flags frequently surrounded a Balmyard; they attracted the spirits or angels who provided healing guidance. Angels were also attracted and entertained by plants or flowers and by offerings of oranges and water placed on a pillar or birdbathlike altar at a Balmyard's front gate. Called a seal, this altar was similar to a West African shrine. Music also served to attract the angels; roused by rhythmic singing, chanting, dancing, and drumming, they visited and sometimes possessed the Mother or her helpers. People sometimes spoke in tongues or wrote messages out in a spirit language.

Before a healing service, a Balmist usually would have "read" each patient in private, divining a general diagnosis and then getting the patient to elaborate on it through an interview. She might have prescribed herbal teas as well as a bath; some Balmists drew a patient's suffering into their own bodies. During a healing service, a Mother might use various actions to drive "destruction" from the church or the body of a sick individual. She might fumigate, wave banners, or use a broom to sweep out evil. She and her helpers might dance in a circle to attract the angels. According to the anthropologist William Wedenoja, treatment was supplemented with

> moralistic admonitions, counseling and the dispensing of herbs ("bush"), prayers, prayer candles, perfumes, oils, patent tonics, and vitamins.

Balmists often wrote what they called "prescriptions" for the articles or medi-

Ecstatic worshipers sing and shout during a religious meeting in Haiti. Their white costumes probably signify purity and cleanliness before the gods. The overwhelmingly female balance of the group is not abnormal; those involved in religious healing churches in the Caribbean are predominantly women.

cines recommended, and patients took these written slips to druggists to be filled.

VODUN In Haiti, unique circumstances meant that the ancestral cults did not whither to the degree that they did in islands such as Jamaica. Vodun religion, which took its name from the African Yoruba god Vodu, emerged in the late 1700s, much as Myalism did in Jamaica. Religious meetings became forums for antislavery activity, and rebel slaves practiced rituals that, like the Myal dance, protected them from death during rebellions or ensured, should they die, their souls would repatriate to Africa.

Gradually, a unified set of ritual standards evolved. For example, snake symbolism took on great importance. The snake represented regeneration; it also symbolized Damballah, the ancient patriarchal deity, whose blessing people sought. For particular favors, other spirits were appealed to (and still are—like Balm, Vodun is actively practiced today). Stones also proved important to Vodun: Round pebbles hurled from the sky by the spirits were worshiped and protected, as was the case in Africa.

Haitians called the spirits *loa*. The *loa* were deified ancestral spirits, and different families worshiped different spirits. In keeping with the violence and instability that plagued life in Haiti, and perhaps through the influence of surviving Carib and Arawak Indians on the island, these deified spirits took on aggressive sides. So, for example, Erzulie, a love goddess, was in one incarnation a woman enamored of beauty, flowers, and finery; in the other incarnation she groaned, screamed, and cried in frustrated rage. Many *loa* also had Catholic counterparts: Under French

Two initiated worshipers bring out the flags of their church at the beginning of a Vodun ceremony. These "standard bearers" are escorted by the la-place (master of ceremonies) who bears a sword. The trio salutes the church and its drums and dignitaries. The latter show their respect by kissing the sword handle and the flagstaffs. After the flag parade, the loa, *or spirits, can be called.*

Catholic influence, Haitians represented them as, or identified them with, saints and sometimes called them by saints' names. People sometimes represented Damballah, for example, as St. Patrick, because of the association with snakes.

Vodun priests and priestesses held ceremonies worshiping the *loa* that asked them to do so. The *loa* appeared after a time of drumming and singing, attracted by the music and by representational drawings, or *vévé*, made on the floor with corn flour. *Loa* joined services by possessing individual worshipers.

The *loa* each had specific personalities, likes, and dislikes, and they acted these out during a possession. They also brought messages and instructions to their worshipers, and advised them on how to behave. In exchange for being worshiped and remembered, they granted favors, including the provision of protection from, or the removal of, misfortune or sickness.

If not propitiated, they withdrew. So Vodun was not, as the popular media would have it, black magic. Rather, it was a complicated religion wherein the powers that be had the ability to cure as well as cause affliction.

Caribbean people were generally poor; their health and the health of their loved ones was all they had. To punish them when they were neglectful, *loa* attacked their health (as did the punishing God of Revival or Myal). Often, this was remedied by making an offering to the offended *loa* of his or her favorite food or a gift of clothing. Loa Sobo, for example, loved goat meat and mutton as well as champagne and cognac. He also loved military apparel, especially in white or lemon yellow. Limba, on the other hand, liked strong liquor and pork.

If not instigated by a neglected *loa*, sickness might have been wrought by sorcery. Like the Myalist and the Balmist, the Vodun priest or priestess could tell when this was so. The priest sometimes searched the sick individual's house for a sorcerer's charm. After determining the nature of the hex, the priest would advise on appropriate protective countermeasures.

Vodun priests and priestesses also recommended charms or guards to protect against evil to begin with. A charm bath, which was much like a balm bath, could offer protection. Another way of preventing harm involved temporarily removing the soul from the body and storing it in a pot or bottle so that it could not be touched.

But in many cases, sickness had natural causes. The Vodun priest or priestess could recognize this and, either directly or through the words of a *loa* that came and possessed them, could recommend forms of treatment or send their charges to others in the village who had fuller knowledge of natural cures.

SHANGO Vodun was similar to Myalism or Balm, but it retained more of an African flavor to its possessions and in the range of spirits who did the possessing. Shango, a Trinidadian cult, was similar to Vodun (and it, too, took its name from a god).

To Cure an Ulcerous Foot

Anthropologist George Eaton Simpson, famous for his work on religious practices in the Caribbean and from whom our details on Shango come, reports the following ulcer remedy given to him by a Trinidadian informant:

> At a Shango ceremony, a follower of Bonzewon (one of the names by which St. Francis is known to some "orisha" people), when possessed, may run into the bush or woods, pick up a frog and bring it to the *palais* [church]. While dancing with the frog, he may approach a person and say, "You have a bad foot. Do you want me to cure it: What will you give me?" The man or woman replies, "Papa, I will give you a cock or a goat or anything you ask for." Bonzewon replies, "Come with me." Bonzewon cuts the skin from the belly of the frog, ties it on the person's foot, and gives an order on what is to be done later. If the sick person fails to do this, Bonzewon comes and does it himself. The frog's skin is kept on the foot two days. When it is taken off, the frog's skin is blue. It is thrown away. A piece of cedar bark is boiled, and the tea is used to wash the sore foot. The backbone of a morocoy (land turtle) killed some time ago is burned to ashes, and the ashes are sprinkled on the ulcer. A castor-oil leaf is heated over a fire and is tied securely over the ulcer. (The frog's skin has drawn out the poison from the foot, and the powder from the morocoy's back has dried the ulcer.) Now the person has to fulfill the promise he made. If Bonzewon is not paid, the foot will break out again.

Possession or a message comes to a man, and fellow worshipers and some onlookers rush forward. The women on the left seem to be chatting and may not be paying close attention to the service. Caribbean healing sessions often go on for hours, and it is not uncommon for people to come and go or to spend time catching up with each other as a session progresses.

The fetish stones of Vodun played a key role in Shango practice; they had to be washed in water infused with certain leaves or herbs, and even fed; blood sacrifices sometimes were performed for them. And as with Vodun *loa,* Shango powers, called *orishas,* possessed worshipers, mostly after prolonged drumming and singing. But perhaps because Trinidad hosted far less violence than Haiti, Shango never developed an aggressive dimension.

As in Vodun, each Shango god expressed his or her own personality when in possession of someone. Shango himself, represented sometimes as St. John, had a mild and peaceful demeanor; he was quiet, spoke carefully, and acted charitably. But Oya, goddess of wind and rain, had a hot temper.

Like Vodun priests or priestesses, and like Myalists or Balmists, Shango leaders, called *amombos,* could conduct ceremonies specifically with healing in mind. Osain, the healing *orisha,* sometimes represented as St. Francis, could be invoked for sickness caused by evil spirits. *Amombos* also could call on the powers that they personally followed. The power possessed the *amombo,* diagnosed the problem, and prescribed the cure. Generally, cures consisted of herbal teas, herbal baths, or rituals. The *amombo* or his or her assistants boiled leaves or crushed them in water and mixed them with oils.

Sometimes, *amombos* cured without possession, with little ritual, and simply used their knowledge of "the leaves." In such cases, smoking pots of incense may have perfumed and purified a room, and the client might have held a candle or two while the *amombo* prayed or gave instructions. But bush doctors were also consulted, especially when no extraordinary aspect to an illness was suspected.

SANTERÍA Santería was, and is, a more Catholic version of the healing religions just described, at least on the surface. It developed in the Spanish-speaking countries of Cuba and Puerto Rico. As in Shango and Vodun, heavy Yoruban influences were evident. Fetish stones also played a key role in Santería: Kept in lidded dishes, rubbed with oil, anointed with blood, and cooled with herbed water, the stones served as the central anchor of the Santería altar.

But colonial teachings on the Catholic saints infused Santería more thoroughly than they did with Shango or Vodun. For example, Santería made greater use of icons in worship and prayer. Altars were decorated with plaster statues, printed pictures of the saints, and rosarylike beads, color coded and numbered to the *orishas.* They also attended with greater interest to the stories of the lives of Jesus, Mary, and the saints, as these stories helped link the various Christian figures with Yoruban ones. Some said that the saints were simply people possessed by the *orishas* and not alternate forms of the *orishas* themselves.

Santería leaders generally worked toward solving problems that could not be solved through regular channels, usually in response to a request for assistance. In this, Santería was a churchless religion or one without a congregation that met regularly, as did practitioners of Shango, Vodun, Balm, and even Myalism. But it did involve possession, divination (with cowry shells or palm nuts), and moral and social counseling or instruction. Sacrifices and gifts were offered to Santería powers as they were in Shango and Vodun to ensure cooperation and to win blessings.

Santería practitioners relied heavily on plants in their rituals. *Omiero*, the sacred liquid used in certain ceremonies, consisted of 101 different herbs thought sacred to the saints. Power infused all plants or herbs, and each had specific healing properties. Sometimes plants alone were used to heal, but practitioners also used a system called *santigüo*, which meant healing through blessing. The practitioner prayed and rubbed the patient's stomach with oil. St. Lazarus, or Babalú-Ayé, patron of the sick, was often called.

Choice of Treatment

When traditional Caribbean peoples were sick, they generally had three choices: (1) to treat themselves, (2) to seek assistance from a naturalistic healer such as a root or bush doctor (or possibly an MD; modern medicine is also a naturalistic system), or (3) to seek healing from a personalistic healer, who knew how to deal with created sicknesses. Both naturalistic and personalistic healers generally used local plants and easily available ingredients to make medicines, but personalistic healers practiced their art in a religious context and drew directly on spiritual forces in making their work effective.

While Santería healers practiced in Cuba or Puerto Rico, Shango healers in Trinidad, Vodun healers in Haiti, and Myalists and later Balmists in Jamaica, the principles of personalistic healing were mostly the same across the Caribbean. They built on naturalistic understandings of how the body functions and involved a religious conviction that spirits and sometimes ancestral ghosts could interact with the living body, for better or for worse. In sickness, the spiritual or physical poison harming the body had to be expelled, and protection or forgiveness had to be secured from the spirit realm. At the same time, the sick individual had to take a long hard look at his or her social relations and moral position and make adjustments accordingly. Bodily (including mental) health followed from healthy social and moral relations.

But some sickness was merely natural, and for that kind of sickness, natural treatment alone would suffice. Not only was this more convenient, it also was less likely to raise suspicion over a sick person's social or moral behavior in his or her neighbor's eyes. For some people, seeking personalistic healing was understood to have problems of the kind that gossip thrived upon: They were sick because they had been in an argument and roused someone's vengeance, or they had lied, cheated, hoarded, committed adultery, or otherwise misbehaved. So some people chose to patronize healers in faraway locations or to make their visits in secret. This was hardly possible, however, because someone would be bound to notice, and talk would eventually find its way back home.

Another solution to such a problem, and perhaps the healthiest option, was to embrace the healing event and to join the healer's group of followers. In this way, Myalism, Revival, Shango, Vodun, Santería, and other healing cults flourished. (Some are still quite active, and healing is one of the Caribbean's most successful cultural exports today.) Moreover, the supportive network provided by fellow followers underwrote and maintained the success of the personalistic healer's work in helping the sick individual to regain health and adjust successfully to trying life conditions.

Some Famous Caribbean Healers

Alexander Bedward (1850–1930): Popular leader of a radical, antiwhite religious sect. Declared insane by colonial officials; committed to an asylum.

Boukman: Leader of Haitian revolt in 1791. Convened a ceremonial meeting during a violent storm, motivating rebellion.

François Duvalier (1907–1971): Medical doctor who ruled Haiti from 1957 until his death; succeeded by his son. Infamous for the violent despotism of his rule; reputed to have taken advantage of his role in Vodun to coerce submission.

Ernesto "Che" Guevara (1928–1967): Argentinian doctor and socialist radical who joined Fidel Castro's expedition against Fulgenico Batista in Cuba in 1963. Physician to Castro's soldiers and unit commander.

Nanny, Cudjoe, and Accompong: Fierce Maroon leaders (sister and brothers). Worked toward achieving Maroon independence in Jamaica from the British (1690–1738).

Growing with Ancient Roots

The various healing systems that evolved in the Caribbean share a common emphasis on harmony, balance, and flow with many healing systems around the world. More specific parallels have to do with the fact that the various African groups, from which the Caribbean slaves originally came, had many ancient religious and healing customs and beliefs in common. The differences that do exist can be understood in terms of the various geographical and ecologic environments in which the systems were created, the diverse endemic diseases and local forms of illness that each system was meant to contend with, and the specific ethnic mix of peoples involved in a given system's creation and practice.

Traditional Caribbean healing systems had ancient roots, but they also had contemporary dimensions. All healing systems evolve over time, incorporating some new practices and discarding some old ones. Customs that fit neatly with knowledge already in place are most likely to be taken up; for example, the use of European purgatives and blood-building tonics made good Creole sense. Foreign healing beliefs and practices continue to be incorporated into Caribbean practices in a similar fashion even today, and likewise Caribbean practices have spread, being carried abroad by emigrants and by others who have seen the enduring value in the ancient healing customs of the Caribbean.

Ancient Treatments

So now that we've seen how the different ancient healing systems were organized and practiced, it's time to see how they treated specific problems. Do the age-old wisdoms apply to health concerns today? Well, yes and no. In some cases, the common sense and herbal expertise of the ancients may be able to help us; however, in many other cases, it's clearly best to let the past stay in the past. The following is a selection of ancient treatments for a few specific health conditions.

Gastrointestinal Problems

THE NEAR EAST The ancient Egyptian medical papyri seem to deal with several intestinal problems; though it is difficult to know whether these treatments were directed at specific intestinal ailments or whether they were aimed at clearing *wekhedu* (a substance they believed to be involved in all diseases; see pages 37–39). For food poisoning, sweet beer left overnight with notched sycamore figs was given for four days to purge the intestines. The *swnw* had to rise early every day "to see what has gone down from his anus." (This is the first known record of a doctor examining a patient's stool.)

The Egyptians also used medicines with laxative effects to clear the bowels: Dates, figs, wormwood, coriander, cumin, juniper, malachite, and other herbs and minerals were combined with things such as honey, dew, wine, milk, or oil. One remedy calls for using the fruits or seeds of the castor-oil plant swallowed with beer.

Although Hebrew scriptures do not discuss the treatment of gastrointestinal problems directly, infections such as dysentery were probably common. Human excrement transferred dysentery by way of water, flies, or contaminated food. Personal hygiene and the safe disposal of human waste away from water sources was essential in preventing the disease. Certain parasites, such as trichinosis and tapeworm, could be carried by food, especially pork. The commandments of the Hebrew Bible show great concern for the disposal of human waste, for dietary restrictions, and for personal hygiene. These practices would have helped prevent the spread of disease, whether or not they were intended to.

EUROPE The Romans had several treatments for intestinal disorders caused by infections. They treated tapeworms, for example, with pomegranate. Dioscorides recommended thyme in the treatment of worms and mint for roundworms. He felt that a small amount of coriander seed in wine had the potential to cure most intestinal infection but cautioned that too much of the herb disturbed the mind.

The Anglo-Saxons practiced a variety of magical healing rites for intestinal problems. Nonsense words written on paper and hung from the neck offered a cure for diarrhea. Amulets made from plants such as betony, vervain, peony, yarrow, mugwort, and plantain were also popular.

The Americas The herbal treatments used by Native Americans obviously varied greatly depending on geographical and climatic conditions. However, several groups used similar remedies for common conditions. The Shoshone, Navajo, and Blackfeet may have treated some cases of diarrhea with the root of the cherry tree and the blackberry as well as the leaves of the horsetail weed. General stomach upset would have called for swamp root, manzanilla buds, or juniper branches.

The Indian Subcontinent According to Ayurveda, indigestion is caused by excess ama (undigested food) in the body (see page 208). In kapha-ama conditions, heavy mucus and congestion accompany the indigestion; in pitta-ama conditions, fever and hyperacidity aggravate the indigestion; in vata-ama conditions, bloating and constipation make the indigestion feel worse. Ayurveda treats indigestion with heat to move the ama out of the body's tissues quickly. Bitters such as gentian or goldenseal help and cayenne is often prescribed.

Yogins, like Indian Ayurvedic practitioners, were also concerned with proper digestion. They viewed a number of ailments as having roots in poor digestion. In ancient times, a number of techniques would be employed to bring the digestive tract into balance: One such technique, called *nauli*, is still used today to help placate gastrointestinal disorders or weaknesses. This practice consists of rigorously pressing the navel back against the spine 100 times without taking a breath. More modern techniques include most forward-bent positions and spinal twists to help relieve constipation.

The Far East In Tibetan medicine, abdominal pain is associated with the liver. This condition was considered to be a "hot" condition and was to be treated with compresses in the region of the liver. Internal medications included *gut gum dun pa*, or saffron of seven ingredients, which consisted of saffron, gypsum, *Disda cordofolia*, gentian, flower of the blue lotus, *Ephedra monosperma*, and myrobalan. In general, indigestion is understood to arise from a disturbance of the phlegm humor, or fault. Because phlegm consists of the earth and water elements, it is heavy and cold. Individuals suffering from phlegm disorders were advised to avoid cold environments and behaviors that would increase phlegm, such as sleeping on the ground. Foods recommended were light and warm in nature and consequently easy to digest. A tea made from ginger, rock salt, myrobalan, and long pepper was given.

The state of the bowels was very important diagnostically in Chinese medicine as they could give a great deal of information concerning the internal condition. Constipation could have been due to a variety of problems, including an insufficiency of *qi* to move the bowels, heat drying up the fluids and causing dry stools, or *qi* stagnation causing blockage. If there was heat, then the stools would often be smelly or there might be a burning sensation. With an insufficiency of *qi*, the problem was simply not enough strength to move the bowels; if there was stagnation, then there would also be pain. Constipation could be treated with many herbs, most notably, *da huang* (rhubarb), which could drain heat and purge the bowels, or *mang xiao* (mirabilite), which could soften hardness and moisten dryness. Also, nuts and seeds, such as *xing ren* (apricot kernels), *yu li ren* (prune pits), and *huo ma ren* (cannabis seeds), were known to help moisten the stools. Acupuncture might include points on the abdomen as well as points on the large intestine and stomach channels.

In Chinese medicine, diarrhea was most commonly thought to be dampness combined with cold or heat, an insufficiency of spleen or stomach *qi*, or an insufficiency of kidney yang. Moxibustion on the lower back and abdomen was frequently used as were herbs such as *ge gen* (peuraria root), *yi yi ren* (coix seed), and *rou gui* (cinnamon bark), combined with herbs such as *huang qi* (astragalus) to supplement the spleen. Acupuncture might be done on the spleen, stomach, and large intestine channels.

An ancient Japanese physician might have chosen the formula *shigyakuto* to treat diarrhea with signs of cold or the absence of yang. This simple but powerful formula contained only three herbs: licorice, ginger, and aconite. The last herb is famous for its warming properties and its beneficial effect on the yang aspects of the body. However, it is exceptionally toxic and so great care was used in the preparation of this herb and the formula itself.

Chinese medicine recognized several causes for nausea and vomiting. Nausea due to pregnancy was usually due to either a spleen and stomach vacuity or a disharmony between the liver and stomach. Herbs such as *sheng jiang* (fresh ginger) were very effective in calming nausea, and the acupuncture point pericardium 6 (*nei guan*, or inner gate) located on the inside of the arm, about two inches above the wrist, was also very useful.

An ancient Japanese formula used to treat a patient with weakness and abdominal pain was *ogikenchuto*, which contained peony root, dates, cinnamon, ginger, astragalus, licorice, and maltose. This was a gentle formula that could be safely used with weak patients and children. It contained herbs that are warming such as cinnamon and ginger, herbs that are strengthening such as astragalus, the soothing herb peony, and two sweet substances—licorice and maltose—to nourish the body and treat pain.

THE CARIBBEAN Belly trouble was perceived as a huge health problem in the Caribbean. The most popular cure-all for constipation—the washout or laxative purge—was taken to eliminate blockages and harmful waste directly from the belly while purifying the blood as well. While washout was taken whenever the need arose, a washout once a month—a schedule modeled on the menstrual cycle—was advised. Every household medicinal supply included, if nothing more, the ingredients for a purge. Recipes for teas from cathartic herbs such as cerasee, licorice, or ramgoat dashalong were well known. People also took oil from the castor plant and physic nut (now known to be poisonous) and what was called salt physic (Epsom salts).

Another one of the most basic belly problems was gas. If the belly was empty too long, excess gas could accumulate. Hot beverages or warm, fermented beverages (especially ginger beer) were useful for helping people to belch off excess gas.

Some mint teas could "turn it down" (turn it into flatulence) and re-empty the stomach. Eating on time could also prevent problems with gas.

Food that did not move down into the belly properly sometimes sat on the stomach, causing nausea or acid stomach. Water mixed with ashes taken from a fire could ease or neutralize stomach trouble. So did eating a roasted ripe banana, burnt peel and all.

Headache

THE NEAR EAST In Egypt, a headache called for an ointment made from cumin, moringa oil, myrrh, lotus flowers, and juniper berries. People also recited magic spells to cure headaches. The pain was treated as if it were a demon, with threats to burn its soul and consume its corpse. Migraines were treated somewhat differently. Because the severe headache of a migraine usually appears on only one side of the head, the "suffering in half the head" mentioned in the Ebers Papyrus is often interpreted as a migraine. The papyrus states, "another remedy for suffering in half the head: the skull of a catfish, fried in oil. Anoint the head therewith."

EUROPE Ancient Romans used massage to relieve headaches, which would have been very effective in the case of stress-induced or tension headaches. The Anglo-Saxons had several approaches. One that combined herbalism with magic was the use of crosswort placed on a red cloth and bound to the head (red was a magical healing color). For severe headaches associated with "the madness of frenzy," the Anglo-Saxons turned to bloodletting, particularly bleeding from the middle of the forehead.

THE AMERICAS In the Americas, by far the most dramatic and advanced medical treatment was surgical removal of parts of the cranial vault, known as *trephining*. We know it was done to repair fractures—a common injury in areas where combat involved mainly the use of clubs. Whether trephining was also used for other ailments, such as brain tumors or to relieve pressure, is not known for sure. Inca doctors especially excelled in the technique.

Maya doctors had a whole series of treatments for headaches. One called for a warm poultice made from several plants, including *Aloe vera* (known in Mexico and Yucatán as *zabila*); a rare unidentified shrub native to the Yucatecan coast; *Desmodium procumens* (called *ne-tab*) or one of its close relatives; and a parasite infesting certain trees. If that didn't do the trick, there were other kinds of poultices: some made of medicinal plants, and others made of *chuy-che*, which means "that which hangs from trees." *Chuy-che* can be either a hanging insects' nest crushed together with the grubs it contained, or a parasitic plant by the same name. Yet another prescription for headache "of a slow continuing kind" called for either a cooling poultice of mashed leaves from a plant in the Agave family, if the headache was caused by exposure to the sun, or a poultice made from the same plant heated by burying it in hot ashes, if the headache was caused by exposure to the cold. For postpartum headache, the Maya doctor used a complex mixture of a dozen different plants, including altinisa (*Parthenium hysterophorus*); the thickly spotted leaves of a vine infesting the trunks and branches of forest trees; a small unidentified shrub;

ortiga; a stinging nettle (known in some parts of Mexico as *tabaco cimarrón*, or wild or bitter tobacco); and a parasite that grows on croton branches. The same complaint was also treated with fumigation with charcoal after the administration of an herbal decoction.

Native North Americans were known to employ poplar or willow bark to combat headaches, both of which contain salicylic acid, the basic ingredient of aspirin.

THE INDIAN SUBCONTINENT As it did in the past, Ayurveda distinguishes headaches by the imbalances that cause them. For example, if a person has an excess of vata (one of the three doshas, see page 196), the headache would be accompanied by anxiety, depression, and perhaps even overly dry skin. There's a good chance that it would have been caused by not getting enough sleep, an irregular diet (poor digestion), or too much mental stimulation. In these cases, Ayurveda would recommend flaxseed in a glass of warm milk or a mixture of ginger powder and warm water applied to the forehead.

An excess of the pitta dosha causes migraine-type headaches accompanied by sensitivity to light, irritability, and a burning sensation around the eyes. Often, these types of headaches are caused by digestive problems (excess pitta in the stomach). Cumin and coriander seeds in warm water would help as would a warm sandalwood oil massage to the head and temples. Kapha headaches are sinus-related and respond well to stimulating herbs, such as a ginger paste spread around the sinuses and between the eyes. These headaches are often accompanied by a sense of heaviness, nausea, and excess phlegm. Calamus or gotu kola powder sniffed up the nose may also be beneficial.

A number of yogic techniques help alleviate headaches, particularly types of headaches brought on by tension or muscular contraction. One technique modern yogin B.K.S. Iyengar teaches is to wrap the head with an elastic bandage (snugly, but not tight enough that it places pressure on the eyes) and practice restorative poses. The supported bridge pose helps postural alignment and relieves tension if you do it daily. This pose involves lying faceup with the back arched and supported by the arms; only the head, neck, shoulders, upper arms, and feet touch the ground.

THE FAR EAST The Chinese believed that headaches had a number of causes. Identifying the location of the headache was crucial so as to determine the channel most affected. Frontal headaches were generally identified with the stomach channel; lateral or one-sided headaches with the gallbladder channel; headaches in the back of the head with the urinary bladder channel; and headaches at the top of the head with the liver. Local acupuncture points would be combined with points farther along the affected channel to move *qi*. *Chuan xiong* (ligisticum root) was well known for its ability to relieve headaches, especially those caused by blood stasis. If headaches were not related to a specific channel, they also might be a symptom of an underlying lack of *qi* or blood.

THE CARIBBEAN In the Caribbean, headaches were thought to have a number of causes: They could be associated with too much pressure, "high blood" (see pages 348–349), tension, stress, or nerve trouble. In the case of nerve trouble, people took medicines to build their white blood and, consequently, their nerves; anything sticky or gluey and whitish would do.

For headaches related to pressure, people wrapped their heads with the leaves of a trumpet, avocado, or breadfruit tree. These leaves are very large; one leaf will cover a normal-sized head. The leaves were thought to draw out the pain or deflect the blood causing it. They might also take tea made from fever grass or aralia.

Heart and Circulatory Problems

THE NEAR EAST Atherosclerosis and calcification of the large arteries have often been found in ancient Egyptian mummies. The medical papyri describe many heart conditions, but scholars cannot identify them all with certainty. Some possible diagnoses include congestive heart failure and ischemic heart disease. The treatment of such conditions involved remedies to cool or refresh the heart or to drive out the heat. One remedy contained melon, sycamore figs, ochre, fresh dates, honey, and water, all left in the dew overnight. It was then strained and drunk the next day. Heart disease caused by a demon called for figs, grapes, sycamore figs, honey, and cow's milk, boiled, strained, and drunk.

EUROPE Although they would have had little knowledge of the workings of the heart, ancient Celtic healers may have used heart tonics to strengthen the blood's constitution, including parts of the yellow cedar, heather, tansy, and hawthorn.

THE INDIAN SUBCONTINENT For centuries yoga has had several ways to address heart ailments. For high blood pressure, certain postures may help. Turning upside down, according to yoga teacher Roger Cole, tricks the body into believing that its blood pressure has risen. The body then takes measures to bring the blood pressure down by relaxing the blood vessels and reducing the hormones that cause the body to retain water and salt. Headstand, shoulder stand, and half-shoulder stand are good postures as are standing forward bends. Deep-breathing yogic techniques also work to lower high blood pressure.

Even in the earliest days of yogic discipline, gurus would encourage their students to perform seated postures for long periods of time to rid themselves of agitation, stress, and preoccupation with aches and pains. Western medical science has long known that stress affects the heart and raises blood pressure. A form of padmasana (the lotus pose) was most often prescribed, coupled with a series of breathing practices that helped the student calm the breath and make its rhythm as slow as possible. Meditation, of course, helped the yogin rid himself of outside distractions that would further agitate him. Sound meditation (audibly chanting or repeating the sound of *Om*) can also have a pacifying effect on the yogin.

THE CARIBBEAN Traditional Caribbean medicine did not view the heart and circulatory system the same way we do, but they did have treatments to address blood-related concerns. "Low blood" was similar to, but not quite the same as, the condition we call low blood pressure. Likewise, "pressure" was not the same as our "high blood pressure." And "high blood" referred to the blood's high location in the body (for example, stuck up in the head). While some of the symptoms matched, the mechanism understood to underlie the conditions differed. So people with pressure drank garlic tea to thin the blood or eliminated blood-building foods such as dark soups from their diets.

Pregnancy, Childbirth, and Fertility

THE NEAR EAST Some Mesopotamian women probably experienced toxemia during pregnancy, since recurring fits of vomiting and edema of the feet and ankles occurred. The practitioners believed that if a pregnant woman's face was yellow, she would give birth to a boy. In fact, she probably suffered from anemia. If a woman had a difficult birth, she took solanum berries. These berries, although poisonous, have antispasmodic properties. If the child died in the womb, the fetus was extracted, probably with some sort of surgical instrument. If the mother died in childbirth and the baby was still alive, a cesarean section might be performed.

EUROPE Greek and Roman writers wrote extensively on obstetric issues, including fertility, birth control, and abortion (see pages 84–85). Folk remedies in northern Europe also addressed the discomforts of pregnancy and childbirth, using both magical and practical methods of facilitating labor (see page 111).

THE AMERICAS Among the Maya, religion and magic were combined with empirical treatment to address pregnancy, birth, and their attendant problems. To ease birth and its pains, a Maya prescription starts with prayer, followed by the administration of a tea made from the root, stock, and leaves of *Lepidium virginicum* (*mastuerzo* in Spanish, cress in English). Along with other members of the genus, it is used as a diuretic and a remedy against gastric and renal complaints. Other ingredients used were *Yerba de la golondrina* (swallow's herb, a species of *Euphorbia*), and the root and trunk of the viny *Ageratum gaumeri*.

To hasten delivery, the Maya doctor prescribed a mash made of the leaves of *Melochia tomentosa* and two peppers. If birth did not occur, sympathetic magic was employed. The inside of the trunk of a *Sabal* tree would be rolled into a ball like a fetus and set up to descend in a manner imitating the descent of the real fetus. Another prescription for delayed delivery involved a mash of a bundle of chili peppers, moss from the mouth of a well, and the soft interior of the young *Crescencia cujete* (gourd tree). Mixing the mash with the juice of a gourd, the practitioner would administer it as an early morning drink after passing it through a sieve.

THE FAR EAST In China, as in the rest of the world, fertility was a major concern. In cases of female infertility, the kidney was usually thought to be involved. The focus of treatment was supplementing the kidney, which is thought responsible for the proper functioning of the reproductive organs. Moxibustion was very commonly used. Male infertility was less understood. Supplementing the kidney essences (the source of the semen) was essential. In general, though, unless the male was impotent or unable to ejaculate, then infertility of the woman was assumed. *Qi gong* exercises might be prescribed along with herbs and acupuncture for sexual dysfunctions.

AFRICA Fertility and successful childbearing have long been emphasized among African cultivators, for whom there is a direct link between wealth in people and wealth in food. Failure to reproduce, uneven reproduction, and infant mortality are the focus of many African therapies. Medications, special foods, the protective isolation of mother and child, herbal formulas to enhance milk production, and community support groups are some of the ways reproduction was encouraged.

Respiratory Ailments

THE NEAR EAST Many pulmonary problems have been identified as occurring in ancient Egypt: emphysema, pleurisy, sand pneumoconiosis, tuberculosis, and bronchopneumonia, among them. Sand pneumoconiosis comes from breathing in blown sand and can turn into pulmonary fibrosis. The medical papyri list many cough remedies, including alum, ochre, salt, bone marrow, honey, milk, tooth of pig, acacia, beer, carob, cumin, dates, figs, lettuce, peas, raisins, bread cooked in oil and honey, and the fat of ox, goose, and pig. A remedy to remove mucus from the chest included myrtle and porridge applied as a bandage for four days.

THE AMERICAS For asthma, colds, coughs, and problems with the lungs and breathing passages, Maya doctors had a whole series of medicines. For example, for a form of asthma called *coc,* the Maya had the following prescription: When convulsions occur, take *Yerba de la golondrina* (swallow's herb), and boil it with a little anise and the belly of a frog. Even if the patient was at the point of death, drinking it down was thought to make him recover.

Other prescriptions for respiratory complaints included the low tropical tree *Leucaena glauca* (lead tree) and the guava (*Psidium guayava*), which could bring on sweating. A more psychosomatic cure involved placing a reddish-colored flint on the fire until it was red hot and then throwing it into cold water; the patient would then drink the water.

For clearing the throat in asthma cases, the Maya doctor prescribed the boiled bark of the tree called *coc-che,* presumably *Conocarpus erecta.* To ease asthmatic breathing, on the other hand, the Maya prescribed frying the fat of a black hen, putting the fat in a beverage, and drinking and eating the mixture before breakfast.

THE INDIAN SUBCONTINENT Ayurvedic physicians treat coughs differently depending on the underlying cause. If the cough is mucous (indicating a kapha excess), the physician will encourage the patient to expel the excess phlegm by drinking an expectorant tea such as one made with ginger, cloves, and cinnamon powder. Turmeric also helps. If the cough is dry (vata cough), demulcents such as ashwagandha and comfrey root are indicated, as well as warm sesame oil dropped into the nose. Pitta coughs generally come with a high fever and sometimes a sore throat, and physicians will prescribe cooling herbs such as burdock root, yellow dock, sandalwood, or peppermint.

In yoga, there are several pranayama, or breathing, techniques that can help to increase lung volume and capacity. Nadishodhana (alternate nostril breathing) has been used successfully to help respiratory problems. It is said that breathing through the right nostril (ruled by the sun) elevates the body's temperature and energizes it. Breathing through the left side (ruled by the moon) calms the body and lowers its temperature. To change from left nostril breathing to right, yogins do the following: Squeeze a hard object against the left armpit; lie down for six minutes on the left side; cross the right leg over the left; and tickle the top of the right ankle.

Some asthma sufferers find the fish pose (matsyasana), a backward stretch that increases lung capacity and helps relieve spasms in the bronchial tubes, to be particularly helpful. The bow pose, which opens and expands the chest, is also said to work well for asthma sufferers.

THE FAR EAST The Chinese believed that a cold or other minor respiratory infections could have been caused either by the invasion of wind and cold evils or by the invasion of wind and heat evils. These would be treated with an herbal formula to warm and release the exterior, which could include such herbs as *ma huang* (ephedra), *gui zhi* (ramulus cinnamomi), *sheng jiang* (fresh ginger), *da zao* (fructus zizyphi jujubae), and *zhi gan cao* (honey fried licorice root). The condition would be treated differently if there was sweating.

Wind heat can invade through the mouth and nose, causing fever, possible slight aversion to cold at the onset, and a floating and rapid pulse. This might have been treated with an herbal formula to cool and release the exterior, which could include such herbs as *jin yin hua* (lonicera flower), *lian qiao* (forsythia fruit), *bo he* (mint), and *dan dou chi* (prepared soybeans). Acupuncture points would include points on the lung, large intestine, and bladder channels.

Because of the care used in differentiating symptoms, the ancient Japanese physician, basing their clinical approach on early Chinese texts, would have many formulas to choose from. For a patient with a cold, fever, chills, stiffness, and soreness in the back and neck, the physician might prescribe the formula *kakonto,* which contains kudzu root, peony, ginger, ephedra, date, cinnamon, and licorice.

THE CARIBBEAN Caribbean people had hundreds of treatments for colds, and although chest ailments might be treated with these, a few bush medicines were known to target the lungs specifically. For example, tea made from ganja (marijuana) was used to treat asthma and other respiratory disorders. Piaba, John Charles, and whiteback also were good. While most chest trouble would probably have been related to colds, some might have been symptomatic of tuberculosis, a disease which the herb fresh cut was known to cure when boiled with love weed and an orange.

Rheumatic Conditions

EUROPE A common problem in ancient Rome was toxicity from lead-adulterated wines, which could cause kidney failure and an increase in uric acid in the blood, known as gout. Uric acid crystals deposited in the joint tissues can lead to the destruction of the joint surfaces, causing swelling, inflammation, pain, and restricted use of hands and feet. To treat it, Celsus prescribed bloodletting, diuretics, emetics, and hot fomentations. During remission, he recommended gentle exercise and a spare diet. Osteoarthrosis is the most common identifiable disease of the Roman world. Over 80 percent of the adult skeletons from the 4th century A.D. cemetery at England's Roman Cirencester suffered from osteoarthrosis, which was probably also the most common disease among the Anglo-Saxons. In this degenerative condition, the joints of the vertebral column were most affected with excess bony outgrowths of the spine. In the arm, the elbow joint was the most common site. *Bald's Leechbook* recommended a mixture of lithwart and honey be applied to the joint. Another remedy given was wormwood mixed with tar and fen cress bound onto the sore joint.

THE INDIAN SUBCONTINENT Ayurveda believes that arthritis is caused by digestive disorders, generally of a vata nature where agni (or digestive fire) is weak. Ama accumulates and, because the colon is unable to function properly, toxins lodge in the joints, causing pain. An Ayurvedic physician may alter a patient's diet, advising him to stay away from heavy, damp foods and foods that produce too much acidity in the body, such as the nightshade family. Typically the physician would prescribe a colon cleansing enema and herbs, such as galangal, turmeric, guggul, and cyperus, that relieve pain.

THE FAR EAST As was the case with many other conditions, the ancient Tibetan physicians categorized rheumatism into a number of distinct conditions. The primary distinction was between "black" and "white" rheumatism. "Black" conditions were of a hot nature and were accompanied by substantial pain, emaciation, a rapid pulse, and a dark complexion. The "white" variety was accompanied by less pain and signs suggesting cold.

Treatment ranged from simple formulas given at the outset to see if the condition could be quickly dispelled to complex formulas using precious compounds including preparations of mercury, minerals, and herbs. One of these—a preparation of detoxified mercury, sulfur, acacia catechu, treacle, saffron, cloves, greater and lesser cardamom, bamboo manna, nutmeg, sal tree resin, cassia tora, cannabis, black pine resin, and garuda of five ingredients—was adjusted to the prevailing temperature of the condition by the addition of long pepper if it was cold and elephant bile if it was hot. Moxibustion and the application of heat was recommended throughout the condition as an external therapy whenever pain was present. Hot springs were also used as a form of external therapy.

In Japan, joint pain, stiffness, and swelling were treated with moxibustion, but acupuncture and herbal formulas would have been used as well. Depending on the areas of the body that were affected, the physician would have burned small amounts of artemisia on the skin at points that were near the affected joints.

Index

Page numbers in *italics* refer to photo captions; those in **boldface** refer to maps.